ABC's of Relationship Selling

THROUGH SERVICE

thirteenth edition

CHARLES M. FUTRELL
Texas A & M University

RAJ AGNIHOTRI
Iowa State University

MICHAEL T. KRUSH
Kansas State University

D1207849

ABC'S OF RELATIONSHIP SELLING THROUGH SERVICE, THIRTEENTH EDITION

Published by McGraw-Hill Education, 2 Penn Plaza, New York, NY 10121. Copyright © 2019 by McGraw-Hill Education. All rights reserved. Printed in the United States of America. Previous editions © 2013, 2011, and 2009. No part of this publication may be reproduced or distributed in any form or by any means, or stored in a database or retrieval system, without the prior written consent of McGraw-Hill Education, including, but not limited to, in any network or other electronic storage or transmission, or broadcast for distance learning.

Some ancillaries, including electronic and print components, may not be available to customers outside the United States.

This book is printed on acid-free paper.
3 4 5 6 QVS 22 21 20 19

ISBN 978-1-260-16982-9 (bound edition)
MHID 1-260-16982-0 (bound edition)

ISBN 978-1-260-31662-9 (loose-leaf edition)
MHID 1-260-31662-9 (loose-leaf edition)

Executive Portfolio Manager: *Meredith Fossell*
Associate Portfolio Manager: *Laura Hurst Spell*
Marketing Manager: *Nicole Young*
Content Project Managers: *Melissa M. Leick, Emily Windelborn*
Buyer: *Sandy Ludovissy*
Design: *Jessica Cuevas*
Content Licensing Specialist: *Ann Marie Jannette*
Cover Image: *©pressmaster/123RF*
Compositor: *SPi Global*

All credits appearing on page or at the end of the book are considered to be an extension of the copyright page.

Library of Congress Cataloging-in-Publication Data
Names: Futrell, Charles, author.
Title: ABC's of relationship selling through service / Charles M. Futrell, Texas A & M University.
Description: Thirteenth edition. | New York, NY : McGraw-Hill, [2019]
Identifiers: LCCN 2018026075 | ISBN 9781260169829 (alk. paper)
Subjects: LCSH: Selling.
Classification: LCC HF5438.25 .F868 2019 | DDC 658.85–dc23
LC record available at https://lccn.loc.gov/2018026075

The Internet addresses listed in the text were accurate at the time of publication. The inclusion of a website does not indicate an endorsement by the authors or McGraw-Hill Education, and McGraw-Hill Education does not guarantee the accuracy of the information presented at these sites.

(dedication)

To Dr. Futrell, his admirable work in enhancing the sales profession, and the legacy of students he impacted.

DR. CHARLES M. FUTRELL The late Dr. Charles M. Futrell was a professor of marketing in the Mays Business School at Texas A&M University in College Station, Texas. Dr. Futrell held a BBA, MBA, and PhD in marketing. Professor Futrell's books, research, and teaching were based on his extensive work with sales organizations of all types and sizes. He was a former salesperson turned professor. Before beginning his academic career, Professor Futrell worked in sales and marketing capacities for eight years with the Colgate Company, The Upjohn Company, and Ayerst Laboratories. This broad and rich background has resulted in numerous invitations to serve as a speaker, researcher, and consultant to industry.

Dr. Futrell's research in personal selling, sales management, research methodology, and marketing management appeared in numerous national and international journals. An article in the summer 1991 issue of the *Journal of Personal Selling & Sales Management* ranked Charles as one of the top three sales researchers in America. He was also recognized in *Marketing Education,* Summer 1997, as one of the top 100 best researchers in the marketing discipline. Professor Futrell served as the American Marketing Association's chair of the Sales and Sales Management Special Interest Group (SIG) for the 1996–97 academic year. He was the first person elected to this position.

Charles received a number of awards as a testament to his work. In 2005, the AMA Sales and Sales Management Special Interest Group (SIG) presented Charles with its Lifetime Achievement Award for commitment to excellence and service in the area of sales. Charles was the recipient of Sales & Marketing Executives International's (SMEI) Educator of the Year in 2007; and the American Marketing Association's Sales Management Special Interest Group awarded Charles the Lifetime Excellence in Teaching Award in 2012.

Dr. Futrell wrote or co-wrote eight successful books for the college and professional audience. Two of the most popular books were Fundamentals of Selling: Customers for Life through Service, and this book, ABC's of Relationship Selling through Service, now in its thirteenth edition, both published by McGraw-Hill/Irwin. Over 300,000 students worldwide learned from Professor Futrell's books.

DR. RAJ AGNIHOTRI is the dean's fellow in marketing and the director of sales initiative at Ivy College of Business, Iowa State University. Previously, Raj held the first John Merrill Endowed Professorship in Consultative Sales at the University of Texas at Arlington and Robert H. Freeman Professor of Sales Leadership and marketing chair at Ohio University. Before entering academia, Raj held a number of sales and marketing positions with start-up ventures to major global corporations. He currently serves on the advisory boards of several technology startups based in the US and Europe. Raj is also involved in executive education and has given sales seminars to industry professionals from North America, Brazil, Europe, and India. He served on the faculty of Samson Global Leadership Program at Cleveland Clinic from 2014 to 2017 and taught health administrators from across the world.

Raj has published over 35 articles in leading scholarly journals and has presented papers at over 50 national and international conferences. He serves on the editorial review board of *Industrial Marketing Management, Journal of Business Research,* and *Marketing Management Journal.* A recipient of the prestigious 2011 James M. Comer Award for the best contribution to selling and sales management theory, Raj's dissertation on salesperson competitive intelligence won the 2010 Best Dissertation Award from American Marketing Association. Raj has also received the 2017 Citation of Excellence Award from Emerald, the 2012 Bright Idea Award from NJPRO Foundation, the 2012 Stanley Hollander Award from Academy of the 2017 Doctoral Students' Mentor of the Year award from College of Business at UT Arlington, the 2012 Advisor of the Year Award from William Paterson University, the 2010 McGraw-Hill/Steven J. Shaw Award from Society for Marketing Advances, and the 2008 Next Gen Award from AMA Sales SIG and University of Houston.

Raj is a passionate teacher, and he was awarded the 2014 Hormel Excellence in Teaching Award for his innovative teaching practices. He has also received Golden M Teaching Award in marketing at Kent State University. A firm believer in experiential learning, Raj launched Maverick Sales Club at UT-Arlington, Consumer Research Center at Ohio University, Professional Sales Club at William Paterson University of New Jersey, among other initiatives.

Raj lives with his beautiful wife, Manusmriti, and their two lovely daughters, Sia and Aarna, in Ames, Iowa. Raj's family is his biggest source for strength, comfort, and inspiration. Raj remains grateful to his parents for teaching him the importance of hard work and kindness.

MIKE KRUSH, DR. MIKE KRUSH (University of Nebraska–Lincoln) serves on the College of Business Administration faculty at Kansas State University and is associated with its National Strategic Selling Institute (NSSI).

Dr. Krush has taught sales and a range of marketing classes at the undergraduate and graduate level at multiple universities including North Dakota State University, St. Cloud State University, and the University of Nebraska–Lincoln.

In terms of sales education, Dr. Krush championed and initiated the Center for Professional Selling Sales Technology at North Dakota State University—the only academic center dedicated to developing the sales skills of college students within the North Dakota University System. The Sales Education Foundation consistently recognized NDSU on its list of top universities for sales education. When serving as its director, Dr. Krush championed the application of the Center for Professional Selling and Sales Technology for full membership within the University Sales Center Alliance, a consortium of sales centers dedicated to advancing the sales profession via teaching, research, and outreach.

Prior to his academic career, Dr. Krush served as a brand manager at the Kimberly-Clark Corporation, one of America's largest publicly held corporations. His responsibilities included areas of strategic marketing for a $600 million brand. In addition, he has conducted marketing and sales operations in the financial services domain, consulted with start-up and existing firms, and written a book on career preparation.

From a research perspective, Dr. Krush was one of three national award winners of the Institute for the Study of Business Market's Doctoral Support Award for his dissertation in business-to-business marketing. Dr. Agnihotri, Dr. Krush, and their colleagues were also recognized by Industrial Marketing Management in 2016 for the Best Article Award.

Dr. Krush's research has been published in a variety of journals, including the *Journal of the Academy of Marketing Science*, the *Journal of Business Research*, the *Journal of Personal Selling and Sales Management*, the *European Journal of Marketing*, *Industrial Marketing Management*, *The Journal of Business Ethics*, and the *Journal of Business and Industrial Marketing*. Mike is blessed with an amazing wife, Joan, and two fantastic kids.

ABC's of Relationship Selling through Service, Thirteenth Edition

With great excitement, we are presenting the thirteenth edition of *ABC's!* As selling continues to grow as a profession, the importance of professional sales education continues to increase in its acceptance and expansion within academia. The thirteenth edition of *ABC's* is specifically focused on the core principles of professional selling. The revisions to the *ABC's* were guided by our conversations with sales students, practitioners, and, more importantly, sales educators.

This edition streamlines the structure and contents to focus on contemporary professional selling, with an emphasis on current practices, and sharpens the focus on the business-to-business realm *along with* business-to-consumer context. Apart from integrating a more contemporary, professional-selling-based approach, the thirteenth edition aims to prepare the student for sales technology utilization.

There Is Much New about *ABC's* Thirteenth Edition

Unique aspects that make this edition of *ABC's* new include the enhanced focus on sales professionalism, the extensive discussion on sales technology such as CRM systems and social media tools, and the exposure to various selling situations and how to react to them. Also important are the changes to many of the main PowerPoints and sections of the Instructor's Manual. Your students will need to use this edition, not a previous one.

Examples of What's New

- Compare this edition's Chapter 1 with the previous edition. You will see the enhanced focus on sales professionalism as we define professional selling and outline a range of core principles. For instance, we include a discussion on how to build a professional reputation as well as the buyer's expectations of professionalism. These changes greatly improve the learning experience.

- Further sharpening the focus on business-to-business selling, we are adding several new sections that distinguish between the organizational and consumer buying process (Chapter 3) and we discuss the role of salespeople as knowledge brokers as well as their value to a range of customers (Chapters 5 and 7).

- Updates regarding the current use of technology have been integrated throughout the book. For example, we replaced the previous edition's contact management section with a section on customer relationship management (CRM). Further we discuss the Internet and the Cloud

(Chapter 5); the means through which CRM technology assists sales-people in prospecting (Chapter 7), in servicing the sale (Chapter 13), and in managing time and territory (Chapter 14) are added to the text.

- We also expanded critical topics such as personality style as well as adaptive selling based upon a buyer's style within Chapter 4 on communication.
- A number of cases at the end of chapters (Chapters 3, 6, 8, 9, 10, and 12) have been expanded and/or added.
- A number of integrated role-plays have been added to the end of Chapter 13. The role-plays can be used as single role-plays or as an ongoing business relationship throughout the semester.
- Materials have been created to help the instructor who is teaching the course for the first time, the professor changing textbooks, as well as the seasoned veteran who has taught the course 20 or more times.
- Significant improvements have been made to this thirteenth edition of *ABC's*. We continue the focus on training readers on a specific, yet generic, step-by-step selling process that is universal in nature. The selling process can be used in selling any type of good or service in any situation—business-to-business, consumer, group, retail, resellers, phone, anywhere where buyer and seller come together. In addition, we add more examples to connect the contents of the textbook to the contemporary business practices and reflect the current business landscape.
- Students have the opportunity to role-play a job interview with the student getting the job and then selling the organization's product involved in the Sell Yourself exercise or in any of the cases at the end of the book. Students love it!
- Students will find it easy to create their class project sales presentation role-play because of knowing what to do first, second, third, and so on.
- Arguably, no other professional selling textbook presents the sales process in such an organized, comprehensive manner—from planning the approach to closing and follow-up for exceptional customer service, all within an ethical framework. Moreover, presenting to current customers, not only to prospects, has been emphasized throughout the book. Such unique aspects distinguish *ABC's* from all other textbooks.

A megatrend in today's business world involves going to extreme efforts to meet consumer needs. Organizations cannot afford to lose customers. It is always easier to sell to a satisfied customer than an unsatisfied one. The cost of acquiring a new customer is higher than keeping a present customer.

This textbook focuses on taking care of the customer through exceptional customer service. Service means making a contribution to the welfare of others. Salespeople exist to help others.

New Additions, Expansions, and Reexaminations to This Edition

Using this textbook each year in our sales classes has resulted in a constant study of the text by students who provide feedback on its content. Present users of the textbook have offered detailed critiques providing direction for revision of the book, as have the reviewers noted in the Acknowledgments. For this edition, we carefully reread the book to ensure that the text better reflects our thoughts and ideas on the subject. The relationships and interactions in the various steps of the selling process have been carefully examined to form a more seamless flow from one chapter to the next, and special emphasis is placed on the importance of ethical behavior in working with prospects and customers.

Scores of sales personnel in the industry today comment on how this textbook reflects what they do on sales calls with prospects and customers. The goal of *ABC's of Selling* has always been to demonstrate to students the order of steps within the selling process; provide numerous examples of what should be in each step; and explain how the steps within the selling process interact with one another. If students understand the sales system by the end of the course, the class has successfully contributed to their education.

Examples of New Additions

ABC's of Selling is a market leader in sales classes worldwide, and its materials can be found in four international versions. Numerous sales trainers around the globe use our selling process to prepare their salespeople.

The Uniqueness of *ABC's of Selling*

The appendix to Chapter 1, "The Core Principles of Professional Selling as Told by a Salesperson," reveals this textbook's unique central focus—serving others unselfishly. To aid in this message, the acclaimed worldwide Core Principles were incorporated in order to stress treating others as you would like to be treated in the marketplace and workplace.

The textbook's foundation is based on service. Its cornerstone is caring of others. *ABC's of Selling*'s values are supported by the pillars of an organization's—and individual's—integrity, trustworthiness, and character (see Exhibit 2.7). The center of business and personal life revolves around personal interactions; as a result, a theme of this textbook is that ethical service, based upon truth between people, builds strong, long-term relationships.

ABC's of Selling seeks to prepare people for the 21st century's demand for ethical treatment—a universal declaration for human rights. It is a calling for a higher standard than what previously exists in many organizations worldwide. The General Assembly of the United Nations has proclaimed that humans possess reason and conscience, and should act toward one another in a spirit of brotherhood. Organizations should not be engaged in war within the marketplace, but committed to serving humankind.

Many people seem to separate their personal life from their business life. Some individuals, when entering the business world, tend to follow the example of others to generate sales. The use of this textbook in your classroom may provide some students with a final opportunity to discuss how to enter the rat race without becoming a rat.

ABC's Approach

ABC's of Selling was conceived as a method of providing ample materials that allow readers to construct their own sales presentations after studying the text. This allows the instructor the flexibility of focusing on the "how-to-sell" approach within the classroom. Covering the basic foundations for understanding the concepts and practices of selling in a practical, straightforward, and readable manner, it provides students with a guide to use in preparing sales presentations and role-playing exercises.

The Philosophy behind This Book

The title should help you understand the philosphy of this book. A student of sales should understand the fundamentals—the basics—of professional selling. All of them. We do not advocate one way of selling as the best route to success! There are many roads to reaching one's goals.

We *do* feel a salesperson should have an assortment of selling skills and should be very knowledgeable, even an expert, in the field. Based on the situation, the salesperson determines the appropriate actions to take for a particular prospect or customer. No matter what the situation, however, the basic fundamentals of selling can be applied.

There is no place in our society for high-pressure, manipulative selling. The salesperson is a problem solver, a knowledge broker, and an adviser to the customer. If the customer has no need, the salesperson should accept that and move on to help another person or firm. If the customer has a need, however, the salesperson should and must go for the sale. All successful salespeople we know feel that once they determine that the customer is going to buy someone's product—and that their product will satisfy that customer's needs—it is their job to muster all their energy, skill, and know-how to make that sale. That is what it's all about!

It is our sincere hope that after the reader has studied this book, he or she will say, "There's a lot more to selling than I ever imagined." We hope many people will feel that this material can help them earn a living and that selling is a great occupation and career.

At the end of the course, we hope all the students will have learned how to prepare and give a sales presentation by visually, verbally, and nonverbally communicating their message. We know of no other marketing course whose class project is so challenging and where so much learning takes place.

Finally, we hope each student realizes that these new communication skills can be applied to all aspects of life. Once learned and internalized, selling skills will help a person be a better communicator throughout life.

Basic Organization of the Book

We worked hard with the publisher to ensure that *ABC's of Selling* would provide students with the basic foundation for understanding all major aspects of selling. The 14 chapters in the text are divided into four parts:

- **Selling as a Profession.** Emphasizes the history, career, rewards, and duties of the professional salesperson and illustrates the importance of the sales function to the organization's success. It also examines the social, ethical, and legal issues in selling.

- **Preparation for Relationship Selling.** Presents the background information salespeople use to develop their sales presentations.

- **The Relationship Selling Process.** At the heart of this book, this part covers the entire selling process from prospecting to follow-up. State-of-the-art selling strategies, practices, and techniques are presented in a "how-to" fashion.

- **Time, Territory, and Self-management: Keys to Success.** The importance of the proper use and management of one's time and sales territory is given thorough coverage.

Special to This Edition

Ethics Emphasized

Unselfish and ethical service to the customer underscores the Core Principles of Professional Selling—a sales philosophy of unselfishly treating others as you would like to be treated without expecting reciprocity. This is how to build long-term relationships with customers.

Sales Call Role-Plays

The role-plays in Chapter 13 are classroom-tested and created from information used by today's top sales forces.

Sell Yourself on a Job Interview

This all-time favorite role-play is in Appendix A with other experiential exercises. For years we have used this student pleaser in both our professional selling and sales management classes. When students see themselves on video, they quickly realize what needs to be done for a professional interview. You have to try this exercise one time!

Student Application Learning Exercises (SALES)

Chapters directly related to creating the role-play have SALES that aid students in better understanding how to construct this popular class project. Students unanimously feel they are great in helping them correctly construct their role-plays. SALES appear at the end of Chapters 3, 5A, 7, 9, 10, 11, and 12.

Sales Careers

Career information has been expanded throughout so students will better understand that there are sales jobs in all organizations—business, service, and nonprofit.

Selling Experiential Exercises

These end-of-chapter exercises help students better understand themselves and/or the text material. Many can be done in class or completed outside and discussed in class.

Technology in Selling

Our goal is to expose students to the existing and emerging technology in sales.

Text and Chapter Pedagogy

Many reality-based features are included in the thirteenth edition to stimulate learning. One major goal of this book is to offer better ways of using it to convey sales knowledge to the reader. To do this, the book includes numerous special features:

Photo Essays

The book features many photographs accompanied by captions that describe sales events and how they relate to chapter materials.

Chapter Topics and Objectives

Each chapter begins with a clear statement of learning objectives and an outline of major chapter topics. These devices provide an overview of what is to come and can also be used by students to see whether they understand and have retained important points.

Sales Challenge/Solution

The text portion of each chapter begins with a real-life challenge that sales professionals face. The challenge pertains to the topic of the chapter and will heighten students' interest in chapter concepts. The challenge is resolved at the end of the chapter, where chapter concepts guiding the salespersons' actions are highlighted.

Making the Sale

These boxed items explore how salespeople, when faced with challenges, use innovative ideas to sell.

Selling Tips

These boxes offer the reader additional selling tips for use in developing their role-plays.

Artwork

Many aspects of selling tend to be confusing at first. "What should I do?" and "How should I do it?" are two questions frequently asked by students in developing their role-plays. To enhance students' awareness and understanding, many exhibits have been included throughout the book. These exhibits consolidate key points, indicate relationships, and visually illustrate selling techniques.

Chapter Summary and Application Questions

Each chapter closes with a summary of key points to be retained. The application questions are a complementary learning tool that enables students to check their understanding of key issues, to think beyond basic concepts, and to determine areas that require further study. The summary and application questions help students discriminate between main and supporting points and provide mechanisms for self-teaching.

Key Terms for Selling/Glossary

Learning the selling vocabulary is essential to understanding today's sales world. This is facilitated in three ways. First, key concepts are boldfaced and completely defined where they first appear in the text. Second, each key term, followed by the page number where it was first introduced and defined, is listed at the end of each chapter. Third, a glossary summarizing all key terms and definitions appears at the end of the book for handy reference.

Ethical Dilemma

These challenging exercises provide students an opportunity to experience ethical dilemmas faced in the selling job. Students should review the definition and explanation of ethical behavior in Chapter 2 before discussing the ethical dilemmas.

Further Exploring the Sales World

These projects ask students to go beyond the textbook and classroom to explore what's happening in the real world. Projects can be altered or adapted to the instructor's school location and learning objectives for the class.

Cases for Analysis

Each chapter ends with brief cases for student analysis and class discussion. These focused cases provide an opportunity for students to apply concepts to real events and to sharpen their diagnostic skills for sales problem solving.

As you see, we have thoroughly considered how best to present the material to readers for maximizing their interest and learning. Teacher, reviewer, and student response to this revision has been fantastic. They are pleased with the readability, reasonable length, depth, and breadth of the material. You will like this edition better than the previous one.

Teaching and Learning Supplements

McGraw-Hill Education has spared no expense to make *ABC's of Selling* the premier text in the market today. Many instructors face classes with limited resources, and supplementary materials provide a way to expand and improve the students' learning experience. Our learning package was specifically designed to meet the needs of instructors facing a variety of teaching conditions and for both the first-time and veteran instructor.

Prof. Agnihotri and Prof. Krush Your Number One Resource

Contact us anytime with questions, comments, or just to say "hello." We talk to instructors, students, and industry sales trainers worldwide. If you are teaching the course, especially for the first time, and want us to look over your syllabus. We are here to serve.

Instructor's Manual

Loaded with ideas on teaching the course, chapter outlines, commentaries on cases, answers to everything—plus much more—the Instructor's Manual is a large, comprehensive time-saver for teachers.

Test Bank

The most important part of the teaching package is the Test Bank. We gave the Test Bank special attention during the preparation of the thirteenth edition because instructors desire test questions that accurately and fairly assess student competence in subject material. The Test Bank provides hundreds of multiple-choice and true/false questions. Each question has been rated for level of difficulty and designated with the page number in the text to locate the correct answer so that instructors can provide a balanced set of questions for student exams.

Connect Library

At **connect.mheducation.com,** you can access downloadable versions of instructor support materials:

- **A PowerPoint Presentation.** A state-of-the-art program offering hundreds of lecture slides. These slides can be customized for any course. They are great!
- **Computerized Test Bank.** The Computerized Test Bank allows instructors to select and edit test items from the printed Test Bank and to add their own questions. Various versions of each test can be custom printed.
- **Electronic Version of the Instructor's Manual.**

Students—study more efficiently, retain more and achieve better outcomes. Instructors—focus on what you love—teaching.

SUCCESSFUL SEMESTERS INCLUDE CONNECT

FOR INSTRUCTORS

You're in the driver's seat.

Want to build your own course? No problem. Prefer to use our turnkey, prebuilt course? Easy. Want to make changes throughout the semester? Sure. And you'll save time with Connect's auto-grading too.

65%
Less Time Grading

They'll thank you for it.

Adaptive study resources like SmartBook® help your students be better prepared in less time. You can transform your class time from dull definitions to dynamic debates. Hear from your peers about the benefits of Connect at **www.mheducation.com/highered/connect**

Make it simple, make it affordable.

Connect makes it easy with seamless integration using any of the major Learning Management Systems—Blackboard®, Canvas, and D2L, among others—to let you organize your course in one convenient location. Give your students access to digital materials at a discount with our inclusive access program. Ask your McGraw-Hill representative for more information.

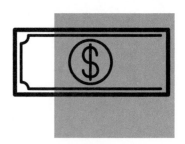

©Hill Street Studios/Tobin Rogers/Blend Images LLC

Solutions for your challenges.

A product isn't a solution. Real solutions are affordable, reliable, and come with training and ongoing support when you need it and how you want it. Our Customer Experience Group can also help you troubleshoot tech problems—although Connect's 99% uptime means you might not need to call them. See for yourself at **status.mheducation.com**

Effective, efficient studying.

Connect helps you be more productive with your study time and get better grades using tools like SmartBook, which highlights key concepts and creates a personalized study plan. Connect sets you up for success, so you walk into class with confidence and walk out with better grades.

©Shutterstock/wavebreakmedia

> **"**I really liked this app—it made it easy to study when you don't have your text-book in front of you.**"**
>
> - Jordan Cunningham,
> Eastern Washington University

Study anytime, anywhere.

Download the free ReadAnywhere app and access your online eBook when it's convenient, even if you're offline. And since the app automatically syncs with your eBook in Connect, all of your notes are available every time you open it. Find out more at **www.mheducation.com/readanywhere**

No surprises.

The Connect Calendar and Reports tools keep you on track with the work you need to get done and your assignment scores. Life gets busy; Connect tools help you keep learning through it all.

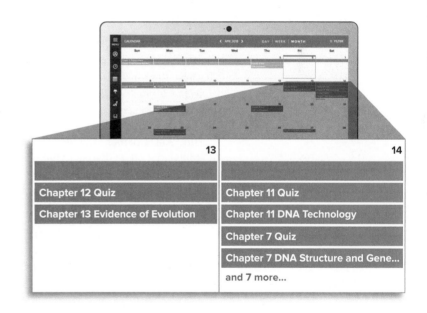

13	14
Chapter 12 Quiz	Chapter 11 Quiz
Chapter 13 Evidence of Evolution	Chapter 11 DNA Technology
	Chapter 7 Quiz
	Chapter 7 DNA Structure and Gene...
	and 7 more...

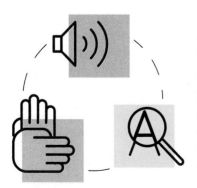

Learning for everyone.

McGraw-Hill works directly with Accessibility Services Departments and faculty to meet the learning needs of all students. Please contact your Accessibility Services office and ask them to email accessibility@mheducation.com, or visit **www.mheducation.com/about/accessibility.html** for more information.

acknowledgments

Working with the dedicated team of professionals at McGraw-Hill/Irwin, who were determined to produce the best personal selling book ever, was a gratifying experience.

We would like to convey our appreciation to MHE team: Laura Hurst Spell, Meredith Fossel, Ann Marie Jannette, and Jennifer M. Blankenship, who oversaw the selection of photographs for this edition. Project managers Melissa Leick and Mithun Kothandath ably guided the manuscript and page proofs through the production process.

Another group of people who made a major contribution to this text were the sales experts who provided advice, reviews, answers to questions, and suggestions for changes, insertions, and clarifications. We want to thank these colleagues for their valuable feedback and suggestions:

- Mark Edward Blake, York College of Pennsylvania
- Richard L. Carter, University of Washington
- John Michael Cicero, Highline College
- Kimberly Annette Fischer, Mid Michigan Community College
- Lukas Forbes, Western Kentucky University
- Thomas F. Frizzell, Massasoit Community College
- Stanton Heister, Colorado Mesa University

We also want to again thank those people who contributed to earlier editions, because their input is still felt in this thirteenth edition. They were Alan Rick, *New England Institute of Technology;* Albert J. Taylor, *Austin Peay State University;* Albert Jerus, *Northwestern College;* Alicia Lupinacci, *Tarrant County College-Northwest Campus;* Alicia Lupinacci, *Tarrant County College;* Allen Schaefer, *Missouri State University;* Ames Barber, *Adirondack Community College;* Balan Nagraj, *Suffolk County Community College;* Barbara Ollhoff, *Waukesha County Technical College;* Becky Oliphant, *Stetson University;* Brian Meyer, *Mankato State University;* Brian Tietje, *California Polytechnic State University;* Bruce Warsleys, *Trend Colleges;* Camille P. Schuster, *Xavier University;* Chris Brandmeir, *Highline Community College;* Christine H. Dennison, *Youngstown State University;* Cindy Leverenz, *Blackhawk Technical College;* Craig A Martin, *Western Kentucky University;* Craig Kelley, *California State University-Sacramento;* Dan Weilbaker, *Northern Illinois University;* David Wiley, *Anne Arundel Community College;* Dawn Bendall-Lyon, *University of Montevallo;* Deborah Jansky, *Milwaukee Area Technical College;* Deborah Kane, Butler County Community College Deborah Lawe, *San Francisco State University;* Dee Smith, *Lansing Community College;* Dennis Elbert, *University of North Dakota;* Dennis Kovach, *Community College of Allegheny County;* Dennis Tademy, *Cedar Valley College;* Dick Nordstrom, *California State University-Fresno;* Don McCartney, *University of Wisonson-Green Bay;* Donald Sandlin, *East Los Angeles College;* Donna Kantack, *Elrick & Lavidge;* Douglas E. Hughes, *Michigan State University;* Duane Bachmann, *Central Missouri State University;* Earl Emery, *Baker Junior College of Business;* Ed Snider, *Mesa Community College;* Eric Newman, *California State University-San Bernardino;* Eric Soares, *California State University-Hayward;* Frances DePaul, *Westmoreland Community*

College; Gary Donnelly, *Casper College;* Gerald Crawford, *University of North Alabama;* Glenna Urbshadt, *British Columbia Institute of Technology;* Greg Gardner, *Jefferson Community College;* Harry Moak, *Macomb Community College;* Herb Miller, *University of Texas–Austin;* Hieu Nguyen, *University of Texas at Arlington;* James E. Littlefield, *Virginia Polytechnic Institute & State University;* James L. Taylor, *University of Alabama;* James Ogden, *Kutztown University;* Jay P. Mulki, *Northeastern University;* Jeff Gauer, *Mohawk Valley Community College;* Jeff Sager, *University of North Texas;* Jim Muncy, *Valdosta State University;* Joan Rossi, *Pittsburgh Technical Institute;* Joe M. Garza, *University of Texas–Pan American;* John R. Beem, *College of DuPage;* John Ronchetto, *University of San Diego;* John Todd, *University of Tampa;* Jon Hawes, *Northern Illinois University;* Joyce Ezrow, *Anne Arundel Community College;* Karen Bilda, *Cardinal Stritch University;* Karen J. Smith, *Columbia Southern University;* Kathy Messick, *J. Sargeant Reynolds Community College;* Keith Steege, *International Academy of Design and Technology-Orlando;* Ken Miller, *Kilgore College;* Kevin Feldt, *University of Akron;* Kevin Hammond, *Community College of Allegheny County;* Leslie E. Martin, Jr., *University of Wisconsin–Whitewater;* Lynn J. Loudenback, *New Mexico State University;* Marilyn Besich, *MSU Great Falls College of Technology;* Marjorie Caballero, *Baylor University;* Michael Discello, *Pittsburgh Technical Institute;* Michael Eguchi, *University of Washington Foster School of Business;* Michael Fox, *Eastern Arizona College;* Mike Behan, *Western Technical College and Viterbo University;* Milton J. Bergstein, *Pennsylvania State University;* Myrna Glenny, *Fashion Institute of Design and Merchandising;* Navneet Luthar, *Madison Area Technical College;* Nicola Thomas Arena, UNC Pembroke Norman Cohn, *Milwaukee Tech;* O. C. Ferrell, *University of New Mexico;* Paul Barchitta, *Queensborough Community College;* Ramon A. Avila, *Ball State University;* Ric Gorno, *Cypress College;* Richard Shannon, *Western Kentucky University;* Robert Piacenza, *Madison Area Technical College;* Robert Smith, *Illinois State University;* Robert Tangsrud, Jr., *University of North Dakota;* Robert Thompson, *Indiana State University;* Robert Weaver, *Fairmont State University;* Rochelle R. Brunson, *Alvin Community College;* Rollie Tilman, *University of North Carolina–Chapel Hill;* Roy Payne, *Purdue University;* Ruth Taylor, *Southwest Texas State University;* Sid Dudley, *Eastern Illinois University;* Suzanne Tilleman, *Montana State University;* Thomas O. Marpe, *Saint Mary's University of Minnesota;* Timothy W. Wright, *Lakeland Community College;* Tracie Linderman, *Horry-Georgetown Technical College;* Trudy Dunson, *Gwinnett Technical College;* William A. Stull, *Utah State University;* William H. Crookston, *California State University–Northridge;* and William J. Cobian, *University of Wisconsin–Stout.*

We would also like to thank the many students who have used the book in their classes and provided feedback. Thanks also to the many instructors who call us each year to discuss the book and what they do in their classes. While we have never met face-to-face, we feel we know you. Your positive comments, encouragement, and ideas have been inspirational.

In addition, salespeople and sales managers have provided photographs, selling techniques, answers to end-of-chapter exercises and cases, and other industry materials that enrich the reader's learning experience. They include the following:

Kim Allen, *McNeil Consumer Products Company;* Alan Baker, *Noxell Corporation;* Michael Bevan, *Parbron International of Canada;* Richard Ciotti, *JC Penney Company;* John Croley, *The Gates Rubber Company;* Terry and Paul Fingerhut, *Steamboat Party Sales, Inc., Tupperware;* Bill Frost, *AT&T Communications;* Steve Gibson, *Smith Barney;* Gary Grant, *NCR;* Jerry Griffin, *Sewell Village Cadillac-Sterling, Dallas;* Martha Hill, *Hanes Corporation;* Debra Hutchins, *Sunwest Bank of Albuquerque;* Mike Impink, *Aluminum Company of America (ALCOA);* Bob James, *American Hospital Supply Corporation;* Morgan Jennings, *Richard D. Irwin, Inc.;* Patrick Kamlowsky, *Hughes Tool Company;* Cindy Kerns, *Xerox Corporation;* Alan Killingsworth, *FMC Corporation;* Santo Laquatra, *SmithKline Beecham;* Stanley Marcus; Gerald Mentor, *Richard D. Irwin, Inc.;* Jim Mobley, *General Mills, Inc.;* George Morris, *The Prudential Insurance Company of America;* Vikki Morrison, *First Team Walk-In Realty, California;* Greg Munoz, *The Dow Chemical Company;* Jeffrey Parker, *Jacksonville State University;* Kathleen Paynter, *Campbell Sales Company;* Bruce Powell, *Richard D. Irwin, Inc.;* Jack Pruett, *Bailey Banks and Biddle;* Joseph Puglisi, *La Roche College;* Emmett Reagan, *Xerox Corporation;* Jeri Rubin, *University of Alaska-Anchorage;* Bruce Scagel, *Scott Paper Company;* Linda Slaby-Baker, *The Quaker Oats Company;* Sandra Snow, *The Upjohn Company;* Matt Suffoletto, *International Business Machines (IBM);* Ed Tucker, *Cannon Financial Group, Georgia.* For the use of their selling exercises and sales management cases, we are especially grateful to these people:

- **Bill Stewart, Gerald Crawford, Keith Absher,** *University of North Alabama*
- **Dick Nordstrom,** *California State University-Fresno*
- **Jeffrey K. Sager,** *University of North Texas*
- **George Wynn,** *James Madison University*

Finally, we wish to thank the sales trainers, salespeople, and sales managers who helped teach us the art of selling when we carried the sales bag full time. We hope we have done justice to their great profession of selling.

We hope you learn from and enjoy the book. We enjoyed preparing it for you. Readers are urged to forward their comments on this text to us. We wish you great success in your selling efforts. Remember, it's the salesperson who gets the customer's orders that keeps the wheels of industry turning. America cannot do without you.

Raj Agnihotri
raj2@iastate.edu
Michael Krush
mikekrush@ksu.edu

contents in (brief)

table of (contents)

Chapter 2
ETHICS FIRST . . . THEN CUSTOMER RELATIONSHIPS   44

PART 2 Preparation for Relationship Selling

chapter 3
THE PSYCHOLOGY OF SELLING: WHY PEOPLE BUY   80

chapter 4

COMMUNICATION FOR RELATIONSHIP BUILDING: IT'S NOT ALL TALK   118

chapter 8
CAREFULLY SELECT WHICH SALES PRESENTATION METHOD TO USE   276

chapter 9
BEGIN YOUR PRESENTATION STRATEGICALLY   311

chapter 12
CLOSING BEGINS THE RELATIONSHIP   430

chapter 13
SERVICE AND FOLLOW-UP FOR CUSTOMER RETENTION   471

The Illustrated Overview of Selling

Even before you begin a formal study of selling, you probably already know a few things about the subject. You know, for example, that selling is about persuading others to buy your product. And you may understand that it is also about helping others satisfy their needs. But that is only part of what you will be studying in selling. The Illustrated Overview of Selling gives you an introduction to the major concepts and issues that are part of selling:

- Selling as a Profession
- Preparation for Relationship Selling
- The Relationship Selling Process
- Time, Territory, and Self-Management: Keys to Success

©Troels Graugaard/Getty Images

Today's salesperson is a professional manager involved in building long-term relationships with customers.

©simonkr/Getty Images

An organization's marketing mix includes its products, prices, distribution, and promotional efforts. Professional selling is one very important element of a firm's promotional activities.

©Hero Images/Getty Images

By tailoring a presentation to an individual or group, the salesperson can better help solve problems and satisfy needs.

©Morsa Images/Getty Images

It takes expertise to sell today's complex goods and services. Whether selling energy drinks or computer chips, salespeople must know their business.

©Kentaroo Tryman/Getty Images

©Tetra Images/Getty Images

From beginning to end, the sales presentation should be a well-planned and well-executed discussion of how to help the prospect.

©Sam Diephuis/Getty Images

The ability to communicate effectively influences a salesperson's success. Using a combination of verbal, nonverbal, and visual communication techniques greatly increases the likelihood of making a sale.

©Ariel Skelley/Blend Images LLC

The sales presentation is a persuasive vocal and visual explanation of a business proposition. The salesperson presents the information needed for the buyer to make a well-informed decision.

©JGI/Tom Grill/Getty Images

Properly managing one's time is essential to being successful. Using sales technology and contacting decision makers at planned intervals help sell and service customers effectively.

©Shutterstock/Monkey Business Images

You are your company's representative. Customers rely on you to provide updated information, suggestions on how to solve their problems, and service. Your employer relies on you to generate sales. As a salesperson you are involved in a highly honorable, challenging, rewarding, and professional career.

ABC's of
Relationship Selling

THROUGH SERVICE

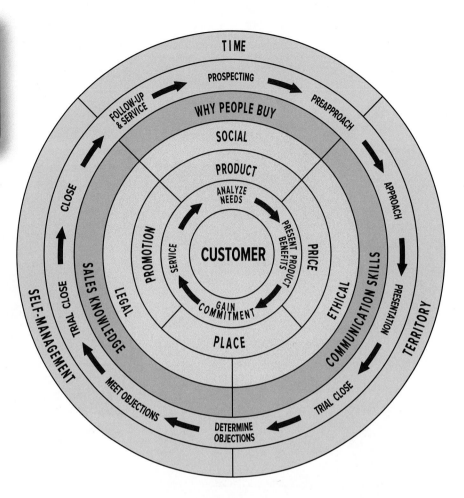

Selling as a Profession

Part I provides an overview of the sales profession and sales presentations. Chapter 1 examines the sales job and introduces the 10-step selling process used throughout the book. Chapter 2 illustrates the impact of social, ethical, and legal issues on a firm's operations.

A central theme of your book involves how sales professionals analyze needs of the customers, present benefits, gain commitment for purchase, and provide service after the sale. The sales firm provides the product to sell, sets price, determines how the customer can receive the product, and promotes the product. All of the activities must take into consideration the many social, ethical, and legal issues that affect how the organization operates.

As you study the two chapters in Part I, continually refer back to the exhibit on the opposite page which shows the abstract view of the entire text. It will help you remember each chapter's core contents and their relationships.

©Monkey Business Images/Shutterstock

The Life, Times, and Career of the Professional Salesperson

Main Topics

What Is the Purpose of Business?

Essentials of a Firm's Marketing Effort

Traditional View of Selling

What Is Professional Selling

The Core Principles of Professional Selling

Everybody Sells!

Sales: A Valued Education Leading to Career Opportunity

What Salespeople Are Paid to Do

Why Choose a Sales Career?

Is a Sales Career Right for You?

Success in Selling—What Does It Take?

C—Characteristics for the Job Examined

Relationship Selling

Sales Jobs Are Different

What Does a Professional Salesperson Do?

The Future for Salespeople

Technology and Information Build Relationships

Selling Is for Large and Small Organizations

The Plan of This Textbook

Building Relationships through the Sales Process

Appendix: The Core Principles of Professional Selling as Told by a Salesperson

Learning Objectives

This chapter introduces you to the professional and rewarding career of selling. After studying this chapter, you should be able to

1-1   Define and explain the term *selling*.

1-2   Explain why everyone sells, even you.

1-3   Define professional selling and explain the Core Principles of Professional Selling.

1-4   Discuss the reasons people might choose a sales career.

1-5   Enumerate some of the various types of sales jobs.

1-6   Describe the job activities of salespeople.

1-7   Define the characteristics that salespeople believe are needed for success in building relationships with customers.

1-8   List and explain the 10 steps in the sales process.

FACING A SALES CHALLENGE

Debra Hutchins majored in French, with a minor in English literature, at Washington University in St. Louis. After graduation she began work as a secretary in the marketing department at Sunwest Bank in Albuquerque, New Mexico.

"I had never considered a sales job while in school, and sales didn't appeal to me when I began work at the bank. I always felt you would have to be an extrovert. I'm more the shy, intellectual type. I don't see myself in the role of a salesperson.

"Someday I *do* want a more challenging job. I'm a very hard worker; long hours don't bother me. I've always had a need to achieve success. One of the things I like about being a secretary is helping customers when they call the bank. It is important to carefully listen to their problems or what they want in order to provide good customer service. Maybe one day I'll find a job that has more challenge, professionalism, and reward."

If you were in Debra's position, what would you do? What types of jobs would you recommend she consider?

Debra Hutchins is like many people in that while she was in school a career in sales did not seem like the thing to do. Most people are unfamiliar with what salespeople do.

As you learn more about the world of sales, a career selling goods or services may become appealing. The salesperson makes valuable contributions to our quality of life by selling goods and services that benefit individuals and industry. Red Motley, former editor of *Parade* magazine, once said, "Nothing happens until somebody sells something." Selling brings in the money and causes cash registers across the country to ring. For centuries, the salespeople of the world have caused goods and services to change hands.

> *Nothing happens until someone sells something.*

More than ever, today's salespeople are a dynamic power in the business world. They generate more revenue in the U.S. economy than workers in any other profession. The efforts of salespeople have a direct impact on such diverse areas as

- Ensuring the success of new products.
- Keeping existing products on the retailer's shelf.
- Constructing manufacturing facilities.
- Opening businesses and keeping them open.
- Generating sales orders that result in the loading of trucks, trains, ships, airplanes, and pipelines that carry goods to customers all over the world.

The salesperson is engaged in a highly honorable, challenging, rewarding, and professional career. In this chapter, you are introduced to the career, rewards, and duties of the salesperson. The chapter begins by relating an organization's business purpose to its marketing efforts.

What Is the Purpose of Business?

The purpose of business is to increase the general well-being of humankind through the sale of goods and services. This requires making a profit in order to operate the business and provide beneficial products to the marketplace. Profit is a means to an end. Reduced to basics, businesses have two major functions: *production* of goods or creation of services and *marketing* those goods and services.[1]

The Primary Goal of Business

The primary goal of business should be to transform the marketplace and workplace into an environment where everyone is treated as they would like to be treated. Business should be fair to all parties involved in both the buying and selling of goods and services.

Marketing's Definition

There are numerous definitions of marketing. Your book will use the American Marketing Association's definition:

> Marketing is the activity, set of institutions, and processes for creating, communicating, delivering, and exchanging offerings that have value for customers, clients, partners, and society at large.[2]

The **marketing concept** is a business philosophy that says the customers' want-satisfaction is the economic and social justification for a firm's existence. Consequently, all company activities should be devoted to determining customers' wants and then satisfying them, while still making a profit.

Essentials of a Firm's Marketing Effort

The essentials of a firm's marketing effort include its ability (1) to determine the needs of its customers and (2) to create and maintain an effective marketing mix that satisfies customer needs. As shown in Exhibit 1.1, a firm's **marketing mix** consists of four main elements—product, price, distribution or place, and promotion—a marketing manager uses to market goods and services. It is the marketing manager's responsibility to determine how best to use each element in the firm's marketing efforts.

Product: It's More than You Think

A **good** is a physical object that can be purchased. A radio, a house, and a car are examples of a good. A **service** is an action or activity done for others for a fee. Lawyers, plumbers, teachers, and taxicab drivers perform services. The term *product* refers to both goods and services.

So, what is a product? When you think of a product, most likely you imagine some tangible object you can touch, such as a radio or automobile. However, there is more to a product than you think.

A **product** is a bundle of tangible and intangible attributes, including packaging, color, and brand, plus the services and even the reputation of the seller. People buy more than a set of physical attributes. They buy want-satisfaction such as what the product will do, its quality, and the image of owning the product.

Price: It's Important to Success

The corporate marketing department also determines each product's initial price. This process involves establishing each product's normal price and possible special discount prices. Since product price often is critical to customers, it is an important part of the

EXHIBIT 1.1

Four elements to the marketing mix and four promotion activities. Where does selling fit into the marketing mix?

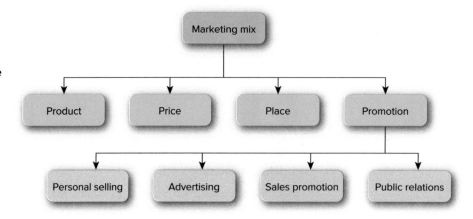

marketing mix. **Price** refers to the value or worth of a product that attracts the buyer to exchange money or something of value for the product.

Distribution: It Has to Be Available

The marketing manager also determines the best method of distributing the product. **Distribution** refers to the channel structure used to transfer products from an organization to its customers. It is important to have the product available to customers in a convenient and accessible location when they want it.

Promotion: You Have to Tell People about It

Promotion, as part of the marketing mix, increases company sales by communicating product information to potential customers. The four basic parts of a firm's promotional effort are (1) **professional selling,** (2) **advertising,** (3) **public relations,** and (4) **sales promotion.** Examples of each marketing mix ingredient are shown in Exhibit 1.2. The company's sales force is one segment of the firm's promotional effort. Salespeople are part of the organization's sales force. So what is the job of the salesperson?

EXHIBIT 1.2

Examples of each marketing mix element.

Product	Price	Place	Promotion
Brand name	Credit terms	Business partners	Advertising
Features	Discounts	Channels	Coupons
Image	List price	Distributors	Customer service
Packaging	Promotional allowances	Inventory	Direct mail
Quality level		Locations	Direct sales
Returns		Retailers	Internet
Services		Transportation	Personal selling
Sizes		Wholesalers	Public relations
Warranties			Social media
			Telemarketing
			Telesales
			Trade shows

©skynesher/Getty Images

In professional selling, a salesperson can tailor a presentation to the needs of an individual customer.

Traditional View of Selling

Many people consider *selling* and *marketing* synonymous terms. However, selling is actually only one of many marketing components. In business, a traditional definition of personal selling refers to the personal communication of information to persuade a prospective customer to buy something—a good, service, idea, or something else—that satisfies that individual's needs.

This definition of selling involves a person helping another person. The salesperson often works with prospects or customers to examine their needs, provide information, suggest a product to meet their needs, and provide after-the-sale service to ensure long-term satisfaction.

The definition also involves communications between seller and buyer. The salesperson and the buyer discuss needs and talk about the product relative to how it will satisfy the person's needs. If the product is what the person needs, then the salesperson attempts to persuade the prospect to buy it.

Unfortunately this explanation of selling does not explain the contemporary nature and practices of the sales profession.

What Is Professional Selling?

As per the definition adapted by American Society of Training and Development (ASTD), professional selling is "the holistic business system required to effectively develop, manage, enable, and execute a mutually beneficial, interpersonal exchange of goods and/or services for equitable value." The National Association of Sales Professionals (NASP) outlines the code of conduct for sales professionals, underscoring their responsibility to customers (acting in the best interest of customers), responsibility to employer (representing the employer in the most professional manner possible), and responsibility to community (serving as a model of good citizenship).

Sales as an occupation has evolved significantly over time and the current focus is on professionalism. Although there is no one explanation of professionalism in sales, we derive the best possible description from the nature of the selling practices. Every salesperson must constantly balance two primary duties that we call the **Core Principles of Professional Selling:** (1) unselfishly serving the buyer or buying organization and (2) professionally representing the selling organization.

Because Professionalism Matters[3]

To Customers: Keeping customers' best interests in mind, sales professionals can bring the creative ideas to improve their businesses and solutions to their business problems. Sales professionals, acting as consultants, can therefore free up resources to let customers focus on their own core competencies.

To Employers: Despite all the money spent on different marketing communication channels, one of the most salient features of the customer buying experience is interaction with the salesperson. In the eyes of a customer, the sales professional is the selling organization. The professionalism displayed by the salesperson is essential in guarding and cementing the company's brand image.

The Core Principles of Professional Selling

When asked, "What would you like to learn in this course?" Steven Osborne, a student in a sales class, said, "I would like to know how to believe in a profession that many people do not trust." We sincerely hope you will be a believer in the value of sales integrity at the end of this sales course and be able to give Steven a positive perspective.

Part of your answer will involve understanding the definition of professional selling discussed earlier and the Core Principles of Professional Selling. These principles will serve as the foundation for conduct or reasoning.

Read the short essay at the back of this chapter in the appendix titled "The Core Principles of Professional Selling as Told by a Salesperson." This short story illustrates the importance of helping people through our jobs and our lives.

Stop a minute and think about how these core principles apply to your life and the business world. These principles will be applied to professional selling throughout the textbook. They are especially effective in explaining differences in salespeople and why so many people may have a negative view of some salespeople and a positive view of other salespeople.

Salesperson Differences

In general, Exhibit 1.3 shows that differences can be explained by the extent of the person's self-interest. As Gallup's survey poll of Americans indicates, people view traditional salespeople as having their self-interest as a priority. This type of salesperson

EXHIBIT 1.3

Interest in serving the customer improves as our self-interest decreases.

← – – – – –	*Continuum of Professionalism*	– – – – – →
Traditional Salesforce		**Modern Salesforce**
Do what they think they can get away with.	Do what they are legally required to do.	Do the right thing.
Guided by self-interests.	Take care of customers.	Find others' interests most important.
Attribute results to personal efforts.	Attribute results to personal efforts, employer, customers, and economy.	Attribute results to others.
Seek recognition for efforts; sharing not important and ego driven.	Enjoy recognition, may share if it suits their purpose. Pride and ego driven.	Feel that an individual's performance is due to others, thus not motived by pride and ego.
Money is life's main motivator.	Money is important, but not to the customer's detriment.	Service most important; money is to be shared.

Every salesperson must constantly balance two primary duties that we call the Core Principles of Professional Selling: (1) unselfishly serving the buyer or buying organization and (2) professionally representing the selling organization.

is preoccupied with his or her own well-being—usually defined in terms of making money—and thus is selfish and cannot be trusted.

The salesperson following the Core Principles of Professional Selling, however, places the interests of others before self-interest. As Exhibit 1.3 illustrates, as interest in serving others improves, a person's self-interest lessens. The more the salesperson considers the customer's interest, the better the customer service.

Everybody Sells!

Your sales class will help make you a better communicator.

If you think about it, everyone sells. From an early age, you develop communication techniques for trying to get your way in life. You are involved in selling when you want someone to do something. For example, if you want to get a date, ask for a pay increase, return merchandise, urge your professor to raise your grade, or apply for a new job, you are selling. You use personal communication skills to persuade someone to act. Your ability to communicate effectively is a key to success in life.

This is why so many people take sales courses. They want to improve their communication skills to be more successful in both their personal and business lives. The skills and knowledge gained from a selling course can be used by a student who plans to go into virtually any field, such as law, medicine, journalism, the military, or his or her own business.

Selling is not just for salespeople; it is a must for everyone. In today's competitive environment, where good interpersonal skills are so valued, the lack of selling capability can put anyone at a disadvantage. So as you read this book and progress through the course, think about how you can use the material both personally and in business.

Sales: A Valued Education Leading to Career Opportunity

The quiet secret is that sales is a large and growing profession. Did you know researchers and studies have found that:[4]

- Sales is the first job chosen by as many as 60 percent of all business majors.
- Sales is the first job chosen by approximately 88 percent of all marketing majors.
- Sales ranks in the top three of the most common professions for undergraduates in economics, liberal arts, and physical sciences.
- Workers across a range of occupations suggest that 41 percent of their time is devoted to sales-like activities.[5]

In fact, many universities have recognized the value of a sales curriculum and created sales centers or sales institutes to provide their students with foundational sales knowledge.

A curriculum in professional selling offers students an incredible opportunity. Sales skills are in demand. Manpower's Talent Shortage Survey indicates that sales representative is one of the top three hardest jobs to fill in the United States.[6] In addition to the demand for applicants with sales skills, students graduating from a sales program learn faster in their sales position than students without a sales education.[7]

In summary, congratulate yourself on taking the first step—a sales education. A sales education provides you with: (a) an excellent opportunity to differentiate yourself from other candidates; (b) knowledge that can hasten your learning within your sales career; and (c) an entryway to organizations that want your skill set.

What Salespeople Are Paid to Do

In the short term, on a day-to-day, week-to-week basis, salespeople are paid to sell—that is their job. When a sales manager sees one of her salespeople, the question is always, "Did you sell anything today?" Salespeople need to sell something "today" to meet the performance goals for

- Themselves, in order to serve others, earn a living, and keep their jobs.
- Their employer, because without the generation of revenues the company fails and thus cannot serve others.
- Their customers, because their products help customers fulfill their needs and help their organizations grow.

In the long run—month to month, year to year—salespeople must build positive long-term relationships with their customers. Why? Because they know, and now you know, that up to 80 percent or more of the future sales of many organizations come from present customers and customer referrals.

Future sales come from present customers and prospects often found by customer referrals.

Salespeople need to close sales and at the same time maintain a great relationship with the buyer. Think about that last sentence. It is a very important thing to understand and learn. Salespeople want to sell to their present customers today, more tomorrow, and even more the day after that. How do you sell someone something and remain his or her business friend? You need to know how professionalism applies to the sales job. That is what this textbook is about.

Why Choose a Sales Career?

Six major reasons for choosing a sales career are (1) service to others; (2) the wide variety of sales jobs available; (3) the freedom of being on your own; (4) the challenge of selling; (5) the opportunity for advancement in a company; and (6) the rewards from a sales career (see Exhibit 1.4).

Service: Helping Others

When asked what she will look for in a career after graduating from college, one of the authors' students, Jackie Pastrano, said, "I'd like to do something that helps other people." The sales career provides the opportunity for service and an emotional purpose in life gained from helping others. That is why this book's central core value is "service." Service is a major reason for choosing a sales career! For many, service is the number one reason.

Service refers to making a contribution to the welfare of others. All of us want to do what Jackie hopes to do—help others! Would you like to help others? There are millions of sales jobs and thus many opportunities to help people and organizations.

A Variety of Sales Jobs Are Available

There are also hundreds, maybe thousands, of different types of sales positions. Look for a firm with a corporate culture that appeals to you.

As members of a firm's sales force, salespeople are a vital element in the firm's effort to market goods and services profitably. Maintaining a professional sales force accounts for major expenditures by most companies. Thus, professional selling presents a large number of career opportunities. There are millions of sales jobs, and the probability that at one time during your life you will have a sales job is high.

There are also hundreds, maybe thousands, of different types of sales positions. Think about this! Almost every good or service you know of has a salesperson who sells it to one or more people in order to get the product to the final user. That is why so many sales jobs are available.

EXHIBIT 1.4

Six major reasons for choosing a sales career.

| Service to others | Variety of sales jobs | Freedom | Challenge | Advancement | Rewards |

Types of Sales Jobs—Which Is for You?

Although there are numerous specific types of sales jobs, most salespeople work in one of three categories: as a wholesale salesperson, a manufacturer's sales representative, or a retail salesperson. These categories are classified according to the type of products sold and the salesperson's type of employer. Please remember, salespersons' roles and responsibilities will differ based on their industry, their firm, and their customer base.

> *There is a sales job perfect for you, but it will require you to research the different roles and responsibilities of salespeople.*

Selling for a Wholesaler. Wholesalers (also called distributors) buy products from manufacturers and other wholesalers and sell to other organizations. A **wholesale salesperson** sells products to parties for

- Resale, such as grocery retailers buying items and selling to consumers.
- Use in producing other goods or services, such as a home builder buying electrical and plumbing supplies.
- Operating an organization, such as your school buying supplies.

Firms engaged in wholesaling are called *wholesaling middlemen*. Classifying wholesaling middlemen is difficult because they vary greatly in (1) the products they sell, (2) the markets to which they sell, and (3) their methods of operation. As there are so many different types, the discussion of types of wholesalers is beyond the scope of this book. However, commonly known wholesalers include SuperValu which buys and distributes products in the grocery domain; Cardinal Health and McKesson in the pharmaceutical wholesaling domain; and Graybar and Border States Electric which distribute electrical parts and components.

Selling for a Manufacturer. Manufacturers' salespeople work for organizations producing the product. The types of **manufacturer's sales representative** positions range from people who deliver milk and bread to the specialized salesperson selling highly technical industrial products. The salesperson working for a manufacturer may sell to other manufacturers, wholesalers, retailers, or directly to consumers. There are five main types of manufacturer sales positions:

1. An account representative calls on a large number of already established customers in, for example, the food, textile, and apparel industries. This person asks for the order.
2. A detail salesperson concentrates on performing promotional activities and introducing new products rather than directly soliciting orders. The medical detail salesperson seeks to persuade doctors, the indirect customers, to specify a pharmaceutical company's trade name product for prescriptions. The actual sale is ultimately made through a wholesaler or directly to pharmacists and hospitals that fill prescriptions.
3. A sales engineer sells products that call for technical know-how and an ability to discuss technical aspects of the product. Expertise in identifying, analyzing, and solving customer problems is another critical factor. This type of selling is common in the oil, chemical, machinery, and heavy equipment industries because of the technical nature of their products.
4. An industrial products salesperson, technical or nontechnical, sells a tangible product to industrial buyers. No high degree of technical knowledge is required or it may be as an engineer.
5. A service salesperson, unlike the four preceding types of manufacturing salespeople, must sell the benefits of intangible or nonphysical products such as financial,

©Monkey Business Images/Shutterstock

A pharmaceutical rep must service and meet the needs of technicians, physicians, and buyers in hospitals that use the company's products.

advertising, or computer repair services. Services, like goods, are either technical or nontechnical in nature.

Selling services is ordinarily more difficult than selling tangibles. The salesperson can show, demonstrate, and dramatize tangible products; the salesperson of intangible products cannot. Intangibles often are difficult for the prospect to comprehend. People cannot feel, smell, see, hear, or taste intangible products. This makes them more challenging to sell.

Selling in Retail. A **retail salesperson** sells goods or services to consumers for their personal, nonbusiness use. Retail selling positions are so numerous that this book has many examples of it. Three common types of sellers who sell at retail are the (1) in-store salesperson, (2) direct seller who sells face-to-face away from a fixed store location, and (3) telephone salesperson.

Look back at the definition of a retail salesperson. Think of all the different types of retail organizations selling something—retailers such as bakeries, banks, caterers, hotels, and travel agents, and stores selling clothes, electronics, flowers, food, and furniture. Each customer contact person takes your money and provides a good or service in return. **Customer contact person** is another name for a salesperson. Although the title may be different, the job is the same—to help you buy.

Direct sellers sell face-to-face to consumers—typically in their homes—who use the products for their personal use. An organization could have one salesperson or 3 million salespeople, like Amway.[8]

As in any type of job—including accountants, mechanics, and politicians—some retail salespeople do very little to help their customers. However, many retail salespeople are highly skilled professionals, commanding exceptionally high incomes for their ability to service their customers. We personally know retail salespeople earning

EXHIBIT 1.5

The complexity and difficulty of these seven sales job categories increase as they move left to right.

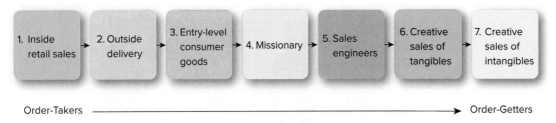

1. Inside retail sales → 2. Outside delivery → 3. Entry-level consumer goods → 4. Missionary → 5. Sales engineers → 6. Creative sales of tangibles → 7. Creative sales of intangibles

Order-Takers ————————————————————→ Order-Getters

$40,000 a year selling shoes; $80,000 selling furniture; $110,000 selling jewelry; and $150,000 selling automobiles.

Order-Takers versus Order-Getters. Sales jobs vary widely in their nature and requirements (see Exhibit 1.5). Some sales jobs require the salesperson only to take orders. **Order-takers** may ask what the customer wants or wait for the customer to order. They do not have a sales strategy and often use no sales presentation. Order-takers must be employed to bring in additional business that the employer probably would not obtain without their efforts. Many never attempt to close the sale. They perform useful services. However, few truly *create* sales.

On the other hand, the creative selling of tangible goods or intangible services in highly competitive lines (or where the product has no special advantages) moves merchandise that cannot be sold in equal volume without a salesperson. These people are **order-getters.** They get new and repeat business using a creative sales strategy and a well-executed sales presentation. The salesperson has an infinitely more difficult selling situation than that faced by the order-taker. In this sense, the individual is a true salesperson, which is why this person usually earns so much more than the order-taker.

This salesperson has two selling challenges. First, the salesperson must often create discontent with what the prospect already has before beginning to sell constructively. Second, the salesperson often has to overcome the most powerful and obstinate resistance. For example, the prospect may never have heard of the product and, at the outset, may have no desire whatsoever to purchase it. The prospect may even be prejudiced against it and may resent the intrusion of this stranger. In other instances, the prospect may want it but may want competing products more. Frequently, the prospect cannot afford it. To meet such sales situations successfully requires creative selling of the highest order.

Creative salespeople often are faced with selling to numerous people to get one order. This is the most difficult selling situation because the representative may have to win over not only the decision maker, the one who can say yes, but also other persons who cannot approve the order but who have the power to veto.

Freedom of Action: You're on Your Own

A second reason why people choose a sales career is the freedom it offers. A sales job provides possibly the greatest relative freedom of any career. Experienced employees in outside sales usually receive little direct supervision and may go for days, even weeks, without seeing their bosses.*

---

*Outside sales usually are conducted off the employer's premises and involve person-to-person contact. Inside sales occur on the premises, as in retail and telephone contact sales.

Job duties and sales goals are explained by a manager. Salespeople are expected to carry out their job duties and achieve goals with minimum guidance. They usually leave home to contact customers around the corner or around the world.

Job Challenge Is Always There

Working alone with the responsibility of a territory capable of generating thousands (sometimes millions) of dollars in revenue for your company is a personal challenge. This environment adds great variety to a sales job. Salespeople often deal with hundreds of different people and firms over time. It is much like operating your own business without the burdens of true ownership.

Opportunities for Advancement Are Great

Successful salespeople have many opportunities to move into top management positions. In many instances, this advancement comes quickly.

A sales personnel **career path,** as Exhibit 1.6 depicts, is the upward sequence of job movements during a sales career. Occasionally, people without previous sales experience are promoted into sales management positions. However, 99 percent of the time, a career in sales management begins with an entry-level sales position. Firms believe that an experienced sales professional has the credibility, knowledge, and background to assume a higher position in the company.

Most companies have two or three successive levels of sales positions, beginning at the junior or trainee level. Beginning as a salesperson allows a person to

Sales skills are in demand by employers.

- Learn about the attitudes and activities of the company's salespeople.
- Become familiar with customer attitudes toward the company, its products, and its salespeople.
- Gain firsthand knowledge of products and their application, which is most important in technical sales.
- Become seasoned in the business world.

When asked why they like their jobs, first-line sales managers say it is because of the rewards. By rewards, they mean both financial rewards and nonfinancial rewards, such as the great challenge and the feeling of making a valuable contribution to their salespeople and the company. Managers also frequently mention that this position represents their first major step toward the top. They have made the cut and are on the management team. Instead of having responsibility for $1 million in sales, as a salesperson does, the manager is responsible for $10 million.

With success, various jobs throughout the sales force and in the corporate marketing department open up. This can include sales training, sales analysis, advertising, and product management. Frequently, traveling the upward career path involves numerous moves from field sales to corporate sales, back to the field, then to corporate, back to the field, and so on. However, sales experience prepares people for more responsible jobs in the company.

Success also creates financial rewards. The larger a company's revenues, the heavier the responsibility of the chief executive, and the larger the compensation. Today, it's common for a CEO of a large national corporation to receive compensation totaling more than $1 million annually.

Leaving aside compensation at the top echelons, both corporate and field sales managers typically receive higher salaries than others (such as production, advertising,

EXHIBIT 1.6

A sales personnel career path.

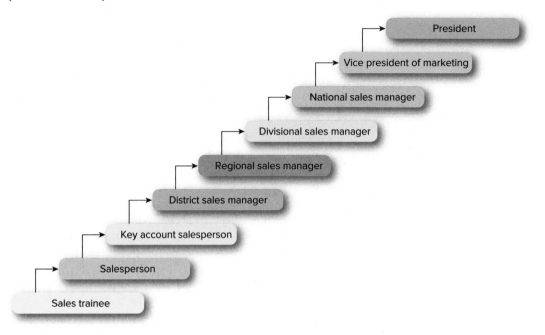

product, or personnel managers) at the same organizational level. Salary is just one part of compensation. Many firms offer elaborate packages that include extended vacation and holiday periods; pension programs; health, accident, and legal insurance programs; automobiles and auto expenses; payment of professional association dues; educational assistance for themselves and sometimes for their families; financial planning assistance; company airplanes; home and entertainment expenses; and free country club membership. The higher the sales position, the greater the benefits offered. In addition to performance, salary typically is related to the following factors:

- Annual sales volume of units managed.
- Number of salespeople managed.
- Length of experience in sales.
- Annual sales volume of the firm.

Rewards: The Sky's the Limit

As a salesperson, you can look forward to two types of rewards—nonfinancial and financial.

Nonfinancial Rewards

Sometimes called psychological income or intrinsic rewards, nonfinancial rewards are generated by the individual, not given by the company. You know the job has been done well—for instance, when you have helped the buyer through the purchase of your product.

Successfully meeting the challenges of the job produces a feeling of self-worth. You realize your job is important. Everyone wants to feel good about their job, and a

Many people appreciate the freedom that a sales career offers.

selling career allows you to experience these good feelings and intrinsic rewards daily. Salespeople often report that the nonfinancial rewards of their jobs are just as important to them as financial rewards.

After training, a salesperson is often given responsibility for a sales territory. The person then moves into a regular sales position. In a short time, the salesperson can earn the status and financial rewards of a senior sales position by contacting the larger, more important customers. Some companies refer to this function as a *key account sales position.*

There Are Two Career Paths

Don't let Exhibit 1.6 mislead you—many salespeople prefer selling over managing people. They want to take care of themselves rather than others. In some companies, a salesperson may earn more money than even the manager, even the firm's president.

Many companies recognize the value of keeping some salespeople in the field for their entire sales career. They do a good job, know their customers, and love what they are doing—so why promote them if they do not want to move up within the organization? However, many other people work hard to move into management.

You Can Move Quickly into Management

The first managerial level is usually the district sales manager's position. It is common for people to be promoted to this position within two or three years after joining the company. From district sales manager, a person may move into higher levels of sales management.

Financial Rewards

Many are attracted to selling because in a sales career financial rewards are commonly based solely on performance. Many professional salespeople have opportunities to earn large salaries. Their salaries average even higher than salaries for other types of workers at the same organizational level.

Is a Sales Career Right for You?

It may be too early in life to determine if you really want to be a salesperson. The balance of this book will aid you in investigating sales as a career. Your search for any career begins with you. In considering a sales career, be honest and realistic. Ask yourself questions such as these:

- Can I manage myself?
- Do I enjoy flexibility?
- What types of problems do I like to solve?
- What are my past accomplishments?
- What are my future goals?
- Do I want to have the responsibility of a sales job?
- Do I mind travel? How much travel is acceptable?
- How much freedom do I want in the job?
- Do I have the personality characteristics for the job?
- Am I willing to transfer to another city? Another state?

> *A sales education provides you with an opportunity to differentiate yourself from other candidates and an entry into organizations that want your skill set.*

Your answers to these questions can help you analyze the various types of sales jobs and establish criteria for evaluating job openings. Determine the industries, types of products or services, and specific companies in which you have an interest.

College placement offices, libraries, and business periodicals offer a wealth of information on companies as well as sales positions in them. Conversations with friends and acquaintances who are involved within selling, or have been in sales, can give you realistic insight into what challenges, rewards, and disadvantages the sales vocation offers. To better prepare yourself to obtain a sales job, you must understand what companies look for in salespeople.

Success in Selling—What Does it Take?

Over the years, We have asked many salespeople and sales managers the question "What helps make a salesperson successful?" The answer is contained in the words *love, success,* and *person,* as in the phrase "a person who loves success." As these words will indicate, to be a good salesperson today it helps to be a good person.

We know students love phrases and acronyms to help them remember. That is why we use them here to help you remember and better understand what selling in today's business environment requires. As Exhibit 1.7 shows, the seven most frequently mentioned characteristics necessary to be successful in sales can be found in the word *success* itself:

S—Service to Others

The successful salesperson is an individual who loves selling, finds it exciting, and is strongly convinced that the product being sold offers something of great value. Today's salespeople make a contribution to the welfare of others through *service.* They are dream makers. They sell solutions to people's needs that make their dreams come true. Salespeople love to help others fulfill their needs through selling their products.

EXHIBIT 1.7

Salespeople should know the meaning of SUCCESS.

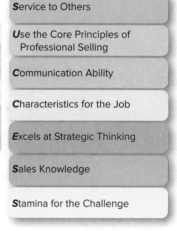

Service to Others

Use the Core Principles of Professional Selling

Communication Ability

Characteristics for the Job

Excels at Strategic Thinking

Sales Knowledge

Stamina for the Challenge

©g-stockstudio/Shutterstock

When things go wrong as they sometimes will,
When the road you're trudging seems all uphill,
When the funds are low and the debts are high,
And you want to smile but you have to sigh,
When care is pressing you down a bit—
Rest if you must, but don't you quit.
Life is queer with its twists and turns,
As every one of us sometimes learns,
And many a person turns about
When they might have won had they stuck it out.

Don't give up though the pace seems slow—
You may succeed with another blow.
Often the struggler has given up
When he might have captured the victor's cup;
And he learned too late
When the night came down,
How close he was to the golden crown.
Success is failure turned inside out—
So stick to the fight when you're hardest hit—
It's when things seem worst that you mustn't quit.[9]

U—Use the Core Principles of Professional Selling

If salespeople do not know how to place the customer's needs first, how can they build a long-term relationship? People like to buy, not be sold. And they like to buy from people they know and trust. That is one reason today's salesperson needs to treat others as he or she would like to be treated.

C—Communication Ability

Good salespeople are good communicators. Great salespeople are great communicators. Whether it involves nonverbal or verbal communications, as discussed in Chapter 4, top salespeople speak the other person's language.

C—Characteristics for the Job

Can anyone be a successful salesperson? It helps to reach that goal if you possess the personal characteristics needed for a sales career. These characteristics are discussed after the remaining work characteristics are introduced. Let's continue our discussion of those work characteristics now.

E—Excels at Strategic Thinking

The sixth work characteristic is that high-performing salespeople tend to be strategic problem solvers for their customers. They can match up their product's benefits with the customer's needs. Strategic customer sales planning is discussed more in Chapter 7.

S—Sales Knowledge at the MD Level

Top professional salespeople have mastered the basic competencies of selling, which include product knowledge (see Chapter 5) and selling skills. As goods and services become more complex, companies place greater emphasis on training their salespeople and on salespeople training themselves. Salespeople must be experts on everything involved with their products, as a medical doctor is an expert. Recent research suggests that salespeople will increasingly assume a role as a knowledge broker.[10] Remember, however, that knowledge is power, but enthusiasm pulls the switch.

S—Stamina for the Challenge of Consistent Adapting

Effective salespeople must be able to adapt to multiple environments, varied types of customers, and distinct business challenges. Today's salesperson needs to be physically, mentally, and spiritually prepared to meet the daily challenges of a sales career. Body, mind, and soul play an important role in the level of a person's stamina. With physical preparedness comes mental strength. Exercise, for example, elevates your mood by increasing energy and simultaneously secreting adrenaline-like substances in the body that act as stimulants and antidepressants, according to the medical community. This increased feeling of well-being transmits itself to the body and mind. In this stressed-out world we all need stress relief. Exercise can help!

Kenneth H. Cooper MD, often referred to as the father of aerobics, says, "It is easier to maintain good health through proper exercise, diet, and emotional balance than to regain it once it is lost."[11] Aerobics, strength training, and stretching are wonderful tools to reduce stress, help you feel better, focus better, and have more energy. If you are not actively using these techniques, try them for three months. Find out how exercise can help you! Be sure to check with your doctor; however, before starting any exercise program.

For many people, personal spirituality or religious beliefs have a great impact upon physical and mental stamina and thus job performance. This is especially true if they feel their sales career is a calling. People's faith may direct everything they do on the job, ranging from how they treat customers to how ethically they act toward their employer.

C—Characteristics for the Job Examined[†]

We skipped over the personal characteristics needed for a sales career earlier. Let's discuss them now. Certainly any discussion of what it takes to be successful in a sales job has to include the person's personal characteristics. As we have described selling, the salesperson wants to help people and thus build a long-term relationship. The question has been asked "How do you sell someone something and remain business friends?" A salesperson can choose to be like the traditional salesperson we all disparage or the salesperson who is truly people oriented.

How do you sell to someone and remain his or her friend? Remember the Core Principles?

Caring, Joy, Harmony

The most important characteristic of a *success*ful salesperson is a **caring** attitude—caring about the customer's best interest. Successful salespeople care about everything connected with their work and life. Without caring, it's difficult—if not impossible—to possess the other eight characteristics of a successful salesperson. See Exhibit 1.8.

There is great **joy** in truly caring for one's customers, and this joy motivates a salesperson to care for customers continuously. Because the salesperson is concerned

[†] See the Glossary at the end of this book for an explanation of key terms in this section.

EXHIBIT 1.8

Triangle showing the nine personal characteristics needed to be a successful sales professional.

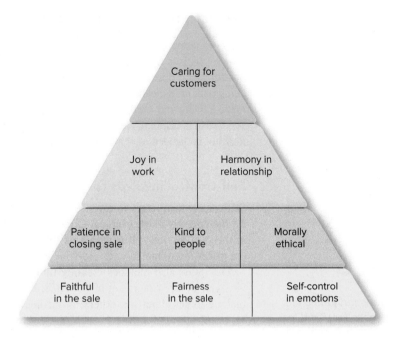

with what is best for the customer, there is a sense of peace or **harmony** in the relationship. The customer can trust the salesperson, so all fear of being taken advantage of is removed.

Patience, Kindness, Moral Ethics

Salespeople are often under pressure to make the sale today! They need to be able to handle the pressure to sell *now* using **patience** in their working relationship with the customer. Let the customer decide when to buy instead of pressuring for a quick decision. A buyer needs information to make an educated decision. Often this takes time and great patience. Patience in closing the sale goes a long way toward building a long-term relationship. Buyers do not like to be pressured into making a quick decision. Do you? We don't! Because people like to buy, not be sold.

Your actions speak louder than your words. People want to see you "walk the talk, not talk the talk." Having patience shows that the salesperson understands the customer's needs and wants to help. This is a display of **kindness.** A kind person is patient and compassionate. Salespeople must be kind to their customers in order to show that they aren't interested solely in making the sale. Remember, we are interested in following the Core Principles of Professional Selling—acting in the best interest of others, not just making sales. A salesperson who follows the Core Principles is a **morally ethical** individual whom the customer can trust.

Faithful, Fair, Self-Control

A salesperson who cares, likes the job, is good to work with, and is patient, kind, and morally ethical is certainly someone who will be **faithful** in taking care of customers. The salesperson will spend the time necessary to help, not just make the sale and never be heard from again until the next sales call. We all want to be thought of as ethical. Faithfulness is an ethical virtue. It shows the employer, customers, and competitors that the salesperson is **fair** to all. Customers can trust this salesperson.

Today's professional salesperson works to be perceived as a consultant, partner, and problem solver for his or her customer. The salesperson's goal is to build a long-term relationship with clients.

Self-Control Is Most Difficult

Now we come to **self-control,** which is the most difficult trait for a salesperson to develop. This is why we discuss it last. Self-control involves restraining our emotions, passions, and desires usually for self-gain. How do salespeople control themselves by being patient in closing the sale, for example? Remember, the salesperson must sell to make a living and keep the job. Thus, there is considerable incentive for the salesperson to use pressure or lie, for example, to compel the customer to buy something that may not be needed or that is falsely represented.

Self-Control Involves Discipline

Self-control also refers to the needed discipline to rise early, work late, and prepare for the next day in the evening. Often the biggest challenge to success is not out there in the sales territory; it is within us. We cannot achieve unless we are willing to pay the price—discipline.

Work and family life balance is critical for success in selling.

Discipline also includes creating time for family—parents, spouse, and children. So often we are caught up in the American way of wanting to be rich and famous that we forget about the others in our life. Instead we must discipline ourselves to set priorities. Setting priorities requires willpower many of us do not have. Misplacing priorities and not balancing work and life demands contributes significantly to a salesperson's failure. Self-control and discipline are thus very important personal characteristics for all of us, no matter what our careers.

As you see, the list of personal characteristics needed to be a good salesperson in today's marketplace is a long one. No doubt your instructor will add to this list, and you undoubtedly will think of other characteristics as well. These characteristics make salespeople good citizens in the business world. However, sadly, it seems that all of us do not have the ability or desire to place the customer first.

One of the Kindest People

Many years ago a man named John Wesley, known as one of the kindest men who ever walked on earth, talked about a simple rule of life. Wesley said he tried to "Do all the good he can by all the means he can in all the places he can at all the times he can to all the people he can as long as ever he can."[12] How would you like to deal with a salesperson who followed both Wesley's rule of life and the Core Principles? We would love to!

Relationship Selling

Salespeople are no longer adversaries who manipulate people for personal gain. They want to be consultants, partners, and problem solvers for customers. Their goal is to build a long-term relationship with clients. Salespeople seek to benefit their employer, themselves, and customers.

In recent years, the distinction between a salesperson and a professional has blurred because the salesperson of today is a pro. Many salespeople know more about their field and product than the buyer. This expertise enables the seller to become the buyer's partner, a counselor on how to solve problems. Today's salesperson professionally provides information that helps customers make intelligent actions to achieve their short- and long-term objectives. Service and follow-up are

EXHIBIT 1.9

The customer is at the center of the sales solar system.

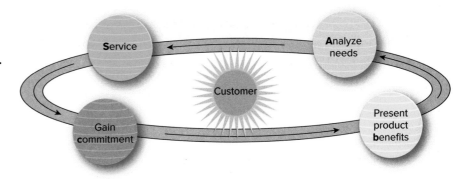

then provided to ensure satisfaction with the purchase. This builds *customer loyalty*—a relationship.

Exhibit 1.9 shows the four main elements in the customer relationship process used by salespeople to build long-term relationships. To help you remember these four elements think of your book's title. The letters *ABCS* stand for **a**nalyze, **b**enefits, **c**ommitment, and service. Salespeople analyze customer needs, present product benefits, and gain commitment for the purchase. They provide excellent service in order to maintain and grow the relationship. Customer product and service satisfactions give the salesperson the opportunity to restart the sales cycle by continuing to analyze customer needs.

Sales Jobs Are Different

As you can see, sales jobs are different from other jobs in several ways. Here are some major differences:

- Salespeople represent their companies to the outside world. Consequently, opinions of a company and its products are often formed from impressions left by the sales force. The public ordinarily does not judge a firm by its office or factory workers.
- Other employees usually work under close supervisory control, whereas the outside salesperson typically operates with little or no direct supervision. Moreover, to be successful, salespeople must often be creative, persistent, and show great initiative—all of which require a high degree of motivation.
- Salespeople probably need more tact, diplomacy, and social poise than other employees in an organization. Many sales jobs require the salesperson to display considerable emotional and social intelligence in dealing with buyers.
- Salespeople are among the few employees authorized to spend company funds. They spend this money for entertainment, transportation, and other business expenses.
- Some sales jobs frequently require considerable traveling and time spent away from home and family. At times, salespeople deal with customers who seem determined not to buy the sellers' products. These challenges, coupled with the physical demands of long hours and traveling, require mental toughness and physical stamina rarely demanded in other types of jobs.

Selling is challenging work! It requires intelligence, the desire to achieve, and the ability to overcome difficulties.

- Customers are the most important people in any business.
- Customers are not dependent on us. We are dependent on them.
- Customers are not an interruption of our work. They are the purpose of it.
- Customers do us a favor in doing business with us. We aren't doing customers a favor by waiting on them.
- Customers are part of our business—not outsiders. Customers are not just money in the cash register.

- Customers are human beings with feelings, and they deserve to be treated with respect.
- Customers are people who come to us with needs and wants. It is our job to fill them.
- Customers deserve the most courteous attention we can give them.
- Customers are the lifeblood of this and every business. Customers pay your salary. Without customers we would have to close our doors.
- Don't ever forget it![13]

What Does a Professional Salesperson Do?

The salesperson's roles or activities can vary from company to company, depending on whether sales involve goods or services, the firm's market characteristics, and the location of customers. For example, a salesperson selling Avon products performs similar, but somewhat different, job activities than the industrial salesperson making sales calls for General Electric.

Most people believe that a salesperson only makes sales presentations, but there is much more to the job than person-to-person selling. The salesperson functions as a **territory manager**—planning, organizing, and executing activities that increase sales and profits in a given territory. A sales territory comprises a group of customers often assigned within a geographical area. Exhibit 1.10 indicates a few typical activities of a salesperson. As manager of a territory, the salesperson performs the following nine functions:

1. **Creates New Customers.** In order to increase sales and replace customers that will be lost over time, many types of sales jobs require a salesperson to prospect. Prospecting is the lifeblood of sales because it identifies potential customers. Salespeople locate people and/or organizations that have the potential to buy their products. The salespeople need the ability to close, or make, the sale.
2. **Sells More to Present Customers.** Tomorrow's sales come from selling to new customers and selling to present customers again . . . and again . . . and again.
3. **Builds Long-Term Relationships with Customers.** Earning the opportunity to sell a present customer more product means the salesperson must have a positive, professional business relationship with people and organizations that trust the salesperson and the products purchased.
4. **Provides Solutions to Customers' Problems.** Customers have needs that can be met and problems that can be solved by purchasing goods or services. Salespeople

EXHIBIT 1.10

A professional salesperson . . .

©Monkey Business Images/Shutterstock

. . . helps meet the needs and solve the problems of the customer.

©Monkey Business Images/Getty Images

. . . makes presentations to new and current customers.

©Erik Isakson/Blend Images LLC

. . . sells to wholesalers and distributors.

©Monkey Business Images/Shutterstock

. . . handles customer complaints.

seek to uncover potential or existing needs or problems and show how the use of their products or services can satisfy needs or solve problems.

5. **Provides Service to Customers.** Salespeople provide a wide range of services, including handling complaints, returning damaged merchandise, providing samples, suggesting business opportunities, and developing recommendations on how the customer can promote products purchased from the salesperson.

   If necessary, salespeople may occasionally work at the customer's business. For example, a salesperson selling fishing tackle may arrange an in-store demonstration of a manufacturer's products and offer to repair fishing reels as a service to the retailer's customers. Furthermore, a manufacturer may have its salespeople sell to distributors or wholesalers. Then, the manufacturer's representative may make sales calls with the distributor's salespeople to aid them in selling and providing service for the distributor's customers.

6. **Helps Customers Resell Products to Their Customers.** A major part of many sales jobs is for the salesperson to help wholesalers and retailers resell the products

that they have purchased. The salesperson helps wholesale customers sell products to retail customers and helps retail customers sell products to consumers.

Consider the Quaker Oats salesperson selling a product to grocery wholesalers. Not only must the wholesaler be contacted but also grocery retailers must be called on, sales made, and orders written up and sent to the wholesaler. In turn, the wholesaler sells and delivers the products to the retailers. The Quaker Oats salesperson also develops promotional programs to help the retailer sell the firm's products. These programs involve supplying advertising materials, conducting store demonstrations, and setting up product displays.

7. **Helps Customers Use Products after Purchase.** The salesperson's job is not over after the sale is made. Often, customers must be shown how to obtain full benefit from the product. For example, after a customer buys a computer system, technical specialists help the buyer learn how to operate the equipment.

8. **Builds Goodwill with Customers.** A selling job is people oriented, entailing face-to-face contact with the customer. Many sales are based, to some extent, on friendship and trust. The salesperson needs to develop a personal, friendly, business-like relationship with everyone who may influence a buying decision. This ongoing part of the salesperson's job requires integrity, high ethical standards, and a sincere interest in satisfying customers' needs.

9. **Provides Company with Market Information.** Salespeople provide information to their companies on such topics as competitors' activities, customers' reactions to new products, complaints about products or policies, market opportunities, and their job activities. This information is so important for many companies that their salespeople are required to send in weekly or monthly reports on activities of the firm's competition in their territory. Salespeople are a vital part of their employers' marketing intelligence system.

Reflect Back

Review the nine functions shown in Exhibit 1.11 to see what they mean and if you could do any or all of them. Carefully think about the second and third functions. To be successful, a salesperson must close sales and build relationships with the same person and/or organization in order to sell more. To do both is challenging to any person. It requires the salesperson to do the other functions: solve problems, provide service, help resell, teach how to use the purchase, build goodwill, and keep your employer up-to-date on customers' needs and feelings toward product and service.

Your book is about these nine functions and much more. When combined and properly implemented, these nine job activities produce increased sales for the

EXHIBIT 1.11

What does a professional salesperson do?

1. Creates new customers.
2. Sells more to present customers.
3. Builds long-term relationships with customers.
4. Provides solutions to customers' problems.
5. Provides service to customers.
6. Helps customers resell products to their customers.
7. Helps customers use products after purchase.
8. Builds goodwill with customers.
9. Provides company with market information.

You are responsible for sales coverage, time, and budget. Help is available and you'll have plenty of marketing and service support; but you're expected to work independently, without constant direction.

Your day is devoted primarily to customer contact. Potential customers may phone the branch and ask to see a Xerox representative. More likely, however, you will acquire customers by making appointments or by visiting businesses to meet the decision-makers, discuss their needs, and offer solutions to their problems. As part of your position, you'll make product presentations, either at the Xerox branch office or at the customer's office. You will also spend a fair amount of time on the telephone following up leads, arranging appointments, and speaking with managers in a variety of businesses and organizations.

In working with customers, you'll need to solve a number of problems. What Xerox product best fits the customer's needs? How do Xerox products compare with the competition? Should the machine be purchased or leased? What's the total cash outlay—and per-copy cost—for the machine and its service? How should the product be financed? Where should the machine be placed for maximum efficiency? What training is needed for employees? How can Xerox products meet future office needs?

You'll also be engaged in a number of customer support activities, such as expediting product deliveries, checking credit, writing proposals, and training customer employees in the use of the product. You also might refer customers to other Xerox sales organizations and make joint calls with representatives from these organizations.

Each day will bring you new challenges to face and problems to solve. Your days will be busy and interesting.[14]

organization and more rewards for the salesperson. An example of how a salesperson integrates these activities will help you better understand the sales job (see the Making the Sale box).

Build a Professional Reputation

This book stresses the concept of sales professionalism. Sales professionalism directly implies that you are a professional person—due the respect and ready for the responsibilities that accompany the title. In speaking before a large class of marketing students, one sales manager for a large college textbook publishing company continually emphasized the concept of sales professionalism. This man stated that a professional sales position is not just an 8-to-5 job. It is a professional and responsible position promising both unlimited opportunity and numerous duties. This veteran sales manager emphasized that a sales job is an especially good vocational opportunity because people are looking for "someone we can believe in; someone who will do what she says—a sales professional."

To be viewed as a professional and respected by your customers and competitors, consider these eight important points:

1. Be truthful and follow through on what you tell the customer. Do not dispose of your conscience when you start work each day.
2. Maintain an intimate knowledge of your firm, its products, and your industry. Participate in your company's sales training and take continuing education courses.

3. Speak well of others, including your company and competitors.
4. Keep customer information confidential; maintain a professional relationship with each account.
5. Never take advantage of a customer by using unfair, high-pressure techniques.
6. Be active in community affairs and help better your community. For example, live in your territory, be active in public schools, and join worthwhile organizations such as the Lions Club, the Chamber of Commerce, environmental organizations, and so forth.
7. Think of yourself as a professional and always act like one. Have a professional attitude about yourself and your customers.
8. Provide service "above and beyond the call of duty." Remember that it is easier to maintain a relationship than to begin one. What was worth attaining is worth preserving. Remember, when you do not pay attention to customers, they find someone who will. The professional salesperson never forgets a customer after the sale.

Understanding Your Buyer's Expectations of Professionalism

Effective sales professionals understand their customers' perceptions. For instance, a survey asked purchasing agents what they did not like salespeople to do during sales calls. The results, shown in Exhibit 1.12, are "the seven deadly sins of business selling."[15]

Purchasing agents want salespeople to act professionally, to be well trained, to be prepared for each sales call, and to keep the sales call related to how the salesperson

EXHIBIT 1.12

The seven deadly sins of business selling.

1. *Lack of product knowledge.* Salespeople must know their own product line as well as the buyer's line or nothing productive can occur.
2. *Time wasting.* Unannounced sales visits are a nuisance. When salespeople start droning on about golf or grandchildren, more time is wasted.
3. *Poor planning.* A routine sales call must be preceded by some homework—see if it's necessary.
4. *Pushiness.* This includes prying to find out a competitor's prices, an overwhelming attitude, and not taking 'no' for an answer.
5. *Lack of dependability.* Failure to stand behind the product, keep communications clear, and honor promises.
6. *Unprofessional conduct.* Knocking competitors, drinking excessively at a business lunch, sloppy dress, and poor taste aren't professional.
7. *Unlimited optimism.* Honesty is preferred to the hallmark of the good news bearers who promise anything to get an order. Never promise more than you can deliver.

Here are a few comments purchasing agents made on these deadly sins:

- They take it personally if they don't get the business; it's as though you owe them something because they constantly call on you.
- I don't like it when they blast through the front door like know-it-alls and put on an unsolicited dog-and-pony show that will guarantee cost saving off in limbo somewhere.
- Many salespeople will give you any delivery you want, book an order, and then let you face the results of their "short quote."
- They try to sell *you,* rather than the product.
- After the order is won, the honeymoon is over.
- Beware the humble pest who is too nice to insult, won't take a hint, won't listen to blunt advice, and is selling a product you neither use nor want to use, yet won't go away.

EXHIBIT 1.13

B. J. Hughes's checklists of do's and don'ts help it to be a customer-oriented company.

Salesperson's Checklist of Do's	Salesperson's Checklist of Don'ts
1. Know the current products/services and their applications in your area. Look for the new techniques/services your customers want.	1. Never bluff; if you don't know, find out.
2. Maintain an up-to-date personal call list.	2. Never compromise your, or anyone else's, morals or principles.
3. Listen attentively to the customers.	3. Don't be presumptuous—never with friends.
4. Seek out specific problems and the improvements your customers want.	4. Never criticize a competitor—especially to a customer.
5. Keep calls short unless invited to stay.	5. Do not take criticisms or turndowns personally—they're seldom meant that way.
6. Leave a calling card if the customer is not in.	6. Do not worry or agonize over what you cannot control or influence. Be concerned about what you can affect.
7. Identify the individual who makes or influences decisions, and concentrate on that person.	7. Do not offend others with profanity.
8. Entertain selectively; your time and your expense account are investments.	8. Do not allow idle conversation to dominate your sales call. Concentrate on your purpose.
9. Make written notes as reminders.	9. Don't try to match the customer drink for drink when entertaining. Drink only if you want to and in moderation.
10. Plan work by the week, not by the clock. Plan use of available time. Plan sales presentations. Have a purpose.	10. Don't be so focused that you use high-pressure tactics.
11. Ask for business on every sales call.	11. Never talk your company down—especially to customers. Be proud of it and yourself.
12. Follow through with appropriate action.	

can help the buyer. Professional selling starts in the salesperson's firm. A professional attitude from the firm employing the salesperson reinforces professionalism among the sales force. One such company is B. J. Hughes, a division of the Hughes Tool Company. B. J. Hughes manufactures and sells oil-field equipment and services to companies in the oil and gas industry. Exhibit 1.13 presents Hughes's checklists of do's and don'ts for its salespeople. By providing these checklists, the company encourages them to act professionally.

The Future for Salespeople

One final thought: In an uncertain and rapidly changing world, how do you learn to be a salesperson? More specifically, how does a course in selling prepare you to become a salesperson ready to face the 21st century?

Learning Selling Skills

Selling is an art and a science.

Selling is both an art and a science. It is an art because many skills cannot be learned solely from a textbook. Selling takes practice, just like golf or tennis. Studying a book helps, but it is not enough. Many skills—such as understanding buyers' nonverbal communication messages, listening, handling objections, and closing—take practice. These skills are learned through experience, training, and the ongoing application of your understanding and skill set.

Selling is also a science because a growing body of knowledge and objective facts describes selling. Becoming a successful salesperson requires a blend of formal learning and practice, of science and art. Practice alone used to be enough to learn how to sell, but no longer. Formal course work in sales can help a salesperson become more competent and be prepared for the challenges of the future. The study of selling helps people see and understand things about sales that others cannot. Training helps salespeople acquire the conceptual, human, and technical skills necessary for selling; this asset results in a salesperson earning more income over a lifetime.

As we see throughout this book, because a salesperson's job is diverse and complex, it requires a range of skills. Although some authors propose a long list of skills, the necessary skills can be summarized in three categories that are especially important: conceptual, human, and technical.

Conceptual Skills

Conceptual skill is the cognitive ability to see the selling process as a whole and the relationship among its parts. Conceptual skill involves the seller's thinking and planning abilities. It involves knowing where one's product fits into the customer's business or how the beginning of a sales presentation relates to asking for the order. Conceptual skills allow the seller to "think strategically"—to understand the product, presentation, buyer, and purchaser's organization.

Although all sellers need conceptual skills, they are especially important for the creative order-getters. They must perceive significant elements in a situation and broad, conceptual patterns.

Human Skills

Human skill is the seller's ability to work with and through other people.

Human skill is the seller's ability to work with and through other people. Salespeople demonstrate this skill in the way they relate to other people, including customers or people within their own organizations. One key human skill is the ability to adapt to the customer. Salesperson adaptability describes the ability of salespeople to understand the appropriateness of their sales actions and the ability to modify their sales actions based on the situation.[16] A seller with human skills likes other people and is liked by them. Sellers who lack human skills often are abrupt, critical, and unsympathetic. Pushy and arrogant, they are not responsive to others' needs.

Technical Skills

Technical skill is the understanding of and proficiency in the performance of specific tasks. Technical skill includes mastery of the methods, techniques, and equipment involved in selling—such as presentation skills and uses for one's products. Technical skill includes specialized knowledge, analytical ability, and the competent use of tools and techniques to solve problems in that specific discipline.

Preparing for a Future in Sales

Over the next few years, new forces will shape sales careers (see Exhibit 1.14). Salespeople will continue to rely heavily on their technical, human, and conceptual skills; however, they will apply them in different ways. Major changes occurring today will continue to occur in the distant future and require salespeople to be knowledgeable in areas they didn't need to know about only a few years ago, including technology.

EXHIBIT 1.14

The American sales force is becoming diversified. Millions of sales jobs provide room for everyone in a sales career!

©digitalskillet/Getty Images

There is one giant megatrend now forming in America you should know about. It will influence your future.

An Ethical Megatrend Is Shaping Sales and Business

Patricia Aburdene's *Megatrends 2010: The Rise of Conscious Capitalism* details new forces that will shape salespeople's jobs. Care to guess what the number one megatrend happening in America is? "Spirituality is today's greatest megatrend," says Aburdene. "Spirituality in business, having quietly blossomed for decades, is an established trend that's about to morph into a megatrend. Where is this taking us?" she asks.

Aburdene says that "if greed, fraud and speculation got America into the crisis of capitalism we see today, it is going to take character, trust and spiritual leadership to get us out. The spirituality in business trend will foster each of those traits—and lift our hearts in the process."[17]

As humans, we have a deep personal need for meaning in our lives and a need to make contributions to society. We should ask ourselves serious, personal questions such as

1. Who am I?
2. Why am I here?
3. What should I do with my life?
4. What do I have to offer?
5. Does anyone else feel like I do?

Recognizing workers' personal needs, organizations are slowly reinventing free enterprise to honor stakeholders and shareholders. They are applying the Core Principles to the workplace to provide employees meaningful work that relates to their personal needs, such as those emphasized by the previous questions. People are eager to work for an organization that markets quality products at fair prices using truthful promotion, and people love to buy from sellers who follow the Core Principles.

Technology and Information Build Relationships

©scanrail/123RF

©Rawpixel.com/Shutterstock

In this textbook you were introduced to the importance that knowledge plays in helping the salesperson fulfill the role of business consultant and how customers expect salespeople to be more knowledgeable than ever before. This creates a tremendous challenge for the salesperson in that the information and knowledge needed to properly sell and service perhaps several hundred customers within the sales territory have expanded well beyond what any individual could possibly know. Salespeople need more information about goods, services, customers, and competitors than ever before.

Often the need to gather and organize information lengthens the sales process. Also, the growing emphasis on team selling and group buying makes it critical to share information quickly and accurately among a wide variety of people who influence the customer's buying decision.

The good news is that technology has exploded the boundaries of today's knowledge frontiers. Salespeople have access to almost any conceivable piece of information or data. Technology is making it possible to improve a person's sales and service performance (see Exhibit 1.15). Laptop computers, tablets, phones, and videoconferencing have become popular sales tools. The salesperson has truly gone high tech. Not only is sales and inventory information transferred much faster, but also specific computerized decision support systems have been created for sales managers and sales representatives.

The goal is to help salespeople increase the speed with which they can find and qualify leads, gather information prior to a customer presentation, reduce their paperwork, report new sales to the company, and service customers after the sale. Computer technology has provided the answer (see Exhibit 1.15).

Technology is expensive. Hardware, software, and training take a large investment. Yet companies believe it is worth the cost because of decreased travel and paperwork,

EXHIBIT 1.15

Technology is enabling salespeople to do a better job selling and servicing their customers.

©Ariel Skelley/Blend Images LLC

Videoconferencing is excellent for presentations and training.

©Anatolii Babii/Alamy Images

Mobile technology is essential for customer relationship management.

more productive sales calls, and better customer service. Chapter 5 has further discussions on the sales automation tools in general and Customer Relationship Management (CRM) technology in particular that salespeople use to build, sustain, and grow relationships.

Selling Is for Large and Small Organizations

©Odua Images/Shutterstock

Many textbook examples are from big business. This is typically because readers recognize Ford Motor Company or McDonald's. Even though America's large organizations are easily recognizable and extremely important to our prosperity, it is easy to overestimate the importance of big business because of its greater visibility. Small firms, even though less conspicuous, are a vital component of our economy.

Small business contributes significantly to our economy. The Small Business Administration classifies approximately 98 percent of all business in the United States—sole proprietorships, partnerships, corporations, part-time businesses, and unincorporated professional activities—as small businesses.

Small enterprises run the gamut from a corner news vendor to a developer of optical fibers. Small business people sell gasoline, flowers, and coffee to go. They publish magazines, haul freight, teach languages, and program computers. They make wines, motion pictures, and high-fashion clothes. They build new homes and restore old ones. They repair plumbing, fix appliances, recycle metals, and sell used cars. They drive taxicabs, run cranes, and fly helicopters. They drill for oil, quarry sand and gravel, and mine exotic ores. They forge, cast, weld, photoengrave, electroplate, and anodize. They also invent antipollution devices, quality control mechanisms, energy-saving techniques, microelectronic systems—a complete list would go on for volumes.

Often, small business entrepreneurs cannot compete head-to-head with giant firms. However, most large firms started small, and then prospered by using many of the concepts, ideas, and practices discussed in this textbook. Because of this fact, we use small business as examples throughout this textbook.

The Plan of this Textbook

Professional selling and the sales job are much more than you might have imagined. The plan of your textbook provides you with the ABC's of what selling is all about. Some of the major topics you will study include

- The social, ethical, and legal issues in selling.
- Why people and organizations buy what they do.
- Verbal and nonverbal communications.
- The importance of knowing your and your competition's products.
- An in-depth discussion of the selling process.
- Self-, time, and sales territory management.

Salespeople are managers of the sales generated from their customers. There is much to know if you want to be a successful sales professional. There is even more to know once you are promoted to the sales manager's job.

Building Relationships Through the Sales Process

*The **sales process:** the salesperson's sequential series of actions that leads toward the customer taking a desired action and ends with a follow-up to ensure purchase satisfaction*

Much of your course will revolve around the sales process. The **sales process** refers to the salesperson's sequential series of actions that leads toward the customer taking a desired action and ends with a follow-up to ensure purchase satisfaction. This desired action by a prospect is usually buying, which is the most important action. Such desired actions also can include advertising, displaying, or reducing the price of the product to their customers.

Although many factors may influence how a salesperson makes a presentation in any situation, following a logical, sequential series of actions can greatly increase the chances of making a sale. This selling process involves 10 basic steps as briefly listed in Exhibit 1.16. The following chapters discuss each of these steps in greater detail.

Before a sales presentation is attempted, several important preparatory activities should occur. This involves prospecting and planning the sales presentation, as shown in Exhibit 1.16.

The following describes a basic sales presentation as shown in Exhibit 1.16. Remember that the person may be ready to buy at any time—such as when you walk into the office, early in the presentation, or sometime in the future. Occasionally, you will not be required to go through your entire presentation, especially if you have had

EXHIBIT 1.16

Ten important steps in the selling process.

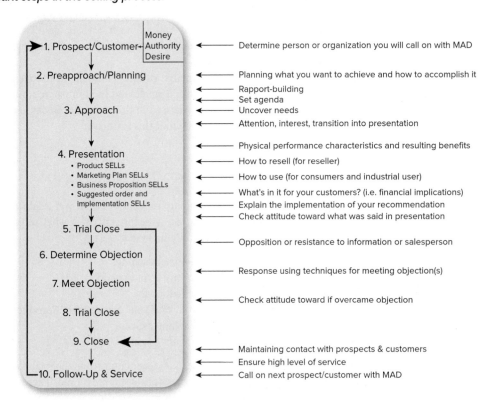

As you come to the end of your presentation, you realize one of your best customers—John Adams—may not buy. John and you have become friends over the last three years. Losing this sale will result in your missing out on a $500 bonus, forfeiting a chance to win a trip to Mexico, and failing to reach your sales quota for the year.

When you finish, John says, "We can't buy." You then explain your situation to John. He says, "Well, why don't you ship the merchandise to me. After the contest is over but before it's time to pay for it, I will ship it back to your company or you can transfer it in small quantities to several of your customers. That way you'll get credit for the sale." You know that your boss will not mind because if you reach your sales quota he will also look good and be rewarded.

What do you do?

1. Accept John's offer without consulting your boss and send the merchandise to his store—in turn, receiving a $500 bonus, a trip to Mexico, and praise from your boss for making the sale and reaching your sales quota.
2. Talk to your boss about the situation and explain John's offer. Let your boss be the ultimate decision maker (taking responsibility instead of you), knowing that he will tell you to take the "sale" from John.
3. Thank John for trying to be a supportive friend but decline his offer because it would not be right to falsify sales for your own benefit.

a long-term relationship with this customer who trusts you. However, most of the time you will go through the entire planned presentation and close using one or more of your textbook's closing methods. Here is an example of a common scenario faced by a salesperson.

Assume you feel it is time to close the sale after discussing the product, marketing plan, and business proposition. Within the presentation, you may ask a final trial close to verify that the person has no objection nor needs more information to make a buying decision, as shown in Exhibit 1.16. Use the person's name in the verification question. "Mr. Jones, you said you like our profit margin, fast delivery, promotional plan and pricing. Is that correct?" "Yes it is," says the buyer.

Since you received a positive response, move toward your close by presenting a suggested purchase order incorporating a closing technique. "Based upon what we discussed, Mr. Jones, I recommend you purchase 100 of the X15 and 350 of the X20. I can have both shipped to you this week or would you prefer next week?" (Alternative close: see Chapter 12).

It is important that you close. Both research and industry sales personnel say that if you are an expert on your product, show and tell while emphasizing benefits, and then close, sales will increase relative to others who use some or none of these important methods to fulfill the needs of the customer. Ask for the order and be quiet. This separates the top performers from the less successful salespeople. You now plan your follow-up and service to this prospect or customer. You are now ready to go see your next prospect or customer.

Before discussing the selling process, Chapter 2 considers the social, ethical, and legal issues in selling. With this background, we are ready to examine what is involved in preparing to meet the customer, followed by an in-depth discussion of how to develop the sales presentation.

SUMMARY OF MAJOR SELLING ISSUES

Selling is an old and honorable profession. It has helped improve this country's standard of living and provided benefits to individual buyers through the purchase of products. Millions of people have chosen sales careers because of the opportunity to serve others, the availability of sales jobs, the personal freedom sales provides, the challenge, the multitude of opportunities for success, and the nonfinancial and financial rewards.

A person can become a successful salesperson through company and personal training and by properly applying this knowledge while developing skills and abilities that benefit customers. Also important are believing in the product or service being sold, working hard, wanting to succeed, and maintaining a positive outlook toward both selling and oneself. In addition, a successful salesperson should be knowledgeable, able to plan, and efficient in using selling time. Effective salespeople are good listeners who provide service to customers. En route to success, salespeople develop a range of skills through study and practice, enhancing their ability to think strategically, relate to others, and understand the technical aspects of their business.

For the future, salespeople will need to be well versed in diverse international markets, able to ethically develop customer partnerships, and ready to utilize technology. The remainder of this book expands on these topics to provide you with the background either to improve your present selling ability or to help you decide if a sales career is right for you.

Quick Review for Students

The quick review sections provide key questions to help you develop a greater level of conceptual understanding. We suggest that after you read the chapter, you ask yourself if you can answer the following questions without looking back at the textbook.

1. What is the definition of professional selling?
2. Why does professional selling play such an important role for business?
3. What are the key differences between sales positions that require the salesperson to be an order-taker versus an order-getter? What specific types of sales positions are more order-takers? What specific types of sales positions are more order-getters?
4. What are seven of the key characteristics of successful salespeople (hint: use the *success* acronym)?
5. What are eight typical salesperson responsibilities?
6. What are the three major categories of selling skills?
7. What are the 10 steps of the sales process?

MEETING A SALES CHALLENGE

As a secretary in Sunwest Bank's marketing department, Debra Hutchins worked closely with the bank's outside salespeople and sales manager. When a sales job opened up, both Alex Romero, the director of marketing, and Rick Mather, the sales manager, asked her if she wanted the job. Debra had seen what salespeople do, so she said, "OK, I'll give it a shot."

Debra was so good as a salesperson she was promoted and now is sales manager, managing three men and one woman. "It's the best decision I've ever made," she says. "If you have not considered a sales career, I highly recommend it."

KEY TERMS FOR SELLING

advertising   6
career path   15
caring   20
common denominator   43
conceptual skill   30
Core Principles of
   Professional Selling   8
Core Principles
   Paradox   43
customer contact
   person   13
denominator   43
direct sellers   13
distribution   6
fair   21

faithful   21
good   5
Great Harvest Law of
   Sales   42
harmony   21
human skill   30
joy   20
kindness   21
manufacturer's sales
   representative   12
marketing concept   5
marketing mix   5
morally ethical   21
order-getter   14
order-taker   14

paradox   42
patience   21
price   6
product   5
professional selling   6
promotion   6
public relations   6
retail salesperson   13
sales process   34
sales promotion   6
self-control   22
service   5
technical skill   30
territory manager   24
wholesale salesperson   12

SALES APPLICATION QUESTIONS

1. The term *salesperson* refers to many types of sales jobs. What are the major types of sales jobs available?
2. Chapter 1 described characteristics of several successful salespeople currently selling goods and services for national companies. Describe those characteristics and then discuss whether or not those same characteristics also are needed for success in other types of jobs.
3. People choose a particular career for many reasons. What are the reasons someone might give for choosing a sales career?
4. What is meant by the term *career path?* What are the various jobs to which a salesperson might be promoted in a company?
5. Describe the Core Principles of Professional Selling and how they relate to the work characteristics of successful salespeople and the personal characteristics needed to sell while building long-term relationships.
6. Return to Exhibit 1.12, the seven deadly sins of business selling. Think of an experience you had with a salesperson who displayed a poor sales image. How did the salesperson's attitude affect your purchase decision?

FURTHER EXPLORING THE SALES WORLD

1. Interview one or more salespeople and write a brief report on what they like and dislike about their jobs; why they chose a sales career; what activities they perform; and what they believe it takes to succeed in selling their products.
2. Contact your college placement office and report on what staff members believe firms recruiting people for sales positions look for in applicants.

NOTES

1. See Paul Hawken, *The Ecology of Commerce* (New York: Harper Business, 1993) for further discussion.

2. American Marketing Association. https://www.ama.org/AboutAMA/Pages/Definition-of-Marketing.aspx

3. Jack Malcolm, "Sales Professionalism: Why Does It Matter?" October 27, 2010, http://customerthink.com/sales_professionalism_why_does_it_matter/

4. Riley Dugan, Ric Sweeney, James Kellaris, *Marketing News* 49, no. 12, (December 2015), pp. 18–19.

5. (http://knowledge.wharton.upenn.edu/article.cfm?articleid=3175)

6. http://www.manpowergroup.us/campaigns/talent-shortage/assets/pdf/2016-Talent-Shortage-Infographic.pdf

7. The Sales Education Foundation, https://salesfoundation.org/

8. For further discussion on direct selling, see Robert A. Peterson and Thomas R. Wotruba, "What Is Direct Selling? Definition, Perspectives, and Research Agenda," *Journal of Personal Selling,* Fall 1996, pp. 1–16; and Richard C. Bartlett, *The Direct Option* (College Station: Texas A&M University Press, 1994).

9. Author unknown.

10. W. Verbeke, B. Dietz, E.Verwaal, "Drivers of Sales Performance: A Contemporary Neta-Analysis. Have Salespeople Become Knowledge Brokers?" *Journal of the Academy of Marketing Science* 39, no. 3 (June 2011), pp. 407–28.

11. www.cooperwellness.com

12. David Jeremiah, *Fruit of the Spirit* (San Diego, CA: Turning Point, 1995), p. 84.

13. Author unknown.

14. Excerpts from Xerox Corporation sales literature.

15. James Lewis, "These Sins Will Kill a Sale," *Selling,* Oct. 1997, p. 6.

16. Baron Weitz, Harish Sujan, and Mita Sujan, "Knowledge, Motivation, and Adaptive Behavior: A Framework for Improving Selling Effectiveness," *Journal of Marketing* 50, October 1986, pp. 174–91.

17. Patricia Aburdene, *Megatrends 2010: The Rise of Conscious Capitalism* (Charlottesville, VA: Hampton Roads, Publishing, 2005), p. 6.

18. *Webster's Eleventh New Collegiate Dictionary* (Springfield, MA: Merriam-Webster, 1973), p. 1076.

19. Kay Author on the radio program "Focus on the Family," July 1, 2002.

20. Barry Farber, "Selling to the Big Ego," *Success Secrets of Sales Superstars,* Irving, CA: Entrepreneur Press, 2011, p. 243–46.

21. E. Dean Gage, "The Biblical Character Traits of Leadership," presentation at Texas A&M University, 2002.

22. www.scruples.org/web/seminars/pssb/chapter2/purpose.htm

The Core Principles of Professional Selling as Told by a Salesperson

Some time ago your present job was offered to you. You researched the company and its products, decided you liked what you found, and became a salesperson. You had heard good and bad things about salespeople. However, these things seem to occur in all occupations.

Your employer produces worthwhile products that will help people. It does not produce things that feed the world's desires. You feel people must always be more important than products, money, or you. You have found an outlet for your life's mission and philosophical goals since you accepted this opportunity.

The Core Principles of Professional Selling

You chose to base your sales philosophy on unselfishly treating others as you would like to be treated and always act professionally. This is what you fondly refer to as the "Core Principles of Selling." Customer needs come before your needs. So each time you make a sales call you ask yourself, "Do I want to build a friendly relationship with this person because I need something from her/him?" You want to help people by providing them with what they actually need. If you do not know how to put other people's needs first, how can you build a true relationship with them?

Sales and Service Are Inseparable

You really do not think of your occupation as work. It's what you do. It defines who you are. It's something you look forward to each day. Going to your job isn't work; it's a chance to be with your friends, because you are all in this together. You want to see your employer's business prosper because it employs many people who use their salary to support their families and the economy. Other people, such as the vendors you buy supplies from, prosper as your company experiences improved sales and profits.

You enjoy business relationships and work wholeheartedly at your job. Yet you enjoy time off from sales to be with your family and to do things within your community.

When pressure is on to sell, you remember the story of a person who also loved his job and talked about how his family was important in his life. Then one Saturday he took his young son to work with him. The boy asked "Daddy, is this where you live?"

Shocked at first, he thought about all the days he leaves home before the child wakes and gets home after the boy is in bed. His behavior revealed what he truly valued. This was a life-changing question coming from a five-year-old child.

You learned long ago that what you do and how you live, more than anything you say, reveals what you truly believe, and value, and that these values are in your life and your relationships with others. Your life's goal of helping others includes your family, friends, boss, co-workers, and community.

You want to do something worthwhile in your life, and your occupation is one of the things that fills that need. This is where you feel you are meant to be in your life. It is your calling. You were put on this Earth to do what you're doing. Some time ago, you stopped to ask yourself, "What is the purpose of my life?" The answer you have discovered is serving others. Service, to you, means making a contribution to the welfare of others.[18] You want to make a difference! And you do make a difference in customers' lives. That is one reason you love sales! You have the opportunity to be with so many people each day. Each day brings wonderful opportunities to improve others' lives.

You have realized that only through service can you find fulfillment in your job and life.[19] Serving others provides you with an emotional purpose in life that helps sustain enthusiasm for getting up each day. Service gives you this daily excitement for life within your heart. But one of the first things you realized in your sales job was that to truly serve others you had to know what you were talking about.

> *What is the purpose of your life?*

To Serve, You Need Knowledge

After much training and experience, you are considered an expert on your industry, competitors, products, and the application of both your products and those of your competitors to customers' needs. Being knowledgeable on products and selling skills is extremely important to you. It allows you to provide a high level of customer service, which can aid you in properly helping your customers fulfill their needs. This knowledge is also valuable in helping your fellow salespeople. In sales, however, you quickly learned people don't care how much you know until they know how much you care.[20]

Customers Notice Integrity

While it did not happen overnight, your customers love to see you! They trust that you are looking out for their best interest because you are a person of integrity and self-control. But to you, integrity is who you are when no one is looking.[21] A sincere desire motivates you to help others by having them purchase your products, and you believe in what you sell. Since your first day of contacting customers, you have realized that they want to buy, not be sold. You have gained genuine happiness from seeing how your products help solve the needs of other people. Because of your gentleness, kindness, and patience, people view you as a role model. Work provides a sense of fulfillment for you, a personal satisfaction from knowing that you are doing something purposeful, meaningful, and worthwhile.

Personal Gain at Any Cost Is Not Your Mantra

Pursuing sales for the sake of self-interest and gain is not your sole goal. Helping others is. You know that you must balance your responsibilities to your firm and your customers. Take care of customers, and customers will take care of you. Your productivity is really not in your hands. Results come in direct proportion to your level of customer service.

It is clear to you that diligence—the willingness to work hard and do your best—is a vital part of your life. You work hard, not to become rich, famous, or admired, although those may be by-products of such a lifestyle, but to help and serve others. Financial rewards result from helping others.

You are proud of what you do. Your intention in life is to accomplish business, sales, and personal goals, such as supplying a better life for your family, selling a quality product, providing good value to the customer, being honest to your employer, and building and strengthening your community through fair business practices and increased employment.[22]

Have an Attitude of Appreciation

You have even built up a reputation as a volunteer in your community by giving your time, money, and effort to projects that help people. Like your job, working for society's benefit provides you with great joy. It is a chance to bring goodness into the community.

While you occasionally think about taking credit, you honestly feel you have had little, if any, direct influence on your accomplishments. You are not a self-made person. Your father and mother, relatives, schoolteachers, friends, spouse, managers, peers, customers, company trainers, and the products you sell are just some of the factors that have molded your life, allowing you to make contributions to the sales growth of your company. This realization of how so many others have helped you over the years has caused you to be aware of how small you are compared to others. Others have provided the means for you and your family to have a wonderful life. For that reason you have a strong affection for every person in your life. Their interests come before yours. That is why you never compare yourself to others; you can let the boss do that.

The Core Principles Are Not

To you, the Core Principles are your action guide. They shape your ethical and moral conduct that people recognize as being of inestimable worth in determining right from wrong, and thus in building relationships between people. The Core Principles are time honored tenets—the codes of conduct to live by for all sales professionals regardless of their individual differences. However, the Core Principles are misunderstood by many. The Core Principles are not (1) corruptible, (2) self-serving, (3) comprehensive, or (4) easy to follow.

Corruptible They Are Not

The Core Principles are composed of pure gold. There are no impurities in it. The Core Principles are not for bad, dishonest, or evil purposes. They do not give someone the license to be bad, dishonest, or immoral. If your sales manager does not mind you falsifying a daily call report when you occasionally take off for a day due to personal reasons, you are both not following the Core Principles. They are not corruptible.

Self-Serving They Are Not

You realize that by the very definition, the Core Principles are not self-serving—doing for someone so they will do for you. In college, you were taught that worldwide marketing practices focus on providing service after the sale to sell customers more in the future. While you realize sales and profits are important to you and your employer and that most come from reselling to current customers, sales and profits are not the focus of the Core Principles. They are a natural outcome of following it in all sales transactions.

The Core Principles do not imply that you should always do to others exactly what you would like done to you or that you do something for someone in order to receive something in return. That would quickly become self-serving. You cannot do something for someone and then insist, or expect, them to do exactly the same thing, or something good, back. Do not treat others as you need to be treated is your motto. Instead, treat them as they need to be treated. There is no reciprocity involved in applying the Core Principles to anything.

People are different. People have individual needs and have to be treated as individuals. How one person wants to be treated in a situation may be different from another person in the same situation. That is why you adjust your communication interaction style to the other person's style. This helps you be a better communicator, increasing the chances the other person will listen to you and consider you trustworthy.

You scratch my back, and I will scratch your back.

Different strokes for different folks.

Comprehensive They Are Not

You have found there is more involved in being a good person than just following the Core Principles. It will not solve every problem you face or tell you what to do for all situations.

Easy to Follow They Are Not

For some salespeople, including yourself, it is hard to follow the Core Principles. It is challenging to place the other person first in every sales transaction. If it is difficult to do with family and friends, it is very hard to do in a business situation.

Everyone has failed at placing other people's best interests before their own. When you fail, go back and correct it—apologize to the customer and make it right.

The Great Harvest Law of Sales

Your mother taught "you reap what you sow." Learning this in sales, you came up with a saying called the **Great Harvest Law of Sales.** It says that how you treat others will often determine how you will be treated. If you treat others generously, graciously, and compassionately, these qualities will come back to you in full measure. Small acts of kindness toward someone over time often result in returns greater than were sown, although the returns may not be immediate but far in the future.

The Core Principles of Professional Selling ask you to treat others as you would like to be treated and act professionally. The Great Harvest Law of Sales says that if you follow the Core Principles, others will often treat you just as you treat them. This is a great mystery or secret revealed to you as to how some people are more successful than others. These are statements that most people see as contradictory or opposed to today's business practices—a **paradox.** Yet they are proven truths. By placing customers first, you often will see increases in sales, greater compensation, and better job

This is a great mystery revealed. A truth that is always true.

opportunities that overlap into a happier life. You actually receive more than you give to the customer or employer. This is the **Core Principles Paradox** in action.

A Corny Example

Your grandfather was a farmer. If he planted corn today, it would be months before the corn would be ready to be harvested. One kernel of corn produces hundreds of kernels. You, the salesperson, like the farmer, must wait to see the fruits of the labor. The farmer receives more corn than planted, as the salesperson often receives more in return for treating customers fairly.

Often, only a person with a deep abiding faith in the truth of the Core Principles of Professional Selling and the Great Harvest Law of Sales will see a bountiful crop. You have seen so many people not able to wait on building trust in the sales relationship. They focus on making the sale today and forget about serving the customer tomorrow.

Your actions have results. What you do comes back to you. If you take care of your customers, they often take care of you. If you do not take care of customers, they leave and do not come back—telling others.

The Common Denominator of Sales Success

The common denominator of sales success is caring.

As a salesperson you are often asked, "What does it take to be successful in sales? Is there one thing?" By now you should know. First, realize that a **denominator** is a common trait. The **common denominator** (trait) of a successful salesperson, compared to those less successful, is unselfishly and sacrificially "caring" for prospects, customers, colleagues, and others by placing their interests before your desires. This is also true of building personal relationships—you care enough to place others first. You love people, your work, and yourself.

©mediaphotos/Getty Images

Ethics First . . . Then Customer Relationships

Main Topics

What Influences Ethical Behavior?

Are There Any Ethical Guidelines?

Management's Ethical Responsibilities

Ethics in Dealing with Salespeople

Salespeople's Ethics in Dealing with Their Employers

Ethics in Dealing with Customers

Managing Sales Ethics

Ethics in Business and Sales

Core Principles of Professional Selling

Learning Objectives

This chapter is one of the most important in this book. Ethical and legal issues for sales personnel are often personal and technical in nature, yet they are essential for understanding how to be an outstanding professional. After studying this chapter, you should be able to

2-1 Explain what influences ethical behavior.

2-2 Define management's ethical responsibilities.

2-3 Discuss ethical dealings among salespeople, employers, and customers.

2-4 Explain what is involved in managing sales ethics.

2-5 Write a short essay on the Core Principles of Professional Selling and how it relates to sales ethics.

FACING A SALES CHALLENGE

As the sales manager of a printing company, you are about to invest in a car-leasing program that involves 18 company cars for your sales staff. Together with your comptroller, you have examined several leasing programs. You have narrowed down your selection to two leasing companies that offer very similar terms. You are meeting with the president of Equilease, a company with which you have never done business. You know from your own prospect files that one of your sales representatives has tried to call on the purchasing manager of Equilease before to get some of the company's printing business; however, he could not sell the account.

As you meet with the president for lunch, you gently steer the conversation in the direction of printing services. Since he is very knowledgeable about printing services and prices, you ask him about ballpark prices charged by his existing supplier. You believe you could provide his company with higher-quality service at a better price.

Since the president of Equilease is in a good mood, you think about setting up a win–win situation. You are considering making this offer: Let's make this a double win. I'll give you 100 percent of our leasing business if you'll consider giving us 50 percent of your printing business. Fair enough?

Is there an ethical conflict in this situation? Would it be ethical to propose such a deal?

Sales personnel constantly are involved with social, ethical, and legal issues. Yet if you think about it, everyone is—including you. If you found a bag full of $100 bills lying on the side of the road, would you keep it? Would you say you were sick to get extra time off work? Would you use the company car to run a personal errand? Have you ever broken the speed limit? Have you ever gone home with one of your employer's pens in your purse or jacket pocket?

These sorts of questions may be difficult for the average person to answer. Some people will respond with an unequivocal yes or no. Others may mull it over a while. Still others may feel compelled to say "it depends" and qualify their response with a "yes, but . . ." or a "no, but . . . ." Maybe that was what you did with the Sales Challenge feature.

Newspapers, radio, and television frequently have news stories of individuals and organizations involved in both good and bad practices. This chapter addresses some of the important ethical and legal issues in selling. It begins by discussing ethical behavior followed by the ethical issues involved in dealing with salespeople, employers, and consumers. The chapter ends by presenting ways an organization can help its sales personnel follow ethical selling practices. What influences ethical behavior?

What Influences Ethical Behavior?

Organizations are composed of individuals. These individuals' morals and ethical values help shape those of the organization. Critical to making decisions in an ethical manner is the individual integrity of the organization's managers, especially those in top management positions. Thus, two major influences on the ethical behavior of sales personnel are employees and the organization itself.

The Individual's Role

All of us, employees and managers alike, bring certain beliefs about the world to a job. These beliefs direct our daily decisions. This "big picture" view of life that directs our behavior is based upon our core belief system. It often is referred to as a person's "worldview."

Personality, religious background, family upbringing, personal experiences, and the situation faced are examples of factors shaping our core belief system. This is why you hear, "no two people are alike." Each one views the world differently than someone else. Your parents probably view many things differently than you do, for example.

Because people have different beliefs about the world around them, referred to as a person's **worldview,** they tend to have different views on ethics and morality.[1] From an early age, you begin a journey down a road to higher moral development. Research has shown that individuals grow or progress in their ability to understand the "truth" or the ability to know what is right or wrong. People's **morals** are their adherence to right or wrong behavior and right or wrong thinking. As one thinks, one does! That includes you and me.

As one thinks, one does!

EXHIBIT 2.1

What is your level of moral development?

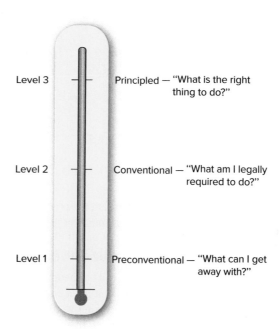

Over time moral development gradually matures in many people. With moral maturity many individuals—but not all—adhere to more truthful or stringent moral principles. Often a person's current moral development can be placed into one of the levels shown in Exhibit 2.1.

- **Level One: Preconventional.** At the **preconventional moral development level,** an individual acts in his or her own best interest and thus follows rules to avoid punishment or receive rewards. This individual would break moral and legal laws. In making an ethical or moral decision, a salesperson at this level might ask, "What can I get away with?"

   Some see them as moral infants with little capacity for self-insight because their genetically installed conscience has hardened over time. They do not see wrong in unethical behavior. If they do, it is rationalized in their favor and quickly forgotten. Whatever happens is someone else's fault.
- **Level Two: Conventional.** At the **conventional moral development level,** an individual conforms to the expectations of others, such as family, friends, employer, boss, or society, and upholds moral and legal laws. A salesperson at this level might ask, "What am I legally required to do?" when making an ethical or moral decision.
- **Level Three: Principled.** At the **principled moral development level,** an individual lives by an internal set of morals, values, and ethics regardless of punishments or majority opinion. The individual would disobey orders, laws, and consequences to follow what he or she believes is right. This person follows the Core Principles. When making an ethical or moral decision a salesperson at this level might ask, "What is the right thing to do?"[2]

The majority of sales personnel, as well as people in general, operate at the conventional level. However, a few individuals are at level 1, and it is estimated that less than 20 percent of individuals reach level 3.

As shown in Exhibit 2.2, the majority (60 to 80 percent) of sales personnel, as well as people in general, behaves at the conventional level—level 2. However, approximately 10 to 20 percent of the people behave at each of the other two levels—levels 1 and 3. Within

People's levels of moral development differ, as does the number of people at each level of moral development. Where are you on your moral development journey?

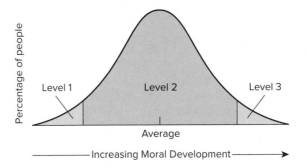

each level, there is a lower and higher level of moral development behavior. Some people at level 2, for example, have behavior closer to level 1 people or level 3 people.

The Organization's Role

If the vast majority of people in our society are at the preconventional or conventional level, it seems that most employees in an organization would feel they must "go along to get along"; in other words, they acquiesce to questionable ethical standards to keep their jobs. At most, they only follow formal policies and procedures.

How will sales personnel handle ethical dilemmas? What if there are no policies and procedures pertaining to some sales practices and a superior directs the salesperson to do something that appears unethical? It is no wonder that radio, television, and newspaper reports frequently feature unethical business practices. Following the hear no evil, see no evil, speak no evil philosophy can create a preconventional or conventional organizational climate.

Are There Any Ethical Guidelines?

The development of sales personnel's moral character can be crucial to a company. The Core Principles of Professional Selling require people whose personal character is at level 3, who have caring attitudes and recognize the rights of others, and who act based on personal, independently defined universal principles of justice and values.

What Does the Research Say?

The question is, "What should an individual base her or his values upon?" In a national survey, the findings revealed that Americans believe by a 3-to-1 margin that truth is always relative to a person's situation. People are most likely to make their moral and ethical decisions on the basis of whatever feels right or comfortable in a situation.[3]

What Does One Do?

Do you face different situations regularly? If the situation is always changing, how do you make a decision over an ethical dilemma? For example, if you found $125,000 in cash that had fallen out of the armored truck at a local bank, would you return it to the bank? But if you found someone's wallet in a parking lot, would you feel compelled to turn it in to a lost-and-found or the police? Why would you decide to keep the $125,000, when you would most likely be willing to turn in the wallet without taking any money from it? Out of class, is it all right to copy someone's homework assignment even when the course syllabus states you have to do your own work? What keeps you from copying on an exam when your professor is out of the room? With your boss's approval, is it all right to offer a customer a $10,000 trip if the customer purchases a $3 million order, even though it is against company policy? Why would you not even question doing so if a $20 lunch was associated with the purchase?

Is Your Conscience Reliable?

Almost every day you have to decide what is the correct thing to do in situations. We all have an internal ultimate moral standard we use to measure good and evil, right and wrong. Some people call that their "conscience." Most of us know we should return the $125,000 or wallet, not copy, or not give someone a bribe. But what would we actually do in these situations?

A person in these situations may feel there is no way to get caught. You could ask the boss about the $10,000, and she might say, "That's what you have to do to get the business. Everyone is doing it." Does that make it all right? Or your college friends cheat. What does it hurt if everyone does it?

What if a person's value system is at the level 2 stage of moral development? This person makes decisions based upon the "situation" and what others, such as friends, family, boss, or competitors, say or do. A person may do the right thing in one situation after talking it over with her mother, yet take the wrong action in some other situation after talking with the boss. Usually people internally rationalize their actions by saying, for example, "I will copy the homework only this one time."

Many people are so used to doing things unethically that they think nothing of it. For example, a woman received a telephone call from her husband's sales manager complaining that he was taking home company office supplies. In a rage his wife replied, "I don't believe that! Why would he do that? He knows I bring enough office supplies home from my job for the both of us."

Yogi Berra, the retired great baseball player, is famous for saying, "When you come to a fork in the road, take it."[4] As shown in Exhibit 2.3, when you come to a fork in the

How will you, as a salesperson, handle ethical dilemmas?

People's morals are their adherence to right or wrong behavior and right or wrong thinking.

"When you come to a fork in the road, take it."

YOGI BERRA

EXHIBIT 2.3

How do you know which fork in the road to take? You need a moral compass!

©olaser/Getty Images

road, how do you know which road is the ethical one? Are your feelings about a situation an accurate measure of its rightness or wrongness? At times, we are not a good judge of what is best to do in a situation because the outcome involves something we want. Thus, we cannot always trust our conscience.

Sources of Significant Influence

Think about this next question for a moment before reading on. What do you use to resolve ethical or moral dilemmas that occur in your life? In the margin, make a list of two or three factors that influence your choices when faced with an ethical or moral issue. What do you base your decisions upon? Do your decision factors include your friends, family, or things you see on television or in the movies? Do their thoughts on what is ethical sometimes change from day to day?

Barna Research is conducting an ongoing study of sources influencing Americans' ethical and moral decision-making processes. In early returns, Barna found the leading influencers in American society to be movies, television, the Internet, books, music, public policy and law, and family.[5]

Wouldn't it be nice to be able to base your decisions on something that never changes, something that can always be depended upon to provide the correct answer in any situation?

Can business and salespeople make ethical choices based on whatever works for them—decisions unique to each situation? We have nothing to help us determine what is really right or wrong no matter what situation you, a businessperson, or a salesperson faces. Or do we?

> "We humans have an infinite capacity for self-justification."
>
> CHARLES COLSON

Three Guidelines for Making Ethical Decisions

What do you need to make a decision about the right or wrong action to take in any situation? You need a never-changing fixed point of reference that is separate from you so you, or anyone else, cannot influence it.[6] The three guidelines to look for in a standard for making ethical decisions, then, are that it never changes, offers a fixed point of reference, and is separate. What does that mean?

A **fixed point of reference** refers to something that provides the correct action to take in any situation and never gets tailored to fit an occasion. This fixed point of reference must be separate from you; otherwise you will be changing the rules based upon your best interest in various situations. This is why your conscience is usually not your best guide to making moral and ethical decisions.

Let's say you are on one of the survivor television shows popular in the early 2000s. You and your teammate are blindfolded, placed in a boat, and set down in the ocean. You are provided a sextant, which is an instrument for measuring angular distances used in navigation to observe altitudes of celestial bodies, such as stars. Your survivor host tells you there is an island directly south of you at a certain latitude and longitude. And luckily, your teammate knows how to work the sextant.

How do you know exactly how to reach this island? You have to have a fixed point of reference that never changes and is 100 percent reliable to point you south to the island. Plus, it cannot connect with you, your teammate, or the boat. What fits these requirements for making the correct decision? The position of the stars fits these three requirements. Stars are fixed points of reference that never change and are separate from the two of you.

Using the sextant and stars allows you to sail directly to the island. The stars have the same fixed location today that they had 2,000 years ago and that they will

©Brand X Pictures/Getty Images

have in the future. The unchanging star locations offer a good example of a fixed point of reference.

How does this relate to a person making ethical, moral decisions in real life? As in the examples of the money, class, and bribe, people need a fixed point of reference separate from them that always provides the same correct ethical answer. What do most people of the world have that fits these three criteria for making the correct decisions in any situation?

Will the Core Principles Help?

Many people of the world make basic right and wrong decisions based upon their religious principles or faith. All of the major religious faiths of the world provide their followers with written doctrine. When these doctrines are compared, it is interesting to discover that similar faith-based principles appear in all religions despite the differences among the various religions. Exhibit 2.4 provides examples of how Christians, Jews, Hindus, Buddhists, and Confucius's followers promote unselfish deeds.[7]

The key to understanding the Core Principles from the perspectives of the religions mentioned in Exhibit 2.4 is to realize that professionalism does not necessarily involve reciprocity. Reciprocity says if you do for me, I will do for you. Many people think of this as a professional act. It is not!

As described in Chapter 1, the Core Principles of professionalism mean doing for others without expecting something in return. In fact, scholars identify professionalism as "an ability to demonstrate ethical choices, values, and practices in decision-making and to commit to the practice of personal and professional values"[8] When studying Exhibit 2.4 think in terms of unselfishly treating others as you would like to be treated.

In her textbook *Perspectives in Business Ethics,* Laura Hartman explores what could serve as a universal, practical, helpful standard for the businessperson's conduct.[9] What do you think could be professional standards for conduct? Former President George W. Bush suggested that true professionalism should guide business decisions. In his April 2002 remarks on faith-based initiatives in America, President Bush talked about people heeding a great call. "A call to love your neighbor just like you'd like to be loved yourself. It's a universal call, and it's a call that has been applicable throughout history. It's really needed right now."[10]

Do you think faith-based perspectives can help people make decisions in an ethical manner? Would you consider your faith a fixed point of reference that never changes and is separate from you? Could your faith's teachings be your moral compass in both your business and your personal life?

"What is the true truth?"

FRANCIS SHAFFER

EXHIBIT 2.4

World religions promote unselfish deeds.

- "This is the sum of duty; do naught unto others what you would have them do to you." The Hindu *Mahabharata* 5:1517
- "Do not do to others what you would not like yourself." Confucius' *Analects* 12:2
- "Hurt not others in ways that you yourself would find hurtful." The Buddhist *Udana Varga* 5:1
- Rabbi Hillel famously told the cynic who demanded that the sage teach him all the Torah while he stood on one foot, "That which is hateful to you do not do unto your neighbor. The rest is commentary."
- "Do to others as you would have them do to you." The Christian Bible, *Matthew* 7:12

Management's Ethical Responsibilities

The concept of ethics, like that of social responsibility, is easy to understand. However, ethics is difficult to define in a precise way. In a general sense, **ethics** are the codes of moral principles and values that govern the behaviors of a person or a group with respect to what is right or wrong. Ethics set standards for what is good or bad in conduct and decision making.[11]

It is very important for supervisors and managers to fulfill their ethical responsibilities and avoid any ethical misconduct. But, is this always the case? Perhaps not. In a 2013 National Business Ethics Survey® of the U.S. Workforce[12], employees reported that that more than half (60 percent) of observed misdeeds involved someone with managerial authority from the supervisory level up to top management. This is alarming as these individuals are often looked upon as role models.

Many companies and their sales personnel get into trouble by making the mistaken assumption that if it's not illegal, it must be ethical. Ethics and moral values are a powerful force for good that can regulate behaviors both inside and outside the sales force. As principles of ethics and social responsibility are more widely recognized, companies can use codes of ethics and their corporate cultures to govern behavior, thereby eliminating the need for additional laws governing right and wrong.

What Is Ethical Behavior?

Sales personnel are frequently faced with ethical dilemmas. **Ethical behavior** refers to treating others fairly. Specifically, it refers to

- Being honest and truthful.
- Maintaining confidence and trust.
- Following the rules.
- Conducting yourself in the proper manner.
- Treating others fairly.
- Demonstrating loyalty to company and associates.
- Carrying your share of the work and responsibility with 100 percent effort.

The definition of ethical behavior, while reasonably specific and easy to understand, is difficult to apply in every situation. In real life, there are always conflicting viewpoints, fuzzy circumstances, and unclear positions. Though difficult, it is critically important to cut through the smoke screen that sometimes exists in such a situation and use 20/20 vision to make an ethical choice.

What Is an Ethical Dilemma?

©DNY59/Getty Images

Because ethical standards are not classified, disagreements and dilemmas about proper behavior often occur. An ethical dilemma arises in a situation when each alternative choice or behavior has some undesirable elements due to potentially negative ethical or personal consequences. Right or wrong cannot be clearly identified. Consider the following examples:

- Your boss says he cannot give you a raise this year because of budget constraints, but because of your good work this past year, he will look the other way if your expense accounts come in a little high.
- Stationed at the corporate headquarters in Chicago, you have 14 salespeople in countries all over the world. A rep living in another country calls to get approval to pay a government official $10,000 to OK an equipment purchase of

$5 million. Such payoffs are part of common business practice in that part of the world.

- An industrial engineer, who is your good friend, tells you three of your competitors have submitted price bids on his company's proposed new construction project. He suggests a price you should submit and mentions certain construction specifications his boss is looking for on the job.

Managers must deal with these kinds of dilemmas and issues that fall squarely in the domain of ethics. Because of their importance, an Ethical Dilemma feature appears in every chapter. In answering the questions at the end of these features, refer both to this chapter and to the chapter in which the feature appears.

Now let's turn to the three main ethical areas sales personnel face most frequently. These involve

1. Salespeople.
2. Employer.
3. Customers.

Although not all-inclusive, our discussion gives you a feel for some of the difficult situations sales personnel encounter.

Ethics in Dealing with Salespeople

Sales managers have both social and ethical responsibilities to sales personnel. Salespeople are a valuable resource; they are recruited, carefully trained, and given important responsibility. They represent a large financial investment and must be treated in a professional manner. Yet, occasionally a company may place managers and/or salespeople in positions that force them to choose among compromising their ethics, not doing what is required, or leaving the organization. The choice depends on the magnitude of the situation. At times, situations arise wherein it is difficult to say whether a sales practice is ethical or unethical. Many sales practices are in a gray area somewhere between completely ethical and completely unethical. Five ethical considerations sales managers face are the level of sales pressure to place on a salesperson, decisions concerning a salesperson's territory, whether to be honest with the salesperson, what to do with an ill salesperson, and employee rights.

Level of Sales Pressure

What is an acceptable level of pressure to place on salespeople? Should managers establish performance goals that they know a salesperson has only a 50–50 chance of attaining? Should the manager acknowledge that goals were set too high? If circumstances change in the salesperson's territory—for example, a large customer goes out of business—should the manager lower sales goals? (See Exhibit 2.5.)

These are questions all managers must consider. There are no right or wrong answers. Managers are responsible for group goals. They have a natural tendency to place pressure on salespeople to reach those goals. Some managers motivate their people to produce at high levels without applying pressure whereas others place tremendous pressure on salespeople to attain sales beyond quotas or set quotas to unattainable levels. However, managers should set realistic and obtainable goals. They must consider individual territory situations. If they do so fairly and sales are still down, then pressure may be applied.

How much pressure should a manager place on salespeople to increase sales?

©stockbroker/123RF

Decisions Affecting Territory

Management makes decisions that affect sales territories and salespeople. For example, the company might increase the number of sales territories, which often necessitates splitting a single territory. A salesperson may have spent years building the territory to its current sales volume only to have customers taken away. If the salesperson has worked on commission, this would mean a decrease in earnings.

Consider a situation of reducing the number of sales territories. What procedures would you use? See if the real-world examples in this section follow the Core Principles of Professionalism. Several years ago, a large manufacturer of health and beauty aids (shaving cream, toothpaste, shampoo) reduced the number of territories to lower selling costs. So, for example, three territories became two. Here is how one of the company's salespeople described it:

> I made my plane reservation to fly from Dallas to Florida for our annual national meeting. Beforehand, I was told to bring my records up to date and bring them to the regional office in Dallas; don't fly, drive to Dallas. I drove from Louisiana to Dallas with my bags packed to go to the national meeting. I walked into the office with my records under my arm. My district and regional managers were there. They told me of the reorganization and said I was fired. They asked for my car keys. I called my wife, told her what happened, and then caught a bus back home. There were five of us in the region that were called in that day. Oh, they gave us a good job recommendation—it's just the way we were treated. Some people had been with the company for five years or more. They didn't eliminate jobs by tenure but by where territories were located.

Companies must deal with their employees in a fair and straightforward manner. It would have been better for managers of these salespeople to go to their hometowns and explain the changes personally. Instead, they treated the salespeople unprofessionally.

One decision affecting a territory is what to do with extra-large customers, sometimes called *key accounts.* Are they taken away from the salesperson and made into house accounts? Here, responsibility for contacting the accounts rests with someone from the home office (house) or a key account salesperson. The local salesperson may not get credit for sales to this customer even though the customer is in the sales-person's territory. A salesperson states the problem:

> I've been with the company 35 years. When I first began, I called on some people who had one grocery store. Today, they have 208. The buyer knows me. He buys all of my regular and special greeting cards. They do whatever I ask. I made $22,000 in commissions from their sales last year. Now, management wants to make it a house account.

Here, the salesperson loses money. It is difficult to treat the salesperson fairly in this situation. The company does not want to pay large commissions, and 90 percent of the 208 stores are located out of the salesperson's territory. Management should care-fully explain this to the salesperson. Instead of taking the full $22,000 away from the salesperson, they could pay a one-time bonus as a reward for building up the account.

To Tell the Truth?

Do not turn from the truth, to the right or left, so you can be successful wherever you go.

Should salespeople be told they are not promotable, that they are marginal perform-ers, or that they are being transferred to the poorest territory in the company so that they will quit? Good judgment must prevail. Sales managers prefer to tell the truth.

Do you tell the truth when you fire a salesperson? If a fired employee has tried and has been honest, many sales managers will tell prospective employers that the person quit voluntarily rather than being fired. One manager put it this way: "I feel he can do a good job for another company. I don't want to hurt his future."

The Ill Salesperson

How much help do you give to a salesperson who is addicted to alcohol or drugs, or who is physically or mentally ill? Many companies require salespeople to seek professional help for substance abuse. If they improve, companies offer support and keep them in the field. Yet, there is only so far the company can go. The firm cannot have an intoxicated or high salesperson calling on customers. Once the illness has a negative effect on business, the salesperson is taken out of the territory. Sick leave and workers' compensation often cover expenses until the salesperson recovers. The manager who shows a sincere, personal interest in helping the ill salesperson greatly contributes to the person's chances of recovery.

Employee Rights

The sales manager must be current on ethical and legal considerations regarding employee rights and must develop strategies for the organization in addressing those rights. Here are several important questions that all managers should be able to answer:

- Under what conditions can an organization fire sales personnel without com-mitting a violation of the law?
- What rights do and should sales personnel have regarding the privacy of their employment records and access to them?
- What can organizations do to prevent sexual and racial harassment and other forms of bias in the workplace?

Employee rights are rights desired by employees regarding their job security and their treatment by employers while on the job, irrespective of whether those rights are cur-rently protected by law or collective bargaining agreements of labor unions. Let's briefly examine three employee-rights questions.

Termination-at-Will

Early in the 20th century, many courts were adamant in strictly applying the common law rule to terminate at will. For example, the **termination-at-will rule** was used in *Boyer v. Western Union Tel. Co.* [124 F 246, CCED Mo. (1903)], in which the court upheld the company's right to discharge its employees for union activities and indicated that the results would be the same if the company's employees were discharged for being Presbyterians.

Later on, in *Lewis v. Minnesota Mutual Life Ins. Co.* [37 NW 2d 316 (1940)], the termination-at-will rule was used to uphold the dismissal of the life insurance company's best salesperson—even though no apparent cause for dismissal was given and the company had promised the employee lifetime employment in return for his agreement to remain with the company.

In the early 1980s, court decisions and legislative enactments moved the pendulum of protection away from the employer and toward the rights of the individual employee through limitations on the termination-at-will rule.

Although many employers claim that their rights have been taken away, they still retain the right to terminate sales personnel for poor performance, excessive absenteeism, unsafe conduct, and poor organizational citizenship. It is crucial, however, for employers to maintain accurate records of these events for employees and to inform employees about where they stand. To be safe, it is also advisable for employers to have an established grievance procedure for employees to ensure that due process is respected. These practices are particularly useful in discharge situations that involve members of groups protected by Title VII, the Rehabilitation Act, or the Vietnam Era Veterans Act.

Privacy

Today it is more important than ever to keep objective and orderly personnel files. They are critical evidence that employers have treated their employees fairly and with respect, and have not violated any laws. Without these files, organizations may get caught on the receiving end of a lawsuit.

Although several federal laws influence record keeping, they are primarily directed at public employers. However, many private employers are giving employees the right to access their personnel files and to prohibit the file information from being given to others without their consent. In addition, employers are casting from their personnel files any non–job-related information and ending hiring practices that solicit such information.

Harassment

Cooperative acceptance refers to the right of employees to be treated fairly and with respect regardless of race, sex, national origin, physical disability, age, or religion while on the job (as well as in obtaining a job and maintaining job security). Not only does this mean that employees have the right not to be discriminated against in employment practices and decisions, but it also means that employees have the right to be free of sexual and racial harassment.

Today, the right to not be discriminated against is generally protected under Title VII, the Age Discrimination in Employment Act, the Rehabilitation Act, the Vietnam Era Veterans Readjustment Assistance Act, and numerous court decisions and state and local government laws. Though the right to be free of sexual harassment is found explicitly in fewer laws, it has been made a part of the 1980 EEOC guidelines, which

Sexual harassment in the workplace wasn't recognized as a legal issue until the 1970s. In 1980, the Equal Employment Opportunity Commission (EEOC) guidelines identified two types of sexual harassment: The first type is quid pro quo, in which an employee who refuses to submit to a superior's sexual advances is threatened with dismissal or other sanctions. The second type is hostile environment harassment; it occurs when jokes, graffiti, and other behavior are directed at persons of the opposite sex. The landmark ruling came in 1986, when the Supreme Court held unanimously that sexual harassment violates Title VII of the 1964 Civil Rights Act if it is unwelcome and "sufficiently severe or pervasive to alter the conditions of the victim's employment and create an abusive working environment."

Some executives believe the courts are being unreasonable about their definitions of sexual harassment. The issue is often awkward or embarrassing to discuss, and no clear-cut definitions of what constitutes offensive behavior exist. For example, a comment about clothing might be considered a compliment by the giver but harassment by the receiver. For these and other reasons, some companies are unwilling to spend time or money educating employees about this issue.

The problem continues to be serious. In 2016, the EEOC received about 6,700 sexual harassment complaints. And new forms of harassment, such as obscene software on company computers and suggestive electronic mail and answering machine messages, keep appearing.

Fortunately, Google, Honeywell, Pepsico, CBS, and a number of other companies have long been concerned about sexual harassment. They distribute booklets that describe inappropriate behavior to employees. They hire consultants or conduct in-house training sessions that include films and role playing. The EEOC has published guidelines to help people understand liability. A key factor in determining liability is whether the employer has an effective internal grievance procedure that allows employees to bypass immediate supervisors (who are often the offenders).[13]

state that sexual harassment is a form of sex discrimination. The designation of sexual harassment as a form of sex discrimination under Title VII also is found in numerous court decisions.

Employers must prevent racial and sexual harassment, which they can do with top management support, grievance procedures, verification procedures, training for all employees, and performance appraisal and compensation policies that reward antiharassment behavior and punish harassment.

Companies must recognize these important strategic purposes served by respecting employee rights:

- Providing a high quality of work life.
- Attracting and retaining good sales personnel. This makes recruitment and selection more effective and less frequent.
- Avoiding costly back-pay awards and fines.
- Establishing a match between employee rights and obligations and employer rights and obligations.

As employees begin to see the guarantees of job security as a benefit, organizations also gain through reduced wage-increase demands and greater flexibility in job assignments.

Salespeople's Ethics in Dealing with Their Employers

Both salespeople and sales managers may occasionally misuse company assets, moonlight, cheat, or steal technology. Such unethical practices can affect co-workers and need to be prevented before they occur.[14]

Misusing Company Assets

Company assets most often misused are automobiles, expense accounts, samples, and damaged-merchandise credits. All can be used for personal gain or as bribes and kickbacks to customers. For example, a salesperson can give customers valuable product samples or a credit for damaged merchandise when there has been no damage.

Moonlighting

Salespeople are not closely supervised and, consequently, they may be tempted to take a second job—perhaps on company time. Some salespeople attend college on company time. For example, a salesperson may enroll in an evening MBA program but take off in the early afternoon to prepare for class.

Cheating

A salesperson may not play fair in contests. If a contest starts in July, the salesperson may not turn in sales orders for the end of June and lump them with July sales. Some might arrange, with or without the customer's permission, to ship merchandise that is not needed or wanted. The customer holds the merchandise until payment is due and then returns it to the company after the contest is over. The salesperson also may overload the customer to win the contest.

Often, the unethical practices of one salesperson can affect other salespeople within the company. Someone who cheats in winning a contest is taking money and prizes from other salespeople. A salesperson also may not split commissions with co-workers or take customers away from co-workers.

Technology Theft

Picture this. A salesperson or sales manager quits, or is fired, and takes the organization's customer records to use for his or her or a future employer's benefit. How is that possible? Well, it's getting easier to do these days because more and more companies provide their sales personnel with computers, software, and data on their customers.

Ethics in Dealing with Customers

"We have formal, ethical policies called business conduct guidelines," says FMC's Alan Killingsworth. "These guidelines thoroughly discuss business conduct and clearly state what is proper conduct and how to report improper conduct. All sales personnel review them and even sign a statement that they understand the guidelines."

Numerous ethical situations may arise in dealing with customers, and sales organizations may create specific business conduct guidelines like FMC's to deal with them. Some common problems sales personnel face include bribes, misrepresentation, price discrimination, tie-in sales, exclusive dealership, reciprocity, and sales restrictions.

Bribes

A salesperson may attempt to bribe a buyer by offering money, gifts, entertainment, and travel opportunities.[15] At times, there is a thin line between good business and misusing a bribe or gift. A $10 gift to a $10,000 customer may be merely a gift, but how do we define a $4,000 ski trip for buyers and their spouses?

Many companies forbid their buyers to take gifts of any size from salespeople. However, bribery does exist. The U.S. Chamber of Commerce estimates that bribes and kickbacks account for $27 billion of the annual $50 billion in white-collar crime.

Buyers may ask for cash, merchandise, or travel payments in return for placing an order with the salesperson. Imagine that you are a salesperson working on a 5 percent commission. The buyer says, "I'm ready to place a $20,000 order for office supplies with you. However, another salesperson has offered to pay my expenses for a weekend in Las Vegas in exchange for my business. You know, $500 tax-free is a lot of money." You quickly calculate that your commission is $1,000. You still make $500. Would it be hard to pass up that $500?

Many large companies have taken steps to control giving and receiving gifts. Bull H. N. Information Systems, a Massachusetts computer manufacturer, prohibits employees from accepting "money, favors, or anything of significance." This does not include, however, bar bills, meals, entertainment, or other small items given as tokens of appreciation.[16]

Misrepresentation

Today, even casual misstatements by salespeople can put a company on the wrong side of the law. Most salespeople are unaware that they assume legal obligations—with accompanying risks and responsibilities—every time they approach a customer. However, we all know that salespeople sometimes oversell. They exaggerate the capabilities of their products or services and sometimes make false statements just to close a sale.

Often, buyers depend heavily on the technical knowledge of salespeople, along with their professional integrity. Yet, sales managers and staff find it difficult to know just how far they can go with well-intentioned sales talk, personal opinion, and promises. They do not realize that by using certain statements they can embroil their companies in a lawsuit and ruin the business relationship they are trying to establish.

A liar has to have a good memory.

When a customer relies on a salesperson's statements, purchases the product or service, and then finds that it fails to perform as promised, the supplier can be sued for **misrepresentation** and **breach of warranty.** Companies around the United States have been liable for million-dollar judgments for making such mistakes, particularly when their salespeople sold high-ticket, high-tech products or services.

You can avoid such mistakes, however, if you're aware of the law of misrepresentation and breaches of warranty relative to the selling function, and if you follow strategies that keep you and your company out of trouble. Salespeople must understand the difference between sales puffery (opinions) and statements of fact—and the legal

"It was my first call as a district manager in Washington, DC," says Alan Lesk, senior vice president of sales and merchandising at Maidenform. "One of the major department stores was not doing a lot of business with Maidenform, and we were looking for more penetration in the market. Surprisingly, the sale took only two sales calls.

"The first person I approached was a buyer. He was completely uncooperative. On the way out of the store, I popped my head into his boss's office and we set up a meeting with some higher level executives later in the week.

"So there I was, a young kid facing a committee of nine tough executives, and I had to make my presentation. I was in the middle of my pitch when the executive vice president stopped me. He told me that this was going to be a big program, about $500,000, and asked me point blank how much of a rebate I was willing to give him to do business with their store, over and above the normal things like co-op ad money. He was actually asking me for money under the table!

"I had to make a decision fast. I stood up and said, 'If this is what it takes to do business here, I don't want anything to do with it.' I then turned to walk out the door, and the guy started cracking up. I guess he was just testing me to see what lengths I'd go to in order to get my sales program into the store.

"This one incident taught me some very important things: You can't compromise your integrity, and you can't let people intimidate you. Most importantly, don't lose your sense of humor. Needless to say, we got the program into the store, and today we do more than $2 million worth of business a year with them."[17]

Bristol Voss, "Eat, Drink, and Be Wary," *Sales & Marketing Management*, January 1991, pp. 49–54. Used by permission.

ramifications of both. There are preventive steps to follow; salespeople must work closely with management to avoid time-consuming delays and costly legal fees.[18]

What the Law Says

Misrepresentation and breach of warranty are two legal causes of action, that is, theories on which an injured party seeks damages. These two theories differ in the proof required and the type of damages awarded by a judge or jury. However, both theories arise in the selling context and are treated similarly for our purposes. Both situations arise when a salesperson makes erroneous statements or offers false promises regarding a product's characteristics and capabilities.

Not all statements have legal consequences, however. When sales personnel loosely describe their product or service in glowing terms ("Our service can't be beat; it's the best around"), such statements are viewed as opinions that the customer, supplier, or wholesaler generally cannot rely on. Thus, a standard defense that lawyers use in misrepresentation and breach of warranty lawsuits is that a purchaser cannot rely on a salesperson's puffery because it's unreasonable to take these remarks at face value.

When a salesperson makes claims or promises of a factual nature regarding a product's or service's inherent capabilities (that is, the results, profits, or savings that will be achieved; what it will do for a customer; how it will perform), the law treats these comments as statements of fact and warranties.

There is a subtle difference between sales puffery and statements of fact; they can be difficult to distinguish. No particular form of words is necessary; each case is analyzed according to its circumstances. Generally, the less knowledgeable the customer,

> *Be a person of 100% truth, not 99% truth. Your proof is in your word.*

Wells Fargo, a financial institution that has traditionally held one of the highest stock market valuations among United States banks and has also appeared multiple times on the Gallup's "Great Places to Work" list, continues to face a business challenge related to ethics. CEO Tim Sloan stated that Wells Fargo needs to work hard "to earn America's trust back." But what created this trust gap between Wells Fargo and the citizens of the United States? The answer involves sales practices and the alleged disregard of ethical responsibilities to the firm's customers.

Based on the information that has been brought forth in news reports,[19] branch managers were given sales quotas that were tied to the number and types of products sold. It appears that when the branch did not meet its daily sales goals, the remaining shortfall was added onto the next day's quota. Further, branch employees may have had financial incentives tied to cross-selling additional financial services to existing customers. As a result of these sales goals and incentives, it seems likely to assume that employees felt a great deal of pressure to sell financial products. News reports allege that some Wells Fargo employees started falsifying documents on behalf of their customers and opening fake accounts to achieve their goals. Employees allegedly shipped their customers' credit cards and other information to the bank instead of the customers' homes. As a result, customers were not aware of the new accounts opened on their behalf. Eventually, customers started noticing the impact of these new accounts on their credit scores. Wells Fargo has found approximately 3.5 million potentially fake bank and credit card accounts.[20] In 2016, the scandal became public and legal implications began to surface. The bank announced it would pay $185 million to settle a lawsuit. Moreover, Wells Fargo's stock price fell and a number of newspaper articles and other press-related stories discussed Wells Fargo in a negative light. It was also reported that Wells Fargo dismissed approximately 5,000 employees due to violations of the firm's ethical standards. Further, some groups of employees allege that they were fired or demoted for acting honestly and for choosing not to resort to unethical practices in order to meet their sales goals. While a number of indiscretions are alleged and will need to be resolved in a court of law, the Wells Fargo situation provides one glimpse into the intersection between sales and ethics. For employees, supervisors, and organizations, the Wells Fargo situation brings forth a number of intriguing challenges and discussions regarding ethics, sales quotas, managerial responsibilities, and individual values.

the greater the chances that the court will interpret a statement as actionable. The following is an actual recent case that illustrates this point:

> An independent sales rep sold heavy industrial equipment. He went to a purchaser's construction site, observed his operations, then told the company president that his proposed equipment would "keep up with any other machine then being used," and that it would "work well in cooperation with the customer's other machines and equipment."

The customer informed the rep that he was not personally knowledgeable about the kind of equipment the rep was selling, and that he needed time to study the rep's report. Several weeks later, he bought the equipment based on the rep's recommendations.

After a few months, he sued the rep's company, claiming that the equipment didn't perform according to the representations in sales literature sent prior to the execution of the contract and to statements made by the rep at the time of sale. The equipment manufacturer defended itself by arguing that the statements made by the rep were

> "People may cheat
> you; be honest
> anyway."
>
> MOTHER TERESA

The real estate salesperson assured the young couple that she would work hard to find them the right house. "Consider me your scout," she said. "I'll find you the best house for the least money." The couple was reassured, and on the way home they talked about their good fortune. They had a salesperson working just for them. With prices so high, it was nice to think they had professional help on their side.

The family selling the house felt the same way. They carefully chose the broker because, they observed, with home prices all over the place these days, they hoped a good salesperson might win them several thousand dollars more. They had another reason to choose carefully: At today's prices, the 6 percent sales commission is a lot of money. "If we have to pay it," they reasoned, "we're better off paying it to the best salesperson."

It happens all the time, and it can have serious consequences. How can both parties expect the best deal? How can a salesperson promise the seller the most for the money and then make the same promise to the buyer?

In the same vein, how can a salesperson whose commission rises or falls with the price of the house being sold be expected to cut into her income? Isn't her total allegiance with the person paying her?

Confusion of this sort has existed in the marketplace for so long that critics are sometimes confounded that regulators haven't made greater efforts to clarify matters.

Two explanations are sometimes offered. First, it is more a human than a legal problem; even if warned, buyers will continue to assume that salespeople work solely for them, rather than for the seller, who pays the salesperson a commission.

Second, a good salesperson sometimes can come close to serving the desires of both parties. The point is arguable, but the justification offered is that the salesperson's compromises may be necessary to save a sale from falling through.

A somewhat similar situation exists in the stock market, where many small investors view their stockbroker as a confidant and adviser.[21]

nonactionable opinions made innocently by the rep, in good faith, with no intent to deceive the purchaser.

The court ruled in favor of the customer, finding that the rep's statements were "predictions" of how the equipment would perform; this made them more than mere sales talk. The rep was held responsible for knowing the capabilities of the equipment he was selling; his assertions were deemed statements of fact, not opinions. Furthermore, the court stated that it was unfair that a knowledgeable salesperson would take advantage of a naive purchaser.[22]

Suggestions for Staying Legal

The following suggestions cover ways that management and sales staff can minimize exposure to costly misrepresentation and breach of warranty lawsuits. Salespeople must always do the following:

1. Understand the distinction between general statements of praise and statements of fact made during the sales pitch (and the legal consequences). For example, the following statements, taken from actual cases, were made by salespeople and were determined legally actionable as statements of fact:
   - This refrigerator will preserve foods in the warmest weather.
   - This tractor has live power-take-off features.

EXHIBIT 2.6

This salesperson must be careful about the claims made in the sales presentation. If she says, "This equipment will increase production 2 percent," and it doesn't, the salesperson and her company may find themselves in court.

©pressmaster/123RF

- ■ Feel free to prescribe this drug to your patients, doctor. It's nonaddicting.
- ■ This mace pen is capable of instantaneous incapacitation for a period of 15 to 20 minutes.
- ■ This is a safe, dependable helicopter.

2. Thoroughly educate all customers before making a sale. Salespeople should tell as much about the specific qualities of the product as possible. The reason is that when a salesperson makes statements about a product in a field in which his or her company has extensive experience, the law makes it difficult for the salesperson to claim it was just sales talk.

   This is especially true for products or services sold in highly specialized areas to unsophisticated purchasers who rely entirely on the technical expertise of the salesperson. However, if the salesperson deals with a customer experienced in the trade, courts are less likely to find that the salesperson offered an expressed warranty, since a knowledgeable buyer has a duty to look beyond the assertions of a salesperson and investigate the product individually.

3. Be accurate when describing a product's capabilities. Avoid making speculative claims, particularly with respect to predictions concerning what a product will do.

4. Know the technical specifications of the product. Review all promotional literature to ensure that there are no exaggerated claims. Keep abreast of all design changes as well. The salesperson shown in Exhibit 2.6, for example, must carefully and honestly explain the technical aspects of her product to her industrial buyers.

5. Avoid making exaggerated claims about product safety. The law usually takes a dim view of such affirmative claims, and these remarks can be interpreted as warranties that lead to liability.

   For example, the Minnesota Court of Appeals ruled that a salesperson's assurances that a used car had a rebuilt carburetor and was a "good runner" constituted an expressed warranty of the vehicle's condition. Someone had bought the car based on the salesperson's assurance of its good quality. The carburetor jammed, causing the car to smash into a tree and injuring the purchaser, who recovered sizable damages.[23]

6. Know federal and state laws regarding warranties and guarantees.
7. Know the capabilities and characteristics of your products and services.
8. Keep current on all design changes and revisions in your product's operating manual.
9. Avoid offering opinions when the customer asks what results a product or service will accomplish unless the company has tested the product and has statistical evidence.

   Statements such as "This will reduce your inventory backlog by 40 percent" can get the company in trouble if the system fails to achieve the promised results. Stay away from that kind of statement. If you don't know the answer to a customer's question, don't lead her on. Tell her you don't know the answer but will get back to her promptly with the information.
10. Never overstep authority, especially when discussing prices or company policy. Remember, a salesperson's statements can bind the company.

One final point: It's generally easy for customers to recover damages on the grounds of misrepresentation and breach of warranty. In many states, this holds even when a salesperson's statement is made innocently.

Price Discrimination

Some customers may receive price reductions, promotional allowances, and support while others do not, even though, under certain circumstances, this violates the **Robinson-Patman Act** of 1936. The act allows sellers to grant what are called *quantity discounts* to larger buyers based on savings in manufacturing costs.

Individual salespeople or managers may practice **price discrimination** to improve sales. *Price discrimination* refers to selling the same quantity of the same product to different buyers at different prices. This can be illegal if it injures or reduces competition. It is certainly unethical and no way to treat customers.

Tie-in Sales

To buy a particular line of merchandise, a buyer may be required to buy other, unwanted products. This is called a **tie-in sale** and is prohibited under the **Clayton Act** when it substantially lessens competition. For example, the salesperson of a popular line of cosmetics tells the buyer, "I have a limited supply of the merchandise you want. If all of your 27 stores will display, advertise, and push my total line, I may be able to supply you. That means you'll need to buy 10 items that you have never purchased before." Is this good business? No—it's illegal.

Exclusive Dealership

When a contract requires that a wholesaler or retailer purchase products from one manufacturer, it is an *exclusive dealership*. If it lessens competition, it is prohibited under the Clayton Act.

Reciprocity

The salesperson says, "I can get my company to buy all of our office supplies from your company if you buy lighting fixtures, supplies, and replacement parts from us." Is this a good business practice?

Reciprocity refers to buying a product from someone if the person or organization agrees to buy from you. The Federal Trade Commission and the Department of Justice consider such a trade agreement illegal if it results in hurting or eliminating competition. Most purchasing agents find this practice offensive. Because reciprocal sales agreements may be illegal, if not unethical, buyers often are afraid to even discuss this with sellers.

Sales Restrictions

To protect consumers against the sometimes unethical sales activities of door-to-door salespeople, there is legislation at the federal, state, and local levels. The Federal Trade Commission and most states have adopted **cooling-off laws.** They provide a cooling-off period (usually three days) in which the buyer may cancel the contract, return any merchandise, and obtain a full refund. The law covers sales of $25 or more made door-to-door. It also states that the buyer must receive from the seller a written, dated contract and/or receipt of the transaction and be told there is a three-day cancellation period.

Many cities require persons selling directly to consumers to be licensed by the city in which they do business if they are not residents and to pay a license fee. A bond also may be required. These city ordinances often are called **Green River ordinances** because the first legislation of this kind was passed in Green River, Wyoming, in 1933. This type of ordinance protects consumers and aids local companies by making it more difficult for outside competition to enter the market.

Both the cooling-off laws and the Green River ordinances were passed to protect consumers from salespeople using unethical, high-pressure sales tactics. These statutes and others were necessary because some salespeople used unethical practices in sales transactions.

Managing Sales Ethics

Over the years, a number of surveys to determine managers' views of business ethics have found the following:

- All managers feel they face ethical problems.
- Most managers feel they and their employers should be more ethical.
- Managers are more ethical with their friends than with people they do not know.
- Even though they want to be more ethical, some managers lower their ethical standards to meet job goals.
- Managers are aware of unethical practices in their industry and company ranging from price discrimination to hiring discrimination.
- Business ethics can be influenced by an employee's superior and by the company environment.

Bad company corrupts good character.

Organizations are concerned about how to improve their social responsiveness and ethical climate. Managers must take active steps to ensure that the company stays on ethical ground. Management methods for helping organizations be more responsive include (1) top management taking the lead, (2) carefully selecting leaders, (3) establishing and following a code of ethics, (4) creating ethical structures, (5) formally encouraging whistle-blowing, (6) creating an ethical sales climate, and (7) establishing control systems.

Follow the Leader

The organization's chief executive officer, president, and vice presidents should clearly champion the efforts for ethical conduct. Others will follow their lead. Their speeches, interviews, and actions need to constantly communicate the ethical values of the organization. The Business Roundtable, an association of chief executives from 250 large corporations, issued a report on ethics policy and practice in companies such as Boeing, Chemical Bank, General Mills, GTE, Xerox, Johnson & Johnson, and Hewlett-Packard. The report concluded that no point emerged more clearly than the crucial role of top management in guiding the social and ethical responsibilities of the organization.

Leader Selection Is Important

Since so few individuals are at the principled level of moral development, it is critical to carefully choose managers. Only people who have the highest level of integrity, standards, and values should assume leadership positions.

Establish a Code of Ethics

A **code of ethics** is a formal statement of the company's values concerning ethics and social issues. It states those values or behaviors that are expected and those that are not tolerated. These values and behaviors must be backed by management's action. Without top management support, there is little assurance that the code will be followed.

The two types of codes of ethics are principle-based statements and policy-based statements. Principle-based statements are designed to affect corporate culture, define fundamental values, and contain general language about company responsibilities, quality of products, and treatment of employees. General statements of principle are often called *corporate credos*. Examples are GTE's "Vision and Values," Johnson & Johnson's "The Credo," and Hewlett-Packard's "The HP Way."

Policy-based statements generally outline the procedures to be used in specific ethical situations. These situations include marketing practice, conflicts of interest, observance of laws, proprietary information, political gifts, and equal opportunities. Examples of policy-based statements are Boeing's "Business Conduct Guidelines," Chemical Bank's "Code of Ethics," GTE's "Code of Business Ethics" and its "Anti-Trust and Conflict of Interest Guidelines," and Norton's "Norton Policy on Business Ethics."

> *"We are all capable of arrogance and folly. Convinced of our own rightness, we don't often listen to others."*
>
> CHARLES COLSON

Create Ethical Structures

An **ethics committee** is a group of executives appointed to oversee company ethics. The committee provides rulings on questionable ethical issues. The ethics committee assumes responsibility for disciplining wrongdoers. This responsibility is essential if the organization is to directly influence employee behavior. An **ethics ombudsperson** is an official given the responsibility of corporate conscience who hears and investigates ethics complaints and informs top management of potential ethics issues. For example, companies like Google, Xerox, and Procter & Gamble have ethics committees reporting directly to the CEO.

Encourage Whistle-Blowing

Employee disclosure of illegal, immoral, or illegitimate practices on the employer's part is called **whistle-blowing.** Companies can provide a mechanism for whistle- blowing as

The prospect must have delivery of the product in four weeks to meet a national advertising rollout. The company has big bucks invested in the ad campaign. After beating the production people about the head and shoulders, the best delivery your company can promise is six weeks. The boss orders you to promise the customer delivery within a four-week deadline. What is the most ethical action to take?

1. Tell your boss that you do not believe that it is right to lie to the customer. State that you will not pass along the four-week lead time but you would be more than happy to tell the customer the true six-week lead time. Tell your boss that you cannot support dishonesty within the company.
2. Do as your boss says and promise the four-week deadline, even though you know there is no possibility of meeting this deadline.
3. Tell your boss to pass along the information to the customer himself. That way you do not have to actually lie.

a matter of policy. All employees who observe or become aware of criminal practices or unethical behavior should be encouraged to report the incident to their superiors, to a higher level of management, or to an appropriate unit of the organization, such as an ethics committee. Formalized procedures for complaining can encourage honest employees to report questionable incidents. For example, a company could provide its employees with a toll-free number that they may call to report unethical activities to top management. This silent witness program could be successful because it allows employees to report incidents without actually having to confront personnel. This program is especially valuable if the employee's own manager is involved in unethical practices. However, with programs such as these, careful verification then becomes necessary to guard against the use of such means to get even with managers or other employees.

Create an Ethical Sales Climate

The single most important factor in improving the climate for ethical behavior in a sales force is the action taken by top-level managers. Sales managers must help develop and support their codes of ethics. They should publicize the code and their opposition to unethical sales practices to their subordinate managers and their salespeople. A stronger level of ethical awareness can be achieved during sales meetings, training sessions, and when contacting customers while working with salespeople.

Establish Control Systems

Finally, control systems must be established. Methods should be employed to determine whether salespeople give bribes, falsify reports, or pad expenses. For example, sales made from low bids could be checked to determine whether procedures have been followed correctly. Dismissal, demotion, suspension, reprimand, and withholding of sales commissions would be possible penalties for unethical sales practices.

Overall, management must make a concerted effort to create an ethical climate within the workplace to best serve customer and organizational goals.

Ethics in Business and Sales

This chapter was a condensed introduction to the subject of social, ethical, and legal issues in selling. There is so much to learn about these three topics. A person can get a law degree or a PhD specializing in each of these three subjects.

From your viewpoint, however, did you learn anything about how an organization might make moral and ethical decisions each day? What about factors you might consider in making the right decisions that guide your life?

Consider this: Take some time now and each day for one week to write down in a diary or journal what guides your thinking and actions, especially those related to moral and ethical issues. Make your journal entries throughout the day and review at the end of each day. Your goal is to see what guides your choices. For example, consider whether you make your moral and ethical decisions based upon

- Whatever will bring you the most pleasing or satisfying results.
- What will make other people happy or minimize interpersonal conflict.
- Values taught by your family.
- Religious principles and teaching or Bible content.
- Something other than the above four reasons.

The most interesting question is, "What is a moral or ethical issue for you?" It is said, "Different strokes for different folks." What's ethical to you may not be ethical to someone else. If you drive five miles per hour over the speed limit, is that all right? What about my telling my wife I like her meatloaf when I do not? What about downloading music from the Internet?

Using the three levels of moral development discussed earlier in the chapter, score each ethical or moral decision you make this week one, two, or three according to the definitions of preconventional, conventional, and principled levels of moral development. Do you have a pattern of using different moral development levels for different decisions, or do you use the same level for each decision?

For one week keep score of your ethical/ moral decisions.

Helpful Hints in Making Career Decisions

As you look at your basic pattern of making moral and ethical decisions, think about this question: Does your personal belief system lend itself to the business or sales profession? This is an important question to answer for your future. As we discussed in Chapter 1, how can you believe in a profession that not many people trust? Here are a few ideas that may help you make a decision about a business or sales career:

- Be involved in businesses/organizations that provide worthwhile products—not just things that feed the world's desires.
- Do what is right according to your beliefs no matter what the cost.
- Do not compromise on your beliefs.
- Remember that people must always be more important than products, finances, fame, power, and position.
- Recognize that good people are desperately needed in all types of businesses/ organizations.

This last point is very important. All occupations need people with good personal integrity, character, and values. You can make a difference by being a role model for others, as a person who wants to unselfishly help other people.

Do Your Research!

Be sure to research any organization in which you are considering a job. Annual reports and the Internet allow you to quickly learn a little about an organization. Talking to people who work there and working for a day with a salesperson also helps you get to know about a company. However, you really have to work for the organization to truly know it. Exhibit 2.7 might provide hints on what to look for when researching an organization.

Exhibit 2.7 shows a hypothetical organization with the slogan of "Preparing People for the 21st Century." The firm's mission is to serve others using the Core Principles of Professionalism as its vision. The foundation upon which the organization is built is service. Integrity, trust, and character provide the upright support for the firm's substructure of values.[24]

Integrity, Trust, and Character

The person of integrity walks securely, but the one who takes crooked paths will be found out.

A person with **integrity** is honest without compromise or corruption. Integrity begins with *I*. It starts with the day-in, day-out ways in which you and I interact with stakeholders. People with integrity have nothing to hide and nothing to fear. Their lives are open books because their behavior agrees with their beliefs.[25]

An organization filled with people of integrity is an ethical organization. The people and organization possess a firm adherence to a code of moral values. From integrity flows confidence that one can trust the other. **Trust** refers to the belief that another will act as he or she is expected to act. This results in the organization and its salespeople having the attributes and characteristics with which one likes to do business.

Character is who you are when no one is looking!

Integrity and trust form the attributes that make up and distinguish the organization and salesperson, often referred to as **character.** Think of character as who you are when no one is looking and what you are willing to stand for when someone is looking.[26]

EXHIBIT 2.7

What do you look for in an employer?

Mission: Is to Serve People

Vision: Is Based Upon the Core Principles of Professionalism

Values: Integrity, Trust, Character

Foundation: Service to Others

An Ethical Sales Organization
Preparing People for the 21st Century
"In God We Trust"

©Photodisc/Punchstock

Character is developed and revealed by tests, and all of life is a test. Major changes in your life, delayed promises, impossible problems, undeserved praise or criticism, senseless tragedies or good fortunes, choices between what is right or wrong and the results of the choices, forgiveness, overcoming temptations, hard and good times are examples of tests we experience in life. Life's testing forms one's character. I have a lot of character. How about you?

Integrity, trust, and character help form the **values** or moral code of conduct toward others. Respect for the dignity of the individual is at the heart of the universal moral code. Please refer back to Exhibit 2.4. This is why salespeople with integrity, trustworthiness, character, and values are so sought after and needed in today's business world.

People who are truly professionals speak the truth. They are **true** to their word and reflect the best of humanity. Truth is consistent with fact or reality.

Core Principles of Professional Selling

Remember the Core Principles of Professional Selling should apply to all aspects of business, marketing, and sales. The center of business life is truth.

Absolute truth sets standards.

What is truth? The **truth** refers to the facts needed to make ethical and moral decisions. But what are true facts? To a person of faith, truth is that which upholds and does not contradict what is fundamental to his or her faith and/or, and frequently dependent on, what is stated in his or her sacred text. How do you determine what is the absolute truth?

"You shall know the truth and the truth shall set you free."

JESUS

The best facts are those that do not change. The best facts are the same yesterday, today, and tomorrow. The best facts are fixed standards, or absolute truths, by which to measure all other facts needed to make any moral or ethical decision. You might want to look over the three guidelines for making ethical decisions again to better understand this term called "truth." You cannot separate personal life from business life. People do, but it is folly. Separation of moral behavior from personal and business life will not work in an individual. Something within the person quietly whispers what is right or wrong in life and business. Service, ethics, relationships, integrity, trustworthiness, and character based upon the truth are at the heart of a person's, and the organization's, moral behavior.

True Professionals Are Ethical

True Professionals Are Ethical

Both ethical behavior and professionalism refer to treating others fairly. Take a moment to look back at their specific definitions.

Notice the title of this brief but important section of this book—true professionals are ethical. The word *ethical* means acting according to moral principles. The word *professionals* here refers to people who follow the Core Principles comes from the Core Principles of Professional Selling. What a powerful phrase—simple but profound: True professionals are ethical. While not always true today, hopefully when you are a business professional ethics will guide your work behaviors and your life.

SUMMARY OF MAJOR SELLING ISSUES

Ethics is a hot topic for managers. Ethical behavior pertains to values of right and wrong. Ethical decisions and behavior are typically guided by a value system. For an individual manager, the ability to make correct ethical choices will depend on both individual and organizational characteristics. An important individual characteristic is one's level of moral development. Corporate culture is an organizational characteristic that influences ethical behavior.

What should an individual base her or his values upon? Could the Core Principles serve as universal, practical, helpful standards for salespeople's conduct? What about your ethical and moral conduct?

Salespeople and managers realize that their business should be conducted in an ethical manner. They must be ethical in dealing with their salespeople, their employers, and their customers. Ethical standards and guidelines for sales personnel must be developed, supported, and policed. In the future, ethical selling practices will be even more important to conducting business profitably.

Quick Review for Students

The quick review sections provide key questions to help you develop a greater level of conceptual understanding. We suggest that after you read the chapter, you ask yourself if you can answer the following questions without looking back at the textbook.

1. What are ethics?
2. What are the two major influences on the ethical behaviors of a salesperson?
3. What is an ethical dilemma? Can you describe a few approaches or considerations that a salesperson could use when confronted by an ethical dilemma?
4. What might be a few ethical responsibilities of a sales manager in regard to their treatment of and interactions with their salespeople?
5. What are the five unethical practices that can affect co-workers and should be avoided by sales professionals?
6. What are the 10 suggestions that salespeople should implement to avoid misrepresentations and breach of warranty issues when dealing with customers?
7. What are the key steps an organization can take to manage sales ethics?

MEETING A SALES CHALLENGE

In essence, the sales manager was seeking reciprocity. The contemplated deal is clearly unethical. In some cases, such a deal may even be unlawful. Companies aware of their legal and ethical responsibilities protect themselves and their employees from unnecessary exposure.

For example, IBM marketing representatives are urged to follow the specific steps set forth in IBM's "Business Conduct Guideline"—a policy-based code of ethics—which states, "You may not do business with a supplier of goods or services." Reasonable? *Yes.* Important? *Absolutely.*

Remember that your career and the future of your company depend on creating values that last. This objective depends on making decisions we can live with tomorrow, not on what we might get away with today.

KEY TERMS FOR SELLING

breach of warranty 59
character 69
Clayton Act 64
code of ethics 66
conventional moral
   development level 47
cooling-off laws 65
cooperative
   acceptance 56
employee rights 55
ethical behavior 52
ethics committee 66

ethics ombudsperson 66
ethics 52
fixed point of
   reference 50
Green River
   ordinances 65
integrity 69
misrepresentation 59
morals 46
preconventional moral
   development level 47
price discrimination 64

principled moral
   development level 47
reciprocity 65
Robinson-Patman Act 64
termination-at-will rule 56
tie-in sale 64
true 70
trust 69
truth 70
values 70
Whistle-blowing 66
worldview 46

SALES APPLICATION QUESTIONS

1. Imagine that you are being encouraged to inflate your expense account. Do you think your choice would be most affected by your individual moral development or by the cultural values of the company for which you worked? Explain.
2. Have you ever experienced an ethical dilemma? Evaluate the dilemma with respect to its impact on other people.
3. Discuss the difference between sales puffery and misrepresentation and how to avoid making mistakes that may prove costly to the firm.
4. Lincoln Electric considers customers and employees to be more important stakeholders than shareholders. Is it appropriate for management to define some stakeholders as more important than others? Should all stakeholders be considered equal?
5. Do you think a code of ethics combined with an ethics committee would be more effective than leadership alone implementing ethical behavior? Discuss.

FURTHER EXPLORING THE SALES WORLD

Talk to a sales manager about the ethical and legal issues involved in the job. Does the manager's firm have

a. A code of ethics?
b. An ethics committee?
c. An ethics ombudsperson?
d. Procedures for whistle-blowing?

Get a copy of any materials relating to topics discussed in this chapter. Report on your findings.

SELLING EXPERIENTIAL EXERCISE

Sales & Marketing Executives International, Inc., was founded in 1935. Today it has over 57,000 members. In 1952 SMEI founded Pi Sigma Epsilon, the only national, coeducational, professional fraternity in marketing, sales management, and selling. PSE has more than 60 chapters nationwide.

Ethical Work Climates

SMEI's five founding principles are (1) professional identification and standards, (2) continuing education, (3) sharing knowledge, (4) assisting students, and (5) supporting free enterprise. Below is SMEI's sales and marketing creed. After studying, determine

A. How the 11 points of SMEI's sales and marketing creed relate to this chapter's section titled "Establish a Code of Ethics."

B. How SMEI's sales and marketing creed relate to the Core Principles of Selling.
   1. I hereby acknowledge my accountability to the organization for which I work and to society as a whole to improve sales knowledge and practice and to adhere to the highest professional standards in my work and personal relationships.
   2. My concept of selling includes as its basic principle the sovereignty of all consumers in the marketplace and the necessity for mutual benefit to both buyer and seller in all transactions.
   3. I shall personally maintain the highest standards of ethical and professional conduct in all my business relationships with customers, suppliers, colleagues, competitors, governmental agencies, and the public.
   4. I pledge to protect, support, and promote the principles of consumer choice, competition, and innovation enterprise, consistent with relevant legislative public policy standards.
   5. I shall not knowingly participate in actions, agreements, or marketing policies or practices which may be detrimental to customers, competitors, or established community social or economic policies or standards.
   6. I shall strive to ensure that products and services are distributed through such channels and by such methods as will tend to optimize the distributive process by offering maximum customer value and service at minimum cost while providing fair and equitable compensation for all parties.
   7. I shall support efforts to increase productivity or reduce costs of production or marketing through standardization or other methods, provided these methods do not stifle innovation or creativity.
   8. I believe prices should reflect true value in use of the product or service to the customer, including the pricing of goods and services transferred among operating organizations worldwide.
   9. I acknowledge that providing the best economic and social product value consistent with cost also includes
      (a) recognizing the customer's right to expect safe products with clear instructions for their proper use and maintenance;
      (b) providing easily accessible channels for customer complaints;
      (c) investigating any customer dissatisfaction objectively and taking prompt and appropriate remedial action;
      (d) recognizing and supporting proven public policy objectives such as conserving energy and protecting the environment.

10. I pledge my efforts to assure that all marketing research, advertising, and presentations of products, services, or concepts are done clearly, truthfully, and in good taste so as not to mislead or offend customers. I further pledge to assure that all these activities are conducted in accordance with the highest standards of each profession and generally accepted principles of fair competition.

11. I pledge to cooperate fully in furthering the efforts of all institutions, media, professional associations, and other organizations to publicize this creed as widely as possible throughout the world.

Used by permission of Sales & Marketing Executives International, Inc., the worldwide professional association for sales and marketing (www.smei.org).

NOTES

1. For an in-depth discussion of worldview, see Charles Colson and Nancy Pearcey, *How Now Shall We Live?* (Nashville, TN: LifeWay Press, 1999).

2. Based on L. Kohlberg, "Moral Stages and Moralization: The Cognitive-Development Approach," *Moral Development and Behavior: Theory, Research, and Social Issues,* ed. T. Lickona (New York: Holt, Rinehart and Winston, 1976). Also see Jerry R. Goolsby and Shelby D. Hunt, "Cognitive Moral Development and Marketing," *Journal of Marketing,* January 1992, pp. 55–68.

3. David Jeremiah, *The New Spirituality* (San Diego, CA: Turning Point, 2002), p. 114. This information is based upon a February 12, 2002 national poll by researcher George Barna of the Barna Research Group (www.barna.org).

4. Yogi Berra and Dave Kaplan, *What Time Is It? You Mean Now?* (New York: Simon & Schuster, 2002), p. 33.

5. Barna Research Group, February 12, 2002 (www.barna.org).

6. The concept of a fixed point of reference separate from oneself comes from a speech made by Frank Peretti titled "What We Believe." A tape recording of the speech can be obtained from James C. Dobson, Focus on the Family (www.family.org).

7. Sam Todd, "World-Changing Lay Ministry," *Texas Episcopalian,* February 2002, p. 8.

8. J. Slomka, B. Quill, M. des Vignes-Kendrick, and L.E. Lloyd, "Professionalism and Ethics in the Public Health Curriculum," *Public Health Reports 2008,* 123 (Suppl 2): 27–35.

9. Laura P. Hartman, *Perspectives in Business Ethics* (Burr Ridge, IL: McGraw-Hill/Irwin, 2002), p. 76.

10. President George W. Bush, *Remarks by the President on Faith-Based Initiative,* April 11, 2002, usinfo.state.gov/usa/faith/s041102.htm

11. Also see Thomas R. Wotruba, "A Comprehensive Framework for the Analysis of Ethical Behavior, with a Focus on Sales Organizations," *Journal of Personal Selling & Sales Management,* Spring 1990, pp. 29–42; and Michael A. Mayo and Lawrence J. Marks, "Empirical Investigation of a General Theory of Marketing Ethics," *Journal of the Academy of Marketing Science,* Spring 1990.

12. National Business Ethics Survey® (NBES®) 2013 Report.

13. Shay Sayre, Mary L. Joyce, and David R. Lambert, "Gender and Sales Ethics: Are Women Penalized Less Severely than Their Male Counterparts?" *Journal of Personal Selling & Sales Management,* Fall 1991, pp. 50–65.

14. Also see Leslie M. Fine and Janice R. Franke, "Legal Aspects of Salesperson Commission Payments: Implications for the Implementation of Commission Sales Programs," *Journal of Personal*

Selling & Sales Management, Winter 1995, pp. 53–68.

15. Richard F. Beltramini, "Exploring the Effectiveness of Business Gifts: A Controlled Field Experiment," *Journal of the Academy of Marketing Science,* Winter 1992, pp. 87–91.

16. Adapted from "Strange Tales of Sales," *Sales & Marketing Management,* June 3, 1995, p. 46.

17. Author unknown.

18. Bristol Voss, "Eat, Drink, and Be Wary," *Sales & Marketing Management,* January 1991, pp. 49–54.

19. Stacy Cowley, "Wells Fargo Workers Claim Retaliation for Playing by the Rules," 26, 2016, https://www.nytimes.com/2016/09/27/business/dealbook/wells-fargo-workersclaim-retaliation-for-playing-by-the-rules.html

20. Matt Egan, "Wells Fargo Uncovers up to 1.4 Million More Fake Accounts," August 31, 2017, http://money.cnn.com/2017/08/31/investing/wells-fargo-fakeaccounts/index.html

21. John Jobs, "Watch Those Buyers," *Sales & Marketing Management,* October 1997, pp. 34–38.

22. Author unknown.

23. Les Andrews, "Watch What You Say," *Distribution,* April 1997, p. 23.

24. Art idea adapted from Gerhard Gschwandtner, "Job 1: What's the Heart of Your Brand?" *Selling Power,* April 2002, pp. 72–76.

25. Adapted from Warren Wiersbe, *The Integrity Crisis* (Nashville, TN: Nelson, 1988), p. 21.

26. Adapted from a talk by E. Dean Gage, 2003.

CASE 2.1

©Ron Chapple Stock/FotoSearch/ Glow Images

Ethical Selling at Perfect Solutions: The Case of the Delayed Product

Scott Patterson is a salesperson for Perfect Solutions, a chemical manufacturing firm. He sells to distributors, sometimes called wholesalers. Distributors buy in large quantities from various manufacturers and sell in smaller quantities to other businesses. Larry Ingram, the CEO of one of Scott's best distributors, called Scott into his office to discuss some concerns he has regarding their business relationship.

Ingram's company has been distributing Perfect Solutions products for over 10 years. In addition, Ingram's company has been the top seller for Perfect Solutions products two of the past three years. However, Scott seems to be doing things that may affect Ingram's sales. Ingram is very upset!

Scott Signs Competitor

Scott recently signed up Barber Distributing to distribute and sell his company's products. Barber Distributing is a competitor of Ingram's. Ingram found out about this relationship when Scott's new client, Barber Distributing, sold to one of Ingram's customers at a price 10 percent under Ingram's normal list price to get the project. Ingram had cut their prices to the bone and still did not win the bid. "Did PS give Barber special price deals?" asks Ingram. Scott says, "No." Ingram wants to know if Barber will bid for the "plant" business coming up. He wants Scott to get him their bid price. Ingram places pressure on Scott to get him the best price for the bid or lose his business.

Ingram feels that his company has been very valuable to Perfect Solutions and demands that Patterson reveal the prices at which he sold products to Barber Distributors. Patterson then promises Ingram that Perfect Solutions has fixed prices that are never altered. Scott told Ingram that he and Barber pay the same price for a particular product.

The Customer Is Upset!

This does not satisfy Ingram and he lets Patterson know that the Dymotzue Company, a competitor of Scott and Perfect Solutions, has quoted Ingram better prices. The price sheets are on Ingram's desk. Ingram says he will not hesitate to leave Patterson for Dymotzue if Scott does not take care of him. Scott asks Ingram what he could do to help ease Ingram's frustration. Ingram says he wants to buy about two truckloads of Bond-do-Perm that Scott promised him but has not yet delivered.

While the Cat Is Away

Ingram is called out of the office. While Ingram is out of his office Patterson calls his manufacturing plant and talks with Jack, the manager. Jack tells him the Bond-do-Perm has some manufacturing problems and will not be available for two months. The company does not want to ship a bad product. Scott gets off the phone as Ingram walks back into his office. Patterson promises Ingram one truckload of the Bond-do-Perm within a few weeks knowing it cannot be delivered at that time. Ingram says he can sell one truckload to his customers as soon as the Bond-do-Perm arrives.

About this time, one of Ingram's salespeople comes into the distribution center's main office and says that Barber Distributing, Ingram's competitor, has just made an offer to sell LubeExcel to one of Ingram's customers at a price 5 percent lower than that of Ingram's price. Ingram is furious, yelling at Scott to do something about this! To help Ingram meet the price, Patterson offers a free drum of LubeExcel to Ingram. Scott is authorized to give free samples only to new customers.

When Ingram leaves the office, Scott decides to look at the Dymotzue price list on Ingram's desk.

Questions

1. Describe the situation faced by both Scott Patterson and Larry Ingram.
2. What would you do if you were Scott Patterson?
3. What would you do if you were Larry Ingram?
4. What are the ethical considerations, if any, in this case?
5. What level of moral development are Patterson and Ingram operating at in this business relationship?

CASE 2.2

©Ron Chapple Stock/FotoSearch/
Glow Images

Sales Hype: To Tell the Truth or Stretch It, That Is the Question

Sally Bateman and Kara McAfree have recently begun working as trainees selling furniture for a large department store. Sally has a very aggressive style, whereas Kara strongly believes in giving the customer the best information possible and then selling them a product that best fits their needs.

Sally Tries to Steal Kara's Customer

One day, two of Kara's customers came in shopping for furniture. Sally told the couple that Kara was out of the store. After Sally determined they were shopping for a new dining table and chairs, she showed them a certain style and told the couple it was brand new. The couple left the store.

Kara happened to overhear the conversation and approached her co-worker with some concerns. Sally initially thought Kara was frustrated because the couple were Kara's customers and she wanted to make sure she got credit for the sale. Kara's main concern, however, was that Sally lied to the customers about the table being new when it was in fact a year old. Sally told Kara that everyone uses "hype" to make sales and if she wants to make her sales figures, she will have to do it too.

Kara Is Concerned about Her Performance

Performance appraisals are quickly approaching, and Kara knows she is getting a poor review because her sales pale in comparison to Sally's. She talks to a co-worker about the review process and asks him if she should tell management that Sally's high numbers are the result of her stealing customers and lying about products. He tells Kara he thinks that would be a bad idea because it might make her look like she is making excuses. He makes it sound as if management may condone the use of sales hype.

Questions

1. Describe the situation faced by Kara.
2. What would you do if you were Kara?
3. What are the ethical considerations, if any, in this case?
4. What level of moral development are Sally and Kara operating at in this business situation?

CASE 2.3

©Ron Chapple Stock/FotoSearch/
Glow Images

Personal Decision Making: Do Ethical Considerations Matter?

Your friend, John, has just told you that he has accepted a job at a major worldwide technology company. You are delighted for your friend for a number of reasons. First, it is only November and John doesn't graduate until May. Therefore, John has landed a great, full-time position six months before graduation. Second, you have met John's soon-to-be supervisor at a recent career fair. She is a really dynamic manager, who is very concerned about building a world-class team. Third, this is an amazing opportunity for your friend, as the technology company is rated as possessing one of the top sales forces in the United States. In addition, the firm has been recognized as being one of the top firms for employee satisfaction.

After Thanksgiving, you and John meet for a quick coffee at the university's student union. While catching up on the holiday, John states that his uncle attended his family's Thanksgiving. His uncle owns a small printing company in John's hometown. John says, "My uncle knows everyone in the area." John's uncle told John that there a number of companies that would be interested in talking with John about sales positions in their firms. John tells you that even though he has signed an employment agreement with the technology company, he thinks he will "test the water a little bit more." John states, "It's a free market isn't it? What could it really hurt to see my options?"

Questions

1. If you were John, how would you handle the opportunity offered by his uncle? What might be three approaches to handle this situation?
2. What are the ethical considerations, if any, in this case?
3. If you were John's soon-to-be supervisor, what might be your thoughts on the situation?
4. What level of moral development is John operating at in this scenario?

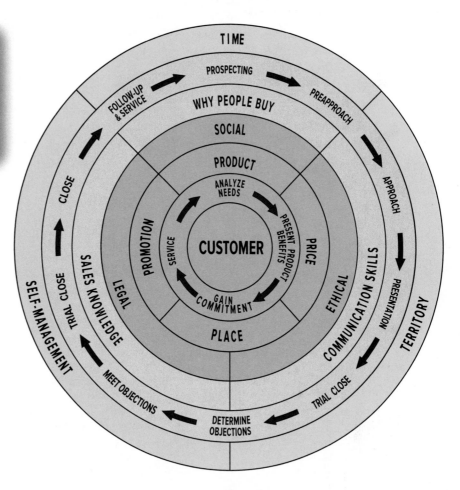

Preparation for Relationship Selling

Part II focuses on the main sales knowledge that salespeople need. Chapter 3 discusses buyer behavior. It begins the discussion of the communication techniques you will use in your sales presentation—salespeople must be excellent communicators. Chapter 4 introduces you to basic verbal and nonverbal communications techniques used by today's salespeople. Chapter 5 provides an overview of sales knowledge required to call on customers. Salespeople use knowledge of buyer behavior, communication skills, and sales knowledge to effectively analyze customer needs, select the proper product benefits to present, gain commitment from the buyer, and provide exceptional service, allowing the opportunity to sell again in the future.

The Psychology of Selling: Why People Buy

Main Topics

The Core Principles: Benefits

Why People Buy—The Black Box Approach

Consumer versus Organizational Buying

Psychological Influences on Buying

Applying Your Understanding of Needs

How to Determine Important Buying Needs—A Key to Success

You Can Classify Buying Situations

Consumer Buying Decision Process

Organizational Buying Decision Process

To Buy or Not to Buy—A Choice Decision

A *FAB*ulous Approach to Buyer Need Satisfaction

The Trial Close—A Great Way to Uncover Needs and SELL

SELL Sequence

Learning Objectives

What do people really buy? They buy the benefits of a product. This chapter examines why and how individuals buy. It emphasizes the need for salespeople to stress benefits in their presentations. After studying this chapter, you should be able to

3–1 Explain the differences between consumer and organizational buying contexts.

3–2 Explain why people buy.

3–3 Enumerate techniques for determining a customer's needs.

3–4 List factors that influence the customer's buying decision.

3–5 Show why buying is a choice decision.

3–6 Explain the differences between a feature, an advantage, and a benefit.

3–7 Be able to construct a SELL Sequence.

3–8 Know when and how to use a trial close.

FACING A SALES CHALLENGE

Five years ago John Salley graduated with a computer science degree from MIT. One year later, he earned his MBA from Texas A&M University with a perfect "A" average. John was on every campus recruiter's list as an outstanding applicant. He had the brains, personality, looks, and motivation of a winner. IBM convinced him to take a sales job.

John was at the top of his class in the IBM sales training program. However, his first two years in sales resulted in an average performance. He could not understand why, because his knowledge of the products was outstanding. John could discuss in great depth the most technical aspects of his products. He was not used to being average. John loved sales but felt things had to change.

If you were in John's position, what would you do?

John Salley is like many people who do everything it takes to be successful in sales. Yet for some reason, they never reach their maximum performance potential. To be successful, salespeople need to be knowledgeable, even experts, on everything discussed in Part II, "Preparation for Relationship Selling."

Chapter 3 examines why and how an individual buys. Numerous influences determine why people buy one product over another. We discuss these reasons and apply them to the various steps in the customer's buying process. This chapter presents selling techniques that will aid you later in developing your sales presentation. They also can help John Salley in his efforts to improve his sales performance. He needs to know why people buy.

The Core Principles: Benefits

As you learn about the psychology of selling, you will better understand why people buy and why the salesperson must emphasize benefits in her sales presentation. Customers want to trust you! They depend upon you to tell the truth. Use your selling skills learned in this chapter to help people by being a better communicator. Periodically asking a person about what you have just said is a great way to find out what they think about your talk. Do the right thing for the person, even if it means a "no sale." After all, you are with the person to unselfishly help that person make the correct buying decision for his or her need, not your need to make a sale. Ethical service builds relationships and is based upon the truth.

Why People Buy—The Black Box Approach

The question of why people buy has interested salespeople for many years. Salespeople know that some customers buy their product after the presentation, yet they wonder what thought process resulted in the decision to buy or not to buy. Prospective buyers are usually exposed to various sales presentations. In some manner, a person internalizes or considers this information and then makes a buying decision. This process of internalization is referred to as a **black box** because we cannot see into the buyer's mind—meaning that the salesperson can apply the stimuli (a sales presentation) and observe the behavior of the prospect but cannot witness the prospect's actual decision-making process.

The classic model of buyer behavior shown in Exhibit 3.1 is called a **stimulus–response** model. A stimulus (sales presentation) is applied, resulting in a response (purchase decision). This model assumes that prospects respond in some predictable manner to the sales presentation. Unfortunately, it does not tell us why they buy or do not buy the product. This information is concealed in the black box.

EXHIBIT 3.1

Stimulus–response model of buyer behavior.

Salespeople seek to understand as much as they can about the mental processes that yield the prospects' responses. We do know

- That people buy for both practical (rational) and psychological (emotional) reasons.
- That salespeople can use specific methods to help determine the prospects' thoughts during sales presentations.
- That buyers consider certain factors in making purchase decisions.

This chapter introduces these three important topics. Each topic emphasizes the salesperson's need to understand people's behavior. However, before we cover these topics, it is important to understand the differences and similarities of the consumer and organizational buying contexts.

Consumer versus Organizational Buying

Consumer buying refers to the purchasing activities of individuals and households for their personal use, consumption or to meet the collective needs of the household unit such as a family or individual.[1] When salespeople (representing a business) sell to consumers (i.e., the end user), this is called B2C, or business-to-consumer selling. B2C selling examples include a salesperson selling financial services, such as life insurance and retirement plans to your grandparents, and home security systems firms selling the system to your family. In B2C selling, the salesperson may only interact or discuss the opportunity with one or two individuals, such as your mother or father, before a decision is made.

Organizational buying includes all of the activities of organizational members as they define a buying situation and identify, evaluate, and choose among alternative brands and suppliers.[2] When salespeople, representing a business, sell to other businesses, this is called B2B, or business-to-business selling. B2B selling examples include apparel manufacturers such as Under Armour® representatives selling the firm's spring apparel line to a sporting goods distributor or a healthcare technology company selling its newest MRI scanner to a hospital system.

Although organizational buying is different from individual buying as shown in Exhibit 3.2,[3] effective salespeople recognize that it is the "human touch" that shapes

EXHIBIT 3.2

Comparison between consumer and organizational buying contexts.

Buying Characteristics	Consumer Context	Organizational Context
Motive	Purposes of the consumer/household	Purposes of the organization
People	Typically an individual	Group of people (e.g., buying center)
Expertise	Decision-maker(s) not expected to possess expertise	Decision-maker(s) expected to possess expertise
Process	Process often impacted by individual's emotions and formal guidelines not necessarily followed	Rationality often recommended as a goal and decision making process may involve formal rules and guidelines
Complexity	Decision tasks more routine in nature and relatively less complex	Decision tasks often complex and significant
Time	Relatively quick decision making	Time-consuming process

and maintains relationships between buying and selling organizations.[4] While the B2B salesperson must understand the customer's processes, the customer's business objectives, the customer's culture, and the buying center's roles and responsibilities, the salesperson also recognizes that buying is an interpersonal process. Regardless of whether the buying situation is your mom purchasing a $10,000 life insurance policy or a chief information officer procuring a multimillion dollar server system, an effective salesperson understands that sales requires interpersonal skills, trust, and adaptability.

Psychological Influences on Buying

Since professional selling requires understanding human behavior, each salesperson must be concerned with a prospective customer's motivations, perceptions, learning, attitudes, and personality. Furthermore, the salesperson should know how each type of behavior might influence a customer's purchase decision.

Motivation to Buy Must Be There

Human beings are motivated by needs and wants. These needs and wants build up internally, which causes people to desire to buy a product—a new car or a new duplicating machine. People's **needs** result from a lack of something desirable. **Wants** are needs learned by the person. For example, people *need* transportation—but some *want* a BMW while others *prefer* a Ford Mustang.

This example illustrates that both practical or rational reasons (the need for transportation) and emotional or psychological reasons (the desire for the prestige of owning a BMW) influence the buying decision. Different individuals have different reasons for wanting to buy. But ultimately, the **motivation to purchase** a product, service, or solution is based on the "lack" of something, otherwise known as a *gap*. For instance, a buyer may be dissatisfied with the current situation. This may occur to you around lunch time. You feel a rumbling in your stomach and start to become a little light-headed. You are hungry (which leads to dissatisfaction with your current situation). In effect, you are motivated to solve a problem. You are motivated to act to enhance your current state and move toward a more desired state. Hence, you visit a local restaurant and purchase a lunch entrée.

In other instances, you may be motivated to act because you discover or are attracted to a future situation (or state). You may be relatively satisfied with your current state and unaware that a better or more desirable state exists. For instance, you and a friend are having a conversation about cell phones. You relay to your friend how happy you are with your cell phone, its accessories, and plan. However, your friend states that her monthly cellphone plan is $15 less than your plan, and she receives a new phone (free of charge) every 16 months. When you learn about your friend's cell phone plan, you realize a more desirable state exists. You are motivated to act to enhance your future, desired state. You visit a new cell phone provider. The salesperson must determine a prospect's needs and then match the product's benefits to the particular needs and wants of the prospect (see Exhibit 3.3).

Economic Needs: The Best Value for the Money

Economic needs are the buyer's need to purchase the most satisfying product for the money. Economic needs include price, quality (performance, dependability, durability), convenience of buying, and service. Some people's purchases are based primarily on economic needs. However, most people consider the economic implications of all their purchases along with other reasons for buying.

EXHIBIT 3.3

Product plus: A product is more than a product.

©Andrea Danti/Shutterstock

We provide a list of economic buying needs commonly associated with business to business purchasing agents:

- Increase my sales.
- Increase the levels of my customers' satisfaction.
- Decrease my expenses, raw materials, and other costs.
- Increase the speed of my manufacturing processes or service delivery.
- Increase the agility or adaptability of a department.
- Increase my profits.
- Aid me in reaching my objectives.
- Aid me in meeting my responsibilities.
- Aid me in understanding my competition or environment.
- Aid me in championing this initiative within my organization.

Many salespeople mistakenly assume that people base their buying decision solely on price. This is not always correct. A higher product price relative to competing goods often can be offset by such factors as service, quality, better performance, friendliness of the salesperson, and convenience of purchase.

In effect, buyers are seeking overall value—the buyer's belief that she is receiving more than the resouces she is investing (i.e., financial, effort, human, and time).

Whatever a person's need might be, it is important for a salesperson to uncover it. Once you determine the individual's need, you are better prepared to develop your sales presentation in a manner relating your product's benefits to that particular need. This is not always easy to do because people may not be fully aware of their needs.

Awareness of Needs: Some Buyers Are Unsure

You have seen that people purchase products to satisfy various needs. Often, however, these needs are developed over such a long period that people may not be fully conscious of their reasons for buying or not buying a product. The buying decision can be complicated by their level of need awareness. Three levels of need awareness have been identified—conscious, preconscious, and unconscious.

©fatihhoca/Getty Images

At the first level, the **conscious need level,** buyers are fully aware of their needs. These are the easiest people to sell to because they know what products they want and are willing to talk about their needs. A customer might say to the salesperson, "I'd like to buy a new car and I want a BMW loaded with accessories. What can you show me?"

At the second level, the **preconscious need level,** buyers may not be fully aware of their needs. Needs may not be fully developed in the conscious mind. They know what general type of product they want but may not wish to discuss it fully. For example, a buyer may want to buy a certain product because of a strong ego need yet be hesitant about telling you. If you don't make a sale and ask why, this buyer may present false reasons, such as saying your price is too high, rather than revealing the real motivation. Falsification is much easier than stating the true reasons for not buying your product—thus getting into a long conversation with you, arguing with you, or telling you that your product is unsatisfactory. You must avoid this brush-off by determining a buyer's real needs first and then relating your product's benefits to these needs.

At the third level, the **unconscious need level,** people do not know why they buy a product—only that they do buy. When people say, "I really don't know what I want to buy," it may be true. Their buying motives might have developed years earlier and may have been repressed. In this case, the salesperson needs to determine the needs that are influential. Often, this is accomplished by skillful questioning to draw out prospective buyers' unconscious needs.

Applying Your Understanding of Needs

Why is it important to understand customer needs? By understanding the customers' needs, you begin to recognize how you can assist the customers and their firms. For example, a salesperson may visit a manufacturing firm. The firm's operations manager may be dissatisfied with the number of items produced every hour by the manufacturing process. The operations manager is unhappy with his firm's current situation (i.e., the quantity of units produced). The operations manager is already aware better options exists. As a salesperson, your goal is to help them reach an improved future situation—the ability to produce more. Therefore, you may discuss a range of options that will assist the buyer to meet the company's production goals.

In other instances, a buyer may not be aware of a better solution or a buyer may be so busy with responsibilities, he has not considered new approaches, processes, or solutions. The customer is not aware of a better future situation. For example, a salesperson may meet with the buyer of the pickles category for a chain of grocery stores. The buyer expresses that she is happy with the annual sales growth of pickles in her store (i.e., around 3 percent). However, the salesperson knows that other grocery stores are stocking a new type of pickle that has captured the interest of grocery consumers. By distributing this new type of pickle, many retailers have increased the sales of the pickle category by another 2 percent. The salesperson's goal is to help the grocery buyer understand that an opportunity exists to increase the sales of pickles by discussing the opportunity of an improved future situation.

As you can see from our examples, understanding the background of needs and how the needs process works is very important for the salesperson. In some instances, the customer may be aware of the needs and is seeking to improve the future situation. However, in other instances, the salesperson will need to create awareness of the opportunity and teach the customer that a better future situation is available. Exhibit 3.4 provides examples of how salespeople help buyers understand a better situation is available.

EXHIBIT 3.4

Examples of how salespeople help buyers understand a better situation is available.

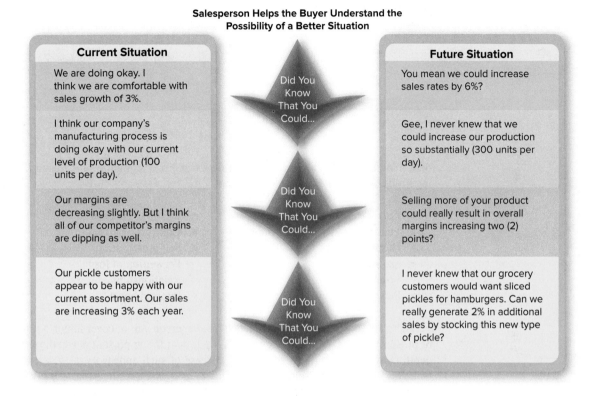

Salesperson Helps the Buyer Understand the Possibility of a Better Situation

Current Situation	Future Situation
We are doing okay. I think we are comfortable with sales growth of 3%.	You mean we could increase sales rates by 6%?
I think our company's manufacturing process is doing okay with our current level of production (100 units per day).	Gee, I never knew that we could increase our production so substantially (300 units per day).
Our margins are decreasing slightly. But I think all of our competitor's margins are dipping as well.	Selling more of your product could really result in overall margins increasing two (2) points?
Our pickle customers appear to be happy with our current assortment. Our sales are increasing 3% each year.	I never knew that our grocery customers would want sliced pickles for hamburgers. Can we really generate 2% in additional sales by stocking this new type of pickle?

(Center arrows: "Did You Know That You Could...")

How to Determine Important Buying Needs—A Key to Success

Your initial task when first meeting the customer is to differentiate between important buying needs and needs of lesser or no importance. Exhibit 3.5 illustrates the concept that buyers have both important needs and needs that are not major reasons for buying a product (relatively unimportant buying needs).

Determine buyers' important needs and concentrate on emphasizing product benefits that will satisfy those needs. Benefits that would satisfy buyers' unimportant needs should be deemphasized in the sales presentation. Suppose your product had benefits involving service, delivery, time savings, and cost reductions. Is the buyer interested in all four benefits? Maybe not. If you determine that delivery is not important, concentrate on discussing service, time savings, and cost reductions. This selling strategy is important to your success in helping the buyer.

Elmer Wheeler, a famous sales speaker, said, "Sell the sizzle, not the steak!" Wheeler is saying that people buy for reasons other than what the product will actually do or its price. They have both practical (rational) and psychological (emotional) reasons for buying. Customers may not buy the product to solve the rational need that the salesperson perceives as important. They may buy to satisfy an emotional need not easily recognized. It is important to understand this sales concept and learn to

The buyer's needs may be economic or psychological.

EXHIBIT 3.5

Match the buyer's needs to the product's benefits and emphasize them in the sales presentation.

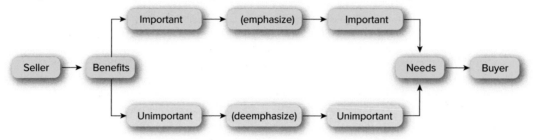

determine the buyer's important buying needs. A list of common psychological buying needs includes these:

- Fear
- Vanity (keep up with the Joneses)
- Desire for gain
- Security
- Love of family
- Personal pleasure

- Desire to succeed
- Comfort or luxury
- Self-preservation
- Prevention of loss
- Relationships
- Internal image

There are several ways through which a salesperson can uncover important needs of prospects. For example, salespeople can pinpoint the important needs through in-depth conversation with prospects. The success of such endeavors, however, would be highly dependent on salespeople's ability to ask good questions and actively listen to prospects' responses to those questions. It is equally imperative for a salesperson to observe a prospect's surroundings and non-verbal expressions to determine the important need. Apart from talking to prospects, a salesperson should also hold interactions with others who are working with the prospect as well as talk to his or her own colleagues within the organization who may have information about the prospect's important needs.

Once you determine the major buying need, you are ready to relate the person's needs to your product's benefits. Like the television camera that transmits images to the television receiver, buyers picture desired products in their minds. Before they focus the picture, buyers often need to be turned on and tuned in. Once you find their real reasons for wanting a particular product or identify major problems that they want to solve, you have uncovered the key to helping them.

Determine your customers' needs and then propose a solution to assist them.

Uncovering these important buying needs is pushing the button that turns on a machine. You have just pushed the customer's hot button. You have awakened a need, and customers realize that you understand their problems. *Basically, this is what selling is all about—determining needs and skillfully relating your product's benefits to show how its purchase will fulfill customers' needs.*

This is not always easy. As we have seen, people have a multitude of different needs and may not understand or see their unconscious needs or problems. In this situation, your challenge is to convert customers' apparently unconscious needs into recognized and understood needs. In the next few sections, we will delve into more into the purchasing process for consumers and organizations. With this understanding, we will then describe one approach that allows you to relate your product's benefits to your customers' needs.

You Can Classify Buying Situations

Some people may appear to make up their minds quickly and easily either to buy or not to buy. This is not always the case. The quickness and ease of deciding the product to buy typically depends on the buying situation. Purchasing a gallon of milk is quite different from buying an automobile. People have more difficulty in selecting, organizing, and interpreting information when purchasing an automobile. Also, their attitudes and beliefs toward the automobile may not be well formed.

True, a few people have the type of personality (and resources) that allows them to quickly purchase an expensive product such as an automobile, but this is unusual. When purchasing some types of products, most people carefully compare competing brands. They talk to salespeople. As they collect information, they form attitudes and beliefs toward each product. People must decide which product has the most desirable features, advantages, and benefits. When considering several brands, people may seek information on each one. The more information they collect, the greater the difficulty they may have in deciding which product to buy.

Purchase decisions can usually be classified as to the difficulty involved in deciding which product to buy. The purchase decision is viewed as a problem-solving activity falling into one of three classifications shown in Exhibit 3.6. These are routine decision making, limited decision making, and extensive decision making.

Some Decisions Are Routine

Many products are purchased repeatedly. People are in the habit of buying a particular product. They give little thought or time to the routine purchase; they fully realize the product's benefits. These are called low-involvement goods because they involve a routine buying decision. People's attitudes and beliefs toward the product are already formed and are usually positive. Office supplies, cold drinks, and many grocery items often are purchased through **routine decision making.**

For a customer making a routine purchase decision, reinforce that this is the correct buying decision. It is important to have the product in stock. If you do not have it, the customer may go to another supplier.

For someone not currently using your product, the challenge is to change this person's product loyalty or normal buying habits. The features, advantages, and benefits of your product should be directly compared to the buyer's preferred brand. Of course, not all purchase decisions are routine.

Some Decisions Are Limited

When buyers are unfamiliar with a particular product brand, they seek more information when making a purchase decision. In this case, there is **limited decision making**—a moderate level of actual buyer involvement in the decision. Buyers know the general qualities of goods in the product class, but they are not familiar with each brand's features, advantages, and benefits. For example, they may perceive that Xerox, 3M, and Canon copiers are the same in performance.

EXHIBIT 3.6

The three classes of buying situations.

These buyers have more involvement in buying decisions in terms of shopping time, money, and potential dissatisfaction with the purchase than in the routine purchase decision. They seek information to aid them in making the correct decision. The sales presentation should provide buyers with the necessary knowledge to make brand comparisons and increase their confidence that the purchase of your product is the correct decision. Occasionally, the purchase of some products requires prospective buyers to go one step further and apply extensive decision making.

Some Decisions Are Extensive

Buyers seeking to purchase products such as insurance, computer servers, or a 3D printer are highly involved in making the buying decision. They may be unfamiliar with a specific brand or type of product and have difficulty in making the purchase decision. This kind of purchase requires more of an investment in time and money than the limited decision. This situation demands **extensive decision making** and problem-solving activities.

In making extensive decisions, buyers believe that much more is at stake relative to other buying decisions. They may become frustrated during the decision-making process, especially if a large amount of information is available. They may be unfamiliar with the products. Buying a technology system or a life insurance policy entails a number of distinct considerations.

Determine all possible reasons why buyers are interested in a product. Then, in a simple, straightforward manner, present only enough information to allow the buyer to make a decision. At this time, you can make product comparisons, if necessary. You also can help the buyer evaluate alternative products.

In summary, your challenge is to *provide buyers with product knowledge that allows them to know if your products fulfill their needs.* Determining what type of decision process a buyer is using is critical to helping the person or organization.

Consumer Buying Decision Process

Today's consumers are constantly exposed to information about various products. What steps do people go through in making a purchase decision?

Typically, the consumer buying decision involves the five basic steps shown in Exhibit 3.7. Consumers recognize a need, collect information through internal and external sources, evaluate that information, decide to buy, and after the purchase, determine whether they are satisfied. This sequence reveals that several events occur before and after the purchase, all of which the salesperson should consider.

As Exhibit 3.7 shows, numerous forces influence a consumer's buying behavior. Rich people or older people, for example, often view purchases differently than lower-income or younger consumers. Psychological factors such as past experience with a salesperson—good or bad—certainly influence buying decisions. Have you ever had a friend or family member cause you to buy one product rather than another? We all have. Thus, whether we realize it or not, numerous factors influence why someone buys something.

Need Arousal

Remember from the first part of this chapter that consumers may experience a need, or the need can be triggered by the salesperson; this is called **need arousal.** It could be psychological, social, or economic; it could be a need for safety, self-actualization, or ego fulfillment. You must determine a person's needs to know what product information to provide. This information should relate the product's benefits to the person's needs.

EXHIBIT 3.7

Personal, psychological, and social forces that influence consumers' buying behavior.

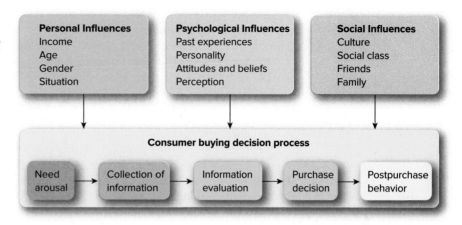

Collection of Information

If consumers know which product satisfies a need, they buy quickly. The salesperson may need only approach them; they already want to buy the product.

However, when consumers are faced with limited or extensive problem solving, they may want to **collect information** about the product. They might visit several retail stores and contact several potential suppliers. They may talk with a number of salespeople about a product's price, advantage, size, and warranty before making a decision.

Information Evaluation

A person's product **information evaluation** determines what will be purchased. After mentally processing all the information about products that will satisfy a need—and this may or may not include your product—a buyer matches this information with needs, attitudes, and beliefs, as discussed earlier, in making a decision. Only then will a **purchase decision** be made.

This evaluation process includes rating preferences on factors such as price, quality, and brand reputation. Attitudes on different products are based on either psychological or rational reasons.

At this stage, a salesperson can be effective. Providing information that matches product features, advantages, and benefits with a buyer's needs, attitudes, and beliefs increases the chances of selling the person the correct product. So, the salesperson is responsible for uncovering the person's needs, attitudes, and beliefs early in the discussion to match the product with the person's needs.

One way to get such information is to determine not only needs, beliefs, and attitudes but also the type of information a person needs before making a decision. Here are some questions you need to know how to answer:

- Which product attributes are important in this decision—price, quality, service?
- Of these attributes, which are *most* important?
- What are the prospect's attitudes toward your products?
- What are the prospect's attitudes toward your competitor's products?
- Which level of satisfaction is expected from buying the product?

This type of questioning not only tells you about the consumer's needs but also involves the consumer in the presentation and may convey the idea that you are truly interested in his or her needs. This attitude toward you is enough to create positive attitudes about your product.

Armed with this knowledge about the prospect, the salesperson is in a better position to provide the information necessary for a decision and also to help the prospect evaluate information in favor of your product. The information should be provided simply, clearly, and in a straightforward manner. It should seek to correct any misinformation about your product. Matching information with a prospect's needs may enable you to

- Impact the person's beliefs about your product, for example, by convincing the customer that your product is priced higher than the competition because it is a quality product.
- Impact the person's beliefs about your competitor's products.
- Change the amount of importance a person attaches to a particular product attribute, for example, by having the customer consider quality and service rather than price alone.
- Show unnoticed attributes of your product.
- Change the search for the ideal product into a more realistic pursuit, such as by substituting a $150,000 home for a $200,000 home.

A company has no better promotional device than having its sales force help prospects and customers to evaluate products on the market—and not merely their own products. The two-way communication between buyer and seller is exceptionally effective in providing the information needed to make the sale on the one hand, and to evaluate the product on the other. Salespeople provide knowledge to aid in their decision-making process. In many respects, salespeople are teachers (professors, if you will) who provide helpful information.

Purchase Decision

Is the sale made once the prospect states an intention to buy? No. Do not consider the sale final until the contract is signed or until you have the buyer's money, because there is still a chance for a change of mind. Even after a buyer has selected a product, purchase intentions can be changed by these four basic factors:

1. The attitude of significant others, such as a relative, spouse, friend, or boss. Consider both the intensity of another person's attitude and the level of motivation the buyer has to comply with or to resist this other person's attitude (see Exhibit 3.8).
2. The perceived risk of buying the product—will it give a return on the money?
3. Uncontrollable circumstances, such as not being able to finance the purchase of a house or to pass the physical examination for a large life insurance policy.
4. The salesperson's actions after the decision has been reached—sometimes it is unwise to continue to talk about a product after this point; something could change the buyer's mind.

The third factor, uncontrollable circumstances, is self-explanatory. However, how can attitudes of others influence a sale? A man may want to buy a dark, conservative business suit, whereas his wife wants him to buy a sport coat and slacks. The buyer's original favorable attitude toward the business suit may have been changed by his wife.

Since buyers may not always be sure that they will be satisfied with a purchase, they may perceive a risk; they may experience tension and anxiety after buying your product. Haven't we all asked ourselves, Have I made the correct decision? The levels of tension and anxiety people experience are related to their perceptions of and attitudes about the products they had to choose from. Uncertainty about differences between your product and those of your competitors can create anxiety,

EXHIBIT 3.8

Other people can influence the prospect's decision to purchase.

©Troels Graugaard/Getty Images

This rep must service and meet the needs of the many people who use his company's products.

©Erik Isakson/Getty Images

This salesperson should sell to all people in the discussion. Otherwise, one person could talk the other out of buying the product.

especially if both products' benefits appear similar, or if your product is more expensive yet promises better benefits. Prospects might see little difference between products or may like them all—and thus can fairly easily change their minds several times before buying.

Finally, many sales have been lost after a buyer has said, "I will buy," and the salesperson continues to talk. Additional information sometimes causes buyers to change their minds. It is important to finalize the sale as quickly as possible after the buyer makes a decision. Once the prospect decides, stop adding information, pack up your bag, and leave.

Postpurchase

> *This is how you follow the Core Principles of Professional Selling.*

No, the decision process does *not* end with the purchase—not for the consumer at least! A product, once purchased, yields certain levels of satisfaction and dissatisfaction. **Purchase satisfaction** comes from receiving benefits expected, or greater than expected, from a product. If consumers' experiences from the use of a product exceed expectations, they are satisfied, but if experiences are below expectations, customers are dissatisfied.

The consumer can experience **purchase dissonance** after the product's purchase. Dissonance causes tension over whether the right decision was made in buying the product. Some people refer to this as *buyer's remorse.* Dissonance increases with the importance of the decision and the difficulty of choosing between products. If dissonance occurs, buyers may get rid of a product by returning it or by selling it to someone else. Alternatively, they may seek assurance from the salesperson or friends that the product is a good one and that they made the correct purchase decision (positively reinforcing themselves).

You can help the consumer be satisfied with the product and lower the level of dissonance in several ways. First, if necessary, show the consumer how to use the product properly. Second, be realistic in making claims for the product. Exaggerated claims may create dissatisfaction. Third, continually reinforce consumer decisions by reminding them how well the product actually performs and fulfills their needs. Remember, in some situations consumers can return the product to the seller after purchase. This cancels your sale and hurts your chances of making future sales to this customer. Fourth, follow up after the sale to determine if a problem exists. If so, help correct it. This is a great way to increase the likelihood of repeat business.

In summary, seek to sell a product that satisfies the consumer's needs. In doing so, remember that the sale is made only when the actual purchase is complete and that you should continue to reinforce the consumer's attitudes about the product at all times, even after the sale. This practice reduces the perceived risk of making a bad buy, which allows buyers to listen to and trust your sales message even though some of your proposals may be out of line with their purchase plans. It also can reduce the buyers' postpurchase dissonance. Buyers who have developed a trust in your product claims believe that you will help them properly use the product.

Organizational Buying Decision Process

Every buying decision aims to satisfy a need or solve a problem. However, the underlying decision process differs when it is made by consumers (i.e., individuals) and firms (i.e., organizations). At the beginning of the chapter (Exhibit 3.2), we discussed the distinctions between the consumer and organizational buying contexts. For the salesperson offering products and services to organizations (such as industrial buyers), it's important to understand how organizations make buying decisions.

Organizational buyers tend to focus on very rational goals such as reducing expenses or increasing sales, and therefore their decision-making process usually incorporates more formal rules, guidelines, and steps. The **organizational buying process** describes the problem-solving procedure the firm uses to meet its goals and objectives, as it relates to making purchases. When the salesperson sells to organizations, she will probably notice that the buying process involves many individuals, multiple goals, and potentially conflicting decision criteria.[5] Generally, firms use a five-step process when making a buying decision. The steps include:

1. Define the problem.
2. Establish the decision criteria.
3. Identify alternatives.
4. Evaluate alternatives.
5. Select appropriate solution.

An **organizational buying situation** begins when the firm perceives a business problem (also called a need). This is very similar to any type of need. The firm perceives that a gap exists between their actual situation and a desired state (or outcome). In order to resolve the business problem (i.e., the need), the firm begins the activities associated with its buying process. As a salesperson, your goal is to work with organizations to help identify and define their gap (i.e., need) and develop a solution that helps the firm meets its objective.

One of the major ways an organizational buying situation differs from the buying process of an individual consumer lies in the number of people involved in the process. In organizational buying situations, a group of employees is usually involved in the decision-making process (establishing the decision criteria, evaluating

Because the organizational buying process differs from the buying process of individuals, the types of questions that the salesperson uses may also be distinct. While this is not a comprehensive list, we provide a few examples of questions that a salesperson may ask members of a buying center in order to understand the firm's needs.

- What are the steps in the buying process for your firm (or for this project)?

- Who are the members of the buying team? What are their specific roles and responsibilities?

- What current challenges is your firm experiencing in this area?

- What are the goals for this project (or product or solution)?

- Can you describe for me your timeline for this project (or decision)?

- What budgets or other resources have been identified for this project?

- What have previous partners (or vendors or other companies) accomplished for you that made them a valued partner?

- What are your expectations of the company that you chose to work with on this project?

alternatives, etc.). This group, often called the **buying center,** comprises all of the people performing different roles in the buying process (e.g., user, buyer, decider, influencer, gatekeeper) based on their expertise and responsibilities within their firm. For example, a salesperson representing a healthcare technology company and selling a new MRI scanner to a hospital system may have to deal with a group of employees in the buying center. The buying center may comprise the doctor that reviews the MRI results (the user), the director of the supply chain (the decider), the chief financial officer (the buyer), the medical technicians that administer the MRI to patients (the influencers), and departmental staff that are responsible for setting meetings and accepting appointments for the doctors and directors (the gatekeepers).

Factors Influencing Organizational Buying Process

When selling to a business customer or an organization, the salesperson must recognize that the organizational buying process is impacted by a variety of factors, including individual, social, and organizational factors.

For instance, the individual influences describe the people in the buying center and their personality characteristics, their roles and responsibilities, and their beliefs and attitudes. All of these characteristics should be considered by the salesperson, as she will be interacting with different members of the buying center and will need to adapt to each individual.

Social influences describe the interpersonal relationships and interactions among and between the members of the buying center. Sometimes employees within the same firm disagree, possess varying levels of trust between one another, and hold different goals for the buying process. A successful salesperson often studies the way the group functions and understands these relational dynamics.

Selling new cars often was difficult, but Linda Martin felt she had a new Cadillac sold. A woman called and said she wanted to buy a new Cadillac exactly like the one parked outside of Linda's office. Linda had another one the same color, but it was fully loaded with the latest high-tech equipment and cost $6,000 more.

The buyer, a 68-year-old widow, listened as Linda described both cars, emphasizing the higher-priced Cadillac. The buyer seemed to become confused over how to work options such as the disk stereo system and cellular telephone. Suddenly the buyer said, "Linda, you seem like a nice person. Which car do you think I should buy?"

What would be the most ethical action to take?

1. Tell the customer to buy the more expensive model. She probably has enough money and you will get more commission.

2. Advise the customer that you think she would be happier with the less expensive model—she does not seem to need or want all of the high-tech gadgets in the more expensive car. Offer to call other dealers in town to see if they have one in stock. You might lose the commission, but at least you have a satisfied customer.

3. Advise the customer that both are equally good options and let her make the decision herself. But do tell her that you only have the more expensive model in stock and that the other car would take six to eight weeks to deliver.

Finally, the organizational buying process is affected by the organization's climate, its goals, and its working environment. Thus, understanding elements, such as the firm's culture and its expectations of its employees as well as the firm's financial objectives is important to understanding the firm's buying process.

To Buy or Not to Buy—A Choice Decision

Salespeople realize that people buy a product because of a need, and that need can be complex due to the influence of perceptions, attitudes, beliefs, and personality. Furthermore, perceptions, attitudes, and beliefs may differ from one purchase to another. How is it possible to state why people buy one product and not another?

Salespeople do not have to be psychologists to understand human behavior. Nor do they need to understand the material covered in courses taken by a psychology major. Furthermore, the average salesperson cannot know all that is involved in the psychological and practical processes that a buyer goes through in making a decision.

What the salesperson *does* need to understand are the various factors that can influence the buying decision, the fact that buyers actually examine various factors that influence these decisions, that buyers actually go through various steps in making decisions, and how to develop a sales presentation that persuades buyers to purchase the product to satisfy needs. To do this, the salesperson should consider the following questions before developing a sales presentation:

- What type of product is desired?
- What type of buying situation is it?
- How will the product be used?
- Who is involved in the buying decision?
- What practical factors may influence the buyer's decision?
- What psychological factors may influence the buyer's decision?
- What are the buyer's important buying needs?

Again, it seems necessary to know a great deal about a person's attitudes and beliefs to answer these questions. Can this be made simpler? Yes. Simply stated, to buy or not to buy is a choice decision. The person's choice takes one of two forms: First, a person has the choice of buying a product or not. Second, the choice can be between competing products. The question salespeople should ask themselves is, "How can I convince a person to choose my product?" The answer to this question involves five things; each is necessary to make the sale. People will buy if

1. They perceive a need or problem.
2. They desire to fulfill a need or solve a problem.
3. They decide there is a high probability that your product will fulfill their needs or solve their problems better than your competitor's products.
4. They believe they should buy from you.
5. They have the resources and authority to buy.

What do you do if you know your product can reduce a prospect's manufacturing costs, saving the firm $5,000 a year, for a cost of $4,000, and the prospect says, "No thanks, I like my present equipment"? This buyer does not perceive a need, and will not buy. Suppose you make your point about reducing operating costs, but for some reason the prospect seems uninterested in reducing costs. Chances are, this person will not buy no matter how persuasively you present your product's benefits—because the prospect does not see high costs as an important problem.

Furthermore, even customers who want to solve a problem, but do not like your product, will not buy. But if you have convinced them, if they want to solve a problem, and if they perceive your product as solving this problem, the question remains, Will these customers buy from you? They will, if they believe you represent the best supplier. If they would rather buy from another supplier, you have lost the sale. Your job is to provide the necessary information so that customers meet each of the five conditions for a sale listed above.

A *FAB*ulous Approach to Buyer Need Satisfaction

An awareness of the types of needs that buyers possess allows you to present your product as a vehicle for satisfaction of those needs. Several methods of presenting a product's benefits are available. A most powerful selling technique used by successful salespeople today is **benefit selling.** In benefit selling, the salesperson relates a product's benefits to the customer's needs using the product's features and advantages as support. This technique is often referred to as the *FAB* **selling technique** (*F*eature, *A*dvantage, and *B*enefit).* These key terms are defined as follows:

- A product **feature** is any *physical characteristic* of a product.
- A product **advantage** is the *performance characteristic* of a product that describes how it can be used or will help the buyer.
- A product **benefit** is a favorable *result* the buyer receives from the product because of a particular advantage that has the ability to satisfy a buyer's need.

The Product's Features: So What?

All products have features or physical characteristics such as the following:

©Jill Braaten/McGraw-Hill Education

Size	Flavor	Shape
Terms	Taste	Uses
Packaging	Price	Delivery
Color	Service	Ingredients
Quantity	Quality	Technology

Descriptions of a product's features answer the question, What is it? Typically, when used alone in the sales presentation, features have little persuasive power because buyers are interested in specific benefits rather than features.

When discussing a product's features *alone,* imagine the customer is thinking, "So what? So your product has this shape or quality; how does it perform and how will it benefit me?" That is why you have to discuss the product's advantages as they relate to the buyer's needs.

The Product's Advantages: Prove It!

Once a product feature is presented to the customer, the salesperson normally begins to discuss the advantages that product's physical characteristics provide. This is better than discussing only its features. Describing the product's advantages, how a product can be used, or how it will help the buyer increases the chances of making a sale. Another way to describe an advantage is that it enables the feature to do something. For instance, advertising enables (or creates) awareness of a product. Examples of product advantages (performance characteristics) follow:

- It is the fastest-selling soap on the market.
- You can store more information and retrieve it more rapidly with our computer.
- This machine will copy on both sides of the pages instead of only one.

How does the prospective customer know that your claims for a product are true? Imagine a prospect thinking, "Prove it!" Be prepared to substantiate any claims you make.

Companies typically train their salespeople thoroughly on the product's physical and performance characteristics. A salesperson may have excellent knowledge of the product yet be unable to describe it in terms that allow the prospect to visualize the benefits of purchasing it. This is because many salespeople present only a product's features and advantages—leaving the buyer to imagine its benefits.

While your chances of helping the customer increase when you discuss both the features and the advantages of your product, you must learn how to stress product benefits that are important to the prospect in your presentation. Once you have mastered this selling technique, your sales will increase.

*Some companies train their salespeople using only features and benefits. They see an advantage and benefit as one and the same. Most companies use *FAB.* This section plus the trial close and SELL Sequence sections are very important for you to learn and use in your sales presentation.

EXHIBIT 3.9

Discuss benefits to fulfill people's needs and to increase sales.

©Jetta Productions/Getty Images

Industrial salespeople work closely with customers to design products and systems that fit their needs.

©Jetta Productions/Getty Images

Consumer goods salespeople can show customers how to increase sales by setting up strategic merchandise displays.

©Patryk Kosmider/Shutterstock

The Product's Benefits: What's in It for Me?

People are interested in what the product will do for them. Emphasizing benefits appeals to the customer's personal motives by answering the question, What's in it for me? In your presentation, stress how the person will benefit from the purchase rather than the features and advantages of your product as shown in Exhibit 3.9.

To illustrate the idea of buying benefits instead of only features or advantages, consider four items: (1) a diamond ring, (2) a vacation, (3) STP motor oil, and (4) movie tickets. Do people buy these products or services for their features or advantages? No; people buy the product's benefits such as these:

- A diamond ring—image of success, investment, or to please a loved one.
- A vacation—memories of places, friends, and family.
- STP motor oil—engine protection, car investment, or peace of mind.
- Movie tickets—entertainment, escape from reality, or relaxation.

As you can see, people are buying benefits—not a product's features or advantages. These benefits can be both practical, such as an investment, and psychological, such as an image of success. The salesperson needs to discuss benefits to answer the prospect's question, What's in it for me?

As you will notice on the examples below, the salesperson translates the advantage into a benefit.

EXAMPLE

Salesperson selling LED lights and sensors: **"I would like to introduce you to our new LED sensors. The sensors are fully customizable and detect each unique individual in your lab areas (feature).** The sensors provide you with an ability to customize your lighting requirements based on the needs of the user. This reduces the need for your employees to adjust the lighting **(advantage).** Hence, your firm will increase its efficiency by reducing the time and labor needed to operate the lighting across your 500 lab settings **(benefit).** How do you think your employees would feel about using the sensors **(trial close)?"**

Sporting goods salesperson to customer: "With this ball, you'll get an extra 10 to 20 yards on your drives **(advantage),** helping to reduce your score **(benefit)** because of its new solid core **(feature).**"

Salesperson to buyer of grocery store health and beauty aids: "Prell's economy size **(feature)** sells twice as fast as all other competitive brands **(advantage)** in stores like yours. You can increase store traffic 10 to 20 percent **(benefit)** and build your sales volume by at least 5 percent **(benefit)** by advertising the product using a feature ad in your weekly sales circular **(feature).**"

New salespeople frequently are not accustomed to using feature, advantage, and benefit phrases. To use them regularly in your sales conversation, a standardized *FAB* Sequence can be used as follows:

The . . . **(feature)** means you **(advantage)** . . . with the real benefit to you being . . . **(benefit).**
Or The . . . **(feature)** enables or allows your firm to . . . **(advantage)** which means the value to you is . . . **(benefits).**
Or The . . . **(feature)** creates/generates . . . for your firm **(advantage)** thereby creating value to your firm by . . . **(benefits).**

The *FAB* Sequence allows you to easily remember to state the product's benefit in a natural, conversational manner. For example, "*The* new solid core center of the Gunshot Golf Ball means *you* could have an extra 10 or 20 yards on your drives, *with the real benefit to you being* a lower score." You can substitute any features, advantages, and benefits between these transition phrases to develop *FAB* sequences. Several sequences can be used one after another to emphasize your product's benefits.

Try it. Out loud, read the golf ball *FAB* Sequence. Then do it again using your own phrasing. Create several variations until finding one you would feel comfortable using in a conversation.

Why should you emphasize benefits? There are two reasons (see Exhibit 3.9). First, by emphasizing benefits customers can better understand if your product will satisfy their need(s). Your primary purpose is to help the person. Second, stressing benefits in your presentation, rather than features or advantages, will bring success. You will satisfy more people's needs and thus your sales will increase.

The success of your sales presentation depends on whether a prospect perceives your product's benefits will satisfy her needs. Therefore, what process can you use to understand the prospect's attitude toward your sales presentation?

The Trial Close—A Great Way to Uncover Needs and Sell

The **trial close** is one of the best selling techniques to use in your sales presentation. It checks the pulse or attitude of your prospect toward the sales presentation. The trial close should be used at these four important times:

1. After making a strong selling point in the presentation.
2. After the presentation.
3. After answering an objection.
4. Immediately before you move to close the sale.

The trial close allows you to determine (1) whether the prospect likes your product's feature, advantage, or benefit; (2) whether you have successfully answered the objection; (3) whether any objections remain; and (4) whether the prospect is ready for you to close the sale. It is a powerful technique to induce two-way communication (feedback) and participation from the prospect. The Selling Tips box gives examples of trial closes. Learn these—you'll use them throughout the course.

If, for example, the prospect says little while you make your presentation, and if you get a "no" when you come to the close, you may find it difficult to change the prospect's mind. You have not learned the real reasons why the prospect says no. To avoid this, salespeople use the trial close to determine the prospect's attitude toward the product throughout the presentation.

The trial close asks for the prospect's *opinion,* not a decision to buy. It is a direct question that can be answered with few words.[*] Look at the trial close examples shown in Selling Tips.

> *The trial close provides an opportunity for your customer to provide feedback.*

Remember the prospect's positive reactions. Use them later to help overcome objections and in closing the sale. Also remember the negative comments. You may need to offset the negatives with the positives later in the presentation. Generally, however, you will not discuss the negative again.

Here is an example of using the prospect's positive comments to ask for the order. Assume that during the presentation you have learned from the prospect that she likes the product's profit margin, fast delivery, and credit policy. You can summarize these benefits in a positive manner such as this:

Salesperson: Ms. Stevenson, you say you like our profit margin, fast delivery, and credit policy. Is that right? [Summary and trial close.]

Prospect: Yes, I do.

Salesperson: With the number of customers coming into your store and our expected sales of the products due to normal turnover, along with our marketing plan, I *suggest you buy.* . . . [State the products and their quantities.] This will provide sufficient quantities to meet customer demand for the next two months, plus provide you with the profit you expect from your products. I can have the order to you early next week. [Now wait for her response.]

Note that the prospect has said there are three things she likes about what you are selling. If the prospect responds favorably to your trial close, then you are in agreement or you have satisfactorily answered an objection. Thus, the prospect may be ready to buy. However, if you receive a negative response, do not close. Either you have not answered some objection or the prospect is not interested in the feature, advantage, or benefit you are discussing. This feedback allows you to better uncover what your prospect thinks about your product's potential for satisfying needs.

SELL Sequence

One way to remember to incorporate a trial close into your presentation is the **SELL Sequence.** Exhibit 3.10 shows how each letter of the word *sell* stands for a sequence of things to do and say to stress benefits important to the customer. By remembering the word *sell,* you remember to *show the feature, explain the advantage, lead into the benefit, and then let the customer talk by asking a question about the benefit (trial close).*

---

*See Chapter 11 for other uses and examples of direct questions.

Using Trial Closes

The trial close is an important part of the sales presentation. It asks for the prospect's opinion concerning what you have just said. The trial close does not ask the person to buy directly. Trial closes can be open-ended questions or close-ended questions. Open-ended questions are preferred as they allow the buyer to provide more feedback. Here are examples:

- How does that sound to you?
- What are your thoughts?
- What other features are you looking for?
- That's great—isn't it?
- How important is this benefit to you?

- What other concerns do you have?
- I have a hunch that you like the money-saving features of this product. Can you share with me your thoughts?
- It appears that you have a preference for this model. What are your thoughts?
- I can see that you are excited about this product. On a scale from 1 to 10, how do you feel it will fit your needs?
- I notice your smile. What do you think about . . . ?
- Am I on the right track with this proposal? What am I missing?

EXHIBIT 3.10

The SELL Sequence: Use it throughout your presentation.

S	E	L	L
Show	**Explain**	**Lead**	**Let**
feature	advantage	into benefit	customer talk

Remember: Your SELL Sequence should provide a solution to a specific buyer need.

EXAMPLE
Industrial salesperson to industrial purchasing agent: "This equipment is made of stainless steel **[feature],** which means it won't rust **[advantage].** The real benefit is that it reduces your replacement costs, thus saving you money **[benefit]**! That's what you're interested in—right **[trial close]?**"

EXAMPLE
Beecham salesperson to consumer goods buyer: "Beecham will spend an extra $1 million in the next two months advertising Cling Free fabric softener **[feature].** Plus, you can take advantage of this month's $1.20 per dozen price reduction **[feature].** The combination of awareness-creating advertising along with a promotional discount provides a revenue-increasing opportunity for you. This means you will sell 15 to 20 percent more Cling Free in the next two months **[advantage],** thus making higher sales and pulling more customers into your store **[benefits].** How does that sound **[trial close]?**"

The trial close asks for an opinion, not to buy!

Once you use a trial close, carefully listen to what the customer says and watch for nonverbal signals to determine if what you said has an impact. If you receive a positive response to your trial close, you are on the right track.

EXHIBIT 3.11

Examples of features, advantages, benefits, and trial closes that form the SELL Sequence.

Features (physical characteristics)	Advantages (performance characteristics feature enables)	Benefits (result from advantage)	Trial Closes (feedback questions)
1. Nationally advertised consumer product	1. Creates greater awareness of product within your target market	1. Increases in-store traffic and shoppers looking to purchase product (i.e., generating sales)	1. What are your thoughts on this marketing strategy?
2. Air conditioner with a high energy-efficiency rating	2. Uses less electricity	2. Saves 10 percent in energy costs	2. How important are energy savings to your firm?
3. Product made of stainless steel	3. Will not rust or deteriorate thereby allowing a greater lifespan	3. Reduces your replacement cost and total cost of ownership	3. How does that sound to you?
4. Supermarket computer system with the IBM 3651 Store Controller	4. Can store more information and retrieve it rapidly by supervising up to 24 grocery checkout scanners and terminals and look up prices on up to 22,000 items	4. Provides greater accuracy, register balancing, store ordering, and inventory management	4. How does this solution align with your objectives?
5. Five percent interest on money in bank checking NOW account	5. Earns interest that would not normally be received	5. The extra money is equivalent to one extra bag of groceries each month. Gives you one extra bag of groceries each month	5. Would you like to earn extra money on your savings?
6. Golf club head made of aerodynamically designed titanium steel	6. Increases club head speed, longer drives	6. Lowers your scores and increases your satisfaction with each round	6. What are your thoughts?

> *SELL Sequences describe how a feature produces a valuable benefit for the buyer.*

Remember, the trial close does not ask the customer to buy or make any type of purchase decision. It asks only for an opinion. The trial close is a trial question to determine the customer's opinion toward the salesperson's proposition to know if it is time to close the sale. Thus, its main purpose is to induce feedback from the buyer.

Exhibit 3.11 presents six examples of SELL Sequences composed of features, advantages, benefits, and trial closes of products. The first column lists features or product characteristics such as size, shape, performance, and maintenance data. The second column shows advantages that arise from respective features. These are the performance characteristics or what the product will do. The third column contains benefits to the customer from these features and advantages.

The last column shows a question—or trial close—related to what the salesperson said. The trial close acts as a feedback method to determine the buyer's opinion about the feature, advantage, and/or benefit. It helps uncover what is important, and what is not important, to the other person. Try using the trial close in your everyday conversations with friends, co-workers, and family members. But remember, more open-ended trial closes will elicit more information and feedback. It works!

For each major product feature, you should develop the resulting advantage and benefit. Then create a trial close to induce feedback for the buyer. You should use the SELL Sequence throughout your presentation.

SUMMARY OF MAJOR SELLING ISSUES

As a salesperson, be knowledgeable about factors that influence your buyer's purchase decision. You can obtain this knowledge, which helps increase the salesperson's self-confidence and the buyer's confidence in the salesperson, through training and practice.

A firm's marketing strategy involves various efforts to create exchanges that satisfy the buyer's needs and wants. The salesperson should understand the characteristics of the target market (consumer or organizational) and how these characteristics relate to the buyer's behavior to better serve and sell to customers.

The individual goes through various steps or stages in the three buying situations of routine decision making, limited decision making, and extensive decision making. Uncover who is involved in the buying decision and the main factors that influence the decision. These factors include various psychological and practical buying influences.

Psychological factors include the buyer's motives, perceptions, learning, attitudes, beliefs, and personality—all of which influence the individual's needs and result in a search for information on what products to buy to satisfy them. Established relationships strongly influence buying decisions, making satisfied customers easier to sell to than new prospects. Customers evaluate the information, which results in the decision to buy or not to buy. These same factors influence whether the buyer is satisfied or dissatisfied with the product.

Realize that all prospects will not buy your products, at least not all of the time, due to the many factors influencing their buying decisions. You need to uncover buyers' needs, solve buyers' problems, and provide the knowledge that allows them to develop personal attitudes toward the product. These attitudes result in positive beliefs that your products fulfill their needs. Uncovering prospects' needs is often difficult because they may be reluctant to tell you their true needs or may not really know what and why they want to buy. You can usually feel confident that people buy for reasons such as to satisfy a need, fulfill a desire, and obtain a value. To determine these important buying needs, you can ask questions, observe prospects, listen to them, and talk to their associates about their needs.

Quick Review for Students

The quick review sections provide key questions to help you develop a greater level of conceptual understanding. We suggest that after you read the chapter, you ask yourself if you can answer the following questions without looking back at the textbook.

1. What is a need and how does it differ from a want? Why is it important for a salesperson to understand the buyer's needs?
2. What are common economic needs and what are common psychological needs? Why might a buyer possess multiple economic and psychological needs?
3. What are the three categories (i.e., classifications) of buying situations? In what major ways are they different from one another?
4. What are the five steps in the buying process? How could a salesperson assist the buyer in each of these steps?
5. Salespeople often ask themselves, "How can I convince a person to choose my product?" What are the five elements that need to be present in order for a customer to purchase a solution?
6. What are the elements of a FAB and SELL Sequence? Why are they valuable?
7. What is the value of a trial close?

MEETING A SALES CHALLENGE

John Salley took the advice of Joe Gandolfo, who has reportedly sold more life insurance than any other person in the world. Joe's philosophy is that "selling is 98 percent understanding human beings and 2 percent product knowledge." Do not let that statement mislead you, for Joe holds the Charter Life Underwriter (CLU) designation as a member of the American College of Life Underwriters. He is extremely knowledgeable about insurance, tax shelters, and pension plans. In fact, he spends several hours a day studying recent changes in pensions and taxation. "But," Joe says, "I still maintain that it's not product knowledge but understanding of human beings that makes a salesperson effective."

John had his sales region's training director work with him two days a week for a month. The director analyzed John's sales presentations and found that they concentrated almost entirely on the technical features and advantages of the products. The training director contacted six of John's customers. Each said they often did not understand him because he was too technical. John immediately began emphasizing benefits and discussing features and advantages in nontechnical terms. Slowly his sales began to improve. Today, John Salley is a true believer in the phrase "It's not what you say, but how you say it."

KEY TERMS FOR SELLING

advantage   98
benefit selling   98
benefit   98
black box   82
buying center   95
collect information   91
conscious need level   86
consumer buying   83
economic needs   84
extensive decision
   making   90

FAB selling technique   98
feature   98
information evaluation   91
limited decision making   89
motivation to purchase   84
need arousal   90
needs   84
organizational buying
   process   94
organizational buying
   situation   94

organizational buying   83
preconscious need level   86
purchase decision   91
purchase dissonance   93
purchase satisfaction   93
routine decision making   89
SELL Sequence   101
stimulus–response   82
trial close   100
unconscious need level   86
wants   84

SALES APPLICATION QUESTIONS

1. What three types of buying situations may the buyer be in when contacted by a salesperson? Briefly describe each type.

2. What are the psychological factors that may influence the prospect's buying decision?

3. While you do not have to be a psychologist or understand exactly how the buyer's mind works, you do need to uncover the buyer's motives.

    a. What techniques can be used to uncover the buyer's motives?

    b. The prospect's intention to buy can be influenced by several things. What information does the salesperson need to obtain concerning the prospect's buying intentions before developing a sales presentation?

4. In the following statements, write down each idea that is a benefit:

    a. Counselor talking to a student: "To improve your science grade, Susie, you must establish better study habits."

    b. Construction supervisor talking to a worker: "That job will be a great deal easier, Joe, and you won't be as tired when you go home nights if you use that little truck over there."

    c. Father talking to his son: "You will make a lot of friends, Johnny, and be respected at school if you learn how to play the piano."

    d. Banker talking to customer: "If you open this special checking account, Ms. Brown, paying your bills will be much easier."

5. In the following statements, determine what parts of each statement are features, advantages, or benefits.

    a. Hardware sales representative to homeowner: "Blade changing is quick and easy with this saw because it has a push-button blade release."

    b. Consumer sales representative to grocery store buyer: "The king-size package of Tide will bring in additional profits because it is the fastest selling, most economical size."

    c. Clothing salesperson to customer: "For long wear and savings on your clothing costs, you can't beat these slacks. All the seams are double-stitched and the material is 100 percent Dacron."

6. Indicate which of the following statements is a feature, advantage, or benefit. Write your answer on a sheet of paper.

    a. Made of pure vinyl.

    b. Lasts twice as long as competing brands.

    c. It's quick-frozen at 30° below zero.

    d. Available in small, medium, and large sizes.

    e. New.

    f. No unpleasant aftertaste.

    g. Saves time, work, and money.

    h. Approved by Underwriters Laboratories (UL).

    i. Gives 20 percent more miles to the gallon.

    j. Contains XR-10.

    k. Baked fresh daily.

    l. Includes a one-year guarantee on parts and labor.

    m. Is packed 48 units, or eight six-packs, to the case.

    n. Guaranteed to increase your sales by 10 percent.

    o. Adds variety to your meal planning.

7. Consider the following information:

The DESKTOP XEROX 2300 copier is a versatile model that delivers the first copy in six seconds. It is also the lowest-priced new Xerox copier available. The 2300 is designed as a general purpose office copier and occupies less than half the top of a standard desk. The new unit copies on a full range of office materials as large as 8½ by 14 inches. A special feature is its ability to reproduce 5½ by 8½-inch billing statements from the same tray used for letter-size or legal-size paper. Selling price of the 2300 will be as low as $3,495 and rentals as low as $60 a month on a two-year contract without a copy allowance.

What are the features, advantages, and benefits of the DESKTOP XEROX 2300 copier? List two additional features, advantages, and benefits that a Xerox salesperson could use in presenting the new copier to a prospective buyer.

8. Several features of a car are listed below. Match each feature with its corresponding benefit(s):

a. Low hoodline:

(1) Better visibility.

(2) Economy.

(3) Quick start-up.

b. Tinted glass:

(1) Reflects sunlight.

(2) Reduces eyestrain.

(3) Reduces glare from sun.

c. Rear window defroster:

(1) Clears rear windshield and thus reduces the danger of driving on a cold, foggy day.

(2) Rear windshield can be deiced or defogged automatically so you do not have to do it yourself.

(3) Increases the cost of the car by $250.

d. Whitewall tires:

(1) Provide better handling and a more stable ride.

(2) Are more appealing to the eye.

(3) Increase the life of your tires.

9. To convince the customers that your product's benefits are important, show how the product benefits will meet their needs. Suppose the customer says: "I need some kind of gadget that will get me out of bed in the morning." Which of the following statements best relates your product feature, the GE clock radio's snooze alarm, to this customer's need?

a. "Ms. Jones, this GE radio has a snooze alarm that is very easy to operate. See, all you do is set this button and off it goes."

b. "Ms. Jones, the GE radio is the newest radio on the market. It carries a one-year guarantee and you can trade in your present radio and receive a substantial cut in the price."

c. "Ms. Jones, since you say you have trouble getting up in the morning, you want an alarm system that will make sure you wake up. Now, GE's snooze alarm will wake you up no matter how often you shut the alarm off. You see, the alarm goes off every seven minutes until you switch off the special 'early bird' knob."

10. A salesperson says: "You expect a pencil sharpener to be durable. Our sharpener is durable because it's constructed with titanium steel bearings. Because of these bearings, our sharpener will not jam up and will last a long time."

    a. In this example, the titanium steel bearings are a

      (1) Benefit.

      (2) Feature.

      (3) Need.

      (4) Advantage.

    b. "Will not jam up" is a

      (1) Benefit.

      (2) Feature.

      (3) Need.

      (4) Advantage.

    c. In the statement "will not jam up" the salesperson has

      (1) Converted a product feature into an advantage.

      (2) Converted benefits into a product feature.

      (3) Related a product feature to the customer's need via benefits.

      (4) Numbers (1) and (2) are correct.

      (5) Numbers (1) and (3) are correct.

    d. The statement "will last a long time" is a

      (1) Benefit.

      (2) Feature.

      (3) Need.

      (4) Advantage.

11. For each of the following products, determine a potential benefit based on their advantages:

Product	Feature	Advantage
a. Diet Coke	*a.* Only one calorie per 16-oz. serving	*a.* Will not increase your body weight when you drink it
b. BIC erasable ink pen	*b.* Erasable ink	*b.* Can erase mistakes
c. Ceiling fan	*c.* Hangs from ceiling, high efficiency	*c.* Out of the way, uses less electricity
d. Sheer panty hose	*d.* No dark patches	*d.* Looks like real skin
e. Drilling an oil well	*e.* Only one engineer for the entire job	*e.* Better service
f. Hefty trash bags	*f.* 2-ply	*f.* Puncture proof, can overstuff them

12. As a salesperson for Procter & Gamble's soap division, you have been asked by your sales manager to determine the features, advantages, and benefits of Tide detergent and to discuss using Tide's benefits in a sales presentation at the next sales meeting. You have determined the following four features of Tide; listed underneath each feature are your ideas of factors that might interest retail grocery buyers. For each feature, determine the benefit that you would emphasize:

    a. Number one selling detergent:

      (1) Best traffic-pulling detergent.

      (2) Great brand loyalty.

      (3) High percentage of market share.

    b. Four sizes:

      (1) Increases your total detergent sales.

      (2) Boxes are standard sizes.

      (3) Case cost is the same.

     c. Heaviest manufacturer-advertised detergent:
        (1) Continues to attract new customers to your store.
        (2) More customers remember this brand's advertising.
        (3) Produces high repeat business.
     d. Distinctive, colorful package:
        (1) Speeds shopping—easy for shoppers to locate on shelves.
        (2) High visual impact stimulates impulse purchases when on special display.
        (3) Familiar package design easy to recognize in store ads.

FURTHER EXPLORING THE SALES WORLD

1. Keep a diary of your purchases for two weeks. Select five or more of the products you purchased during that period and write a short report on why you purchased each product and what you feel are the features, advantages, and benefits of each product.
2. This week examine the television advertisements of three different products or services and report on the features, advantages, and benefits the commercials use to persuade people to buy each product.
3. Shop for a product costing over $100. Report on your experience. Find out if the salesperson is on a commission pay plan.

STUDENT APPLICATION LEARNING EXERCISES (SALES)

At the end of appropriate chapters beginning with this chapter, you will find Student Application Learning Exercises (SALES). SALES are meant to help you construct the various segments of your sales presentation. SALES build on one another so that after you complete them, you will have constructed the majority of your sales presentation.

SALE 1 of 7—Chapter 3

Now you are ready to begin developing your sales presentation. To make **Sale 1:**

1. State what you will sell.
2. Briefly describe the individual and/or organization to which you will sell.
3. List three features of your product, including each feature's main advantage and benefit. Refer back to the *FAB* definitions. *FAB*s should discuss your product, not your marketing plan or business proposition. We'll do that later.

Feature	Advantage	Benefit
a.	*a.*	*a.*
b.	*b.*	*b.*
c.	*c.*	*c.*

4. Now create a SELL Sequence for each *FAB* (see page 101). Label each of the components of the SELL Sequence using brackets as shown on page 103.

SELLING EXPERIENTIAL EXERCISE

You have learned much about selling in this course. Let's find out how much, and at the same time better understand your attitude toward selling. Three of the following 10 statements are false. Which are the false statements? Please first cover the answers.

Is Organizational Selling for You?

1. Dealing with customers is less exciting than the work involved in most other jobs.
2. Selling brings out the best in your personality.
3. Salespeople are made, not born; if you don't plan and work hard, you'll never be exceptional at selling.
4. Attitude is more important in selling positions than most other jobs.
5. Those good at selling often can improve their income quickly.
6. Learning to sell now will help you succeed in any job in the future.
7. In your first sales job, what you learn can be more important than what you earn.
8. Selling is less demanding than other jobs.
9. You have less freedom in most selling positions.
10. A smile uses fewer muscles than a frown.[6]

False statements: 1, 8, and 9.

NOTES

1. David Mothersbaugh and Delbert Hawkins, *Consumer Behavior: Building Marketing Strategy,* 13th ed. (New York: McGraw-Hill, 2016).

2. F. E. Webster, Jr. and Y. Wind, "A General Model for Understanding Organizational Buying Behavior," *Journal of Marketing,* 1972, pp. 12–19.

3. Elina Jaakkola, "Purchase Decision-Making within Professional Consumer Services: Organizational or Consumer Buying Behaviour?" *Marketing Theory,* March 2007, pp. 93–108.

4. R. Agnihotri, M. Krush, and R. K. Singh, "Understanding the Mechanism Linking Interpersonal Traits to Pro-Social Behaviors among Salespeople: Lessons from India,"

Journal of Business & Industrial Marketing 27, no. 3 (February 2012), pp. 211–27.

5. F. E. Webster, Jr. and Y. Wind, "A General Model for Understanding Organizational Buying Behavior," *Journal of Marketing,* 1972, pp. 12–19.

6. Adapted from J. R. Schermerhorn, J. G. Hunt, and R. N. Osborn, "Managing Organizational Behavior" (New York: Wiley, 1991), p. 123.

7. Mary E. Shoemaker, "A Framework for Examining IT-Enabled Market Relationships," *Journal of Personal Selling & Sales Management* 21, no. 2 (2001), pp. 177–85.

CASE 3.1

©Ron Chapple Stock/FotoSearch/
Glow Images

Economy Ceiling Fans, Inc.

As a salesperson for Economy Ceiling Fans, you have been asked to research and determine customers' attitudes and beliefs toward your brand of ceiling fans. With this information you will determine if your company has the correct product line and suggest selling points for the company's salespeople when discussing fans with customers who come into their chain of retail stores.

You decide to hold an open house on a Sunday in one of your typical stores located in an upper-income neighborhood and advertise your special prices. During that time, you ask everyone to be seated, thank them for coming, and ask them to discuss their attitudes toward your company and ceiling fans.

Some people felt that they should shop for ceiling fans without considering brands, but once they selected a brand, they should go to the stores carrying that particular brand and buy from the store with the best price. Most people had collected information on fans from personal sources (such as friends), commercial sources (such as advertising, salespeople, company literature), and public sources (such as consumer rating organizations). Sixty percent had narrowed their choice to fans from Hunter, Casablanca, and Economy, and they seemed to look for three things in a ceiling fan: price, quality, and style.

Questions

1. Given this information about why people buy ceiling fans, what should salespeople be instructed to do when a customer enters their store?
2. The research suggests that some customers will be focused on varying areas, such as price, quality, and style. How might a salesperson change their conversation with a customer that is focused on style versus a customer focused on price? Similarly, how might the salesperson's conversation changes between a customer focused on price versus a customer focused on quality?

CASE 3.2

©Ron Chapple Stock/FotoSearch/
Glow Images

Jackson Ceiling Fans

You work as a salesperson for Jackson Ceiling Fans, a manufacturer of ceiling fans for households and apartments. As a salesperson, you work with retailers across the United States. These retailers buy directly from your firm (i.e., the manufacturer) and then resell your products to an end consumer. The retailer's consumers may be homeowners, remodeling businesses, general contractors, and maintenance personnel.

Your supervisor has asked you to research your retailers' buying processes for ceiling fans. With this information, you will determine if your company has the correct selling strategy for your company's salespeople.

After one of the major home décor trade shows, you hold a focus group discussion with three groups of retailers. You have nine representatives attend the discussion:

- Three representatives work for major, big-box, home improvement retailers. These retailers are nationwide and provide a range of fan products. They operate very large stores (i.e., greater than 100,000 square feet). They have a range of customers. They serve homeowners, contractors, and even maintenance personnel for apartments.
- Three representatives own multiple hardware stores (i.e., 5 to 15 stores). These hardware stores tend to be located in suburban strip malls or stand-alone buildings in neighborhoods. They charge premium prices. They are known for providing a great deal of guidance and advice to their consumers (i.e., homeowners).
- The third group of three representatives are owners of lumberyards. This group of retailers work solely with general and specialty contractors. They provide a variety of fans often based on price, style, or brand.

Your meeting has provided an abundance of research. You have developed a summary table (see next page). Now, you must discern the differences in the buying processes and the benefits that are important to each type of business buyer.

Questions

1. Explain the different needs that a salesperson would have to address for each type of customer?
2. For each type of customer, describe what the salesperson would need to consider regarding the timing of meetings.
3. For each type of customer, describe how the amount sold would be different.
4. What would be the key difference in meeting preparation for a salesperson who is meeting with a buying committee for a big-box retailer versus a meeting with the buyers for the lumberyard?

	Big-box, home improvement retailers	Suburban, neighborhood-based hardware stores	Local lumberyards
Buying process (cycle)	We purchase twice per year. We have set times for meetings (specific days, times, weeks) every year.	We consistently review opportunities for products. We review products once per quarter for sell-through. This allows us to know whether we will continue rebuying the product or discontinue it.	We allow our managers to purchase products when they see a need in the market, due to contractor requests. The system is pretty fluid.
What is the buying process?	We place orders 6 months ahead of time. For stocking in Spring (March), we begin the process of reviewing products in September.

You will meet with a buying committee of three individuals. You should share with us any new product introductions ahead of time (i.e., 12 months if possible). | Our buyers for the fan category are located at our headquarters.

We review new items once per year (October) and then place orders in November.

You will meet with our buyer. The buyer will provide a recommendation to our general manager. | The manager of each lumberyard and their home décor manager is responsible for all purchases for their store.

You would meet with both of those individuals. |
| **Quantity of units ordered** | We order eight (8) SKUs of the 15 best-selling styles for placement in each store.

We will offer all styles online.

We would purchase for all of our stores (2,000). | We tend to order four (4) of the most general SKUs to be placed in each store.

We also offer additional styles online.

We would purchase for all of our stores (5 to 15). | We hold one unit of 20 different styles in-store.

We offer our customers a catalog (in-store) for different styles.

We also offer an unlimited amount of styles online. |
| **Consumers (who are the retailers' customers?)** | We serve homeowners (50%), contractors (30%), maintenance personnel (20%). | We serve homeowners primarily (90%) and some specialty contractors (10%). | We serve contractors (95%) and some walk-in consumer traffic (5%) |
| **What are the retailers' top three buying needs?** | 1. MSRP (price on shelf needs to be competitive with our competitors).

2. Margins. The ceiling category should yield 20% overall.

3. Invoice terms. We prefer net 90 if possible. | 1. Margin. We require a margin exceeding 55%.

2. Training of our salespeople on the product.

3. Product assortment that is aligned with contemporary decorating needs. | 1. Delivery speed. Once we order something from you, we would like to receive it within 72 hours.

2. Margins exceeding 40% for products stocked in the store.

3. A strong assortment of products that can be displayed on our website. |
| **What types of assistance do the retailers' require?** | 1. We expect you to promote your products in our promotional circular twice per year. You are responsible for "buying-down" the price and placing your product on sale by a minimum of 10%.

2. We expect you to create national awareness of your brand.

3. We need market share data on your product. This should be provided to us on a quarterly basis. | 1. We expect your team to provide quality training to our salespeople once per year (i.e., in-store).

2. We expect co-op advertising opportunities.

3. We need to understand the key trends in homeowner décor as it relates to ceiling fans. | 1. We expect great follow-up after the order and the ability to track the order and shipment.

2. We expect 100% of your products that we display online will be available within 72 hours (i.e., received in our stores).

3. We expect 24-hour customer support for the installation of your products (via phone). |

CASE 3.3

Tech Corporation

©Ron Chapple Stock/FotoSearch/
Glow Images

After completing a rigorous product training and spending one year in an inside sales position in Dallas, you are now a field sales executive for Tech Corporation, a sales and Customer Relationship Management (CRM) technology provider to small and midsize organizations. Recently, you received an update from your inside sales team who qualified a new lead in your territory, Power Solution Inc., a company that provides power solutions to manufacturing units throughout the Midwest as well as few Southern states.

After doing some additional research using LinkedIn®, you decided to call on Mr. Tom Smith, the purchasing manager of the company, whose contact information was given to you by the inside sale team. You called and spoke with Mr. Smith and he acknowledged the need for customer relationship management software primarily for the salespeople working for the company. He also suggested you set an initial meeting with their VP-sales, Mr. Mike Morris. Mr. Smith mentioned that Mr. Morris travels a great deal. He suggested you contact Mr. Morris's administrative assistant, Ms. Olson, and determine if you can find a mutually convenient time to meet.

After the call, you thought of your Professional Selling class where you learned about the buying center and its importance in organizational buying situations. You felt good because you were ready to use that learning in this situation!

Product Background for This Case

CRM is a technology system that helps companies manage information about existing and potential customers. Many CRM systems include contact management technology, a listing of all the customer contacts that a salesperson makes in the course of conducting business. The form of the technology is like an electronic collection of business cards and includes such information as the contact's name, title, company, address, phone number, fax number, and e-mail address. It also may include additional information such as the particular industry, date of last order, name of administrative assistant, other key decision makers, and so on.

The value of a CRM system lies in its ability to manage knowledge. CRM software often combines sales, marketing, and customer service data into one information technology platform.[7] For example, the CRM system may include insight from the salesperson's colleagues. In some firms, the customer service department may have had interactions with a customer and documented the communication, or the marketing department may have sent the customer an invitation to a webinar and captured this information within the CRM system. Hence, CRM technology not only provides a tracking mechanism, it also allows salespeople and their colleagues to share critical information throughout their organization and more effectively collaborate.

Questions

1. First, review the list of the key roles in a buying center. Consider who would be the person or people who would fulfill each role and write it down. Please keep in mind that one person can perform different roles and several individuals may occupy the same role.

   Users (person/people who actually use the software tools)   _____
   Buyer(s) (person/people who have the authority for
   contracting with suppliers)   _____
   Influencer(s) (person/people who influence the
   decision process)   _____
   Decider(s) (person/people who have the authority to
   finalize the purchase)   _____
   Gatekeeper (person who may control the flow of information) _____

2. Because each person in the buying center will have distinct needs, write down the specific needs—as it pertains to the customer relationship management system—for users, buyers, influencers, deciders, and gatekeepers. Please consider writing multiple needs including economic needs, psychological needs, and any other applicable need for each individual.

3. Now, write at least one benefit that the customer relationship management system would need to provide in order to meet each person's need(s).

CASE 3.4

©Ron Chapple Stock/FotoSearch/
Glow Images

McDonald's Ford Dealership

In this case, you are presented with two different scenarios. Read and evaluate each scenario.

Scenario 1: The used car salesperson for McDonald's Ford, John Alexander, approaches a woman, June Miller, in the car lot:

Seller: Can I help you?

Buyer: 20,000 miles on this one—I'll bet a little old lady owned this lemon! What was it, really, before you set it back?

Seller: That is the actual mileage. Hi, I'm John Alexander and you are? . . . *[He waits for reply.]*

Buyer: June Miller.

Seller: June, what can I help you with?

Buyer: Oh, I don't know. Something that runs and will get me around.

Seller: Do you travel out of town or just drive back and forth to work?

Buyer: I drive everywhere! I'm even getting in a car pool with my boss.

Seller: Good mileage is important then.

Buyer: Sure is. [*She walks over and looks at a full-size, four-door Ford.*] Say, I like this one! $6,500! You have to be kidding.

Seller: Do you need that much room?

Buyer: Not really, there is just me.

Seller: June, are you saying you need a car that is dependable, gets good gas mileage, not too big, and not too expensive?

Buyer: How did you guess?

Seller: Follow me. . . . *[He shows her five cars that he feels have those features. Then he asks:]* Which one of these do you like? [June provides feedback on each car.].

Buyer: Well, they are OK, but I really don't like them. Thanks for your time. I'll shop around a little more. Give me your card and I'll get back to you later.

Questions

1. Describe the situation and the buyer's apparent needs.
2. What has the salesperson done well in this scenario?
3. How could the salesperson learn more about the buyer's needs?
4. What should the seller do now that the buyer has said no to the cars he has shown her and is about to leave the car lot?

Scenario 2: The used car salesperson for McDonald's Ford, John Alexander, approaches a woman, June Miller, in the car lot:

Seller: Can I help you?

Buyer: 20,000 miles on this one—I'll bet a little old lady owned this lemon! What was it, really, before you set it back?

Seller: That is the actual mileage. Hi, I'm John Alexander and you are? . . . [*He waits for reply.*]

Buyer: June Miller.

Seller: June, what can I help you with?

Buyer: Oh, I don't know. Something that runs and will get me around.

Seller: Can you tell me about how much you travel. For instance, some folks primarily drive to their workplace while others commute 10 or more miles per day?

Buyer: I drive everywhere!

Seller: I can appreciate that. How many miles a year do you drive?

Buyer: Probably 20,000. But that may be less. I'm getting in a car pool with my boss.

Seller: That sounds like a great way to reduce miles. Will you be driving in the car pool?

Buyer: Probably not. [*She walks over and looks at a full-size, four-door Ford.*] Say, I like this one! $6,500! You have to be kidding.

Seller: What do you like about this one, June?

Buyer: I like that it looks sleek. I also like Ford cars.

Seller: What are the elements that concern you?

Buyer: The price. $6,500 is a lot.

Seller: June, would you be willing to sit in the car and tell me what you like most about it and what you like least about it?

Buyer: I guess so. But, I'm not going to get it at this price.

Seller: I totally understand. I'm not looking for a commitment. I'd just like to learn what would make a car good for you. [*June and John open the doors and enter into the car.*]

Seller: June, what are the three major items you need in a car, and does this car have any of them?

Buyer: I need a car I can afford. This one definitely isn't it. I want something that looks nice and sleek, and it doesn't really need to be so big. There's just me.

Seller: Okay June. That makes a lot of sense. Would you like to see a few cars that might meet your needs? Then, you can tell me if we're getting closer to what you are thinking?

Buyer: I guess so.

Seller: Follow me. . . . [*He shows her five cars that he feels have those features. After each car, John asks June*] What do you like and not like about his one?

Buyer: Well, I'm still thinking. Thanks for your time. I'll shop around a little more. Give me your card and I'll get back to you later.

Questions

1. Describe the situation and the buyer's apparent needs. What differences did you see between the scenarios?
2. What has the salesperson done well in the second scenario versus the first scenario?
3. How could the salesperson learn more about the buyer's needs in the second scenario?
4. What should the seller do now that the buyer has said no to the cars he has shown her and is about to leave the car lot?
5. Now that you have reviewed both scenarios, what three keys would you suggest a salesperson remember when trying to learn about a buyer's needs?

©Monkey Business Images/Getty Images

Communication for Relationship Building: It's Not All Talk

Main Topics

The Core Principles: Communication

Communication: It Takes Two

The Buyer's Personality Should Be Considered

Adaptive Selling Based on Buyer's Personality Style

Nonverbal Communication: Watch for It

Communication: Improve Your Encoding and Decoding

Learning Objectives

The ability to effectively communicate both verbally and nonverbally is crucial to sales success. This chapter introduces this important sales skill. After studying this chapter, you should be able to

4–1   Present and discuss the salesperson–buyer communication process.

4–2   Determine a person's personality type.

4–3   Discuss and illustrate the importance of using nonverbal communication when selling.

4–4   Define and recognize acceptance, caution, and disagreement nonverbal signals.

4–5   Explain ways of developing persuasive communication.

FACING A SALES CHALLENGE

Amos Skaggs, purchasing professional, stands as a salesperson enters his office. "Hi, Mr. Skaggs," the salesperson says, offering his hand. Skaggs returns a limp, one-second handshake and sits down behind his desk. He begins to open his afternoon mail, almost as though no one else were in the room.

The salesperson sits down and begins his canned sales talk by saying, "Mr. Skaggs, I'm here to show you how your company can lower manufacturing costs by 10 percent." Skaggs lays his mail down on his desk, leans back in his chair, crosses his arms, and with a growl says: "I'm glad to hear that. You know something, young fellow, pretty soon it won't cost us anything to manufacture our products." "Why is that?" the salesman mumbles, meekly looking down to the floor. "Well, you are the ninth person I've seen today who has offered to save us 10 percent on our costs."

Skaggs stands up, leans over the table, and while peering over his glasses says slowly, "I believe I've heard enough sales pitches for one day." The initially enthusiastic salesperson now apologetically says, "If this is not a good time for you, sir, I can come back at a later date."

The problem facing this salesperson is common. The buyer has been seeing salespeople all day. Basically, they say the same thing: "Buy from me and I'll save you money." The buyer has communicated his feelings toward the salesperson both verbally and nonverbally. What message has Skaggs sent to the salesperson? If you were the salesperson, what might you do now?

Although many other factors are crucial to sales success, the ability to communicate effectively is of prime importance. To convincingly convey this important sales skill, this chapter directly applies a basic communication model to the buyer–seller interaction. We describe several factors influencing communication, along with possible barriers to effective communication. We also examine the often ignored—though always critical—topic of nonverbal communication. The balance of this chapter relates some techniques to improve sales communication.

The Core Principles: Communication

What if you could read someone's mind? What if you could tell what he or she is thinking? Wow, wouldn't that be cool! How would you use the knowledge of what is going on in a person's mind about what you are saying—for helping or selling purposes? For the other person's best interest or your best interest? People have ears, but cannot hear. People have eyes, but cannot see. People have two ears and one mouth but do more talking than listening. What are your answers for these four questions? How do the three "People have . . ." sayings relate to your life?

This chapter and the last chapter provide several of the little known secrets about how to read people's minds. Body language, coupled with asking questions periodically as you talk with someone and listening to his or her replies, is a great way to better understand what is going on in someone's mind. Questioning, watching nonverbals, listening, and talking as needed are secrets to successfully helping others in a sales situation. They also work in your everyday life. Try them! Use these secrets of effective communication for building long-term relationships.

Communication: It Takes Two

Communication, in a sales context, is the act of transmitting verbal and nonverbal information and understanding between seller and buyer. This definition presents communication as an exchange process of sending and receiving messages with some type of response expected between seller and buyer.

This sounds simple, right? But have you ever had someone talk to you and realize you did not hear what was said? "You have eyes but do not see; you have ears but do not hear" is a saying that dates back thousands of years. This wise saying is important to all of us, including salespeople, in our daily living. Salespeople have to understand the many ways people communicate with them.

Communication channels during the sales presentation take many forms. Ideas and attitudes can be effectively communicated by media other than language. Actually, in a normal two-person conversation, less than 35 percent of the social meaning utilizes verbal components. Said another way, much of the social meaning in a conversation is conveyed nonverbally. Furthermore, what you say verbally is not always what you actually mean. Exhibit 4.1 expands on this point by illustrating the psychological thought processes of both the speaker and the listener.

Research has found that face-to-face communication is composed of *verbal, vocal,* and *facial* communication messages. One equation presents the total impact of communicated messages as equal to 7 percent verbal, 38 percent tone of voice, and 55 percent nonverbal expressions.[1] If one recognizes these findings as a reasonable approximation of the total communicative process, then uninformed salespeople actually ignore a major part of the communication process that occurs during buyer–seller interaction. How the sales message is given can be as important to making the sale

Nonverbal communication constitutes 55% of the total impact of communicated messages.

EXHIBIT 4.1

"What you say verbally is not what you always hear."

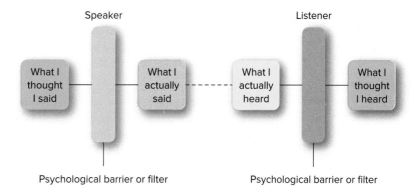

as what is said. Thus, nonverbal communications are important in communication between buyer and seller. An awareness of nonverbal communication is a valuable tool in successfully making a sale.

Vocal communication includes such factors as voice quality, pitch, inflection, and pauses. A salesperson's use of vocal factors can aid in sales presentation, too. Along with verbal, vocal, and nonverbal communication, many other elements also are involved in sales communication.

Salesperson–Buyer Communication Process Requires Feedback

A basic communication model that depicts how the salesperson–buyer communication process works is shown in Exhibit 4.2. Basically, communication occurs when a sender transmits a message through some type of medium to a receiver who responds to that message. Exhibit 4.2 presents a model that contains eight major communication elements. These elements are defined as

- **Source.** The source of communication (also called the communicator); in our case, it's the salesperson.
- **Encoding process.** The salesperson's conversion of ideas and concepts into the language and materials used in the sales presentation.
- **Message.** The information intended to be conveyed in the sales presentation.
- **Medium.** The form of communication used in the sales presentation and discussion; most frequently words, visual materials, and body language.
- **Decoding process.** Receipt and translation (interpretation) of the information by the receiver (prospective buyer).
- **Receiver.** The person the communication is intended for; in our case, it's the prospect or buyer.

EXHIBIT 4.2

The basic communication model has eight elements.

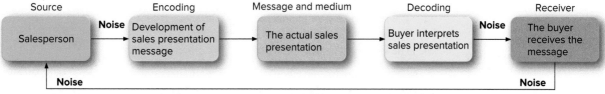

- **Feedback.** Reaction to the communication as transmitted to the sender. This reaction may be verbal, nonverbal, or both.
- **Noise.** Factors that distort communication between buyer and seller. Noise includes barriers to communication, which we will discuss later.

This model portrays the communication process. A salesperson should know how to develop a sales presentation (encoding) so that the buyer obtains maximum understanding of the message (decoding). The salesperson should use communication media that most effectively communicate a specific sales message. Clear verbal discussion, visual aids such as pictures or diagrams, and models or samples of the product are several types of media a salesperson might use in communicating a sales message.

Studies have shown that people retain 10 percent of what they read, 20 percent of what they see, 30 percent of what they hear, and 50 percent of what they hear and see. If possible, it is important to incorporate into your presentation communication that appeals to all five senses (sight, hearing, smell, feel, taste). This is challenging to do!

One-way communication occurs when the salesperson talks and the buyer only listens. The salesperson needs a response or feedback from the buyer to know if communication occurs. Does the buyer understand the message? Once feedback or interaction and understanding between buyer and seller exist in a communication process, two-way communication has been established.

Two-way communication is essential to make the sale. The buyer must understand your message's information to make a buying decision. Two-way communication gives the salesperson the ability to present a product's benefits, instantly receive buyer reactions, and answer questions. Buyers usually react both verbally and nonverbally to your presentation. Guidelines to identifying buyers' personality style help guide you in your talk with the prospect or present customers.

Two-way communication is essential to make the sale. Communication positively impacts trust and relationship quality.

The Buyer's Personality Should Be Considered

People's personalities also can affect buying behavior by influencing the types of products that fulfill their particular needs. **Personality** can be viewed as the individual's distinguishing character traits, attitudes, or habits. Although it is difficult to know exactly how personality affects buying behavior, it is generally believed that personality has some influence on a person's perceptions, attitudes, and beliefs, and thus on buying behavior.

Self-Concept

One of the best ways to examine personality is to consider a buyer's **self-concept,** the view of one's self. Internal or personal self-evaluation may influence a buyer's attitude toward the products desired or not desired. Some theorists believe that people buy products that match their self-concept. According to self-concept theory, buyers possess four images:

1. The **real self**—people as they actually are.
2. The **self-image**—how people see themselves.
3. The **ideal self**—what people would like to be.
4. The **looking-glass self**—how people think others regard them.

One of the best ways to examine personality is to consider a buyer's self-concept, the view of one's self.

As a salesperson you should attempt to understand the buyer's self-concept, because it may be the key to understanding the buyer's attitudes and beliefs. For example, if a man is apparently unsatisfied with his self-image, he might be sold through appeals to his ideal self-image. You might compliment him by saying, "Mr. Buyer, it is obvious that the people in your community think highly of you. They know you as an ideal family man and good provider for your family [looking-glass self]. Your purchase of this life insurance policy will provide your family with the security you want [ideal self]." This appeal is targeted at the looking-glass self and the ideal self. Success in sales is often closely linked to the salesperson's knowledge of the buyer's self-concept rather than the buyer's real self.

Adaptive Selling Based on Buyer's Personality Style

Adaptive selling describes the salesperson's ability to adjust and modify their behaviors to better align with their customers' needs.[2] The salesperson uses his or her actions, communication, and behaviors to demonstrate to the buyer that he or she is similar to the buyer and compatible with the buyer

In order to build a long-term, trust-filled business relationship, the buyer must perceive the salesperson as a compatible business associate. As you will learn in Chapter 7, compatibility increases the potential for the buyer to like and trust the salesperson. Likeability describes the customer's perception that the salesperson is welcoming, friendly, and good-natured.[3] Research demonstrates that as the degree of liking increases, people are more willing to share information[4] and even collaborate.[5]

So how do you create compatibility? You need to adapt your personal style to best relate to the people with whom you interact. For example, the customer (or person) that you best relate to, the one you find it easiest to call upon, probably has a primary personality style similar to yours (i.e., you are compatible). The other side of the coin states that the person hardest for you to call on usually has a primary style that differs from yours. Because the salesperson is in the relationship business, she must understand how to relate to various types of personalities (i.e., she must adapt). A salesperson who can adapt adjusts his or her sales approach to best meet the needs (and personality style) of the customer. One way to accomplish this is through the study of personality types.

Personality Typing

Carl Gustav Jung (1875–1961), with Sigmund Freud, laid the basis for modern psychiatry. Jung divided human awareness into four functions: (1) feeling, (2) sensing, (3) thinking, and (4) intuiting.* He argued that most people are most comfortable behaving in one of these four groups. Each group, or personality type, has certain characteristics formed by past experiences.

Exhibit 4.3 provides some guidelines you can use to identify someone's personality style. You can determine styles by identifying the key trait, focusing on time orientation, and identifying the environment, and by hearing what people say. Imagine that four of your buyers say the following things to you:

  a. "I'm not interested in all of those details. What's the bottom line?"
  b. "How did you arrive at your projected sales figure?"
  c. "I don't think you see how this purchase fits in with our whole operation here."
  d. "I'm not sure how our people will react to this."

How would you classify their personality styles?[†]

---

*There are numerous methods of personality typing, each of which is due to the method's conceptual theory. Currently, personality typing is a popular sales training technique. We use Jung's classification because of his scientific reputation.

[†]Answers: (*a*) Senser, (*b*) Thinker, (*c*) Intuitor, and (*d*) Feeler.

EXHIBIT 4.3

Guidelines to identifying personality style.

Guideline	Thinker	Intuitor	Feeler	Senser
How to describe this person	A direct, detail-oriented person. Likes to deal in sequence on *his/her time.* Very precise, sometimes seen as a nitpicker. Fact oriented.	A knowledgeable, future-oriented person. An innovator who likes to abstract principles from a mass of material. Active in community affairs by assisting in policy making, program development, etc.	People oriented. Very sensitive to people's needs. An emotional person rooted in the past. Enjoys contact with people. Able to read people very well.	Action-oriented person. Deals with the world through his/her senses. Very decisive and has a high energy level.
The person's strengths	Effective communicator, deliberative, prudent, weighs alternatives, stabilizing, objective, rational, analytical, asks questions for more facts.	Original, imaginative, creative, broad-gauged, charismatic, idealist, intellectual, tenacious, ideological, conceptual, involved.	Spontaneous, persuasive, empathetic, grasps traditional values, probing, introspective, draws out feelings of others, loyal, actions based on what has worked in the past.	Pragmatic, assertive, directional results oriented, technically skillful, objective—bases opinions on what he/she actually sees, perfection seeking, decisive, direct and down to earth, action oriented.
The person's drawbacks	Verbose, indecisive, overcautious, overanalyzes, unemotional, non-dynamic, controlled and controlling, overserious, rigid, nitpicking.	Unrealistic, far-out, fantasy-bound, scattered, devious, out-of-touch, dogmatic, impractical, poor listener.	Impulsive, manipulative, overpersonalizes, sentimental, postponing, guilt-ridden, stirs up conflict, subjective.	Impatient, doesn't see long range, status-seeking, self-involved, acts first then thinks, lacks trust in others, nitpicking, impulsive, does not delegate to others.
Time orientation	Past, present, future.	Future.	Past.	Present.
Environment				
Desk	Usually neat.	Reference books, theory books, etc.	Personal plaques and mementos, family pictures.	Chaos.
Room	Usually has a calculator and computer output, etc.	Abstract art, bookcases, trend charts, etc.	Decorated warmly with pictures of scenes or people. Antiques.	Usually a mess with piles of papers, etc. Action pictures or pictures of the manufacturing plant or products on the wall.
Dress	Neat and conservative.	Mod or rumpled.	Current styles or informal.	No jacket; loose tie or functional work clothes.
Application				
What will rapport likely be like?	Rapport will probably be minimal. They will probably be very business-like and formal in their rapport.	Some level of rapport. It will probably be professional and polite.	Rapport may be the lengthiest of any communication type. It will probably more socially oriented vs. business oriented. You might expect laughter or humor.	Rapport will probably be pretty limited. The individual may understand that rapport is part of the interaction but will want to get to the point of the discussion.

Guideline	Thinker	Intuitor	Feeler	Senser
What should you remember about this type of person?	Think logic and details. They probably have high expectations of themselves and the choices they make. They don't like to make bad decisions or make mistakes. Accuracy and attention to detail are important. They tend to be perfectionists. Don't make silly mistakes or spelling errors. It will impact your credibility.	Think creativity, new ideas. They might seem guarded and reserved. You may have to work very diligently to receive feedback. They enjoy learning new things and stretching their capacities. They probably won't tell you they are upset or frustrated, but rather keep it to themselves.	Think about the relationship. They probably enjoy networking; they might appreciate building their network, and receiving virtual introductions to others. They may look somewhat disorganized.	Think about action and pragmatism. They are action-oriented and might seem impatient. They might be seen as focused or assertive. It's probably a good idea not to dive into the minutia of details. They are probably pragmatic. You need to earn their trust. You will not receive it immediately.
What should you remember when you are preparing your presentation?	They will probably desire • Being presented with many precise options • To understand the details • An option that meets all of their criteria. • An organized, detailed discussion and presentation. It's okay to be detailed. They probably enjoy being immersed in data, analytics or ensuring they understand any new system or process.	They probably desire to • Have a salesperson who can provide knowledge they can learn from • Understand how you can help them with their goals or vision • Evaluate multiple options • Be a little guarded and not provide a great deal of helpful feedback. • Be presented with unique solutions that may be difficult to execute.	They probably desire • Some level of social proof or recommendations from others (i.e., testimonials, colleagues and peers, market leaders). • A sales conversation that is more socially based and passionate, with strong storytelling elements.	They probably desire • An agenda and action plan for the meeting • Logical recommendations • Conversations that don't dive into non-strategic minutia • A discussion that helps facilitate a decision • A recommendation or set of recommendations that are tied to action plans, follow-ups, and assurance you can make progress
What should you remember when you want them to make a decision on your solution?	They will probably be more methodical and deliberative in decision making. They will be quite cautious in making decisions due to their goal of optimizing. They will want time to evaluate multiple options and weigh pros and cons.	They probably will need time to evaluate options and make a decision based on their own. They may be cautious in making decisions. They will want to evaluate multiple options. It may appear that they are procrastinating or delaying the decision. You may need to follow-up to ensure everyone (you and the intuitor) are on task.	They probably will want input from others before making a decision. They probably will consult peers or confidantes to test ideas and receive feedback.	They want a path forward and to feel they are making progress. They might be impatient with you for not moving quick enough. They probably are the most likely to make a decision. But they will expect the action steps to begin . . . now.

Adapt Your Presentation to the Buyer's Style

The objective is to increase your skill at recognizing the style of the people you deal with. Once you recognize the basic style of a buyer, it is possible to modify and adapt your presentation to the buyer's style to achieve the best results. Although this method

Creating compatibility is essential to developing and maintaining a relationship. As you discover your buyer's personality and self-concept, your goal is to adapt the sales conversation to the style they appreciate. We provide a few communication practices to consider when structuring the sales conversation:

- **Rapport:** Does the buyer appreciate more relationship-building rapport to learn about one another (i.e., chit-chat) or does the buyer prefer to be more focused and move directly to the objectives of the meeting?

- **Presenting information:** Does the buyer prefer more detailed data (i.e., charts and graphs or other quantitative data) or a more descriptive discussion (i.e., testimonials from other customers, or white papers and case studies providing a more story-based discussion about a problem and the solution)?

- **Challenging or facilitating:** Does the buyer appreciate someone who challenges beliefs and assumptions or someone who acts as a guide through a variety of potential solutions?

- **Closing:** Does the buyer want to make a decision immediately, or will the buyer need time to think through the alternatives or consult with other individuals in the organization or family?

is not foolproof, it does offer an alternative way of presenting material if you are not succeeding. Let's examine a suggested tailored selling method based on the prospect's personality type preferences.

The Thinker Style

This person places high value on logic, ideas, and systematic inquiry. Completely preplan your presentation with ample facts and supporting data and be precise. Present your material in an orderly and logical manner. When closing the sale be sure to say, "Think it over, Joe, and I'll get back to you tomorrow," whenever the order does not close on the spot.

The Intuitor Style

This person places high value on ideas, innovation, concepts, theory, and long-range thinking. The main point is to tie your presentation into the buyer's big picture or overview of this person's objectives. Strive to build the buyer's concepts and objectives into your presentation whenever possible. In presenting your material, be sure you have ample time.

In closing the sale, stress time limitations on acting. A good suggestion is to say, "I know you have a lot to do—I'll go to Sam to get the nitty-gritty handled and get this off the ground."

The Feeler Style

This person places high value on being people oriented and sensitive to people's needs. The main point to include in your presentation is the impact your idea will have on people. The feeler likes to small talk with you, so engage in conversation and wait for this person's cue to begin your presentation. The buyer will usually ask,

"What's on your mind today?" or something similar. Use emotional terms and words, such as, "We're *excited* about this!"

In your presentation, start with something carried over from your last call or contact. Keep the presentation on a personal note. Whenever possible, get the buyer away from the office (lunch, snack, etc.) on an informal basis; this is how this person prefers to do business. Force the close by saying something such as, "OK, Joe, if there are no objections, let's set it up for next week." Even if the buyer says no, you are not dead. The key with a feeler is to push the decision.

The Senser Style

This person places high value on *action*. The key point with a senser is to be brief and to the point. Graphs, models, and samples help the senser visualize your presentation. With a senser, verbal communication is more effective than written communication.

In presenting, start with conclusions and results and have supporting data to use when needed. Suggest an action plan—"Let's move *now*"—the buyer has to feel you know what to do.

In closing, give one best way. Have options, but do not present them unless you have to. An effective senser close is, "I know you're busy; let's set this up right *now*."

Watch for Clues

Exhibit 4.4 shows two buyers' environments. Look at the environment guidelines listed in Exhibit 4.3 to identify each buyer's personality style.

The neatness of the desk and dress of the buyer on the left indicates she may be a thinker, whereas the buyer on the right appears to be a senser. The salesperson should alternate the presentation to fit each person's style. However, determining a buyer's personality style is not always as easy as the example shown in Exhibit 4.4.

EXHIBIT 4.4

Environment provides clues to the buyer's style. What are the personality styles of the buyers who sit at these desks?

©AVAVA/Shutterstock

©Exactostock/SuperStock

What Is Your Style?

What is your personality style? It only takes a few minutes to find out by completing the short questionnaire at the end of this chapter.

At least six messages are involved in the communication process:

1. What you mean to say.
2. What you really say.
3. What the other person hears.
4. What the other person thinks is heard.
5. What the other person says about what you said.
6. What you think the other person said about what you said.

It gets complicated, doesn't it? Sue and I were looking at a gorgeous moon together under romantic circumstances. As we shared the moment, how was I actually feeling? I was feeling romantic. If we followed the six messages, that incident would have looked something like this:

We can miss each other's wavelengths completely by the time the six messages are completed without even realizing what has happened. All of us are constantly in the process of encoding and decoding messages.

1. What you mean to say	("The moon puts me in a romantic mood.")
2. What you really say	("Isn't that a brilliant moon?")
3. What the other person hears	("The moon is bright.")
4. What the other person thinks she hears.	("Yes, it's bright enough for a walk.")
5. What the other person says about what you said.	("Yes, it's bright enough to hit a golf ball by.")
6. What you think the other person said about what you said.	("I don't feel romantic.")

We need to learn to ask questions or restate the point to clarify meaning. To say what we mean straightforwardly must be our constant goal in order for those around us to discard all decoding devices.[6]

Determining Style Can Be Difficult

Each of the four styles is present, in some degree, in all of us. However, one style is usually dominant, and another complementary style is used as a backup. The primary style an individual employs often remains the same in both normal and stress situations, whereas the secondary style is likely to vary.

Some individuals do not have a primary or secondary style, but have a personal style comprising all four types. Dealing with this individual requires strong rapport to isolate the prospect's predominant personal likes and dislikes.

Nonverbal Communication: Watch for It

Recognition and analysis of nonverbal communication in sales transactions are relatively new. The presence and use of nonverbal communication, however, has been acknowledged for years. In the early 1900s, Sigmund Freud noted that people cannot keep a secret even if they do not speak. A person's gestures and actions reveal hidden feelings about something.

People communicate nonverbally in several ways. Four major **nonverbal communication** channels are the physical space between buyer and seller, appearance, handshake, and body movements.

Concept of Space

The concept of **territorial space** refers to the area around the self that a person will not allow another person to enter without consent. Early experiments in territorial space dealt with animals. These experiments determined that higher-status members of a group often are afforded a freedom of movement that is less available to those of lower status. This idea has been applied to socially acceptable distances of space that human beings keep between themselves in certain situations. Territorial space can easily be related to the selling situation.

Space considerations are important to salespeople because violations of territorial space without customer consent may set off the customer's defense mechanisms and create a barrier to communications. A person (buyer) has four main types of distance to consider—intimate (up to 2 feet); personal (2 to 4 feet); social (4 to 12 feet); and public (greater than 12 feet).

Intimate space of up to 2 feet, or about arm's length, is the most sensitive zone, since it is reserved for close friends and loved ones. To enter intimate space in the buyer–seller relationship, for some prospects, could be socially unacceptable—possibly offensive.

During the presentation, a salesperson should carefully listen and look for signs that indicate the buyer feels uncomfortable—perhaps that the salesperson is too close. A buyer may deduce from such closeness that the salesperson is attempting to dominate or overpower the buyer. This feeling can result in resistance to the salesperson. If such uneasiness is detected, the salesperson should move back, which reassures the customer.

Personal space is the closest zone a stranger or business acquaintance is normally allowed to enter. Even in this zone, a prospect may be uncomfortable. Barriers, such as a desk, often reduce the threat implied when someone enters this zone.

Social space is the area normally used for a sales presentation. Again, the buyer often uses a desk to maintain a distance of 4 feet or more between buyer and seller. Standing while facing a seated prospect may communicate to the buyer that the salesperson seems too dominating. Thus, the salesperson should normally stay seated to convey a relaxed manner.

A salesperson should consider beginning a presentation in the middle of the social distance zone, 6 to 8 feet, to avoid the prospect's erecting negative mental barriers. This is especially true if the salesperson is not a friend of the prospect.

Public space can be used by the salesperson making a presentation to a group of people. It is similar to the distance between teacher and student in a classroom. People are at ease, and thus easy to communicate with, at this distance because they do not feel threatened by the salesperson.

Four major nonverbal communication channels are the physical space between buyer and seller, appearance, handshake, and body movements.

Space Threats

The territorial imperative causes people to feel that they should defend their space or territory against **space threats.** The salesperson who pulls up a chair too close, takes over all or part of the prospect's desk, leans on or over the desk, or touches the objects on the desk runs the risk of invading a prospect's territory. Be careful not to create defensive barriers. However, should you sense a friendliness between yourself and the prospect, use territorial space to your benefit.

Space Invasion

The prospect who allows you to enter or invade personal and intimate space is saying, "Come on into my space; let's be friends." Now you can use space to your advantage.

In most offices, the salesperson sits directly across the desk from the prospect. The prospect controls the space arrangement. This defensive barrier allows the prospect

EXHIBIT 4.5

Office arrangements and territorial space.

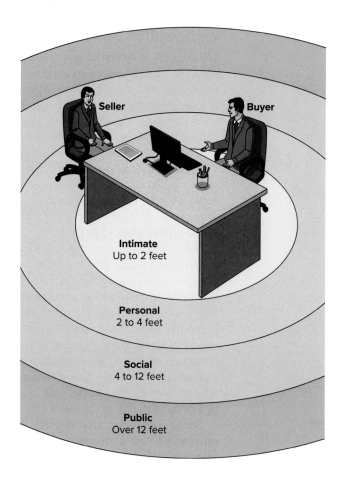

Intimate
Up to 2 feet

Personal
2 to 4 feet

Social
4 to 12 feet

Public
Over 12 feet

to control much of the conversation and remain safe from **space invasion.** Often, seating is prearranged and it could be a space threat if you moved your chair when calling on a prospect for the first time.

However, if you have a choice between a chair across the desk or beside the desk, take the latter seat, as shown in Exhibit 4.5. Sitting beside the prospect lowers the desk communication barrier. If you are friends with the buyer, move your chair to the side of the desk. This helps create a friendly, cooperative environment between you and the buyer.

Communication Through Appearance

Other common methods of nonverbal communication are signals conveyed by a person's physical appearance and handshake. Once territorial space has been established, general appearance is the next medium of nonverbal communication a salesperson conveys to a customer. Appearance not only conveys information such as age, sex, height, weight, and physical characteristics, but it also provides much data on personality. For instance, hairstyle is one of the first things a buyer notices about a salesperson.

Style Hair Carefully

You have only one chance to make a favorable first impression.

Hairstyle traditionally has been important in evaluating personal appearance. Today's salespeople must consider the type of customer they call on and adjust their hairstyles accordingly.

Salespeople should carefully consider their grooming and its impact on customers' perceptions. Some companies leave grooming up to each individual. Your grooming objective is to eliminate communication barriers. Your grooming can convey a favorable first impression. Should your company not have a policy on grooming, examine your customers' grooming before deciding on your style.

Dress as a Professional: Adapting to the Customer

While the long-held belief in sales was to "suit up," today's salespeople must adapt to the occasion and their customer's environment. Historically, the choice of the salesperson's business professional clothing was considered a major determinant of sales success. Books on the subject of professional attire suggested that sales representatives should wear conservative, serious clothing that projects professionalism, just the right amount of authority, and a desire to please the customer. Further, many companies described rules for every major clothing item and accessory; the rules often were derivatives of one basic commandment—dress in a simple, elegant style. This practice was designed to project a conservative, stable corporate image to both customers and the general public.

However, a number of companies have eased their dress code policies. In some companies, business casual is the norm, while other firms specify that one's dress depends on where you are located (i.e., inside the firm or outside of the firm) and the work you are performing (i.e., working with a customer or returning e-mails in your office).

Sales managers may also suggest to their salespeople that it's important to choose attire based on your customer and the location of the meeting. Imagine a scenario in which a salesperson visits a construction site. The salesperson is wearing a formal suit while everyone else is wearing jeans and work wear. Would the salesperson's dress create compatibility? Perhaps not. Further, imagine the salesperson in the technology sector. At the headquarters of your technology company, it is perfectly acceptable to wear a pair of jeans and a T-shirt. However, what happens when the technology salesperson wears jeans and a T-shirt when she meets with a CEO and CFO of a financial services company? Has she set herself up for success?

Ultimately, your business wardrobe will depend on your firm's dress code, the work you are conducting, whether you are meeting with a customer, and the dress code and culture of your customer. Depending on the day and your responsibilities, you might expect to wear a formal suit and tie for Tuesday's meeting; and a pair of nice jeans and a button-down shirt for Thursday's meetings. Therefore, your professional wardrobe might be varied and require you to own a wide range of apparel.

Exhibit 4.6 and the "Dress for Success" appendix at the end of this chapter illustrate several key considerations for appropriate dress and grooming. Before reading on, look over the appendix at the end of this chapter to better prepare you for the business world. If you are uncertain about what to purchase, consider visiting visit several specialty clothing retailers. They will have the latest styles and spend time with you. Tell the salespeople what you are looking for and see what they say. Think of this as an investment in yourself because it is expensive to build a wardrobe. However, you are worth it!

The nonverbal messages that salespeople emit through appearance should be positive in all sales situations

In summary, the nonverbal messages that salespeople emit through appearance should be positive in all sales situations. Characteristics of the buyer, cultural aspects of a sales territory, and the type of product being sold all determine a mode of dress. In considering these aspects, create a business wardrobe that sends positive, nonverbal messages in every sales situation.

EXHIBIT 4.6

Dress for success.

Business Professional Clothing (Men)

Suit and tie
- Often conservative colors (i.e., black, blue, and gray)

Suit jacket and tailored pants

Shirts
- Usually an Oxford cloth
- Usually a neutral color or white shirt

Accessories
- Socks: Matching colors
- Shoes and belts are in matching colors

Shoes
- Polished, leather shoes

©Andrey Popov/Shutterstock

Business Professional Clothing (Women)

Suits and pant suits
- Often conservative colors (i.e., black, blue, and gray)

Dress and jacket
- Often conservative colors (i.e., black, blue, and gray)

Accessories
- Scarfs: Neutral and conservative colors
- Hosiery: Neutral colored hosiery
- Fewer and more subdued accessories

Shoes
- Lower heels or flats
- Closed toe pumps

©wavebreakmedia/Shutterstock

Business Casual Clothing (Men)

Sports coat, long-sleeved shirt, and dress pants/slacks
- Jacket and pant color can match, or
- Jacket and pant color do not necessarily have to match

Dress pants or slacks with long-sleeved shirt (tie optional)

Shirts
- Pressed long-sleeve shirt

- Collared shirts
- Button-down shirts

Accessories
- Socks: Matching colors or more trendy
- Shoes and belts are in matching colors

Shoes
- Polished, leather shoes
- More contemporary and trendy shoes (probably still leather or suede)

©elwynn/Shutterstock

Business Professional Clothing (Women)

Blazers and dress pants
Blazers and skirt (knee length and below)
Skirts (knee length and below)
Dresses (knee length and below)
Dress pants
Blouse with a skirt
A greater number of accessories

Shirts
- Blouse
- Sweater
- Button-down blouse
- Blazer
- Cardigan

Shoes
- Closed-toe shoes
- Flats
- Heels (wedges)

©Pepsco Studio/Shutterstock

Conservative Casual to Casual Clothing (Men)

More conservative casual

Tops:
- Long-sleeved shirts (trendy colors)
- Sweaters
- Ironed cotton shirts (golf or polo-style)

Pants
- Flat-front cotton pants such as khakis
- Microfiber pants

Shoes
- More contemporary and trendy shoes (probably still leather or suede)

More casual
- Sports coat, long-sleeved shirt and jeans
- Sports coat, sports shirt, and jeans

©Quality Master/Shutterstock

Conservative Casual to Casual Clothing (Women)

More conservative casual

Tops
- Silk blouses
- Sweaters
- Knit shirts

Pants
- Casual skirts (knee-length)
- Cotton pants
- Microfiber pants
- Seasonal dress

Shoes
- Shoes that cover most of your foot

More casual
- Blazer and jeans
- T-shirt layered with something fashionable
- Shoes: Casual shoes (probably not tennis shoes), sandals, heels, boots

©Gyorgy Barna/Shutterstock

Refrain From Wearing The Following (Better Check with Your Company for Policy on These Items): Men & Women

Workout clothing
Shorts
Types of Material
- Leather • Spandex

Anything that is too tight (such as polyester workout shirts) or revealing shirts

Tops
- Sleeveless shirts or muscle T-shirts
- T-shirts (especially ones that you wore in college)
- Tank tops or halter tops

Shorts
- Faded jeans (due to wear)
- Jeans with holes in them (due to wear)

White socks

Shoes
Such as running shoes or beach flip-flops

©Fanya/Shutterstock

You have only one chance to make a favorable first impression. Impressions of you are based, in part, upon your appearance. How you are dressed makes a first and lasting impression on those you meet in any situation. We provide some general dress guidelines below.

Overall guidelines:

- **Clean and pressed is always best.** From blouses, dress shirts to t-shirts, please iron out the wrinkles or consider using commercial laundry or dry cleaning establishment.

- **Even if it's mussed, make sure it's styled.** Ensure your hair is combed and styled appropriately.

- **If you aren't sure, just ask.** In some instances, it may be difficult to understand the dress code for your company or your customer's company. If you aren't sure what is expected, never be afraid of asking for clarification.

- **Tattoos and piercings.** Policies in some areas tend to be fluid based on business norms. Depending on the company and the interaction, certain policies may apply. Again, don't be afraid to ask about policies regarding tattoos (covered or uncovered during business meetings) as well as understanding what types of piercings are acceptable.

- **First impressions are important.** Knowing that everyone makes automatic judgments, remember that you only have one opportunity to make a great first impression. If you aren't sure of the dress code, consider the saying, "It is better to be over dressed than under dressed." Only a rare customer has stated, "That salesperson was so unprofessional by wearing that suit." When in doubt, consider the +1 rule we discussed earlier in the chapter.

Communication Through The Handshake

Today, a handshake is the most common way for two people to touch one another in a business situation, and some people feel that it is a revealing gesture. A firm handshake is more intense and is indicative of greater liking and warmer feelings. A prolonged handshake is more intimate than a brief one, and it could cause the customer discomfort, especially in a sales call on a new prospect. A loosely clasped, cold, handshake is usually interpreted as indicating that someone is aloof and unwilling to become involved. This cold fish handshake is also perceived as unaffectionate and unfriendly.

General rules for a successful handshake include extending your hand first—if appropriate. Remember, however, a few people may be uncomfortable shaking hands with a stranger. At times, you may want to allow your customer to initiate the gesture. Maintain eye contact with the customer during the handshake, gripping the hand firmly. These actions allow you to initially establish an atmosphere of honesty and mutual respect—starting the presentation in a positive manner.[7]

General handshake rules:

1. Demonstrate your interest. If possible, align your body position with the buyer.
2. Step or lean ever-so-slightly forward and initiate the handshake.
3. Maintain eye contact with the buyer.
4. Show a positive attitude by smiling.
5. Use a positive tone when introducing yourself or saying hello.

Body Language Gives You Clues

From birth, people learn to communicate their needs, likes, and dislikes through nonverbal means. The salesperson can learn much from a prospect's raised eyebrow, a smile, a touch, a scowl, or reluctance to make eye contact during a sales presentation. The prospect can communicate with you literally without uttering a word. An ability to interpret these signals is an invaluable tool to the successful sales professional. In conjunction with interpretation of body language, the salesperson's skillful use and control of physical actions, gestures, and overall body position also are helpful.

The buyer can send nonverbal signals via five communication modes. They are the body angle, facial expression, hand movements or position, arm movement or position, and leg position. (Exhibit 4.7 shows examples.) These modes generally send three types of messages: (1) acceptance, (2) caution, and (3) disagreement.

Acceptance signals indicate that your buyer is favorably inclined toward you and your presentation. These signals give you the green light to proceed. While this may not end in a sale, at the least the prospect is saying, "I am willing to listen." What you are saying is both acceptable and interesting. Some common acceptance signals include these:

- *Body angle.* Leaning forward or upright at attention.
- *Face.* Smiling, pleasant expression, relaxed, eyes examining visual aids, direct eye contact, positive voice tones.
- *Hands.* Relaxed and generally open, perhaps performing business calculations on paper, holding on as you attempt to withdraw a product sample or sales materials, firm handshake.
- *Arms.* Relaxed and generally open.
- *Legs.* Crossed and pointed toward you or uncrossed.

Salespeople frequently rely only on facial expressions as indicators of acceptance. This practice may be misleading since buyers may consciously control their facial expressions. Scan each of the five key body areas to verify your interpretation of facial signals. A buyer who increases eye contact, maintains a relaxed position, and exhibits positive facial expressions gives excellent acceptance signals.

Acceptance signals indicate that buyers perceive that your product might meet their needs. You have obtained their attention and interest. You are free to continue with your planned sales presentation.

Caution signals should alert you that buyers are either neutral or skeptical toward what you say. Caution signals are indicated by these characteristics:

- *Body angle.* Leaning away from you.
- *Face.* Puzzled, little or no expression, averted eyes or little eye contact, neutral or questioning voice tone, saying little, and then asking only a few questions.
- *Hands.* Moving, fidgeting with something, clasped, weak handshake.

©Monkey Business Images/
Shutterstock

EXHIBIT 4.7

Which of the five communication modes can a salesperson look for with these customers?

©iStockphoto/Getty Images

©Michael Goldman/Getty Images

©Image Source

- *Arms.* Crossed, tense.
- *Legs.* Moving, crossed away from you.

Caution signals are important for you to recognize and adjust to for two main reasons. First, they indicate blocked communication. Buyers' perceptions, attitudes, and beliefs regarding your presentation may cause them to be skeptical, judgmental, or uninterested in your product. They may not recognize that they need your product or that it can benefit them. Even though you may have their attention, they show little interest in or desire for your product.

Second, if caution signals are not handled properly, they may evolve into disagreement signals, which causes a communication breakdown and makes a sale difficult. Proper handling of caution signals requires that you

- Adjust to the situation by slowing down or departing from your planned presentation.
- Use open-ended questions to encourage your buyers to talk and express their attitudes and beliefs. "How might we improve the efficiency of your workforce"? and "What do you think about this benefit?" are examples of open-ended questions.
- Carefully listen to what buyers say, and respond directly.
- Project acceptance signals. Be positive, enthusiastic, and smile. Remember, you are glad to be there to help buyers satisfy their needs. Refrain from projecting caution signals even if a buyer does so. If you project a positive image in this situation, there is greater probability that you will change a caution light to a green one and make the sale.

Your objective in using these techniques is to change the yellow caution signal to the green go-ahead signal. If you continue to receive caution signals, proceed carefully with your presentation. Be realistic and alert to the possibility that the buyer may begin to believe that your product is not beneficial and begin sending disagreement or red-light signals.

Disagreement signals tell you immediately to stop the planned presentation and quickly adjust to the situation. Disagreements, or red-light signals, indicate that you are dealing with a person becoming uninterested in your product. Anger or hostility may develop if you continue the presentation. Your continuation can cause a buyer to feel an unacceptable level of sales pressure, resulting in a complete communication breakdown. Disagreement signals may be indicated by these signs:

©Westend61/Getty Images

- *Body angle.* Retracted shoulders, leaning away from you, moving the entire body back from you, or wanting to move away.
- *Face.* Tense, showing anger, wrinkled face and brow, little eye contact, negative voice tones, or sudden silence.
- *Hands.* Motions of rejection or disapproval, tense and clenched, weak handshake.
- *Arms.* Tense, crossed over chest.
- *Legs.* Crossed and away from you.

You should handle disagreement signals as you did caution signals, by using open-ended questions and projecting acceptance signals. There are four additional techniques to use. First, stop your planned presentation. There is no use in continuing until you have changed disagreement signals into caution or acceptance signals. Second, temporarily reduce or eliminate any pressure on the person to buy or to participate in the conversation. Let the buyer relax as you slowly move back to your presentation. Third, let your buyer know you are aware that something upsetting has occurred. Show that you are there to help, not to sell at any cost. Finally, use direct questions to determine a buyer's attitudes and beliefs such as "What do you think of . . . ?" or "Have I said something you do not agree with?"

Your Voice: What Does It Communicate to Your Customer?

A very rapidly growing trend within the sales industry is the use of an inside sales department. Inside sales people sell remotely.[8] In these positions, salespeople are located together in a central location instead of dispersed across a territory. Inside salespeople leverage different forms of technology (such as web conferencing, social media, hosted webinars, and telephones) to qualify prospects, convene sales meetings, present demonstrations, and serve their customers. One of the inside salesperson's tools lies in selling using video technology, web conferences, and the phone. As such, it is increasingly important to consider your vocal characteristics. This selling tip provides a few thoughts to consider regarding your vocal characteristics and the impact it could have on your customers.

- *Inflection:* Your vocal inflection helps create a positive perception. Imagine someone who calls you and never uses any inflection (i.e., monotone). Would you infer, perhaps, the person was apathetic or just didn't care? Similarly, what vocal characteristics demonstrate that the person is happy to talk with you? What vocal elements do you notice?

- *Volume:* Have you ever experienced a friend who was nervous about an interaction? Did the volume change in the person's voice? Did the volume become louder than normal? Perhaps you could barely hear your friend. Based on your friend's vocal volume, when did you perceive him or her as frustrated, assertive, scared, or meek? What might be the customer's perception?

- *Rate or Pace:* Perhaps you have a friend who became nervous and stopped talking or made long, uncomfortable pauses. Or, perhaps when your friend became nervous, he or she rambled or talked very rapidly or even talked over someone or couldn't stop talking. How would a customer perceive this?

- *Emphasis or Enunciation:* Do you have friends who mumble? They speak softly. It almost seems as if they barely open their mouth when they speak. Do you have a difficult time understanding them? How would a customer perceive their level of professionalism?

Body Guidelines

Over time, you will know customers well enough to understand the meaning of their body movements. Although a prospect may say no to making a purchase, body movement may indicate uncertainty.

Exhibit 4.8 relates some common nonverbal signals that buyers may project.[9] The interpretation of most body language is obvious. Be cautious in interpreting an isolated gesture, such as assuming that little eye contact means the prospect is displeased with what you are saying. Instead, concentrate on nonverbal cues that are part of a cluster or pattern. Let's say your prospect begins staring at the wall. That is a clue that may mean nothing. You continue to talk. Now, the prospect leans back in the chair. That is another clue. By itself, it may be meaningless, but in conjuction with the first clue, it begins to take on meaning. Now, you see the prospect turn away, legs crossed, brow wrinkled. You now have a cluster of clues forming a pattern. It is time to adjust or change your presentation.

In summary, remember that nonverbal communication is well worth considering in selling. A salesperson ought to

Understanding nonverbal communication is a critical skill to develop.

- Be able to recognize nonverbal signals.
- Be able to interpret them correctly.

EXHIBIT 4.8

What nonverbal signals are these buyers giving to you?

©JUPITERIMAGES/Comstock
Images/Alamy Stock Photo

©Purestock/Superstock

©Caia Image/Glow Images

1. When you mention your price, this purchasing agent tilts her head back, raises her hands, and assumes a rigid body posture. What nonverbal signals is she communicating, and how would you move on with the sale?

2. As you explain your sales features, this buyer looks away, clasps his hands, and crosses his legs away from you. What nonverbal signals is he communicating, and how would you move on with the sale?

3. As you explain the quality of your product, this company president opens his arms and leans toward you. What nonverbal signals is he communicating, and how would you move on with the sale?

©Jim Barber/
Shutterstock

Answers

1. Your buyer is sending red signals. That means you are facing nearly insurmountable barriers. You've got to stop what you are doing, express your understanding, and redirect your approach.
2. This buyer is sending yellow signals that warn you to exercise caution. Your own words and gestures must be aimed at relaxing the buyer, or the prospect may soon communicate red signals.
3. This buyer is sending green signals that say everything is "go." With no obstacles to your selling strategy, simply move to the close.

- Be prepared to alter a selling strategy by slowing, changing, or stopping a planned presentation.
- Respond nonverbally and verbally to a buyer's nonverbal signals.

Effective communication is essential in making a sale. Nonverbal communication signals are an important part of the total communication process between buyer and seller. Professional salespeople seek to learn and understand nonverbal communication to increase their sales success.

Mirroring and Mimicry

Have you ever watched two friends interact? Did you ever notice how engaged they appeared? Did they look relaxed or comfortable with the other person? When you looked at them, did you notice that they looked as if they were the mirror image of one another? Or has a stranger ever smiled at you and you immediately smiled back

Mirroring Exercise

In this Selling Tips exercise, you will practice your mirroring skills. Why are mirroring skills important? Mirroring is one of the behaviors you can practice to create compatibility with a buyer; and compatibility serves as a key element in developing trust within a relationship.

In this two-person exercise, you will have a buyer and a seller, who should sit across from one another. The buyer begins the exercise by telling the seller about her background. As the buyer is talking, she intermittently changes her nonverbal expressions, including her body position, her body movement, her level of eye contact, and even the expressions on her face.

The individual who is playing the seller should mirror the actions and movements of the buyer (and also continue the conversation by asking the buyer questions). After one or two minutes, each person switches roles, (i.e., the buyer becomes the seller and the seller assumes the buyer's role).

After each partner plays both roles, it's time to do the opposite actions. As the buyer makes a facial expression, changes her body position, or makes a movement, the seller should perform the opposite action. After one or two minutes, end the exercise and discuss the differences when the partners mirror one another and when the partners perform the opposite action.

at the individual? This type of behavior is not unusual. In fact, it's a way that we blend into a social environment. It's called *mimicry* or *mirroring*.

Mirroring or mimicry happens when people take part in similar actions at relatively the same time (i.e., within three to five seconds). People might mimic one another's actions, such as shrugs, their body position, such as their posture, other actions or expressions, such as smiling, and even vocal inflections and accents.[10] For the salesperson, understanding the value of mimicry is important, as it may assist in creating greater levels of compatibility, thereby leading to liking, trust, empathy and helping behaviors.[11]

In Chapter 7, you will learn about the drivers of trust and the value of trust. One of the key ways to generate trust in a relationship is through similarity and compatibility. Therefore, mirroring is one approach to enhancing similarity and trust.

Many of our students have relayed the value of mirroring an interviewer during a job interview. They noticed how engaged everyone became in the conversation. In many sales classes and in training, instructors create exercises to practice mirroring. In this chapter's Selling Tips, we provide one opportunity to practicing your similarity-building skills with a buyer through mirroring.

Communication: Improve Your Encoding and Decoding

To become a better communicator, consider two major elements of communication. First, always strive to improve the message and its delivery in the sales presentation. You need to be a capable encoder. Second, improve your ability to determine what the buyer is communicating to you. To do so, you need to be a good listener or decoder. A good sales communicator knows how to effectively encode and decode during a presentation.

Encoding: The Sender's Professional Communication

As you learned earlier, the communication process includes the sender encoding the message properly. Encoding describes the salesperson converting ideas into language. In the following section, we introduce a few best practices to ensure your sales communication is encoded effectively.

1. **Reduce vocalized pauses.** Vocalized pauses are the words and phrases that speakers inject between words when they speak.[12] You may have heard speakers place words such as "umm," "uhh," "like," "awesome," "great," or "and" throughout a conversation. In some instances, vocalized pauses may be so rampant in a conversation that the listener's attention focuses on the number of vocalized pauses rather than the content of the message.

   To enable effective, professional communication, a salesperson should aim to reduce the use of vocalized pauses. How can you reduce your vocalized pauses? You could consider watching a video of your sales role play. Many students become more aware of their vocalized pauses when they watch their video role play. In other instances, salespeople join professional development organizations, such as Toastmasters International, to hone their communication skills.

2. **Use positive, specific, professional language.** Using professional language is important for building your credibility and communication effectiveness. By using *specific language,* you create the opportunity for greater understanding by your buyer. By using *positive language,* you potentially create greater levels of enthusiasm and interest within the buyer; and by using *professional language,* you help create a perception of credibility and expertise. Exhibit 4.9 provides a few common areas that entry-level salespeople often confront in enhancing their positive, specific, professional language. Please note that we use a little hyperbole in the exhibit to demonstrate our point.

3. **Use transitions to maintain conversational flow.** Sales conversations should have a natural flow. Transitions help relate or link two ideas or sections of the conversation in a natural way. One easy method to create transitions within a sales

EXHIBIT 4.9

The use of professional language is an important element of your professional credibility.

Instead of stating	Consider using the word(s)
Cost	Expenses or investment or value
Loss	Opportunity cost
What were you thinking?	Share with me your decision process?
Why would you do that?	Can you explain to me what led to those actions?
Worries or problems?	Concerns?
What should we do now?	How would you like to proceed?
	What might the next steps be?
We are absolutely the cheapest.	We are pleased to offer you an investment that requires a minimal financial commitment.
I have two ways we could go.	May I submit two potential solutions for you to consider?
I'd like to throw a couple of ideas your way.	May I suggest three ideas for you to consider?
I will need you to okay this.	Would you be comfortable reviewing and approving this?
Are you ready to do the deal?	Could we please move forward with the purchase agreement?
Yep or You Bet	Yes.
	Absolutely. We can move forward.

conversation is by replaying the buyer's needs. You will learn that during the approach section, the buyer will communicate their needs. In order to transition between the sections in your sales presentation, you could reiterate a need. By reiterating the need, you foreshadow the value of the upcoming information. For instance, a transition between the product section and the marketing plan section might start with, "And Mr. Jones, you mentioned that all new products introduced into your store required incremental promotional support *[replaying the need]*. I'm happy to report that our multitiered marketing plan provides over $3 million in consumer promotions. . . ."

4. **Use proof statements to create credibility in your communication.** Salespeople have known for years that using highly credible sources can improve the effectiveness of the sales presentation message. **Proof statements** are statements that substantiate the salesperson's claims. Pharmaceutical companies often quote research studies performed by outstanding physicians at prestigious medical schools to validate claims of product benefits. These proof statements add credibility to a sales message.

   Salespeople sometimes quote acknowledged experts in a field on the use of products. By demonstrating that other customers or respected individuals use the products, they encourage customer belief in the validity of information presented in a sales presentation. People place greater confidence in a trustworthy, objective source (particularly one not associated with the salesperson's firm) and are therefore more receptive to the salesperson's communication.

5. **Express enthusiasm through vocal tone and vocal inflection.** Great salespeople use various forms of **enthusiasm** to show their excitement toward helping their customer. When you demonstrate a positive, willing attitude you can create genuine interest in other people. For some people, this means using varied levels of inflection in their voice. For others, it means their vocal tone demonstrates an excitement in the other person.

6. **Express empathy when appropriate. Empathy** is the ability to identify and understand the other person's feelings, ideas, and situation. As a salesperson, you need to be interested in what the buyer is saying—not just in giving a sales presentation.

No one is perfect. We all have some bad listening habits that we get away with when we talk to our family and friends. In a business context, however, leave these bad habits behind and practice active listening. To gain insight into your listening habits, read through this list of common irritating listening habits and be honest with yourself; notice what you are guilty of and use this awareness to begin eliminating them:

1. You do all the talking.
2. You interrupt when people talk.
3. You never look at the person talking or indicate that you are listening.
4. You start to argue before the other person has a chance to finish.
5. Everything that is said reminds you of an experience you've had, and you feel obligated to digress with a story.
6. You finish sentences for people if they pause too long.
7. You wait impatiently for people to finish so that you can interject something.
8. You work too hard at maintaining eye contact and make people uncomfortable.
9. You look as if you are appraising the person talking to you, looking him or her up and down as if considering the person for a modeling job.
10. You overdo the feedback you give—too many nods of your head and "uh-huh's."

Many of the barriers to communication mentioned earlier can be overcome when you place yourself in the buyer's shoes. Empathy is saying to a prospect, "I'm here to help you," or "Tell me your problems and needs so I can help *you.*"

Empathy is also evidenced by a salesperson's display of sincerity and interest in the buyer's situation. This may mean acknowledging at times that a prospect may not need your product. Take, for example, the Kimberly-Clark Corporation salesperson who finds that the customer still has 90 percent of the paper towels purchased three months ago. There is no reason to sell this customer more paper towels. It is time to help the customer sell the paper towels now on hand by suggesting displays, price reductions, and formats for newspaper advertisements. It is always wise to adopt your customer's point of view to best meet the customer's needs.

7. **Keep the message simple.** Simplicity in communication often demonstrates the speaker's discipline. That is, great speakers invest a great deal of time and effort to distill complex subjects into readily understandable elements. You may hear the acronym KISS. This stands for the old sell philosophy of **K**eep **I**t **S**imple, **S**alesperson. The story is told of an elderly lady who went into a hardware store. The clerk greeted her and offered her some help. She replied that she was looking for a heater. So the clerk said, "Gee, are you lucky! We have a big sale on these heaters, and a tremendous selection. Let me show you." So after maybe 30 or 45 minutes of discussing duothermic controls, heat induction, and all the factors involved with how a heater operates, including the features and advantages of each of the 12 models, he turned to the little old lady and said, "Now, do you have any questions?" To which she replied, "Yes, just one, Sonny. Which one of these things will keep a little old lady warm?"

> *"Try honestly to see things from the other person's point of view."*
>
> DALE CARNEGIE

An overly complex, technical presentation should be avoided when it is unnecessary. Be specific and concise, but use words and materials that the buyer can understand easily. The skilled salesperson can make a prospect feel comfortable with a new product or complex technology through the subtle use of nontechnical information and a respectful attitude.

8. **Use feedback to guide your communication.** Learn how to generate feedback to determine whether your listener has received your intended message. Feedback does not refer to any specific type of listening behavior by the buyer but rather to a recognizable response. A shake of the head, a frown, or an effort to say something are all signals to the salesperson. If the salesperson fails to notice or respond to these signals, no feedback can occur, which means faulty or incomplete communication. A salesperson's observation of feedback is like an auto racer's glances at the tachometer. Both aid in ascertaining a receiver's response.

   Often, feedback must be sought openly because the prospect does not always give it voluntarily. By interjecting into the presentation questions that require the customer to give a particular response, you can stimulate feedback. Questioning, sometimes called *probing,* allows the salesperson to determine the buyer's attitude toward the sales presentation. **Probing** refers to gathering information and uncovering customer needs using one or more questions

   A telecommunications company included this type of feedback in their sales training sessions. Their sales trainers suggested to their salespeople that they use questions in their presentations. Potential questions that could be used in such training include

   - Would you be willing to share your thoughts on your current investment in your firm's telecommunications equipment?
   - On a scale of 1 to 100, how would you rate the level of service your firm is being provided?
   - What is your current satisfaction level with the equipment you presently have installed and use?

These questions were intended to draw responses from the customers concerning the relationship with their present supplier. They provided the salespeople with a method of determining how the prospect felt about the current provider. These responses allowed the salesperson to discuss the specific features, advantages, and benefits of the salesperson's products relative to the products the prospect used at that time. Future chapters will fully discuss questioning techniques to use during your presentation.

9. **Generate feedback on your communicated benefits through a trial close.** In planning your presentation, it is important to predetermine when and what feedback-producing questions to ask. Remember to use the trial close as part of your SELL Sequence, as discussed in Chapter 3. The use of a question after discussing a benefit is a great method of obtaining feedback.

Decoding a Sales Conversation: Listen Carefully

Hearing refers to being able to detect sounds. **Listening** is deriving meaning from sounds that are heard. Everything you hear is not worth your undivided attention; for the salesperson, however, listening is a communication skill critical to success.

Salespeople often believe that their job is to talk rather than to listen. If they both talk *and* listen, their persuasive powers increase. Since people can listen (about 400 words per minute) roughly twice as fast as the average rate of speech, it is understandable that a person's mind may wander while listening or that the salesperson may tune out a prospect. Once you ask a question, carefully listen to the response. In fact, a relative rule of thumb for sales is an 80:20 ratio of listening to speaking. That is, the goal of the salesperson is to spend 80 percent of the meeting listening and 20 percent of the meeting talking.

The Three Levels of Listening

Whenever people listen, they are at one of three basic levels of listening. These levels require various degrees of concentration by the listener. As you move from the first to the third level, the potential for understanding and clear communication increases.

Marginal Listening. Marginal listening, the first and lowest level, involves the least concentration, and typically listeners are easily distracted by their thoughts. During periods of marginal listening, a listener exhibits blank stares, nervous mannerisms, and gestures that annoy the prospect and cause communication barriers. The salesperson hears the message but it doesn't sink in. There is enormous room for misunderstanding when a salesperson is not concentrating on what is said. Moreover, the prospect cannot help but feel the lack of attention, which may be insulting and diminishes trust. It may be funny when family members continually patronize each other with "Yes dear" regardless of what is said. In real life, however, it is not funny.

Why do you have one mouth and two ears?

> **Prospect:** What I need, really, is a way to reduce the time lost due to equipment breakdowns.
>
> **Salesperson:** Yeah, OK. Let's see, uh, the third feature of our product is the convenient sizes you can get.

Salespeople of all experience levels are guilty of marginal listening. Beginners who lack confidence and experience may concentrate so intensely on what they are supposed to say next that they stop listening. Old pros, by contrast, have heard it all before. They have their presentations memorized and want the prospect to hurry and finish talking so the important business can continue. These traditional salespeople forget that the truly important information lies in what the prospect says.

Evaluative Listening. Evaluative listening, the second level of listening, requires more concentration and attention to the speaker's words. At this level, the listener actively tries to hear what the prospect says but isn't making an effort to understand the intent. Instead of accepting and trying to understand a prospect's message, the evaluative listener categorizes the statement and concentrates on preparing a response.

The evaluative listening phenomenon is a result of the tremendous speed at which a human can listen and think. It is no surprise that evaluative listening is the level of listening used most of the time. Unfortunately, it is a difficult habit to break, but it can be done with practice.

> **Prospect:** What I need, really, is a way to reduce the time lost due to equipment breakdown.
>
> **Salesperson:** (defensively) We have tested our machines in the field, and they don't break down often.

In this example, the salesperson reacted to one aspect of the prospect's statement. Had the salesperson withheld judgment until the end of the statement, he could have responded more objectively and informatively.

In evaluative listening, it is easy to be distracted by emotion-laden words. At that point, you aren't listening to the prospect. Instead, you are obsessed with the offensive word and wondering what to do about it. This is a waste of time for both you and the prospect. It increases personal and relationship tension and throws your communication off course. To avoid the problems of marginal and evaluative listening, practice active listening.

Active Listening. Active listening is the third and most effective level of listening. The active listener refrains from evaluating the message and tries to see the other person's point of view. Attention is not only on the words spoken but also on the thoughts, feelings, and meaning conveyed. Listening in this way means the listener puts herself into someone else's shoes. It requires the listener to give the other person verbal and nonverbal feedback.

> **Prospect:** What I need is a way to reduce the time lost due to equipment breakdowns.
>
> **Salesperson:** Could you tell me what kind of breakdowns you have experienced?

In this example, the salesperson spoke directly to the prospect's concerns—not around them. Her desire to make a presentation was deferred so she could accomplish a more important task—effectively communicating with the prospect.

Active listening is a skill that takes practice in the beginning, but after a while, it becomes second nature. The logic behind active listening is based on courtesy and concentration.

Active listening is sometimes difficult to do, especially for the novice salesperson. The novice may continue to talk about a particular situation or problem. However, the salesperson must *learn to listen.* It is a key to sales success. People like and appreciate a listener, as this poem says so well:

> His thoughts were slow,
> His words were few,
> And never made to glisten,
> But he was a joy
> Wherever he went.
> You should have heard him listen.
>
> —*Author Unknown*

Active Listening: Listen to Words, Feelings, and Thoughts

This may seem obvious, but when someone speaks to you, the person is expressing thoughts and feelings. Despite the logic of this statement, most of us listen only to the words. Spoken language is an inexact form of communication, but it is the best we have in this stage of human evolution. If you come back 2,000 years from now, perhaps you will communicate with your prospects via mental telepathy. For now, given the limitations of words, look beyond them to hear the entire story.

Listen *behind* the words for the emotional content of the message. This is conveyed in the nuances of voice and body language. Some people, such as sensers (discussed in Chapter 3), give you little emotional information. That's all right, because you deal with them in a factual, business-only style. Feelers, on the other hand, reveal their emotions, and in turn, they appreciate your acknowledgment of their feelings. It is appropriate to discuss their feelings and treat them more as friends than as strict business associates.

Tips on listening actively:

1. *Pay attention.*
2. *Ask yourself, "How can I assist this person?"*
3. *Take essential notes. Interpret the key areas of the message in three to five words.*
4. *Summarize the buyer's thoughts and replay them.*

"You can be a good conversationalist by being a good listener."

DALE CARNEGIE

Here are several things to do to improve your listening skills:

- Stop talking.
- Your goal is to listen for 80% of the conversation and talk for only 20%.
- Show the prospect you want to listen.
- Pay active attention.
- Watch for nonverbal messages and project positive signals.
- Recognize feelings and emotions.
- Ask questions to clarify meaning.

- If appropriate, restate the prospect's position for clarification.
- Listen to the full story.
- Take notes. Summarize key points in three to five words.
- Use appropriate body language, such as leaning forward and nodding.
- Keep interpreting. Ask yourself, "Where is the person experiencing challenges, pains, and opportunities?"
- Keep asking yourself, "How can I assist this person?"

> *Silence creates:*
> - *Room for listening*
> - *Freedom to observe*
> - *Time to think*

You can hear the emotions behind the words in several ways. First, look for changes in eye contact. After establishing a comfortable and natural level of eye contact, any sudden deviations from the norm tip you off to emotional content in the message. People tend to look away from you when they talk about something embarrassing. When this happens, make a quick mental note of what it pertained to and treat that subject delicately. Also, give a person the courtesy of looking away momentarily yourself—as if you are saying, "I respect your privacy."

Listen *between* the words for what is not said. Some people reveal more in what they don't say. Part of this is due to the emotional content of the message and part is due to the information they give you. A story illustrates this point.

A salesperson was talking to the president of a large paper mill. "I simply asked him what kind of training he had for his salespeople. He went into a long discourse on all the seminars, training films, videotapes, and cassettes they had from the parent company, suppliers, industry associations, and in-house programs. I sat, listened, and took notes. At the end of his speech I said to him, 'I noticed you didn't mention anything about time management for salespeople.' He raised his voice and emphatically said, 'You know, just this morning I was talking to a guy and I told him we have to have some time-management training for our salespeople.'"

> *Sales is 2% what happens to you, 98% your attitude to it!*

The lesson here is to get the prospect talking and listen actively—concentrate. Take notes, look for clues to emotions, and don't interrupt or start thinking about your next question (see Exhibit 4.10).

Technology Helps to Remember

A distinction must be drawn between listening and remembering. Listening is the process of receiving the message the way the speaker intended to send it. **Memory** is recall over time. Listening and time have profound effects on memory. An untrained listener is likely to understand and retain only about 50 percent of a conversation.

You are part of a sales district containing six salespeople. At least once a month, everyone gets together for dinner and sometimes entertainment. This is an aggressive group, very spirited in their discussion of any topic.

Tonight you sit and listen to one of the salespeople maliciously and wrongfully attack your company and your boss. You can tell that this person is serious and has strong feelings about what is being said.

What would be the most ethical action to take?

1. Interject with your opinion. This might start a heated debate, but at least you did not compromise your ideals.
2. Interject with your opinion during dinner and leave dinner if the negative conversation continues. Sit down with your boss the next day and suggest that he bring the other salesperson in to discuss what the underlying problems are and how they might be resolved.
3. Let him talk. Everybody is entitled to his/her own opinions.

> *"Do this and you'll be welcome anywhere—become genuinely interested in other people."*
>
> DALE CARNEGIE

After 48 hours, the retention rate drops to 25 percent. Think of the implications. Memory of a conversation that occurred more than two days ago may be incomplete and inaccurate.

After you leave the prospect's office, take a few minutes to write down, or log in your computer, what occurred during the sales call. This is valuable information for doing what you promised and planning the next sales call. Chapter 6 will discuss much more about the use of technology in communicating with customers.

EXHIBIT 4.10

Active listening is important to your sales success. Concentrate, take notes, look for clues, don't interrupt!

©Eric Audras/Getty Images

SUMMARY OF MAJOR SELLING ISSUES

Communication is defined as transmission of verbal and nonverbal information and understanding between salesperson and prospect. Modes of communication commonly used in a sales presentation are words, gestures, visual aids, and nonverbal communication.

A model of the communication process is composed of a sender (encoder) who transmits a specific message via some medium to a receiver (decoder) who responds to that message. The effectiveness of this communication process can be hampered by noise that distorts the message as it travels to the receiver. A sender (encoder) can judge the effectiveness of a message and media choice by monitoring the feedback from the receiver.

Barriers, which hinder or prevent constructive communication during a sales presentation, may develop or already exist. These barriers may relate to the perceptional differences between the sender and receiver, cultural differences, outside distractions, or how sales information is conveyed. Regardless of their source, these barriers must be recognized and either overcome or eliminated if communication is to succeed.

Nonverbal communication has emerged as a critical component of the overall communication process within the past 10 or 15 years. Recognition of nonverbal communication is essential for sales success in today's business environment. Awareness of the prospect's territorial space, a firm and confident handshake, and accurate interpretation of body language are of tremendous aid to a salesperson's success.

Overall persuasive power is enhanced through development of several key characteristics. The salesperson who creates a relationship based on mutual trust with a customer by displaying true empathy (desire to understand the customer's situation and environment), a willing ear (more listening, less talking), and a positive attitude of enthusiastic pursuit of lasting solutions for the customer's needs and problems increases the likelihood of making the sale.

Quick Review for Students

The quick review sections provide key questions to help you develop a greater level of conceptual understanding. We suggest that after you read the chapter, you try to answer the following questions without looking back at the textbook:

1. What is the definition of communication, in a sales context? What are eight elements of a basic communication model?
2. What is the definition of adapting selling? What are the four communication practices that may help a salesperson in adapting to a buyer?
3. What are four key guidelines to identify personality style?
4. What are four major nonverbal communication channels?
5. Why is listening important in a sales context and what are the three levels of listening?
6. What is mirroring and how it can help a salesperson?
7. What are the eight best practices to ensure your sales communication is encoded effectively?

MEETING A SALES CHALLENGE

In this imaginary sales call, buyer and seller communicated both verbal and nonverbal messages. Here, nonverbal messages conveyed both parties' attitudes better than the actual verbal exchange. The salesperson's negative reactions served to increase Amos Skaggs's hostile attitude. He could sense that the salesperson did not understand his problem and was there only to sell him something—not to solve his problem. This impression caused a rapid breakdown in communication. The end result, as in this case, is usually **NO SALE.**

The salesperson may have reacted correctly to Skaggs. Since he is in a bad mood, coming back another day may be best. If the salesperson cannot come another day, then the salesperson needs to stop the planned presentation and let the buyer know he understands. He should show that he is there to help. But most of all, he must project a positive attitude and not be frightened by Skaggs.

KEY TERMS FOR SELLING

acceptance signals   134
adaptive selling   123
caution signals   134
communication   120
decoding process   121
disagreement signals   135
empathy   140
encoding process   121
enthusiasm   140
feedback   122
hearing   142
ideal self   122

intimate space   129
listening   142
looking-glass self   122
medium   121
memory   145
message   121
mirroring   138
noise   122
nonverbal
    communication   128
personal space   129
personality   122

probing   142
proof statements   140
public space   129
real self   122
receiver   121
self-concept   122
self-image   122
social space   129
source   121
space invasion   130
space threats   129
territorial space   129

SALES APPLICATION QUESTIONS

1. Draw the salesperson–buyer communication process. Describe each step in the process. Why is two-way communication important in this process?
2. This chapter outlined several forms of nonverbal communication.
   a. Give an example of a salesperson making a good first impression through the proper use of an introductory handshake.
   b. What signals should the salesperson look for from a buyer's body language? Give several examples of these signals.
3. A salesperson may spend hours developing a sales presentation and yet the buyer does not buy. One reason for losing a sale is that the salesperson and the buyer do not communicate. What barriers to communication may be present between seller and buyer during a sales presentation?
4. When two people are talking, they want the listener to understand what they are saying. They both want to be effective communicators. The same is true of the salesperson who wants the buyer to listen to a sales presentation. What can the salesperson do to help ensure that the buyer is listening?
5. You arrive at the industrial purchasing agent's office on time. This is your first meeting. After you have waited five minutes, the agent's secretary says, "She will see you." After the initial greeting, she asks you to sit down.
   For each of these three situations determine:
   a. What nonverbal signals is she communicating?
   b. How would you respond nonverbally?
   c. What would you say to her?
      (1) She sits down behind her desk. She sits up straight in her chair. She clasps her hands together and with little expression on her face says, "What can I do for you?"
      (2) She sits down behind her desk. She moves slightly backward in her chair, crosses her arms, and while looking around the room says, "What can I do for you?"
      (3) She sits down behind her desk. She moves slightly forward in her chair, seems hurried, yet is relaxed toward your presence. Her arms are

uncrossed. She looks you squarely in the eye, and with a pleasant look on her face says, "What can I do for you?"

6. In each of the following selling situations determine:
   a. What nonverbal signals is the buyer communicating?
   b. How would you respond nonverbally?
   c. What would you say?
      (1) The buyer seems happy to see you. Because you have been calling on him for several years, the two of you have become business friends. In the middle of your presentation, you notice the buyer slowly lean back in his chair. As you continue to talk, a puzzled look comes over his face.
      (2) As you begin the main part of your presentation, the buyer reaches for the telephone and says, "Keep going; I need to tell my secretary something."
      (3) As a salesperson with only six months' experience, you are somewhat nervous about calling on an important buyer who has been a purchasing agent for almost 20 years. Three minutes after you have begun your presentation, he rapidly raises his arms straight up into the air and slowly clasps his hands behind his head. He leans so far back in his chair that you think he is going to fall backward on the floor. At the same time, he crosses his legs away from you and slowly closes his eyes. You keep on talking. Slowly the buyer opens his eyes, uncrosses his legs, and sits up in his chair. He leans forward, placing his elbows on the desk top, propping his head up with his hands. He seems relaxed as he says, "Let me see what you have here." He reaches his hand out for you to give him the presentation materials you have developed.
      (4) At the end of your presentation, the buyer leans forward, his arms open, and smiles as he says, "You really don't expect me to buy that piece of junk, do you?"

FURTHER EXPLORING THE SALES WORLD

Using questions is an effective method for a salesperson to obtain feedback from a buyer. This statement applies to conversation between two people. For the next two days, try using questions in your conversations with other people and report on your results. These questions should reflect an interest in the person you are conversing with and the topic being discussed. Use of the words *you* and *your* should increase feedback and create an atmosphere of trust.

For example, you can use questions such as "What do you mean?" "What do you think?" and "How does that sound?" in your conversation to have other people participate and to help determine how they feel toward the topic of conversation.

Asking people's opinions also can result in a positive response because they may feel flattered that you care about their opinion. Questions can help you guide the direction of topics discussed in conversation. Try to determine people's reactions to your questions and report your findings in class.

SELLING EXPERIENTIAL EXERCISE

Instructions: Read the following questions and write *yes* or *no* for each statement on a separate sheet of paper. Mark each answer as truthfully as you can in light of your behavior in the last few meetings or gatherings you attended.

Listening Self-Inventory

	Yes	No
1. I frequently attempt to listen to several conversations at the same time.	____	____
2. I like people to give me only the facts and then let me make my own interpretation.	____	____
3. I sometimes pretend to pay attention to people.	____	____
4. I consider myself a good judge of nonverbal communications.	____	____
5. I usually know what another person is going to say before he or she says it.	____	____
6. I usually end conversations that don't interest me by diverting my attention from the speaker.	____	____
7. I frequently nod, frown, or whatever to let the speaker know how I feel about what he or she is saying.	____	____
8. I usually respond immediately when someone has finished talking.	____	____
9. I evaluate what is being said while it is being said.	____	____
10. I usually formulate a response while the other person is still talking.	____	____
11. The speaker's delivery style frequently keeps me from listening to content.	____	____
12. I usually ask people's points of view.	____	____
13. I make a concerted effort to understand other people's points of view.	____	____
14. I frequently hear what I expect to hear rather than what is said.	____	____
15. Most people believe that I have understood their points of view when we disagree.	____	____

According to communication theory, the correct answers are as follows: no for questions 1, 2, 3, 5, 6, 7, 8, 9, 10, 11, 14; and yes for questions 4, 12, 13, 15. If you missed only one or two questions, you strongly approve of your own listening habits, and you are on the right track to becoming an effective listener in your role as a salesperson. If you missed three or four questions, you have uncovered some doubts about your listening effectiveness, and your knowledge of how to listen has some gaps. If you missed five or more questions, you probably are not satisfied with the way you listen, and your friends and co-workers may not feel you are a good listener either. Work on improving your active listening skills.[13]

WHAT'S YOUR STYLE—SENSER, INTUITOR, THINKER, FEELER?

Individuals differ in the way they interact with others and the way they gather and evaluate information for problem solving and decision making. Four psychological functions identified by Carl Jung are related to this process: sensation, intuition, thinking, and feeling.[14]

Before you read further, complete the Problem-Solving Diagnostic Questionnaire (Part A) and then check the scoring key that appears in Part B.[15] It has no right or wrong answers; just read each item carefully and then give your answer.

Part A: Questionnaire to Determine Your Style

Indicate your responses to the following questionnaire on a separate sheet of paper. None of these items has right or wrong responses.

I. Write down the number and letter of the response that comes closest to how you usually feel or act.
1. I am more careful about
   a. People's feelings.
   b. Their rights.
2. I usually get along better with
   a. Imaginative people.
   b. Realistic people.

3. It is a higher compliment to be called
   a. A person of real feeling.
   b. A consistently reasonable person.
4. In doing something with many people, it appeals more to me
   a. To do it in the accepted way.
   b. To invent a way of my own.
5. I get more annoyed at
   a. Fancy theories.
   b. People who do not like theories.
6. It is higher praise to call someone
   a. A person of vision.
   b. A person of common sense.
7. I more often let
   a. My heart rule my head.
   b. My head rule my heart.
8. I think it is a worse fault
   a. To show too much warmth.
   b. To be unsympathetic.
9. If I were a teacher, I would rather teach
   a. Courses involving theory.
   b. Fact courses.

II. Write down the letters of the words in the following pairs that appeal to you more.

10.	*a.* compassion	*b.*	foresight
11.	*a.* justice	*b.*	mercy
12.	*a.* production	*b.*	design
13.	*a.* gentle	*b.*	firm
14.	*a.* uncritical	*b.*	critical
15.	*a.* literal	*b.*	figurative
16.	*a.* imaginative	*b.*	matter of fact

According to Jung, only one of the four functions—sensation, intuition, thinking, or feeling—is dominant in an individual. However, the dominant function is usually backed up by one of the functions from the other set of paired opposites. Part C shows the four problem-solving styles that result from these matchups.

Part B: Scoring Key to Determine Your Style

The following scales indicate the psychological functions related to each item. Use the point-value columns to arrive at your score for each function. For example, if you answered *a* to the first question, your I*a* response in the feeling column is worth 0 points when you add up the point-value column. Instructions for classifying your scores follow the scales.

Classifying Total Scores

■ Write *intuition* if your intuition score is equal to or greater than your sensation score.
■ Write *sensation* if your sensation score is greater than your intuition score.
■ Write *feeling* if your feeling score is greater than your thinking score.
■ Write *thinking* if your thinking score is greater than your feeling score.

According to Jung, gathering information and evaluating information are separate activities. People gather information by either *sensation* or *intuition* but not by both simultaneously. People using *sensation* would rather work with known facts and hard data and prefer routine and order while gathering information. People using *intuition* would rather look for possibilities than work with facts and prefer solving new problems and using abstract concepts.

Sensation	Point Value	Intuition	Point Value	Thinking	Point Value	Feeling	Point Value
2b_____	1	2a_____	2	1b_____	1	1a_____	0
4a_____	1	4b_____	1	3b_____	2	3a_____	1
5a_____	1	5b_____	1	7b_____	1	7a_____	1
6b_____	1	6a_____	0	8a_____	0	8b_____	1
9b_____	2	9a_____	2	10b_____	2	10a_____	1
12a_____	1	12b_____	0	11a_____	2	11b_____	1
15a_____	1	15b_____	1	13b_____	1	13a_____	1
16b_____	2	16a_____	0	14b_____	0	14a_____	1
Maximum Point Value:	(10)		(7)		(9)		(7)

Part C: The Four Styles and Their Tendencies

Personal Style	Action Tendencies
Sensation-thinking	Emphasizes details, facts, certainty
	Is decisive, applied thinker
	Focuses on short-term, realistic goals
	Develops rules and regulations for judging performance
Intuitive-thinking	Shows concern for current, real-life human problems
	Is creative, progressive, perceptive thinker
	Emphasizes detailed facts about people rather than tasks
	Focuses on structuring organizations for the benefit of people
Sensation-feeling	Prefers dealing with theoretical or technical problems
	Is pragmatic, analytical, methodical, and conscientious
	Focuses on possibilities by using interpersonal analysis
	Is able to consider a number of options and problems simultaneously
Intuitive-feeling	Avoids specifics
	Is charismatic, participative, people oriented, and helpful
	Focuses on general views, broad themes, and feelings
	Decentralizes decision making; develops few rules and regulations

Information evaluation involves making judgments about the information a person has gathered. People evaluate information by *thinking* or *feeling*. These represent the extremes in orientation. *Thinking* individuals base their judgments on impersonal analysis, using reason and logic rather than personal values or emotional aspects of the situation. *Feeling* individuals base their judgments more on personal feelings, such as harmony, and tend to make decisions that result in approval from others.

Questions

1. Look back at your scores. What is your personal problem-solving style? Read the action tendencies. Do they fit?
2. Studies show that the sensation-thinking (ST) combination characterizes many managers in Western industrialized societies. Do you think the ST style is the best fit for most jobs in today's society?
3. Also look at Exhibit 4.3: "Guidelines to Identifying Personality Style". Compare yourself and others you know to the guidelines. Do you find a match between you and the individual style? What about your roommate, spouse, parents, or siblings?
4. How can you use this information to improve your communication ability?

NOTES

1. Gerhard Gschwandtner, *Nonverbal Selling Power* (Englewood Cliffs, NJ: Prentice Hall, 1995), p. 3.

2. Barton A. Weitz, Harish Sujan, and Mita Sujan, "Knowledge, Motivation, and Adaptive Behavior: A Framework for Improving Selling Effectiveness," *Journal of Marketing* 50, no. 4 (October 2 1986), pp. 174–91.

3. P. M. Doney and J. P. Cannon, "An Examination of the Nature of Trust in Buyer–Seller Relationships," *Journal of Marketing* 61, 2 (April 3 1997), pp. 35–51.

4. N. Collins and L. Miller, "Self-Disclosure and Liking: A Meta-Analytic Review," *Psychological Bulletin* [serial online], November 1994;116(3):457. Available from: Business Source Premier, Ipswich, MA. Accessed November 27, 2017.

5. Niels J. Pulles and Paul Hartman, "Likeability and Its Effect on Outcomes of Interpersonal Interaction," *Industrial Marketing Management* 66 (October 5 2017), pp. 56–63.

6. Author unknown.

7. Also see Dana Ray, "Every Guest Leaves Satisfied," *Selling Power* (April 1997), p. 37; and Robert A. Peterson, Michael P. Cannito, and Steven P. Brown, "An Exploratory Investigation of Voice Characteristics and Selling Effectiveness," *Journal of Personal Selling & Sales Management,* Winter 1995, pp. 1–16.

8. Jeff Green, "Sales Moves beyond Face-to-Face Deals, onto the Web," *Bloomberg.Com*, January 11, 2013, p. 4.

9. Text of figure reproduced from the sales training course, "The Languages of Selling," Gerhard Gschwandtner & Associates, Falmouth, Virginia. Photos by Professor Futrell.

10. Tanya L. Chartrand and Jessica L. Lakin, "The Antecedents and Consequences of Human Behavioral Mimicry," *Annual Review of Psychology* 64 (January 3, 2013), pp. 285–308.

11. Ibid.

12. G. R. Miller and M. A. Hewgill, "The Effect of Variations in Nonfluency on Audience Ratings of Source Credibility," *Quarterly Journal of Speech* 50 (1964). pp. 36–44.

13. Source: Ethel C. Glenn and Elliott A. Pood, "Listening Self-Inventory," *Supervisory Management*, January 1996, pp. 12–15.

14. Carl Jung, *Psychological Types* (London: Routledge and Kegan Paul, 1923).

15. Adapted from I. Myers, *The Myers-Briggs Type Indicator* (Princeton, NJ: Educational Testing Service, 1962).

16. Adapted from *Marketplace Ethics: Issues in Sales and Marketing* (Westport, CT: J/S Productions, 1990), pp. 73–92.

CASE 4.1

Skaggs Manufacturing

John Andrews arrived promptly for his 10 A.M. meeting with Martha Gillespie, the buyer for Skaggs Manufacturing. At 10:15, when she hadn't arrived, John asked her secretary if she was out of the office for the morning. The secretary smiled and said, "She'll probably be a few minutes late." John resented this delay and was convinced that Martha had forgotten the appointment.

Finally, at 10:20, Martha entered her office, walked over to John, said hello, and promptly excused herself to talk to the secretary about a tennis game scheduled for that afternoon. Ten minutes later, Martha led John into her office. At the same time, a competing salesperson entered the office for a 10:30 appointment. With the door open, Martha asked John, "What's new today?" As John began to talk, Martha began reading letters on her desk and signing them. Shortly after that, the telephone began to ring, whereupon Martha talked to her husband for 10 minutes.

As she hung up, Martha looked at John and suddenly realized his frustration. She promptly buzzed her secretary and said, "Hold all calls." She got up and shut the door. John again began his presentation when Martha leaned backward in her chair, pulled her golf shoes out of a desk drawer, and began to brush them.

About that time, the secretary entered the office and said, "Martha, your 10:30 appointment is about to leave. What should I tell him?" "Tell him to wait; I need to see him." Then she said, "John, I wish we had more time. Look, I think I have enough of your product to last until your next visit. I'll see you then. Thanks for coming by."

John quickly rose to his feet, did not shake hands, said "OK," and left.

Questions

1. What nonverbal cues did the salesperson, John Andrews, experience when contacting Martha Gillespie?
2. If you were John Andrews, how would you have handled the situation?
3. If you were John Andrews, what might be a few options to gain the buyer's attention?
4. Place yourself in Martha Gillespie's role? Why do you think that she communicated in this manner? What might be her perception of John Andrews, his firm, and his products?

CASE 4.2

©Ron Chapple Stock/FotoSearch/ Glow Images

Alabama Office Supply

Judy Allison sells cellular telephones with a unique messaging technology for Alabama Office Supply in Birmingham. Today she is calling on Bill Taylor, purchasing agent for a large manufacturing firm. Two weeks earlier, she had made her first sales call and had left a demonstrator for the company executives to try out. The previous evening, Bill had called Judy and asked her to come in so he could give her an order. After their initial hellos, the conversation continued:

Buyer: Judy, thanks for coming by today. Our executives really like your equipment. Here is an order for four phones. When can you deliver them?

Salesperson: Is tomorrow too soon?

Buyer: That is perfect. Leave them with Joyce, my administrative assistant. Joyce [*Bill says over the intercom*], Judy will deliver the phones tomorrow. Joyce, I want you to go ahead and take them to Sally, Anne, and Sherri. Our younger staff sure understand the use of modern technology. It's too bad that more of our purchasing executives are hesitant to use this new technology. I'm happy with four folks but we have at least 30 more people who could really leverage this technology.

Salesperson: Bill, thanks for your help.

Buyer: Forget it Judy, I wish I could have helped more. Your cell phones can reduce the "telephone tag" we play with each other and customers. Customers are leaving us because they can't reach our salespeople when they are out on the road contacting customers. I really appreciate the new messaging technology integrated into your phones. I could see this making some impact. Our purchasing staff continues to grow. It looks like we'll probably hire 20 more folks in the next three months. But oh well, sometimes we need to take small steps.

Salesperson: You're right; many of my customers are going to them for that very reason.

Buyer: I know, but some of our more experienced executives still feel they don't want them. They don't want their phone to ring when they're in with a customer. Plus, some of our executives still believe that cell phones have some tie to cancer and that has them worried. I wish the older purchasing executives in our company felt the same way the younger executives do about using these things.

Questions

1. Analyze and describe the conversation between Judy Allison and Bill Taylor.
2. What questions might be going through Judy's mind as she is listening to Bill?
3. From the conversation, what potential sales opportunities exist?
4. If you were Judy Allison, what questions might you ask Bill?
5. What type of information might Judy be planning to input into her firm's CRM (customer relationship management) system about this interaction?

CASE 4.3

©Ron Chapple Stock/FotoSearch/
Glow Images

Vernex, Inc.

Samantha Wells (Sam), a marketer at Vernex, is discussing shipping dates with Duke Stillwell, the shipping manager. Sam notices that Duke is shipping 300,000 HS200 fire alarm sensor circuits out of inventory. Sam asks Duke why the company is finally writing them off this inventory, especially before the merger is finalized. Duke informs Sam that Ed Naughton, the director of marketing, sold the sensor circuits to Executron, apparently at full price. Sam is confused by Executron's purchase and also questions why Ed would charge them full price when the new HS300s are about to be introduced. Duke assures Sam that Ed knows what he is doing and comments that he is grateful for the much needed warehouse space.

Ed is talking with Carrie Ventana, the administrative manager, in the lobby when Sam joins them. Sam asks Carrie if she is going to attend the Dallas conference. Ed remarks that this is a conference they would not miss and that management has been going over the records carefully and should be announcing the merger and the new director of marketing then. Carrie tells Ed that he is a shoo-in for the job, especially since he just made the big Execu-tron sale. Sam congratulates Ed on the sale and asks him why he did not notify her about it. Ed claims that he forgot and suggests a promotion for Sam if he becomes director of marketing.

After Ed leaves, Sam tells Carrie that she wanted to talk to her about the Exec-utron sale. Sam asks Carrie whether Executron has ever bought sensor circuits from Vernex before. Carrie offers to go to her office to check the computer's central customer file. The computer verifies that this is the first time Executron has bought from this division. Sam explains that she is concerned because marketing over estimated the market for these circuits and now, suddenly, Ed sells the circuits to a company that appears to have no use for them. Carrie comments that the president of Executron is Ed's good friend, so he would not do anything to hurt them. Carrie adds that she knows that Executron is doing well financially because Ed told her to invest in them years ago when he did, and now she regrets not following his advice. Sam still questions why Ed did not give Executron a discount for the old circuits. Carrie defends Ed's reputation and asks Sam why it is wrong for Ed to make himself look better, get rid of a liability, and beef up the bottom line. Sam admits nothing is wrong, if it is a legitimate sale. But what if Executron returns the circuits right after Ed's promotion?[16]

Questions

1. What are the main ethical issues, if any, in the Vernex, Inc., case?
2. What are Samantha (Sam) Wells's options?
3. How do the three levels of moral development relate to Sam's situation?
4. What would you do?

Dress for Success . . . and to Impress for Business Professional and Business Casual Occasions!

You have only one chance to make a favorable first impression. Impressions of you are based upon your appearance. How you are dressed makes a first and lasting impression on those you meet in any situation. The following dress guidelines for men and women provide the basic guidelines for both business professional and business casual attire.

Women

- Clean and pressed clothing.
- Wear a pantsuit, or a jacket and coordinating knee- or calf-length skirt.
- Appropriate colors for interviews are black, gray, navy blue, tan, and brown. Pinstripes also work well, as long as they are small and conservative.
- Tailored blouse in a color that complements your suit. A small print also might work, but stay away from trends, and stick to traditional styles and colors.
- No dresses.
- Leave your purse in your vehicle, or use a small purse.
- Clear or neutral nail polish; stay away from red, pink, or any other bright colors.
- One set of conservative earrings.
- Conservative watch.
- One ring per hand or less.
- Conservative closed-toe shoes; pumps are acceptable, but avoid high heels and stilettos.

©Getty Images/Hemera
Example for formal interview.

- Clean makeup that looks natural and fresh.
- Skin tones for hosiery; no bare legs.
- Cover tattoos if possible.
- Apply little to no perfume, hairspray, or other scents that might offend or cause allergic reaction to others.
- A good rule of thumb is that if you could wear it to a club or bar, don't wear it to the interview.
- Hair should be clean, neat, and out of your eyes.
- No book bags or bulky briefcases.
- No gum, candy, food, or cigarettes. Refrain from smoking prior to the interview in the clothes you plan to wear. The interviewer cannot legally ask you if you smoke, but may smell it.
- You can take a bottle of water.
- Bring a padded portfolio with a legal pad and nice pen.

©Sam Diephuis/Getty Images
Example for business casual.

Men

- Clean and pressed clothing.
- Wear a suit and tie, unless business casual is accepted. It is not recommended that you wear jeans to an interview.
- Good colors for interviews are black, gray, navy blue, tan, and brown.
- Silk necktie with a conservative pattern.
- Nails should be short and clean.
- Only a wedding band or college class ring.
- Cover tattoos if possible.
- Little to no cologne.
- Hair should be clean, neat, and out of your eyes.
- No book bags or bulky briefcases.

©moodboard/SuperStock
Example for formal interview.

- No gum, food, candy, or cigarettes. Refrain from smoking prior to the interview in the clothes you plan to wear. The interviewer cannot legally ask you if you smoke, but may smell it.

- You can take a bottle of water.

- Facial hair should be neat and trimmed.

- Bring a padded portfolio with a legal pad and nice pen.

©Jetta Productions/Blend Images LLC

Example for business casual.

Sales Knowledge: Customers, Products, Technologies

Learning Objectives

Successful salespeople are knowledgeable individuals. Many salespeople are experts in their field. After studying this chapter, you should be able to

5–1 Explain why it is so important to be knowledgeable.

5–2 Discuss the major body of knowledge needed for increased sales success.

5–3 Illustrate how to use this knowledge during the sales presentation.

5–4 Explain the main technologies used by salespeople.

FACING A SALES CHALLENGE

You are proud of the products you sell and tell everyone they are, the best on the market, light-years ahead of the competition. Of course you have worked for the company for only two weeks. But the sales training course you took last week clearly convinced you that your products are much better than any others on the market. During one presentation on a new washing machine detergent, you concentrated on discussing the quality of the product: how well it cleans, its environmental safety factor, how much users like its pleasant scent on their clothes. The grocery store buyer said, "I could care less about the quality of your products."

Why did the buyer respond in a negative way to you? What is the buyer interested in?

Salespeople need to know many things. Features, advantages, and benefits are important to discuss, but which *FAB*s are of interest to the buyer? The above situation is a sales challenge all salespeople face. The salesperson was apparently talking about the wrong things. What would be of interest to a retailer, wholesaler, manufacturer, or consumer? Chances are they are interested in similar, but also different, *FAB*s. This chapter examines the basic body of knowledge essential to the success of all salespeople.

The Core Principles: Knowledge

In Chapter 1 you learned salespeople need knowledge at the medical doctor M.D. level. Salespeople must be experts on everything involved with their products. Although you need facts, it is more important to have the wisdom necessary to apply the knowledge. Again, just as the medical doctor does when treating people for health problems, and just as you rely on the medical doctor to have the knowledge, wisdom, and skills needed to help you, so do customers rely on the help of salespeople. The salesperson may be the expert or have the most current information about a product or situation. The customer relies on the salesperson to provide information—truthfully.

This is why a person's integrity and character, as discussed in Chapter 2, are so important in building long-term relationships. Placing the customer's welfare before one's own welfare is key to having a successful sales career. Please remember, however, that people do not care how much you know until they know how much you care. They want you to follow the Core Selling Principles: treat customers as you would like to be treated by a salesperson.

Sources of Sales Knowledge

Knowledge for selling is obtained in two ways: First, most companies provide some formal sales training that teaches information through preliminary training programs and sales meetings. Second, the salesperson learns by being on the job. Experience is the best teacher for the beginning salesperson.

Sales training is the effort an employer puts forth to provide the opportunity for the salesperson to receive job-related culture, skills, knowledge, and attitudes that result in improved performance in the selling environment.

Successful companies thoroughly train new salespeople and maintain ongoing training programs for their experienced sales personnel. Companies are interested in training primarily to increase sales volume, salesperson productivity, and profitability.

Like many professional careers, selling is a skill that is truly developed only through *experience*. Sales knowledge obtained through education, reading, formalized sales training, and word-of-mouth is helpful in enhancing overall sales ability, but actual experience is the critical source of sales knowledge. Some sales managers hire only experienced people to fill entry-level selling slots. Indeed, some corporations do not allow people to fill marketing staff positions unless they have had field sales experience with the company or a major competitor.

Sales experience improves a salesperson's abilities by showing how buyers perceive a product or product line, revealing unrecognized or undervalued product benefits or shortcomings, voicing a multitude of unanticipated protests and objections, showing a great number of prospect moods and attitudes over a short period, and generally providing a challenge that makes selling a skill that is never mastered, only improved.

No author or sales trainer can simulate the variety of situations that a salesperson confronts over the span of a career. Authors and trainers can provide only general guidelines as a framework for action. Only actual selling experience gives a person direct feedback on how to function in a specific selling situation. The sales knowledge gained through periodic sales training and actual experience benefits the salesperson, the firm, and the customers.

Only through possessing a high level of knowledge can the salesperson provide excellent service. This leads to "S—success" as discussed in Chapter 1. Knowledge is part of the Core Principles of Professional Selling. Knowledge based upon wisdom and conveyed to the buyer truthfully builds relationships.

> *"I am still learning."*
>
> MICHEL ANGELO

Why Is Salesperson Knowledge Important?

Salespeople today must be knowledgeable to be effective in their jobs. Four important reasons for the salesperson to have selling knowledge are (1) to increase the salesperson's self-confidence, (2) to build the buyer's confidence in the salesperson, (3) to build relationships through truly caring about the needs of others, and (4) to meet the buyer's expectations. These reasons are, for the salesperson, the major need for acquiring sales knowledge.

Knowledge Increases Confidence in Salespeople

Salespeople who call on, computer systems engineers, university professors, or aerospace experts may be at a disadvantage. In many cases, they have less education and experience than prospects in their fields of expertise.

Imagine making a sales call on Dr. Michael DeBakey, the distinguished heart surgeon. Can you educate him in the use of your company's synthetic heart valves? Not really, but you can offer help in supplying product information from your firm's medical department. This personal service, your product knowledge, and his specific needs are what will make the sale. Knowledge about your company, its market, and your buyer enables you to acquire confidence in yourself, which results in increased sales.

A Knowledgeable Salesperson Creates Confidence in the Buyer

Furthermore, prospects and customers want to do business with salespeople who know their business and the products they sell. When a prospect has confidence in the salesperson's expertise, a sales presentation becomes more acceptable and believable to the prospect.

Strive to be the expert on all aspects of your product. Knowledge of your product and its uses also allows you to confidently answer questions and field objections that prospects raise. You can explain better how a product suits a customer's needs. But product knowledge alone may not be enough to convince every buyer.

Knowledge Demonstrates That the Salesperson Cares about the Buyer's Needs

Often within minutes buyers can tell if salespeople know what they are talking about. You have experienced it yourself. You ask questions and quickly form an impression of a salesperson. A relationship begins to build; knowledge builds relationships and results in sales for the seller. Typically, the more knowledge you have and the more you care about the other person, the higher your sales.

The Buyer Expects a Highly Knowledgeable Salesperson

Most buyers want to interact with a qualified, knowledgeable salesperson. For salespersons who are consistently learning, the investment in increasing their knowledge yields a number of benefits. For instance, the salesperson's expertise helps create trust in a relationship (Chapter 7); and interestingly, sales-related knowledge is a key individual quality that positively impacts salesperson performance.[1]

However, don't be fooled that salesperson knowledge is simply about a product or service. Buyers expect a great deal from today's salesperson. Buyers want salespeople to aid them in meeting their professional, organizational, and personal goals. For instance, buyers want salespeople who are (1) well-versed in building a relationship as well as providing the ongoing service needed to maintain the relationship,[2] (2) able to furnish important information on the environment and help interpret the information,[3] and (3) able to demonstrate important interpersonal qualities, such as effective communication and other relationship-building behaviors.[4]

In summary, knowledge is critical to meet the buyer's expectations. In the next section, we review the many forms of salesperson knowledge.

Know Your Customers

How can you match your product's benefits with a buyer's needs if you don't know your customers? If you are selling to someone you've never seen before you have to ask about the buyer's needs. Business-to-business selling also requires asking numerous questions, sometimes spending weeks with a customer.

In fact, salespeople are increasingly expected to be knowledge brokers[5] for their buyers. That means, the salesperson must possess a range of information, including knowledge about: (a) their customers, (b) their customer's business and industry, (c) their customer's organization, and (d) key dynamics and trends that can impact their customer. We offer a few questions in Exhibit 5.1 (i.e., what, who, and when/how) that salespeople commonly ask themselves to better understand their customers.

Know Your Company

Knowledge of your firm usually helps you project an expert image to the prospect. Company knowledge includes information about the history, policies, procedures, distribution systems, promotional activities, pricing practices, and technology that have guided the firm to its current position.

The type and extent of company knowledge to use depends on the company, its product lines, and the industry. In general, consumer-goods salespeople require less information about the technical nature of their products; however, selling high-technology products (computers, rocket-engine components, complex machinery, etc.) to highly knowledgeable industrial buyers requires extensive knowledge.

General Company Information

All salespeople need to know the background and current operating policies of their companies. These policies are your guidelines, and you must understand them to do your job effectively. Information on company growth, policies, procedures, production, and service facilities is often used in sales presentations. Exhibit Follows.

EXHIBIT 5.1

Questions that salespeople should ask to better understand their customers.

What	Who	When and How
What are the key needs of your buyer?	Who has a role in the purchasing process? What are their respective roles in the process?	How might the buyer prioritize needs? Which need(s) is absolutely essential to meet? Which need(s) might not be required to be met exactly?
What are your customer's personal objectives or goals?	Who is the buyer (i.e., who purchases the product) versus who is the user of the product? Are they the same individual(s)? What influence do they have on the decision?	When does your customer make decisions (e.g., seasonal, specific buying times, during certain life transitions, anytime)?
What are your customer's roles and responsibilities? How does each impact the buying decision?	Who makes the final decision for the purchase?	How often does your customer expect contact or progress updates from you?
What is the buying process? What are the stages in the buying process? Who plays a role in each stage?	Who currently serves the customer's needs (i.e., competitors)?	When might key dynamics in your customer's industry impact your customer's firm? Which of these trends offer opportunities and challenges?
What is your customer's perception of your firm and its products or services?	Who might be able to provide you with a referral or recommendation that the customer would perceive as credible?	How would the customer pay for your solution (financing terms, cash terms, etc.)?
What policies and procedures do salespeople have to follow in order to sell to the customer?	Who does the customer seek for guidance (formally or informally)?	How long does the buying process last (hours, days, months, years)?
What specific information is required in order for the buyer to make a decision?	If a purchase is made, who will be your key daily contact(s)?	When are the key deadlines for meeting with your customer or providing proposals?
What are key concerns or risks that the customer considers when making this type of purchase?	Who will need to be aware of any implementation steps or play a role in the implementation process?	How should you communicate with your customer (i.e., e-mail, text, instant message, phone call, face-to-face)? When should you use each type of communication media?

Company Growth and Accomplishment

Knowledge of your firm's development since its origin provides you with promotional material and builds your confidence in the company. A technology salesperson might say to a buyer:

> In 1952, our firm placed its first commercial electronic computer on the market. That year, our sales were $342 million. Currently, our sales are projected to be over $95 billion. We have reached these high sales figures because our advanced, technological office equipment and information processors are the best available at any price. Our newest product, the "I-Execution and Artificial Intelligence" system I am showing you, is the most advanced piece of equipment on the market today. It is five years ahead of any other technology on the market.

Policies and Procedures

Effective salespeople are always enhancing their knowledge.

To give good service, you should be able to tell a customer about policies: how an order is processed, how long it takes for orders to be filled, your firm's returned goods policy, how to open a new account, and what to do in the event of a shipping error. When you handle these situations quickly and fairly, your buyer gains confidence in you and the firm.

Production Facilities

Many companies require their new salespeople to tour their production facilities to give them a firsthand look at the company's operations. This is a good opportunity to gain product knowledge. For example, the Bigelow-Sanford Carpet Company salesperson can say, "When I was visiting our production plant, I viewed each step of the carpet-production process. The research and development department allowed us to watch comparison tests between our carpets and competitors' carpets. Our carpets did everything but fly . . . and they are working on that!"

Service Facilities

Many companies, such as Intel, Xerox, and 3M, have both service facilities and service representatives to help customers. Being able to say, "We can have a service representative there the same day you call our service center," strengthens a sales presentation, especially if service is important for the customer (as it is in the office copier and technology industries).

Know Your Product

Knowledge about your company's product and service and your competitors' solutions is a major component of sales knowledge. Become an expert on your company's products. Understand how they are produced and their level of quality. This type of product knowledge is important to the buyer. Product knowledge may include such technical details as

- Performance data.
- Physical size and characteristics.
- How the product operates.
- Specific features, advantages, and benefits of the product.
- How well the product is selling in the marketplace.

The salesperson's knowledge creates value for customers.

Many companies have their new salespeople work in the manufacturing plant (for example, on the assembly line) or in the warehouse (filling orders and receiving stock). This hands-on experience may cost the salesperson a lot of sweat and sore muscles for a few of weeks or months, but the payoff is a world of product knowledge and help in future selling that could not be earned in any other way. In some manufacturing and distribution firms, their new salespeople spend several weeks in a production plant. Often, new salespeople in the oil and gas industry roughneck and drive trucks during the first few months on the job. A sales representative for one chemical company spends the first two or three weeks on the job in a warehouse unloading freight cars and flatbed trucks and filling 55-gallon drums with various liquid chemicals.

Salespeople also can learn much at periodic company sales meetings. At sales meetings, a consumer-goods manufacturer, such as Frito-Lay, may concentrate on developing sales presentations for the products to receive special emphasis during the coming sales period. Company advertising programs, price discounts, and promotional allowances for these products are discussed. Although little time is spent on the technical aspects of consumer products, much time is devoted to discussing the marketing mix for these products (product type, promotion, distribution, and price).

Sales managers for firms selling technical products, such as Merck, Alcoa, and Emerson Electric, might spend as much as 75 percent of a sales meeting discussing product information. The remaining time might be allotted to sales techniques.

Know Your Channels of Distribution

It is essential to understand the channel of distribution your company uses to move its products to the final consumer. Knowledge of each channel member (also called reseller or middleman) is vital. Wholesalers and retailers often stock thousands of products, and each one may have hundreds of salespeople from a multitude of companies calling on its buyers. Know as much about each channel member as possible. Some important information you will need includes the following:

Who plays a role in your buyer's business?

- Likes and dislikes of each channel member's customers.
- Product lines and the assortment each one carries.
- When each member sees salespeople.
- Distribution, promotion, and pricing policies.
- What quantity of which product each channel member has purchased in the past.

Although most channel members will have similar policies concerning salespeople, keep abreast of the differences.

Know Your Product's Pricing and Discount Policies

An important part of a comprehensive marketing strategy for a product is establishing its price. **Price** refers to the value or worth of a product that attracts the buyer to exchange money or something of value for the product. A product has some want-satisfying attributes for which the prospect is willing to exchange something of value. The person's wants assign a value to the item offered for sale. For instance, a golfer who wants to purchase a dozen golf balls already has conceived some estimated measure of the product's value. Of course, the sporting goods store may have set a price higher than estimated. This could diminish *want* somewhat, depending on the difference between the two. Should the golfer then find the same brand of golf balls on sale at a discount store, at a price more in line with a preconceived idea of the product's value, the want may be strong enough to stimulate a purchase.

Many companies offer customers various types of discounts from normal prices to entice them to buy. These discounts become an important part of the firm's marketing effort (see Exhibit 5.2). They are usually developed at the corporate level by the firm's marketing managers. Immediately before the sales period when the product's promotion begins, the sales force is informed of special discounts that they may offer to customers. This discount information becomes an important part of the sales presentation. It is important for salespeople to familiarize themselves with the company's price, discount, and credit policies so that they can use them as a competitive advantage and enhance their professional image with the buyer.[6]

The appendix at the end of this chapter discusses the various pricing issues that salespeople should be able to explain to their buyers. It also has useful information for developing a sales presentation for your class project role-play.

EXHIBIT 5.2

Examples of prices and discounts salespeople discuss in their sales presentations.

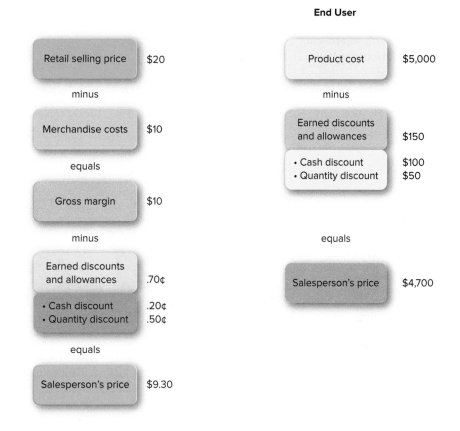

End User

Retail selling price	$20

minus

Merchandise costs	$10

equals

Gross margin	$10

minus

Earned discounts and allowances	.70¢
• Cash discount	.20¢
• Quantity discount	.50¢

equals

Salesperson's price	$9.30

Product cost	$5,000

minus

Earned discounts and allowances	$150
• Cash discount	$100
• Quantity discount	$50

equals

Salesperson's price	$4,700

Know Your Competition, Industry, and Economy

What would the salesperson shown in Exhibit 5.3 need to know about his competition? She needs to be knowledgeable about his products, her firm's service and credit policies, and the price of the products. She also needs to know what her competition is doing in each of these areas.

Today's successful salespeople understand their *competitors'* products, policies, and practices as well as their own. It is common for a buyer to ask a salesperson, "How does your product compare to the one I'm currently using?" If unable to confidently answer such a question, a salesperson will lose ground in selling. A salesperson needs to be prepared to discuss product features, advantages, and benefits in comparison to other products and confidently show why the salesperson's product will fulfill the buyer's needs better than competing products.

One method to obtain information on competitors is through advertisements. From a competitor's online advertising, Joe Mitchell, a salesperson representing a small business machines firm, developed a chart for comparing the sales points of his machines against the competition. Joe does not do this for fun, nor does he name the competitive equipment on the chart. Instead, he calls them Machine *A,* Machine *B,* and Machine *C.* When he finds a claimed benefit in one of the other machines that his product does not have, he works to find a better benefit to balance it.

Salespeople never stop learning.

What does this salesperson need to know about the competition?

©goodluz/Shutterstock

"Maybe the chart isn't always useful," Joe says, "but it certainly has prepared me to face a customer. I know just what other machines have—and what they do not have—that my prospect might be interested in. I know the principal sales arguments used in selling these machines and the benefits I must bring up to offset and surpass competition. Many times a prospect will mention an online advertisement of another company and ask about some statement or other," Joe says. "Because I've studied those ads and taken the time to find out what's behind the claims, I can give an honest answer and I can demonstrate how my machine has the same feature or quality and then offer additional benefits. Of course, I never run down a competitor's product. I just try to run ahead of it."

The salesperson selling industrial goods and an industrial buyer work for different companies but are both in the same industry. The industrial buyer often seeks information from salespeople on the *industry* itself and how economic trends might influence the industry *and* both of their companies. Thus, the salesperson should be well informed about the industry and the economy. The salesperson can find this information in the company records, newspapers, television, radio, *The Wall Street Journal,* industrial and trade periodicals, and magazines such as *Bloomberg Businessweek* and *U.S. News & World Report.* The salesperson who is well informed is more successful than the poorly informed salesperson.

Know How to Help Your Customers Resell Your Product

In some industries, salespeople assist their customers to resell their product to the end-user. For example, let's assume a salesperson is selling a new type of mouthwash to a grocery-store chain. The buyer for the grocery stores may ask the salesperson, "How will your firm create awareness of your product and incent grocery consumers to visit my store and purchase your mouthwash?"

The salesperson will need to develop a promotional plan for the grocery-store buyer. The promotional plan's goal is to help sell the mouthwash to consumers that visit the grocery store. The main ingredients of a firm's promotional effort may include personal selling, advertising, publicity, and sales promotion. Therefore, an understanding of marketing is often essential for the salesperson.

In our example, the plan may integrate promotions within the grocery store, such as in-store sampling, along with national initiatives conducted by the mouthwash manufacturer, such as national advertising and social media programming. This means the salesperson must keep abreast of her company's advertising and sales promotion activities. By incorporating these data into a sales presentation, the salesperson can provide customers with a world of information that they may know little about and that can secure the sale. Exhibit 5.4 illustrates an example of advertising and sales promotion that may be used when making a sales presentation for a mouthwash called Fresh Mouth.

Suppose Fresh Mouth is a new product that just emerged from the test market. As a lead-in to the information in Exhibit 5.4, you might say:

> Ms. Buyer, Fresh Mouth was a proven success in our Eastern test markets. Fresh Mouth had a 9.8 percent market share only nine months after the start of advertising. Laboratory tests proved that the Fresh Mouth formula is superior to the leading competition.
>
> Consumer panels significantly preferred Fresh Mouth to leading competing brands. There was a repurchase rate of 50 percent after sampling. The trade [retailers] gave enthusiastic support in the test-market areas.

Next, you would discuss the information contained in Exhibit 5.4.

Types of Advertising Differ

The development and timing of an advertising campaign for a product or service are handled by a firm's advertising department or by an outside advertising agency. The result of this effort is the television commercial, radio spot, print media (newspaper or magazine), or other form of advertisement (billboard, transit placard, etc.). Following development of the ad, the firm must establish and coordinate a plan for tying in sales force efforts with the new ad campaign. There are six basic types of advertising programs that a company can use: national, retail, cooperative, trade, industrial, and direct-mail advertising.

National advertising is advertising designed to reach all users of the product, whether consumers or industrial buyers. These ads are shown across the country. In some cases, national advertisers may restrict their expenditures to the top 100 markets. Top 100 refers to the 100 largest major metropolitan areas where most of the U.S. population is concentrated. Therefore, the advertiser gets more punch per ad dollar. Giant marketing companies such as Procter & Gamble, IBM, Ford, Holiday Inn, and Coca-Cola commonly use national advertising.

Retail advertising is used by a retailer to reach customers within its geographic trading area. Local supermarkets and department stores regularly advertise nationally distributed brand products. National-brand advertising may be totally paid by the retailer or partially paid by the manufacturer.

Cooperative, or **co-op, advertising** is advertising the retailer conducts with the cost paid for by the manufacturer or shared by the manufacturer and retailer. It is an attractive selling tool for the salesperson to give the buyer an advertising allowance to promote a firm's goods. An advertising agreement between a retailer and a manufacturer often provides for these aspects:

- The duration of the advertisement. How long the advertisement will appear.
- The product(s) to be advertised.

EXHIBIT 5.4

Advertising and sales promotion information the salesperson provides the buyer.

1. **Massive Sampling and Couponing:**
   - There will be blanketing of the top 300 markets with 4.4-oz samples plus 80¢-off coupons. Your market is included.
   - There will be a 75% coverage of homes in the top 100 markets. Your market is included.
2. **Heavy Advertising:**
   - Nighttime network TV.
   - Daytime network TV.
   - Saturation spot TV.
   - Newspapers.
   - The total network and spot advertising will reach 85 percent of all homes in the United States five times each week based on a four-week average. This means that in four weeks, Fresh Mouth will have attained 150 million home impressions—130 million of these impressions will be women.
   - There will be half-page, two-color inserts in local newspapers in 50 markets, including yours. This is more than 20 million in circulation. Scheduled to tie in with saturation sampling is a couponing program.
   - $80 million will be spent on promotion to ensure consumer acceptance.
3. **TV Advertising Theme** (the salesperson would show pictures or drawings of the advertisement):
   - The commercial with POWER to sell!
   - "POWER to kill mouth odor—POWER to kill germs—POWER to give FRESH MOUTH."
   - The commercial shows a young man, about 20 years of age, walking up to a young woman saying, "Hi, Susan!" They kiss and she says, "My, you have a fresh mouth, Bill!" He looks at the camera with a smile and says, "It works!" The announcer closes the commercial by saying, "FRESH MOUTH—it has the POWER!"
4. **Display Materials:**
   - Shelf display tag.
   - Small floor stand for end-of-aisle display—holds 24 12-oz bottles.
   - Large floor stand—holds 48 12-oz bottles.

- The amount of money paid to the retailer for advertising purposes.
- The type of advertising—radio, television, newspaper, magazine.
- Proof by the retailer that the product has been advertised as agreed upon (a copy of the advertisement).

Generally, national and retail advertising are aimed at the final consumers. Trade and industrial advertising are aimed at other members in the channel of distribution and other manufacturers.

Trade advertising is undertaken by the manufacturer and directed toward the wholesaler or retailer. Such advertisements appear in trade magazines serving only the wholesaler or retailer. (Exhibit A in the appendix to this chapter is an example of manufacturer advertising to retail pharmacies in the popular trade magazine *American Druggist.*)

Industrial advertising is aimed at individuals and organizations that purchase products used in manufacturing other products. General Electric may advertise small electric motors in magazines read by buyers employed by firms such as Whirlpool or Sears.

Direct-mail advertising is mailed directly to the consumer or industrial user; it is an effective method of exposing these users to a product or it reminds them that the product is available to meet a specific need. Often, trial samples or coupons accompany direct-mail advertising.

Direct-mail advertising can solicit a response from a current user of a product. For example, the user may be asked to fill out and mail in a questionnaire. In return, the manufacturer sends the user a sample of the product or information about the product.

Why Spend Money on Advertising?

Why would a company spend money on advertising? Companies advertise because they hope to

- Increase overall sales and sales of a specific product.
- Give salespeople additional selling information for sales presentations.
- Develop leads for salespeople through mail-ins, ad response, and so on.
- Increase cooperation from channel members, such as retailers or distributors, through co-op advertising and promotional campaigns.
- Educate the customer about the company's products.
- Inform prospects that a product is on the market and where to buy it.
- Reduce cognitive dissonance over the purchase.
- Create sales or presell customers between a salesperson's calls.

Advertising serves various purposes depending on the nature of a product or industry. The majority of top advertisers are well-known manufacturers of consumer goods. This indicates that advertising dollars are lavished on consumer items. Because industrial advertising has more specified channels of communication (such as trade periodicals and trade shows) and a smaller number of potential customers, advertising costs tend to be lower. In either case, carefully employed advertising benefits both a firm and its sales force. Sales promotion is another potential aid to a company and its sales force.

Sales Promotion Generates Sales

Sales promotion involves activities or materials other than personal selling, advertising, and publicity used to create sales for goods or services. Sales promotion can be divided into consumer and trade sales promotion. **Consumer sales promotion** includes free samples, coupons, contests, and demonstrations to consumers. **Trade sales promotion** encourages resellers to purchase and aggressively sell a manufacturer's products by offering incentives like sales contests, displays, special purchase prices, and free merchandise (e.g., buy 10 cases of a product and get 1 case free).

The company's promotional efforts can be a useful sales tool for an enterprising salesperson. Sales promotion offers may prove to the retailer or wholesaler that the selling firm will assist actively in creating consumer demand. This, in turn, improves the salesperson's probability of making the sale. Next, we discuss some popular sales promotion items: point-of-purchase displays, shelf positioning, and consumer and dealer premiums such as contests and sweepstakes.

Point-of-Purchase Displays: Get Them Out There

Point-of-purchase (POP) displays allow a product to be seen easily and purchased. A product POP display may include photographs, banners, drawings, coupons, a giant-size product carton, reduce end cap displays, counter displays, or floor stands. POP displays greatly increase product sales. It is up to the salesperson to obtain the retailer's cooperation to allow the POP display in the store. People are attracted to

©Andrew Resek/McGraw-Hill Education

displays. They catch the customer's attention and make products easy to purchase, which results in increased product sales.

In-store product demonstrations, sampling programs, and cross-merchandising are also popular. Many grocery chains offer samples of food and drinks. They particularly like to cross-merchandise, such as placing cookies in the dairy section. Employees retail and clothing stores offer to spray men and women with fragrances as they shop. Each of these methods is an effective way to sell products.

Shelf Positioning Is Important to Your Success

Another important sales stimulator is the shelf positioning of products. **Shelf positioning** refers to the physical placement of the product within the retailer's store. **Shelf facings** are the number of individual products placed beside each other on the shelf. Determine where a store's customers can easily find and examine your company's products and place products in that space or position with as many shelf facings as the store allows (see Exhibit 5.5).

The major obstacle faced when attempting to obtain shelf space for products is limited space. A retail store has a fixed amount of display space and thousands of products to stock. You compete for shelf space with other salespeople and with the retailer's brands.

It is often up to the salesperson to sell the store manager on purchasing different sizes of a particular product. Also, the salesperson may want a product displayed at several locations in the store. A Johnson & Johnson salesperson may want the company's baby powder and baby shampoo displayed with baby products and adult toiletries.

Premiums

The premium has come a long way from being just a trinket in a Cracker Jack box. Today, it is a major marketing tool. American businesses spend billions of dollars on consumer and trade premiums and incentives. Premiums create sales.

©Education & Exploration 4/
Alamy Stock Photo

EXHIBIT 5.5

Sales reps know that good shelf positioning and shelf facings boost sales.

©Andrew Resek/McGraw-Hill Education

A **premium** is an article of merchandise offered as an incentive to the user to take some action. The premium may act as an incentive to buy, to sample the product, to come into the retail store, or to stir interest so the user requests further information. Premiums serve a number of purposes: to promote consumer sampling of a new product, to introduce a new product, to encourage point-of-purchase displays, and to boost sales of slow products. Three major categories of premiums are contests and sweepstakes, consumer premiums, and dealer premiums.

Technology and Selling

The use of a wide range of technology and software applications by sales personnel indicates the need to learn about certain forms of sales technology and their use. Today's technology and software applications are quickly and effectively training people and providing easy-to-use opportunities to serve customers.

Sales personnel find technology serves as a valuable tool for increasing productivity within the sales force. The 10 most widely used applications are shown in Exhibit 5.6. Here are several major reasons for salespeople to use varying forms of technology:

- Provides more effective management of sales leads and better follow-through on customer contacts. Software applications provide a permanent lead file.
- Improves customer relations due to more effective follow-ups. This leads to greater productivity.
- Improves organization of selling time. Software help reps monitor and organize everything.
- Provides more efficient account control and better time and territory management. There is a better awareness of each account's status, which provides more time for customer contacts.
- Increases number and quality of sales calls.
- Offers faster speed and improved accuracy in finishing and sending reports and orders to the company.
- Helps develop more effective proposals and persuasive presentations (see Exhibit 5.7).

If you have little knowledge about various forms of sales technology, start learning!

Knowledge of Technology Enhances Sales and Customer Service

Technology is at the heart of salespeople's ability to provide top-quality customer service by receiving and sending out information. Technology is advancing at a rapid pace, and affecting people—including salespeople—in all aspects of their lives (see Exhibit 5.8).

EXHIBIT 5.6

Top 10 software applications.

Software applications are focused on the customer. Here are the top 10 applications in order of use:

1. Customer/prospect profile.	6. Sales presentation.
2. Lead tracking.	7. Time/territory management.
3. Call reports.	8. Order entry.
4. Sales forecasts.	9. Travel and expense reports.
5. Sales data analysis.	10. Checking inventory/shipping status.

EXHIBIT 5.7

The tablet has numerous applications.

©Monty Rakusen/Image Source

EXHIBIT 5.8

By using technology, this salesperson can sell and serve customers no matter what her location.

©Dougal Waters/Getty Images

Technology helps salespeople increase their productivity and effectiveness, and allows them to gather and access information more efficiently. You can use computer technology to improve communication to the home office, with others on your sales force, and with customers. Salespeople also use technology to create better strategies for targeting and tracking clients. Sales force automation breaks down into three broad areas of functionality covering (1) personal productivity, (2) communications, and (3) order processing and customer service.[7]

Personal Productivity

Many programs can help a salesperson increase **personal productivity** through more efficient data storage and retrieval, better time management, and enhanced presentations. Remember that you do business with the one you trust and you trust the one you know. So keep in touch with customers. Let's discuss some of the more popular uses of technology.

Customer Relationship Management (CRM) Technology

Customer relationship management (CRM) is a technology system that helps companies manage information about existing and potential customers. Many CRM systems include contact management technology, a listing of all the customer contacts that a salesperson makes in the course of conducting business. The form of the technology is like an electronic collection of business cards and includes such information as the contact's name, title, company, address, phone number, fax number, and e-mail address. It also may include additional information such as the particular industry, date of last order, name of administrative assistant, other key decision makers, and so on (see Exhibit 5.9).

> *You do business with the one you trust and you trust the one you know. So keep in touch with your customers.*

Customer Relationship Management Technology

You may not be acquainted with the term CRM, but you may be aware of many of the leading providers of CRM technology systems. CRM is the combination of a customer-centered philosophy in the organization supported by technology that often combines sales, marketing and customer service into one.
Common vendors of CRM software include:

- Salesforce

- Microsoft dynamics

- Netsuite

The value of a CRM system lies in its ability to manage knowledge. CRM software often combines sales, marketing, and customer service data into one information technology platform.[8] For example, the CRM system may include insight from the salesperson's colleagues. In some firms, the customer service department may have had interactions with a customer and documented the communication, or the marketing department may have sent the customer an invitation to a webinar and captured this information within the CRM system. Hence, CRM technology not only provides a tracking mechanism, it also allows salespeople and their colleagues to share critical information throughout their organization and more effectively collaborate.

Her cell phone provides information needed about a prospect.

©Ariel Skelley/Blend Images LLC

Calendar Management

As a salesperson, the most vulnerable asset you have to manage is time. Improvement of time management directly increases productivity. Electronic **calendar management,** as a part of sales force automation, can make time management easier and less prone to errors or oversights.

When a salesperson schedules appointments, telephone calls, or to-do lists on an electronic calendar, the system automatically checks for conflicts, eliminating the need for rescheduling. An electronic calendar can assign a relative priority to each item. It also can create an electronic link between a scheduled event and a particular contact or account so that the appointment or call information is accessible as part of the salesperson's calendar, and as part of the contact or account history. Once it can be viewed from different perspectives, the information contained in the calendar becomes much more useful.

For the sales manager, electronic calendar management automatically consolidates information concerning the whereabouts of the entire sales force. Weekly or monthly calendars, which quickly become outdated, have been improved. Now information can be automatically generated when salespeople schedule their appointments. The system also allows salespeople to instantly update their appointments and schedules directly from the field.

Automated Sales Plans, Tactics, and Ticklers

Sales strategies often fall in a sequence of events that can be identified and plotted. A traditional example involves a thank-you letter sent immediately after an initial sales call and a follow-up telephone call three days later. In the sales world, it may be difficult for busy salespeople to track all the details. As a result, important follow-up items sometimes get overlooked. If this happens, a salesperson's diligent prospecting efforts become wasted and valuable prospects are squandered.

A sales force automation system begins working as soon as the initial meeting is entered into the system. A few simple commands tell it to remind you to send a thank-you letter and schedule a follow-up phone call. It also can notify the sales manager if these follow-ups are not completed.

Another sales situation might call for a regular follow-up every year or two after the sale, depending on the sales cycle associated with your product. It is particularly easy for follow-up calls like this to be neglected because of the long lead time involved. The problem becomes more apparent if the salesperson who made the original sale leaves the company or is promoted. When that happens, the customer often falls through the cracks, becoming an orphan. Automated sales tactics and ticklers prevent this from happening.

Geographic Information Systems

A **geographic information system (GIS)** allows salespeople to view and analyze customer and/or prospect information on an electronic map. This may be extremely useful if you are visiting an area for the first time. It also can be helpful in a familiar area. Customer information can be accessed directly from contact-management data and sorted accordingly, allowing you to plan sales calls geographically and make the most efficient use of your time. Also, a GIS may reveal customer buying patterns that otherwise may not be apparent.

Computer-Based Presentations

Computer-based presentations can be a powerful presentation tool. PowerPoint presentations with short product video clips provide a means of creating a customized dynamic video and sound discussion of the product.

Tablets Improve Sales

Tablets allow salespeople to show data and videos about specific products in their presentations to buyers. Likewise, podcasts and other forms of e-learning modules are an excellent way to train salespeople on product knowledge and selling skills. They can provide coaching and practical advice at a moment's notice.[9] Imagine a salesperson preparing to call on a major customer. The video clip enables the seller to review such things as objection handling and closing techniques, as well as a video sales presentation role-play of the product being presented to the buyer while sitting in the customer's waiting room. What a great way for getting mentally prepared to help someone minutes before being called into the buyer's office.

Communications with Customers and Employer

In the 21st century, a company's success hinges on its ability to deliver information quickly to customers and employees. Today's most popular sales force automation systems involve written communication and e-mail.

Written Communication

Written communication plays a large part in the lives of most salespeople. Particularly important is the need for written communication with customers. A thank-you letter or e-mail mailed immediately after an initial sales call can often mean the difference between a favorable impression and one that is not as favorable. Sometimes it can make or break a sale. In spite of its potential impact, salespeople frequently overlook this simple task because they lack an easy way to get it done. There always seem to be other, more pressing things to do.

E-mail (Electronic Mail)

Electronic mail (e-mail) allows messages to be sent electronically through a system that delivers them immediately to any number of recipients worldwide.

In creating an e-mail to customers, use the same professional writing skills you would in a business letter. Correct grammar, sentence structure, spelling, and content are extremely important in building customer relationships. Also, make sure you send the e-mail to the correct person.

An e-mail sent to the wrong customer may surprise and upset the customer. Take care in writing and sending e-mails.

Customer Order Processing and Service Support

The process of obtaining, generating, and completing an order is much more complicated than it may actually sound. The many steps involved in a manual system may take several days or even weeks to complete and confirm. Automated systems shorten the sales-and-delivery cycle. While in the office with your customer, you can use the Internet to access information and make things happen more efficiently. You can check the inventory status of merchandise on the sales order, receive approval for your client's credit status, and begin the shipping process immediately. Salespeople's automated order entries directly update the company computer without having to be reentered at the home office.

Salespeople's Virtual Offices

Due to the availability, processing speeds, and expanding reach of technology, salespeople are able to conduct business in a variety of venues that effectively serve as **virtual offices**. For salespeople who need to be constantly in touch with their clients, technology allows a functioning virtual office in the salesperson's home, vehicle, hotel room, or even local coffee shop. Laptops, tablets, cell phones, printers, data services, and Wi-Fi allow salespeople to stay in constant contact with their customers even when driving between cities or states. Jeff Brown, an agent manager with U.S. Cellular, frequently uses a mobile office. "If I arrive at a prospect's office and they can't see me right away," Brown says, "then I can go outside to work in my office until they're ready to see me."[10]

©Dave and Les Jacobs/Blend Images LLC

The Value of Mobile Technology

Technology has enabled mobility for the salesperson. The average salesperson's cell phone often includes mapping/GPS technology, CRM technology, capabilities for phone and web conferencing,and access to marketing and sales collaterals. Let's use 3M salesperson Bob Barr to demonstrate the value of mobile technology used in sales. Headquartered in Houston, Texas, Bob's sales territory is composed of seven states. He travels 25,000 miles by car each year and frequently flies by airplane if the drive is greater than five hours. Bob, like many salespeople worldwide, relies on mobile technology.

Sales: Internet and the Cloud

The Internet provides salespeople with access to research, data, people, and vast amounts of information. Sales organizations are spending millions of dollars on software, hardware, and training for their salespeople to use the Net. It is a great sales tool. Let's briefly discuss the Internet.

EXHIBIT 5.10

Websites can provide valuable information to salespeople.

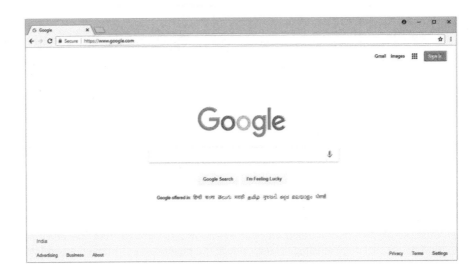

The Internet

The **Internet,** often referred to as the Net, is a global network of computers. It is a worldwide, self-governed network, connecting thousands of smaller networks, and millions of computers and people, to megasources of information. Similar in some ways to the telephone system, it reaches every country in the world. Just as you can call people anywhere in the world, so too can you contact their computers as long as they are connected to the Net. Salespeople, by using an Internet search engine system such as Google, Bing, or Yahoo (see Exhibit 5.10), can get access to valuable information in few minutes.

The Cloud

What is the **cloud?** You are probably already using it. Do you use Google docs, Dropbox, or Office 365? These are all online, cloud-based applications.

Previously, firms and their employees needed to have software downloaded on their computers, or firms managed their own servers. Now, firms contract with companies who are responsible for the software applications and hardware technology. Thus, employees only need to access the Internet, enter their username and password, and open the appropriate software application.

The cloud has enabled a more mobile, portable opportunity for salespeople. The cloud allows access to software anywhere, as long as the individual is connected to the Internet. Today's salesperson can access CRM technology, order processing, and other important purchasing and background data from their tablet, smartphone, or other computing device.

Global Technology Provides Service

The ability to access information is a valuable asset. We are in an era in which corporate strategy relies on efficiency; it can make or break a business. When salespeople travel far from home, the need for the right information, at the right time, in the right place becomes critical. Increased worldwide interaction requires access and exchange of data on a global basis.

As technology solves problems, it presents new opportunities. For example, advances in mobile data collection and wireless data communications have dramatically increased the amount of data that need to be collected, managed, stored, and accessed. Organizations that harness this information can maximize the level of service they offer, resulting in increased sales.

A salesperson in Europe, for example, can send information to America electronically. The information is stored in the organization's main computer database. A salesperson in Florida has access to the information and can send additional data to the database. Even a Texas salesperson in a customer's office can send and receive information to and from the same database using a wireless communication.

Technology Etiquette

With so much technology available, salespeople have many options when it comes to communicating with customers and placing orders. For salespeople to use this technology properly, they must be aware of the proper etiquette that comes along with these various channels of communication.

Netiquette

Netiquette is the term used for etiquette on the Internet.[11] Since the Internet changes so rapidly, netiquette does also. No matter how quickly it changes, netiquette is still based on the Core Principle, of "do unto others as you would have done to you." In sales, the need for netiquette mostly arises when sending or distributing e-mail.

Many practices should be considered when sending an e-mail to a customer, a prospect, or your manager. According to Mary Mitchell, author of *The Complete Idiot's Guide to Business Etiquette,* people seem to express rudeness a lot more than they used to—especially online. In her opinion, one of the reasons for increased rudeness is that electronic communication has reduced the amount of human-to-human contact. "This not only makes it easier to be rude, but we lose regular practice in being mannerly," says Mitchell.

Mitchell also believes that rudeness produces more rudeness. Since rudeness tends to multiply, each individual act of politeness also has a ripple effect. Workplace expert, executive coach, and Hall of Fame speaker Marjorie Brody who is also the President/CEO of BRODY Professional Development outlines some do's and don'ts when it comes to e-mail communication:[12]

Do

- Use clear, descriptive and current subject headings; if topics change, rewrite the subject line
- Be clear & concise in your message
- Use dates, salutations, proper punctuation/spelling, and a friendly closing
- Read & edit a message in an e-mail "chain" before forwarding or replying to all
- Ensure you include a signature (sig) file—your contact information at the end
- Respond as quickly to an e-mail as you would a telephone message

Don't

- Use all capital letters, which is the online equivalent to SHOUTING
- Make comments or requests in an e-mail that you would not make in person
- Send repeat messages; pick up the phone if you don't get a reply in a timely manner
- Send bad news (i.e., "You're fired.")

The best thing to remember in sending e-mail is to treat customers in the same courteous manner in which you would treat them in person. Your customers cannot see you through your e-mail, and the only way that they can judge you is by the way in which you represent yourself.

©Roberto Westbrook/Blend Images LLC

Cell Phones

Hundreds of millions of people subscribe to wireless services. With the convenience that cell phones bring, including wireless service that allows you to check your e-mail and surf the Web from your phone, some problems emerge as well. When salespeople do not understand the courteous use of their phone, meetings and sales calls can be interrupted and ruined.

A salesperson can prevent distractions caused by his or her cell phone in many ways. These guidelines should be kept in mind at all times:[13]

- **The person you are with is the most important person to talk to.** Whether you are with a customer, potential buyer, or your supervisor, utilize the Caller ID feature for screening options. You may decide to let your voice mail take the call and return the call at a more appropriate time.
- **Turn off your phone during meetings, sales calls, and presentations.** Talking on the phone during any of these can be disruptive and violate basic courtesy. If you are expecting an important call, use text messaging or silence your ringer.
- **Don't engage in cell yell.** Yelling on a cell phone can be offensive to a customer and unnecessary. Most phones have sensitive microphones that can pick up even a whisper. There is no need to speak louder on your cell phone than you would on any other phone.

Voice Mail

Voice mail is a convenient way for salespeople to receive messages in their office or on their cell phone when they are unavailable. It is important to always change your outgoing message to let your customers know where you are and your availability. It also lets them know when you will return their calls. You should always leave a contact name and the phone number of someone who can help in case a customer needs immediate assistance.

Please, please repeat your telephone number s-l-o-w-l-y!

It is also important to be courteous when leaving a voice message for someone else. You should say your name and phone number slowly at the beginning and ending of the message. This keeps the recipient from having to replay your message. You should also be specific and concise when leaving a message; you do not want to ramble. I frequently outline the key points in my message before the call. Standing while talking helps the message be like a natural conversation.

Speakerphones and Conference Calls

It may be necessary to conduct a meeting over the telephone through a conference call. This should be the only reason a salesperson uses a speakerphone in an office setting. This prevents private information from being heard. People participating in a conference call should identify themselves while speaking, and one person should act as the meeting leader to prevent confusion from people talking over one another.

SUMMARY OF MAJOR SELLING ISSUES

Company knowledge includes information about a firm's history, development policies, procedures, products, distribution, promotion, and pricing. A salesperson also must know the competition, the firm's industry, and the economy. This knowledge can even be used to improve one's self-concept. A high degree of such knowledge helps the salesperson build a positive self-image and feel thoroughly prepared to interact with customers.

Wholesalers and retailers stock thousands of products, which often makes it difficult to support any one manufacturer's products as the manufacturer would like. This situation may result in conflicts between members of the channel of distribution.

To reduce these conflicts and aid channel members in selling products, manufacturers offer assistance in advertising, sales promotion aids, and pricing allowances. Additionally, many manufacturers spend millions of dollars to compel consumers and industrial buyers to purchase from channel members and the manufacturer.

National, retail, trade, industrial, and direct-mail advertising create demand for products and are a powerful selling tool for the salesperson in sales presentations. Sales promotion activities and materials are another potential selling tool for the salesperson to use in selling to consumer and industrial buyers. Samples, coupons, contests, premiums, demonstrations, and displays are effective sales promotion techniques employed to help sell merchandise.

Price, discounts, and credit policies are additional facts the salesperson should be able to discuss confidently with customers. Each day, the salesperson informs or answers questions customers pose in these three areas. Customers always want to know the salesperson's list and net price, and if there are any transportation charges. Discounts (quantity, cash, trade, or consumer) represent important buying incentives the manufacturer offers to the buyer. The buyer wants to know the terms of payment. The salesperson needs to understand company credit policies to open new accounts, see that customers pay on time, and collect overdue bills. See the appendix at the end of this chapter for additional discussions on pricing.

Finally, success in sales requires knowledge of the many technologies used to sell and serve customers. Computers, written communication, e-mail, cell phones, the Internet, and CRM systems have quickly become part of the professional's sales kit. Proper knowledge of the courteous manner in which these many technologies should be used is a necessity.

Quick Review for Students

The quick review sections provide key questions to help you develop a greater level of conceptual understanding. We suggest that after you read the chapter, you try to answer the following questions without looking back at the textbook.

1. What are four important reasons for the salesperson to have selling knowledge?
2. What is a major component of sales knowledge?
3. What type of information should salespeople possess to act as knowledge brokers?
4. What are five key technical details that are included in product knowledge?
5. What does *price* refer to?
6. What does CRM stand for? How does CRM technology help salespeople?
7. What are some do's and don'ts when it comes to e-mail communication?

MEETING A SALES CHALLENGE

To be successful, salespeople need to be knowledgeable about many things. However, being an expert on the product is only part of what it takes to be a top performer. You also need to know how to use good communication and selling skills.

Sure, this grocery buyer wants to sell his customers a good product, but the reseller is possibly more interested in whether he can sell the product once he buys it and how much money he will make. Resellers are "bottom-line" oriented; because they want to know what's in it for them, they concentrate on discussing return on investment.

KEY TERMS FOR SELLING

calendar management   178
cloud   181
computer-based
    presentations   179
consumer sales
    promotion   173
cooperative (co-op)
    advertising   171
direct-mail advertising   172
e-mail (electronic mail)   180

geographic information
    system (GIS)   179
industrial advertising   172
Internet   181
national advertising   171
netiquette   181
personal productivity   177
point-of-purchase (POP)
    displays   173
premium   175

price   168
retail advertising   171
sales training   163
shelf facings   174
shelf positioning   174
trade advertising   172
trade sales promotion   173
virtual office   180
written
    communication   179

SALES APPLICATION QUESTIONS

1. A salesperson's knowledge needs to extend into many areas such as general company knowledge; product knowledge; knowledge of upcoming advertising and promotional campaigns; knowledge about company price, discount, and credit policies; and knowledge about the competition, the industry, and the economy. These are all vital for sales success. For each of these categories, explain how a salesperson's knowledge can lay the groundwork for successful selling.

2. How do salespeople generally acquire their sales knowledge?

3. Explain how a salesperson's knowledge can be converted into selling points used in the sales presentation. Give two examples.

4. A salesperson must have a good understanding of the competition, customers, and everything connected with the company. Why, however, should a salesperson take time to be up-to-date on facts about the economy and the industry?

5. What is the difference between a product's shelf positioning and its shelf facings? How can a salesperson maximize both shelf positioning and shelf facings? Why is this important?

6. Companies use numerous premiums in their efforts to market products. Why? What types of premiums do they use? How can a salesperson use a premium offer in a sales presentation to a wholesaler or a retailer?

7. What are the major types of advertising that a manufacturer might use to promote its products? How can a salesperson use information about the company's advertising in a sales presentation?

8. Before firms such as General Foods and Quaker Oats introduce a new consumer product nationally, they frequently place the product in a test market to see how it will sell. How can a salesperson use test information in a sales presentation?

9. What is cooperative advertising? Explain the steps involved.

10. Why do companies advertise?

11. Consumer sales promotion and trade sales promotion try to increase sales to consumers and resellers, respectively. Several promotional techniques follow; classify each item as a consumer or trade promotional technique and give an

example for each one. Can any of the promotions be used for both consumers and the trade?

a. Coupons on or inside packages.
b. Free installation (premium).
c. Displays.
d. Sales contests.
e. Drawings for gifts.
f. Demonstrations.
g. Samples.

12. What is *netiquette,* and when does the need for it mostly arise in sales?
13. Cell phones are a convenient way for salespeople to keep in touch with customers even when they are out of their office. Although cell phones are useful, they can be a distraction. List four things that salespeople can do to make sure that they are using their phones in a courteous manner.

SELLING EXPERIENTIAL EXERCISE

You may think you have a good attitude for sales, but if you do not have the confidence to meet customers and prospects you do not know, all is lost. This exercise can help you measure your self-confidence. Read each statement and then, on a separate sheet of paper, write the number you believe best fits you.

How Is Your Self-Confidence?

	High				Low
I can convert strangers into friends quickly and easily.	5	4	3	2	1
I can attract and hold the attention of others even when I do not know them.	5	4	3	2	1
I love new situations.	5	4	3	2	1
I'm intrigued with the psychology of meeting and building a good relationship with someone I do not know.	5	4	3	2	1
I would enjoy making a sales presentation to a group of executives.	5	4	3	2	1
When dressed for the occasion, I have great confidence in myself.	5	4	3	2	1
I do not mind using the telephone to make appointments with strangers.	5	4	3	2	1
Others do not intimidate me.	5	4	3	2	1
I enjoy solving problems.	5	4	3	2	1
Most of the time, I feel secure.	5	4	3	2	1
			Total Score _____		

Add up the numbers to get your score. If you scored more than 40, you may really enjoy selling as a profession. If you rated yourself between 25 and 40, you may simply need more experience in dealing with people and exposing yourself to the wide variety of sales roles. A score of less than 25 indicates that you might need to place yourself in new situations and continue to develop your personal interaction skills.[14]

NOTES

1. Willem Verbeke, Bart Dietz, and Ernst Verwaal, "Drivers of Sales Performance: A Contemporary Meta-Analysis. Have Salespeople Become Knowledge Brokers?" *Journal of the Academy of Marketing Science* 39, no. 3 (June 2011), pp. 407–28.

2. Raj Agnihotri, Jorge Fernando, Colin B. Gabler, Omar Itani, and Michael Krush, "Salesperson Ambidexterity and Customer Satisfaction: Examining the role of Customer Demandingness, Adaptive Selling, and Role Conflict," *Journal of Personal Selling and Sales Management* 37, no. 1 (2017), pp. 27–41.

3. M. T. Krush, R. Agnihotri, K. J. Trainor, and E. L. Nowlin, "Enhancing Organizational Sensemaking: An Examination of the Interactive Effects of Sales Capabilities and Marketing Dashboards," *Industrial Marketing Management* 42, no. 5 (July 2013), pp. 824–835.

4. Raj Agnihotri, Michael Krush, Rakesh K. Singh, "Understanding the Mechanism Linking Interpersonal Traits to Pro-Social Behaviors among Salespeople: Lessons from India," *Journal of Business and Industrial Marketing* 27, no. 3 (February 2012), pp. 211–227.

5. Willem Verbeke, Bart Dietz, and Ernst Verwaal, "Drivers of Sales Performance: A Contemporary Meta-Analysis. Have Salespeople Become Knowledge Brokers?" *Journal of the Academy of Marketing Science* 39, no. 3 (June 2011), p. 407.

6. Also see Sanjay K. Dhar and Stephen J. Hoch, "Price Discrimination Using In-Store Merchandising," *Journal of Marketing,* January 1996, pp. 17–30.

7. Portions of this section were adapted from George W. Colombo, *Sales Force Automation* (New York: McGraw-Hill, 1994).

8. Mary E. Shoemaker, "A Framework for Examining IT-Enabled Market Relationships," *Journal of Personal Selling and Sales Management* 21, no. 2 (January 2001), pp. 177–85.

9. Lauren Hahn, "Tuning Up Sales Skills," *Sales and Marketing Management,* March 2006, p. 17.

10. Andy Cohen, "Going Mobile, Part 2," *Sales and Marketing Management,* June 1994, p. 5.

11. Shari Cauldron, "Virtual Manners," *Workforce,* February 2000, pp. 31–32.

12. Courtesy of Hall of Fame speaker Marjorie Brody who is also an executive coach, President/CEO of BRODY Professional Development (Philadelphia), and a workplace expert and author.

13. Susan Golding, "City of San Diego Mayor's Press Release," July 10, 2000.

14. Adapted from Elwood N. Chapman, *Sales Training Basics* (Menlo Park, CA: Crisp Publications, 1992), p. 11.

15. Adapted from *Marketplace Ethics: Issues in Sales and Marketing* (Westport, CT: J/S Productions, 1990), pp. 55–72.

CASE 5.1

©Ron Chapple Stock/FotoSearch/ Glow Images

Claire Cosmetics

Jane Thompson was hired recently by a national cosmetics manufacturer. She just graduated from college. Having no previous work experience, she always felt nervous about making sales presentations. Her largest customers made her especially nervous. However, for the month she was in her territory, Jane only took orders, which relieved much of the pressure, and the salespeople whom Jane replaced did an excellent job; customers seemed to accept Jane because of this.

In today's e-mail, Jane receives information on products the company wants the sales force to emphasize next month. She is instructed to review the material and come to next week's sales meeting prepared to discuss the information. Of the four products to concentrate on, one product will receive special emphasis. Claire Super Hold hair spray will have the following sales promotion aids and price allowances:

- Floor stand containing 12 8-ounce and 36 12-ounce sizes.
- Counter display containing 6 8-ounce and 6 12-ounce sizes.
- $1 floor stand and counter display off-invoice allowance.
- 10 percent co-op advertising allowance requiring proof of advertising.
- 10 percent off-invoice discount for each dozen of each size purchased.

The 8-ounce size has a suggested retail price of $1.39 and has a normal invoice cost of 83¢, or $9.96 a dozen. The more popular 12-ounce size retails for $1.99 and costs $1.19 each, or $14.28 a dozen. Jane knows that she, like each salesperson, will be called on at the meeting to give her ideas on how to sell this product in front of the 10 salespeople in her district. Her boss will be there and, it is rumored, the national sales manager will be in the area and may attend. This makes her really nervous.

Questions

1. What can Jane do to prepare herself for the meeting and reduce her nervousness?
2. If you were attending the meeting, what ideas would you present?

CASE 5.2

©Ron Chapple Stock/FotoSearch/
Glow Images

McBath Women's Apparel

Getting a new, improved product into a chain of stores that has never carried her line of women's apparel is a new experience for Lynn Morris. Lynn has been promoted to key account sales representative for McBath Women's Apparel in the past month.

She has worked for McBath since graduating from college three years earlier. As a novice salesperson in a large metropolitan market, she inherited a sales territory where all of the major department stores in her area carried the popular McBath line. By displaying a service attitude, Lynn kept all her original accounts and managed to help several outlets increase sales of McBath products, but she was never given the opportunity to sell to new accounts.

Now, she has accepted the key account (a key account is one that generates a large volume of sales for the company) sales position in another region of the country. Also, she has the responsibility of selling to a large chain of department stores (Federale) that has never carried McBath products. Maurice Leverett, vice president of marketing at McBath, is counting heavily on adding the Federale chain because James McBath, the company's president, is intent on continuing McBath's rapid sales growth.

Lynn firmly believes that her products are the best on the market. She is concerned, however, about the sales interview she has scheduled with the chief purchasing agent at Federale, Mary Bruce. Despite McBath's high-quality image and its reputation for having a dependable, hard-working sales force, Mary Bruce has turned down other McBath salespeople several times over the past six years, saying, "We already stock four manufacturers' lingerie. We are quite happy with the lines we now carry and with the service their salespeople provide us. Besides, we only have so much floor space to devote to lingerie and we don't want to confuse our customers with another line."

Lynn has decided to make her company's new display system her major selling point for several reasons:

- Several high-ranking McBath executives (including vice president of marketing Maurice Leverett) are strong supporters of the new display and want it in all retail outlets.
- The stores currently using the display for test marketing purposes have shown an increase in sales for McBath products of 50 percent.
- Federale will not have to set aside much space for the new system, and it can be installed, stocked, and ready for use in less than one hour.
- The display will increase shopping convenience by allowing shoppers easy access to the well-known, trusted line of McBath products with the aid of clear, soft-shell plastic packaging and easy-to-understand sizing.
- A new advertising campaign will start in a few weeks and will emphasize the revolutionary display. Other promotions, such as coupons and special introductory sales, will also be tried.

Questions

1. Lynn believes a good presentation will be critical for her to sell Bruce the new display. How should she structure her presentation? What are the key selling points to discuss?
2. Assume you are Maurice Leverett (vice president of marketing for McBath). Give an example of each of the four major types of discounts discussed in this chapter that your salespeople could use to help put the new display into retail stores. What type of discount will be most effective, and what will be least effective? Explain your reasoning.
3. How can Lynn use quantity (cumulative and noncumulative), cash, trade, and consumer discounts to her advantage?

CASE 5.3

©Ron Chapple Stock/FotoSearch/
Glow Images

Electric Generator Corporation

The Electric Generator Corporation was founded in the early 1970s to develop and market electrical products for industrial and commercial markets. Recently, the company has developed a new electric generator, the EGI, with a revolutionary design. Although its initial cost is $2,000 higher than any competing generator, reduced maintenance costs will offset the higher purchase price within 18 months. The Electric Generator sales force has been instructed to concentrate all effort on selling this new generator, as the company believes it has a sales potential of $500 million.

Sandy Hart, the company's South Texas salesperson, has as her main customer the E. H. Zachary Construction Company of San Antonio, which is the largest nonunion construction firm in the world. Because of the importance of potential Zachary purchases of the EGI (estimated at $1 million), Sandy's boss asks her to take two days off and develop a plan for contacting and selling to Zachary. Monday morning, she is expected at the Houston regional sales office to present this plan to her boss, the regional sales manager, and the divisional sales manager. These two people will critique the presentation, and then the four of them will finalize a sales plan that Sandy will present to Zachary's buying committee.

Questions

1. If you were Sandy, what would be your suggested sales plan?
2. How would a value analysis enter into your presentation?

CASE 5.4

©Ron Chapple Stock/FotoSearch/
Glow Images

Frank's Drilling Service

Frank's Drilling Service specializes in drilling oil and gas wells. Scott Atkinson, one of its salespeople, was preparing to contact the drilling engineer at Oilteck, an independent oil company. Scott has learned that Oilteck plans to drill approximately 12 new wells in the next six months.

Scott estimates that each oil well will require a drilling depth of approximately 10,000 feet. The drilling service the company currently uses charges 90¢ a foot, plus $1,200 per hour for personnel to operate the equipment. The service takes about 16 days to drill each well.

Frank's charges $1,200 per hour for personnel, and its costs are $1 a foot. Scott believes his drilling crews save customers time and money because they can drill a 10,000-foot well in 12 days.

Questions

1. Using the above information, develop a value analysis that Scott could use to sell to his customer.
2. What are several features, advantages, and benefits Scott should discuss with Oilteck's drilling engineer?
3. Consider a few concerns the buyer might communicate after Scott presents the value analysis.

CASE 5.5

©Ron Chapple Stock/FotoSearch/
Glow Images

FruitFresh, Inc.

Perry Ackerman, a product manager for FruitFresh, is visiting with his wife Dee, a member of the Town Recycling Committee, outside the local grocery store. Perry is upset because his new product line is losing market share to FruitFresh's major competitor, Cainer. Dee mentions that Cainer's new slogan "Nature Knows Best" is a good one, but Perry explains Cainer is not being truthful because they are using artificial coloring in its juice. Dee recalls that Cainer has previously been in trouble for inappropriately advertising its packaging as biodegradable and comments that maybe someone will report them again. Dee then asks Perry about progress on FruitFresh's plan to use recycled packaging materials. Perry explains that it is a very difficult and expensive process, but that there is a project team meeting on Tuesday that should give them some answers.

In the Tuesday meeting Perry tells the other employees on the team that people care about the environment and that they will spend their money to prove it. Lynn Samuels, the marketing director, agrees that the market exists and instructs Mike Stritch, from its advertising agency, to begin his presentation. Mike informs the group that the agency recommends building a campaign around recycled packaging. He goes on to explain that FruitFresh can make their cartons with better than 50 percent recycled products, the highest percentage that any company has been able to achieve, and suggests the slogan "FruitFresh. Good for you, good for your world." Lynn and the other employees like the idea, but Perry is concerned. Perry questions whether they would be misrepresenting its product by claiming that the container is recycled when only half of the packaging comes from recycled products.

Defending his idea, Mike comments that Cainer, FruitFresh's competitor, would have no problem making such a claim. When Perry counters that Cainer might copy their campaign, Mike argues that the public may not believe them because of their previous record in the environmental area. Perry inquires why they do not publicize that Cainer is using artificial coloring in its "natural" juice. Mike does not think that this would have the same impact and stresses that they would have to be careful before they began making accusations. Lynn also stresses that FruitFresh has a sizable investment in this product line and explains that they cannot raise their prices enough to offset the increased manufacturing costs of going above 50 percent recycled material because of the tight market. She comments that she is interested in keeping plastics out of the waste stream, but that FruitFresh also needs to make a profit. Mike then assures Perry that he has done his research and that they have to determine which plastics are recycled in laminated products. Lynn reminds Perry that it is his decision since he is the brand manager. Perry contemplates his decision.[15]

Questions

1. What are the main ethical issues, if any, in the FruitFresh case? Describe each ethical issue.
2. What are Perry's options?
3. How do the three levels of moral development relate to Perry's situation?
4. What would you do?

©NicoElNino/Shutterstock

Appendix

Sales Arithmetic and Pricing

Salespeople want to exchange something for something—usually their products for the customer's money. Organizations and consumers (even you) want the answer to the question "How much is this going to cost?" Salespeople have to be prepared to discuss all aspects of costs and prices. Consequently, some knowledge of the rudiments of sales arithmetic and pricing is essential for you.

Since most students taking this course will create a sales presentation as their class project, this information will benefit you. Some students will have had a course in accounting, marketing, or retailing, and therefore this information is intended as a review. This appendix discusses sales arithmetic and pricing concepts that are useful in sales to (1) resellers, such as wholesalers and retailers and (2) end-users, such as businesses and nonprofit organizations.

TYPES OF PRICES

Although a firm may engage in many pricing practices, all companies have a list price, net price, and prices based on transportation terms. Five of the most common types of prices are

- **List price**—the standard price charged to customers.
- **Net price**—the price after allowance for all discounts.
- **Zone price**—the price based on geographic location or zone of customers.
- **FOB shipping point**—FOB (free on board) means the buyer pays transportation charges on the goods—the title to goods passes to the customer when they are loaded on shipping vehicles.
- **FOB destination**—the seller pays all shipping costs.

These prices are established by the company. Normally, the salesperson is not involved in pricing the product. This type of pricing allows the salesperson to quote prices according to company guidelines.

Selling the same quantity of similar products at different prices to two different industrial users or resellers is illegal. Laws such as the Robinson-Patman Act of 1936 forbid price discrimination that injures competition in *interstate* commerce. Although the law does not apply to sales within a state (intrastate sales), a majority of states have similar laws.

A company can justify different prices if it can prove to the courts that its price differentials do not substantially reduce competition. Often, companies justify price differentials by showing the courts one of two things. First, take the case of one customer buying more of a product than another. For the customer purchasing larger quantities, a firm can manufacture and market the products at a lower cost. These lower costs are passed on to the customer in the form of reduced prices. Second, price differentials can be justified when a company must lower prices to meet competition. Thus, if justified, companies can offer customers different prices. They typically do this through discounts.

DISCOUNTS LOWER THE PRICE

Discounts are a reduction in price from the list price. In developing a program to sell a product line over a specified period, marketing managers consider discounts along with the advertising and personal selling efforts the firm engages in. The main types of discounts allowed to buyers are quantity, cash, trade, and consumer discounts.

Quantity Discounts: Buy More, Pay Less

Quantity discounts result from the manufacturer's saving in production costs because it can produce large quantities of the product. As Exhibit A shows, these savings are

EXHIBIT A

Various promotional allowances available to resellers.

Great New Deal!						
Four double-strength sizes to strengthen your profits!						
Promotional Allowances						Promotional Support
Free-Goods Allowance*	Plus Advertising Allowance†		Plus Merchandising Allowance			
	Option A	Option B‡	Reduced Price Feature	Display		
12-oz liquid 8½% off invoice	Up to $1.25 per dozen	$1.00 per dozen	75¢ per dozen reduced price feature	75¢ per dozen floor or end cap display		Direct to consumer national TV promotion . . . 1.705 GRPs
5-oz liquid 8½% off invoice	Up to 75¢ per dozen	50¢ per dozen	50¢ per dozen reduced price feature	50¢ per dozen floor or end cap display		88% reach 1.7 billion impressions
60s tablets 8½% off invoice	Up to 75¢ per dozen	$1.00 per dozen	75¢ per dozen reduced price feature	75¢ per dozen floor or end cap display		Year-round physician detailing and sampling
24s tablets 8½% off invoice	Up to 75¢ per dozen	50¢ per dozen	50¢ per dozen reduced price feature	50¢ per dozen floor or end cap display		Major trade and medical journal advertising support

Also available—up to 2% billback allowance for four-color roto advertising or consumer coupon programs.

Unlimited purchases allowed for claiming billback allowances.

Retail buy-in period: July 15 through August 30, 2018.

Advertising performance period: July 15 through November 8, 2018.

Claim deadline: 45 days following appearance of ad.

Contact your representative for complete details.

*Through participating wholesaler.

†All ads should feature both liquid and tablets.

‡ Provided advertising coverage is in at least 75% of the applicant's trading area.

passed on to customers who buy in large quantities using discounts. Quantity discounts are either noncumulative or cumulative.

One-time reduction in prices are **noncumulative quantity discounts,** which are commonly used in the sale of both consumer and industrial goods. For example, the list price for a computer might be $6,000. If a business buys 9 or fewer the price would be $5,800; 10 to 29 units, $5,500; and any number of computers over 30, $5,000. The Schering salesperson might offer the buyer of Coricidin D a 16.6 percent price reduction. The Colgate salesperson may offer the retailer 2 dozen king-size Colgate tubes of toothpaste free for every 10 dozen purchased.

The salesperson is expected to use these discounts as inducements for the retailer to buy in large quantities. The sales goal is to have the prospect display and locally advertise the product at a price lower than normal. Ideally, the retailer's selling price should reflect the price reduction allowed because of the quantity discount.

Cumulative quantity discounts are discounts the customer receives for buying a certain amount of a product over a stated period, such as one year. Again, these discounts reflect savings in manufacturing and marketing costs.

To receive a 10 percent discount, a buyer may have to purchase 12,000 units of the product. Under the cumulative discount, buyers would not be required to purchase the 12,000 units at the same time—they could purchase 1,000 units each month, for example. As long as the agreed-on amount is purchased within the specified time, the 10 percent discount on each purchase applies. A cumulative discount allows the buyer to purchase the products as needed rather than in a single order.

Cash Discounts Entice the Customer to Pay on Time

Cash discounts are earned by buyers who pay bills within a stated period. For example, if the customer purchases $10,000 worth of goods on June 1 and the cash discount is $2/10$ net 30, the customer pays $9,800 instead of $10,000. Thus, $2/10$ net 30 translates into a 2 percent discount if the bill is completely paid within 10 days of the sale. If the payment is not made within 10 days, the full $10,000 is due in 30 days. Buyers should understand that 2 percent can mean extra money.

Trade Discounts Attract Channel Members' Attention

The manufacturer may reduce prices to channel members (middlemen) to compensate them for the services they perform. These are **trade discounts.** The trade discount is usually stated as a percentage off the list retail price. A wholesaler may be offered a 50 percent discount and the retailer offered a 40 percent discount off list price. The wholesaler's price to its retail customers is 10 percent above its cost or 40 percent off the list price. The wholesaler earns a 10 percent gross margin on sales to retail customers. Channel members are still eligible to earn the quantity and cash discounts.

Consumer Discounts Increase Sales

Consumer discounts are one-time price reductions the manufacturer passes on to channel members or directly to the consumer. Cents-off product labels are price reductions passed directly to the consumer. A package marked 15¢ off each product or $1.80 a dozen uses a consumer discount (see Exhibit B).

EXHIBIT B

Types and examples of discounts.

Types of Discounts	Discount Examples
Quantity discount	
Noncumulative (one-time)	■ Buy 11 dozen, get 1 dozen free.
	■ 20 percent off on all purchases.
	■ $5-off invoice for each floor-stand purchase.
Cumulative (yearly purchases)	■ 5 percent discount with purchase of 8,000 units.
	■ 8 percent discount with purchase of 10,000 units.
	■ 10 percent discount with purchase of 12,000 units.
Cash discounts	■ $2/10$ end of month.
	■ $2/10$ net 30.
Trade discounts	■ 40 percent off to retailers.
	■ 50 percent off to wholesalers.
Consumer discounts	■ 15¢ off regular price marked on product's package.
	■ 10¢-off coupon.

The manufacturer expects channel members to reduce the price from their normal price. A mass merchandiser might normally sell a product with a list price of $2.50 for $1.98. The manufacturer would want salespeople to persuade the retailer to price the product 15¢ lower than the $1.98, or at a price of $1.83.

Cents-off coupons that the consumer brings to the retail store are another example of a temporary price discount. In both the cents-off label and coupon examples, the manufacturer ensures that the price reduction is passed on to the consumer. This occurs because channel members may not have promoted the product or reduced the price, keeping the quantity or off-invoice savings for themselves. The salesperson uses an offer of a cents-off product label and coupons to sell larger quantities to customers. For a summary of discounts and examples of each, see Exhibit B.

Resellers: Markup and Profit

Markup is the dollar amount added to the product cost to determine its selling price. Markup often is expressed as a percentage and represents gross profit, not net profit. **Gross profit** is the money available to cover the costs of marketing the product, operating the business, and profit. **Net profit** is the money remaining after the costs of marketing and operating the business are paid.

Exhibit C presents an example of markup based on a product's selling price for each channel-of-distribution member. Each channel member has a different percentage markup. The product that costs the manufacturer $3 to produce eventually costs the consumer $12. The manufacturer's selling price represents the wholesaler's cost. Price markups enable the wholesaler to pay business operating costs, to cover the product's cost, and to make a profit. The wholesaler's selling price of $6 becomes the retailer's cost. In turn, the retailer marks up the product to cover its cost and the associated costs of doing business (such as stocking the product and allocation of fixed costs per square foot), and to maintain a desired profit level.

The percentage markup is based on either the product's selling price or its cost. It is important to know the method of determining markup. Using the manufacturer's cost of $3, a markup of $2, and a selling price of $5 shown in Exhibit C, the methods of determining percentage markup can have different results:

$$\text{Percentage markup on selling price} = \frac{\text{Amount added to cost}}{\text{selling price}} = \frac{\$2.00}{\$5.00} = 40 \text{ percent}$$

$$\text{Percentage markup on cost} = \frac{\text{Amount added to cost}}{\text{cost}} = \frac{\$2.00}{\$3.00} = 66.6 \text{ percent}$$

Channel members want to buy goods at low prices and establish selling prices at a competitive level that allows for a reasonable profit. Such objectives result in retailers having different markups on different goods. For example, a retailer may have

EXHIBIT C

Example of markup on selling price in channel of distribution.

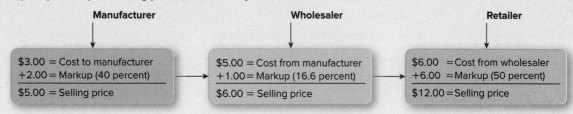

Manufacturer	Wholesaler	Retailer
$3.00 = Cost to manufacturer +2.00 = Markup (40 percent) $5.00 = Selling price	$5.00 = Cost from manufacturer +1.00 = Markup (16.6 percent) $6.00 = Selling price	$6.00 = Cost from wholesaler +6.00 = Markup (50 percent) $12.00 = Selling price

markups of 10 percent on groceries, 30 percent on cameras, and 50 percent on house-ware items. Based on the type of store (discount–high volume; specialty–low volume; department–high service), markups may vary greatly depending on the volume of sales and degree of service rendered.

In preparing the sales presentation for an individual customer, the salesperson should consider all the discounts available to suggest a promotional plan for the retailer. For example, the advertisement shown in Exhibit A illustrates several of the discounts a retailer can receive with the purchase of four decongestants. The salesperson can use these discounts in the sales presentation by suggesting that the retailer advertise the products at a reduced price and place the promotional displays by each of the store's cash registers.

Markup and Unit Price

Sellers, especially consumer goods salespeople, like to talk in terms of the cost and profits earned from an individual unit. However, wholesalers and retailers do not buy one product at a time. Depending on the customer's size, manufacturers may sell resellers several dozens or thousands of dozens at a time. The cost and profits of an individual unit may not be useful for wholesalers, but it becomes extremely important to retailers because their customers buy the product one at a time.

Here is how it works: Assume you are selling a consumer product to a large chain of grocery stores. As shown in Exhibit D, each unit normally costs $1.80 and the retailer sells it for $2.19, 10¢ less than the manufacturer's $2.29 suggested selling price. This gives a normal profit of 39¢, or an 18 percent markup [($2.19 − $1.80 = 39¢); then divide by $2.19 (39¢ ÷ $2.19 = 18 percent)]. Subtracting the 53¢ promotional allowance gives a deal cost of $1.27.

The normal profit, or markup, is 18 percent. If the product is sold at $1.89 for an additional two weeks, the markup reflecting the 53¢ promotional allowance equals 33 percent. If the retailer buys the product and does not reduce the price, the manufacturer is throwing away 53¢ a unit, or $6.36 a dozen.

EXHIBIT D

Example of using unit cost.

Consumer goods salespeople often break down costs and talk of unit costs and profits. Here is the arithmetic one salesperson used in her presentation:

$1.80 = Regular cost of each unit

−.53 = Special promotional allowance

$1.27 = Deal cost

$2.29 = Manufacturer's suggested selling price

$2.19 = Normal retail selling price

18% = Retailer's normal profit ($2.19 − $1.80 = 39¢ markup) (39¢ ÷ $2.19 = 18% markup)

$1.39 = 3-day special price suggested for retailer to advertise product

8.6% = 3-day sale profit margin ($1.39 − $1.27 = 12¢) (12¢ ÷ $1.39 = 8.6% markup)

$1.89 = 2-week special price suggested for in-store promotion

33% = After-sale profit margin ($1.89 − $1.27 = .62) (62¢ ÷ $1.89 = 33% markup)

18% = Normal profit ($2.19 − 1.80 = 39¢) (39¢ ÷ $2.19 = 18%)

The above information (except for the arithmetic in parentheses) was on a sheet of paper with the buyer's company name at the top. The seller showed how the buyer could purchase a large quantity and make 9 percent profit by selling each item for $1.39 instead of the normal $2.19. The retailer's customers save 80¢ ($2.19 − $1.39 = 80¢). After the three-day sale, the retailer increases the price to $1.89 for two weeks and makes 33 percent instead of the 18 percent markup. Some numbers are rounded up.

What are the salesperson's objectives? To have the retailer (1) buy a larger quantity than normal; (2) reduce the price for a three-day $1.39 advertised promotion; and (3) run a two-week, in-store promotion at $1.89. The retailer's sale price of $1.39 would provide an 8.6 percent profit and the $1.89 produces a 33 percent profit margin. The manufacturer, retailer, and the retailer's customers all win in this deal.

Markup and Return on Investment

Consumer goods salespeople also can use return on investment (ROI) in their presentations. **Return on investment (ROI)** refers to an additional sum of money expected from an investment over and above the original investment. ROI is often expressed as a percentage; however, salespeople can also use a dollar return on investment. The information shown in Exhibit E illustrates the actual ROI a salesperson used. Continuing the previous example shown, the salesperson wants the customer to have a three-day advertised special; offer a two-week, in-store price reduction; and buy a large quantity for normal stock. The purchasing agent buys for a chain of 100 grocery stores.

Normally, the chain averages selling 1,500 dozen during a six-week period. The salesperson feels the promotion and price reduction will increase sales to 3,000 dozen (500 + 1,000 + 1,500). As seen in Exhibit E, the salesperson asks the retailer to invest $55,262 ($7,620 + $15,240 + $32,400). Sales are projected to be $70,440 ($8,340 + $22,680 + $39,420) with profits of $15,180 ($720 + $7,440 + $7,020). The retailer's return on investment is 27.5 percent as shown here:

$70,440 = total gross sales
−55,260 = total investment
$15,180 = total gross profit
27.5% = ROI ($15,180 ÷ $55,260)

	3-Day Special	2-Week Special	Normal
Total stores	100	100	100
Deal dates	June 1 through June 30		
Regular cost per dozen	$21.60	$21.60	$21.60
Less allowance (53¢)			
Deal cost per dozen	$15.24	$15.24	$21.60
Feature price	1.39	1.89	2.19[f]
Cases purchased	500[a]	1,000	1,500
Total investment	$7,620[b]	$15,240	$32,400
Total gross sales	$8,340[c]	$22,680	$39,420
Total gross profit	$720[d]	$7,440	$7,020
Return on investment (ROI)	9.0%[e]	49%	22%[g]

[a]5 cases per store
[b]500 × 15.24 = $7,620
[c]500 × 12 = 6,000; 6,000 × $1.39 = $8,340
[d]$8,340 − $7,620 = $720
[e]$720 ÷ $7,620 = 9%
[f]$21.60 12 @ case = $1.80 (regular cost)
[g]$7,020 ÷ $32,400 = 22%

Discounts, payment plans, markups, unit prices, and return on investment are important for salespeople to understand thoroughly. Customers are extremely interested in listening to this information during the salesperson's presentation.

ORGANIZATIONS: VALUE AND ROI

Business salespeople often include a value analysis in the sales presentation. A **value analysis** determines the best product for the money. It recognizes that a high-priced product may sometimes be a better value than a lower-priced product. Many firms routinely review a value analysis before deciding to purchase a product (see Exhibit F).

The value analysis evaluates how well the product meets the buying company's specific needs. It addresses such questions as

- How do your product's features, advantages, and benefits compare to the product currently being used?
- Can your product do the same job as your buyer's present product at a lower price?
- Does the buyer's current equipment perform better than required? (Is equipment too good for present needs?)
- On the other hand, will a higher-priced, better-performing product be more economical in the long run?

As you can see from the examples in this chapter, frequently you must analyze the buyer's present operation carefully before suggesting how your product might improve efficiency, enhance the quality or quantity of the product produced, or save money.

In discussing how to present a value analysis to a buyer, Patrick Kamlowsky, who sells drilling bits for oil and gas wells, said this:

> It's not as simple as it may appear to make a recommendation and have the oil company adhere to it. You must be thorough in the presentation and present the facts in an objective manner. After all, their money is at stake. The presentation must be logical and based on facts that are known; it must be made with as little speculation as possible.
>
> What is difficult is presenting a recommendation to one who has spent 30 or more years in the oil field and has drilled all over the world. I am confronted with the challenge of explaining to this man that the methods he has employed for years may not be the best application where he is currently drilling. The presentation of the recommendation must therefore be thorough and to the point. When talking to him, I do not imply that his method is outdated or wrong, but that I believe I can help him improve his method. To be successful, I must establish two things very quickly—his respect and my credibility. Showing him my proposal and supporting evidence, and permitting him the time to evaluate it, are vital. I don't wish to come on to him too strong, just show him that I genuinely want to help.

EXHIBIT F

This salesperson presents a value analysis to help her customers determine the best buy for their investment.

©Chris Ryan/age fotostock

A salesperson can develop numerous types of value analyses for a prospective buyer. Three types frequently used are (1) product cost versus true value, (2) unit cost, and (3) return on investment.

Compare Product Costs to True Value

All buyers want to know about costs. The value analysis developed for a customer should present cost in a simple, straightforward manner. A product's costs are always relative to something else; thus, cost must be judged in value and results. The base cost of your product should never be the determining factor of the sale. Buying a product based solely on cost could cause a customer to lose money.

Never discuss costs until you have compared them to the *value* of a product. In this manner, the customer intelligently compares the true worth of the proposed investment in your product to its true monetary cost. In effect, a good purchase involves more than initial cost; it represents an investment, and you must demonstrate that what you sell is a good investment.

Exhibit G provides an example of how a salesperson might compare the cost of a copier (Product X) with a competitive copier (Product C). It illustrates how you can demonstrate to a buyer that your product is a better value than one would think from looking only at purchase price. Another value analysis technique is to further break down a product's price to its unit cost.

Unit Costs Break Down Price

One method of presenting a product's true value to a buyer is to break the product's total costs into several smaller units, or the **unit cost.** Assume you sell a computer system that costs $1,000 per month and processes 50,000 transactions each month. The cost per transaction is only 2¢.

Return on Investment Is Listened To

Return on investment refers to an additional sum of money expected from an investment over and above the original investment. Buyers are interested in knowing the percentage return on their initial investment. Since the purchase of many business products is an investment in that it produces measurable results, salespeople can talk about the percentage return that can be earned by purchasing their products.

Again, assume you sell computer equipment requiring a $10,000 per month investment. Benefits to the buyer are measured in hours of work saved by employees, plus the resulting salary savings. First, have the buyer agree on an hourly rate, which

EXHIBIT G

Cost versus value of a small copier.

	Product C	Product X
Initial cost	$2,695	$3,000
Type of paper	Treated paper	Plain paper
Copy speed	12 copies per minute	15 copies per minute
Warm-up time	Instant	Instant
Cost of each copy	3¢ a copy	1¢ a copy
Monthly cost (assuming 10,000 copies)	$300	$100

Conclusion: The difference in the purchase price of the two copiers is $305 ($3,000 − $2,695). Product X saves $200 on monthly copy costs. The savings on monthly copy costs pays for the higher-priced Product X in one and one-half months. In 15 months, savings on the monthly copy equal the purchase price of Product X. Therefore, Product X is less expensive in the long run.

includes fringe benefit cost; let's say salaries average $5 an hour for employees. The hours saved are then multiplied by this hourly rate to obtain the return on investment. If hours saved amounted to 2,800 per month, the savings would be $14,000 per month (2,800 hours × $5 hourly rate). You could develop a table to show the potential return on investment:

> *The more I know, the more I realize the need to know more.*

Value of hours saved	$14,000 per month
Cost of equipment	−10,000 per month
Profit	$ 4,000 per month
Return on investment ($14,000 ÷ $10,000)	140 percent

Subtracting the $10,000 cost per month from the return of $14,000 per month provides a $4,000 a month profit or a 140 percent return on investment. This is taken one step further by considering return on investment after taxes—calculated like this:

$$\frac{\$14,000\,(1 - \text{Tax rate})}{\$10,000}$$

This return on investment presents the buyer with a logical reason to buy. Remember to let the customer make the cost estimates. The buyer must agree with the figures used for this to be effective in demonstrating the real value of buying your product.

KEY TERMS FOR SELLING

cash discounts   196
consumer discounts   196
cumulative quantity
   discounts   195
FOB destination   194
FOB shipping point   194
gross profit   197

list price   194
markup   197
net price   194
net profit   197
noncumulative quantity
   discounts   195

return on investment
   (ROI)   199
trade discounts   196
unit cost   201
value analysis   200
zone price   194

SALES APPLICATION QUESTIONS

1. Many companies offer customers various discounts from their normal or list price to entice them to buy. Discuss the main types of discounts offered.
2. Should the salesperson mention a discount at the beginning, middle, or end of a sales presentation? Why?
3. It cost a company $6 to manufacture a product that it sold for $10 to a wholesaler who sold it to a retailer for $12. A customer of the retailer bought it for $24. What was the markup on selling price for each member of this product's channel of distribution?
4. Determine the markup of a product that costs your customer $1 with the following potential suggested resell prices: $1.25, $1.50, $2. How much profit would the wholesaler or retailer make selling your product at each of the three suggested resell prices?
5. Assume you sell hardware supplies to grocery, drug, and hardware retailers. Tomorrow, you plan to call on the Ace Hardware chain—your largest customer. To reach your sales quota for this year, you must get a large order. You know Ace will buy something; however, you want it to purchase an extra amount. Furthermore,

you know it is 120 days overdue on paying for what you shipped months ago, and your company's credit manager will not ship more merchandise until Ace pays the bill. How would you handle the sales call? Include in your answer where you would discuss the overdue bill problem in your sales presentation. Also include what you would do if the buyer said, "I haven't paid for my last order yet! How can I buy from you today?"

6. List and define five commonly quoted types of prices.

7. The following examples are several types of discounts. In each situation: (*a*) explain what type of discount is used, (*b*) determine by what percentage the *cost* of the product has been reduced, as well as savings per unit, and (*c*) answer other questions asked for each situation.

   a. Bustwell Inc., a regional business computer firm, is attempting to sell a new computer-operated gasoline pump meter to a convenience store chain, Gas 'N' Go. The device will help reduce gasoline theft, give an accurate record of each sale, and aid in determining when Gas 'N' Go should order more gasoline. Gus Gas, of the convenience chain, seems interested in your initial proposal but believes the price may be too high. The cost of each computer is $1,000, but you could sell Gas 50 computers for $45,000. The Gas 'N' Go chain owns 43 stores and is building eight more that will open in about one month.

   b. The Storage Bin Warehouse in your territory has reported a number of break-ins in the past three months. As a salesperson for No-Doubt Security Products, you believe your extensive line of alarm systems and locks could benefit the warehouse greatly. You make an appointment with the manager at the Storage Bin for early next week. During your preparation for the sales call, you discover that the warehouse currently uses poor-quality locks and has no security system. You plan to offer the manager a security package consisting of 150 Sure-Bolt dead-bolt locks (for their 150 private storage rooms) at a price of $10 each and a new alarm system costing $5,000. The terms of the sale are $\frac{2}{10}$ net 30. How would the total cost change if the terms of the alarm system alone were changed to $\frac{5}{10}$ net 30 (and the locks remained $\frac{2}{10}$ net 30)? What is the cost of the security package if the Storage Bin takes 25 days to pay for the purchase?

   c. You are a salesperson for Madcap Arcade Games, selling video games and pinball machines. A local business wants to open an arcade and would like to buy a new game about every two weeks. A new game costs $3,000. You can offer a 5 percent discount (an end-of-year rebate) if at least 25 games are purchased from you during the next year. What will the discount be in dollars?

   d. The XYZ company is having its year-end sales push. As a salesperson for XYZ, a manufacturer of consumer goods like toothpaste, shampoo, and razor blades, you have been instructed to give a "buy 11 get 1 free" discount to half of your accounts. The remainder of your accounts, because of their small volume, are offered 10 percent off on all purchases. Compare the two situations. Which is the better deal?

8. As a salesperson for the Electric Generator Corporation, you have decided to attempt to sell your EG 600 generator to the Universal Construction Corporation. The EG 600 costs about $70,000. You estimate that operating and maintenance costs will average $3,000 a year and that the machine will operate satisfactorily for 10 years. You can offer a $65,000 price to Universal if it purchases 10 to 20 machines. Should it purchase more than 21 machines, the cost would be $58,000 per generator. The generators currently used originally cost $65,000, have a life

of seven years, and cost $5,000 each year to operate. As far as you know, Universal's present supplier cannot offer a quantity discount.

    a. Develop a value analysis table comparing the two generators.

    b. In your presentation, what are the selling points you would stress?

9. Value analysis is an effective sales tool. Define value analysis and describe its use in a selling situation.

STUDENT APPLICATION LEARNING EXERCISES (SALES)

At the end of appropriate chapters beginning with Chapter 3, you will find Student Application Learning Exercises (SALES). SALES are meant to help you construct the various segments of your sales presentation. SALES build on one another so that after you complete them, you will have constructed the majority of your sales presentation.

SALE 2 of 7—Chapter 5

An important part of your presentation is the discussion of price to your buyer. To make **SALE 2,** first review pages 193–202.

Your assignment is to construct one or more pages that show the prices you will discuss with your buyer. This page—or pages—will serve as a visual aid that you show and discuss with your buyer during the business proposition phase of your sales presentation.

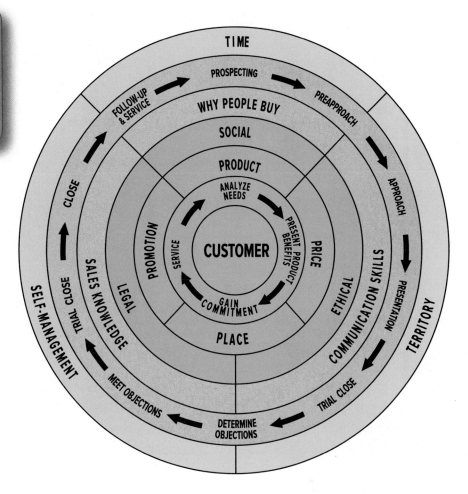

The Relationship Selling Process

We are now prepared to study the selling skills that successful salespeople use. These skills help salespeople find prospects, analyze their needs, create a presentation that emphasizes benefits of the salesperson's products, and show how needs will be fulfilled. Successful salespeople address potential objections in order to gain commitment—in other words, close the sale. They provide exceptional service to earn the privilege of repeating the cycle to help the customer in the long term. These salespeople follow the Core Principles throughout the sales process in order to sell today and build a long-term business friendship.

©Abel Mitja Varela/Getty Images

Prospecting—The Lifeblood of Selling

Main Topics

The Core Principles: Prospecting

The Sales Process Has 10 Steps

Steps Before the Sales Presentation

Prospecting—The Lifeblood of Selling

Prospecting Is an Ongoing Process

Planning a Prospecting Strategy

Prospecting Methods

Prospecting Guidelines

The Referral Cycle

Call Reluctance Costs You Money!

Obtaining the Sales Interview

Applying CRM Technology to Prospecting

How Is Prospecting Changing?

Learning Objectives

Here we begin to discuss the steps within the sales process. This chapter examines the first step—prospecting. After studying this chapter, you should be able to

6–1 Define the sales process, and list and describe its 10 steps in the correct sequence.

6–2 State why it is important to prospect.

6–3 Describe the various prospecting methods.

6–4 Ask for a referral anywhere during the referral cycle.

6–5 Make an appointment with a prospect or customer in person or by telephone or by e-mail.

FACING A SALES CHALLENGE

Joe, a business graduate, and two of his friends, Alex and Kathryn, engineering graduates, participated in a university innovation competition during their last semester in college. Building on the applications of IOT (Internet of Things), they pitched an idea for a home security system. The idea met with such positive feedback, the team started the business the following summer. With much excitement they started developing the business plan. The product was suitable for folks who are not ready for an expensive dedicated security system. Their proposed system lets people monitor their homes including indoor and outdoor security cameras, video doorbells, and smart locks from anywhere using routine gadgets such as a phone or tablet. However, as they moved forward, things were not looking so simple anymore!

All three partners, on a fine Thursday afternoon, sat down for their weekly business planning meeting when Joe said, "Selling a new technology-enabled home security system in our market will not be easy for us. The city has only 45,000 households; the county has 55,000. Yet there are eight or more companies offering home security systems in the area. I'm not sure where to begin."

Kathryn joined the conversation: "Moreover, many homes in the area already have home security systems in place. So, I'm not sure we can count on promoting to them. We're going to have to explore new territories, knock on doors, and dial-for-dollars to even come up with leads."

Alex broke in with, "Let's go after the market leader. They have the biggest market share in our area. We need to hit them head-on."

"No way," replied Joe. "We could get creamed if we got into a war by attacking the biggest competitor or any of our other competitors. But with easy-to-use features," Joe continued, "excellent service and support, and our fair price on a state-of-the-art home security system, we can develop our market share."

"Hold it, hold it," Kathryn said. "Let's start over and develop a plan that will allow us to uncover as many prospects as quickly as we can. After all, we need to push this new product and get the competitive edge before the competition knows what hit 'em."

If you were one of these young entrepreneurs, how would you respond? What would be your sales plan?

The first two parts of this book give much of the background a salesperson needs for making an actual presentation. However, you can be the most knowledgeable person on topics such as buyer behavior, competitors, and product information, yet still have difficulty being a successful salesperson unless you are thoroughly prepared for each part of the sales call. Part III of this book examines the various elements of the sales process and sales presentation. It begins by explaining what the sales process means. Then we discuss methods of prospecting that may help Joe, Alex, and Kathryn plan their sales program.

The Core Principles: Prospecting

Many types of selling require prospecting. Without previous knowledge of who might purchase a product, the salesperson locates individuals and/or organizations that have the money, authority, and the desire to buy. Because people tend to do business with the people they know, and that they feel are honest and ethical, prospecting is not easy. Buying from a stranger is getting harder and harder. People want to trust the person they buy from and they buy from people they know.

All salespeople who begin their sales careers prospecting look forward to the day when most of their sales come from present customers. Frequently, these salespeople gain new customers through referrals from customers. Referrals are earned by demonstrating your integrity, trustfulness, and character to the customer who eventually provides you the referral. Ethical service builds relationships and is based upon the truth.

The Sales Process Has 10 Steps

As discussed in Chapter 1, the **sales process** refers to a sequential series of actions by the salesperson that leads toward the prospect or customer taking a desired action and ends with a follow-up to ensure purchase satisfaction. Although many factors

EXHIBIT 6.1

The selling process has 10 important steps.

may influence how a salesperson makes a presentation in any one situation, a logical, sequential series of actions exists that, if followed, can greatly increase the chances of making a sale. This selling process involves 10 basic steps, as listed in Exhibit 6.1. Step one is discussed in this chapter, and all steps are discussed in greater detail in the following chapters. Before a sales presentation can be attempted, several important preparatory activities should be carried out.

Steps before the Sales Presentation

As indicated in Exhibit 6.2, a successful salesperson begins with prospecting—obtaining an appointment with the prospect and planning the sales interview prior to ever actually meeting with the prospect or customer. Like a successful lawyer, the salesperson does a great amount of background work before meeting the judge—the prospect. One rule of thumb states that a good sales process involves 20 percent presentation, 40 percent preparation, and 40 percent follow-up, especially when selling

EXHIBIT 6.2

Before the sales presentation.

large accounts. However, even that varies from account to account. At Xerox, the national account manager will spend up to 18 months preparing a detailed description of a potential national account. This report, which can easily end up being 50 pages long, is basically a business plan for selling the prospect. Thus preparation time for this sales call would be greater than the 40 percent rule of thumb.[1] As in most professions, success in selling often requires as much or more preparation before and between calls than is involved in actually making the calls themselves.

In Chapter 1 we said, "Nothing happens until someone sells something." However, even selling requires a preceding step: Nothing happens until someone does some prospecting.

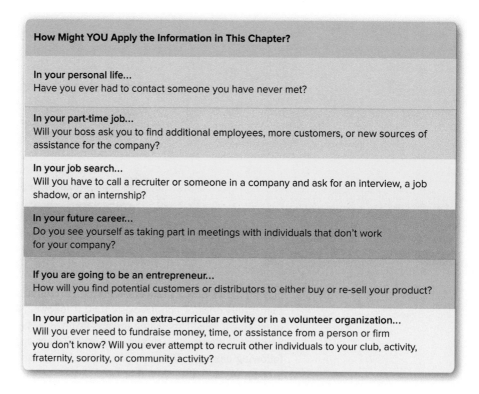

How Might YOU Apply the Information in This Chapter?

In your personal life...
Have you ever had to contact someone you have never met?

In your part-time job...
Will your boss ask you to find additional employees, more customers, or new sources of assistance for the company?

In your job search...
Will you have to call a recruiter or someone in a company and ask for an interview, a job shadow, or an internship?

In your future career...
Do you see yourself as taking part in meetings with individuals that don't work for your company?

If you are going to be an entrepreneur...
How will you find potential customers or distributors to either buy or re-sell your product?

In your participation in an extra-curricular activity or in a volunteer organization...
Will you ever need to fundraise money, time, or assistance from a person or firm you don't know? Will you ever attempt to recruit other individuals to your club, activity, fraternity, sorority, or community activity?

Prospecting—The Lifeblood of Selling

Prospecting is the first step in the selling process. A **prospect** is a qualified person or organization that has the potential to buy your good or service. **Prospecting** is the lifeblood of sales because it identifies potential customers. A salesperson must look constantly for new prospects for two reasons:

1. To increase sales.
2. To replace customers that will be lost over time.

Why Is Prospecting Important to a Business?

Before we delve into the first step in the sales process, let's review why this stage is so important to a business.

As we discussed previously, prospecting aids our firm because it's a source to: (a) increase sales and (b) to replace lost customers. From a business standpoint, developing new customers plays an important role because customers purchase our firm's products and services and thereby create revenue. Revenue is defined as the number of products sold multiplied by the price of the product.

Ultimately a business needs to sell its products and services. Revenue is the key to ensuring the business is an ongoing entity. Therefore, it makes sense that revenue is often called the "topline of the business" as it is the first line on the firm's profit and loss statement and keeps the business running. But why is revenue so important? Revenue is used to fund the organization's strategies and activities. It is often considered the lifeblood of the organization. As you can see in the profit and loss statement (Exhibit 6.3), it is the amount from which everything else, such as expenses and salaries, is subtracted.

Revenue pays for the cost of goods sold (i.e., the materials used to manufacture or provide your firm's products or services); it pays for the ongoing expenses that the organization incurs in conducting business. And most importantly of all, revenue pays for the salaries of everyone in the organization, including the salespeople.

Yet have you ever stepped back and asked, "What or who generates revenue?" Can a product or service by its mere existence generate revenue? We would suggest that salespeople and their activities of locating customers and then developing long-term relationships with these customers help create revenue. Hence, salespeople serve an important role in organizations; they help a firm develop its stream of revenues.

Through prospecting, salespeople secure understanding about a customer and potential business opportunities that could evolve into sales in a later stage. Therefore, it is essential for a salesperson to acknowledge the importance of prospecting. Although the process of prospecting differs across organizations and industries, there are certain key elements that a salesperson learns to identify to enhance the possibility of finding new customers. It is also important to know that finding the prospects is one of the more challenging stages of selling process, especially in the business-to-business selling context. But, with a proper approach, planning and dedicated level of effort, salespeople will find that they can excel at the prospecting phase, similar to other phases of sales.

The Prospecting Process

Step 1: Lead generation and development

For many firms, the first step in the prospecting process lies in developing a list or pool of viable prospects. A **lead** is the person or a firm that has the potential to become a customer. The first step in the prospecting process is to populate a list of leads—that is, to generate a list of names, addresses, e-mail addresses, and other contact information of plausible customers. **Lead generation** focuses on establishing a group of firms and individuals that may be in the target market for your solution (i.e., product or service).

Step 2: Qualifying a Lead

A prospect should not be confused with a lead. The transformation of a lead to a prospect occurs through an evaluation process, called the lead qualification process. The **lead qualification** refers to the steps that the salesperson uses to evaluate the lead. In the qualifying process, the salesperson uses some set of predefined criteria to determine whether the lead possesses an interest in the product as well as an ability to buy

Revenue is often called the "topline of the business" as it is the first line on the firm's profit and loss statement.

Salespeople serve an important role in firms; they help a firm develop its stream of revenues.

Your Business Income Statement For Year Ending Dec. 31, 20xx		
Revenue:		
Gross Sales		0.00
Less: Sales Returns/Allowance		0.00
Net Sales		0.00
Cost of Goods Sold:		
Purchases	0.00	
Delivery Charges	0.00	
Cost of Goods Sold:		0.00
Groos Sales Profit(Loss)		0.00
Expenses:		
Expense #3	0.00	
Expense #4	0.00	
Expense #5	0.00	
Expense #6	0.00	
Expense #7	0.00	
Expense #8	0.00	
Expense #9	0.00	
Expense #10	0.00	
Total Expenses:		0.00
Net Operating Income:		0.00
Other Income:		
Income #2		0.00
Income #3		0.00
Total Other Income:		0.00
Net Income (Loss):		0.00

©Design Pics/Darren Greenwood

As a salesperson, you can ask yourself three questions to determine if an individual or organization is a

QUALIFIED PROSPECT.

the product. The goal of qualifying a lead is to help understand which leads have the potential to truly become a buyer.

For example, let's review a quick example of a basic lead qualification process. A very straightforward approach is to ask yourself the three following questions to determine if an individual or organization (i.e., lead) is a **qualified prospect:**

1. Does the lead have the _m_oney to buy?
2. Does the lead have the _a_uthority to buy?
3. Does the lead have the _d_esire to buy?

A simple way to remember this qualifying process is to think of the word *mad* for *m*oney, *a*uthority, and *d*esire. A true prospect must have the financial resources, money, or credit to pay and the authority to make the buying decision. The prospect also should desire your product. Sometimes an individual or organization may not recognize a need for your product. Once the lead has been qualified, it becomes a prospect.[2]

Lead Qualification and Lead Scoring The qualifying process assists salespeople to understand which group of lead holds the greatest potential to become customers. Often, firms use a **lead scoring system** as part of their lead qualifying process. In very basic terms, a lead scoring system grades each lead based on a range of criteria. The lead scoring system (a) helps salespeople understand which leads become prospects and (b) categorizes prospects into groups. Depending on the firm, these classifications might be presented as

1. Points on scale. Each prospect would receive an overall score from 1 to 100.
2. Categories, such as letters: A, B, C, D. The group of prospects with the greatest likelihood to purchase would be placed in the A category.
3. Classifications, such as platinum, gold, and silver. The group of prospects with the greatest likelihood to purchase would be placed in the platinum category.

As you can see, the categories of a lead scoring help the salesperson in: (a) prioritizing their efforts and (b) focusing upon the prospects that have the greatest potential to purchase. They help the salesperson prioritize which prospects to initially cultivate.

Locating leads and qualifying prospects are important activities for salespeople. Take, for example, technology salesperson Matt Suffoletto's comments on prospecting:

> Prospecting is the process of acquiring basic demographic knowledge of potential customers for your product. Lists that are available from many vendors break down businesses in a given geography by industry, revenue, and number of employees. These lists can provide an approach to mass marketing, via either mailings or telephone canvassing. That canvassing is either done by the salesperson or through an administrative sales support person. No matter who performs the canvas or how it is done, it is an important element in increasing sales productivity. The next step of qualifying the potential customer is often included in the prospecting process. Qualification is a means of quickly determining two facts. First, is there a potential need for your product? Second, is the prospect capable of making a purchase decision? Specifically, does he or she have the decision authority and the financial ability to acquire your product?

Prospecting Is an Ongoing Process

It is also important to know that finding prospects is a continuous process, even for established companies and experienced salespeople. Obtaining new customers and selling more products to present customers are the ways to increase sales revenue.

Customer attrition—the loss of customers over time—also creates a critical need for prospecting. In the United States, companies are expected to have attrition rates of 20 percent (on average). In Europe, the customer attrition rate goes up to 30 percent per year. In many instances, customer attrition is not controllable. For example, customers may believe a competitor's services create more value; some customers may literarily go out of business; and other customers may merge or be acquired and no longer need the salesperson's services. That means, most firms are always prospecting.

Planning a Prospecting Strategy

Frequently salespeople, especially new ones, have difficulty prospecting. Meeting strangers and asking them to buy something can be uncomfortable for people. Many salespeople prefer to see others who have characteristics similar to their own—although in most cases, the similarity need not go this far!

Identifying prospects is one of the more challenging stages of the selling process, and the process of prospecting differs across organizations, industries, and selling context as shown in Exhibit 6.4. Nonetheless, the overall goal is to identify and enhance the possibility of finding new customers.

To be successful, prospecting requires a strategy. Prospecting, like other activities, is a skill that can be constantly improved by a dedicated salesperson. Some salespeople charge themselves with finding X number of prospects per week. Indeed, Xerox asks its sales force to allocate a portion of each working day to finding and contacting several new prospects. A successful salesperson continually evaluates prospecting methods, comparing results and records with the mode of prospecting used in pursuit of a prospecting strategy that will result in the most effective contact rate.[3]

Prospecting Methods

The actual method by which a salesperson obtains prospects may vary. Exhibit 6.5 shows several of the more popular prospecting methods.

EXHIBIT 6.4

Prospecting strategy depends upon the type of industry, organization, and selling context.

Let's Compare

B2B Prospecting	B2C Prospecting
In the technology sector... You or a marketing representative may develop content on certain subjects that may interest potential prospects. This may include e-books, white papers, and newsletters. When a firm or individual downloads these items, it provides an opportunity for a follow-up email or phone call.	**In some areas, such as financial services...** Some firms may ask that you lead seminars on topics, such as financial planning. In some firms, you may be asked to reach out to family and friends first and parlay these acquaintances into referrals of other prospects.
In the medical sector... You may ask an existing client, such as a purchasing manager, for a referral with one of her colleagues.	**In some areas, such as banking...** You may attend and become active in civic organizations and banking to meet other individuals and create networks and awareness of you, personally, and your firm's services.
In some industries... You may be tasked with a pregenerated list of firms that meet certain qualifications. Your goal may be to find a decision maker that would be willing to discuss with you or another representative your product or service.	

EXHIBIT 6.5

Prospecting methods that work!

Prospecting is the lifeblood of selling. While some salespeople don't have to prospect, most rely on prospecting to increase sales and make money. Here are 13 popular methods:

- Prospecting on the Web
- Cold canvassing
- Endless chain customer referrals
- Orphaned customers
- Sales lead clubs
- Prospect lists
- Getting published

- Public exhibitions and demonstrations
- Center of influence
- Direct mail
- Telemarketing
- Observation
- Networking

Which methods use referrals from customers and other people?

Prospecting on the Web

The most recent advancement in prospecting is the use of the Internet to find and learn about potential buyers. This is a fast and easy way to find information about individuals or businesses by using technology.

E-mail Marketing

In order to generate leads, firms may purchase lists of potential contacts, including their e-mail addresses. Then, the firm e-mails opportunities, offers, and invitations to potential customers. If the e-mail garners interest, the customer may respond to the firm. The salesperson then contacts the lead.

Social Media Platforms

The most recent advancement in prospecting is the use of social media tools and platforms such as LinkedIn, Facebook, and others to find potential buyers. Social media platforms provide great opportunities to learn about potential customers, their firms, and their decision makers. For example, a salesperson working in the construction industry can learn that a civil engineering company has secured a large account via the search updates feature in LinkedIn. At this point, the salesperson may decide to send a congratulatory note to the engineering firm and also initiate a communication regarding a new product line for the construction industry that the company may find useful. In another instance, a salesperson working at a pharmaceutical firm can reach out to social network connections and promote business by tweeting deals and promotions that may generate some interest among connections.

Also, salespeople could utilize social media to communicate product and service reviews and showcase testimonials to enhance their credibility. Salespeople should join LinkedIn groups that have a common interest within an industry or area of interest. In this way, they may start a discussion topic that is pertinent to the group or join an existing discussion. In some instances, the salesperson may have information that can assist in the discussion and therefore post a pertinent link to access the firm's website, a white paper, or recent content. When the interested group members visit the information and download it, they complete a form to access the data. This form provides you with their respective contact information.

Online Events

To generate interest and create awareness of their products and services, many firms offer online events. This may include webinars, demonstrations, insight on trends, or easily accessible on-demand videos. It is important to note that such events may create a variety and depth of customer information on the leads. However, the key for the salesperson is to prioritize the information in a method that can be readily acted upon.

When developing online events such as a webinar, it's important to be customer focused and work diligently to make sure the webinar is perceived as valuable to the attendees. For example, a salesperson working for a company that sells technology services may use webinars to generate leads. That being said, the salesperson should be well versed in the technology and its application in a customer setting. To demonstrate credibility, the salesperson should be able to answer questions that may get asked during the webinar. It is also a smart move to make yourself available via social media platforms and e-mail after the webinar to answer additional questions. This way, a salesperson could continue the conversation with webinar attendees. However, it's probably not advisable to sell the product during the webinar. Instead, view the webinar as an opportunity to focus on issues and solutions that are important to your prospects.

Cold Canvassing

The **cold canvass prospecting method** is based on the law of averages. For example, if past experience reveals that 1 person out of 10 will buy a product, then 50 sales calls could result in five sales. Thus, the salesperson contacts in person, by phone, and/or by mail as many leads as possible, recognizing that a certain percentage of people approached will buy. There is generally no knowledge about the individual or business the salesperson calls on. This form of prospecting relies solely on the volume of cold calls made.

The salesperson building a new customer base often employs cold canvass prospecting. For example, a home security salesperson may be given responsibility for a new geographic area. In this instance, canvassing may mean visiting neighborhoods and introducing herself and her firm's services. In industries such as third party logistics providers, the salesperson may cold-call small and medium-sized businesses to introduce the firm and its shipping services. Many office supply salespeople do the same thing, going from one business to another. Real estate, insurance, and stock brokerage firms are other businesses that use cold calls.

Endless Chain Customer Referral

Cold calling is tough! Contacting strangers day after day is challenging even for the most motivated individuals. Yet many new salespeople have to begin their sales careers cold calling to get customers. Once someone is sold, the salesperson has two possibilities for future sales.

First, satisfied customers are likely to buy again from the salesperson. That is why we stress the importance of building a relationship with the customer. It is critical to your success. Second, the customer often refers the salesperson to someone she knows. This is known as the **endless chain referral method** of prospecting. This is a very effective method for finding customers. *Customers* and *customer referrals* are the two best sources of future sales, with repeat sales from customers being better. A **referral** is a person or organization recommended to you by someone who feels that this person or organization could benefit from you or your product.

Don't ask current customers, "Do you know anyone else who could use my product?" Rarely are clients eager to judge whether colleagues are prepared to make a purchase. Instead, ask whether your customer knows any other individuals or organizations that might be interested in finding out about your product.

Customers and customer referrals are your future.

If you sense hesitation from customers to give out referrals, it's probably because they are afraid that their associates may not want to be pestered. Say, "Let me tell you what I'm going to do with any names you give me. I will make one phone call to each party, indicate that you were nice enough to give me their names, and give them a brief outline of what we do. If they express an interest, we will get together and I will give them the same professional service I've given you. If, on the other hand, they express no interest, I will thank them for their time and never call them again." This approach puts your customers at ease and moves solid, new prospects onto your lead list.

Don't forget that your prospects are friends, neighbors, relatives—anyone and everyone you know or come into contact with. They may know people who are looking for your product and the great service you provide your customers. Everyone is a prospect!

Orphaned Customers

Orphaned **customers** are customers whose salesperson has left the company. Salespeople often leave their employers to take other jobs; when they do, their customers are orphaned. These orphans are great prospects. A salesperson should quickly contact such customers to begin developing relationships. You can turn orphans into a lead-generating gold mine.

In addition, if you've been selling for a while, you've surely built up a backlog of inactive accounts. Weed out the names who for whatever reason will never buy. The rest are solid prospects. Call them again and find out why they're not buying from you anymore. What would it take to change that? They may have stopped ordering your type of product altogether, or they may have gone with a competitor because of a special one-time offer, or there may have been a management change and therefore a change in buying patterns. You have to determine why the customer stopped buying from you. After you do that, reestablishing contact and turning that prospect into a customer again is *standard sales procedure.*

Sales Lead Clubs

Organize a group of salespeople in related but noncompetitive fields to meet twice a month to share leads and prospecting tips. To get started, write a formal mission statement, charge dues to ensure commitment, and grant membership to only one salesperson from each specific field. Next, set up administrative procedures and duties to keep the club on track and committed to its stated mission.

Finally, establish guidelines for what constitutes a good lead, and track prospect information and effectiveness. Group the leads by effectiveness so members can better understand which leads can help the rest. You may even have every member who closes a lead contribute to a kitty. Each month the winner can be the member who provided the most closed leads.

Prospect Lists

Make a list of what your ideal prospect looks like. This may differ depending whether you are targeting individuals (households) or businesses. Ask yourself the following questions:

- Who are my ideal prospects?
- What is their economic bracket (household) or business size (revenue, profits or employees) do they usually fall into?
- What kinds of organizations (household) or industries (business) do they belong to?
- What characteristics do most of my existing customers share?
- What changes, transitions, trends are they potentially confronting?

- Do they have children (household) or how many employees do they employ (businesses)?
- Do they use certain technologies, systems or processes?
- Do they have similar occupations, educations, hobbies, illnesses, transportation needs, or family concerns (household) or belong to certain trade organizations and groups (businesses)?

And the key question:

- Where am I most likely to find the greatest conglomeration of people or businesses who fit my prospect's profile?

List Number One. Take the information you have accumulated and apply it. Go to the library and look up the Standard Industrial Classification (SIC) code number for your ideal prospects' businesses. Ask a librarian for help if you need it. Every type of business has a specific SIC code. Related industries have similar numbers; scan the directory to locate the numbers that fit the profile. This should provide you with an excellent prospect list. In addition, literally hundreds of other business directories can help you generate lists based on corporate profiles.

List Number Two. What kinds of publications do your ideal prospects likely read? Find out whether these publications sell lists of subscribers. If a publication's readership matches your prospect profile well enough, this list should be well worth the cost.

List Number Three. A number of firms sell lists. These companies offer a variety of criteria that you can use to generate a quality prospect list. Dun & Bradstreet is an example of such a company. For your convenience, the information may even be available online.

Getting Published

Although you may give away your services as a writer for free, the residual benefits make your efforts well worth the time. Submit articles about your field or industry to journals, trade magazines, newspapers, and social media sites, such as LinkedIn. You, or a team of your colleagues, can develop and maintain a blog in the format of an online journal. Such blogs are useful for writing opinions, educating prospects, and initiating discussions regarding your product and its usefulness. Your submissions or blogs don't have to be glossy and expensive; just fill them with information that people can genuinely use, then make sure you have no spelling or grammatical mistakes. Instead of getting paid, ask the publication to include your address and telephone number at the end of the article and to write a little blurb about your expertise.

By demonstrating your knowledge and expertise in your field, you can enhance your credibility in your potential prospects' eyes. Once prospects think of you as a credible expert, you may be the one they contact when they're ready to buy. In addition, prospects who call you for advice can come to depend on you and your product. Thus, you attract prospects without having to go out prospecting.

Research Publications and Insights

In some industries, firms create e-books, white papers, executive summaries, or research overviews that provide useful and timely insights into the customers' industries, consumers, processes, and technology. In this area, the firm and salesperson's goal is to develop credibility, disseminate knowledge, and position the firm as a resource and knowledge broker for potential customers.

The short answer: Customers often have distinct needs.

For the salesperson, this means that your solution may not always be suitable for every business or every industry. It is important to remember that a greater number of leads may not always be better for the company. The time that a salesperson invests with an ill-qualified lead—that does not convert into a customer—consumes financial resources. Unqualified leads also result in frustration and missed opportunities for salespeople.

Relatedly, a highly qualified lead means an opportunity for revenue for the firm and a greater return on the salesperson's time investment.

As a salesperson, your goal is to find the segments, or groups of prospects, that you can best assist. Simply put, the salesperson must ask herself, "Which group of customers can I provide the most value for?" As such, a reliable method to qualify leads into prospects is an important step in this process.

Public Exhibitions and Demonstrations

Exhibitions and demonstrations frequently take place at trade shows and other types of special interest gatherings. Many times, related firms sponsor a booth at such shows and staff it with one or more salespeople.[4] As people walk up to the booth to examine the products, a salesperson has only a few minutes to qualify leads and get names and addresses in order to contact them later at their homes or offices for demonstrations. Although salesperson–buyer contact is usually brief, this type of gathering gives a salesperson extensive contact with a large number of potential buyers over a brief time. Remember, however, that success at trade shows stems from preparation. Here are several things to do:

- Set up an interesting display to get people's attention. A popcorn machine, local celebrity, or inexpensive giveaway are good ideas.
- Write down your message so that it fits on the back of a business card.
- Practice communicating two or three key points that get your message across succinctly. Get it down pat but don't memorize your sales pitch to make it sound overly canned.
- Make a list of the major buyers at the show you want to pursue for contacts.
- Set up to maximize your display's visibility based on the flow of traffic.
- Be assertive in approaching passersby. Instead of the common "Hello" or "How are you?" try "Do you use [product or service] in your operations?" or "Have you seen [product or service]? If I can show you how to be more profitable, would you be interested?" Next offer them a sample to handle, but not to keep. Don't let them take the item and move on without talking to you.
- Use lead cards to write down prospect information for efficient and effective postshow follow-up.
- Be prepared for rejection. Some buyers will ignore you. Don't take it personally. Be brief but professional. Your time is too valuable to waste on nonprospects.
- Become part of an expert panel or deliver a presentation during the trade show, as these can give a salesperson credibility and exposure to an even broader audience. An effective participation in a trade show may create a buzz for the

MAKING THE SALE

Successful Selling Secrets:
Vikki Morrison

There are no secrets to successful selling. There is only hard work from 7:00 in the morning to 10:00 at night. The biggest secret is total honesty at all times with all parties. You should act with integrity and treat clients with the same respect you want from them.

"Never call clients with anything but calm assurance in your voice, because if they feel you are panicked, they will become panicked. Your walk, speech, mannerisms, and eye-to-eye contact say more about you than you'll ever know, so practice all forms of your presentation every day in every way. I suppose a secret is to save the best house for last. I just try to do the best job for the client, even when it means turning them over to another agent who would have a more suitable property in a different area."

Morrison does not work alone; she uses her available resources in selling. A computer terminal in her office gives her up-to-date information on listings and an analysis of proposed transactions. She personally employs three assistants to help her keep up with the listings and shoppers. Vikki Morrison knows the value of the real estate in her area and can give free market analysis with less than one hour's notice.

"An important part of my job is providing customers personal service via constant follow-up, before the appointment, during, and after the sale. I have periodic follow-ups to see how they like their new home or investments. Anniversary flowers and cards on their birthday are a specialty of mine. I try to eliminate any and all of their buying fears when I can and be available to reassure them.

"I sell on emotional appeal. No matter what the facts, most people still buy based on emotion. The triggers for someone's emotional side can be quite varied. For example, for some men, their families are their hot button; for others, the greed appeal of a good deal is more important. Every person is different and should be handled as the very important individual that they are.

"Another factor in my selling is that I care about my clients. They know it, I know it, and they feel it when I'm working with them and long after the escrow is closed. These people are my good friends and we have fun together."

salesperson's product but that interest could fade away in a short time as your prospect gets in touch with many suppliers and sales reps during the trade show. Therefore, it is critical for you to follow up quickly to reap the benefits.

Center of Influence

Prospecting via the **center of influence method** involves finding and cultivating people in a community or territory who are willing to cooperate in helping to find prospects. They typically have a particular position that includes some form of influence over other people, as well as information that allows the salesperson to identify good prospects. For example, a person who graduates from college and begins work for a local real estate firm might contact professors and administrators at his alma mater to obtain the names of teachers who have taken a job at another university and are moving out of town. He wants to help them sell their homes.

Clergy, salespeople who are selling noncompeting products, officers of community organizations like the chamber of commerce, and members of organizations such as the Lions Club or a country club are other individuals who may function as a center of influence. Be sure to show your appreciation for this person's assistance. Keeping such influential persons informed on the outcome of your contact with the prospect helps to secure future aid.

Direct Mail

In cases where there are a large number of prospects for a product, **direct-mail prospecting** is sometimes an effective way to contact individuals and businesses. Direct-mail advertisements have the advantage of contacting large numbers of people, who may be spread across an extended geographical area, at a relatively low cost when compared to the cost of using salespeople. People who request more information from the company subsequently are contacted by a salesperson.

Telemarketing

Telemarketing is a marketing communication system using telecommunication technology and trained personnel to conduct planned, measurable marketing activities directed at targeted groups of consumers. The internal process of a telemarketing center is shown in Exhibit 6.6. For some telemarketing campaigns, the salesperson makes outbound calls. The salesperson is provided a list of potential prospects or utilizes dialing technology, in which a computer and telephony system are integrated. The system provides a list of prospects and begins dialing them. Once someone answers, the system alerts the salesperson. The salesperson takes the call. After the call, the system allows the salesperson to track the results.

In other instances, firms attempt to incentive consumers to call into their call center. Potential customers may also take it upon themselves to call your firm. How might this happen? Firms often place their phone numbers on their websites, e-mails, or white papers. As the customer reads this information, they become more and more interested and seek out additional information. Firms are also enabling their mobile apps with click-to-call abilities; and phone numbers are begin placed on advertisements using Google AdWords. This allows quick access to a live information source and expertise and enables the lead generation process. Another means by which to initiate telemarketing ventures is by featuring an 800 phone number in print, Internet, or television advertisements. When the viewer or reader responds, the call comes into a call center and a trained specialist handles it. This person may take an order (in the case of a telephone call) or transfer the person to a telephone selling or teleselling unit. The specialist may provide information or service. The specialist also can determine whether the customer has sufficient potential to warrant a face-to-face sales call. The duties of a telemarketing specialist are based

EXHIBIT 6.6

The processing system within a telemarketing center.

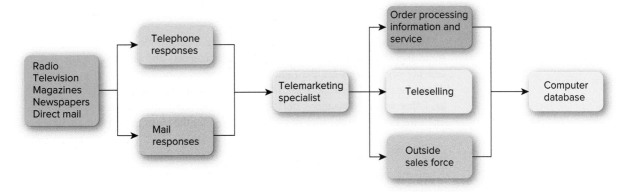

on the type of product being sold and to whom it is sold. As you probably have experienced, telemarketers tend to rely on memorized or formula selling, which tends to be a much more structured conversation in which the buyer does 70 percent or more of the talking. You will learn more about the types of sales presentation in Chapter 7.

Teleprospecting

As relational selling continues to evolve, many firms are adopting an approach named teleprospecting, as an element within their lead generation process. **Teleprospecting** could be described as a process to qualify a prospect and to determine if an organization is the right fit for their product. Hence, it often involves a number of calls and discussions with the lead. Unlike telemarketing, teleprospecting applies critical sales behaviors, such as listening and attempting to diagnose customer needs rather than using a script.[5] In many instances, teleprospecting requires more sales training than what is traditionally provided to a telemarketer, as the assessment of business needs and the communication of potential options is required for success.

Like direct marketing, use of **telephone prospecting** to contact a large number of prospects across a vast area is far less costly than use of a canvassing sales force, though usually more costly than mailouts.[6] This person-to-person contact afforded by the telephone allows for interaction between the lead and the caller—enabling a lead to be quickly qualified or rejected.

A firm's marketing and sales departments may collaborate to develop a list of targeted leads. While the potential customers may not be expecting a call from the teleprospector, the background research assists the teleprospector in generating greater levels of customer interest and attention than conventional telemarketing processes. In other instances, the lead may have requested more information or made direct contact with the selling firm through a website or other response method. In this example, the teleprospector generates a "warm-call" because the prospect is already aware of the product and has demonstrated interest in learning more about it.

Inside Sales

Due to the cost of face-to-face interactions, many firms are seeking more cost-effective means of enabling the customer–salesperson interaction. As such, firms are centralizing many elements of their sales force. Rather than have a national canvassing sales force, firms introduce inside sales centers that focus on working remotely with customers from a regional or national headquarters.[7]

This trend continues to increase due to the enhanced quality of technology such as telephony, web conferencing, and webinars. As such, the salesperson's skill sets must expand beyond simply using the phone. Today's inside sales representatives must be able to leverage a wide range of technology—whether it is the phone, webinars, web conferencing, or video demonstrations.

While many inside sales centers have salespeople with the full range of sales skills, some also employ lead specialists who qualify prospects and determine if the customer and her organization are the right fit for the salesperson's solution. If the prospect is deemed viable, the lead specialist transfers the customer to an inside sales account specialist. Other sales organizations start the sales conversation through an inside sales rep to make the process more efficient (and less costly) for the buyer as well as the selling firm.

Observation

A salesperson often can find prospects by constantly watching what is happening in the sales area—the **observation method.** Office furniture, computer, and copier salespeople look for new business construction in their territories. New families moving into town are excellent leads for real estate and insurance salespeople. No matter what prospecting method you use, you must always keep your eyes and ears open for information on who needs your product.

Networking

For many salespeople, prospecting never ends. They are always on the lookout for customers. Everyone they meet may be a prospect, or that person may provide a name that could lead to a sale. The term given to making and using contacts is **networking.**

Of the many ways to find new prospects, networking can be the most reliable and effective. People want to do business with, and refer business to, people they know, like, and trust. The days of the one-shot salesperson are over; the name of the game today is relationship building.

Building a network is important, but cultivating that network brings sales. The key is positioning, not exposure. The goal of cultivating your network is to fill a niche in the mind of each of your contacts so when one of those contacts, or someone he or she knows, needs your type of product or service, you are the *only* possible resource that would come to mind.

Here are several tips for cultivating your network to dramatically increase your referral business:

1. Focus on meeting *center-of-influence* people. These people have established a good reputation and have many valuable contacts. A few places to find the key people in your industry are trade association meetings, trade shows, or any business-related social event.
2. Ninety-nine percent of your first conversation with a networking prospect should be about his or her business. People want to talk about *their* business, not yours.
3. Ask open-ended, feel-good questions like "What do you enjoy most about your industry?"
4. Be sure to ask, "How would I know if someone I'm speaking with would be a good prospect for you?" If you're on the lookout to find this person new business, he will be more inclined to do the same for you.
5. Get a networking prospect's business card. It's the easiest way to follow up with your new contact.
6. Send a handwritten thank-you note that day: "It was nice meeting you this morning. If I can ever refer business your way, I certainly will."
7. When you read newspapers and magazines, keep the people in your network in mind. If you find an article one of your contacts could use or would enjoy, e-mail it.
8. Stay on your contacts' minds by sending them something every month; notepads with your name and picture are perfect. They will keep these pads on their desks and be constantly reminded of you and your product or service.
9. Send leads. The best way to get business and referrals is to give business and referrals.
10. Send a handwritten thank-you note whenever you receive a lead, regardless of whether it results in a sale.

When meeting someone, tell her what you sell. Ask what she does. Exchange business cards and periodically contact the person. Eventually, you may build a network of people talking to each other, sharing ideas, and exchanging information. Also, you can use several of the previously discussed methods of prospecting, such as the endless chain and center of influence methods, to build your network.

Don't wait for your ship to come in . . . swim out to it.

Prospecting Guidelines

Like many other components of the selling process, prospecting methods should be chosen in light of the major factors defining a particular selling situation. As in most other optional situations discussed in this book, there is no one optimal mode of prospecting to fit all situations. Generalizations can be made, however, regarding the criteria used in choosing an optimal prospecting method for a particular selling situation. Three criteria you should use in developing the best prospecting method require you to take these actions:

1. *Customize* or choose a prospecting method that fits the specific needs of your individual firm. Do not copy another company's method; however, it's all right to adapt someone's method.
2. Concentrate on *high-potential* customers first, leaving for later prospects of lower potential.
3. Always *call back* on prospects who did not buy. With new products, do not restrict yourself to present customers only. A business may not have purchased your present products because they did not fit their present needs; however, your new product may be exactly what they need.

Always keep in contact with your prospects and customers to help them solve problems through the purchase of your product. Only in this way can you maximize your long-term sales and income.

Referrals Used in Most Prospecting Methods

Referrals can be directly used in (1) cold canvassing, (2) endless chain customer referrals, (3) orphaned customers, (4) sales lead clubs, (5) public exhibitions and demonstrations, (6) centers of influence, (7) telephoning, and (8) networking. Eight of the thirteen popular prospecting methods directly ask someone if he or she knows others who might be interested in their product.

Many salespeople using these methods are reluctant to ask for referrals. Yet if they would, sales would increase. Try it! If done correctly, people will give referrals. Here are some ideas on getting referrals to increase your prospect pool.

The Prospect Pool

Referrals come from prospects. Different sources of prospects form the prospect pool. The **prospect pool** is a group of names gathered from various sources. Your source, for example, may be a mailing list, telephone book, referrals, orphans, or existing customers. As Exhibit 6.7 shows, a prospect pool is usually created from four main sources.[8]

1. *Leads*—people and organizations you know nothing, or very little, about.
2. *Referrals*—people or organizations you frequently know very little about other than what you learned from the referral.
3. *Orphans*—company records provide your only information about these past customers.
4. *Your customers*—the most important prospects for future sales.

Most salespeople required to create customers through prospecting do not like to cold call. They have the goal of a prospect pool composed of customers, referrals, and, when available, orphans. The secret to reaching this goal is the referral cycle.

EXHIBIT 6.7

Components of the prospect pool.

The Referral Cycle

Obtaining referrals is a continuous process without beginning or end. The salesperson is always looking for the right opportunity to find a referral. The **referral cycle** provides guidelines for a salesperson to ask for referrals in four commonly faced situations, as shown in Exhibit 6.8.

If you have a sales presentation at 10 a.m., you can begin the referral cycle in the presentation phase. If you are delivering a product to a client, you can start the cycle in the product delivery phase. If you are planning to make telephone calls to leads, referrals, orphans, or customers tonight, you can begin in the preapproach phase.

Regardless of where you are in the referral cycle, you can begin at that point. Perfect your techniques so that you will be working on every phase of the cycle simultaneously. Direct any contact with the prospect toward presenting yourself and your product in such a way as to overcome any objections you could face later when asking for referrals and, of course, when making a sale.

The Parallel Referral Sale

Salespeople must sell the product, plus sell the prospect on providing referrals. This is known as the **parallel referral sale.** Equal emphasis must be given to both the product sale and the referral sale. You must nurture a parallel referral sale from the time of the initial contact, such as when making an appointment. The referral sale should receive equal importance, effort, and emphasis as the product sale. This is the key to the referral cycle.

The Secret Is to Ask Correctly

Many salespeople do not ask for referrals. If they do ask, they often do so infrequently and incorrectly. Understand that if others—even customers—never had objections to

EXHIBIT 6.8

The referral cycle: when to ask for referrals.

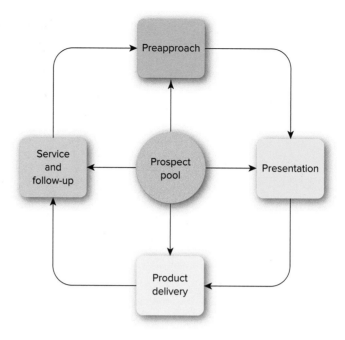

giving referrals there would be no problem in getting them. A salesperson could simply ask for referrals and live happily ever after. Unfortunately, this is not the case. Here are examples of why some clients may not wish to give referrals:

- Clients are afraid of upsetting friends and relatives.
- Clients do not want friends to think they're talking about them.
- Clients may believe in the product but not in the salesperson.
- Clients fear the salesperson may not be around years down the road.
- Clients do not feel they can benefit from giving the salesperson referrals.

It is absolutely essential that you consider these objections when asking for referrals. By doing so, you will obtain more referrals, get more appointments, and make more sales.

When to Ask

Properly asking for referrals can greatly improve a person's sales. Sounds simple, doesn't it? All one needs to do is ask others for referrals. It's simple, but not as simple as it first sounds. It is important to ask professionally at each phase of the referral cycle.

The Preapproach

Great care must be taken during the preapproach contact phase of the referral cycle. Whether the initial contact is face-to-face or via telephone, the effectiveness of your approach will be the deciding factor in determining whether you are given the opportunity to make a sales presentation.

Many prospects will hang up the phone as soon as they suspect an attempt is being made to sell them something. If, in the first several seconds, you fail to overcome their initial feelings of discomfort and intrusion, your chances of developing a relationship are slim.

Mentioning that a firm or business acquaintance of theirs recommended that you call helps alleviate some of the initial anxiety in dealing with quick objections. This is one of the reasons why working on referrals is so effective. Certainly, people are willing to listen a bit longer if they know a person they trust is the reason for this personal contact. Here's an example:

> Hello, is this John? . . . Hi, John, my name is Charles Futrell from Merrill Lynch. George and Barbara Smith are clients of mine. I met with them last week and helped them set up their retirement program. They were really pleased with both my products and service. *And since I work primarily through referrals,* they were kind enough to mention that you might be interested in learning about the value I have to offer.
>
> I'd like to set up a time to stop by your home or office and share some ideas that you may find of great benefit. *It's not really important to me that we do business;* all I ask is if you appreciate the time we share together, if you feel that you benefit from the time we spend together, and, most important, if you respect my integrity, *you would be willing to pass my name on to a friend or business associate who may also benefit from my services,* just as George and Barbara did. Is that fair enough?

> *The harvest can be bountiful, but people who will ask are few.*

We have begun the process of selling the prospect—and hopefully the customer—on giving us one or more referrals. We are telling John that it is not important for me to make a sale. We are asking if he feels it is reasonable, if and only if he is happy with me, that he pass my name on just as his friends did. It is easy for John to answer yes. I have presented my offer in a nonthreatening manner that was endorsed by his friends George and Barbara.

To say "It's not really important to me that we do business" is very unusual. People are not accustomed to hearing a salesperson say that it is not important to make a sale.

The Presentation

Depending on the particular industry you represent, the situation in which you present your product for sale may be called by a variety of names. It could be a meeting, appointment, interview, or presentation. Hereafter, we refer to it as the *presentation*.

During the presentation you have the greatest opportunity to influence your prospect. It is important to understand that your prospect will scrutinize everything you say and do, whether it be through words, expressions, or body language. During this presentation you also must be conscious of presenting your desire to get referrals.

The presentation phase of the referral cycle actually begins when you sit down with your prospects for the purpose of making a sales presentation. As comfortably as possible, you should make a conscious effort to mention the referring person. This may be a remark as simple as "George told me that you like to golf. Did you get a chance to get out this week?" or "Barbara mentioned that you like to garden. Did the last frost we had affect your plants at all?"

This initial contact plants the seed for the beginning of the parallel referral sale. During the next 10 or 15 minutes there should be no discussion about the product or service being offered. This time is best used to build rapport and help break down any barriers between the prospects and their perception of you as a salesperson. To accelerate this process you should mention the referring person as often as possible. It is easy to tell when the barriers begin to come down. The walls of resistance have fallen when you begin to feel comfortable with your prospects. If you do not feel comfortable with your prospects, they certainly will not feel comfortable with you.

Once you establish rapport, you should take a moment to explain to your prospects what will occur during the time you will be together. It doesn't matter what good or service you are selling; this approach should be used regardless. Then when appropriate, mention the referrals. Here are two examples:

> John and Nonnie, if you're happy with my service, I hope you will be willing to pass my name on to other people who would appreciate the same honesty and integrity I have extended to you. I don't do this because I'm a good person, I do it because it makes good business sense. If I take care of you, you'll take care of me. And my livelihood depends on getting referrals. My success and the success of my business is totally dependent on getting quality referrals from my client. I realize that you will introduce me to your friends, family, and business associates only if the quality and integrity of the service I provide surpasses that to which you've grown accustomed. This I pledge.

Product Delivery

Almost every selling profession has some type of product delivery phase. The delivery phase is more obvious with some products than others. For example, in the life insurance industry it involves the agent physically handing the policy to the client. In real estate, it would be the day the sale closes on the home or property. With computers, it would be the day that the system is installed and usable. In advertising, it would be the day that the ad runs in the publication. Automobile buyers go to the dealership or have the salesperson deliver the vehicle to them. Whatever your profession, you should identify the precise moment that your product becomes of value to your customer, and at this point the product delivery phase begins. Here's an example of how to make the referral sale:

> I'm sure by now, John, you realize that I work strictly through referrals. I am constantly striving to bring my clients even greater service by improving my business. I have a very important question for you and would appreciate your giving this some thought. Is there any one thing that you would like to see me change or improve that would increase the likelihood of my getting referrals from you in the future?

This is only an example to get you thinking about how to properly ask for the referral. And you do need to always ask!

Service and Follow-Up

Customer service is the performance of any helpful or professional work or activity for a person, family, or organization. The service and follow-up phase of the referral cycle provides you with ongoing opportunities to maintain contact with your clients. Anytime that you have contact with your clients you encounter the possibility of getting more referrals. The quality and quantity of service will help enhance the quality and quantity of the referrals you receive. High-quality service helps create a very professional and caring image that clients are not afraid of sharing with their friends, family, and business associates; a high quantity of service helps keep you and your product fresh in the client's mind. Service is one of the key components of the Core Principles. Service shows you have a servant heart and care about the customer rather than solely the money you make from the sale.

For many salespeople, the product delivery phase represents the end of the relationship with their clients. There are three reasons why this happens. First, the nature of the business may not require any additional service. Second, although there may be a need for continued service, salespeople are so preoccupied with prospecting or selling that they cannot devote adequate time to providing adequate service. Third, salespeople may not realize that providing their clients with quality service can benefit them in expanding the quality and quantity of their business. What it comes down to is no need, no time, or no benefit. Here is an example of what might be said during a typical annual follow-up:

> Hello, John. This is Charles Futrell. As I promised when we first did business, this is my "official" once-a-year call to let you know that I am thinking about you. Do you have any questions? Is there anything I can do for you? . . . I also want to make sure you and Nonnie have received your birthday cards and quarterly newsletters. What do you think of my newsletters? . . . Terrific. I'll let you go now. Don't forget, you've got my number if you need any help. Please keep me in mind when talking to your friends and business associates. As you know, John, I depend on quality clients like you and Nonnie to keep me in business. One of the reasons I work so hard to help my customers is because of the people you refer to me. Your referrals are really appreciated. (Pause) John, is there anyone you or Nonnie feel I should help? (Pause) Thank you very much! I look forward to seeing you soon. Goodbye.

We like to share the story of little Steve with our sales students! During one of the practice sessions of little league baseball, Steve, a six-year-old player said, "Coach, I've never hit the ball." Coach replied, "Well, Steve, you never swing at the ball." Steve was afraid the pitcher would hit him with the ball. Like Steve, salespeople are afraid to swing or rather ask someone for a referral. People are not going to hit you if you ask with a smile on your face. Have you ever had a salesperson ask you for a referral? What a shame it is not to ask someone if they know who could use your help. The secret of obtaining referrals is to always professionally ask people. The main times to ask for referrals are shown in Exhibit 6.8.

Don't Mistreat the Referral

One final thought on referrals—don't mistreat them! The salesperson who mistreats a referral can lose the referring customer and the prospect. Like dropping a rock into a pool of water, it can have a ripple effect. Be sure to treat the referral in a professional manner. Always follow through on what you have told the referral.

Once you have sold the referral, and gotten more referrals, ask the *new* customer to contact the *referring* customer on her experience with the salesperson. Now you have two customers giving you referrals. This can create an *endless chain* of referrals, helping to quickly fill your prospect pool with only customers and referrals.

Tracking Referrals

Keeping track of referrals is just as important as staying in contact with customers. Whether you use index cards or a computerized contact system, it's important to keep detailed records on all information you collect on the prospect/customer. (See the discussion of the customer profile in Chapter 7 and the review of computerized customer contact programs in Chapter 5.)

Call Reluctance Costs You Money!

What good is knowing how to prospect if you won't prospect? All salespeople seem to have call reluctance from time to time. An estimated 40 percent of all salespeople suffer a career-threatening bout of call reluctance at some point. In its milder forms, call reluctance keeps countless salespeople from achieving their potential. Research indicates that 80 percent of all first-year salespeople who don't make the grade fail because of insufficient prospecting.

Call reluctance refers to not wanting to contact a prospect or customer. This tricky demon assumes a dozen faces and comes disguised as a salesperson's natural tendencies.

In basketball you'll always miss 100 percent of the shots you don't take.

Countermeasures for call reluctance are numerous and depend on the type of reluctance experienced by the person. But the initial step is always the same: You must admit you have call reluctance and that your call reluctance is keeping you from helping others and earning what you're worth. For many salespeople, owning up to call reluctance is the most difficult part of combating it.[9]

Salespeople must seek out prospects to find them. In basketball, as in sales, you'll always miss 100 percent of the shots you don't take. If you do not call on people, you cannot make a sale. So in sales you must knock, so the door will be opened for you. Before you knock you often need an appointment.

Obtaining the Sales Interview

Given a satisfactory method of sales prospecting and an understanding of the psychology of buying, a key factor in the selling process that has yet to be addressed is obtaining a sales interview. Although cold calling (approaching a prospect without prior notice) is suitable in a number of selling situations, industrial buyers and some other types of individuals may have neither the time nor the desire to consult with a sales representative who has not first secured an appointment.

The Benefits of Appointment Making

The practice of making an appointment before calling on a prospect can save a salesperson hours in time wasted traveling and waiting to see someone who is busy or even absent. When the salesperson makes an appointment, a buyer knows someone is coming. People are generally more receptive when they expect someone than when an unfamiliar salesperson pops in. Appointment making is often associated with a serious, professional image and is sometimes taken as an outward gesture of respect toward a prospect.

From the salesperson's point of view, an appointment provides a time set aside for the buyer to listen to a sales presentation. This is important because adequate time to explain a proposition improves the chance of making the sale. In addition, a list of appointments aids a salesperson in optimally allocating each day's selling time. Appointments can be arranged by telephone, by sending an e-mail, or by contacting the prospect's office in person.

Telephone Appointment

For obvious time and cost benefits, salespeople usually phone to make sales appointments. Though seemingly a simple task, obtaining an appointment over the telephone is frequently difficult. Business executives generally are busy and their time is scarce. However, these practices can aid in successfully making an appointment over the telephone:

- Plan and write down what you will say. This helps you organize and concisely present your message.
- Clearly identify yourself and your company.
- State the purpose of your call and briefly outline how the prospect may benefit from the interview.
- Prepare a brief sales message, stressing product benefits over features. Present only enough information to stimulate interest.
- Do not take no for an answer. Be persistent even if there is a negative reaction to the call.

The owner of an oil field supply house in Kansas City was Jack Cooper's toughest customer. He was always on the run, and Jack had trouble just getting to see him, much less getting him to listen to a sales presentation. Jack would have liked to take him to lunch so he could talk to him, but the owner never had time. Every day he called a local hamburger stand and had a hamburger sent to his office so he wouldn't have to waste time sitting down to eat.

Jack wanted to get the owner interested in a power crimp machine that would enable him to make his own hose assemblies. By making them himself, the owner could save about 45 percent of his assembly costs—and Jack would make a nice commission.

The morning Jack was going to make his next call, his wife was making sandwiches for their children to take to school. Jack had a sudden inspiration. He asked his wife to make two deluxe bag lunches for him to take with him.

Jack arrived at the supply house just before lunchtime. "I know you're too busy to go out for lunch," he told the owner, "so I brought it with me. I thought you might like something different for a change."

The owner was delighted. He even took time to sit down and talk while they ate. After lunch, Jack left with an order for the crimper—plus a standing order for hose and fittings to go with it!

- Ask for an interview so that you can further explain product benefits.
- Phrase your appointment request as a question. Your prospect should be given a choice, such as: "Would nine or one o'clock Tuesday be better for you?"

Successful use of the telephone in appointment scheduling requires an organized, clear message that captures interest quickly. Before you dial a prospect's number, mentally or physically sketch out exactly what you plan to say. While on the telephone get to the point quickly (as you may have only a minute), disclosing just enough information to stimulate the prospect's interest. For example:

> Mr. West, this is Sally Irwin of On-Line Computer Company calling you from Birmingham, Alabama. Businessmen such as yourself are saving the costs of rental or purchase of computer systems, while receiving the same benefits they get from the computer they presently have. May I explain how they are doing this on Tuesday at nine o'clock in the morning or would one o'clock in the afternoon be preferable?

One method for obtaining an appointment with anyone in the world is for you to have someone else make it for you. Now, that sounds simple enough, doesn't it? However, do not just have anyone make the appointment. It should be a satisfied customer. Say, "Listen, you must know a couple of people who could use my product. Would you mind telling me who they are? I'd like you to call them up and say I'm on my way over." Or, "Would you just call them up and ask them if they would meet with me?" This simple technique frequently works. In some situations, an opportunity to make an appointment personally arises or is necessitated by circumstances.

Asking for an Appointment by E-mail

Although seeking an appointment over the phone has many advantages, it may not be ideal in all the situations. Phone calls require immediate responses and that is why it

Yogi Berra has been quoted as saying, "Whatever you do in life, 90 percent of it is half mental." What does that mean to you? What do the following statements from famous motivational writers over the last 70 years mean to you? Have you ever been reluctant to do something? How does this relate to prospecting?

- "Positive mental attitude governs your life and mind and it is the starting point of all riches."—Napoleon Hill
- "I will greet this day with love in my heart."—Og Mandino

- "Let's fill our minds with thoughts of peace, courage, health, and hope for our life is what our thoughts make it."—Dale Carnegie
- "Count your blessings—not your troubles."—Dale Carnegie
- "When fate hands us a lemon, let's try to make lemonade."—Dale Carnegie
- "I will persist until I succeed."—Og Mandino
- "Sharpen the saw—renew the physical, spiritual, mental, and social/emotional dimensions of your nature."—Stephen Covey

may be a turnoff to a prospect who does not like to make decisions in haste. Sending an e-mail seeking an appointment could be a good option in such cases. E-mails offer flexibility to both the salesperson and a prospect.

E-mailing your prospects to schedule a sales meeting is not a bad idea at all. This way you are respectful of your prospects' time rather than trying to "catch" them over the phone, as they could be busy when you make a call.

How you send e-mails and how you keep track of your e-mail messages are critical business practices that salespeople should pay attention to. Writing a winning e-mail message requires your attention to details including a promising subject line, proper greeting, rich contents, and professional format and style. A professionally written e-mail message that clearly and succinctly outlines the background and presents the reasons for the meeting surely captures a prospect's attention as shown in the example given below.

Subject: McGraw-Hill Education

Dear Dr. Agnihotri,

By way of introduction, my name is Rhonda White and I am the Learning Technology Consultant for the business courses at McGraw-Hill; my team and I are responsible for helping faculty members here at Iowa State University. We had the briefest of introductions the last time I was on campus but I have no expectation of you recalling that. I am writing to you on the recommendation of your colleague Dr. Michael Krush who said you may be interested in learning about new technologies available to enhance the educational experience for students in your sales classes. I would love to talk with you about it and get your thoughts on where you are with the idea plus answer any questions you might have. I am available next Wednesday (11/20) or Friday (11/22) at 1pm CST, if that works for you.

I look forward to hearing from you.

Thanks,
Rhonda

According to a study by Behavioral Sciences Research Press, the problem of call reluctance in sales is widespread and costly.[10] Among the findings of the Dallas research and sales training firm:

- Some 80 percent of all new salespeople who fail within their first year do so because of insufficient prospecting activity.
- Forty percent of all sales veterans experience one or more episodes of call reluctance severe enough to threaten their continuation in sales. It can strike at any time.

- The call-reluctant salesperson loses more than 15 new accounts per month to competitors.
- Call-reluctant stockbrokers acquire 48 fewer new accounts per year than brokers who have learned to manage their fear.
- In some cases, the call-reluctant salesperson loses $10,800 per month in gross sales.
- In others, call reluctance costs the salesperson $10,000 in lost commissions per year.

Personally Making the Appointment

Many business executives are constantly bombarded with an unending procession of interorganizational memos, correspondence, reports, forms, and *salespeople*. To use their time optimally, many executives establish policies to aid in determining whom to see, what to read, and so on. They maintain gatekeepers (secretaries or receptionists) who execute established time-use policies by acting as filters for all correspondence, telephone messages, and people seeking entry to the executive suite. Successful navigation of this filtration system requires a professional salesperson who (1) is determined to see the executive and believes it can be done; (2) develops friends within the firm (many times including the gatekeepers); and (3) optimizes time by calling only on individuals who make or participate in the purchase decision.

Believe in Yourself. As a salesperson, believe that you can obtain interviews because you have a good offer for prospects. Develop confidence by knowing your products and by knowing prospects—their business and needs. Speak and carry yourself as though you expect to get in to see the prospect. Instead of saying, "May I see Ms. Vickery?" you say, while handing the secretary your card, "Could you please tell Ms. Vickery that Ray Baker from XYZ Corporation is here?"

Develop Friends in the Prospect's Firm. Successful salespeople know that people within the prospect's firm often indirectly help in arranging an interview and influence buyers to purchase a product. A successful Cadillac salesperson states:

> To do business with the boss, you must sell yourself to everyone on his staff. I sincerely like people—so it came naturally to me. I treat secretaries and chauffeurs as equals and friends. Ditto for switchboard operators and maids. I regularly sent small gifts to them all. An outstanding investment.

233

The little people are great allies. They can't buy the product. But they can kill the sale. Who needs influential enemies? The champ doesn't want anyone standing behind him throwing rocks. In many cases, all you do is treat people decently—an act that sets you apart from 70 percent of your competitors.

Matt Suffoletto, the computer salesperson mentioned earlier, says it another way:

I have observed one common distinction of successful salespeople. They not only call on the normal chain of people within the customer's organization, but they have periodic contact with higher-level decision makers to communicate the added value which their products and services have provided. This concept, when exercised judiciously, can have a tremendous impact on your effectiveness.

Respect, trust, and friendship are three key elements in any salesperson's success. Timing is also important.

Call at the Right Time on the Right Person. Both gatekeepers and busy executives appreciate salespeople who do not waste their time. By using past sales call records or calling the prospect's receptionist, a salesperson can determine when the prospect prefers to receive visitors. Direct questions, such as asking the receptionist, "Does Mr. Smith purchase your firm's office supplies?" or "Whom should I see concerning the purchase of office supplies?" can be used in determining whom to see.

Do Not Waste Time Waiting. Once you have asked the receptionist if the prospect can see you today, you should (1) determine how long you will have to wait, and whether you can afford to wait that length of time; (2) be productive while waiting by reviewing how you will make the sales presentation to the prospect; and (3) once an acceptable amount of waiting time has passed, tell the receptionist, "I have another appointment and must leave in a moment." When politely approached, the receptionist will usually attempt to get you in. If still unable to enter the office, you can ask for an appointment as follows: "Will you please see if I can get an appointment for 10 on Tuesday?" If this request does not result in an immediate interview, it implies the establishment of another interview time. If you establish a positive relationship with a prospect and with gatekeepers, waiting time normally decreases while productivity increases.

Applying CRM Technolgy to Prospecting

As you learned about the CRM system and its ability to manage knowledge in Chapter 5, now you will learn how it can assist the firm and its salesforce in the prospecting process. The system serves as a repository for varying information about potential leads, provides tools to segment this pool of potential customers, and enables scoring of these prospects to help the salesperson prioritize her efforts.

Lead Generation and Tracking via Marketing Automation

In some CRM systems, you can develop a marketing campaign (i.e., you automate it within the CRM system). The campaigns can involve a number of marketing tactics, including trials of products and services, direct mail, e-mail, and other promotions.

You are a new life insurance agent and have just made a sale to an old family friend who is the personnel manager for a large manufacturing company in your town. To help you in your prospecting, he offers you a large file of personnel data on the employees of the company, including income, family size, phone numbers, and addresses.

This information would be very valuable. You are sure to make 5 to 10 sales from this excellent prospect list. As he hands you the material, you notice it is stamped, "Not for Publication, Company Use Only!"

What would be the most ethical action to take?

1. Take the information. It could really help you get started.
2. Thank your friend for the offer but refuse the information. It would not be right to accept something that is marked confidential.
3. Refuse the information and tell your friend that it was not good practice for him to offer it. Let him know that if anything like this were to happen again, you would have to report him to the proper people in his company.

For instance, a marketing campaign could target a set of potential customers in the hopes of generating sales leads. Additionally, the CRM technology allows the firm to track the behavior of leads. For instance, CRM technology can examine how much time prospects spent on the firm's websites, blogs, or social media. Then, the marketing automation technology allows the firm to customize and target each prospect with customized communication strategies, such as e-mails, e-newsletters, invitations to webinars, and other social events to assist the prospect learn more about the firm's solution. Finally, the technology allows the firm to measure the results and activities of the campaigns. This type of information allows the salesperson and the firm to allocate resources more efficiently.

Contact Management

Imagine your phone's address and e-mail list, the business cards of prospects you recently met, notes about potential customers, and any additional information about leads. The CRM system combines all of this information. A CRM system allows the salesperson to create a central storage area for each prospect's information. This accessibility allows each salesperson to learn about the prospect.

Lead Scoring

The CRM system allows the selling firm to input qualifying criteria for the lead scoring process. Then, the CRM system can automatically calculate each lead's score. This allows the sales team to prioritize their efforts and resources quickly and efficiently.

Data Integration and Learning

Not only can a CRM system integrate all of the information about leads, it can also integrate best practices for prospecting and nurturing relations, and it can share this learning across the organization.

Pipeline Management

Firms consider the pipeline as the number of prospects and customers in each stage of the sales process. The goal of pipeline management is to understand the potential for business in the immediate term (current customers) and future term (prospects).

A CRM technology's pipeline management function helps salespeople generate reports to better understand the movement of prospects through the sales process. This information is critical to helping salespeople plan their time.

How Is Prospecting Changing?

Social Selling

You are undoubtedly aware of the term social media. Social media has also impacted sales. **Social sales technology** is defined as any social interaction–enhancing technology that can be deployed by sales professionals to generate content (e.g., blogs, microblogs, wikis) and develop networks (e.g., social networks, online communities).[11]

The use of social sales technology has impacted the interactions of buyers and sellers on a daily basis. For instance, the seller's organization communicates a wide range of information about their firm's company, their products, services, and capabilities on websites; social media posts, such as Twitter, LinkedIn, and Facebook; blogs; white papers; etc. Buyers often initiate their own search for product and service information. They visit websites, join LinkedIn groups and follow perceived thought-leaders in their industries, and download information and documents to enhance their understanding of potential solutions.

LinkedIn, a popular social networking website for businesses and their employees, has emerged as a method to assist in the prospecting process. InMail, LinkedIn's internal e-mail system, makes it possible for a sales representative to e-mail any LinkedIn user without an introduction. LinkedIn also assists salespeople, as it tracks the users who view your profile—including potential leads. But most importantly, LinkedIn allows the salesperson to learn about the needs and of prospects and their firms. Salespeople are able to access comments and posts of prospects, download documents and white papers, and learn background information about their potential customers.

Social Listening

With LinkedIn and other social media, salespeople can better understand buyers and their activities. Further, a salesperson has an opportunity to monitor new and existing customers who are accessing the seller's information, posting comments, and downloading documents. In some industries, the monitoring, interpreting, and seeking understanding of buyer-based actions and communication is called *social listening.* Social listening provides one means of understanding customer needs and is becoming increasingly important to integrate into the selling process.

SUMMARY OF MAJOR SELLING ISSUES

The sales process involves a series of actions beginning with prospecting for customers. The sales presentation is the major element of this process. Before making the presentation, the salesperson must find prospects to contact, obtain appointments, and plan the entire sales presentation.

Prospecting involves locating and qualifying the individuals or businesses that have the potential to buy a product. A person or business that might be a prospect is a *lead*. These questions can determine if someone is qualified: Is there a real need? Is the prospect aware of that need? Is there a desire to fulfill the need? Does the prospect believe a certain product can be beneficial? Does the prospect have the finances and authority to buy? And, Are potential sales large enough to be profitable to me?

Several of the more popular prospecting methods are cold canvassing, endless chain customer referrals, orphaned customers, sales lead clubs, public exhibitions, demonstrations, centers of influence, telephoning, and networking. To obtain a continual supply of prospects, the salesperson should develop a prospecting method suitable for each situation.

Once a lead has been located and qualified as a prospect, the salesperson can make an appointment with that prospect by telephone or in person. At times, it is difficult to arrange an appointment, so the salesperson must develop ways of getting to see the prospect. Believing in yourself and feeling that you have a product the prospect needs are important.

Quick Review for Students

The quick review sections provide key questions to help you develop a greater level of conceptual understanding. We suggest that after you read the chapter, you try to answer the following questions without looking back at the textbook.

1. What is prospecting? What are two key reasons for salespeople to look out for prospects?
2. What are three three questions to determine if an individual or organization is a qualified prospect (hint: use the *MAD* acronym)?
3. List any four of the prospecting methods a salesperson may use.
4. What are four commonly faced situations where a salesperson may ask for referrals?
5. What are four main sources for a salesperson to create a prospect pool?
6. In what ways does CRM technology help in prospecting?
7. What is social selling? What is social listening?

MEETING A SALES CHALLENGE

Joe, Alex, and Kathryn analyzed the proposed prospecting systems fairly well. Finding customers is difficult for startups, however. You need a customer base and prospecting is the only way to get there. You can't stay in business for long by just coming up with an innovative and cost-effective product.

Just because a customer buys one thing from a company does not mean that the customer would not be open to learn about the innovations happening in the field. Remember, there is always room for improvement when it comes to serving customers! Moreover, big companies often are fooled by their corporate egos into thinking that their existing customers will keep buying from them forever.

Going after the market leader seems to scare Joe for some reason. However, think a minute. Exactly what will big companies do that they won't do competitively anyway? Competition exists on all sides by many firms. If the company has a good cost story to tell, then go after the big users to whom the cost savings will be significant.

In short, all the systems have virtues and none should be excluded from consideration.

So much depends, however, on the particular territory. Some territories may have more young families—those who are more willing to explore high-tech security systems and would want more control compared to others. The salesperson must adapt to the characteristics of the territory.

KEY TERMS FOR SELLING

call reluctance   229
center of influence
    method   220
cold canvass prospecting
    method   216
customer service   228
direct-mail prospecting   221
endless chain referral
    method   216
exhibitions and
    demonstrations   219

lead   211
lead generation   211
lead qualification   211
lead scoring system   213
networking   223
observation method   222
orphaned customers   217
parallel referral sale   225
prospect   210
prospect pool   224
prospecting   210

qualified prospect   212
referral   216
referral cycle   225
sales process   208
social sales technology   236
telemarketing   221
telephone prospecting   222
teleprospecting   222

SALES APPLICATION QUESTIONS

1. What is the difference between a lead and a prospect? What should you, as a salesperson, do to qualify a potential customer?
2. This chapter termed prospecting the *lifeblood of selling.*
   a. Where do salespeople find prospects?
   b. List and briefly explain seven prospecting methods discussed in this chapter. Can you think of other ways to find prospects?
3. Assume that you have started a business to manufacture and market a product line selling for between $5,000 and $10,000. Your primary customers are small retailers. How would you uncover leads and convert them into prospects without personally contacting them?
4. Assume you had determined that John Firestone, vice president of Pierce Chemicals, was a prospect for your paper and metal containers. You call Mr. Firestone to see if he can see you this week. When his secretary answers the telephone, you say, "May I speak to Mr. Firestone, please?" and she says, "What is it you wish to talk to him about?" How would you answer her question? What would you say if you were told, "I'm sorry, but Mr. Firestone is too busy to talk with you"?
5. You are a new salesperson. Next week, your regional sales manager will be in town to check your progress in searching for new clients for your line of industrial chemicals. You have learned that Big Industries, Inc., a high-technology company, needs a supplier of your product. Also, a friend has told you about 12 local manufacturing firms that could use your product. The sales potential of each of these firms is about one-tenth of Big Industries. Knowing that your sales manager expects results, explain how you will qualify each lead (assuming the 12 smaller firms are similar).

FURTHER EXPLORING THE SALES WORLD

Contact several salespeople in your community and ask them to discuss their prospecting system and the steps they use in planning their sales calls. Write a short paper on your results and be prepared to discuss it in class.

SELLING EXPERIENTIAL EXERCISE

To measure your attitude toward selling, complete the following exercise. Circle a 5 to indicate that your attitude could not be better in this area; circle a 1 to indicate that you definitely do not agree. Circle a 2, 3, or 4 if you are saying something in between disagree and agree.

Your Attitude toward Selling

	Disagree				Agree
1. There is nothing demeaning about selling a good or service to a prospect.	1	2	3	4	5
2. I would be proud to tell friends that selling is my career.	1	2	3	4	5
3. I can approach customers, regardless of age, appearance, or behavior, with a positive attitude.	1	2	3	4	5
4. On bad days—when nothing goes right—I can still be positive.	1	2	3	4	5
5. I am enthusiastic about selling.	1	2	3	4	5
6. Having customers turn me down does not cause me to be negative.	1	2	3	4	5
7. The idea of selling challenges me.	1	2	3	4	5
8. I consider selling to be a profession.	1	2	3	4	5
9. Approaching strangers (customers) is interesting and usually enjoyable.	1	2	3	4	5
10. I can always find something good in a customer.	1	2	3	4	5

Total Score _____

Add up your score. If you scored more than 40, you have an excellent attitude toward selling as a profession. If you rated yourself between 25 and 40, you appear to have serious reservations. A rating under 25 indicates that another type of job is probably best for you.[12]

NOTES

1. Also see Malcolm Fleschner, "High-Level Selling," *Selling Power,* February, 2, 2010. Online at: https://www.sellingpower.com/2010/02/01/4423/high-level-selling

2. Al Paul Lefton, Jr., "The Lucky Seven: How to Roll into Sales," *Business Marketing,* August 1987, pp. 86–89; and David H. Sandler, "Prospecting . . . for Profit," *Personal Selling Power,* September 1990, p. 40.

3. Donald L. Brady, "Determining the Value of an Industrial Prospect: A Prospect Preference Index Model," *Journal of Personal Selling & Sales Management,* August 1987, pp. 27–32; and Roger Pell, "It's a Fact . . . Qualified Referrals Bring More Sales in Your Company," *Personal Selling Power,* March 1990, p. 30.

4. "Trade Shows: Creating Sales Leads," *Marketing Communications,* November 1993, pp. 36–40.

5. http://www.bizjournals.com/boston/blog/mass-high-tech/2012/05/teleprospecting-versus-telemarketing.html

6. Also see Herbert E. Brown and Roger W. Brucker, "Telephone Qualifications of Sales Leads," *Industrial Marketing Management,* August 1987, pp. 185–90.

7. Ken Krogue, "What Is Inside Sales? The Definition of Inside Sales," February 26, 2013 @ 01.29 a.m. https://www.forbes.com/sites/kenkrogue/2013/02/26/what-is-inside-sales-the-definition-of-inside-sales/#5d061cc566d8

8. Portions of this section have been adapted from Scott Krammick, *Expecting Referrals: The Resurrection of a Lost Art* (Fredericksburg, VA: Associate Publishing, 1994).

9. Also see George W. Dudley and Shannon L. Goodson, *Earning What You're Worth? The Psychology of Sales Call Reluctance* (New York: Behavioral Sciences Research Press, 1992).

10. Ibid.

11. R. Agnihotri, P. Kothandaraman, R. Kashyap, and R. Singh, "Bringing 'Social' into Sales: The Impact of Salespeople's Social Media Use on Service Behaviors and Value Creation," *Journal of Personal Selling & Sales Management* 32, no. 3, (June 2012), pp. 333–48.

12. Adapted from Donald R. Rice, *What I Think about Selling* (Menlo Park, CA: Crisp Publications, 2000), p. 33.

CASE 6.1

©Ron Chapple Stock/FotoSearch/
Glow Images

Canadian Equipment Corporation

You work for the Canadian Equipment Corporation selling office equipment. Imagine entering the lobby and reception room of a small manufacturing company. You hand the receptionist your business card and ask to see the purchasing agent. "What is this in reference to?" the secretary asks, as two other salespeople approach.

Question

Which of the following alternatives would you use, and why?

a. Give a quick explanation of your equipment, ask whether the secretary has heard of your company or used your equipment, and again ask to see the purchasing agent.
b. Say, "I would like to discuss our office equipment."
c. Say, "I sell office equipment designed to save your company money and provide greater efficiency. Companies like yours really like our products. Could you help me get in to see your purchasing agent?"
d. Give a complete presentation and demonstration.

CASE 6.2

©Ron Chapple Stock/FotoSearch/
Glow Images

Montreal Satellites

As a salesperson for Montreal Satellites, you sell television satellite dishes for homes, apartments, and businesses. After installing a satellite in Jeff Sager's home, you ask him for a referral. Jeff suggests you contact Tom Butler, his brother-in-law.

Mr. Butler is a well-known architect who designs and constructs unique residential homes. Your objective is to sell Mr. Butler a satellite for his office and home in hopes that he will install them in the homes he builds. Certainly he is a center of influence and a good word from him to his customers could result in numerous sales. Thus, another objective is to obtain referrals from Mr. Butler.

Questions

1. After eight attempts, you now have Mr. Butler on the telephone. What would you say in order to get an appointment and set the stage for getting referrals?
2. You get the appointment and are now in Mr. Butler's office trying to get him to buy a satellite for his home and office. Sometime during the presentation you are going to ask for a referral. What would you say?
3. Mr. Butler buys a satellite for his home but not his office. You install the satellite yourself and then spend 15 minutes showing Mr. and Mrs. Butler and their two teenagers how to use it. Before you leave, how would you ask for a referral?
4. Three months after the installation you are talking to Mr. Butler. How would you ask for a referral?

CASE 6.3

PizzaMunch and Social Listening Part 1

©Ron Chapple Stock/FotoSearch/
Glow Images

Because social listening and social selling continue to evolve, we believe the best way to understand it is by examining an example of how it may occur in the marketplace.

You are a salesperson for an entrepreneurial, emerging company in the consumer packaged goods world, Ag-Kru Foods. Your flagship product is called the PizzaMunch, a portable, healthy pizza product. Because the product is new, your sales team has worked with the marketing department to provide a whole portfolio of online marketing materials. This includes

- An e-book on the changing needs of the pizza category.
- A series of white papers on the evolution of American eating habits.
- A contact form for a webinar presentation of how to merchandise the PizzaMunch in different channels of retail, including grocery stores, convenience stores, and retail warehouses.
- Weekly podcast of retail and consumer trends that impact retail food categories.

Your analytics department sends a message to you. A potential prospect, Shari Karkin, just downloaded a number of white papers and has signed up for a webinar—all last night. It appears that Shari may have an interest in Pizza-Munch. Now your objective is to take action to assist Shari. But what should you do?

Questions

1. What are your options to contact Shari? What communication mode would you use to contact her (i.e., phone, e-mail, instant message, LinkedIn)? Explain why you chose this mode of communication.
2. What would be your communications goals in the message to Shari? Write down the actual communication message that you would use.

Social Listening Part 2

Your firm offers the PizzaMunch. Because this product is new, your sales team is trying to discover prospects that may be interested in the product. The sales team believes a primary target customer is involved in the convenience store industry. As such, your sales team has been following a number of groups on LinkedIn, including

- One group involved in the purchasing of pre-made food for convenience stores.
- One group involved in the understanding business trends for convenience stores.
- One group involved in understanding food consumption trends in convenience stores.
- One group made up of individuals who own convenience stores (i.e., three or fewer convenience stores).

You notice that Jane Sterling, a participant in one of these groups, occasionally posts a question about selling pizza within convenience stores. Jane operates a convenience store outside a strip mall. The strip mall contains a major gym and a national retailer that specializes in workout clothing. Therefore, Jane's store receives a great deal of customer traffic from those who frequent the gym and the retailer. In one of her posts, sent to the group made up of individuals who own convenience stores, she relays that one of her consistent frustrations lies in her inability to find a pizza option that would cater to her customers. Many of her customers have asked her if she can provide a more healthy pizza. She wonders if any other convenience store owners face the same type of customer requests.

Questions

1. What are two specific options that you could use to respond to Jane?
2. Write down the communication you would send Jane. What specific results would you want to achieve by sending this communication to Jane?

CASE 6.4

©Ron Chapple Stock/FotoSearch/
Glow Images

Conducting Research to Learn about Leads

You are a salesperson for an entrepreneurial, emerging company in the consumer packaged goods world, Ag-Kru Foods. Your flagship product is called the PizzaMunch, a portable, healthy pizza product.

Ag-Kru Foods has gained distribution in a number of well-known grocery stores and mass merchandisers. However, the next step for sales growth targets convenience stores. Your firm has very little experience in this channel of trade.

Background

Your supervisor has informed you, via e-mail that she would like you to conduct research on two leads (i.e., convenience store chains) in your territory. She has provided you with an information template. Her directions are as follows:

1. Choose two convenience stores in your geographic area. I would like to know as much about the leads as possible. My plan would be to meet with their top management group in the next 6 to 8 weeks.
2. Use a number of the following resources to conduct research and complete the background information for the two leads.
3. Submit the typed, completed information sheet within the next 72 hours. You may modify the information sheet as you deem appropriate.
4. Please ensure the format and content is professional as your document will be submitted to our chief operating officer as well.
5. Please include the citation for each source of information.
6. You can use any data source that is available to you. Per our research vendor, using a basic search engine, such as Google, may be somewhat ineffective. I know that you are currently taking some college classes. Consider consulting databases available on your library website. Also, please consider using the following websites and databases, if available:
   - LinkedIn (client)
   - InfoUSA
   - D&B Hoovers
   - Google Finance or Yahoo Finance
   - Social media sites of client, including LinkedIn, Twitter, and Facebook
   - The client's website, including its "About Us" and "Press" pages
   - LexisNexis
   - Online industry trade publications, including magazines focusing on convenience stores

	Your Information	Source of information

1. Name of firm
2. NAIC or SIC Number
3. Number of employees
4. Description of business
5. Headquarters address
6. Headquarters phone number
7. Key management (names)
   (top 3 managers and titles)
8. How long has each member of
   management been employed in firm
9. Contact information for the
   three top managers
   a. E-mail addresses (if possible)
   b. Phone numbers
10. Revenue (income) for most recent year
11. Profits for most recent year
12. Recent news about the firm (what
    could you discuss)
13. Awards/honors for the firm and
    any of its top management
14. Other information that would assist in
    starting a conversation/creating rapport
15. Three key industry trends affecting
    convenience stores and its prepared
    food sections/sales

Questions

1. Now that you have completed the information template, what websites did you find most valuable?
2. What was the most difficult information to find and why?
3. Now having done this exercise, how would your approach change? Why?

©ESB Professional/Shutterstock

Planning the Sales Call Is a Must!

Learning Objectives

Planning the sales call is the second step in the selling process. It is extremely important to spend time planning all aspects of your sales presentation. After studying this chapter, you should be able to

7–1 Explain the importance of sales call planning.

7–2 List the four planning steps in order and understand them.

7–3 Develop a customer benefit plan.

7–4 Describe the prospect's five mental steps in buying.

FACING A SALES CHALLENGE

After being hired, trained, and given a sales territory, you have been assigned by your boss to work with three of your company's salespeople. You immediately notice they are not doing what you've been trained to do. They walk into an office, introduce themselves, and ask if the customer needs anything today. Prospects rarely buy, and customers tell them what they need. This doesn't seem like selling to you. It's order taking, and that type of job is not for you.

The problem is, how do you get someone to listen to you? How do you know what they think of your product? How do you know when they're ready to buy? Next Monday, you call on your first customer. What are you going to do?

The Core Principles: Planning

A sales manager was working with his new salesperson one day. The boss asked, "What is your purpose for calling on this prospect today?" The salesperson replied, "To sell them something?" The sales manager said, "That's great, but what is your purpose?"

Begin Your Plan with Purpose and Passion Will Follow

The sales manager's question is forcing the new salesperson to create a broad philosophical statement toward a business meeting with a customer or prospect. Purpose is broad in scope. Purpose is not a list of plans, goals, or objectives that differ from one sales call to another. Purpose is a constant truth that guides your business life.

Purpose directs how you approach each sales call. It defines success for you. Purpose classifies your relationships. It helps define who you are as a sales professional.

Knowing your purpose focuses your sales efforts to serve others. It concentrates your effort and energy on what is important. Knowing your purpose motivates your life and is your reason to get out of bed in the morning. Purpose produces passion. Nothing energizes like a clear purpose. Conversely, passion evaporates like smoke in the wind without purpose.

Hopefully your **sales call purpose** is to make a contribution to the welfare of the person or organization. You want to help someone reach his goals or solve his business problems. Could you be enthusiastic and passionate about asking someone to buy something that would help him? You want to make a contribution to the welfare of others—don't you? So how do you help someone? You need a plan that is related to your purpose.

Plan to Achieve Your Purpose

Your tomorrow is today! Your today was yesterday's tomorrow! Concentrate on today. Do not worry about tomorrow. There are enough worries for today.

What does that mean? How you think, how you act, what you accomplish today will determine your future—your tomorrow. To an overwhelming degree, you can control your future by what you do today.[1] Today's test score is based upon yesterday's studying. What you sell today is based on preparation done yesterday. Does that make sense to you?

So plan each day, do the best you can to carry out your plan and adjust to circumstances as you go, and then at the end of each day evaluate your day to ensure you are on your way toward a successful tomorrow.

Everyone knows this, yet the difference between successful people and less successful people is that successful people plan, implement their plans, and evaluate the day's sales results in order to know what to do tomorrow. Less successful people think about planning but seldom do it.

Do you plan how to prepare for a test? Once you have taken the test (implemented your plan), do you evaluate how and what you studied versus your test results? Few students do, but the ones who plan, work their plan, and then evaluate their results do much better on the next test. Try it! It works in a class, just as it does in sales.

A plan is a method of achieving an end. A plan involves what you want to accomplish and how you will do it

What's a Plan?

A **plan** is a method of achieving an end. A plan involves what you want to accomplish and how you will do it. Before ever making the sales call, the salesperson reviews the purpose for the meeting. Now the salesperson plans how to help solve problems and fulfill the needs of the person or organization. Careful planning of every aspect of the sales call helps the salesperson be organized and prepared to interact with the customer. For each prospect or customer, a salesperson is often faced with a specific, unique set of problems to solve or needs to fulfill. As a result, each sales call requires a specific solution from the salesperson. You plan in order to help. Planning is part of ethical service which leads to building relationships with the customer. The foundation of your plan must be based upon building a trust-based business relationship.

What is the importance of truth? From your honesty (integrity), people realize you can be trusted. Your honesty and trustworthiness form your character or who you are to others. Your use of facts (truth) without distortion by personal feelings or prejudices makes you like a superhero, a super salesperson. How?

You want to help someone in need! How? Sell her something? Why? It will help her meet her need. You can do that!

What Is Success?

With purpose comes a plan; with a plan comes success. What will be a successful sales call? How do you define success? For example:

Purpose

↓

Plan

↓

Success

- A baseball coach might define success as winning more games than losing. Her or his boss might define success as winning the national championship or the World Series.
- You might define success as making an A or just passing this course.
- A salesperson might define success as making sales quota this year or being the top salesperson in the company.

But what about calling on the individual customer? What is a success for you? It goes back to purpose. **Success** is setting a goal and accomplishing it. You are meeting with someone with the purpose of helping him or her. Your purpose, plan, and goal do not center on selling but helping. Can you fail?

Successful but No Sale

How could you *not* make a sale and still have a successful sales call? What if your customer did not have a need? You did not fail. What if your product would not help meet the needs of the person? How could you say you were not successful?

Now consider this. There are reasons you may not make a sale. Agreed? But there should never be a reason that you do not meet the "purpose" of your business meeting. Why? What is your purpose? To help someone!

> *Trust serves as the glue that enables relationships. Without trust, it is difficult to develop and maintain a relationship.*

The Gap: Trust Building in a Sales Relationship

Many people do not trust salespeople. Some salespeople are self-centered, only wanting to make a sale for their own benefit. However, you can help eliminate this negative stereotype of salespeople by exhibiting honesty and trust-building actions and communication.

There can be no long-term relationships between two parties without trust based upon truth. One lie, one misrepresentation, can lead to separation, even divorce, between seller and buyer. Has that ever happened to you in your life?

Why Is Trust Important?

Some suggest that trust serves as the glue that enables relationships. Without trust, it is difficult to develop a relationship. Without trust, your buyers may not confide in you. The buyers may not disclose key details regarding their needs. By not revealing this important information, your ability to develop a worthy solution may be hindered.

> *A secret of successful people! Plan, implement, evaluate.*

For instance, you probably experience a lack of trust on a consistent basis with certain salespeople. Consider the last time you entered a retail store. Did the retail associate ask, "Is there anything I can help you with?" If so, what was your answer? Perhaps you stated, "No, I'm just looking" or "No thanks." If this was your response, it appears that you communicated an objection to the salesperson in the hopes they would leave you alone.

But, what if you visited the store for a specific reason. Perhaps you needed to find a daring piece of fashion that you were sensitive to ask about. Or, perhaps you visited a hardware store, but you weren't sure of the name of the product. You didn't want to look silly, so you chose to meander the aisles and look for the product rather than ask for help.

Why didn't you accept the retail associate's assistance? We might suggest it was due to a lack of trust. You chose to not share your needs because you did not trust that person.

As you can see from our example, trust is an important facet in a business relationship. As a salesperson, your goal is to develop a trusting relationship with the buyer. But what builds trust? According to research, trust building elements include[2]

- Communication.
- Similarity and compatibility.
- Expertise.
- Investing resources into the relationship, such as time and effort.
- Providing benefits such as saving the buyer time or helping to make a decision(s).
- Reducing conflict or opportunities for conflict.

Salespeople who want to build trusting relationships with their clients should develop their personal communication and interaction skills; enhance their ability to adapt to the buyers in order to create compatibility; work to develop their knowledge of their own business and the buyers' business; diligently serve their customers; and ensure the customers are able to attain their goals and objectives. You should also note that conflict is often detrimental to a trusting relationship. As you see in Exhibit 7.1, we present a number of ideas to build trust. The exhibit identifies specific actions that a salesperson could use to enhance key trust-building elements.

EXHIBIT 7.1

A salesperson could take specific actions to build trust.

How could the salesperson build trust in the following areas?	The salesperson could ask, "Do I...?"
Communication	Do I listen well? Do I express myself clearly? Do I use specific, professional language? Do I work to reduce my vocalized pauses (i.e., umm, uhh)? Do I practice my presentations before I speak to a group? Do I summarize my buyer's needs to ensure I understand the individual?
Similarity and compatibility	Do I build similarity during rapport (i.e., find common values, topics, interests etc.)? Do I use customer-oriented language (you or we vs. me or I)? Do I mirror the buyer when appropriate?
Expertise	Do I share my knowledge with the buyer? Do I study my industry? Do I learn about the intricacies of my customers' businesses? Do I continually learn about my firm, my customers and my industry (i.e., am I a lifelong learner)? Do I try to help my buyer by sharing my understanding of their business or industry?
Investing resources into relationship	Do I prepare adequately (i.e., invest the needed time) for my meetings? Do I work diligently to find resources and solutions for my customers? Do I seek and find other internal resources (i.e., colleagues) that can also assist my buyer?
Providing benefits, such as time savings or decision making	Do I attempt to understand my buyer's problems and help them solve them? Do I understand my buyer's personal goals, career goals and business goals? Do I provide multiple solutions to my buyer? Do I work to understand my buyer's industry and how they can become more effective? Do I follow up with my buyer and ensure high-quality post-sales service?

Strategic Customer Sales Planning—The Preapproach

Once the prospect has been located, or the salesperson determines which customer to call on, the salesperson is ready to plan the sales call. Planning is often referred to as the preapproach (see Exhibit 7.2). This chapter discusses the many aspects of planning a sales call. Let's begin by learning why salespeople should consider the customer's needs in order to recommend a creative solution that will benefit both the buyer and the seller.

High-performing salespeople tend to be strategic problem solvers for their customers (refer back to Exhibit 1.7). **Strategic** refers to programs, goals, and problems of great importance to customers. The top salespeople who are effective strategic problem solvers have the skills and knowledge to be able to

- Uncover and understand the customer's strategic needs by gaining in-depth knowledge of the customer's organization.
- Possess the needed knowledge about the customer's organization, the customer's industry, and the firm's product or service.

EXHIBIT 7.2

The preapproach involves planning the sales presentation.

Buyer expectations are increasing, especially when it comes to solutions. But how should we think about a solution? Sales research suggests the following four key elements comprise a solution:[3]

1. Defining the customer's needs and must-haves: This includes (a) a strong needs inquiry to understand the customer's needs (i.e., needs that lay at the conscious, preconscious, and unconscious levels), (b) familiarity and understanding of the customer's business, including its business and operating structure, and the trends in its industry, and (c) identifying and understanding the difference between the customer's present-day needs and the customer's upcoming needs.
2. Developing a customized solution that (a) meets the customer's needs and will align with the customer's circumstances (marketplace, business model, facilities, etc.) and (b) is made of a number of well-organized elements that work well together.
3. Being able to integrate, set up, and implement the solution within the customer's environment (facilities, locations, operational processes, etc.). This might mean modifying the solution during its implementation and providing training to ensure the customer can fully utilize the solution.
4. Providing support after the solution has been implemented within the customer's business. In this stage, the salesperson's firm may need to provide consistent support and assistance (i.e., post-sales service, training, trouble-shooting, and recognition of ongoing opportunities for enhancement).

- Develop solutions that demonstrate a creative approach to addressing the customer's strategic needs in the most efficient and effective manner possible.
- Arrive at a mutually beneficial agreement.
- Create value—as perceived by the customer.

Strategic needs, creative solutions, and mutually beneficial agreements are critical to strategic problem solving. When properly executed by the salesperson, they create a **strategic customer relationship** or a formal relationship with the customer, the purpose of which is joint pursuit of mutual goals. Strategic goals for a customer typically include reducing costs and/or increasing productivity, responsiveness, sales, and profits. The sales organization has goals of increasing sales and profits.

> *A strategic customer relationship—the purpose of which is joint pursuit of mutual goals.*

Strategic Needs

The salesperson who understands the full range of the customer's needs is in a much better position to provide a product solution that helps the customer progress more efficiently and effectively toward achieving his or her organization's strategic goal. "The top salespeople have an in-depth understanding of our needs," said one business purchasing professional. "They can match up their products with these needs to help us reach our goals."

Needs of the Buyer

A critical element of the salesperson's knowledge lies in understanding the buyer's strategic needs. However, needs may be elusive. As we discussed in Chapter 3, many buyers may or may not be totally aware of their needs. Therefore, we provide a list of needs that are commonly associated with buyers. The table includes needs for business-to-business markets (i.e., very economic-based and important to a firm), the human needs of business buyer (i.e., the needs of humans that are responsible for buying in a business-to-business environment), and business-to-consumer markets (i.e., the needs of the everyday consumer). The table provides you with a tool for your pre-approach document. As you begin to forecast your buyer's needs, you can ask yourself whether the buyer possesses any of the following needs.

Business-to-Business Needs	Personal Needs of the Business-to-Business Buyer	Business-to-Consumer Needs
Help increase my firm's revenues (sales)	Help me reach my business objectives and other responsibilities	Help me reach my personal and/or professional goals and objectives
Help increase my firm's net profits	Help me feel competent with my team, colleagues, and supervisors	Help me feel secure (financially, emotionally, relationally)
Help increase my firm's gross margins (price – cost of goods sold)	Help me with my relationships with my team, colleagues, and supervisors	Help me reduce my perceived risk regarding a change
Help increase the speed in which my firm sells its product(s) (i.e., inventory turnover)	Help me reduce my concerns about a change in my business, business plans, or responsibilities	Help me take care of those I love or who are important to me
Help increase the pace of my firm's production processes	Help me become more insightful about my industry	Help me feel secure about my actions
Help increase the satisfaction of my firm's or my business unit's customers	Help me become more insightful about my competition	Help me feel competent in front of others whom I perceive are important
Help reduce my firm's or business unit's expenses (costs)	Help me understand key trends that will impact my firm or my responsibilities	Help me with my personal personal responsibilities
Help enhance my firm's or business unit's cash flow	Help me champion an idea to my team, my supervisor, or my colleagues	Help me become more efficient with my time (i.e., save me time)
Help enhance my firm's or business unit's working capital	Help me reduce my workload	Help me reduce the effort needed to make a decision
Help my firm to use less materials (inputs) and maintain or increase our production	Help me become more efficient with my responsibilities	Help me with my relationships (I.e., personal and/or professional)
Help my firm's ability to adapt to competition	Help me advance professionally within my firm	Help me feel better about myself
Help my firm's ability to retain customers or develop new customers	Help me generate influence within my organization	Help me enjoy certain aspects of my life that I perceive are important

Creative Solutions

For each customer, a salesperson is often faced with a specific, unique set of problems to solve. As a result, each customer requires a specific solution from the sales organization. The ability of a salesperson to tailor a "custom" solution for each customer is critical today. The salesperson needs to follow a three-stage creative problem solving process: (1) finding the problem, (2) solving the problem, and (3) implementing the solution. Instead of one product, the salesperson often must create the solution from a mix of goods and services. Usually, the solution represents one of two options:

1. A customized version or application of a product and/or service that efficiently addresses the customer's specific strategic needs.

2. A mix of goods and services—including, if appropriate, competitors' products and services—that offers the best possible solution in light of the customer's strategic needs.

The better a salesperson is at creatively marshaling all available resources to address a customer's strategic needs, the stronger the customer relationship becomes. Today's salespeople need to be **creative problem solvers** who have the ability to develop and combine nontraditional alternatives to meet the specific needs of the customer. In order to become a creative problem solver, the salesperson must invest a significant amount of effort into delving into the buyer's true needs, interpreting the needs, and creating a meaningful solution.

But what is a meaningful solution? A meaningful solution solves the buyer's problems and creates value for the buyer. Value occurs when the buyer perceives that what she has received from the salesperson's solution is greater than what she invested in order to attain the solution (i.e., time, effort, money, or other resources). However, value is perceptual—it is defined by the buyer. The buyer determines the elements, processes, efforts, products, and services that she appreciates. For instance, a buyer may believe a salesperson is extremely valuable because he always inputs orders correctly and communicates when he has finished key actions (i.e., follow-up). The buyer may believe the salesperson's company provides exactly the same product as does his competition. However, the competitive firm does not create value because its salesperson always makes mistakes during the ordering process.

Let's review another example. A buyer for a sporting goods firm may believe that one of its manufacturers creates value because it is very innovative. While the manufacturing firm may not always introduce the best-selling products, the manufacturer is always introducing new products in an attempt to garner increased sales for its sporting good distributors. Hence, the buyer may believe that the absolute sales numbers for each new product not is as important as the manufacturer's consistent effort to introduce new products and bring new sales to its sporting goods distributors. As you can see, the perception of value may not always be tied directly to the price of the product. Each buyer will perceive value differently.

As the examples suggest, the salesperson needs to understand how to create value for the customer—through understanding the customer's needs and developing meaningful solutions tied directly to those needs.

Mutually Beneficial Agreements

Salespeople and customers say that a significant shift has occurred in their expectations of the outcome of sales agreements—from the adversarial win-lose to the more collaborative win-win arrangement. To achieve a mutually beneficial agreement, salespeople and customers must work together to develop a common understanding of the issues and challenges at hand.

Information about an organization's business strategies and needs is often highly confidential. But more and more customers, in the interest of developing solutions that will help achieve their strategic goals, are willing to let salespeople cross the threshold of confidentiality.

The Customer Relationship Model

The customer relationship model shown in Exhibit 7.3 brings together the main elements of consultative selling. It shows that customers have strategic needs that salespeople must meet through creative solutions. In doing so, both buyer and seller

EXHIBIT 7.3

Consultative selling—customer relationship model.

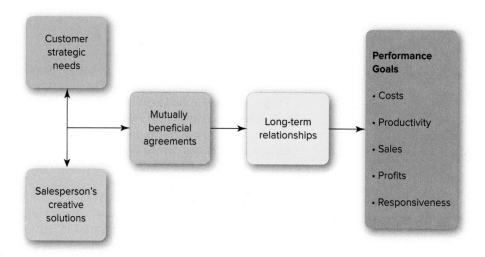

benefit. The customer reaches his or her goal, as does the seller. This results in the seller being able to sell the customer again and again and again—building a long-term relationship. Strategic customer sales planning is extremely important to the success of today's salespeople. Let's examine the important aspects of the second step in our customer relationship process, called the preapproach. The **preapproach** refers to *planning the sales call* on a customer or prospect.

Why Does Preparation Matter?

Planning the sales call is the key to success (see Exhibit 7.4). Salespeople say there are numerous reasons for planning the sales call, and four of the most frequently mentioned reasons are (1) planning aids in building confidence; (2) it develops an atmosphere of goodwill between the buyer and seller; (3) it reflects professionalism; and (4) it generally increases sales because the salesperson understands better the buyer's needs.

Builds Self-Confidence

In giving a speech before a large group, most people are nervous. You can greatly reduce this nervousness and increase self-confidence by planning what to say and practicing your talk. The same is true in making a sales presentation. By carefully planning your presentation, you increase confidence in yourself and your ability as a salesperson. This is why planning the sales call is especially important.

Develops an Atmosphere of Goodwill

The salesperson who understands a customer's needs and is prepared to discuss how a product will benefit the prospect is appreciated and respected by the buyer. Knowledge of a prospect and concern for the prospect's needs demonstrate a sincere interest in a prospect that generally is rewarded with an attitude of goodwill from the prospect. This goodwill gradually builds the buyer's confidence and results in a belief that the salesperson can be trusted to fulfill obligations.

©Yuri_Arcurs/Getty Images

Creates Professionalism and Credibility

Good business relationships are built on your knowledge of your company, industry, and customer's needs. Show prospects that you are calling on them to help solve their problems or satisfy their needs. These factors are the mark of a professional salesperson, who uses specialized knowledge in an ethical manner to aid customers.

Increases Sales

A confident salesperson who is well prepared to discuss how products address particular needs always will be more successful than the unprepared salesperson. Careful planning ensures that you have diagnosed a situation and have a remedy for a customer's problem. Planning ensures that a sales presentation is well thought out and appropriately presented.

Like other beneficial presales call activities, planning is most effective (and time efficient) when done logically and methodically. Some salespeople try what they consider planning, later discarding the process because it took too much time. In many cases, these individuals were not aware of the basic elements of sales planning.

Elements of Sales Call Planning

Exhibit 7.5 depicts the four components of **sales call planning**: (1) determining the sales call objective; (2) developing or reviewing the customer profile; (3) developing a

The four components of sales call planning are (1) determining the sales call objective; (2) developing or reviewing the customer profile; (3) developing a customer benefit plan; and (4) developing the individual sales presentation.

EXHIBIT 7.5

Steps in the preapproach: planning the sale.

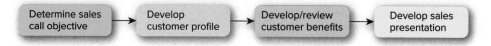

customer benefit plan; and (4) developing the individual sales presentation based on the sales call objective, customer profile, and customer benefit plan.

Always Have a Sales Call Objective

The **sales call objective** is the main purpose of a salesperson's contact with a prospect or customer.

Is it possible to make a sales call without having a sales call objective in mind? Why can't salespeople just go in and see what develops? They can: In fact, a survey call is a legitimate sales technique. However, when all the calls that salespeople make are survey calls, they should be working exclusively for the market research department.

The Precall Objective Selling is not a very complex process. It's just difficult to do on a consistent basis. That's why, whether you regard it as an art or a science, the discipline of selling starts with setting a precall objective.

If anyone doubts this, remember that, by definition, a sales call must move systematically toward a sale or the next step toward a decision to purchase. Often, we're not talking about elaborate planning. Sometimes it takes only a few seconds before a call. But on every occasion, it's vital for the sales representative to answer one simple question: "If this call is successful, what will result?"

Taking the time to do this starts the selling process in motion. Before every sales call, ask yourself, "What am I going in here for? What is the result I'm trying to make happen? If they give me the opportunity, what am I going to recommend?"

Focus and Flexibility Writing down your precall objective increases the focus of your efforts. Given today's rising costs and the investment made in the salesforce, this focus is essential. If salespeople are just going around visiting customers to see what develops, they are merely well-paid tourists. If they are professional sales representatives, they should be moving their customers toward a predetermined goal.

Knowing where you are going definitely increases the likelihood of getting there. Obviously, if the precall objective turns out to be inappropriate as the sales call develops, it's easy to switch tactics. Often, such changes involve a simple redirection.

The more specific the objective of each sales meeting, the greater the likelihood for success.

Making the Goal Specific When asked the purpose of a call, some salespeople say enthusiastically, "It's to get an order. Let's go!" However, this is too broad of a goal. Goals are much more attainable when they provide concrete direction. While everyone's in favor of getting orders, it is more likely to happen if salespeople stop and ask themselves questions such as these: What need of this prospect can I serve? Which good or service is best for this account? How large an order should I suggest? The more specific the objective, the better.

Moving toward Your Objective Just because a salesperson isn't making a formal presentation doesn't mean that the call shouldn't be planned. Sometimes the sales call has a limited objective. Guiding the customer in the direction of that preplanned outcome is what I see experienced salespeople doing on most sales calls. They do it with such simple questions as these:

- If we can meet the spec, can you set up a trial?
- How soon will the vice president be available to make a decision?
- Can you schedule a demonstration before the end of the month?

How to Set a Sales Call Objective Don't let anyone tell you that selling is so repetitive that the next step becomes a matter of rote. Knowing where you are going may be rote, but getting there requires thinking and skill. Set a **SMART** call objective that is

Set a SMART call objective. Specific—to get an order is not specific.

Measurable—quantifiable (number, size, etc.).

Achievable—not too difficult to fulfill.

Realistic—not too easy to fulfill.

Timed—at this call or before the end of the financial year.

Specific—to get an order is *not* specific.

Measurable—quantifiable (number, size, etc.).

Achievable—not too difficult to fulfill.

Realistic—not too easy to fulfill.

Timed—at this call or before the end of the financial year.

It's amazing how often even veteran salespeople skip the precall objective step in favor of just seizing whatever opportunities present themselves. As a professional, it's your responsibility to avoid this kind of behavior. Commit to having an objective for every call, and after a call check your results against that objective. This is a simple truth that the best sales professionals have known all along. Often the most important step in a sale takes place without the customer even being there.

In addition, the sales call objective should be directly beneficial to the customer. For example, the Colgate salesperson might have the objectives of checking all merchandise, having the customer make a routine reorder on merchandise, and selling promotional quantities of Colgate toothpaste.

The Colgate salesperson might call on a chain store manager with the multiple objectives of making sure that Colgate products are placed where they sell most rapidly, replenishing the store's stock of Colgate products so that customers will not leave the store disgruntled due to stockouts, and aiding the manager in deciding how much promotional Colgate toothpaste and Rapid Shave shaving cream should be displayed.

Industrial salespeople develop similar objectives to determine if customers need to reorder or to sell new products. In the next section, we provide a few examples of effective SMART objectives and a few examples of less effective SMART objectives.

Examples of an Effective SMART Call Objective

To meet with the Joe's Retail Grocery buyer with responsibilities in the cleaning category on March 15, 2019_____ and sign an agreement on March 15, 2019_____ (specific) to purchase 55 cases of the new Kragni product solution (measurable) and distribute it within 50 of their 100 stores (achievable and realistic) by June 1, 2019_____ (realistic and time-based).

To present XMZ Electrical Distribution with two specific solutions that provide long-term cost reductions based on their stated needs of reducing their annual energy expenses (specific). The goal of each solution is to meet XMZ Electrical Distribution's stated objective of a payback period less than three years (measurable). My goal is to gain approval by the buyer of both solutions at the August 12, 2019, meeting (achievable and realistic) and begin implementing the solution in XMZ's 10 largest distribution centers by December 1, 2019_____ (specific and time-based).

Example of an Ineffective SMART Call Objective

To set a meeting with the customer sometime in the next few months (not very specific) and talk to them about some of our products (not measurable) with the hopes they will buy many of the products from our product line (hard to determine if this is realistic or achievable) in the next year or so (not time-based).

To meet with John S. of Alley Grocery within January or February (not very specific) and discuss a few ideas on a promotional plan (not measurable). My goal is to have John S. consider the opportunities and potentially get back to me sometime soon (may not be very realistic or timely).

Customer Profile Provides Insight

A customer profile sheet, as shown in Exhibit 7.6, can be a guide for determining the appropriate strategy to use in contacting each customer. The salesperson should review as much relevant information as possible regarding the firm, the buyer, and the

EXHIBIT 7.6

Information used in a profile and for planning.

Customer Profile and Planning Sheet
1. Name: _____
Address: _____
2. Type of business: _____
Name of buyer: _____
3. People who influence buying decisions or aid in using or selling our product: _____
What mode of communication does the buyer prefer (face-to-face, e-mail, text, phone, instant message, etc.)
4. Buying hours and best time to see buyer: _____
5. Mode of communication the buyer prefers (face-to-face, e-mail, text, phone, instant message, etc.): _____
6. Administrative assistant's name: _____
7. Buyer's profile: _____
8. Buyer's personality style: _____
9. Sales call objectives: _____
10. What are customer's important buying needs: _____
11. Major industry pressures faced by the buyer's firm: _____
12. Sales presentation: _____
a. Sales approach: _____
b. Features, advantages, benefits: _____
c. Method of demonstrating *FAB:* _____
d. How to relate benefits to customer's needs: _____
e. Trial close to use: _____
f. Anticipated objections: _____
g. Trial close to use: _____
h. How to close this customer: _____
i. Hard or soft close: _____
13. Sales made—product use/promotional plan agreed on: _____
14. Post–sales call comments (reason did/did not buy, what to do on next call; follow-up promised): _____

individuals who influence the buying decision—before making a sales call—to properly develop a customized presentation. The salesperson also must consider the material discussed in Chapter 5 concerning why the buyer buys at this time.

A **customer profile** should tell you such things as these:

■ Who makes the buying decisions in the organization—an individual or committee?

■ What is the buyer's background? The background of the buyer's company? The buyer's expectations of you?

■ What are the desired business terms and requirements of the account, such as delivery, credit, technical service?

■ What competitors successfully do business with the account? Why?

■ What are the purchasing policies and practices of the account? For example, does the customer buy special price offer promotions, or only see salespeople on Tuesdays and Thursdays?

■ What is the history of the account? For example, past purchases of our products, inventory turnover, profit per shelf foot, our brand's volume sales growth, payment practices, and attitude toward resale prices.

■ What are the buyer's critical needs?

■ What pressure(s) is the buyer facing within their organization and their competitive environment?

Determine this information from a review of records on the company or through personal contact with the company.

How Do I Find the Information for a Customer Profile?   The available amount of customer information will vary based on the salesperson's firm and industry. For example, some firms have integrated their customer relationship management software into their sales process. In these firms, salespeople can access a range of information about the customer or prospect including the history of the customer account, industry information, social media trends, contact history, and overviews of key discussions.

However, other firms may be limited in their resources. Therefore, the salesforce must be able to efficiently find information about prospects and customers on their own. In these cases, the salesperson can use a range of online sources. We highlight a few resources widely available to salespeople and their firms. In some instances, access may be free or require some level of an investment. We only highlight a few examples (without endorsement) to provide you with an idea of the variety of information available to you:

LinkedIn is one of the premier social networks for business. It provides an opportunity for individuals and businesses to network. A salesperson can learn an organization's background as well as its decision-makers' background, such as employment history, educational background, educational experience, training, and general interests.

D&B Hoovers provides a range of information about businesses, industries, and markets. While this is a paid service, it provides opportunities to better understand firms, decision makers, and their market environment.

Manta.com tends to focus on small businesses. One of the firm's stated goals is to assist small businesses with their marketing needs. Many companies use Manta.com to provide information about their products, services, locations, and so on. By doing so, it provides a litany of information that can help the salesperson understand the firm.

Bizstats.com provides a quick financial overview that provides a salesperson with a general, financial understanding of companies that operate within a certain industry. For instance, a salesperson could use this information to understand the average industry performance on metrics such as net income, balance sheet metrics, return on sales, and inventory turnover.

Place Yourself in the Buyer's Shoes Great preparation means that a salesperson conducts research in order to better understand the buyer's potential needs. One method to understand the buyer's perspective is to imagine yourself in his/her role. Based on your understanding of the buyer's firm and industry, you could ask yourself, "Which of the following areas are placing pressure on the buyer?" and "Which of the following areas might be causing the buyer to seek a solution?" We provide a number of questions that a salesperson might use to better understand the professional buyer and the buying organization.

- Is the buyer under pressure to meet certain personal goals (i.e., on the performance evaluation)? What might be the key challenges facing the buyer in meeting personal performance objectives?
- Is the buyer under pressure to meet certain financial objectives or obligations? What specific financial metrics does the buyer need to assist the firm in meeting?
- Is the buyer and her firm impacted by the competition? In what specific ways is the competition creating challenges to the buyer and her firm?
- Is the buyer confronting technological challenges or trends that are impacting her firm? What are the specific challenges tied to technology? What specific type of assistance might the buyer be seeking?
- Is the buyer confronting certain internal challenges, such as a manufacturing constraint or departmental conflicts? In what specific areas might the buyer be seeking assistance to overcome such internal challenges?
- Is the buyer facing economic dynamics, such as inflation, discretionary income or other economic-based challenges? What specific types of assistance might the buyer be seeking to alleviate this type of economic or financial pressure?
- Are regulations or political challenges impacting the buyer's firm? What type of assistance might the buyer be seeking to confront or overcome such challenges?
- Is the buyer experiencing challenges in serving her customers? What types of assistance might the buyer be seeking?
- What specific area of the buyer's business is being impacted? Is it a specific business unit or a category of business?

A similar approach could be used by the salesperson to understand the buyer's personal or psychological needs. The salesperson could ask herself if it is possible that the buyer confronts any of the following situations:

- Is the buyer attempting to meet certain personal goals related to family matters or pressures?
- Is the buyer attempting to change the perceptions that others have of him or her?
- Is the buyer attempting to change their personal perception of something in his or her life or career?
- Is the buyer attempting to avoid a topic or situation that may negatively impact him or her?
- Is the buyer attempting to meet certain personal financial goals?
- Is the buyer confronting some type of challenge based on the economy or some sort of public policy?

Creating a Foundation for Your Customer Benefit Plan

Earlier you placed yourself in the buyer's role, and you asked a range of questions related to the pressures confronting the buyer. This exercise provided insight into the buyer's potential needs.

The next step combines your understanding of the potential pressures and needs confronting the buyer with an overview of potential solutions. This summary creates a brief outline for developing the Customer Benefit Plan. The following example provides one approach for developing this summary.

"Based on the buyer's key challenges that include (*insert the specific key challenges*), the buyer will need help finding solutions for the following needs including: (*insert needs*). I can assist the customer by providing a solution that will (*insert your benefits that are directly tied to the buyer's needs*). My buyer will undoubtedly want to discuss areas that are important to him/her. Therefore, I need to specifically discuss metrics or topics such as (*insert key metrics or key topics*). The buyer may also be somewhat leery of change. In fact, many of the common concerns that the buyer might express as objections may include (*insert potential areas of concern, risk or worries regarding a change*).

Customer Benefit Plan: What It's All About!

Beginning with your sales call objectives and what you know about your prospect, you are ready to develop a **customer benefit plan.** The customer benefit plan contains the nucleus of the information used in your sales presentation; thus it should be developed to the best of your ability. The customer benefit plan incorporates this four-step process:

Step 1. Once you have outlined the potential needs of your prospect, select the features, advantages, and benefits of your product to present to your prospect. (See Chapter 3.) This addresses the issue of why the buyer should purchase your product. The main reason the prospect should purchase your product is that its benefits fulfill certain needs or solve certain problems. Carefully determine the benefits you wish to present. Again, we would like to stress to you that the benefits you select should align with the buyer's most important needs.

Step 2. Develop your marketing plan. If selling to wholesalers or retailers, your marketing plan should include how, once they buy, they will sell your product to their customers. An effective marketing plan includes suggestions on how a retailer, for example, should "promote" the product through displays, advertising, proper shelf space and positioning, and pricing.

Did you hear the story of the guy who went into a small grocery store and asked the owner if he had any salt? "Do I have salt!?" shouted the grocer. He showed the shopper shelves full of salt and then took him to the storeroom and showed him boxes of salt, saying, "Do I have salt!?" Next they went to the basement to see more boxes, where the grocer again exclaimed, "Do I have salt!?"

Do you think the grocer will buy more salt when the salesperson returns? Chances are he will want to return salt, not buy it. To help this grocer generate revenue to pay his rent and employees, the salt salesperson must help him sell salt. How? Well, maybe give away a box of 39¢ salt with each purchase over $5. This might draw more customers into the store. In consumer sales with national companies it is often easy to sell to the customer. If the customer cannot sell what you sold, you will not sell anything. Provide strategies on selling through to the reseller's customers.

For an end-user of the product, such as the company that buys your manufacturing equipment, computer, or customer relationship management software, develop a program showing how your product is most effectively used or coordinated with existing equipment.

Exhibit 7.7 has other examples of topics often discussed in the marketing plan segment of your sales presentation. Many of these topics were discussed in Chapter 5.

Step 3. Develop your business proposition. The business proposition provides the buyer with an understanding of the important financial metrics. The business proposition includes items such as price, percent markup, forecasted profit per square foot of shelf space, return on investment, and payment plan. Value analysis is an example of a business proposition for an industrial product. Other examples of topics discussed in the business proposition segment of your sales presentation are shown in Exhibit 7.7.

Step 4. Develop a suggested purchase order based on a customer benefit plan. The suggested purchase order and implementation plan provides a recommendation to the buyer. In effect, this section helps the buyer understand the potential action steps that are required. A proper presentation of your customer needs analysis and your product's ability to fulfill these needs, along with a satisfactory business proposition and marketing plan, allows you to justify to the prospect what product and/or how much to purchase. This suggestion may include, depending on your product, such things as what to buy, how much to buy, what assortment to buy, and when to ship the product to the customer.

You should also develop visual aids to effectively communicate the information developed in these four steps. The visuals should be organized in the order you discuss them. Your next step is to plan all aspects of the sales presentation. Finally, you will want to plan the steps for implementation. For instance, you will need to consider how often you contact the buyer and provide progress updates.

The Sales Presentation: An Overview of the Process

It is now time to plan your **sales presentation** from beginning to end. This process involves developing steps 3 to 9 of the sales presentation described in Exhibit 7.2: the approach, presentation, and trial close method to uncover objections; ways to overcome objections; additional trial closes; and the close of the sales presentation. Each step is discussed in the following chapters.

New salespeople often ask their sales trainers to be more specific on how to construct the sales presentation. In addition to the 10 steps in the selling process shown in Exhibit 7.2, they ask, "What's involved in the presentation itself?" Exhibit 7.8 summarizes the major phases within the sales presentation. Before briefly discussing them, let's review a few things.

Before developing your presentation, you need to determine the prospect or customer to call on, make an appointment, and then plan the sales call. This process is shown in Exhibit 7.2. The steps in planning the call are shown in Exhibit 7.5. Now that we know whom we will call on and what our objective will be, it's time to plan out and prepare the sales presentation itself.

The major phases within the presentation are shown in Exhibit 7.8. Please understand that Exhibit 7.8 is more specific than Exhibit 7.2 in showing the selling process

EXHIBIT 7.7

What Topics Should I Consider in My Planning?

In your Customer Profile and Planning Sheet, you develop a sales presentation strategy as part of the fourth step (developing your sales presentation). However, the question for many entry-level salespeople is "What do I include in each section?" In this exhibit, we provide potential topics that you might discuss with the buyer. Please remember, you will focus your presentation on the elements that will solve the buyer's problems and help them with their needs. Therefore, you will need to be selective with your planned presentation topics.

Marketing Plan Topics		Business Proposition Topics	
For Resellers: Helps the reseller understand how you will support them in reselling your product or solution)	**For End-Users: Helps the end-user understand how you will help them integrate the solution into their company, products, and processes)**	**For Resellers: Helps the reseller understand "what is in it for them" by reselling your product or solution**	**For End-Users: Helps the end-user understand "what is in it for them" by integrating the solution into their company, products, and processes**
1. Investment and implementation of awareness activities including: • Geographic reach: National advertising, regional, local, or co-op advertising • Types of advertising, including (social media, television, radio, outdoor, other internet initiatives) 2. Investment and implementation of sales promotion strategies including: • Samples • Point of Purchase displays • In-store signage • Contests • Coupons • Demonstrations • In-store promotions and initiatives 3. Investment and implementation of training the reseller's salesforce or personnel • Online training seminars • In-person training seminars • Training manuals or online reference materials • Training videos • Webinars • Timing of training 4. Investment in trade shows 5. Investment in trade promotion • Promotions in sales circulars • Displays • On-shelf price reductions • End-cap displays	1. Availability • Timelines • Seasonality 2. Delivery • Timelines • Locations 3. Installation • Who does it • When • How • Timelines 4. Training on use or integration • Online training sessions • In-person training seminars • Training manuals or online reference materials • Training videos • Webinars • Timing of training 5. Integration timelines 6. Ongoing service • Monitoring • Evaluation 7. Guarantees 8. Warranty • Length • Terms 9. Maintenance and Service agreements	1. Projected Sales • Units • Dollars 2. Projected Profits • Annual • Reseller's Fiscal Year 3. List price 4. Margins: • Gross margin (percentage and absolute amount) • Markup on cost (percentage and absolute amount • Markup on price (percentage and absolute amount) 5. Discounts • Cash • Consumer • Quantity • Trade 6. Financing • Payment plans • Interest rates • Terms 7. Incremental sales growth of product category due to your product 8. Potential inventory turnover 9. Projected market share 10. Slotting allowances	1. List price 2. ROI 3. Payback period 4. Discounts • Cash • Quantity 5. Shipping costs • Terms • Timelines • Mode (rail, long-haul truck, etc.) 5. Financing terms • Payment plans • Terms • Interest rate 6. Value analysis 7. Cost of ownership (long term) 8. Expected carrying cost • Day of inventory 9. Working capital investment 10. Reduction in expenses 11. Increased productivity • Units • Personnel (hours) • Personnel (sales rates) 12. Projected impact on quality levels • Reduced defects

EXHIBIT 7.8

Major phases in your presentation: a sequence of events to complete in developing a sales presentation.

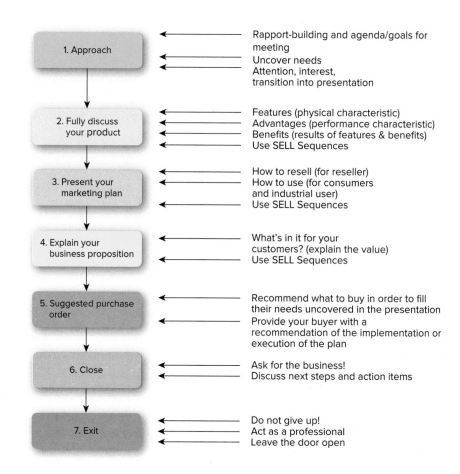

steps. You should plan out everything that is included in Exhibit 7.8. You should also do each phase in the exact order shown in Exhibit 7.8 in order to create a well-organized presentation.

Here's how you create the presentation. Based on the homework you have done on the prospect or customer, create the opening (approach) of the presentation. This section usually comprises a rapport-building opportunity, an agenda, and a discovery section that helps you learn about the buyer's needs. This section is further discussed in Chapter 9. Then prepare your product's *FAB*s, marketing plan, and business proposition. They were discussed earlier in this chapter and in previous chapters. Now, consider the solution that best meets the buyer's needs. Prepare a suggested purchase order and choose a closing method that feels natural for you to use when asking for the business. Should you make the sale or not make the sale, it is important to know how to exit the buyer's office. Thanking the customer for the order and discussing the key next steps in the process are two of the critical areas in this section. Closing the sale and the exit are discussed in Chapter 12.

Visual aids and demonstrations should be used to help create an informative and persuasive sales presentation. As mentioned earlier, the *last step* in planning your sales call is the development and rehearsal of the sales presentation.

In developing the sales presentation, think of leading the prospect through the five steps or phases that salespeople believe constitute a purchase decision. These phases are referred to as the prospect's mental steps.

The Prospect's Mental Steps

In making a sales presentation, consider the **prospect's mental steps:** quickly obtain the prospect's full attention, develop interest in your product, create a desire to fulfill a need, establish the prospect's conviction that the product fills a need, and, finally, promote action by having the prospect purchase the product. As shown in Exhibit 7.9, these steps occur in the following order.

Attention

From the moment you begin to talk, quickly capture and maintain the prospect's **attention.** This may be difficult at times because of distractions, pressing demands on the prospect's time, or lack of interest. Carefully plan what to say and how to say it. Since attention-getters have only a temporary effect, be ready to quickly move to step 2, sustaining the prospect's interest.

Interest

Before meeting with prospects, determine their important buying motives. These can be used in capturing **interest.** If you don't do this ahead of time, you may have to determine them at the beginning of your presentation by asking questions. Prospects enter the interest stage if they listen to and enter into a discussion with you. Quickly strive to link your product's benefits to prospects' needs. If this link is completed, prospects usually express a desire for the product.

Desire

Attempt to gain the prospect's full attention, develop interest in your product, create a desire to fulfill a need, establish the prospect's conviction that the product fills a need, and, finally, promote action by having the prospect purchase the product.

Using the *FAB* formula (Chapter 3), strive to bring prospects from lukewarm interest to a boiling **desire** for your product. Desire is created when prospects express a wish or wanting for a product like yours.

To better determine if they should purchase the product, prospects may have questions for you and may present objections to your product. Anticipate prospects' objections and provide information to maintain their desire.

Conviction

While prospects may desire a product, they still have to be convinced that your product is best for their needs and that you are the best supplier of the product. In the **conviction** step, strive to develop a strong *belief* that the product is best suited to prospects' specific needs. Conviction is established when no doubts remain about purchasing the product from you.

Purchase or Action

Once the prospect is convinced, plan the most appropriate method of asking the prospect to make a **purchase** or take some **action.** If each of the preceding steps has been implemented correctly, closing the sale is the easiest step in the sales presentation.

EXHIBIT 7.9

The prospect's five mental steps in buying.

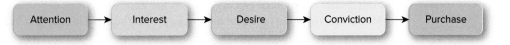

You have been working part-time for a large national department store chain for the past year. Your store, like others in the mall, has been experiencing a higher than normal amount of shoplifting. Store management has hired off-duty police wearing street clothes to walk around the store as if shopping and arrest thieves. The store manager strongly enforces the store policy that all people caught will be arrested.

For several months, you have suspected a fellow salesperson of taking office supplies home on a frequent basis. You have overlooked these discrepancies because she helped you learn the ropes when you started, and you believe that everyone takes a supply or two on occasion. Today, you saw the person take a damaged jogging suit, give the customer credit, and then put it in a store bag and place it under the counter. That night, as you were both leaving, the person had the bag with something in it. It could be the jogging suit or just something that your co-worker purchased earlier. You want to know if the jogging suit is in the bag, but you also know that if it is the jogging suit, the store manager will prosecute her.

What would be the most ethical action to take?

1. Take your manager aside and tell him/her what you witnessed. Let your manager handle the situation from there since it is potentially dangerous.
2. Do nothing. It is not your responsibility to investigate the situation. Let your manager find out him/herself.
3. Pull the person aside and explain that you thought you saw her put something in the bag. Let your co-worker know that you aren't going to tell anyone if it is true, but that the person should really stop to avoid jeopardizing her job.

Overview of the Selling Process

We have briefly discussed the various steps in the selling process, reviewed the sales presentation, and examined the five mental steps a prospect moves through while purchasing a product. Each step will be examined in more depth later, along with methods and techniques that successful salespeople use to lead the prospect to make the correct purchase decision.

The presentation's approach gets the prospect's attention and interest by having the prospect recognize a need or problem and state a wish to fulfill the need or solve the problem. The presentation constantly maintains interest in the information you present and generates desire for the product.

Uncovering and answering the prospect's questions and revealing and meeting or overcoming objections results in more intense desire. This desire is transformed into the conviction that your product can fulfill the prospect's needs or solve problems. Once you have determined that the prospect is in the conviction stage, you are ready for the close.

Empathizing with the Buyer.
Learning from an Experienced Buyer, Matthew Leiseth

Matthew Leiseth knows consumer packaged goods. Matthew serves as the president of Hornbacher's, a regional grocery chain in the Red River Valley of North Dakota and Minnesota. He began his experience in the grocery industry in 1991 and has continued in a variety of positions with increasing responsibility. For more than 25 years, Matthew has met and worked with salespeople in a variety of buying and merchandising capacities covering both tactical execution and the development of major strategies.

Matthew was kind enough to share some of his thoughts on the interactions between salespeople and buyers.

What makes a salesperson really impactful? As a grocer, our goal is to grow sales and profitability in all of our categories. Therefore, the really impactful salespeople consider the category (i.e., the broad grouping of products serving consumers, such as coffee) and the role their product plays in the category. We have worked with salespeople who present opportunities that provide benefits to the overall category as well as their brand. This group of salespeople consider how their products and brands are performing as well as the overall category in which they compete. This type of long-term business understanding is really important to us. By helping us drive sales and profitability, everyone wins.

Impactful salespeople also understand that buyers have multiple options. The salespeople who use a partnership attitude demonstrate a genuine understanding that our consumers make a daily decision to buy or not to buy. It's important to deliver the products and services that our consumers want each day. Therefore, we need to have multiple options from which our consumers can choose. The impactful salespeople understand that we need to find the products that will delight our customers and meet their needs. This type of salesperson works diligently to understand the market and how it changes, and provides solutions in terms of products, services, and knowledge.

Impactful salespeople understand the various roles their products can play. Many of the salespeople that work with us represent a range of products. Sometimes products play various roles in our categories. This understanding and knowledge is essential to our business discussions and our strategy. Salespeople build trust through their knowledge, their understanding, their insight, and their ability to leverage their firm's resources and expertise. They know how to find answers and bring forward solutions.

You mentioned that trust is important. In your perspective what are some of the key sales behaviors that help build a trusting relationship with buyers?

- *Effective salespeople focus on the relationship and understand all of the elements that help build a business relationship.* The helpful salesperson really listens to the buyer's needs and works to build the business together. They understand that they may not close absolutely every sale or promotional opportunity, but by being a business partner that works to improve our overall categories, they open up a long-term business opportunity.
- *Effective salespeople understand each customer's specific buying process.* The really effective salespeople work to understand the customer's processes such as (a) when do we make purchases (i.e., our buying cycle), (b) what format of information is important to us and when do we need this information, (c) how does our business work, and (d) what are our business objectives.
- *Effective salespeople value the buyer's time.* It's great when salespeople let us know about news ahead of time. It's great to send a meeting agenda one week ahead of time to the buyer. Let the buyer understand the purpose of the meeting. When you e-mail the buyer an agenda, it allows the buyer to understand the meeting's goals and also to provide feedback regarding the goals. Similarly, when you are presenting to a buyer, focus on the question, "What's the most productive use of our time today?"
- *Effective salespeople are specific.* Don't be ambiguous or overgeneralize business issues. Try to really understand the buyer's business objectives and work diligently to provide solutions to these business needs. This allows us to focus our ongoing conversations in two ways: (a) what do we talk about and (b) how do we talk about it.

- *Effective salespeople are proactive and confront the difficult issues.* We understand that market conditions may change. Be transparent and let the buyer know about the changes as soon as possible. If you expect changes in production, strategy, promotional funding, back orders, or price increases, bring the news to us. Your willingness to be proactive with both the great news and the not-so-great news is important to the business relationship.
- *Effective salespeople make sure we all understand the next steps.* At the end of each meeting, make sure to recap each party's actions steps. We need to confirm our next steps as well as the next steps to which the salesperson has committed.
- *Effective salespeople follow up.* We need to make sure everyone makes good on their commitments. As a salesperson, you often are the one who recommends a timeline for implementation. Make sure you recommend a timeline that is reasonable—a timeline that you and your team can deliver upon.

Courtesy of Hornbacher's

SUMMARY OF MAJOR SELLING ISSUES

Most salespeople agree that careful planning of the sales call is essential to success in selling. Among many reasons why planning is so important, four of the most frequently mentioned are that planning builds self-confidence, develops an atmosphere of goodwill, creates professionalism, and increases sales. By having a logical and methodical plan, you can decide what to accomplish and then later measure your accomplishments with your plan.

There are four basic elements of sales call planning. First, you must always have a sales call objective—one that is specific, measurable, and beneficial to the customer. Second, as a salesperson you must also develop or review the customer profile. By having relevant information about your customer, you can properly develop a customized presentation. You can find information on the background, needs, and competitors of your potential buyer by reviewing your company's records or by personally contacting the buyer and the company.

The third step in planning your sales call involves developing your customer benefit plan. To do this, look at why the prospect should purchase your product and develop a marketing plan to convey those reasons and the benefits to your prospect. Then, develop a *business proposition* by listing your price, percent markup, return on investment, and other quantitative data about your product in relation to your prospect. Last, develop a *suggested purchase order* and present your analysis, which might include suggestions on what to buy, how much to buy, what assortment to buy, and when to ship the product.

Finally, plan your whole sales presentation. Visual aids can help make your presentation informative and creative. In making your call, think in terms of the phases that make up a purchase decision—the mental steps: capturing the prospect's attention, determining buying motives, creating desire, convincing the person that your product is best suited to her or his needs, and then closing the sale.

By adhering to these guidelines for planning your sales presentation, you may spend more time planning than on the actual sales call. However, it will be well worth it.

Quick Review for Students

The quick review sections provide key questions to help you develop a greater level of conceptual understanding. We suggest that after you read the chapter, you try to answer the following questions without looking back at the textbook.

1. What are the elements of trust? For each element of trust, please describe a specific salesperson action that could help create it.
2. Why is it important that the salesperson serves as a problem solver for the customer?
3. Why is it important for the salesperson to tailor a custom solution for each customer? What are the major elements of the consultative selling model?
4. What are the four components of sales call planning? What specific actions would a salesperson conduct in each step of the process?
5. What are the specific elements of a SMART goal? Why is it important that a salesperson write a SMART goal before meeting with a customer?
6. What is the value of understanding the buyers' needs? Describe a few approaches salespeople could use to better understand their buyers' needs? What are a few common needs of buyers?
7. What are the four elements of a customer benefit plan? Why is preparing a customer benefit plan important?

MEETING A SALES CHALLENGE

The purpose of your sales presentation is to provide information so the prospect can make a rational, informed buying decision. You provide this information using your *FAB*s, marketing plan, and business approval.

The information you provide allows the buyer to develop positive personal *beliefs* toward your product. The beliefs result in *desire* (or *need*) for the type of product you sell. Your job, as a salesperson, is to convert that need into a want and into the *attitude* that your product is the best product to fulfill a certain need. Furthermore, you must convince the buyer not only that your product is the best but that you are the best source to buy from. When this occurs, your prospect has moved into the *conviction* stage of the mental buying process. Listen and watch for it.

When a real need is established, the buyer will want to fulfill that need, and there is a high probability that he or she will choose your product. Whether to buy or not is a "choice decision," and you provide the necessary information so that the customer chooses to buy from you.

When you are prepared, the prospect or customer recognizes it. This gives you a better chance of giving your presentation and thus increases your sales, because the more presentations given, the more people sold. Veteran salespeople have a tendency not to prepare. Many get lazy and fall into a bad habit of "winging it." Top sales professionals rarely are unprepared. Do you want to be an order-taker or an order-getter? Your success is entirely up to you!

KEY TERMS FOR SELLING

action 265	interest 265	sales call purpose 255
attention 265	plan 247	sales presentation 262
conviction 265	preapproach 254	SMART 257
creative problem solvers 253	prospect's mental steps 265	strategic 250
customer benefit plan 261	purchase or action 265	strategic customer
customer profile 259	sales call objective 256	relationship 251
desire 265	sales call planning 247	success 248

SALES APPLICATION QUESTIONS

1. What are the elements to consider when planning a sales call? Explain each one.
2. An important part of planning a sales call is the development of a customer benefit plan. What are the major components of the customer benefit plan? What is the difference in developing a customer benefit plan for a General Foods salesperson selling consumer products versus an industrial salesperson selling products for a company such as IBM?
3. Many salespeople feel a prospect goes through several mental steps in making a decision to purchase a product. Discuss each one of these steps.
4. Outline and discuss the sequence of events in developing a sales presentation.
5. Some salespeople feel a person should not be asked to buy a product until the prospect's mind has entered the conviction step of the mental process. Why?
6. What is the difference, if any, between the selling process and the sales presentation?
7. Define the term *selling process.* Second, list the major steps in the selling process on the left side of a piece of paper. Third, beside each step of the selling process, write the corresponding mental step that a prospect should experience.
8. Below are 13 situations salespeople commonly face. For each situation, determine the mental buying stage that your prospect is experiencing. Give a reason why the prospect is at that stage.
    a. "Come on in; I can only visit with you for about five minutes."
    b. "That sounds good, but how can I be sure it will do what you say it will?"
    c. "Yes, I see your copier can make 20 copies a minute and copy on both sides of the page. Big deal!"
    d. The buyer thinks, "Will the purchase of this equipment help my standing with my boss?"
    e. "I didn't know there were products like this on the market."
    f. The buyer thinks, "I'm not sure if I should listen or not."
    g. "I wish my equipment could do what yours does."
    h. "Well, that sounds good, but I'm not sure."
    i. "What kind of great deal do you have for me today?"
    j. "When can you ship it?"
    k. You discuss your business proposition with your buyer, and you receive a favorable nonverbal response.
    l. "I like what you have to say. Your deal sounds good. But I'd better check with my other suppliers first."
    m. You have completed your presentation. The buyer has said almost nothing to you, asking no questions and giving no objections. You wonder if you should close.
9. Think of a product sold through one of your local supermarkets. Assume you were recently hired by the product's manufacturer to contact the store's buyer to purchase a promotional quantity of your product and to arrange for display and advertising. What information do you need for planning the sales call, and what features, advantages, and benefits would be appropriate in your sales presentation?

FURTHER EXPLORING THE SALES WORLD

Ask a buyer for a business in your community what salespeople should do when calling on a buyer. Find out if the salespeople that this buyer sees are prepared for each sales call. Ask why or why not the buyer purchases something. Do salespeople use the *FAB* method as discussed in this chapter? Does the buyer think privately, "So what?" "Prove it!" and "What's in it for me?" Finally, ask what superiors expect of a buyer in the buyer's dealing with salespeople.

SELLING EXPERIENTIAL EXERCISE

Do you set objectives for each of your classes? Are your course objectives SMART—specific, measurable, achievable, realistic, and timed? Salespeople set objectives for each customer. Would you consider setting objectives for each class, constantly measuring your performance, and reevaluating your progress toward the objective? You can do this by answering the questions in Exhibit 7.10.

SMART Course Objective Setting

Enough time has passed in your selling course that you have one or more grades. Let's assume you want to make an A in the class. Ask your instructor or see your class syllabus for the total points you can earn in your sales course. Assuming no curve, multiply the maximum points by 0.9. If you can earn a maximum of 1,000 points, then you only need 900 points for an A. Your goal now becomes a total score of 900 points on all graded activities.

Subtract the total points you have earned so far from the number of points needed to reach your objective—900 points. How many remaining test(s) and assignment(s) are ahead? Determine if you can reach your course grade objective by making an 80, 90, or 95 percent average on all remaining test(s) and assignment(s). Each time you receive a grade for a major assignment, recalculate your progress toward scoring 900 points and making your A.

As in sales, usually a person's class performance is a function of their ability and motivation. This is why class performance is a function (f) of an individual's ability times motivation, or

$$\text{Class performance} = f(\text{Ability} \times \text{Motivation})$$

Now for the most important question of all. The answer to this question will determine your future grade in this or any class. "How hard are you willing to work in reaching your course grade objective?" On a scale of 1 to 10—with 10 being the maximum effort—how hard are you willing to work in this course to reach your objective?

EXHIBIT 7.10

SMART course objective setting.

- What grade do you want to make in this course? Write on this line _____
- How many points do you have to earn in this class to reach your objective?_____ (Total points multiplied by 0.9. See your syllabus for total course points.)
- How many points do you now have in the course? _____
- How many points do you need to earn to reach your objective? _____
- Can you reach your objective? _____Yes _____ No
- On a scale of 1 to 10—with 10 being the maximum effort—how hard are you willing to work in this course to reach your objective? Be honest with yourself. My "effort score" will be_____.
- In your class notes, write a statement explaining how you will reach your grade objective.

Be honest with yourself! Write it down! This is important; write it down, please.

My effort score is ————— (1 to 10).

Each time you recalculate your progress toward your goal of making an A in this class, reconsider your "effort score." Write down all future "effort scores." See if over time your "effort score" begins to decline, increase, or stay the same.

STUDENT APPLICATION LEARNING EXERCISES (SALES)

At the end of appropriate chapters beginning with Chapter 3, you will find Student Application Learning Exercises (SALES). SALES are meant to help you construct the various segments of your sales presentation. SALES build upon one another so that after you complete them, you will have constructed the majority of your sales presentation.

SALE 3 of 7—Chapter 7

In planning the sales presentation, it is necessary to create a marketing plan. Review the section beginning on page 261 titled "Customer Benefit Plan: What It's All About." The marketing plan is described in step 2 on page 261. Carefully study Exhibits 7.7 and 7.8. Review the advertising and sales promotion sections contained in pages 263–264. To make **SALE 3:**

1. List three *FAB*s you could discuss in your marketing plan.

Feature	Advantage	Benefit
a.		
b.		
c.		

2. Write out one **SELL Sequence** using the *FAB*s. Label each of the components of the **SELL Sequence** using parentheses.

NOTES

1. Adapted from Robert H. Schuller, *Success Is Never Ending, Failure Is Never Final* (New York: Bantam, 1988), p. 227.

2. Robert W. Palmatier, Rajiv P. Dant, Dhruv Grewal, and Kenneth R. Evans, "Factors Influencing the Effectiveness of Relationship Marketing: A Meta-Analysis," *Journal of Marketing* 70, no. 4 (October 2006), pp. 136–53.

3. Kapil R., Tuli, Ajay K. Kohli, and Sundar G. Bharadwaj, "Rethinking Customer Solutions: From Product Bundles to Relational Processes," *Journal of Marketing* 71, no. 3 (July 2007), pp. 1–17.

4. Adapted from *Marketplace Ethics: Issues in Sales and Marketing* (Westport, CT: J/S Productions, 1990), pp. 35–54.

CASE 7.1

©Ron Chapple Stock/FotoSearch/
Glow Images

Ms. Hansen's Mental Steps in Buying Your Product

Picture yourself as a Procter & Gamble salesperson who plans to call on Ms. Hansen, a buyer for your largest independent grocery store. Your sales call objective is to convince Ms. Hansen that she should buy the family-size Tide detergent. The store now carries the three smaller sizes. You believe your marketing plan will help convince her that she is losing sales and profits by not stocking Tide's family size.

You enter the grocery store, check your present merchandise, and quickly develop a suggested order. As Ms. Hansen walks down the aisle toward you, she appears to be in her normal grumpy mood. After your initial greeting and handshake, your conversation continues:

Salesperson: Your sales are really up! I've checked your stock in the warehouse and on the shelf. This is what it looks like you need. [You discuss sales of each of your products and their various sizes, suggesting a quantity she should purchase based on her past sales and present inventory.]

Buyer: OK, that looks good. Go ahead and ship it.

Salesperson: Thank you. Say, Ms. Hansen, you've said before that the shortage of shelf space prevents you from stocking our family-size Tide—though you admit you may be losing some sales as a result. If we could determine how much volume you're missing, I think you'd be willing to make space for it, wouldn't you?

Buyer: Yes, but I don't see how that can be done.

Salesperson: Well, I'd like to suggest a test—a weekend display of all four sizes of Tide.

Buyer: What do you mean?

Salesperson: My thought was to run all sizes at regular shelf price without any ad support. This would give us a pure test. Six cases of each size should let us compare sales of the various sizes and see what you're missing by regularly stocking only the smaller sizes. I think the additional sales and profits you'll get on the family size will convince you to start stocking it regularly. What do you think?

Buyer: Well, maybe.

Questions

1. Examine each item you mentioned to Ms. Hansen, stating what part of the customer benefit plan each of your comments is concerned with.
2. What are the features, advantages, and benefits in your sales presentation?
3. Examine each of Ms. Hansen's replies, stating the mental buying step she is in at that particular time during your sales presentation.
4. At the end of the conversation, Ms. Hansen said, "Well, maybe." Which of the following should you do now?

   a. Continue to explain your features, advantages, and benefits.
   b. Ask a trial close question.
   c. Ask for the order.
   d. Back off and try again on the next sales call.
   e. Wait for Ms. Hansen to say, "OK, ship it."

CASE 7.2

©Ron Chapple Stock/FotoSearch/
Glow Images

Machinery Lubricants, Inc.

Ralph Jackson sells industrial lubricants to manufacturing plants. The lubricants are used to lubricate the plant's machinery. Tomorrow, Ralph plans to call on the purchasing agent for Acme Manufacturing Company.

For the past two years, Ralph has been selling Hydraulic Oil 65 in drums to Acme. Ralph's sales call objective is to persuade Acme to switch from purchasing oil in drums to a bulk oil system. Last year, Acme bought approximately 364 drums or 20,000 gallons at a cost of $1.39 a gallon or $27,800, with a deposit of $20 for each drum. Traditionally, many drums are lost, and one to two gallons of oil may be left in each drum when returned by customers. This is a loss to the company.

Ralph wants to sell Acme two 3,000-gallon storage tanks at a cost of $1,700. He has arranged with Pump Supply Company to install the tanks for $1,095. Thus, the total cost of the system will be $2,795. This system reduces the cost of the oil from $1.39 to $1.25 per gallon, which will allow it to pay for itself over time. Other advantages include having fewer orders to process each year, a reduction in storage space, and less handling of the oil by workers.

Question

If you were Ralph, how would you plan the sales call?

CASE 7.3

©Ron Chapple Stock/FotoSearch/
Glow Images

Telemax, Inc.

Ellen St. James, a marketing director for Telemax, Inc., is walking through an antique store with Monica, a customer and friend. Ellen is in charge of a project called Stardust, a new telecommunication product in which her company has invested heavily. Monica informs Ellen that she has learned from a marketer at PCI, one of Telemax's major competitors and the industry leader, that they are planning to introduce a product similar to Stardust. Ellen is immediately upset, but tries to hide this fact from Monica. Ellen states that she has heard about this product and asks Monica if she was able to find out when the product will be introduced. Monica states that she had asked the marketer this question, but he did not give her a straight answer.

Ellen is having lunch with Carl, her former subordinate at Telemax. Ellen and Carl start talking about work and Ellen confides to Carl that Stardust will be available in 90 days. Ellen explains that she needs to know when PCI is introducing its product because, if Stardust is introduced after or at the same time as PCI's product, Telemax probably will not be able to gain the needed market share. Ellen asks Carl for advice on how to get this information and he gives her several suggestions, including putting someone on PCI's payroll, asking her customers for information, hiring a private investigator, and pushing Stardust through Telemax's quality assurance department. Ellen, however, does not feel comfortable using any of these tactics. Carl recalls that Ellen hired an ex-PCI employee, Frank Cilento, and recommends that she finds out what he knows or can find out. Ellen remarks that Frank is up for a promotion. As the vignette closes, Ellen is left to consider whether to use the possibility of promotion as leverage with Frank.[4]

Questions

1. What are the main ethical issues, if any, in the Telemax, Inc., case? Describe each ethical issue.
2. What are Ellen's options?
3. How do the three levels of moral development relate to Ellen's situation?
4. What would you do?

©Inti St Clair LLC/Blend Images

Carefully Select Which Sales Presentation Method to Use

Main Topics

The Core Principles: Presentation

Sales Presentation Strategy

Sales Presentation Methods—Select One Carefully

Areas to Consider in Any Sales Presentation Method

The Group Presentation

Negotiating So Everyone Wins

Sales Presentations Go High-Tech

Select the Presentation Method, Then the Approach

The Parallel Dimensions of Selling

The Sales Presentation and Techniques (A Review of the Process)

Practice and Time

Learning Objectives

To know the best way to begin the sales presentation, first determine the type of sales presentation to use for each prospect or customer. After studying this chapter, you should be able to

8–1   State why you first select a sales presentation method and then select the approach.

8–2   Describe the different sales presentation methods, know their differences, and know the appropriate situation for using a particular method.

8–3   Know the key areas that you can consider in any sales presentation method.

8–4   Better understand how to give a presentation to a group of prospects.

8–5   Understand why negotiations can be an important part of the presentation.

8–6   Be able to discuss the structure and contents of a sales presentation based on the parallel dimensions of selling.

FACING A SALES CHALLENGE

It took you four hours to plan, prepare, and practice your sales presentation to the largest manufacturer in your sales territory. Although the manufacturer has never purchased before, you feel your product will benefit the company. You arrive on time for your appointment with Juan Gomez.

Mr. Gomez's administrative assistant takes you into a large conference room, saying, "They'll be with you in a few minutes." "They," you think. "Who is coming?" you ask. "The head of accounting, production, and two engineers—and the president wants us to call her once the meeting gets under way." As she leaves, you become dizzy, your stomach gets upset, and you feel weak in the knees. "I've never given a presentation to a group—let alone experts. And the president of the company. Oh, my—what am I going to do?" What would you do?

Salespeople, sales trainers, and sales managers agree that the most challenging, rewarding, and enjoyable aspect of the buyer–seller interaction is the **sales presentation.** An effective sales presentation completely and clearly explains all aspects of a salesperson's proposition as it relates to a buyer's needs. Surprisingly, attaining this objective is not as easy as you might think. Few successful salespeople will claim that they had little trouble developing a good presentation or mastering the art of giving the sales presentation. How, then, can you as a novice, develop a sales presentation that will improve your chances of making the sale?

You must first select a sales presentation method according to your prior knowledge of the customer, your sales call objective, and your customer benefit plan. Once you have made the selection, you are ready to develop your sales presentation. The particular sales presentation method that you select will make an excellent framework on which to build your specific presentation.

Once you select the presentation method for a specific prospect or customer, it is time to determine how to open or begin the sales presentation. Steps 3 through 9 of the sales process comprise the seven steps within the sales presentation itself. The sales opener, or approach, as shown in Exhibit 8.1, is the first major step in the sales presentation. The approach is discussed in Chapter 9.

This chapter discusses the four different sales presentation methods, including how to conduct a group presentation. Negotiations are also introduced in this chapter, since they are often necessary regardless of the presentation method used. One of the most important parts of your textbook is "The Parallel Dimensions of Selling" discussed on page 298 of this chapter.

The Core Principles: Presentation

Salespeople face various types of prospects, customers, and organizations each day, requiring the skill to use different presentation methods based upon the situation. What is not different from one sales call to another is the purpose of meeting with someone. You want to help the person or organization. From your honesty within the presentation, people will realize you can be trusted.

The heart of the sales presentation is the discussion of the product, marketing plan, and business proposition. The question is, "To whom is the presentation being given?" Once this question is answered, the salesperson can choose the type of sales presentation method best suited to the prospect or customer. That is what this chapter is about. Your selection of the best presentation method for the situation will allow you to improve the chances of helping the customer. Thus, you must master the art of delivering a good sales presentation. This will lead to solving the customer's problems. With great presentations you can ethically serve others, building long-term relationships, based upon the truth. As you travel from place to place, helping others you touch, you improve their lives. What a wonderful calling this will be if you truly love to sell and help your business neighbors in the community.

Sales Presentation Strategy

Salespeople work with customers in different ways. They face numerous situations, including

- **Salesperson to buyer:** A salesperson discusses issues with a prospect or customer in person or over the phone.
- **Salesperson to buyer group:** A salesperson gets to know as many members of the buyer group as possible.

©monkey business images/Getty Images

EXHIBIT 8.1

The third step in the sales process is the first step in the sales presentation. The sales presentation method determines how you open your presentation.

- **Sales team to buyer group:** A company sales team works closely with the members of the customer's buying group.
- **Conference selling:** The salesperson brings company resource people to discuss a major problem or opportunity.
- **Seminar selling:** A company team conducts an educational seminar for the customer company about state-of-the-art developments.

Each customer contact represents a unique challenge for the salespeople. Thus, the salesperson needs to understand the various sales presentation methods.

Sales Presentation Methods—Select One Carefully

The sales presentation involves a persuasive verbal and visual explanation of a business proposition. Of the many ways of making a presentation, four methods are presented here to highlight the alternatives available to help sell your products.

The most common method involves a need-satisfaction or problem–solution approach.

As shown on the continuum in Exhibit 8.2, the four sales presentation methods are (1) memorized, (2) formula, (3) need-satisfaction, and (4) problem–solution selling methods.[1] The basic difference in the four methods is the percentage of the conversation controlled by the salesperson. In the more structured memorized and formula selling techniques, the salesperson normally has a monopoly on the conversation, whereas the less structured methods allow for greater buyer–seller interaction; both parties participate equally in the conversation. Transactional selling generally is more structured, whereas partnering requires a more customized presentation, with relationship selling typically somewhere in between (see Exhibit 8.2).

The Memorized Sales Presentation

The memorized sales presentation would not be appropriate for more relational or consultative selling.

The **memorized presentation** is based on either of two assumptions: that a prospect's needs can be stimulated by direct exposure to the product, via the sales presentation, or that these needs have already been stimulated because the prospect has made the effort to seek out the product. In either case, the salesperson's role is to develop this initial stimulus into an affirmative response to an eventual purchase request.

The salesperson does 80 to 90 percent of the talking during a memorized sales presentation, only occasionally allowing the prospect to respond to predetermined questions, as shown in Exhibit 8.3. Notably, the salesperson does not attempt to determine the prospect's needs during the interview, but gives the same canned sales talk

EXHIBIT 8.2

The structure of sales presentations.

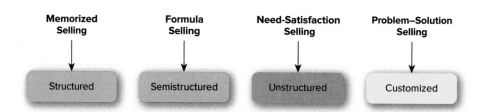

EXHIBIT 8.3

Participation time by customer and salesperson during a memorized sales presentation.

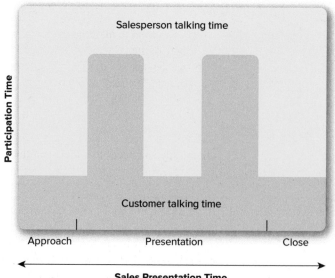

to all prospects. Since no attempt is made at this point to learn what goes on in the consumer's mind, the salesperson concentrates on discussing the product and its benefits, concluding the pitch with a purchase request. The seller hopes that a convincing presentation of product benefits will cause the prospect to buy.

Actually, parts of any presentation may be canned, yet linked with free-form conversation. Over time, most salespeople develop proven selling sentences, phrases, and sequences for discussing information. They tend to use these in all presentations.

Despite its impersonal aura, the canned or memorized sales presentation has distinct advantages, as seen in Exhibit 8.4.

- It ensures that the salesperson gives a well-planned presentation and that all of the company's salespeople discuss the same information.
- It both aids and lends confidence to the inexperienced salesperson.
- It is effective when selling time is short, as in door-to-door or telephone selling.
- It is effective when the product is nontechnical—such as books, cooking utensils, and cosmetics.

As may be apparent, the memorized method has several major drawbacks:

- It presents features, advantages, and benefits that may not be important to the buyer.
- It allows for little prospect participation.
- It is impractical to use when selling technical products that require prospect input and discussion.
- It proceeds quickly through the sales presentation to the close, requiring the salesperson to close or ask for the order several times, which may be interpreted by the prospect as high-pressure selling.

The story is told of the new salesperson who was halfway through a canned presentation when the prospect had to answer the telephone. When the prospect finished the telephone conversation, the salesperson had forgotten the stopping point and started over again. The prospect naturally became angry.

In telling of his early selling experiences, salesperson John Anderson remembers that he was once so intent on presenting his memorized presentation that halfway through it the prospect yelled, "Enough, John, I've been waiting for you to see me. I'm ready to buy. I know all about your products." Anderson was so intent on giving his canned presentation, and listening to himself talk, that he did not recognize the prospect's buying signals.

For some selling situations, a highly structured presentation can be used successfully. Examine its advantages and disadvantages to determine if this presentation is appropriate for your prospects and products.

Some situations may seem partially appropriate for the memorized approach but require a more personal touch. Such circumstances warrant the examination and use of formula selling.

The Formula Presentation

The **formula presentation,** often referred to as the *persuasive selling presentation,* is akin to the memorized method: It is based on the assumption that similar prospects in similar situations can be approached with similar presentations. However, for the formula method to apply, the salesperson must first know something about the prospective buyer. The salesperson follows a less structured, general outline in making a presentation, allowing more flexibility and less direction.

EXHIBIT 8.4

Dyno Electric Cart memorized presentation.

Situation: You call on a purchasing manager to elicit an order for some electric carts (like a golf cart). The carts would be used as transportation around the buildings and grounds of a manufacturing plant. The major benefit to emphasize in your presentation is that the carts save time (i.e. reduce transit time between building for personnel).; you incorporate this concept in your approach. For this product, you have chosen to use the memorized stimulus–response presentation.[2]

Salesperson: Hello, Mr. Pride, my name is Karen Nordstrom, and I'd like to talk with you about how to save your company executives' time. By the way, thanks for taking the time to talk with me.

Buyer: What's on your mind?

Salesperson: As a busy executive, you know time is a valuable commodity. Nearly everyone would like to have a few extra minutes each day and that is the business I'm in, selling time. While I can't actually sell you time, I do have a product that is the next best thing . . . a Dyno Electric Cart—a real time-saver for your executives.

Buyer: Yeah, well, everyone would like to have extra time. However, I don't think we need any golf carts. [First objection.]

Salesperson: Dyno Electric Cart is more than a golf cart. It is an electric cart designed for use in industrial plants. It has been engineered to give comfortable, rapid transportation in warehouses, plants, and across open areas.

Buyer: They probably cost too much for us to use. [Positive buying signal phrased as an objection.]

Salesperson: First of all, they cost only $2,200 each. With a five-year normal life, that is only $400 per year plus a few cents for electricity and a few dollars for maintenance. Under normal use and care, these carts require only about $100 of service in their five-year life. Thus, for about $50 a month, you can save key people a lot of time. [Creative pricing—show photographs of carts in use.]

Buyer: It would be nice to save time, but I don't think management would go for the idea. [Third objection, but still showing interest.]

Salesperson: This is exactly why I am here. Your executives will appreciate what you have done for them. You will look good in their eyes if you give them an opportunity to look at a product that will save time and energy. Saving time is only part of our story. Dyno carts also save energy and thus keep you sharper toward the end of the day. Would you want a demonstration today or Tuesday? [Alternative close.]

Buyer: How long would your demonstration take? [Positive buying signal.]

Salesperson: I only need one hour. When would it be convenient for me to bring the cart in for your executives to try out?

Buyer: There really isn't any good time. [Objection.]

Salesperson: That's true. Therefore, the sooner we get to show you a Dyno cart, the sooner your management group can see its benefits. How about next Tuesday? I could be here at 8:00 and we could go over this item just before your weekly management group meeting. I know you usually have a meeting Tuesdays at 9:00 because I tried to call on you a few weeks ago and your secretary told me you were in the weekly management meeting. [Close of the sale.]

Buyer: Well, we could do it then.

Salesperson: Fine, I'll be here. Your executives will really be happy! [Positive reinforcement.]

The salesperson generally controls the conversation during the sales talk, especially at the beginning. Exhibit 8.5 illustrates how a salesperson should take charge during a formula selling situation.[3] For example, the salesperson might make a sales opener (approach), discuss the product's features, advantages, and benefits, and then start to solicit comments from the buyer using trial closes, answering questions, and handling objections. At the end of the participation curve, the salesperson regains control over the discussion and moves in to close the sale.

EXHIBIT 8.5

Participation time by a customer and salesperson during a formula sales presentation.

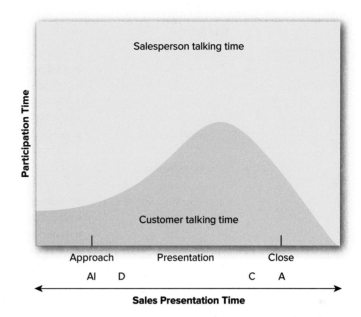

The formula selling approach obtains its name from the salesperson using the attention, interest, desire, and action (AIDA) procedure of developing and giving the sales presentation. We earlier added conviction (C) to the procedure because the prospect may want or desire the product, yet not be convinced this is the best product or the best salesperson from whom to buy.

Straight rebuy situations, especially with consumer goods, lend themselves to this method. Many prospects or customers buy because they are familiar with the salesperson's company. The question is, how can a salesperson for Quaker Oats, Revlon, Gillette, Procter & Gamble, or any other well-known manufacturer develop a presentation that convinces a customer to purchase promotional quantities of a product, participate in a local advertising campaign, or stock a new, untried product?

SmithKline Beecham Products, a consumer goods manufacturer, has developed a sequence, or formula, for its salespeople to follow. The company refers to it as the *10-step productive retail sales call.* The SmithKline Beecham salesperson sells products such as Cling Free Sheets and Aquafresh toothpaste. The 10 steps and their major components are shown in Exhibit 8.6.

Formula selling is effective for calling on customers who currently buy and for prospects about whose operations the salesperson has learned a great deal. In such situations, formula selling offers significant advantages:

- It ensures that all information is presented logically.
- It allows for a reasonable amount of buyer–seller interaction.
- It allows for smooth handling of *anticipated* questions and objections.

When executed in a smooth, conversational manner, the formula method of selling has no major flaws, as long as the salesperson has correctly identified the prospect's needs and wants. The Procter & Gamble formula sales presentation given as an example in Exhibit 8.7 can be given to any retailer who is not selling all available sizes of Tide (or of any other product). In this situation, a formula approach is used in calling on a customer the salesperson has sold to previously. If, on the other hand, the salesperson did not know a customer's needs and used this Tide presentation, chances are

EXHIBIT 8.6

The 10-step productive retail sales call.

Step Number	Action
1. Plan the call.	■ Review the situation. ■ Analyze problems and appointments. ■ Set objectives. ■ Plan the presentation. ■ Check your sales materials.
2. Review plans.	■ Before you leave your car to enter the store, review your plans, sales call objectives, suggested order forms, and so on.
3. Greet personnel.	■ Give a friendly greeting to store personnel. ■ Alert the store manager for sales action.

4. Check store conditions.	■ Note appearance of stock on shelf.
	■ Check distribution and pricing.
	■ Note out-of-stocks.
	■ Perform a quick fix by straightening shelf stock.
	■ Report competitive activity.
	■ Check back room (storeroom):
	  Locate product to correct out-of-stocks.
	  Use reserve stock for special display.
	■ Update sales plan if needed.

5. Make the approach.	■ Keep it short.
6. Present.	■ Make it logical, clear, interesting. ■ Tailor it to dealer's style. ■ Present it from dealer's point of view. ■ Use sales tools.
7. Close.	■ Present a suggested order (ask for the order). ■ Offer a choice. ■ Answer questions and handle objections. ■ Get a real order.
8. Merchandise.	■ Build displays. ■ Dress up the shelves.
9. Record and report.	■ Complete them immediately after the call.

10. Analyze the call.	■ Review the call to spot strong and weak points.
	  How could the sales call have been improved?
	  How can the next call be improved?

customer objections would arise early in the presentation—as they sometimes do with the memorized sales presentation method. The formula technique is not adaptable to all complex selling situations; a number of them require other sales presentations.

The Need-Satisfaction Presentation

The television remote is a powerful tool in many homes. It determines which show is watched, how high the sound is, and whether a program plays or stops. The person who holds it has control.[4]

In a similar way, we like to be in charge of the sales presentation—determining the starts, stops, pauses, and rewinds. A sales presentation requiring questions, comments, and long discussions by the buyer challenges the seller to set aside the planned

EXHIBIT 8.7

A formula approach sales presentation.

Formula Steps	Buyer–Seller Roles	Sales Presentation
Summarize the situation for *attention and interest*.	**Salesperson:**	Ms. Hansen, you've said before that the shortage of shelf space prevents you from stocking our family-size Tide—though you admit you may be losing some sales as a result. If we could determine *how much* volume you're missing, I think you'd be willing to *make* space for it, wouldn't you? [Trial close.]
State your marketing plan for *interest*.	**Buyer:**	Yes, but I don't see how that can be done.
	Salesperson:	Well, I'd like to suggest a test—a weekend display of all four sizes of Tide.
	Buyer:	What do you mean?
Explain your marketing plan for *interest* and *desire*.	**Salesperson:**	My thought was to run all sizes at regular shelf price *without* any ad support. This would give us a pure test. Six cases of each size should let us compare sales of the various sizes and see what you're missing by regularly stocking only the smaller sizes. I think the additional sales and profits you'll get on the family size will convince you to start stocking regularly. [Reinforce key benefits.] What do you think? [Trial close.]
Buyer appears to be in *conviction* stage.	**Buyer:**	Well, maybe. [Positive reaction to trial close.]
Suggest an easy next step or *action*.	**Salesperson:**	May I enter the six cases of family-size Tide in the order book now? [Close.]

presentation to allow conversational interaction. The rookie salesperson finds this situation nerve-racking, while the seasoned veteran finds this an exhilarating experience. The need-satisfaction and problem–solution presentation methods share the control between buyer and seller.

The **need-satisfaction presentation** is different from the memorized and the formalized approach; it is designed as a flexible, interactive sales presentation. It is the most challenging and creative form of selling.

The salesperson typically starts the presentation with a probing question such as, "What are you looking for in investment property?" or "What type of technology needs does your company have?" This opening starts a discussion of the prospect's needs and also gives the salesperson an opportunity to determine whether any of the products being offered might be beneficial. When something the prospect has said is not understood by the salesperson, it can be clarified by a question or by restating what the buyer has said. The need-satisfaction format is especially suited to the sale of industrial and technical goods with stringent specifications and high price tags.

Often, as shown in Exhibit 8.8, the first 50 to 60 percent of conversation time (referred to as the **need-development** phase) is devoted to a discussion of the buyer's needs.[5] Once aware of the prospect's needs (the **need-awareness** phase), the salesperson begins to take control of the conversation by restating the prospect's needs to clarify the situation. During the last stage of the presentation, the **need-fulfillment** (or need-satisfaction) phase, the salesperson shows how the product will satisfy mutual

A common goal: Structure the sales conversation to allow the buyer to talk 80% of the time.

EXHIBIT 8.8

Participation time by customer and salesperson during need-satisfaction and problem–solution sales presentations.

EXHIBIT 8.9

A need-satisfaction presentation.

Salesperson: Mr. Pride, you really have a large manufacturing facility. How large is it?

Buyer: We have approximately 50 acres under roof, with our main production building almost 25 acres under one roof. We use six buildings for production.

Salesperson: How far is it from your executives' offices to your plant area? It looks like it must be two miles over to there.

Buyer: Well, it does, but it's only one mile.

Salesperson: How do your executives get to the plant area?

Buyer: They walk through our underground tunnel. Some walk on the road when we have good weather.

Salesperson: When they get to the plant area, how do they get around in the plant?

Buyer: Well, they walk or catch a ride on one of the small tractors the workers use in the plant.

Salesperson: Have your executives ever complained about having to do all that walking?

Buyer: All the time!

Salesperson: What don't they like about the long walk?

Buyer: Well, I hear everything from "It wears out my shoe leather" to "It's hard on my pacemaker." The main complaints are the time it takes them and that some older executives are exhausted by the time they get back to their offices. Many people need to go to the plant but don't.

Salesperson: It sounds as if your executives are interested in reducing their travel time and not having to exert so much energy. By doing so, doesn't it seem they would get to the plant as they need to, saving them time and energy and saving the company money?

Buyer: I guess so.

Salesperson: Mr. Pride, on the average, how much money do your executives make an hour?

Buyer: Maybe $30 an hour.

Salesperson: If I could show you how to save your executives time in getting to and from the plant, would you be interested?

Buyer: Yes, I would. [Now the salesperson moves into the presentation.]

needs. As seen in Exhibit 8.9, the salesperson selling the Dyno Electric Cart begins the interview with the prospect by using the planned series of questions to uncover problems and to determine whether the prospect is interested in solving them.[6]

Should you have to come back a second time to see the prospect, as is often the case in selling industrial products, you would use the formula sales presentation method in calling on the same prospect. You might begin with a benefit statement such as this:

> Mr. Pride, when we talked last week, you were interested in saving your executives time and energy in getting to and from your plant, and you felt the Dyno Electric Cart could do this for you. (You could pause to let him answer or say, "Is that correct?")

From the buyer's response to your question, you can quickly determine what to do. If the buyer raises an objection, you can respond to it. If the buyer requests more information, you can provide it. If what you have said about your product has pleased the buyer, you simply ask for the order.

Be cautious when uncovering a prospect's needs. Too many questions can alienate the prospect. Remember, initially many prospects do not want to open up to salespeople. Actually, some salespeople are uncomfortable with the need-satisfaction approach because they feel less in control of the selling situation than with a canned or formula presentation. A good point to remember is that you are not there to perform on a stage but rather to learn about your prospect's needs—not your own. Eventually, you can learn to anticipate customer reactions to this presentation and learn to welcome the challenge of the interaction between you and the buyer.

The Problem–Solution Presentation

In selling highly complex or technical products such as insurance, industrial equipment, accounting systems, manufacturing equipment, and technology, salespeople often are required to make several sales calls to develop a detailed analysis of a prospect's needs. After completing this analysis, the salesperson arrives at a solution to the prospect's problems and usually uses both a written analysis and an oral presentation. The **problem–solution presentation** usually consists of six steps:

1. Convincing the prospect to allow the salesperson to conduct the analysis.
2. Making the actual analysis.
3. Agreeing on the problems and determining that the buyer wants to solve them.
4. Preparing the proposal for a solution to the prospect's needs.
5. Preparing the sales presentation based on the analysis and proposal.
6. Making the sales presentation.

The problem–solution presentation is a flexible, customized approach involving an in-depth study of a prospect's needs, and it requires a well-planned presentation. Often, the need-satisfaction and problem–solution presentations are used when it is necessary to present the proposal to a group of individuals.

Comparison of Presentation Methods

Exhibit 8.10 illustrates differences in the four sales presentation methods. It also shows the wide variety of sales jobs available for you to choose from if you are seeking a career. Hopefully you will see that selling different products in different industries has similarities but many differences in salespeople's job activities.[7]

Some of the students in our professional selling classes say, "I do not want to have a sales career." We ask "Why?" "I do not want to do any cold-call type of prospecting and no straight commission" they might reply. We describe sales jobs with straight salaries and bonuses with no cold calling and then ask, "What about working for these companies?" "That sounds fine," they may say.

Learn about your customer's needs . . . always.

EXHIBIT 8.10

Important characteristics of types of sales calls.

Characteristics	Memorized (Structured)	Formula (Semistructured)	Need-Satisfaction (Unstructured)	Problem–Solution (Customized)
Relationship	Transactional	Relationship	Partnering	Partnering
When Used	New customer door-to-door; telesales	Repeat customer	New customer; new opportunity	New customer; new opportunity
Opening	Canned	Reminder of past status	Questions	Request for study
Presentation Time	Minutes	Half hour(s)	Day(s)	Week(s)
Multiple Calls?	No	Sometimes	Frequently	Always
Type of Negotiations	None	Several variables	Multiple variables	Complex
Script Flexibility	None	Modest	No script	No script
Assumed Interest Level	Already established, or can be generated	Already established	Not established, or not known	Not known
Prior Contact with Buyer?	Not usually	Usually	Not necessarily	Not necessarily
Type of Product	Trivial; simple	Simple; previously sold	Industrial/technical	Complex
Sample Product	Vegetable dicer; vacuum cleaner; cosmetics	Premium cable channel; consumer goods; cars	Home entertainment center	Information technology solutions warehouse system
			Computer real estate	Company insurance
Salary ($)	30–50K	40–70K	50–90K	80–200K

What are the main things you are looking for in a job? Well, there is a sales job that has what you are looking for somewhere. Remember the chapter's introductory sales challenge of the salesperson faced with meeting with a group?

What Is the Best Presentation Method?

Each of these sales presentation methods is the best one when the method is properly matched with the *situation.* For example, the memorized presentation method can be used when time is short and the product is simple. Formula selling is effective in repeat purchases or when you know or have already determined the needs of the prospect.

The need-satisfaction method is most appropriate when you must gather information from the prospect, as is often the case in selling industrial products. Finally, the problem–solution presentation is excellent for selling high-cost technical products or services, and especially for system selling involving several sales calls and a business proposition. To help improve sales, the salesperson should understand and be able to use each method based on each situation. Remember the chapter's introductory sales challenge of the salesperson faced with meeting with a group?

Areas to Consider in Any Sales Presentation Method

Salespeople should be aware of critical elements that can enhance the rate of success during any type of sales presentation. Specifically, four key areas that can be considered in any sales presentation methods are (1) questioning, (2) listening, (3) combining your listening and questioning skills, and (4) storytelling.

Asking Great Questions

Regardless of the sales presentation method, we'd like to stress the value of questions. Each presentation method involves some level (i.e., quantity and quality) of questions because questions play a critical role in every sales conversation.

As a salesperson, every interaction provides you with an opportunity to learn about your customer. Great questions enable this learning; they allow the customer to respond at some length and share critical information with you. Questions allow you to discover buyer needs, organizational needs, previously used processes, and customer perspectives. By asking questions, you demonstrate your interest in the customer, and you help provide yourself with the needed understanding to craft a solution.

As an entry-level salesperson, it's important to plan your questions, to test them and to learn which questions elicit the information you need and which do not elicit quality information. For each sales discussion, proactively prepare a range of open-ended questions. Begin integrating words such as "How," "What," "Who," "Describe," "Can you share," and "Explain to me" into your questions. Next, practice the sequence of your questions. For instance, are your questions asked in a logical manner? Do you prepare follow-up questions that can be used when the customer provides an ambiguous answer? Do you have questions to use to better understand the buyer's concerns or objections? We believe your effectiveness as a salesperson will depend on your ability to ask questions and listen thoughtfully to your buyer's answers.

Listen More Than You Talk

Listening serves as an essential element of any sales presentation method. Listening is an extremely important skill but it is often an underrated skill. Listening allows you to engage the buyer and learn about their business objectives, their personal goals, and their expectations. Great listening skills allow the salesperson to develop a solution that matches the buyer's needs.

Within sales, it is important to consistently develop your listening skills. Great salespeople practice their listening skills by taking notes, interpreting the buyer's nonverbal messages and body language, recognizing the customer's feelings and emotions, restating the customer's perspective to ensure they understand the customer's point-of-view, and actively interpreting the customer's communication. In Chapter 4, you will learn even more about listening and how to practice your listening skills.

Combining Your Listening and Questioning Skills

When you combine your listening skills with your ability to ask effective questions, you will find that you will need to talk less during your sales conversations. As a result, the buyer might talk 80 percent of the time and you might talk 20 percent of the time during a sales conversation. How can this occur? Your questions will allow the buyer to explain their perspectives and goals, and your listening skills will allow you to better understand their needs. Further, you will be more equipped to identify opportunities for your buyer and to analyze potential pitfalls in their current processes. You will transition from simply offering alternatives to providing solutions, proposing strategies, and advising your buyer on approaches to help them reach their goals. Your advice and knowledge may become indispensable to your buyer and provide you with an advantage over the competition. Therefore, it's essential to practice your listening skills and your ability to ask effective questions.

Storytelling in Sales

When we describe storytelling in sales, it may be tied to a few misconceptions. Storytelling doesn't mean the salesperson starts their sales conversation with "Once upon a time . . ." However, **storytelling in sales** describes the approach that the salesperson uses to communicate and create understanding by describing some sort of sequence of events or a narrative. Stories are interesting. They create interest. People like stories because the communication moves beyond facts and statistics. Stories integrate emotions, and descriptions, and stories convey interesting situations or challenges.

Consider some of your recent class experiences. Have you had an instructor that taught you how to calculate a metric by writing the formula on the board? How much did you remember? Now, have you ever had an instructor who taught you the formula for calculating a metric, but they began the lesson by describing a challenge commonly faced in business? Then, they described the metric and its value, how the metric is used by professionals, why the metric is important to understand, and why understanding the metric makes you valuable? Which approach was more interesting? Which approach helped you understand how to calculate the metric and understand its importance? Our hunch is the instructor that told you a story created a more impactful opportunity to learn.

Effective salespeople understand that stories are an important way to help their customers understand, to help their customers learn, and to help their customers advance toward their goal. In fact, research shows that storytelling helps an audience member understand the speaker's key points as well as remember them longer.[8]

In all probability, you have met or worked with someone who is a great storyteller. Instead of simply relaying facts or statistics, they use language and stories to communicate in an interesting and relevant manner. Within sales, you could use stories to describe the competitive challenges facing your customer and how your product can help your customer overcome them. Or instead of simply relaying statistics, you could use a case study that describes the impact of these statistics on users or employees.

In the next section, we review a few common best practices used in communicating sales stories.

> **Remember the elements of your favorite stories:** Every story has a hero and a challenge. Is the hero your product, your solution, or your company? What challenge is the hero facing? Or is someone, such as a customer, facing a challenge and the hero actually helps them overcome the challenge? How does the hero help them overcome the challenge? And what is the result of overcoming the challenge? Common story themes include moving from rags to riches, from little to big, from challenger to champion.

> **Remember to use the customer's language:** Use familiar terminology and buzzwords in a conversational tone.

> **Use metaphors:** A **metaphor** is an *implied* comparison that uses a contrasting word or phrase to evoke a vivid image. Metaphors are a powerful communication tool because they can make it easier to understand something that is complicated. For instance, when Apple CEO Steve Jobs announced the IPhone, he used the following metaphor (i.e., leapfrog). "What we wanna do is make a leapfrog product that is way smarter than any mobile device has ever been, and super-easy to use."[9]

Figures of speech such as metaphors have a similar effect on the brain as the actual interaction with an object.[10] For instance, if a speaker states that "That product is like touching sandpaper," the metaphor may actually activate the same region in the brain that helps you "feel" texture.

Think about a parable: A **parable** is a brief story used to illustrate a point. Parables compare something familiar to something unfamiliar. For example, a salesman might tell his client, "I have a daughter, and before she started school this year I took her to the doctor and got her immunized so she wouldn't catch any diseases from the other kids at school. This virus protection software does the same thing for your network. The software immunizes your network against computer diseases."

Incorporate analogies: The **analogy** compares two different situations that have something in common such as "Our new training system allows your new employees to learn about your products and retain the knowledge. It's like riding a bike. Once you learn how to do it, you never forget it."

> *Stories are powerful because they transport us into other people's worlds but, in doing that, they change the way our brains work and potentially change our brain chemistry — and that's what it means to be a social creature.*[11]
>
> PAUL ZAK, IN A 2012 TED TALK

The Group Presentation

At times you will meet with more than one decision maker for a group presentation.[12] Many group presentation elements are similar to other types of presentations. The primary difference is that either you or your team presents the proposal to a group of decision makers.

The group presentation, depending on size, may be less flexible than a one-on-one meeting. The larger the group, the more structured your presentation. It would not work if everyone jumped in with feedback and ideas simultaneously, so a semblance of order has to be arranged. As the salesperson in charge, you can structure the presentation and provide a question-and-answer period at the end of or during the presentation.

The ideal situation is to talk with most or all of the decision makers involved during the analysis phase. That way, they will have contributed to determining what is needed. The points you discuss will hit on thoughts they have expressed regarding the problems at hand. In the initial part of the presentation, you should accomplish the following steps:

Give a Proper Introduction

State your name and company name, and explain in a clear, concise sentence the premise of your proposal. For example, your statement might sound like this: "Good morning. I'm Jeff Baxter from International Hospitality Consultants. I'm here to share my findings, based on research of your company and discussions with Mary Farley, that suggest my company can help increase your convention bookings by 15 to 30 percent."

Establish Credibility

Give a brief history of your company that includes the reason the business was started, the company philosophy, its development, and its success rate. Mention a few companies that you have worked with in the past, especially if they are big names. This reassures the client by letting the group know who you are and the extent of your experience and credibility.

Provide an Account List

Have copies of an account list available for everyone in attendance. It would be monotonous to say each company that you've worked with. Instead, hand out copies either in advance or while you talk. This list shows the various sizes, locations, and types of companies you've helped in the past.

State Your Competitive Advantages

Right up front you can succinctly tell the group where your company stands relative to the competition. Don't get into a detailed analysis of comparative strengths and weaknesses; just make it clear that you can do better than the competition.

Give Quality Assurances and Qualifications

Get the group on your side by stating guarantees in the beginning. This shows pride in your product and that you don't skirt the issue of guarantees. Also, give your company's qualifications and credentials. For example, "We are certified by the United States government and licensed in 48 states to treat or move toxic waste," or "I have copies of the test reports from an independent lab." If your company has an impressive money-back guarantee or an extended warranty, mention it.

Cater to the Group's Behavioral Style

Every group comprises individuals with personal styles. However, a group also exhibits an overall or dominant style; that is, it has a decision-making mode that characterizes one of the four behavioral styles (see Chapter 3). If you can quickly determine the group style, you will hold their attention and give them what they want more effectively. Some people are more impatient than others. If you don't address their needs, you will lose their attention.

Get People Involved

After establishing the credibility of your company, involve the group in the presentation. The first thing to do is go around the room asking for everyone's input into the decision-making criteria for making the purchase. Preface this with, "I spoke to Fred, Sally, and Sue and learned their views on what your company would like to see changed in this area. In my research, I discovered it would also benefit you to have X, Y, and Z improved. I'd like to hear all of your thoughts on this matter." Ask each person to add to the list of benefits and the decision-making criteria. Take notes, perhaps on a flip chart, of what everyone says to help shape your presentation.

After everyone has had a chance to speak, go through your presentation exactly as in a one-on-one presentation. The primary difference is that you want to answer all the questions, fears, and concerns in the group. Meet each person's specific needs with a specific proposal.

When using this method, it is essential during your preparation to brainstorm all possible concerns and questions the decision makers may have. This information comes from talking to people within the company, other salespeople, and people in the industry. Be so well prepared that there is nothing they could come up with as decision-making criteria that you haven't already thought of and answered.

> *"The only place where success comes before work is in a dictionary."*
>
> VIDAL SASSOON

The Proposal

When you prepare for a group, write a proposal document that ranges from one page to an entire notebook with data, specifications, reports, and solutions to specific problems. The proposal document is a reference source that tells your customer what she bought if she said yes and what she didn't buy if the answer was no. This document addresses everything you and your prospect discussed in the analysis phase: problems, success criteria, decision-making criteria, and how your product or service answers each. At the end, include relevant documents and copies of testimonial letters from satisfied customers.

During your presentation, do not read from the document. It is not the presentation; it is strictly a resource of facts to give your prospect after a decision is made. In addition, when making your presentation, do not expect to cover every point in the proposal unless you are brief. Your presentation will focus on the issues that relate to the customer's specific need gap; tangential information should be left in the document. Remember that proposal documents don't sell products; people sell products. The document is no substitute for a first-rate presentation.

No Prices

The best way to present a proposal document is without prices. There are several reasons for this. First, some people will go directly to the prices without reading through the document. Second, prices tend to prejudice non–decision makers—who should not be concerned with prices. If the decision maker asks why the prices are missing, tell him, "I thought you would prefer the flexibility of showing the document to other people without their knowing prices. It's a matter of confidentiality." The third reason is politics. Imagine a board of directors that has not had a raise in two years looking at a document that proposes a $2 million computer for the company. This may stir up problems.

Make it clear that you are not trying to hide the prices and that you would be more than happy to talk about them with the appropriate people, the decision makers. It is important to present prices in the proper perspective and context.

When you share the proposal, address each problem and give specific information about your solutions. Make sure you discuss features, advantages, and benefits—and get feedback from the group. Ask trial closes like these:

- "Can you see any other advantages to this?"
- "How do you feel about that? Do you think that would solve the problem?"

Summarize Benefits

At the end, summarize your proposal by giving a benefits summary: "Here is what benefits your firm will receive if you accept my proposal." Talk about how the benefits will address their specific problems.

Before your presentation, find out from your primary contact in the company if the group will make a decision while you are there or if they will discuss it and inform you later. You also should know if they are responsible for dealing with the financial aspects of the purchase. If so, you will have to talk about the costs and the benefits they will receive in relation to the costs. If they will not be concerned with prices, don't discuss them.

When you have completed the benefits summary, solicit impressions from the group. Ask if they agree that the solution you proposed would solve their problem or meet their needs. Without asking for it, get a feeling for the disposition of the group. If you are working with one person, it is easier to ask for an impression.

At the end of your summary, ask if there are any questions. At this point, you are close to the end of your allotted time. When someone asks a question that is answered in your proposal document, refer him to the appropriate section of the document and assure him that a complete answer is provided.

Negotiating So Everyone Wins

No matter what type of presentation method you use, or whether you talk to one person or a group of people, be prepared to negotiate. Many salespeople negotiate during the confirming phase of the sale. Their products or services are big-ticket items with many negotiable details. The negotiating process during the sale confirmation becomes a critical point that can affect the business relationship.

There are many negotiating styles with various names. For example, there are cooperative, competitive, attitudinal, organizational, and personal modes of negotiating. Most inexperienced negotiators operate in the competitive mode because they mistakenly think the shrewd businessperson is one who wins at the other's expense. With a win–lose attitude in mind, they "don't show all their cards" and use other strategies to gain the upper hand. Often this is done at the expense of the business relationship.

If you see prospects as adversaries rather than business partners, you will have short-term, adversarial relationships. The tension, mistrust, and buyer's remorse created are not worth the small gains you may win using this negotiating style. There is a better way.

Professional salespeople negotiate in a way that achieves satisfaction for both parties. They rely on trust, openness, credibility, integrity, and fairness. Their attitude is not "How can I get what I want out of this person?" It's "There are many options to explore that will make both of us happy. If two people want to do business, the details will not stand in the way." It is important *not* to negotiate the details before your customer has made a commitment to your solution.

"A successful salesperson has expertise in the products he or she sells, as well as an in-depth knowledge of the customer's business. The salesperson often makes recommendations which alter the mainstream of the customer's business process. Recognizing the requirement of business skills, IBM provides training in both the technical aspects of our products, as well as their industrial application.

"My territory consists of manufacturing customers; hence, I pride myself in understanding concepts such as inventory control, time phased requirements planning, and shop floor control. Typically, I work with customer user department and data processing people to do application surveys and detailed justification analysis. After the background work is completed, I make proposals and presentations to educate the chain of decision makers on the IBM recommendations.

"Selling involves the transformation of the features of your product into benefits to the customer. The principal vehicles for that communication are the sales call, formal presentations, and proposal. The larger the magnitude of the sale, the more time and effort is spent on presentations and proposals. A proposal may range from a simple one-page letter and attachment with prices, terms, and conditions, to multivolume binders with detailed information on the product, including its use, detailed justification, implementation schedules, and contracts. The wide range of comprehensiveness implies an equal range in time commitment of the salesperson.

"Very few sales are made in a single call. At the first sales call, the salesperson generally searches for additional information that needs to be brought back, analysis that needs to be done, or questions to be answered. These are opportunities to demonstrate responsiveness to the customer. Getting back to the customer in a very timely and professional manner is a way to build trust and confidence into a business relationship."

Phases of Negotiation

If your product or service requires negotiating on a regular basis, set the stage for negotiation early in the sales process. There are things you can do to prepare for negotiation from the beginning.

Planning

The number one asset of a strong negotiator is preparation. During the planning phase, after completing a competition analysis, you know how your company compares with the competition for price, service, quality, reputation, and so on. This knowledge is important at negotiation time. You may be able to offer things the competition cannot. It is advantageous to point out these advantages to your prospect when the time is right.

Before you make a proposal to a client, search your company's sales records to find any reports of previous sales to your prospect or similar businesses. If these records documented the successes and failures of negotiating, you will learn from other salespeople's experience. For this reason, your call reports should include details of what transpired during any negotiation. The knowledge gained from these records is not a strategy per se, but insight into the priorities of this market segment. For example, businesses in a certain industry segment may value service more than price, or they may care more about help in training and implementation than a discount.

To Fix the Mistake . . . or Not

A favorite customer of yours, Dick Sargent, has been having trouble lately paying his bills. Dick owns a small manufacturing plant. He employs six people. Bad economic conditions in his area severely hurt Dick's small business. Thus, sales for this account have dropped 60 percent.

Last week, you arranged for him to buy a six-month supply of plastic pipe he uses to manufacture his best-selling product. Due to the quantity purchased, your company's credit manager said he could pay for it in equal payments over the next four months.

Today, Dick calls you to thank you for the extended credit and for the extra $100 discount. You realize there has been a billing error on his $15,000 order.

What would be the most ethical action to take?

1. Apologize to Dick and tell him that there has been an error. Offer to go and talk to your boss to see if there is a way to get him some type of discount.
2. Nothing. It's only $100—chances are that nobody will notice and you like helping out your favorite customer.
3. Tell Dick that there has been an error but that you will keep it quiet if he does. Let Dick decide if he is comfortable with that.

During your preparation, review the various bargaining chips available to you. Some of the questions to answer include these:

- What extra services can you offer?
- How flexible is the price or the payment plan?
- Are deposits and cancellation fees negotiable?
- Is there optional equipment you can throw in for free?
- Can you provide free training?
- What items in the negotiation will be inflexible for you?
- How can you compensate for these items?

Meeting

When you meet a prospect, you start building the relationship by proving you are someone who is credible, trustworthy, and, it is hoped, the type of person your prospect likes to do business with. If you are all these things, you will eliminate tension from the relationship and thereby ease the negotiation process.

As proof of this concept, imagine selling your car to a friend. Now imagine selling it to a stranger. Who would be easier to negotiate with? The friend, of course. For both of you, the top priority is the relationship; the secondary priority is the car deal.

Studying

When you study a prospect's business, look at the big picture. As mentioned earlier in the book, don't focus on features; look for benefits you can provide. Look behind a prospect's demands for reasons. You can ask, "What are you trying to accomplish by asking for this?" After the prospect answers, you may be able to say, "We can accomplish that another way. Consider this alternative . . ." The more options for providing benefits, the more flexible the negotiation.

"Do not fear going forward slowly; fear only to stand still."

CHINESE PROVERB

During this phase, you must find out what other competitors' products or services your prospect is considering. This gives insight into what they are looking for and willing to pay. If you are selling a half-million-dollar CAT scanner and your prospect is also considering a three-quarter-million-dollar CAT scanner, you know your product is not priced too high. If, however, your prospect is looking at a lot of lower-priced units, it may be an uphill struggle to get the prospect to spend what you're asking. Knowing who your competitors are will help you assess bargaining strengths and weaknesses.

Every purchase is made with decision-making criteria in mind, either consciously or subconsciously. Find out what they are for your prospect and the prospect's company. Within those criteria, there are usually three levels of desire: must have, should have, and would be nice to have. Be clear about these levels and how they create limits for negotiations. Obviously, "must haves" are much less flexible than "would be nice to haves."

Proposing

Proposing is another phase that indirectly affects subsequent negotiations. What you do in the presentation sets the stage for what may come later. During your presentation, tie features and advantages to benefits and emphasize unique benefits. In this way, your product or service and company are positioned above the competition. It is important to position yourself as well. Don't be afraid to let your prospect know she is getting you and everything you have promised to do after the sale.

The successful resolution of a negotiation starts with a commitment to do business together. It is then necessary for both parties to maintain common interests and resolve any conflicts cooperatively. The key to selling and negotiating is to always seek a win–win solution in which both buyer and seller are happy.

Sales Presentations Go High-Tech

Whether in transactional, relationship, or partnering situations, salespeople are finding high-tech sales presentations effective in providing customers with the necessary information to make informed decisions. Chapter 10 discusses these important selling tools further.

Select the Presentation Method, Then the Approach

Before developing the presentation, you must know which presentation method you will use. Once you determine which presentation method is best for your situation, plan what you will do when talking with your prospect. Your initial consideration should be how to begin your sales presentation.

The Parallel Dimensions of Selling

So what have you learned from your textbook? You have come a long way, in a short time, in understanding the many challenges facing today's salesperson. It is a big job—one full of personal and financial rewards.

Before moving on to learning specific sales communications techniques used in the selling process, take a look at Exhibit 8.11.[13] You have learned about the discussion sequence, the buyer's mental steps, and a little about the selling process.

Top-performing salespeople use the parallel dimensions of selling to plan, create, and execute their presentations. One of the main reasons to study and understand Exhibit 8.11 is to learn how the three dimensions of selling—discussion sequence, selling process, buyer's mental steps—interact, often at the same time, to form a specific sales presentation.

First Column

First, let's briefly look at the parallel dimensions of selling exhibit. Look now! The far left column shows the order that your discussion should take within the presentation. Discuss the product, then the marketing plan, the business proposition and then close.

Second Column

The second column the left shows the same discussion sequence with examples of each part of the presentation. When you present your product, discuss its features,

EXHIBIT 8.11

The parallel dimensions of selling. When you understand their sequences and interactions, you are ready to go sell something!

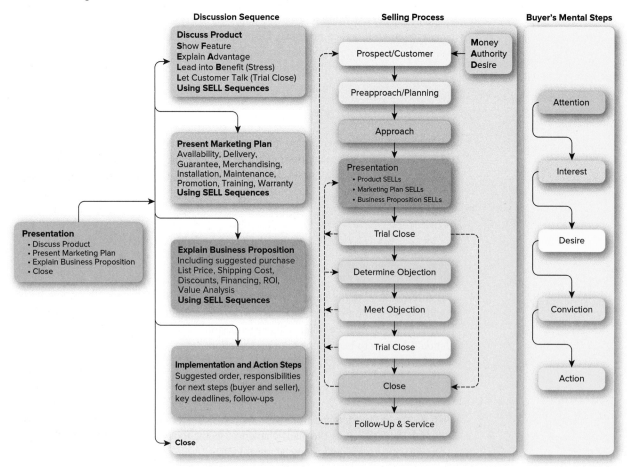

advantages, and benefits followed with a trial close for each major benefit. The marketing plan is next in your presentation. Now discuss your business proposition incorporating the SELL Sequences. As discussed in Chapter 3, the SELL Sequence is an acronym for **showing** your feature, **explaining** its advantage, **leading** into the benefit, and then **letting** the person give feedback on what you have said by asking a trial close question. Present what you suggest should be purchased by the customer or prospect followed by one or more trial closes. Now close, asking for the order using one of the closing techniques in your textbook. Look and listen to the buyer's response to your trial close question. They are important. Learn the definitions and meanings of both a close and trial close.

Third Column

The third column shows the 10-step selling process beginning with the prospect or customer you plan to contact in your business meeting and ending with service and follow-up of that prospect or customer.

Fourth Column

The last column illustrates the buyer's mental steps as the salesperson moves down the steps of the presentation, which begins with the approach and ends with the close. Thus, there are parallel dimensions occurring at the same time between the selling process and the buyer's mental stages. The approach gets the buyer's attention and interest. The presentation continues to hold interest and convinces the buyer this product will take care of their need or solve their problem. Their desire to buy begins to rise. When the seller feels the person has entered the conviction stage of the buyer's mental state, it is time for action.

The Sales Presentation and Techniques (A Review of the Process)

Now let's take a closer look at the 10-step selling process. Once you have determined your contact (whether a prospect, customer, or past customer who has not bought anything for some time), make an appointment and then plan your business meeting strategy and tactics in the preapproach or planning step of the 10-step selling process. Determine your sales call objectives and review or develop a customer profile with information about the prospect or customer and the organization. Now develop a list of potential questions to understand your prospect's needs. Next, create the main features, advantages, and benefits that most likely align to your prospect's needs. Now you are ready to develop and polish your sales presentation, as discussed later. Practice it until it sounds natural, as if talking to a friend.

Think about how you will dress to project a professional appearance. Remember to think through the positive creative imagery that you will use as you wait in the person's office before the meeting. You envision everything that will occur during your business meeting that will end in a sale and a new business friendship. Review your customer relationship management (CRM) data information in the preapproach and before entering the person's office. Be sure to know such things as past purchases, everyone's name, hobbies, family, what you talked about at the previous meeting, personality type, and likes and dislikes in interacting with salespeople. This research will aid you in developing conversation topics for the rapport section.

While waiting to see the buyer, meet and talk with everyone possible, especially the buyer's administrative assistant. Learn about things such as family, hobbies, and pets. These people can help get you in to see the buyer and provide valuable information on what is going on in the company that might impact you. Input this information into your CRM system.

Your Sales Presentation

Create a presentation that adapts to the buyer's personality style. Choose your presentation method and then select your approach technique. This is based on your product and knowledge of the person and of the organization. Practice more than one approach if you are unsure of the situation you will face. Be prepared to improvise, adapt, and overcome any obstacles in your way.

The Approach

The approach begins when you first see the prospect or customer and ends when you begin discussing your product. In the approach, you meet, greet, build rapport, and use one of the approach techniques to capture the person's attention and interest and to provide a transition into the sales presentation.

We provide a few key areas to remember in the approach:

Great First Impressions. First, focus on making a great first impression. Slow up. Do not rush to sit down and begin your presentation. If this is the first time meeting with the buyer, introduce yourself and your firm. Be sure to have a firm handshake, align with the person, look the person in the eyes, and smile projecting positive green signals. You are excited to meet with the person!

Business Materials and Nonverbal Communication. If this is the first time you are meeting a buyer, consider providing a business card to your buyer and also asking the buyer for a business card. If the buyer does not offer you a seat, ask, "May I sit here?" If possible, sit in the buyer's personal space across the desk. Here you can observe angles of body, face, arms, hands, and legs so you can easily watch for green, yellow, and red nonverbal communication signals discussed in Chapter 4 that can direct the way your presentation should proceed (see Exhibit 8.12).

Before setting any materials on your buyer's desk, always ask for permission. If small enough, place your product on the buyer's desk during the approach or when you start discussing the product. If selling large equipment, you might show a picture or video from your tablet or laptop.

EXHIBIT 8.12

Nonverbal signals can direct your presentation.

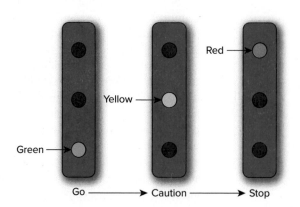

Consider an Agenda. Depending on the particular situation, you may want to communicate an agenda for the meeting. The agenda allows you to confirm the objective(s) for the meeting. Consider using customer-focused language. This type of language reduces the word "I" and uses language such as "you," "your," and "we." You should also confirm with the buyer whether the agenda's objective(s) are correct. You can accomplish mutual understanding by asking the questions, "What am I missing?" or "What are your thoughts on the objectives for today's meeting?"

Ask Great Questions and Listen Carefully. The approach also allows you to understand your buyer's needs by asking open-ended questions as well as listening carefully to your buyer's answers. To ensure your approach is effective, planning your questions is extremely important. Plus, it takes practice to consistently use open-ended questions. Conduct as much research as possible on your buyer's potential needs during the preapproach stage and structure your questions to carefully draw out and confirm potential needs. Remember, the answers communicated by your customer are equally important. Therefore, you should ask your buyer if you can take notes about your conversation. If the buyer is amenable to note-taking, you should take out your note pad and capture key information about the buyer's needs. At the end of the needs inquiry portion of the approach, you should summarize your buyer's needs. Again, ask your buyer whether your summary is correct or whether you have left anything out.

Elements of the Presentation

In the presentation, your goal is to link the buyer's needs with your potential solution. We provide a few key areas to remember in the presentation:

Communication Style. After the approach, you move into the core of your presentation. Remember that similarity is one of the critical ways to create trust. Therefore, pace your talking pattern based on such things as the buyer's energy level, speed of talk, breathing pattern, personality type, and time available. Mention the person's name several times during the presentation after discussing an important benefit. Throughout, watch the buyer's nonverbal signals. No matter what happens while you are in the buyer's office, always project green signals. Eliminate all of your ticks, such as saying "uh" or "um."

Top salespeople are great storytellers. Rather than simply relaying information, great salespeople create a narrative, a meaningful context to explain the value of their product. In order to tell a great story, you can draw from a number of elements to improve your communication with the buyer, to make your solution more memorable, and create greater attention and interest.

Within the sales conversation, use one or more of the following sales presentation elements: proof statements, visual aids, demonstrations, dramatization, and persuasive communication. These elements are not mutually exclusive. For example, a demonstration can also involve participation, proof, and dramatization. Inserting a simile, metaphor, analogy, parable, or story at the appropriate place can aid you in painting an enticing picture of how your product will fulfill the needs of the buyer.

Sections of Sales Presentation. There are three parts of the presentation that should be discussed in the correct order. Each element should focus on pertinent benefits that help solve the buyer's needs.

First present the product, second the marketing plan, and third the business proposition. The product section provides an overview of the service, solution, or product.

EXHIBIT 8.13

Examples of distribution channels for consumer and industrial products.

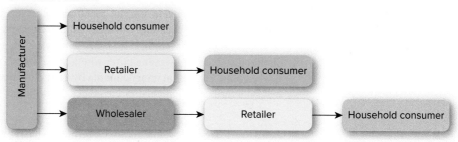

Consumer Products

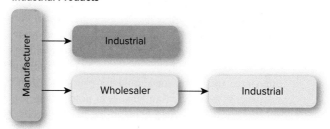

Industrial Products

There are two types of marketing plans. For the reseller, you will discuss how they will sell the product after purchase. Examples of a reseller would be a retailer, distributor, or wholesaler. For an end user, such as a manufacturing plant or government institution, you will explain how the product will fit into their present operation. Pertinent topics include delivery, guarantee, installation, maintenance, and training. The business proposition section details the financial benefits of your product, service, or solution. It may include elements such as gross margin, markup, ROI, payback period, investment returns, or cost savings. The final stage, often integrated into the business proposition, is to discuss the implementation steps, or the steps to put your solution into action.

Communicating the Benefits. To communicate your solution's benefits, please consider using SELL Sequences. The use of SELL Sequences allows you to focus on the product's benefits, rather than on its features and advantages. Yes, you do need to discuss features and advantages, but you want to emphasize benefits. Benefits solve problems and represent the elements of your solution that are important to your buyer. Remember, the benefit is the value your solution provides to the buyer. You can ask yourself, "Why would this feature be important to the buyer?" and "How will this help my buyer meet objectives?"

The trial close is one of your best communication tools. It asks for an opinion, not a decision. Therefore, it's often asked in the form of an open-ended question. "What are your thoughts on our proposed promotional plan?" is a trial close that might be used somewhere in the presentation.

A positive response to your trial close tells you the benefit is important to the person. You use this information later in your close. For example, you might say, "Earlier you said that you like our profit margin, fast delivery, and credit policy. Are there any areas in which you have concerns?" A positive response verifies the buyer's feelings to your product and may prompt you to close. Should the buyer give a positive response such as "That sounds great!" or "That's what I've been looking for in a product," you may not need to ask a trial close. It is your decision. You know what the person thinks about what you have said concerning your product fulfilling the need or solving the problem. If the person gives green signals, such as a smile or nodding the head after you have said something, you cannot always take that as a positive response. Many buyers are taught to make positive comments or use positive gestures during a sales presentation. Again it is your judgment, but generally you should go ahead and ask your trial close.

Welcome Objections!

Objections, resistance, concerns, or questions can occur anywhere in the presentation. Welcome an objection, resistance, concern, or question! This helps you understand what the buyer is thinking about relative to you, your sales conversation, and your product. Objections may occur due to concerns about the salesperson, the product, the salesperson's company, or other pertinent areas.

Before you answer any objection, it's always important to listen carefully and even ask questions to ensure you understand the customer's point of view. This also takes practice. We often want to answer a concern immediately. Instead, practice on listening to objections and then using follow-up questions to ensure you understand the customer's point of view. Then, address and answer any objections as they arise, except when they pertain to price (as discussed later). While we provide a number of techniques, we suggest that the critical steps to overcoming objections include listening carefully to the objection, acknowledging it, gaining further understanding about the objection, answering the objection, and seeking feedback via a trial close.

Price Objections. Pricing questions are one of the most common objections. In the ideal sales conversation, you will have discussed thoroughly your product and marketing plan so that the person knows the value of your solution's business proposition. However, if asked about price early in the presentation, you may choose to postpone the answer until later in the discussion. You may choose to postpone your answer by stating, "I'd be delighted to discuss the value of the product in a minute. Would you be amenable to this approach?" or "If it's okay, I'd love to discuss price, but I'd like to first share a few key elements that will aid in that discussion." This is a judgment situation. Only you will know when to discuss price. If the person persists in wanting to discuss price during the presentation, then you should talk about the product's price. To help make the decision you should judge if the person has gone from sending out green signals to sending yellow or red (see Exhibit 8.14). If the nonverbal signals are yellow or red, you should discuss price. One possibility for the person's action is that the individual has a type of personality that doesn't want to hear the background; he or she just wants to get to the bottom line. Remember, one of the best approaches to overcome a pricing objection is to stress the solution's value. For instance, does your solution provide long-term advantages, such as increased revenues, reduced expenses, less maintenance, greater quality improvements, or elevated customer satisfaction?

EXHIBIT 8.14

Watch for yellow and red signals.

Closing

How does this align with your goals? says the salesperson in her trial close

Closing is the process of helping people to make a decision that will benefit them. You aid people with their decision to help themselves by asking them to buy. Effective closing techniques include summarizing the benefits that were important to the buyer and then directly asking for the sale. After the sale, if needed, review your notes with the person to make sure you remember accurately what to do in the follow-up or service areas. Since some salespeople who continue to visit after the close experience a change of mind by the buyer, leave as soon as possible.

Does Not Buy

Should the person not buy, do not take it personally. Try to discover why before leaving. This helps you prepare for your return visit. However, chances are the reason for not buying will come out in your presentation.

Act as a professional. Leave the door open for a return visit. You might conclude by saying, "Mr. Smith, would you do one thing for your company? Would you please think about what we discussed? Please look over this material and the price sheet. I know (product name) is needed by your organization. Please call me if you have any questions. Would it be all right, Mr. Smith, if I come by in a month or so to see what you think about (product name)?" Stand, smile, and compose yourself. While looking the buyer in the eyes and giving a firm handshake, say something like, "Thank you very much, Mr. Smith. I really enjoyed visiting with you! I look forward to seeing you next month!" Do not leave the room as if it is on fire. Leave slowly, professionally with a smile on your face, a song in your heart, and a spring in your step. Be friendly with everyone you pass as you go to your vehicle. Call them by name if known.

Follow-Up and Service

Follow-up and service are extremely important to your success in keeping the person as a customer and in gaining referrals. Before you leave, discuss the key actions steps that you and the buyer have agreed upon. Review your notes once out of the buyer's office. Input information and data on the business meeting into your CRM system as soon as possible. This enables you to do a great job in preparing for the next business meeting with this person. See if the reason for the purchase or rejection is similar to other business meetings. This can help you improve your next sales presentation. In addition, provide consistent communication with the buyer. E-mail or call the buyer and provide information updates on important aspects of the order, such as deadlines, shipments, deliveries, and other information. Communicate judiciously but ensure the buyer knows that you are following up on your commitments.

Solving a Buyer's Problem Makes Sense

Place yourself in the buyer's shoes. What if you were in that role? If you were a purchasing professional for a business, wouldn't you want to have salespeople who have planned a presentation containing all of the information about the product, marketing plan, and business proposition based upon your needs? You bet you would! And wouldn't you want the salesperson to meet your objections or answer all of your questions truthfully? Yes! And most important, wouldn't you want the salesperson to place your needs first, over making a sale. Absolutely!

By imagining yourself as the buyer, you create a means to differentiate yourself. Its use sets you apart from all of the other salespeople who only want to make a sale and a fast dollar, often by using high-pressure tactics or not caring about a long-term relationship. Treat your prospects and customers as your business neighbors. If you care, they will care!

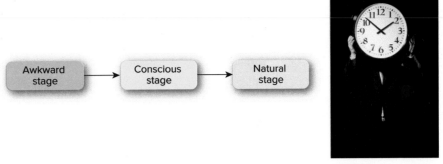

EXHIBIT 8.15

Training usage phases over time.

Awkward stage → Conscious stage → Natural stage

©Kelly Redinger/Design Pics

Practice and Time

Both new and experienced salespeople go through a learning process consisting of three phases of usage before true behavioral changes occur as a result of sales training. Many salespeople feel awkward at first. In the second phase of training usage, the salesperson consciously uses the training more and more, slowly becoming better at its application on the job. In the third phase of training usage, the new techniques become a natural part of the day-to-day job (Exhibit 8.15). Habits are difficult to change. It takes regular, on-the-job reinforcement to change a salesperson's habits. As the new training begins to produce more sales, people master the sales techniques and they become natural to use. This may relate to what you are experiencing in your sales class. It is very common!

SUMMARY OF MAJOR SELLING ISSUES

To improve your chances of making a sale, you must master the art of delivering a good sales presentation. An effective presentation will work toward specifically solving the customer's problems. The sales presentation method you select should be based on prior knowledge of the customer, your sales call objective, and your customer benefit plan.

Because prospects want to know how you and your product will benefit them and the companies they represent, you must show that you have a right to present your product because it has key benefits for them. Many different sales presentation methods are available. They differ from one another depending on what percentage of the conversation is controlled by the salesperson. The salesperson usually does most of the talking in the more structured memorized and formula selling techniques, while more buyer–seller interaction occurs in the less structured methods.

In the memorized presentation, or stimulus–response method, the salesperson does 80 to 90 percent of the talking, with each customer receiving the same sales pitch. Although this method ensures a well-planned presentation and is good for certain nontechnical products, it is also somewhat inflexible, allowing little prospect participation. The formula presentation, a persuasive selling presentation, is similar to the first method, but it takes the prospect into account by answering questions and handling objections.

The most challenging and creative form of selling uses the need-satisfaction presentation. This flexible method begins by raising questions about what the customer specifically needs. After you are aware of the customer's needs, you can then show

how your products fit these needs. You must be cautious because many people don't want to open up to the salesperson.

When selling highly complex or technical products like computers or insurance, a problem–solution presentation consisting of six steps is a good sales method. This method involves developing a detailed analysis of the buyer's specific needs and problems and designing a proposal and presentation to fit these needs. This customized method often uses a selling team to present the specialized information to the buyer.

In comparing the four presentation methods, there is no one best method. Each one must be tailored to meet the particular characteristics of a specific selling situation or environment. That is why you should managing the parallel dimension of selling.

Quick Review for Students

The quick review sections provide key questions to help you develop a greater level of conceptual understanding. We suggest that after you read the chapter, you try to answer the following questions without looking back at the textbook.

1. What are the four sales presentation methods discussed in this chapter? Briefly define each method.
2. What are the similarities and differences among different sales presentation methods?
3. What are the four key areas that can be considered in any sales presentation methods?
4. How would you describe storytelling in sales? What are the common communication tools that can be used in communicating sales stories?
5. What kind of attitude should a professional salesperson have while negotiating? List and briefly define different phases of negotiation.
6. What are the three dimensions of selling? How do these dimensions interact to form a sales presentation?

MEETING A SALES CHALLENGE

Don't panic! You've done everything you could have done. You have worked hard on this presentation, and you are prepared. This will be a challenge you can handle. As all pros know, on any sales call you have to be prepared to adapt to the situation. They must be very interested, or they would not have these executives attend the meeting.

This presentation is similar to the one-on-one you practiced but less flexible. Once the group has assembled, they will ask you to begin—so first introduce yourself and explain in a clear, concise sentence the premise of your proposal. Follow the remaining five group-presentation suggestions in this chapter. Invite everyone to ask questions throughout your talk.

KEY TERMS FOR SELLING

analogy   291
formula presentation   281
memorized
   presentation   280
metaphor   290

need-awareness   285
need-development   285
need-fulfillment   285
need-satisfaction
   presentation   285

parable   291
problem–solution
   presentation   287
sales presentation   278
storytelling in sales   290

SALES APPLICATION QUESTIONS

1. One salesperson profiled in this book stated that he concentrates on the need-fulfillment phase of the sales presentation. Is he correct in his approach? Why or why not?
2. Assume that a salesperson already knows the customer's needs. Instead of developing the customer's needs as a part of the sales presentation, she goes directly to the close. What are your feelings on this type of sales presentation?
3. To properly use the formula sales presentation, what information does the seller need?
4. What steps are required to develop and use the need-satisfaction presentation?
5. Assume you are selling a product requiring you to typically use the problem-solution sales presentation method. You have completed your study of a prospect's business and are ready to present your recommendation to her. What is your selling strategy?
6. According to Exhibit 8.11, what should be occurring in the buyer's mental state during the "Approach" step of the selling process?
7. Assume that you are a salesperson for a cable company. You have a repeat customer that has already established interest level in your product. What type of sales call should you use?

FURTHER EXPLORING THE SALES WORLD

Assume that you are a salesperson selling a consumer item such as an Apple iPad. Without any preparation, make a sales presentation to a friend. If possible, record your sales presentation on your phone or tablet. Analyze the recording and determine the approximate conversation time with your prospect. On the basis of your analysis, which of the four sales presentation methods discussed in this chapter did you use? How early in the sales presentation did your prospect begin to give you objections?

SELLING EXPERIENTIAL EXERCISE

The following 10 personal characteristics necessary to successful negotiation can help you determine the potential you already possess and also identify areas where improvement is needed. On a separate piece of paper, write the number that best reflects where you fall on the scale. The higher the number, the more the characteristic describes you. When you have finished, total the numbers.

What Are Your Negotiation Skills?

1. I am sensitive to the needs of others. 1 2 3 4 5 6 7 8 9 10
2. I will compromise to solve problems when necessary. 1 2 3 4 5 6 7 8 9 10
3. I am committed to a win–win philosophy. 1 2 3 4 5 6 7 8 9 10
4. I have a high tolerance for conflict. 1 2 3 4 5 6 7 8 9 10
5. I am willing to research and analyze issues fully. 1 2 3 4 5 6 7 8 9 10
6. Patience is one of my strong points. 1 2 3 4 5 6 7 8 9 10
7. My tolerance for stress is high. 1 2 3 4 5 6 7 8 9 10
8. I am a good listener. 1 2 3 4 5 6 7 8 9 10
9. Personal attack and ridicule do not unduly bother me. 1 2 3 4 5 6 7 8 9 10
10. I can identify bottom-line issues quickly. 1 2 3 4 5 6 7 8 9 10

If you scored 80 or more, you have characteristics of a good negotiator. You recognize what negotiating requires and seem willing to apply yourself accordingly. If you scored between 60 and 79, you should do well as a negotiator but have some characteristics that need further development. If your evaluation is less than 60, you should go over the items again carefully. You may have been hard on yourself, or you may have identified some key areas on which to concentrate as you negotiate. Repeat this evaluation again after you have had practice negotiating.[14]

NOTES

1. Adapted from G. M. Grikscheit, H. C. Cash, and W. J. E. Crissy, *Handbook of Selling: Psychological, Managerial, and Marketing Bases* (New York: Wiley, 1981).

2. Example provided by Professor Richard D. Nordstrom, California State University–Fresno.

3. Adapted from Grikscheit, Cash, and Crissy, *Handbook of Selling: Psychological, Managerial, and Marketing Bases.*

4. Adapted from Charles F. Stanley, *In Touch* (Atlanta, GA: In Touch), March 2006, p. 44.

5. Adapted from Grikscheit, Cash, and Crissy, *Handbook of Selling: Psychological, Managerial, and Marketing Bases.*

6. Example provided by Professor Richard D. Nordstrom, California State University–Fresno.

7. David Fitzpatrick, IBM Executive in Residence, Howard University, Washington, DC, and Charles M. Futrell, 2004.

8. Zak, Paul J. "Why Your Brain Loves Good Storytelling," *Harvard Business Review* (2014): 1–5.

9. https://thenextweb.com/apple/2015/09/09/genius-annotated-with-genius/.

10. Annie Murphy Paul, "Your Brain on Fiction," *New York Times,* March 18, 2012, SR6.

11. Empathy, Neurochemistry, and the Dramatic Arc: Paul Zak at the Future of StoryTelling 2012. TED https://www.youtube.com/watch?time_continue=17&v=q1a7tiA1Qzo.

12. Also see Tony Alessandra, Phil Wexler, and Rich Barrera, *Nonmanipulative Selling* (Englewood Cliffs, NJ: Prentice Hall, 1997).

13. David Fitzpatrick, IBM Executive in Residence, Howard University, Washington, DC, and Charles M. Futrell, 2001.

14. Adapted from Robert B. Maddax, *Successful Negotiation* (Menlo Park, CA: Crisp Publications, 1988), p. 19.

CASE 8.1

Cascade Soap Company

Mike Bowers sells soap products to grocery wholesalers and large retail grocery chains. The following presentation occurred during a call he made on Bill Reese, the soap buyer for a grocery store.

Salesperson: Bill, you have stated several times that the types of promotions or brands that you appreciate are ones that carry the best profit. Is that right?

Customer: Yes, it is. I'm under pressure to increase my profit-per-square-foot in my department.

Salesperson: Bill, I recommend that you begin carrying the king size of Cascade. Let's review the benefits and economics of this proposal. King-size Cascade would cost you 86.8¢ a box. The average resale in this market is 99¢. That means that you would make 12.2¢ every time you sell a box of king-size Cascade. Based on my estimated volume for your store of $40,000 per week, you would sell approximately two cases of king-size Cascade per week. That is $19.80 in new sales and $2.44 in new profits per week for your store. As you can see, the addition of Cascade 10 to your automatic dishwashing detergent department will increase your sales and, even more importantly, increase your profits—and this is what you said you wanted to do, right? Are there any elements that I'm missing?

Customer: Yes, I am interested in increasing profits.

Salesperson: That sounds great. We can begin the implementation very quickly. Let me ask you for your thoughts on two potential options to make this happen? Do you want me to give this information to the head stock clerk so that she can make arrangements to put Cascade 10s on the shelf? Or would you like me to put it on the shelf on my next call?

Questions

1. What sales presentation method was Mike using?
2. Evaluate Mike's handling of this situation. What areas of improvement might you suggest to Mike? In what specific areas did Mike do well?

CASE 8.2

Presenting to an Organizational Buyer

Roberto Garcia is a sales executive at MarketPulse, a Kansas City–based firm that offers full-scale marketing research services to business customers. MarketPulse primarily serves customers in the food industry. At this time, its operations have been limited to Midwestern states. However, the company aspires to expanding its customer base and grow its reach beyond the heartland.

Roberto is busy preparing for his third meeting with Mr. Ajay Gupta, the VP-Product Management at ABC Tech Inc. based in Silicon Valley. ABC Tech is in the process of developing its new product BaNCS, a banking solution system suitable for small and midsize community banks and credit unions. ABC Tech is a well-known name for IT services and outsourcing. However, this is the first time that they have introduced their own product in the United States; they are very sensitive (and cautious) about the success of the product.

During the first meeting, Roberto conducted a lengthy needs-discovery conversation. From the conversation, he gained a better understanding about ABC Tech, its services, and the product in question—BaNCS. Mr. Gupta made it clear to Roberto that his firm wants to partner with a marketing research company with the capabilities to capture trends within states and across the United States. Roberta also learned that ABC Tech was aware that the company will be perceived as an outsider within the financial services industry; and therefore ABC Tech is very interested in a detailed understanding of customer preferences.

During the second meeting, Mr. Gupta discussed the dynamics of the technology industry. Because technology products need to evolve constantly and incorporate customer feedback to do so, ABC Tech wants to partner with a market research firm that can work with ABC's product development team. The marketing research vendor should also be able to provide market information to the product development team to allow it so forecast potential sales of their existing and upcoming software products.

In the proposed third meeting, Roberto will be presenting to a decision-making group including Mr. Gupta and two other executives: the director of product development and the senior project engineer for the BaNCS product. Roberto is diligently preparing his sales presentation and is writing a list of questions that he anticipates Mr. Gupta and his team will ask during the presentation. Roberto worries about the fact that the MarketPulse has never worked with a technology company.

Questions

1. What do you believe are three of Mr. Ajay Gupta's objectives?
2. What do you believe are Roberto's main objectives for the presentation and sales conversation?
3. What sales presentation method would be most appropriate for this situation? Explain why you chose this option.
4. What are the key points that Roberto should be highlighting during his presentation?
5. What are two possible points of compromise?
6. What are likely to be two points of concern within the sales conversation? Why do you believe that these concerns might arise?

Begin Your Presentation Strategically

Main Topics

The Core Principles: The Approach

What Is the Approach?

The Right to Approach

The Approach—Opening the Sales Presentation

Be Flexible in Your Approach

Using Questions Results in Sales Success

Is the Prospect Still Not Listening?

Transitions: Maintain Conversational Flow

Learning Objectives

You have selected your prospect, planned the sales call, and determined the appropriate presentation method. Now, you must determine how to begin the sales presentation. This step in the selling process is called the *approach*. After studying this chapter, you should be able to

9–1   Explain the importance of using an approach and provide examples of approaches.

9–2   Describe why questions are the most important element of the approach.

9–3   Describe the various types of questioning techniques for use throughout the presentation, and give an example of each technique.

9–4   Understand the importance of being flexible in your approach.

9–5   Explain the value of agendas and transitions within the approach section of the selling process.

FACING A SALES CHALLENGE

You are making a cold call on the operating manager of a local bank—Citizen's National. You assume one of the manager's responsibilities consists of purchasing technology, such as mobile applications (apps). Based on your experience with other banks, you suspect an opportunity exists for an order and ongoing service throughout the year.

As a salesperson for Mobile Banking Apps, Inc., you especially want to sell your new banking application that helps small banks serve their customers. Since this is a small bank, you decide to go in cold, relying on your questioning ability to uncover potential problems and make the prospect aware of them.

You are now face-to-face with the manager. You have introduced yourself, and after some small talk you feel it is time to begin your presentation. Many salespeople face this situation several times each day. What would you do? What type of presentation would you use? How would you begin the presentation?

Have you ever been told, "You get only one opportunity to make a good first impression"? If the first minute of talking with a prospect creates a bad impression, it can take hours to overcome it—if you ever do. Many times, salespeople get only one chance to sell a prospect.

The approach—or beginning—of your presentation is essential to the prospect's allowing you to discuss your product. If done incorrectly the prospect may stop you from telling your sales story. You need to have a good beginning in order to have a good ending to your sales presentation.

This chapter introduces you to the *do's* and *don'ts* of beginning your sales presentation. Many salespeople are nervous about contacting prospects. Let's begin our discussion of the approach by discussing its overall importance and value.

The Core Principles: The Approach

World-renowned author, Stephen Covey, wrote the worldwide best-selling book *The 7 Habits of Highly Effective People*. Within the book, Covey shared seven habits related to professional and personal effectiveness. One of these habits is beginning with an end in mind. Salespeople should begin their sales presentations knowing the key benefits to be discussed and having a reasonable idea of what to suggest that the prospect or customer buy to solve his or her needs. But an even more important point made by Covey is that in order to be successful you should seek first to understand, then to be understood. This is great advice for salespeople. Salespeople should understand the customer's needs in order to suggest solutions. Undoubtedly, this means salespeople must be great at asking questions and solving problems.

Knowing you can help solve a customer's problem(s) provides great caring, confidence, and excitement in your mind, body movements, and speech. You are there to help the person. Wow, what a wonderful feeling you will experience by knowing your career is focused on solving problems, providing knowledge, and assisting your clients. By demonstrating a genuine interest in learning about the customer's needs, helping others, and cooperatively working together toward a goal you are building the foundation for a long-term relationship. It is clear you are there for the other person—not yourself.

The care shown at the beginning of your conversation allows you to give your presentation. This often results in a sale.

Ethical service after the sale builds true long-term relationships. The beginning of the sales presentation is called the *approach.*

What Is The Approach?

A golf shot from the fairway toward the green is referred to as the approach. The golfer is effectively preparing and taking preliminary steps before attempting to be successful.

The salesperson is similar to the golfer. Imagine this: The salesperson locates a prospect or identifies a customer to contact, gets an appointment, plans the presentation, and arrives at the prospect's/customer's business. The salesperson is called into the office. The approach phase of the selling process begins. The salesperson begins the preliminary steps toward getting the buyer to listen to the sales presentation.

For salespeople, the **approach** refers to the time from when they first see the buyer to when they begin to discuss the product. The approach could last seconds or minutes depending upon the time it takes to meet, greet, build rapport, and go through one of the approach communication techniques discussed later in this chapter.

EXHIBIT 9.1

The approach begins the sales presentation.

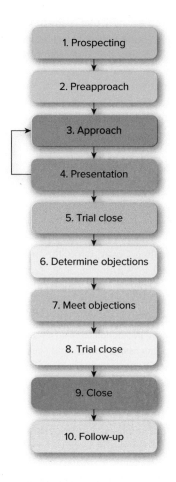

1. Prospecting
2. Preapproach
3. Approach
4. Presentation
5. Trial close
6. Determine objections
7. Meet objections
8. Trial close
9. Close
10. Follow-up

The approach refers to the time from when the salesperson first see the buyer to when the salesperson begins to discuss the product.

As you see in Exhibit 9.1, the approach, the third step in the selling process, is the first step in the actual sales presentation. We caution you not to take the approach step in the selling process lightly—it is very serious. Many sales trainers feel that it can be the most important step toward helping customers solve their needs through buying your products. If the approach is unsuccessful, you may never get the opportunity to give your product presentation.

Take a minute now to consider and study Exhibit 9.1 and the actions taken by the salesperson in the approach. It may help you see the importance of the approach in the sales presentation. Certainly it will help you understand this and the next chapter better.

The Right To Approach

Focus on the customer

You have the right (or duty) to present your product if you can show that it will definitely benefit the prospect. In essence, you have to prove *you* are worthy of the prospect's time and serious attention. You may earn the right to this attention in a number of ways:

- By being faithful to the sales call objective—helping others.
- By exhibiting specific product or business knowledge.
- By expressing a sincere desire to solve a buyer's problem and satisfy a need.

- By stating or implying that your product will save money or, increase the firm's profit margin, or provide another important benefit.
- By displaying a service attitude.

Basically, prospects want to know how you and your product will benefit *them* and *the companies* they represent. Your sales approach should initially establish, and thereafter concentrate on, your product's key benefits for each prospect.

This strategy is especially important during the approach stage of a presentation because it aids in securing the prospect's interest in you and your product. At this point, you want this unspoken reaction from the prospect: "Well, I'd better hear this salesperson out. I may hear something that will be of use to me." Now that you have justified your right to sell to a prospect, determine how to present your product.

The Approach—Opening The Sales Presentation

Raleigh Johnson spent days qualifying the prospect, arranging for an appointment, and planning every aspect of the sales presentation; and in the first 60 seconds of the sales presentation, he realized his chance of selling was excellent. He quickly determined the prospect's needs and evoked attention and interest in his product because of the technique he used to begin the sales interview.

A buyer's reactions to the salesperson in the early minutes of the sales presentation are critical to a successful sale. This short period is so important that it is treated as an individual step in selling, referred to as the approach. Part of any approach is the prospect's first impression of you.

Your Attitude During the Approach

It is common for a salesperson to experience tension in various forms when contacting a prospect. Often this is brought on when the salesperson has preconceived ideas that things may go wrong during the sale. Prospects may be viewed as having negative characteristics that make the sales call difficult.

All salespeople experience some degree of stress at times. Yet successful salespeople have learned a relaxation and concentration technique called **creative imagery** that allows them to better cope with stress. The salesperson envisions the worst that can happen. Then preparation is made to react to it and even accept it if need be. The best that can happen is also envisioned. Furthermore, contingency plans are mentally prepared should the planned sales presentation need to be abandoned.

> *A buyer's reactions to the salesperson in the early minutes of the sales presentation are critical to a successful sale.*

The last question the salesperson should ask herself is, "What are the chances that things will go wrong?" Chances are the answer involves a low probability. Usually, there is less than a 1 percent chance that things will go wrong, especially when careful planning has taken place before the sales call. A greater than 99 percent probability that things will go as planned should dim fears of the most worrisome salespeople.

Why Are First Impressions Important?

Have you ever met someone and instantly knew they would be a friend. Similarly, have you ever been in a situation in which you knew you couldn't trust someone? Think about how quickly you came to this judgment. Perhaps you called it gut instinct, intuition, or first impressions. Science demonstrates that these judgments occur all of the time.

In fact, within psychology, first impressions are often related to a research term, *thin-slice judgments.*[1] This means that our decisions or judgments about someone or something occur automatically. Some research suggests that we are not consciously aware of the vast majority of our decisions (90 percent or more).[2] But while we are not aware of these processes, we are actually processing information quite rapidly.

How do thin-slice judgments apply to sales? Because customers are automatically and quickly judging the salesperson, the first seconds and minutes of a sales interaction matter. During this time a customer may be deciding whether a salesperson can be trusted, can provide the needed assistance, and can provide the level of needed expertise. Therefore, it's important to be self-aware of one's nonverbal and verbal communication, one's mannerisms, and one's interaction style. Ultimately, you want to ensure your first impression is perceived as extremely positive by the buyer.

How To Make A Good First Impression

You have only one chance to make a good first impression.

When you meet your prospect, the initial impression you make is based on a number of aspects: your appearance, your mannerisms, your communication, and your interaction style. If this impression is favorable, your prospect is more likely to listen to you; if it is not favorable, your prospect may erect communication barriers that are difficult to overcome.

Here are some suggestions for making a favorable first impression:

Preparation

- If possible, before the sales conversation, learn how to pronounce your prospect's name correctly and use it throughout the discussion.
- If you have a pre-set meeting, arrive 5 to 15 minutes before the meeting.
- Confirm you have all of your needed materials.
- If you plan on using technology in your discussion, practice using the technology beforehand. In addition, develop a contingency plan if the technology doesn't work.

Nonverbal language

- Be enthusiastic and positive throughout the discussion.
- Maintain eye contact with the prospect.
- Smile, always smile! (Try to be sincere with your smile; it will aid you in being enthusiastic and positive toward your prospect.)
- Refrain from chewing gum, or drinking when in your prospect's office.
- Keep an straight posture to project confidence.
- If the prospect offers to shake hands, do so with a firm, positive grip while maintaining eye contact.
- If you are waiting to meet with the prospect, refrain from taking out your cell phone and checking texts and e-mails or playing games.

Dress

- Dress +1: In your preapproach, research the firm's culture. Attempt to dress one step above the corporate culture. For instance, if you are meeting at an industrial setting, such as a manufacturing plant, a full suit may not allow you to create rapport. If everyone wears jeans and t-shirts, you may choose to wear jeans or khakis and a collared shirt.

- If you are not aware of the corporate culture, wear business clothes that are suitable and fairly conservative. Rarely will a prospect perceive you negatively if you are overdressed.
- Be neat in dress and grooming.

Materials and Technology

- Leave all unnecessary materials outside the office (coat, umbrella, or newspaper).
- Ensure your cell phone's volume control is set to airplane mode or vibrate.
- Ensure you have all of your needed materials (sales collaterals, business cards, order forms, etc.)
- Order all of your needed materials in a sequence in which you would likely use them.
- Ensure all of your needed materials are professionally organized.

Manners

- If possible, sit down. Should the prospect not offer a chair, ask, "May I sit here?"
- Always ask if you can place materials on the workspace of the customer or prospect.
- Do not apologize for taking the prospect's time.
- Do not imply that you were just passing by and that the sales call was not planned.
- Should the prospect introduce you to other people, remember their names by using the five ways to remember names shown in Exhibit 9.2.

A salesperson must learn how to project and maintain a positive, confident, and enthusiastic first impression no matter what mood the prospect is in when the salesperson arrives.

To ensure you are confident, preparation is key. Your diligent effort in the preapproach stage of the sales process will provide you confidence. Before you meet with your customer, review the following three important facets of the sales process:

- Your sales call *objective.*
- The *type of approach* that will be well received.
- Your *customer benefit plan.*

This approach selection process can greatly aid in making a positive first impression.

©Caia Images/Glow Images

A person's name is music to his ears.

EXHIBIT 9.2

Five ways to remember a prospect's name.

1. Be sure to hear the person's name and use it: "It's good to meet you, Mr. Firestone."
2. Spell it out in your mind, or if it is an unusual name, ask the person to spell the name.
3. Relate the name to something you are familiar with, such as relating the name Firestone to Firestone automobile tires or a hot rock/stone.
4. Use the name in the conversation.
5. Repeat the name at the end of the conversation, such as "Goodbye, Mr. Firestone."

Sales Presentation Methods	Approach Techniques		
	Statement	Questions	Demonstration
Memorized (canned)	✓	✓	✓
Formula (persuasive selling)	✓	✓	✓
Need-satisfaction		✓	

Approach Techniques and Objectives

Approach techniques that follow the initial small talk are grouped into three general categories: (1) opening with a statement; (2) opening with one or more questions; and (3) opening with a demonstration.

Your choice of approach technique depends on which sales presentation method you have selected based on your situation and sales presentation plan. Exhibit 9.3 presents one way of determining the approach technique to use. Using questions in a sales approach is feasible with any of the presentation methods, whereas statements and demonstrations typically are reserved for either the memorized or formula sales presentation methods. Because of their customer-oriented nature, the need-satisfaction and problem–solution sales presentation methods always employ questions at the outset. This chapter reviews each of the approach techniques with examples of their uses and benefits.

Overall, the three approach techniques have three basic objectives:

1. To capture the prospect's *attention*.
2. To stimulate the prospect's *interest*.
3. To provide a *transition* into the sales presentation.

Imagine the prospect silently asking three questions: (1) "Shall I see this person?" (2) "Shall I listen, talk with, and devote more time to this person?" and (3) "What's in it for me?" The answers to these questions help determine the outcome of the sale. If you choose to use either of these two approaches, create a statement or demonstration approach that causes the prospect to say yes to each of these three questions.

Small Talk Warms 'em Up

In most, if not all, sales calls the approach consists of two parts. First is usually a "small talk" or rapport-building phase. The goal of rapport is to help develop trust by creating a connection (i.e., you and the buyer demonstrate some level of similarity).

Rapport often consists of the introductory elements of the discussion, such as the greeting, or introduction, and learning about each other. For instance, assume you are meeting a client for the first time. Your rapport may include introducing yourself and your firm, asking how the client's day has progressed, confirming how long the client can meet, or even providing a compliment about the customer or her business.

If this is the second meeting or an ongoing series of meetings, you could discuss something the buyer expressed at a previous meeting, such as a project's progress, a personal activity or interest, or the status of their business. Please remember, the rapport section is to demonstrate similarity not to demonstrate differences. Your goal is to find some element that the buyer has shared with which you align. For instance, if your buyer states they will attend a professional football game in a few days, your goal is to reaffirm your interest in football, or how fun it is to attend any type of

EXHIBIT 9.4

Topics for building rapport.

Rapport Topics: First Meetings	Rapport Topics: Ongoing Meetings
Ask about their interests (hobbies, sports, activities, etc.)	Ask about the progress on a project that the buyer previously shared with you
Ask about work history	Ask about the buyer's progress on his or her objectives or responsibilities
Ask for perceptions about a business topic or trend	Ask about an interest area (hobbies, sports, etc.) the buyer shared with you
Ask about the activities over a period of time (vacation, previous weekend, etc.)	Ask about a vacation, trip or activity the buyer previously shared with you

professional sporting event. Please refrain from telling the buyer that your favorite team is a noted rival or you dislike all sports. Exhibit 9.4 provides a few examples of rapport topics.

Please keep in mind that you will need to adapt your rapport to the customer's style. This is especially true when calling on a prospect who has a feeler, intuitor, or thinker personality style.* The senser, however, may want to get directly to business. We provide a few examples of rapport building below. As you will note, the rapport section often integrates other elements of the approach, including that of statements and questions.

Rapport Building Example (Consumer Packaged Goods Sales)

Salesperson: Hello, Mr. Jones. My name is Joe Smith and I represent USA Grocery Products. Thank you so much for the time to meet with you today.

Buyer: It's very nice meeting you as well.

Salesperson: Before our meeting, I had the opportunity to walk through your stores on Main Avenue and Center Street. The attractiveness of the merchandising displays and the in-stock levels really impresses me. Both elements appear to be on the cutting edge of industry trends.

Rapport Building Example (Financial Services Sales)

Salesperson: Hello Ms. Johnson, I'm Jason Smith with First Savings Bank. You previously worked with my colleague Erin. How are you this morning?

Buyer: I'm great. Thanks for asking. How are you?

Salesperson: I'm doing great. Do you mind if I set my materials for today on your desk?

Buyer: Please feel free. Please have a seat.

Salesperson: I noticed all of the soccer memorabilia in your office. Could I guess that you have a strong interest in the sport?

Buyer: Why yes. I absolutely love everything about the sport.

Salesperson: I totally agree, it is so popular worldwide. Now tell me, did you play it, coach it, or attend some great matches?

*Refer to Chapter 2 for the discussion on personality styles.

In some instances, you may have previously met with the buyer. In those situations, the more appropriate rapport method may be: (a) to focus on a discussion point from the previous meeting; (b) to ask the buyer about an interest expressed at the previous meeting; or (c) to relay good news or progress about a project, service, or other business-related matter.

The second part of the approach is the planned, formal selling technique used as a lead-in to the upcoming discussion of the product. It consists of using a statement, demonstration, or one or more questions. Which of these three to use is based on the situation.

The Situation Determines the Approach

The situation you face determines which approach technique you use to begin your sales presentation. The situation is dictated by a number of variables that only you can identify. Some of the more common situational variables are

- The type of *product* you are selling.
- Whether this is a *repeat call* on the same person.
- Your degree of knowledge about the *customer's needs.*
- The *time* you have for making the sales presentation.
- Whether the customer is *aware of a problem.*

The sales approach can be a frightening, lonely, heart-stopping experience. It can easily lead to ego-bruising rejection. Your challenge is to move the prospect from an often cold, indifferent, or sometimes even hostile frame of mind to an aroused excitement about the product. By quickly gaining the prospect's attention and interest, the conversation can make a smooth transition into the sales presentation, which greatly improves the probability of making the sale.

In addition to creating attention, stimulating interest, and providing for transition, using questions in your approach includes the following objectives:

1. To *uncover* the needs or problems *important* to the prospect.
2. To determine if the prospect wishes to *fulfill* those needs or *solve* these problems.
3. To have the prospect *tell you* about these needs or problems, and the intention to do something about them.

> The use of questions in your approach is preferable to statements or demonstrations.

Because people buy to fulfill needs or solve problems, ***the use of questions in your approach is preferable to statements or demonstrations.*** Questions allow you to uncover needs, whereas statements and demonstrations are appropriate when you assume knowledge of the prospect's needs. However, the salesperson can use all three approach techniques in the proper situation. Exhibit 9.5 shows the three basic approach techniques and examples of each technique you will study, beginning with opening statements. Be sure to remember to build long-term trust when creating your approach.

EXHIBIT 9.5

Approach techniques for opening the presentation.

Statements	Demonstrations	Questions
■ Introductory	■ Product	■ Customer Benefit
■ Complimentary	■ Showmanship	■ Curiosity
■ Referral		■ Opinion
■ Premium		■ Shock
■ Agenda		■ Multiple Question (SPIN)

Be Flexible in Your Approach

Picture yourself as a salesperson getting ready for coming face-to-face with an important prospect, Ellen Myerson. You have planned exactly what you are to say in the sales presentation, but how can you be sure Myerson will listen to your sales presentation? You realize she is busy and may be indifferent to your presence in the office; she probably is preoccupied with her own business-related situation and several of your competitors already may have seen her today.

You have planned to open your presentation with a statement on how successful your medical billing software has been in helping save time and eliminate errors with accounts receivable. When you enter the office, Myerson comments on how efficient her billing associates are and how they produce error-free work. From her remarks, you quickly determine that your planned statement approach is inappropriate. What do you do now?

You might begin by remarking how lucky she is to have such conscientious billing associates, and then proceed into the SPIN question approach, first asking questions to determine general problems that she may have, and second using further questions to uncover specific problem areas she might like to solve. Once you have determined specific problems, you could ascertain whether they are important enough for her to want to solve them in the near future. If so, you can make a statement that summarizes how your product's benefits will solve her critical needs, and test for a positive response. A positive response allows you to conditionally move into the sales presentation.

> *No matter what, always smile! Show you care.*

Build Long-Term Trust

Many salespeople are tempted to exaggerate their product's benefits in the approach. Why? Because of what you just read. Should the salesperson not get a person's attention and interest quickly, that person may not allow the presentation. This is well known by top salespeople. So, there can be temptation in one's own interest to exaggerate a product's benefits. People do not want to be taken advantage of by salespeople. Promising too much can lose the sale and destroy the relationship, so follow long-term trust by placing the other person's interest before your self-interest. Let's see how to open the presentation with attention-getting statements.

Opening with Statements

Opening statements are effective if properly planned, especially if the salesperson has uncovered the prospect's needs before entering the office. Four statement approaches frequently used are (1) the introductory approach, (2) the complimentary approach, (3) the referral approach, and (4) the premium approach. As you will quickly note, many of the opening statements may be integrated in the rapport section.

The **introductory approach** is the most common and the least powerful because it does little to capture the prospect's attention and interest. It opens with the salesperson's name and business: "Hello, Ms. Crompton, my name is John Gladstone, representing the Pierce Chemical Company."

The introductory approach is needed when meeting a prospect for the first time. In most cases, though, the introductory approach should be used in conjunction with another approach. This additional approach could be the complimentary approach.

Everyone likes a compliment. If the **complimentary approach** is sincere, it is an effective beginning to a sales interview:

- Ms. Rosenburg, you certainly have a thriving restaurant business. I have enjoyed many lunches here. I'm interested in learning if there might be an opportunity to assist you with additional restaurant products and services that might make things easier for you and your employees.
- Mr. Davidson, I was just visiting with your boss, who commented that you were doing a good job in keeping your company's printing costs down. I am interested in learning more about your business's needs in the hopes of helping you reduce your costs further.

Sometimes a suitable compliment is not in order or cannot be generated. Another way to get the buyer's attention is to mention a mutual acquaintance as a reference (see Exhibit 9.6).

The use of another person's name, the **referral approach,** is effective if the prospect respects that person; it is important to remember, however, that the referral approach can have a negative effect if the prospect does not like the person you refer to:

- Ms. Rosenburg, my name is Carlos Ramirez, with the Restaurant Supply Corporation. When I talked to your brother last week, he wanted me to give you the opportunity to see Restaurant Supply's line of paper products for your restaurant.
- Hello, Mr. Gillespie—Linda Crawford with the Ramada Inn suggested that I contact you concerning our new Xerox table copier.

One salesperson tells of having a customer send a brief introductory text message to a friend. When calling on the friend, the salesperson placed his cellphone on the desk and said," Did Amos McDonald send this text to you, Ms. James . . . could we review it?"

> The use of another person's name, the **referral approach,** is effective if the prospect respects that person.

EXHIBIT 9.6

The referral approach.

Salespeople can integrate technology when using the referral approach. A salesperson could ask a current customer to text a referral message to a colleague.

©Mark Edward Atkinson/Blend Images LLC

Few people can obtain a reference for every prospect they intend to contact (this may be especially true for a beginning salesperson). Even if you don't know all the right people, you can still get on track by offering the buyer something for nothing–a premium.

A **premium approach** is effective because everyone likes to receive something free. When appropriate, use free samples and novelty items in a premium approach.

- Early in the morning of her first day on a new campus, one textbook salesperson makes a practice of leaving a dozen doughnuts in the faculty lounge with her card stapled to the box. She claims that prospects actually come looking for her!
- Mr. Jones, here is a beautiful desk calendar with your name engraved on it. Every month it displays key industry trends and one of our products that can assist you leveraging these trends. This month's calendar, for example, features our newest product.
- Ms. Rogers, please try this complimentary set of automotive tools at one of your stations. Once you use them, my hunch is that many of your technicians will be asking for them.
- Ms. McCall [handing her the product to examine], I want to leave samples for you, your cosmetic representative, and your best customers of Revlon's newest addition to our perfume line.

Creative use of premiums is an effective sales approach.

Agenda Statements

An agenda is the plan or a brief framework of the goals of the meeting or the targeted discussion areas.

Our buyers, like most professionals, face time constraints. Meetings pack their collective schedules. Therefore, the salesperson must be aware and respectful of the customer's time and schedule. An agenda serves as an effective method to demonstrate your respect and professional credibility. An **agenda** is the plan or a brief framework of the goals of the meeting or the targeted discussion areas.

In order to build trust, an agenda should use customer-focused language. An effective agenda uses words including "you" and "your" or "we" rather than "me," "mine" and "I." The agenda helps demonstrate that you want to assist the customer with his or her goals, challenges, and/or responsibilities. Please remember that while we proactively plan and attempt to predict our customer's needs in the preapproach, we never assume we understand all of the goals for the meeting. We always provide an open-ended question (i.e. a trial close) at the end of the agenda to ask whether we missed any elements or goals for the meeting. The following are a few examples of customer-focused agendas.

Business-to-Business Agenda Example (Technology Sales)

Salesperson: "Thank you so much for e-mail yesterday. It really helped in setting the goals for today's 30-minute discussion. First, may we start with some questions so that I may learn more about your company's needs in terms of cloud-based technology? Then, we can clarify potential opportunities regarding how XYZ Technology may be able to help move you and your company toward its objectives. Finally, you mentioned discussing the financial implications of implementing any solutions. Can you share with me any other goals that I might have missed for today's meeting?"

Business-to-Business Agenda Example (Industrial Sales)

Salesperson: "I'm really excited about our discussion. Before we begin, I'd like to confirm that I meet your objectives for today's meeting. First, you mentioned that you have scheduled 45 minutes for today's conversation. In your e-mail, you also mentioned that you would like to learn more about our supply chain solution system and the potential opportunities to integrate it into your operations. What other key discussion points would you envision for today's meetings?"   Now, before we begin, would you be amenable before we begin, would you be amenable if I asked a few questions to learn more about your firm's needs, your responsibilities and goals, and even some of your current supply-chain challenges?

Business-to-Consumer Agenda Example (Financial Services Sales)

Salesperson: "Thank you so much for being able to meet today. In our earlier phone conversation, you had mentioned a number of goals for today's meeting. Before we begin, I thought it would be nice to confirm I captured all of them correctly. You had mentioned that you would like to review all of your financial goals for retirement. Then, based on your goals, we could review the options that might best suit your goals. Finally, you were interested in learning about the fees associated with implementing these options as well as the timeline. You also stated we had about one hour to discuss these issues. What did I miss that you would like to discuss?"

Using an Agenda to Overcome Existing Issues

If you have met previously with the buyer, your may want to ensure the buyer's attention is not focused on a business issue you have not identified. For example, perhaps one of your team members in the customer service area did not fully meet the expectations of your buyer. Your buyer may be very upset with your firm, and you may not be aware of this service failure. Therefore, you may want to include an agenda item that focuses upon any underlying issues. An example is provided below.

Business-to-Consumer Underlying Issues Agenda Example (Industrial Sales)

Salesperson: "It's great to see you today. For the goals of today's meeting, you mentioned that you would like to understand the progress of our project and the next steps in terms of your investment in the project. However, before we begin with the full discussion, I'm also interested in your thoughts regarding the current state of service and affairs. Are there any critical issues you'd like to discuss before we move forward with today's agenda?"

Opening with Questions

Questions are the most common openers because they allow the salesperson to better determine the prospect's needs and force the prospect to participate in the sales interview. The salesperson should use questions only that experience and preplanning have proven receive a positive reaction from the buyer, since a negative reaction is hard to overcome.

Like opening statements, opening questions can be synthesized to suit a number of selling situations. The following sections introduce several basic questioning approaches. This listing is by no means exclusive, but it introduces you to a smattering

> *Questions are the most common openers because they allow the salesperson to better determine the prospect's needs.*

of questioning frameworks. With experience, a salesperson develops a knack for determining what question to ask what prospect.

Multiple-Question Approach (SPIN)

In many selling situations, it is wise to use questions to determine the prospect's needs. A series of questions is an effective sales interview opener. Multiple questions force the prospect to immediately participate in the sales interview and quickly develop two-way communication. Carefully listening to the prospect's needs aids in determining what features, advantages, and benefits to use in the sales presentation (see Exhibit 9.7).

A popular method of using multiple questions is the **multiple-question approach (SPIN),** which involves using a series of four types of questions in a specific sequence.[3] SPIN stands for (1) Situation, (2) Problem, (3) Implication, and (4) Need-payoff questions. Since SPIN requires questions asked in their proper sequence, its parts are carefully described in the following four steps.

Questions encourage others to talk. Be a good listener.

Step 1

Situation questions. Ask about the prospect's general situation as it relates to your product.

Industrial Examples

- Dyno Electric Cart salesperson to purchasing agent: "How large are your manufacturing plant facilities?"
- Medical billing technology salesperson to purchasing agent: "How many billing agents do you have in your company?"

Consumer Examples

- Real estate salesperson to prospect: "How many people do you have in your family?"
- Appliance salesperson selling a microwave oven to prospect: "How often do you like to cook?" "How often do you and your family eat out?"

EXHIBIT 9.7

The SPIN approach first determines needs.

In the SPIN approach, the sales rep uses a specific sequence of questions to effectively open a sales interview.

©Monkey Business Images Ltd/Getty Images

> *"Become genuinely interested in other people—ask questions."*
>
> DALE CARNEGIE

As the name of this question implies, the salesperson first asks a situation question that helps provide a general understanding of the buyer's needs. Situation questioning allows the salesperson to move smoothly into questions on specific problem areas. Also, beginning an approach using specific questions may make the prospect uncomfortable and unwilling to talk to you about problems—the prospect may even deny them. These are warm-up questions that enable you to gain a better understanding of the prospect's business.

Step 2

Problem questions. Ask about specific problems, dissatisfactions, or difficulties the prospect perceives relative to your situation question.

Industrial Examples

- Dyno Electric Cart salesperson to purchasing agent: "Have your executives ever complained about having to do so much walking in and around the plant?"
- IBM computer salesperson to purchasing agent: How would you describe the major challenges, in terms of accuracy, experienced by your billing agents? (You may have previously asked the billing agents this question and know that they are dissatisfied.)

Consumer Examples

- Real estate salesperson to prospect: "How has your family grown and in what areas do you need more space?"
- Appliance salesperson selling microwave oven to prospect: "How happy are you with your present oven?" "How many times a week must you quickly prepare meals?"

> *The SPIN question method stands for (1) Situation, (2) Problem, (3) Implication, and (4) Need-payoff questions.*

Problem questions are asked early in the presentation to bring out the needs or problems of the prospect. Your goal is to have the prospect admit, "Yes, I do have a problem."

To maximize your chance of making the sale, determine which of the prospect's needs or problems are important (explicit needs) and which are unimportant. The more explicit needs you can discover, the more vividly you can relate your products' benefits to areas the prospect is actually interested in and, thus, the higher your probability of making the sale.

In this step, the prospect recognizes an important or explicit need or problem, along with a desire to fulfill the need or solve the problem. Problem questions are useful in developing explicit needs.

If the prospect should state a specific need after your situation or problem questions, do not move directly into your sales presentation. Continue with the next two steps to increase your chances of making the sale. A prospect may sometimes not appreciate all the ramifications of a problem.

Step 3

Implication questions. Ask about the implications of the prospect's problems or how a problem affects various related operational aspects of a home, life, or business (see Exhibit 9.8). Please remember to use open-ended questions for implication questions. Allow the buyer to describe the problem's impact.

EXHIBIT 9.8

A popular multiple-question approach is the SPIN.

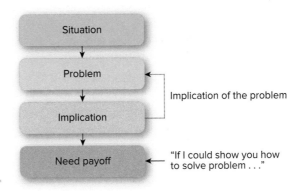

Situation

Problem

Implication of the problem

Implication

Need payoff ← "If I could show you how to solve problem . . ."

Industrial Examples

- Dyno Electric Cart salesperson to purchasing agent: "It sounds as if your executives would have an interest in reducing their travel time and not having to exert so much energy in transit. How much time, energy, and company resources would you envision might be saved if they could get to the plant as quickly as they desire?"
- Medical billing technology salesperson to purchasing agent: "Does this problem mean your administrative assistants are not as efficient as they should be, thus increasing your costs per page created?"

Consumer Examples

Implication questions describe the impact a problem has on the buyer (i.e., due to this problem, the result or impact on us is _____).

- Real estate salesperson to prospect: "So with the new baby and your needing a room as an office in your home, what problems does your current residence create for you?"
- Appliance salesperson to prospect: "With both of you working, does your present kitchen oven mean . . . inconvenience for you? . . . that you have to eat out more than you want to? . . . that you have to eat junk foods instead of well-balanced meals?"

Implication questions seek to help the prospect realize the true dimensions of a problem. The phrasing of the question is important in getting the prospect to discuss problems or areas for improvement, and it fixes them in the prospect's mind. In this situation, the prospect is motivated to fulfill this need or solve this problem.

If possible, attach a bottom-line figure to the implication question. You want the prospect to state, or agree with you, that the implications of the problem are causing such things as production slowdowns of 1 percent, resulting in increased cost of 25 cents per unit; increased reproduction costs of 1 cent per copy; loss of customers; or the need to hire added personnel to make service calls costing an extra $500 per week.

Use these hard data later in your discussion of the business proposition. Using the prospect's data, you can show how your product can influence the prospect's costs, productivity, or customers.

S-P-I questions do not have to be asked in order, and you can ask more than one of each type. You will generally begin with a situation question and follow with a problem question. However, you could ask a situation question, a problem question, and another situation question, for example. Similarly, you may ask many implication questions to better understand the impact of the problem. In many instances, your SPIN question sequence may actually be S-P-I-I-I-N. See Exhibit 9.9 for suggestions for developing implication questions. The need-payoff question, however, is always last.

EXHIBIT 9.9

Developing implication questions.

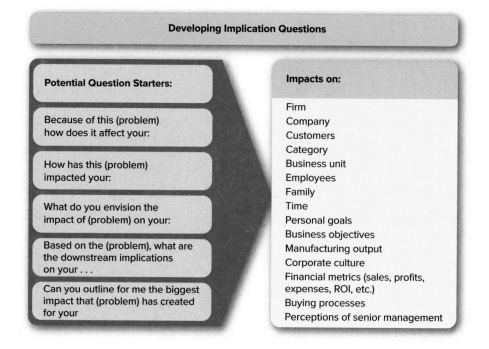

Developing Implication Questions

Potential Question Starters:

Because of this (problem) how does it affect your:

How has this (problem) impacted your:

What do you envision the impact of (problem) on your:

Based on the (problem), what are the downstream implications on your . . .

Can you outline for me the biggest impact that (problem) has created for your

Impacts on:

Firm
Company
Customers
Category
Business unit
Employees
Family
Time
Personal goals
Business objectives
Manufacturing output
Corporate culture
Financial metrics (sales, profits, expenses, ROI, etc.)
Buying processes
Perceptions of senior management

Step 4

Need-payoff question. Ask if the prospect has an important, explicit need.

Industrial Examples

- Dyno Electric Cart salesperson to purchasing agent: "If I could show you how you can solve your executives' problems in getting to and from your plant, and at the same time save your company money, would you have an interest?"
- Medical billing technology salesperson to purchasing agent: "Would you be interested in a method to improve your billing agents' accuracy at a lower cost than you now incur?"

Consumer Examples

- Real estate salesperson to prospect: "If I could show you how to cover your space problems at the same cost per square foot, would you be interested?"
- Appliance salesperson to prospect: "If I could show you an appliance that would provide a convenient way to prepare well-balanced, nutritious meals at home, would you be interested?"

Phrasing the need-payoff question is the same as opening with a benefit statement. However, in using the SPIN approach, the prospect defines the need. If the prospect responds positively to the need-payoff questions, you know this is an important (explicit) need. You may have to repeat the P-I-N questions to fully develop all of the prospect's important needs.

The Procter & Gamble and Tide sales presentation in Exhibit 8.7 was an example of using the P-I-N approach for a customer with whom you are familiar. Let's say your customer says yes to the need-payoff question: "If we could determine how much volume you're missing, I think you'd be willing to make space for the larger size, wouldn't you?" Then, you move directly into a brief sales presentation.

If the answer is no, this is not an important need. Start over again by asking Problem, Implication, and Need-payoff questions to determine important needs.

Product Not Mentioned in SPIN Approach As you see from SPIN examples, the product is not mentioned in the approach. This allows you to develop the prospect's need without revealing exactly what you are selling.

When a salesperson first walks into the buyer's office and says, "I want to talk about Product X," the chances of a negative response greatly increase because the buyer does not perceive a need for the product. SPIN questions allow you to better determine the buyer's needs before starting the presentation. In addition, by integrating open-ended questions throughout the SPIN, you allow customers to provide you with their perceptions of the problem and its impact.

Questions Added to the SPIN Salespeople may append questions or additional categories of questions to the SPIN. We offer two distinct examples of customizing the SPIN to serve the needs of the salesperson.

The first method is to integrate a detailed **needs-summary section** before the needs-payoff section of the SPIN. This section's goal is to ensure the salesperson totally understands the buyer's needs. To ensure mutual understanding, the salesperson replays the buyer's needs to him. Then, once the buyer states that the salesperson has correctly relayed all of the needs, the salesperson moves to the needs payoff. We provide a few examples of this approach.

Needs Summary Example 1: "If I may, I'd like to ensure I totally understand your needs. You shared with me that your company is seeking a solution that will provide greater investment income in the short-term, enhanced financial security in the next three years, and reduced paperwork and processing time over the long term. What elements did I miss?"

Needs Summary Example 2: "Thank you so much for sharing your thoughts. Would it be acceptable to say that your firm's challenges are that you have experienced a 10% decrease in sales over the past month? Similarly you noted that your competitors have continued to increase their promotional frequency over the past 12 months, and that's placing pressure on you as you have an annual objective of 6% growth in sales to meet? What other needs did I not capture?"

The second method is to integrate a **needs-prioritization section** before the needs-payoff section of the SPIN. This section's goal is to allow the buyer to prioritize needs. Again, the goal is to ensure mutual understanding. For instance, imagine the salesperson has just used a detailed needs-summary section. Once the buyer has stated that the salesperson understands the needs, the salesperson asks the buyer to prioritize them. The buyer's answers allow the salesperson to better understand the ranking of each need relative to one another.

We provide two examples of the needs-prioritization section.

Salesperson needs summary: "Thank you so much for sharing your thoughts. Would it be acceptable to say that your firm's challenges are that you have experienced a 10% decrease in sales over the past month? Similarly you noted that your competitors have continued to increase their promotional frequency over the past 12 months, and that's placing pressure on you as you have an annual objective of 6% growth in sales to meet? What other needs did I not capture?"

Buyer: "I think you are there. That really captures my situation and my current needs."

Salesperson needs-prioritization example 1: "Great, knowing that these are the three major needs you confront, how would you rank them? Which one is the most pressing and which one is least pressing?"

Salesperson needs-prioritization example 2: "Okay, now that we know these are your three major needs, how would you rate each one? While I understand each need is important, which one must be addressed immediately; and which need might be able to be prioritized and addressed in a slightly longer time period?"

Customer Benefit Approach

Using this approach, the salesperson asks a question that implies the product will benefit the prospect; if it is their initial meeting, the salesperson can include both his (her) and the company's name. This customer benefit approach may also serve as a useful method when prospecting for customers using the telephone. Because the approach is focused on a benefit, it may enhance the prospect's attention and interest.

■ Hi. I'm Charles Foster of ABC Shipping and Storage Company! Mr. McDaniel, would you be interested in a new storage and shipping container that will reduce your transfer costs by 10 to 20 percent?

■ Were you aware that your firm could save 20 percent on the purchase of our tablet computers?

■ Ms. Johnson, did you know that several thousand companies—like yours—have saved 10 to 20 percent of their manufacturing cost as described in the *Industrial Times* article? [Continue, not waiting for a response.] They did it by installing our computerized assembly system! Is that of interest to you?

> *Consider using the Customer-Benefit Approach when tele-prospecting.*

Your **customer benefit approach** question should carefully be constructed to anticipate the buyer's response. However, always be prepared for the unexpected, as when the salesperson said, "This office machine will pay for itself in no time at all." "Fine," the buyer said; "as soon as it does, send it to us."

A customer benefit approach can also be implemented through the use of a direct statement of product benefits. Although the customer benefit approach begins with a question, it can be used with a statement showing how the product can benefit the prospect. The three customer benefit questions shown earlier can be converted into benefit statements:

■ Mr. McDaniel, I want to talk with you about our new storage and shipping container, which will reduce your costs by 10 to 20 percent.

■ I'm here to show you how to save 20 percent on the purchase of our tablet computers.

■ Ms. Johnson, several thousand companies—like yours—have saved 10 to 20 percent on their manufacturing cost by installing our automated assembly system! I'd like 15 minutes of your time to show how we can reduce your manufacturing costs.

Benefit statements are useful in situations in which you know the prospect's or customer's critical needs and have a short time to make your presentation. However, to ensure a positive atmosphere, you can follow statements with a short question—"Is that of interest to you?"—to help ensure that the benefits are important to the buyer. Even if you know of the buyer's interest, a positive response—"Yes"—to your question is a commitment: The buyer will listen to your presentation because of the possible benefits your product offers.

Furthermore, you can use the buyer's response to this question as a reference point throughout your presentation. A continuation of an earlier example illustrates the use of a reference point:

■ Mr. McDaniel, earlier you mentioned interest in reducing your shipping costs. The [now mention your product's feature] enables you to [now discuss your product's advantages]. And the benefit to you is reduced manufacturing costs.

Sometimes, salespeople have to prepare an approach that temporarily baffles a prospect. One common method of baffling entails the exploration of human curiosity.

Curiosity Approach

The salesperson asks a question or does something to make the prospect curious about the product or service (see Exhibit 9.10). The salesperson may integrate a trend, unique research findings, or other insights that could impact the customer's business into the question. By doing so, the salesperson shares her expertise with the buyer and creates interest in the services or products sold by the firm. For example, a salesperson for McGraw-Hill, the company that publishes this book, might use the **curiosity approach** by saying:

- Do you know why college professors such as yourself have made this [as she hands the book to the prospect] the best-selling book about how to sell on the market?
- Do you know why a recent *Industrial Times* article described our new automated assembly system as revolutionary? [The salesperson briefly displays the *Industrial Times* issue, then puts it away before the customer can ask to look at the article. Interrupting a sales presentation by urging a prospect to review an article would distract the prospect's attention for the remainder of the interview.]

Opinion Approach

People are usually flattered when asked their opinion on a subject. Most prospects are happy to discuss their needs if asked correctly. Here are some examples:

- I'm new at this business, so I wonder if you could help me? My company says our Model I-1000 copier, printer, and scanner is the best on the market for the money. What do you think?
- Mr. Jackson, I've been trying to sell you for months on using our products. What is your honest opinion about our line of electric motors?

The salesperson may share a unique insight that could create interest and curiosity within the customer.

©Robert Kneschke/Shutterstock

The **opinion approach** is especially good for the new salesperson because it shows that you value the buyer's opinion. Opinion questioning also shows that you will not challenge a potential buyer's expertise by spouting a memorized pitch. Additionally, opinion questions may reveal previously unexplored opportunities for your product to meet even more of the prospect's needs.

Shock Approach

As its title implies, the **shock approach** uses a question designed to make the prospect think seriously about a subject related to the salesperson's product. In many instances, you could again bring forward a trend, a statistic, or other valuable research that the prospect may not know. Again, the value of the shock approach is to generate interest and position the salesperson as providing credible knowledge to the prospect. For example:

- Did you know that individuals your age have a 20 percent chance of having a heart attack this year? (Life insurance)
- Did you know that home burglary, according to the FBI, has increased this year by 15 percent over last year? (Alarm system)
- Shoplifting costs store owners millions of dollars each year! According to industry research, there is a good chance you have a shoplifter in your store right now? (Store cameras and mirrors)

This type of question must be used carefully, as some prospects may feel you are merely trying to pressure them into a purchase by making alarming remarks. Please remember, the shock approach is to use interesting, valuable information that is related to the salesperson's product. Further, the information is often not known by customers. Therefore, you are bringing them valuable knowledge to consider their existing situation.

Using Questions Results in Sales Success

Because asking questions to a prospect or customer is important to sales success it's time to introduce you to a few additional categories of questions.

Asking questions, is an excellent technique for (1) obtaining information from the prospect, (2) developing two-way communication, and (3) increasing prospect participation.

Questions show you care!

When using questions in selling, you need to know or anticipate the answer you want for a question. Once you know the desired answer, you can develop the question. This procedure can be used to request information you do not have and to confirm information you already know.

An ideal question is one a prospect is willing and able to answer. You should ask questions wisely. Therefore, preparing questions is important. In fact, practicing the sequence of questions as well as practicing a variety of questions allows you to adapt to your buyer and situation.

Why would asking a question get the prospect's attention? To give an answer, a prospect must think about the topic. You can use four basic categories of questions at any point during the presentation. These categories are (1) nondirective (open-ended), (2) directive (closed-ended), (3) rephrasing, and (4) redirect questions.

Often, our first inclination is to ask a closed-ended question within a conversation. However, effective salespeople are always focused on understanding the buyer's needs. One of the best ways to learn about the buyer's needs is through open-ended questions. The following examples demonstrate how you can transform a closed-ended question into an open-ended question. In addition, we provide a few examples of probing (also known as follow up) questions that help you learn even more about the buyer's needs.

Ultimately, our goal is to transition away from questions that begin with "Don't, Does, Doesn't, How Many, Is, Are, and Was" and consider other methods to start questions that allow the buyer to communicate more information.

Closed-ended	Open-ended	Probing
Don't you agree?	**What are** your thoughts about. . .?	**Can you explain** to me more about. . .?
Are those the type of decisions you are typically responsible for?	**Would you describe to me** the types of decisions you make and how the process works?	For that portion of the process, **can you tell me** who is involved and what is their respective role?
Is there a problem?	**What elements of this** (product/service) are creating challenges?	**Can you lead me through** any other challenges we need to address?
Do you always use that type of process?	**How would you describe** the key steps in your process?	You mentioned the proposal stage. **What are you expecting from** your vendors during that part of the process?
Is this the type of information you need for ordering an item?	**Can you share with me** the type of information you need to make this as easy as possible for your ordering system?	**What formats** of information would be helpful to you and your ordering system?
Is this our only option?	**What options are** available to move forward?	**Can you compare for me** what you see as the best options available?
When did you begin using that technology?	**What led you to** begin using that type of technology?	Would you be willing to **share with me** what you see as the major benefits of integrating systems like this one?
Do you use many vendors in this process?	**How do you integrate** your vendors into your processes? How many vendors are typically used in this type of process?	In your eyes, **how does** a vendor become valuable in this part of the process?
Do you like those type of features?	**Which elements do you like** most about the product?	**How does** that element impact your customer service levels?
How many items do you normally order?	**What quantities and assortment** of products do you usually order?	When you say a "tremendous amount," **how would you quantify** that to me?
Is this the way you want the issue handled?	**What are a few different ways** that you would like to see this handled?	**What would make** one of these options more optimal than the other alternatives?
Did the website provide you with the needed information?	Now that you've viewed the website, **what questions can I** answer for you?	You also mentioned the shipment terms are important to you? **What are your firm's** goals for product turnaround (from order to receiving)?
Was our service okay during the past quarter?	**How would you describe** our service for the past quarter?	You mentioned the word "mediocre." **Can you share with me** what specific elements should be improved?
Does this problem occur often?	**Would you describe to me** when this problem occurs?	**Can you explain** to me what happens when this problem occurs?

One of the most difficult challenges for many entry-level salespeople is asking open-ended questions. While the common approach is to ask When, How, What, Where, Who questions, other alternatives exist. In this selling tip, we provide a number of potential ways in which to begin open-ended questions.

How would describe. . . . ?

What are your greatest. . . . ?

Can you share with me the three most important. . . . ?

How would you rank your top three. . . . ?

What are the roles and responsibilities of. . . . ?

Can you lead me through the process of. . . . ?

How does that impact. . . . ?

How would you compare this . . . . with. . . . ?

What does this vendor do to ensure they are. . . . ?

What upsets you the most about. . . . ?

How will this affect your personal. . . . or your organization's . . . . or your financial. . . .

Can you describe for me the reasons that. . . . ?

What criteria would you use to evaluate. . . . ?

What led you to. . . . ?

The Nondirective Question

To open up two-way communication, the salesperson can use an open-ended or **nondirective question** by beginning the question with one of six words: *who, what, where, when, how,* or *why.* Examples include the following:

- Who is involved in the buying process and what are their roles?
- Who else might find this information important?
- Who would you consider to be your major competitors?
- What features are you looking for in a product like this?
- What do you consider your three most important financial goals?
- What types of challenges do you experience in using this older machinery?
- Where will you use this product?
- Where would you envision integrating this product?
- When will you need the product?
- How often will you use the product?
- How is a product like this used within your manufacturing facility?
- Why do you need or want to buy this type of product?

One-word questions such as *Oh?* or *Really?* also can be useful in some situations. One-word questions should be said with emphasis: *Oh?!* This prompts the customer to continue talking. Try it—it works.

To practice using the open-ended questioning technique, ask a friend a question—any question—beginning with one of these six words, or use a one-word question, and see what answer you get. Chances are, the response will consist of several sentences. In a selling situation, this type of response allows the salesperson to better determine the prospect's needs.

The purpose of using a nondirective question is to obtain unknown or additional information, to draw out clues to hidden or future needs and problems, and to leave the situation open for free discussion of what is on the customer's mind. Situation and implication questions are examples of the nondirective question.

One type of open-ended question is the probing question. Probing refers to gathering information and uncovering customer needs using one or more questions. Probing questions help the salesperson understand more about a topic. For instance, if a customer provides a vague or ambiguous answer, a probing question can help delve deeper into the topic. Probing questions can assist the salesperson understand more of the details of the customers' buying processes, responsibilities, goals and needs. Two examples of probing questions follow:

Example 1:

Salesperson: Would you describe to me how the buying process works? (open-ended question)

Buyer: Well, basically we involve a lot of people and get a lot of feedback.

Salesperson: For this size of an investment, that makes total sense. Would you be willing to share with me who specifically is involved and what each person's respective role is? (probing question)

Example 2:

Salesperson: Since this is our quarterly review, I'm interested in your thoughts on how the technology performed for your company. How would you describe our service in this area for the past quarter? (open-ended question)

Buyer: Tough question. But overall, probably okay to slightly mediocre in terms of results.

Salesperson: You mentioned the word *mediocre.* Can you share with me what specific elements should be improved? (probing question).

The Direct Question

The **direct question,** or closed-ended question, can be answered with very few words. A simple yes or no answers most direct questions. They are especially useful in moving a customer toward a specific topic. Examples the salesperson might use include questions such as these: "Mr. Berger, are you interested in saving 20 percent on your manufacturing costs?" or, "Reducing manufacturing costs is important, isn't it?" You can anticipate a yes response to these questions.

Never phrase the direct question as a direct negative–no question. A *direct negative–no question* is any question that can be answered in a manner that cuts you off completely. The retail salesperson says, "May I help you?" and the reply usually is, "No, I'm just looking." It's like hanging up the telephone on yourself. You are completely cut off.

Other types of direct questions ask "What kind?" or "How many?" The questions also ask for a limited, short answer from the prospect.

However, the answer to a direct question does not really tell you much, because there is little feedback involved. You may need more information to determine the buyer's needs and problems, especially if you could not determine them before the sales call. That's why salespeople work hard to develop a variety of open-ended questions.

The Rephrasing Question

The third type of question is called the **rephrasing question.** At times, the prospect's meaning is not clearly stated. In this situation, if appropriate, the salesperson might say:

- Would it be correct to say that price is the most important thing you are interested in? [sincerely, not too aggressively]
- Earlier in the conversation, you shared that delivery times are of the utmost importance. Can you tell me more about your expectations in this area?
- So to provide a quick recap of our discussion, if I can improve the delivery time, you would be interested in buying?
- So if I've captured this correctly, you are looking for a product that has strong brand awareness and ongoing levels of innovation? Is there anything that I'm missing?

This form of restatement allows you to clarify meaning and determine the prospect's needs.

The Redirect Question

The fourth type of question is the **redirect question.** This is used to redirect the prospect to selling points that both parties agree on. There are always areas of agreement between buyer and seller even if the prospect is opposed to purchasing the product. The redirect question is an excellent alternative or backup opener. This example clarifies the concept of redirective questioning:

Imagine you walk into a prospect's office, introduce yourself, and get this response: "I'm sorry, but there is no use in talking. We are satisfied with our present suppliers. Thanks for coming by." Respond by replacing your planned opener with a redirecting question. You might say:

- Do we agree that having a supplier who can reduce your costs is important?
- You would agree that manufacturers must use the most cost-efficient equipment to stay competitive these days, wouldn't you?
- Wouldn't you agree that you continually need to find new ways to increase your company's sales?

Using a redirect question moves the conversation from a negative position to a positive or neutral one while reestablishing communication between two people. The ability to redirect a seemingly terminated conversation through a well-placed question may impress the prospect simply by showing that you are not a run-of-the-mill order-taker, but a professional salesperson who sincerely believes in the beneficial qualities of your product.

Three Rules for Using Questions

The first rule is to carefully plan your questions. You may want to rehearse the questions you will ask so that you are able to anticipate the answer. By framing a question in a certain manner, you may be able to generate unique or valuable information. However, if you do not plan your questions or the sequence of your questions, you may confuse the customer or you may lead yourself into a situation from which you cannot escape. Although questions are a powerful selling technique, they can easily backfire.

The second rule in using a question is to pause or wait after submitting a question to allow the prospect time to respond to it. Waiting for an answer to a well-planned

Dennis DeMaria, a branch manager for Westvaco from Folcroft, Pennsylvania, says, "One of the biggest single weapons you as a salesperson can use in getting an order from a customer or prospect is keeping quiet and patiently waiting for the buyer to answer your questions. The information obtained from asking questions is the necessary knowledge you use to find the buyer's likes, dislikes, hot buttons, and areas to avoid. This valuable information also informs the salesperson whether the customer is ready to buy or whether he or she could continue selling.

"Experience has shown that salespeople *do* ask questions but they forget the most important part of this sales principle: *After you ask a question, you must be patient, don't talk, and let the buyer answer.* It does not matter how long it takes for the buyer to respond; keep quiet and wait for the answer. Remember, the first person to speak after a question has been asked, loses."[4]

Question. Anticipate answer, wait for reply, listen, really listen.

question is sometimes an excruciating process—seconds may seem like minutes. A salesperson must allow the prospect time to consider the question, and hope for a response. Failing to allow a prospect enough time defeats the major purpose of questioning, which is to establish two-way communication between the prospect and the salesperson.

The third rule is to listen. Many salespeople are so intent on talking that they forget to listen to what the prospect says (or they disregard nonverbal signals). Salespeople need to listen consciously to prospects so that they can ask intelligent, meaningful questions that aid both themselves and their prospects in determining what needs and problems exist and how to solve them. Prospects appreciate a good listener and view a willingness to listen as an indication that the salesperson is truly interested in their situation.

Is the Prospect Still Not Listening?

What happens when, using your best opening approach, you realize that the prospect is not listening? What about prospects who open mail, who fold their arms while looking at the wall or beyond you into the hallway, who make telephone calls in your presence, or who may even doze off?

This is the time to use one of your alternative openers that tune the prospect in to your message. Perhaps, the prospect might participate in the sales conversation if you use either the question or the demonstration approach. By handing the person something, showing something, or asking a question, you can briefly recapture attention, no matter how indifferent a prospect is to your presence.

If you can overcome such preoccupation or indifference in the early minutes of your interview by quickly capturing the prospect's attention and interest, the probability of your making a sale will greatly improve. This is why the approach is so important to the success of a sales call.

It is crucial to never become flustered or confused when a communication problem arises during your approach. As mentioned earlier, the salesperson who can deftly capture another person's imagination earns the right to a prospect's full attention and interest. Your prospect should not be handled as an adversary, for in that type of situation you seldom gain the sale.

Demonstration Openings

Openings that use demonstrations and drama are especially effective because of their ability to force the prospect into participating in the sales conversation. Of the two methods discussed here, the product approach is more frequently used alone or in combination with statements and questions.

In the **product approach,** the salesperson places the product on the counter or hands it to the customer, saying nothing. The salesperson may wait for the prospect to begin the conversation. The product approach is useful if the product is new, unique, or colorful, or if it is an existing product that has changed noticeably.

If, for example, Pepsi-Cola completely changed the shape of its bottle and label, the salesperson would simply hand the new product to the retail buyer and wait for a reaction. In marketing a new financial calculator for college students, the Texas Instruments salesperson might simply lay the product on the buyer's desk and wait. Another form of the product approach is to lead the buyer through a demonstration. This approach may be useful for introducing a new product, process, or system. We highlight a few examples in which a salesperson integrates technology into a demonstration.

Technology in the Demonstration

How can a salesperson quickly capture a prospect's attention and interest? If technology can be incorporated into a demonstration approach, it can be a powerful attention-grabber!

Imagine a salesperson asking a grocery store's purchasing agent to follow her to a conference room to "see something." The salesperson doesn't discuss the product until after the prospect has entered a conference room that uses virtual reality to stimulate a new method to display products in the customer's grocery store.

In other industries, a salesperson could place a new tablet computer on the purchasing agent's desk. Then, the salesperson could open with a demonstration of her new cloud-based software.

Technology can be a wonderful way to creatively and professionally begin a sales presentation and enhance a demonstration. Sounds, visuals, and touch cause the prospect's mind to instantly focus on the salesperson's words and actions. However, the key to any demonstration is to keep customer-focused. Ensure your demonstration focuses on a key benefit that is important to the buyer. When planning a demonstration, it's always important to ask yourself, "How would this assist the buyer?" or "Why would the buyer consider this benefit important?"

The **showmanship approach** involves doing something unusual to catch the prospect's attention and interest; this should be done carefully so that the approach does not backfire, which can happen if the demonstration does not work or is so flamboyant that it is inappropriate for the situation. Please remember, the showmanship approach should focus on a customer-centered benefit. While features are important, creative methods to demonstrate benefits will enhance your sales effectiveness.

- "Ms. Rosenburg, our paper plates are the strongest on the market, making them drip-free, a quality your customers will appreciate." [The salesperson places a paper plate on her lap and pours cooking grease or motor oil onto it while speaking to the prospect.]
- As she hands the buyer a plate from a new line of china, she lets it drop to the floor. It does not break. While picking it up, she says, "Our new breakthrough in treating quality china will revolutionize the industry. Your customers, especially newlyweds, will love this feature. Don't you think so?"
- The salesperson selling Super Glue would repeat the television advertisement for the prospect. In the prospect's office, the salesperson glues two objects together, such as a broken handle onto a coffee cup, waits one minute, hands the cup to the buyer for a test, and then begins the sales presentation. The mended cup can be left with the buyer as a gift and a reminder.
- The life insurance salesperson hands the prospect multiple stacks of mocked-up currency, such as monopoly bills, that roughly equate to the amount of a life insurance policy payout, saying, "Steve, if you suffer an unfortunate accident, imagine being able to care for your family by providing them with this level of financial security."

Transitions: Maintain Conversational Flow

Have you ever experienced a conversation in which an awkward silence occurred? The flow of the conversation is important. In some instances, the awkward pauses occur between the different elements of the sales process. **Transitions** help relate or link two ideas or sections of the conversation. For instance, how do you eloquently link the rapport section with the agenda section? How do you link the agenda section to the needs discovery section? You need to practice transitions to ensure the conversation flows. The following example demonstrates a transition between the rapport section and the agenda section.

Business-to-Business Scenario (Industry: Business Insurance)

Salesperson: Absolutely, the summer is flying by. So have you had the opportunity to play much golf recently?

Buyer: A few rounds. It helps me to relax after especially busy days at work. The exercise and camaraderie really allows me to settle down and think about the major issues in my business. Do you play?

Salesperson: Absolutely. I really enjoy golf as well. It's a great way to exercise and focus on the big picture, which actually bring me to why we're meeting today, to discuss the major financial elements of your business, especially business risk and liability (**transition**). Your note last week suggested that the goal for today's meeting is to learn about your business's key area of liability and risk and evaluate potential solutions to minimize this risk. What are your thoughts of this business outline? Are there any other areas we should add? (**agenda**)

SUMMARY OF MAJOR SELLING ISSUES

As the first step in your sales presentation, the approach is a critical factor. In the majority of sales-oriented situations in which you and the prospects must agree on needs and problems, a questioning approach (SPIN, for instance) is in order. Generally, in developing your approach, imagine your prospects asking themselves, "Do I have time to listen to, talk with, or devote to this person? What's in it for me?"

Words alone will not ensure that you are heard. The first impression that you make on a prospect can negate your otherwise positive and sincere opening. To ensure a favorable impression in most selling situations, consider your attire, and act as though you are truly glad to meet the prospect.

Your approach statement should be especially designed for each prospect. Your ability to adapt to the buyer and the selling situation is critical to your success. You can choose to open with a statement, question, or demonstration by using any one of the techniques. You should have several alternative approaches ready in case you need to alter your plans for a specific situation.

Carefully phrased questions are useful at any point in a sales presentation. Questions should display a sincere interest in prospects and their situations. Skillfully handled questions employed in a sales approach can wrest a prospect's attention from distractions and center it on you and your presentation. Questions are generally used to determine prospect wants and needs, thereby increasing prospect participation in the sales presentation. Four basic types of questions discussed in this chapter are direct, nondirective, rephrasing, and redirect questions.

In using questions, practice not only the type of questions you will ask but also anticipate the potential answers to your questions. Also, remember to allow prospects time to completely answer the question. Listen carefully to their answers for a guide as to how well you are progressing toward selling to them. Should you determine that your prospect is not listening, do something to regain attention. Techniques such as offering something or asking questions can refocus the prospect's attention long enough for your return to the presentation.

Quick Review for Students

The quick review sections provide key questions to help you develop a greater level of conceptual understanding. We suggest that after you read the chapter, you try to answer the following questions without looking back at the textbook.

1. What is the goal of the approach section of the selling process? What are the various categories of approaches that a salesperson may use?
2. What is the goal of the rapport section? What topics could be incorporated within the rapport building section of the approach?
3. What is the value of incorporating an agenda into the approach section of the sales process? Why might a buyer appreciate the use of an agenda by the salesperson?
4. What are the elements of the acronym "SPIN?" Why might some salespeople believe that using multiple "I" questions within the SPIN process is very useful?
5. What is the value of using transitions within the approach section?
6. Why might salespeople incorporate a needs summary and a needs prioritization section within the SPIN process?
7. Why are open-ended questions one of the most important tools that can be used in the approach section of the sales process?

MEETING A SALES CHALLENGE

Questions are important tools for salespeople. They help uncover needs and problems, obtain valuable selling information, and qualify the prospect's interest and buying authority. So it pays to ask good ones.

Because you may need to first develop an analysis of the bank's operation, the need-satisfaction or problem–solution presentation methods would work well for this situation. Begin with questions that are direct, well aimed, and, most importantly, force the prospect to talk about a specific problem. Questions that cannot be answered yes or no provide the most information. A multiple-question approach, such as SPIN, would be appropriate for this situation.

KEY TERMS FOR SELLING

agenda   323
approach   313
complimentary
   approach   322
creative imagery   315
curiosity approach   331
customer benefit
   approach   330
direct question   335

introductory approach   321
multiple-question approach
   (SPIN)   325
needs-prioritization
   section   329
needs-summary
   section   329
nondirective question   334
opinion approach   332

premium approach   323
product approach   338
redirect question   336
referral approach   322
rephrasing question   336
shock approach   332
showmanship
   approach   339
transitions   339

SALES APPLICATION QUESTIONS

1. Explain the reasons for using questions when making a sales presentation. Discuss the rules for questioning that the salesperson should follow.
2. What are three general categories of the approach? Give an example of each.
3. What is SPIN? Give an example of a salesperson using SPIN.
4. Discuss each of the four types of questions. In each of the following instances, determine if a direct, nondirective, rephrasing, or redirect question is being used.
   a. "Now let's see if I have this right; you are looking for a high-quality product and price is no object?"
   b. "What type of clothes are you looking for?"
   c. "Are you interested in Model 101 or Model 921?"
   d. "Well, I can appreciate your beliefs, but you would agree that price is not the only thing to consider when buying a copier, wouldn't you?"
   e. "When would you like to have your new Xerox 9000 installed?"
   f. "Are you saying that *where* you go for vacation is more important than the cost of getting there?"
   g. "You would agree that saving time is important to a busy executive like yourself, wouldn't you?"
5. Which of the following approaches do you think is the best? Why?
   a. "Ms. Jones, in the past, you've made it a practice to reduce the facings on heavy-duty household detergents in the winter months because of slower movement."
   b. "Mr. Brown, you'll recall that last time I was in, you expressed concern over the fact that your store labor was running higher than the industry average of 8 percent of sales."
   c. "Hi! I'm Jeanette Smith of Procter & Gamble, and I'd like to talk to you about Cheer. How's it selling?"
6. Assume you are a salesperson for NCR (National Cash Register Corporation) and you want to sell Mr. Johnson, the owner/manager of a large independent supermarket, your POS terminals. You have just met Mr. Johnson inside the front door of the supermarket, and after your initial introduction, the conversation continues:

Salesperson: Mr. Johnson, your customers are really backed up at your cash registers, aren't they?

Buyer: Yeah, it's a real problem.

Salesperson: Do your checkers ever make mistakes when they are in a rush?

Buyer: They sure do!

Salesperson: Have you ever thought about shortening checkout time while reducing checker errors?

Buyer: Yes, but those methods are too expensive!

Salesperson: Does your supermarket generate over $1 million in sales each month?

Buyer: Oh, yes—why?

Salesperson: Would you be interested in discussing a method of decreasing customer checkout time by 100 percent and greatly reducing the number of errors made by your checkers, if I can show you that the costs of solving your problems will be more than offset by your savings?

    a. Using the framework of the SPIN approach technique, determine whether each of the above questions asked by the salesperson is a Situation, Problem, Implication, or Need-payoff question.

    b. If Mr. Johnson says yes to your last question, what should you do next?

    c. If Mr. Johnson says no to your last question, what should you do next?

7. As a salesperson for Gatti's Electric Company, Cliff Defee is interested in selling John Bonham more of his portable electric generators. John is a construction supervisor for a firm specializing in constructing large buildings such as shopping centers, office buildings, and manufacturing plants. He currently uses three of Cliff's newest models. Cliff just learned that John will be building a new manufacturing plant. As Cliff examines the specifications for the new plant, he feels John will require several additional generators. Two types of approaches Cliff might make are depicted in the following situations:

Situation A:

Salesperson: I see you got the Jonesville job.

Buyer: Sure did.

Salesperson: Are the specs OK?

Buyer: Yes.

Salesperson: Will you need more machines?

Buyer: Yes, but not yours!

Situation B:

Salesperson: I understand you have three of our electric sets.

Buyer: Yes, I do.

Salesperson: I'm sure you'll need additional units on your next job.

Buyer: You're right, I will.

Salesperson: Well, I've gone over your plant specifications and put together products just like you need.

Buyer: What I don't *need* are any of your lousy generators.

Salesperson: Well, that's impossible. It's a brand-new design.

Buyer: Sorry, I've got to go.

    a. Briefly describe the approaches in situations A and B. In both situations, Cliff is in a tough spot. What should he do now?

    b. What type of approach could Cliff have made that would have allowed him to uncover John's dissatisfaction? Would the approach you are suggesting also be appropriate if John were satisfied with the generators?

8. This is a cold call on the warehouse manager for Coats Western Wear, a retailer with four stores. You know most of the manager's work consists of deliveries from the warehouse to the four stores. Based on your experience, you suspect that the volume of shipments to the warehouse fluctuates; certain seasons of the year are extremely busy.

    As a salesperson for Hercules Shelving, you want to sell the manager your heavy-duty-gauge steel shelving for use in the warehouse. Since this is a relatively small sale, you decide to go in cold, relying only on your questioning ability to uncover potential problems and make the prospect aware of them.

You are now face-to-face with the warehouse manager. You have introduced yourself, and after some small talk it is time to begin your approach. Which of the following questions would be best?

a. "Have you had any recent storage problems?"
b. "How do you take care of your extra storage needs during busy seasons such as Christmas?"
c. "Can you tell me a little about your storage problems?"

FURTHER EXPLORING THE SALES WORLD

1. Television advertisements are constructed to capture the viewer's attention and interest to sell a product or service quickly. Examine at least five commercials and report on the method each one used to get your attention, stimulate your interest, and move you from this attention–interest phase into discussing the product. Determine whether the first few seconds of the commercial related to the product's features, advantages, or benefits, and if so, how? Using a tape recorder may help you.

2. Assume that you have a 30-minute job interview next week with a representative of a company you are really interested in. How would you prepare for the interview, and what could you do during the first few minutes of the interview to get the recruiter interested in hiring you? Can you see any differences between this interview situation and the environment of a salesperson making a sales call?

STUDENT APPLICATION LEARNING EXERCISES (SALES)

To make **SALE 4** first select the method you will use for your presentation. Please review Chapter 8. Next, write down the name of the approach technique you will use for this presentation method. Please see Exhibit 9.5.

Presentation method: _____
Approach technique: _____

SALE 4 of 7–Chapter 9

Now write out what you will actually say in your approach, including what the buyer should say. Relate your approach to your *FAB*s developed in **SALE 1** so you have a smooth transition into discussing your product.

Seller:

Buyer:

Imagine you have now finished the approach. Write out the buyer–seller dialogue for the first two **SELL Sequences.** Refer back to **SALE 1.** Create an imaginary response by the buyer to each of your trial closes.

SELL 1

Seller:

Buyer:

SELL 2

Seller:

Buyer:

Role-play your approach and **SELL Sequences** with someone to see if you are satisfied. If available, use a tape recorder to listen to your speed, voice inflections, phrases, and any unwanted mannerisms, such as frequently repeating "uh" or "I see."

NOTES

1. Laura A. Peracchio and David Luna, "The Role of Thin-Slice Judgments in Consumer Psychology." *Journal of Consumer Psychology* (Lawrence Erlbaum Associates) 16, no. 1 (2006), pp. 25–32.

2. M. Szegedy-Maszak, Mysteries of the Mind (Cover story), *U.S. News & World Report,* 138, no. 7: February 28, 2005, pp. 52–61.

3. For a complete discussion, see Neil Rackham, *SPIN Selling* (New York: McGraw-Hill, 1988).

4. Dennis DeMaria, "Keep Quiet and Get the Order," *Personal Selling Power,* March/April 1993, p. 17.

CASE 9.1

©Ron Chapple Stock/FotoSearch/
Glow Images

The Thompson Company

Before making a cold call on the Thompson Company, you did some research on the account. Barbara Thompson is both president and chief purchasing officer. In this dual capacity, she often is so rushed that she is impatient with salespeople. She is known for her habit of quickly turning down the salesperson and shutting off the discussion by turning and walking away. In looking over Thompson's operation, you notice that the inefficient metal shelving she uses in her warehouse is starting to collapse. Warehouse employees have attempted to remedy the situation by building wooden shelves and reinforcing the weakened metal shelves with lumber. They also have begun stacking boxes on the floor, requiring much more space.

However, you know that these make-shift wooden supports are against federal regulations. If the warehouse was inspected, fines between $1,000–$3,000 per metal shelf could be imposed. Next, you understand that if the shelves collapsed and injured someone, the average worker's compensation claim exceeds $10,000. From your research, you know that the Thompson Company owns 10 warehouses. Further, each warehouse has a minimum of 30 shelving units, and each shelving unit has a minimum of 8 shelves. Plus, each shelving unit stores between $10,000–$30,000 worth of goods. Many of these goods are fragile.

You recognize the importance of getting off to a fast start with Thompson. You must capture her attention and interest quickly or she may not talk with you.

Questions

1. Develop three questions that have the greatest possibility of gaining Ms. Thompson's attention.
2. You've gained Ms. Thompson's attention and she has granted you a 20-minute meeting. Write down an agenda statement that you could convey to her.
3. Develop three open-ended questions you would use to begin to understand Ms. Thompson's needs regarding shelving.

CASE 9.2

©Ron Chapple Stock/FotoSearch/
Glow Images

The Copy Corporation

Assume you are contacting the purchasing agent for office supplies of a large chain of retail department stores. After hearing that the company is opening 10 new stores, you determine that they will need a copier for each store. Three months earlier, you had sold this purchasing agent a lease agreement on two large machines. The buyer wanted to try your machines in the company's new stores. If they liked them, you would get the account. Unknown to you, one of the machines was broken, which caused the purchasing agent to be pressured by a store manager to replace it immediately. Unfortunately, the replacement procedure was not very efficient and it caused the purchasing agent a great deal of time and effort. They have sent your customer service department a number of e-mails. However, most of the e-mails were not answered in a satisfactory manner. As you walk into the purchasing agent's office, you say:

Salesperson: Congratulations. I understand you are opening 10 new stores in the next six months.

Buyer: I don't know who told you, but you seem to know!

Salesperson: If you'll let me know when you want a copier at each store, I'll arrange for it to be there.

Buyer: Look, I don't want any more of your lousy copiers! When the leases expire, I want you here to pick them up, or I'll throw them out in the street! I've got a meeting now. I want to see you in three months.

Questions

1. What are three steps that the salesperson could have taken before the interaction in order to be better prepared for the meeting?

2. Describe this situation, commenting on what the salesperson did correctly and incorrectly.
3. Now challenge yourself. Develop a strategy in which the salesperson asks only questions within this portion of the meeting. What specific questions would you ask?
4. Develop another approach the salesperson could use to uncover the problems experienced by the purchasing agent.

CASE 9.3

Electronic Office Security Corporation

Ann Saroyan is a salesperson for the Electronic Office Security Corporation. She sells industrial security systems that detect intruders and activate an alarm. When Ann first began selling, she used to make brief opening remarks to her prospects and then move quickly into her presentation. Although this resulted in selling many of her security systems, she felt there must be a better method.

Ann began to analyze the reasons prospects would not buy. Her conclusion was that even after her presentation, prospects still did not believe they needed a security alarm system. She decided to develop a multiple-question approach that would allow her to determine the prospect's attitude toward a need for a security system. If the prospect does not initially feel a need for her product, she wants her approach to help convince the prospect of a need for a security system.

Ann developed and carefully rehearsed her new sales presentation. Her first sales call using her multiple-question approach was with a large accounting firm. Ann used LinkedIn™ and other resources to conduct research on the company. She learned the accounting firm employed 22 accountants and 12 support staff. It appeared to be growing its client base by about 10% each year. In addition, it appeared the firm had approximately 400 clients. According to an accounting database, she found that on average, an accounting client relationship is worth approximately $8,000 per year. While these are averages, Ann felt quite confident about the research she had conducted.

Ann also brought with her a list of office materials and their estimated value. While Ann knew each firm and their purchasing process is distinct, she was happy to have a reference regarding average purchase prices for items commonly used in offices. Information on this list included:

Item (per piece)	Estimated Replacement Cost
Industrial sofa	$1,800
Desk	800
Artwork (average)	450
Artwork (custom)	1,200
Lobby chair	250
Chair for desk	375
Smart-boards	$2,800
Server	4,000
Laptops (business)	1,250
Tablets	800
Cell phones (business)	650
External hard drives (1 TB and above)	280

She asked the receptionist whom she should see and was referred to Joe Bell. After she waited 20 minutes, Bell asked her to come into his office. The conversation went like this:

Salesperson: This is a beautiful old building, Mr. Bell. Have you been here long?

Buyer: About 10 years. Before we moved here, we were in one of those ugly glass and concrete towers. Now, you wanted to talk to me about office security.

Salesperson: Yes, Mr. Bell. Tell me, do you have a security system at present?

Buyer: No, we don't. We've never had a break-in here.

Salesperson: I see. Could you tell me what's the most valuable item in your building?

Buyer: Probably our technology, specifically our server systems and all the technology that we run through the system. We have a series of laptops, tablets, touch monitors, and smart-boards integrated throughout the building.

Salesperson: Are those items fairly portable and mobile?

Buyer: Yes, amazingly, it's not much bigger than a typewriter. we can relocate monitors and smart-boards based our needs, meetings, and work goals.

Salesperson: Would it be difficult to run your business without these items—if it were stolen, for example?

Buyer: Oh, yes, that would be quite awkward.

Salesperson: Could you tell me a bit more about the problem you would face without this type of hardware?

Buyer: It would be detrimental to our people and their productivity, but I suppose we could manage until our insurance gave us a replacement.

Salesperson: But without the access to this type of integrated technology, wouldn't your customer service levels suffer?

Buyer: Not if we got the replacement quickly.

Salesperson: You said the server and related hardware is insured. Do you happen to know if the software—the programs, your customer files—are also insured?

Buyer: I don't believe so; our insurance covers the equipment only.

Salesperson: And do you keep backup records somewhere else—in the cloud, for example?

Buyer: No, we don't. We have some secondary backup on-site—basically on external hard drives.

Salesperson: Mr. Bell, in my experience, software isn't left behind after a theft. Wouldn't it be a serious problem to you if that software were taken?

Buyer: Yes, you're right, I suppose. Redevelopment would certainly cost a lot. The software applications were expensive.

Salesperson: And even worse, because software development can take a long time, wouldn't that hold up your billings to customers?

Buyer: While it isn't ideal, we are financial professionals and could always do that manually.

Salesperson: What effect would that have on your processing costs?

Buyer: I see your point. It would certainly be expensive to run a manual system, as well as being inconvenient.

Salesperson: And if you lost your software, wouldn't it also make it harder to serve your customers?

Buyer: Yes. I don't have much contact with that part of the business. While I'm in charge of the technology as the owner of the firm, it's not something I enjoy dealing with. But without order processing and stock control I'm sure we would grind to a halt in a matter of days.

Salesperson: Are there any other items in the building that would be hard to replace if stolen?

Buyer: Some of the furnishings. I would hate to lose this antique clock, for example. In fact, most of our furnishings would be very hard to replace in the same style.

Salesperson: So, if you lost them, wouldn't it hurt the character of your office?

Buyer: Yes, it would be damaging. We've built a really fun, productive image here, and without it we would be like dozens of other people in our business—the glass and concrete image.

Salesperson: This may sound like an odd question, but how many doors do you have at ground level?

Buyer: Let me see . . . uh . . . six.

Salesperson: And ground-level windows?

Buyer: About 10 or a dozen.

Salesperson: So there are 16 or 18 points where a thief could break in, compared with 1 or 2 points in the average glass and concrete office. Doesn't that concern you?

Buyer: Put that way, it does. I suppose we're not very secure.

Questions

1. Based on your reading of the case, how would you describe the dialogue between the buyer and seller?
2. What were the positive aspects of the questions asked by the salesperson? What questions would you have changed or altered? What would you have asked instead?
3. Analyze each of the salesperson's questions and state whether it is a situation, problem, implication, or need-payoff type of question.
4. Analyze each of the buyer's responses to the salesperson's questions and state what type of need the salesperson's question uncovered. Was it an implied or minor need response or was it an explicit or important need response? Why?
5. How would you improve on this salesperson's approach?
6. After the buyer's last statement, which of the following would you do?
   a. Move into the presentation.
   b. Ask a problem question.
   c. Ask a need-payoff question.
   d. Ask for an appointment to fully discuss your system.
7. After having read the dialogue, write a series of questions that you believe may be more effective in gaining the needed information from the buyer.

CASE 9.4

Needs Discovery

You work for Lamps, Lights & Illumination, LLC, an industrial leader in providing lighting solutions to businesses. Your firm is known for a wide variety of lighting products and quality services—all related to lighting and illumination. Your firm has 200 plus branches on the East and West Coasts and is now focusing on opening branches in the Midwest United States. Each branch consists of a lighting center in which industrial customers can view various lighting fixtures. Each branch is also equipped with a small distribution center, located in the rear of the building. The distribution serves two purposes. First, it serves as a small, efficient warehouse that stocks the fastest-moving goods and supplies. Second, it serves as a pick-up center that allows customers to pick up the goods that were ordered.

From a service standpoint, the headquarters of your firm provides many customer-focused departments, including: (a) a centralized electrical engineering department providing assistance for customer projects, (b) a centralized customer-call center specializing in assisting electricians with installation, (c) a lighting blueprint and design center that assists customers with planning major projects, (d) a centralized lighting décor center with expertise in decorating trends and ideas for projects, such as building multi-unit apartment complexes, luxury homes exceeding one million dollars, and industrial lighting such as manufacturing plants, and (e) a centralized energy efficiency center stocked with experts well-versed in reducing energy usage via lighting and lighting-based equipment.

Sales Scenario: You are a territory representative for Lamps, Lights and Illumination, LLC. You will be calling on a large electrical contractor, Pete's Quality Electrical Contracting. Pete's Quality Electrical Contracting has developed an array of relationships with major local, regional and national multi family homebuilders. You have learned that Pete's Quality Electrical Contracting has been awarded a large contract to wire four multifamily apartment complexes in your area. Each apartment complex will have 250 apartments. Hence, the total number of units is 1,000.

This is a very unique contract. Two of the four units will only offer two bedroom apartments. Similarly, the remaining two units will only offer three bedroom apartments. The owners will change the aesthetics of the apartment complex, such as granite countertops, wood or vinyl flooring, or wall coverings. However, each two bedroom apartment will have the same electrical design, including lighting. Similarly, each three-bedroom apartment will have the same electrical design, including lighting. You believe this presents a fantastic opportunity for Lamps, Lights and Illumination, LLC.

You have called many of your colleagues within the construction industry. They have heard that the apartment contractor is very interested in reducing energy to run the complex. In addition, you have heard that this is the largest lighting contract in the history of Pete's Quality Electric Contracting.

Meeting 1: Needs Discovery

You have set a meeting with Pat Smith, the head of procurement for Pete's Quality Electrical Contracting. Originally, you believed both Pat Smith and Ryan Jones, the chief financial officer would be attending the meeting. However, you learned recently that Ryan will not be able to attend.

Your goal for the meeting is to understand the company's lighting needs, as it relates to the project. You will meet with the procurement official to learn about the varied needs (procurement and financial) of the firm. You will need to ask a series of probing questions to understand both the needs of the procurement individual and the potential needs of the financial officer.

The questions should help you understand the needs of the electrical contractor as it pertains to lighting, the perceptions of the procurement official, and the financial officer. At the end of the meeting, your goal is to summarize the needs. If you have outlined the needs well, you can request the official set up a meeting to present your solution to the financial officer.

Questions

1. What would you predict as some of the major needs for the procurement officer? Please write three to five needs.
2. What would you predict as some of the major needs of the financial officer? Please write three to five needs.
3. What would you prepare as your sequence of needs discovery questions? Write down the questions you would ask the procurement officer during the approach.

Elements of a Great
Sales Presentation

Main Topics

Building a Trusting, Long-Term Relationship

An Overview of the Presentation Section of the Sales Process

Three Essential Steps within the Presentation

The Sales Presentation Mix

Visual Aids Help Tell the Story

Dramatization Improves Your Chances

Demonstrations Prove It

Technology Can Help!

The Sales Presentation Goal Model

The Ideal Presentation

Be Prepared for Presentation Difficulties

Learning Objectives

The fourth step in the sales process is the presentation. Here, you discuss with the buyer the product's features, advantages, and benefits, your marketing plan, and the business proposition. After studying this chapter, you should be able to

10–1 Discuss the purpose and essential steps of the sales presentation.

10–2 Give examples of the six sales presentation mix elements.

10–3 Describe difficulties that may arise during the sales presentation and explain how to handle them.

10–4 State how to handle a discussion regarding the competition.

10–5 Explain the need to properly diagnose the prospect's personality to determine the design of the sales presentation.

FACING A SALES CHALLENGE

You are a salesperson representing Superior Carpets. You have been talking about several of your new carpet's features, advantages, and benefits to a retailer. You have just told your customer that because of Superior's new technology, the synthetic fibers in your new product will not fade even if exposed to direct sunlight. Your customer then says, "That sounds great, but I don't know. I've had too many customers complain about fading."

What do you do in this situation? As you see, the customer doubts whether your carpet will resist fading; and whether a fade-resistant carpet is an important benefit. How do you prove the carpet will not fade? What if the customer will not take your word?

The presentation part of the selling process is a persuasive vocal and visual discussion of a business proposition. In developing your presentation, consider the elements you will use to provide the information a buyer needs to make a buying decision. At any

EXHIBIT 10.1

The presentation is the heart of the sale. An effective approach allows a smooth transition into discussing your product's features, advantages, and benefits. Use the various sales presentation mix items to tell your story.

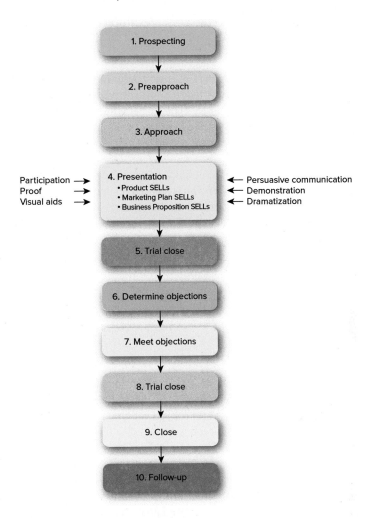

time, a customer may mention a concern, as in "Facing a Sales Challenge" above. A proper response is needed to make the sale.

This chapter discusses the elements of the presentation—the fourth step in the sales process (see Exhibit 10.1). We examine the purpose and essential steps in the presentation. Next, we review and expand on the presentation techniques salespeople use and how to handle the customer in the sales challenge. The chapter ends by discussing the importance of the proper use of trial closes and difficulties that may arise in the presentation, along with the need to design your presentation around an individual situation and buyer. Let's first see what business life is about following the Core Principles.

Building a Trusting, Long-Term Relationship

Visualize you are in front of a purchasing professional for a company. Across the desk from you is a 50-year-old person who has been a buyer for this company for 20 years. Do you think this person would know his or her organization and its needs? Would this person have experience in dealing with salespeople? If the buyer sees 5 to 10 salespeople a day, over 40,000 salespeople may be sitting where you are in this imaginary business meeting.

Purchasing professionals are busy people. You may have a 30-minute appointment. This is why preparation may take hours for a few-minute presentation. You are expected to know your products, something about his or her organization, and how your product can help the company before ever walking into the buyer's office. You are expected to present your product, marketing plan, and business proposition in a clear, concise, organized manner so that it is easy to determine if the product is of value to the buyer.

Truthfully discussing your product shows you are a person with integrity and character who is focused on unselfishly helping this person. Should there be a hint of exaggeration, the buyer may not buy. Yet after several business meetings over time with Superior Carpets, mentioned in "Facing a Sales Challenge," the buyer may believe you about the product not fading, especially if you have been truthful in the past and you use a proof statement as discussed in this chapter. Ethical service will build true relationships between buyer and seller.

> *Customers are busy people and they possess high expectations of salespeople. This is why a salesperson may prepare many hours for a meeting that takes less than one hour.*

An Overview of the Presentation Section of the Sales Process

A young salesperson was disappointed about losing a big sale. As he talked with his sales manager after the sales call, he said, "I guess it just proves you can lead a horse to water but you can't make him drink." The manager replied, "John, take my advice: Your job is not to make him drink. Your job is to make him thirsty."[1]

The main goal of your presentation is to provide information and knowledge to the prospect/customer. This knowledge includes the discussion of your product, marketing plan, and business proposition. Once you have given your presentation, the customer is in a much better position to know if your product should be purchased. However, we know that a prospective buyer considers many things before making a decision about what product to buy. As we have seen, the approach or first few minutes of the sales conversation should be constructed to determine the prospect's need, capture attention and interest, and allow for a smooth transition into the presentation. Once you have determined the customer's needs, your goal is to logically tie your product's benefits to them. Salespeople accomplish this goal through the use of the presentation.

> *Salespeople should demonstrate the value their product, their firm, and they personally will create for customers.*

The presentation is a continuation of the approach. What is the purpose of the presentation. It communicates *knowledge* via the features, advantages, and benefits of your product, marketing plan, and business proposal in a way that aligns to the needs of your customer. This allows the buyer to develop positive personal *beliefs* toward your product. These beliefs result in *desire* (or *need*) for the type of product you sell. Your job, as a salesperson, is to convert that need into a want and into the *attitude* that your product is the best option to fulfill a certain need. You make the buyer thirsty. Furthermore, you must convince the buyer not only that your product is the best but also that you are the best source to buy from. When this occurs, your prospect has moved into the *conviction* stage of the mental buying process. The buyer is very thirsty.

When a real need is established, the buyer wants to fulfill that need, and there is a high probability that your product is best. This results in your you making a sale, as shown in Exhibit 10.2. Whether or not to buy is a choice decision, and you have provided the necessary information so that the customer chooses to buy from you.

Assume, in our hypothetical example, that you are a salesperson for Microsoft and you wish to sell 10 cloud-based subscriptions for your new edition of Microsoft Office, costing $15 per month per user to a company. The prospect's company uses your competitor's products, which cost $8 each. How should you conceptualize the prospect's thought processes regarding whether or not to buy from you (as shown in Exhibit 10.1) to develop your presentation?

Begin by realizing that the prospect has certain attitudes toward her current productivity software. The prospect's job performance is judged by her management of certain responsibilities. Thus, improving the performance of company employees is important. However, the prospect knows little about you, your new cloud-based product, or your product's benefits. The prospect may feel that her current software products are good, high-quality, products. However, you cannot be sure about the buyer's current attitudes.

Dale Carnegie stressed that an easy way to become a good conversationalist is to be a good listener and encourage others to talk about themselves. You might develop a SPIN approach to determine the buyer's attitudes toward business productivity in general and your software specifically. Once you have addressed each of the four SPIN questions, and you feel more information about your product is needed, begin the presentation.

Present the product information that meets the needs of your buyer and allows the buyer to develop a positive attitude toward your product. Next, possibly using a value-analysis proposal, show how your product can increase efficiency, reduce costs, and pay for itself in one year, using a return-on-investment (ROI) technique. A positive reaction from your prospect indicates that she has reached the desire stage of the mental buying process. There is a need for some brand of office productivity software.

Now, show why your Microsoft cloud-based productivity software is the best solution to the buyer's need and show that you will provide service after the sale. A positive response on these two items indicates that the prospect believes your product is best and that the conviction stage has been reached. The prospect wants to buy the Microsoft cloud-based productivity software.

Up to this point, you have discussed your product's features, advantages, and benefits, your marketing plan, and your business proposition. You have *not* asked the prospect to buy. Rather, you have developed a presentation to lead the prospect through four of the five mental buying steps: the attention, interest, desire, and conviction steps. It may take you five minutes, two hours, or several weeks of repeat calls to move the prospect into the conviction stage.

> "An easy way to become a good conversationalist is to be a good listener and encourage others to talk about themselves."
>
> DALE CARNEGIE

You must move the prospect into the conviction stage before a sale is made. So hold off asking the prospect to buy until the conviction stage. Otherwise, this usually results in objections, failure to listen to your whole story, and fewer sales. The sales presentation has seven major steps. Each step is taken in order to logically and sequentially move the prospect into the conviction stage of the buying process.

When a person buys something, did you ever stop to think about what is actually purchased? Is the customer really buying your product? No. What the customer is actually buying is a mental picture of the future in which your product helps to fulfill some expectation. The buyer has mentally conceived certain needs. Your presentation must create mental images that move your prospect into the conviction stage.

Three Essential Steps Within the Presentation

No matter which of the four sales presentation methods is used, your presentation must follow these three essential steps, shown in Exhibit 10.3.* In Chapter 3, we discussed features, advantages, and benefits. However, this element of the sales process is so important, a review is worthwhile.

Step 1

Fully discuss the *features, advantages,* and *benefits* of your product. Tell the whole story.

Step 2

Present your marketing plan. For wholesalers and retailers, this is your suggestion on how they should *resell* the product. For end users, it is your suggestion on how they can *use* the product. Again, consider using the feature, advantages, benefit approach to communicate the marketing plan to the buyer.

EXHIBIT 10.3

Three essential steps within the presentation.

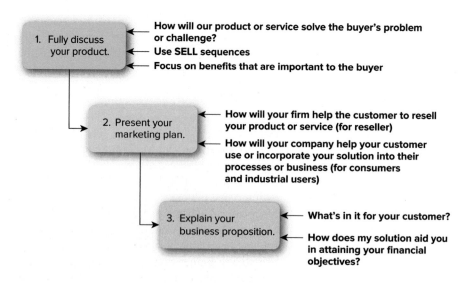

1. Fully discuss your product.
- How will our product or service solve the buyer's problem or challenge?
- Use **SELL** sequences
- Focus on benefits that are important to the buyer

2. Present your marketing plan.
- How will your firm help the customer to resell your product or service (for reseller)
- How will your company help your customer use or incorporate your solution into their processes or business (for consumers and industrial users)

3. Explain your business proposition.
- What's in it for your customer?
- How does my solution aid you in attaining your financial objectives?

*The three steps are discussed in Chapter 7 under "Customer Benefit Plan: What It's All About!"

Step 3

Explain your business proposition. This step relates the *value* of your product to the *cost* or the investment required. It should be discussed last, since you always want to present your product's benefits and marketing plan relative to your product's price. The business proposition is another opportunity to use the features, advantages, benefits approach to communicate to the buyer.

Remember Your *FAB*s!

It is extremely important to emphasize benefits throughout the presentation. Using the *FAB* Sequence communication technique when discussing the product, marketing plan, and business proposition greatly improves your chances of making the sale.

While you have read briefly about *FAB*s, it is important to understand each element. Therefore, we provide a quick review and a few examples.

A feature is any characteristic of the product. This may be a tangible or intangible characteristic. An advantage is the performance characteristic of the product or service. It describes how the feature will help the buyer. One way to think about an advantage is it serves as the enabler. The advantage describes how the feature enables the benefit. A benefit is the favorable result the buyer receives from the product or service because the particular advantage has the ability to satisfy a buyer's need. Remember, buyers possess unique needs. Therefore, you will need to select specific features that allow the buyer to attain the benefits he or she covets.

The *FAB* Sequence allows you to communicate concisely the value of your product or service. However, great *FAB* Sequences require preparation and knowledge about your firm, its services, policies, and procedures as well as a high level of customer understanding. Therefore, construct your *FAB* Sequences with care and effort.

Ideally, the salesperson should present information in each of the steps shown in Exhibit 10.3 to create a logical conversation with the buyer. That is, the salesperson should discuss the product and its benefits before moving to the marketing plan or business proposition.

Assume you sell food products to hotels and food retail chains, and one of your products is a pancake mix. Notice in Exhibit 10.4 the *FAB*s for each of the three essential steps within the presentation. Even for a product like pancake mix, salespeople should use benefits to paint a visual picture in the minds of the buyers of how this product will fulfill their needs. This is what professional selling is all about—relating your product's benefits to a customer's needs in a truthful and ethical manner. To ensure your *FAB* Sequences are effective, we provide a few best practices and examples below.

1. **FAB Sequences should be logical.** The feature should logically enable some type of benefit. For example, a feature describing product quality is probably unlikely to cause profitability. Instead, we know that either pricing or expenses (investments) generally drive profitability. Therefore, we would probably discuss the investment (or cost) of our product as a feature and then communicate that the initial investment allows the retailer to price the product at a suitable margin, which effectively increases profitability.

2. *FAB* **Sequences should use specific language.** As we mentioned previously, buyers are extremely busy. An effective salesperson uses professional, business language to convey their *FAB* Sequences. For instance, rather than describe a benefit as "high profit," "good quality," or "a lot more margin," you might state a specific number, such as "12% more profit," a comparison such as "quality exceeds the leading competitor by 13%," or "margins 5 points greater than your industry average."

EXHIBIT 10.4

Salespeople use these FABs in their presentations.

Features, Advantages, and Benefits of Bix Buckwheat Pancake Mix (Customer: Restaurants)		
Features	**Advantages (enables or produces)**	**Benefits**
Product		
1. Traditional "farmhouse" recipe, with freshest ingredients; fortified with vitamins A, B, C, and D; no preservatives	1. Great tasting, fluffy, and light; highly nutritious; strongly favored in taste test vs. competition	1. Provides an appealing item; expands breakfast menu; increases breakfast business through greater customer satisfaction
2. User needs only to add water, stir, and cook	2. Quick and easy for your cooks and chefs to prepare	2. Requires minimal kitchen time and labor; reduces time invested in making pancakes by 10% (on average)
Marketing Plan		
3. Just-in-time delivery: weekly or as needed	3. No need to store large quantities	3. Requires minimal inventory space; reduces inventory carrying costs by 6%
4. Local distribution center	4. Additional orders can be filled quickly	4. Prevents out-of-stock situations
5. An experienced sales representative with over 20 years of experience in food-service industry	5. Provides consulting and a partnership to assist you and your firm	5. Immediately accessible for questions; provides knowledge and research for solving business problems and helping you meet your business goals
Business Proposition		
6. Quantity discounts	6. Reduces costs on average by 3%	6. Increases your profits by reducing your investment in product
7. Extended payment plans	7. Reduces initial up-front costs	7. Increases your cash flow

3. **Structure and convey your *FAB* Sequences as you would in a business conversation.** Many entry-level people communicate *FAB* Sequences by relaying information rather than knowledge. This approach makes the salesperson appear rather robotic and the discussion sounds relatively memorized or scripted to the buyer.

4. **Integrate a trial close after your *FAB* Sequences.** A professional salesperson never assumes the buyer understands every benefit. Buyers possess unique experiences and perspectives; and therefore, buyers will interpret information in distinct ways. Effective salespeople work diligently to confirm understanding via trial closes. You will learn about the value of trial closes in the next section and their value in confirming understanding.

5. **Generate credibility of your *FAB* Sequences by incorporating proof statements.** We will introduce proof statements in the next few sections. However, it is important to mention the integration of proof statements provides credibility and supports your benefits.

For additional guidance, we provide five examples of *FAB* Sequences for business-to-business and business-to-consumer settings. As you review the sequences, examine their logic, their specific language, and their conversational tone.

Example 1: **FAB Sequence for Product Section (business-to-business example)**

Salesperson: "This product uses all natural materials and is baked rather than fried. [Feature] This will appeal to health conscious customers that you stated are a critical target market for your prepared foods category [Advantage]. By providing this product in your prepared health foods section, you begin to draw more traffic into the aisle and move forward in achieving your revenue goals of 3%. [Benefit]. Does the uniqueness of the product align with what you had envisioned for your health food category? [Trial Close]

Example 2: FAB Sequence for Marketing Plan (business-to-business example)

Salesperson: Now, I would like to share with you how our marketing plan will support you and our new product. We will invest $3 million in a television campaign to support our new cleaning product, CleanExtreme. [Feature] This level of advertising will increase local and national product awareness of our product because it will be shown during 8 out of the next 12 months. [Advantage] This increased awareness will help drive customers into your store seeking to buy the CleanExtreme product and ultimately increase the revenues by 2% in your cleaning section. [Benefit] In your experience, how does this level of marketing support compare to other new products? [Trial Close]

Example 3: FAB Sequence for Marketing Plan Section (business-to-consumer example)

Salesperson: We also offer a four-year extended warranty service on all of our appliances. [Feature] The warranty offers additional coverage that extends significantly beyond the original manufacturer's two-year warranty. [Advantage] By purchasing our extended warranty, your appliances are protected for six full years, thereby eliminating any risk or costly repair bills in the immediate future. [Benefit] Considering the average repair costs $75 per hour, what are your thoughts on eliminating any notion of this risk for the next six years? [Trial Close]

Example 4: FAB Sequence for Business Proposition Section (business-to-business example)

Salesperson: Now I would like to discuss one pricing strategy that we suggest for our new products. Our products are shipped in cases. Each case of product contains six bottles of our cleaning spray. Our price to you is $12 per case or an investment of $2 per unit [Feature]. We recommend a manufacturer's suggested retail price of $2.89. At this MSRP, your margin is $.089 per unit [Advantage]. Using this pricing strategy, your firm receives a markup on cost of 44.5 percent, which is 4.5 points greater than the average product in your cleaning category [Benefit]. What are your thoughts on the suggested pricing strategy? (Trial Close]

Example 5: FAB Sequence for Business Proposition Section (business-to-consumer example)

Salesperson: If you are comfortable with moving on, I would like to discuss the value of our investment advisory services. If you choose to move forward with our Classic Service option, we will manage all of your investments for a low fee of .25% of all assets. [Feature] In comparison to your current fee structure, the Classic Service option is 75 basis points lower in investment fees. [Advantage] For you, this means you are able to increase your share of all of your investment returns by 75 basis points. [Benefit] What are your thoughts on lowering your investment fees and still receiving a high quality of service? [Trial Close]

Ideally, the salesperson should present information in each of the FAB steps to create a visual picture in the prospect's mind of the benefits of the purchase. To do this, use persuasive communication and participation techniques, proof statements, visual aids, dramatization, and demonstrations as you move through each of the steps during the presentation.

The SELL Sequence and Trial Close: The FAB + Trial Close

When a question is coupled with discussing a product's feature, advantage, and benefit, it forms the SELL Sequence

When a question (i.e., trial close) is integrated with the product's feature, advantage, and benefit (FAB), it forms the SELL Sequence. The SELL Sequence is a great method of determining if the FAB is of interest to the buyer.

The use of a question to induce feedback is also a persuasive communication technique, and therefore part of the salesperson's presentation mix. Thus, the SELL Sequence is an effective form of persuasive communication.

As a salesperson, your goal is to understand the customer and their perceptions. The trial close serves as an excellent method to ensure the customer understands the benefits of your services and products. An effective trial close, most often, takes the form of an open-ended question. By using open-ended trial-close questions, you provide buyers with an opportunity to explain their understanding of the benefit, their risks or concerns, or other issues that are present.

As illustrated in Exhibit 10.1, the trial close should be used after making a strong selling point in the presentation, after the presentation itself, after answering an objection, and immediately before you move to close the sale.

Trial closes take many forms. We provide a few examples of open-ended trial closes below.

- What are your thoughts thus far on the product/service?
- How does this margin align your objectives?
- What concerns do you have with the project thus far?
- What are other key items you need from our firm?
- How does this align with your initial goals?
- How does this meet your timelines?
- Who else would find this information important?
- Who else should be included in these steps?
- What other areas are of concern to you?
- In what areas of your business can you see this affecting?
- Where else do you think this might aid in your business?
- What other areas would you consider?
- What other items were you envisioning?
- What are your initial impressions thus far?
- How do you think this initiative will affect your business?
- What concerns do you have with the marketing plan?
- How could the increased margins impact your objectives?
- What are your thoughts on how this process would affect your current manufacturing system?
- How well does this align to the goals we discussed?

In the next section, we will delve into additional persuasive factors to consider in the presentation—logical reasoning, persuasive suggestions, a sense of fun, communicating your personal value, trust, body language, a controlled presentation, diplomacy, conversation style, and using words as selling tools.

The business proposition answers the buyer's question, "What's in it for me or my firm?" In business-to-business sales, this usually means a range of financial or quantitative benefits (i.e., economically based). For the business-to-consumer sector, the business proposition could meet the buyer's economic or psychological needs.

In this example, we incorporate a few representative buyer needs in the first column. In the second column, we identify potential solutions that could be incorporated into the business proposition. The final column provides a SELL sequence that could be used by the salesperson in the business proposition section of the sales process.

Buyer's Need(s)	Examples of Solutions to Include in the Business Proposition	Example of Business Proposition SELL SEQUENCE
Help increase my firm's profits (i.e., margins)	Explain how the results of the suggested pricing strategy will align with the buyer's business objectives. Discuss the amount of margin and compare it to the average gross margin percent that the customer receives for all products.	Further, we would like to ensure that the product is not only driving sales, but it is also meeting your margin expectations. As you can see (salesperson shows buyer the list price sheet), the list price for our product is $1.29 (feature). We suggest a retail price on-shelf of $1.99, which provides you with a 70 cent margin (advantage). What this means to you is that this product produces a 54.3% markup on cost (i.e. gross margin), which is 14 points greater than the average product in your category (benefit). How would a gross margin at this level assist you in making your annual profit objective? (trial close)
Help me feel secure (financially, emotionally, relationally) Help me take care of those I love or are important to me	Discuss the legacy that the buyer is creating by purchasing your product. Discuss the lack of financial distress often exhibited by those who do purchase your product or service.	With this 10-year long-term disability policy (feature), you'll provide yourself with annual protection against the income losses that commonly occur with long-term disabilities (advantage). What this means is that if an accident occurs, you will receive $55,000 of income per year that allows you to provide for your needs and the needs of your family (benefit). Doesn't this type of protection sound like a great way to take care of your family? (trial close)
Help my firm use less in energy (i.e., reduce my expenses)	Discuss the amount of cost savings that can be realized by incorporating your product in the buyer's warehouse. Discuss the potential savings provided by making an initial investment.	As we review our analysis of your warehouse's heating system, you'll note that our heating system uses 40% less energy than your current system (feature). And while the investment in our system is $42,000 (feature), you'll find the energy efficiency provides you with a substantial cost savings (advantage). At a current rate of $.18 per heating unit, we project savings of approximately $1,500 per month (benefit). With this cost savings, you'll be able to pay for the system in 29 months, and then receive the ongoing savings of $1,500 each month thereafter (benefit). What are your thoughts on such a short payback period and ongoing savings? (trial close)
Help increase the pace of my firm's production processes	Discuss the profit impact of increasing productivity.	Now, let's compare the projected results against the annual business goals that you shared with me. When customers integrate our hardware into their manufacturing process, our data indicates that they have received an average increase in productivity of 8 percent per machine (feature). Now, each of your manufacturing sites has four manufacturing lines and each line produces 30 units per hour. Our hardware enables 2.4 additional units produced per machine (advantage). When we project this increase across your 12 manufacturing sites and 48 total machines, integrating our hardware provides you with an additional 2,764 units produced per day (advantage). If we use the average margin you receive per unit, the annual increase in production could yield your firm $230,000 in additional profit. What are your thoughts on making this type of investment in order to reach these new production and profit levels? (trial close)

The Sales Presentation Mix

Salespeople sell different products in different ways, but all salespeople use six classes of presentation elements to some degree in their presentations to provide meaningful information to the customer. These elements are called the *presentation mix.*

The **sales presentation mix** refers to the elements the salesperson assembles to sell to prospects and customers. While all elements should be part of the presentation, it is up to the individual to determine how much each element is emphasized. This determination is primarily based on the sales call objective, customer profile, and customer benefit plan. Let's examine each of the six elements, as shown in Exhibit 10.5.

Persuasive Communication

To be a successful salesperson, do you need to be a smooth talker? No, but you do need to consider and use factors that promote clear communication of your messages. In Chapter 1, we discussed seven factors that help you be a better communicator:

1. Using questions.
2. Being empathic.
3. Keeping the message simple.
4. Creating mutual trust.
5. Listening.[2]
6. Having a positive attitude and enthusiasm.
7. Being believable.

Logical Reasoning

The application of logic through reasoning is an effective persuasive technique that appeals to prospects' common sense by requiring them to think about the proposition and to compare alternative solutions to problems. It can create excellent results when applied to selling computers, heavy equipment, and communication systems. This is

EXHIBIT 10.5

The salesperson's presentation mix. Choose some or all of these ingredients for a great presentation.

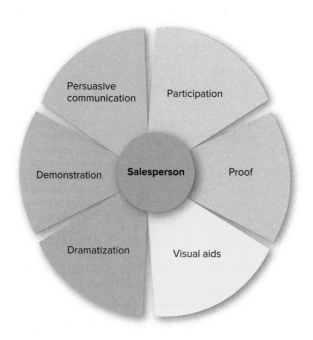

especially true when selling complicated proposals involving comparative cost data, when price versus benefits must be judged, and when the product is a radically new concept.

Logical reasoning involves a presentation constructed around three parts: a major premise, a minor premise, and a conclusion. Here is an example:

1. *Major premise:* All manufacturers wish to reduce costs and increase efficiency.
2. *Minor premise:* My equipment will reduce your costs and increase your efficiency.
3. *Conclusion:* Therefore, you should buy my equipment.

If presented exactly in this straightforward manner, the logical formula may be too blunt; the prospect may raise defenses. However, you can develop the framework or presentation outline to determine if the prospect is interested in reducing costs and increasing manufacturing efficiency. If so, then present a value analysis that shows the benefits of your product over alternatives. Information such as performance data, costs, service, and delivery information can be presented in a persuasive manner using various elements of the presentation mix.

Persuasion through Suggestion

Suggestion, like logical reasoning, is used effectively to persuade prospects. The skilled use of suggestions can arouse attention, interest, desire, conviction, and action. Types of suggestions that may be considered for the presentation are listed below.

1. **Suggestive propositions** imply that the prospect should act now, such as, "Shouldn't you go ahead and buy now before the price goes up next month?" Prospects often like to postpone their buying decisions, so the suggestive approach can help overcome this problem.
2. **Prestige suggestions** ask the prospect to visualize using products that famous people, companies, or persons the prospect trusts use, such as "The National Professional Engineers Association has endorsed our equipment. That's the reason several hundred Fortune 500 manufacturers are using our products. This elite group of manufacturers finds that the equipment helps increase their profits, sales, and market share. Is this of interest to you?"
3. **Autosuggestion** attempts to have prospects imagine themselves using the product. Television advertisements frequently use this form of suggestion. The salesperson visualizes the product, saying, "Just imagine how this equipment will look and operate in your store. Your employees will perform much better and they will thank you."
4. The **direct suggestion** is used widely by professional salespeople in all industries because it does not "tell" but suggests buying, which does not offend the buyer. Such a suggestion might state: "Based on our survey of your needs, I suggest you purchase. . . ." or "Let's consider this: We ship you three train carloads of Whirlpool washers and dryers in the following colors and models. . . ."
5. The **indirect suggestion** is used at times for some prospects when it is best to be indirect in suggesting a recommended course of action. Indirect suggestions help instill in prospects' minds factors such as doubt about a competitor's products or desire for your product, which makes it seem as if it is their idea: "Should you buy 50 or 75 dozen 12-oz cans of Revlon hairspray for your promotion?" or "Have you talked with anyone who has used that product?"
6. The **countersuggestion** evokes an opposite response from the prospect: "Do you really want such a high-quality product?" Often, the buyer will begin expanding on why a high-quality product is needed. This is an especially effective technique to include in the presentation if you have already determined that the prospect wants a high-quality product.

Selling is fun, not a battle between the prospect and salesperson, so loosen up and enjoy the presentation. Be a problem-solver and an ally.

Make the Presentation Fun

Selling is fun, not a battle between the prospect and salesperson, so loosen up and enjoy the presentation. This is easy to do once you believe in yourself and what you are selling—so sound like it! Have the *right mental attitude* and you will be successful.

Communicate Your Personal Value

When Dr. Futrell worked for a large national industrial manufacturer, his sales manager taught him to personalize the presentation. He would say, "Charles, you are enthusiastic; you believe in yourself, your products, your company; and you give a very good presentation. To improve, however, you need to personalize your relationship with each of your customers. In some manner, let them know during your presentation that you have their best interests at heart." He would always say, "Show 'em that you love 'em."

Dr. Futrell came up with the short phrase "You have me." Once he incorporated this into his presentation at the appropriate time, he saw a significant increase in his total sales and sales-to-customer call ratio. Dr. Futrell communicated personal value by saying something like: "You are not only buying my products but me as well. You have me on call 24 hours a day to help you in any way I can."

Yes, it sounds corny, but it helped show customers that he cared for them and that they could believe in him. This helped build trust. You might choose a different way, yet be sure to demonstrate that you look out for their interests.

Build Trust

Two of the best and easiest ways to build your persuasive powers with prospects are *being honest* and *doing what you say you will do*. This builds trust, which increases sales. Most professional buyers have long memories that can be used to your advantage if you follow through after the sale as you said you would when presenting the proposal.

> *Two of the best and easiest ways to build your persuasive powers with prospects are being honest and doing what you say you will do. This builds trust, which increases sales.*

Honesty is always the best policy, and it is an effective way to build trust. The salesperson should never claim more than the product can accomplish. If the product does not live up to expectations, apologize, return the product for credit, or trade for another product. This action is important in obtaining repeat sales. It builds trust; the next time the prospect is reluctant to buy, you say, "Haven't I always taken care of you? Trust me, this product is what you need. I guarantee it!"[3]

Remember that you do business with the one you trust and you trust the one you know. Trust develops over time. This would be a good time to review Chapter 1's discussion of the characteristics needed for the sales job shown in Exhibit 1.8. They are

- Caring for customers.
- Joy in your work.
- Harmony in relationships.
- Patience in closing the sale.
- Kindness to all you contact.

- Morally ethical.
- Faithful to your word.
- Fairness.
- Self-control.

People having these personal traits easily build trust with others. So can you!

Use Body Language—Send Green Signals

> *The salesperson's nonverbal communication must project a positive image to the prospect.*

Just as you watch for buying signals from a prospect, the prospect watches your facial expressions and body movements. The salesperson's nonverbal communication must project a positive image to the prospect, one that shows you know what you are talking about and understand the buyer's needs. Your customer will think, "I can trust this person."

The best nonverbal selling technique is the smile. As a sales manager once said, "It's often not what you say but how you say it, and you can say almost anything to anyone if you do it with a smile. So, practice your facial expressions and smile—always smile."

As discussed in Chapter 3, project "green" signals. If you are excited about helping the other person, it will show nonverbally. Your whole body will radiate a form of light through your eyes showing that you care. Your eyes are the lamps of your thoughts. People can tell you care.

Control the Presentation

In making the presentation, direct the conversation to lead the prospect through the presentation and proposal. The salesperson often faces difficulties on how to maintain control and what to do if the prospect takes control of the conversation. For example, what do you do if the prospect likes to talk about hobbies, attacks your company or products for poor service or credit mix-ups, or is a kidder and likes to poke fun at your products?

When this happens, the salesperson should stay with a planned presentation if possible. If there is some complaint, this should be addressed first. If the prospect likes to talk about other things, do so briefly. When the prospect's attention and interest are hard to maintain, questions or some manner of eliciting participation in the presentation are the two best methods to rechannel the conversation.

Be sure to control the visual aids and any materials you use in the presentation. New salespeople often make the mistake of handing prospects their catalog, price list, or brochures showing several products. When buyers are looking through these items, chances are that they are not listening. Too much information can cause frustration, and they will not buy. So, keep your product materials and discuss the information you wish to present while prospects look at and listen to you.

Be a Diplomat

> Dale Carnegie once said that a sure way of not making an enemy is to show respect for the other person's opinions. Never tell a person he or she is wrong.

All salespeople face the situation in which prospects feel they are right or know it all, and the salesperson has different opinions. For example, the salesperson previously may have sold the prospect's company a machine that always breaks down because of its operator, not the equipment, yet the salesperson's company is blamed. What to do?

The salesperson has to be a diplomat in cases in which tempers rise and prospects are wrong but feel they are correct and will not change their opinions. Retreat may be the best option; otherwise, you risk destroying the relationship. If you challenge the prospect, you could win the battle only to lose the war. This is a decision that the salesperson must make based on individual situations.

Dale Carnegie once said that a sure way of not making an enemy is to show respect for the other person's opinions. Never tell a person he or she is wrong. Would this apply to both your customers and others in your life?

Use a Pleasant Dialogue: Make the Conversation Interesting

Pleasant words are like honey, sweet to the ears. Construct your presentation to incorporate excellent speech, delivery, and particularly building of suspense into your stories. With these techniques, your talk comes alive rather than sounding like a dull, memorized presentation spoken in a monotone voice.

Participation Is Essential to Success

The second major part of the presentation involves techniques for motivating the prospect to participate in the presentation. Four ways to induce participation are

1. Questions
2. Product use
3. Visuals
4. Demonstrations

We have already discussed the use of questions and will discuss the use of visuals and demonstrations later, so let's briefly consider having prospects use the product:

- If you sell equipment let them see, hear, and use it!
- If you sell food, let them see, smell, and taste it!
- If you sell clothes, let them touch and wear them!

By letting prospects use the product, you can appeal to their senses: sight, sound, touch, smell, and taste. The presentation should be developed with appeals to the senses, since people often buy because of emotional needs and the senses are keys to developing emotional appeals.

By letting prospects use the product, you can appeal to their senses: sight, sound, touch, smell, and taste.

Proof Statements Build Believability

Prospects often say to themselves, before I buy, you must *prove it.* "Prove it" is a thought everyone has at times. Salespeople must prove that they will do what they promise, such as helping to make product displays when the merchandise arrives. Usually, prove it means proving to a prospect during a presentation that the product's benefits and the salesperson's proposal are legitimate.

Because salespeople often have a reputation for exaggeration, at times prospects are skeptical of the salesperson's claims. By incorporating **proof statements** into the presentation, the salesperson can increase the prospect's confidence and trust that product claims are accurate. Several useful proof techniques are the customer's past sales figures, the guarantee, testimonials, company proof results, and independent research results.

Past Sales Help Predict the Future

Salespersons frequently use customers' past sales proof statements when contacting present customers. Customers keep records of their past purchases from each of their suppliers; the salesperson can use these to suggest what quantities of each product to purchase. For example, the Colgate salesperson checks a customer's present inventory of all products carried, determines the number of products sold in a month, subtracts inventory from forecasted sales, and suggests the customer purchase that amount. It is difficult for buyers to refuse when presentations are based on their own sales records. If they are offered a price discount and promotional allowances, they might purchase 3 to 10 times the normal amount (a promotional purchase).

"Give the world the best you have, and it may never be enough; give the world the best you've got anyway."

MOTHER TERESA

Assume, for example, that a food store normally carries 10 dozen of the king-size tubes of Colgate toothpaste in inventory with 3 dozen on the shelf, and sells approximately 20 dozen a month. The salesperson produces the buyer's past sales record and says, "You should buy 7 to 10 dozen king-size Colgate toothpaste." If offering promotional allowances, the salesperson might say:

The Colgate king-size is your most profitable and best-selling item. You normally sell 20 dozen Colgate king-size each month with a 30 percent gross profit. With our 15 percent price reduction this month only, and our advertising allowances, I suggest, based on your normal sales, that you buy 80 to 100 dozen, reduce the price 15 percent, display it, and advertise the discount in your newspaper specials. This will attract people to your store, increase store sales, and make your normal profit.

The salesperson stops talking to see the buyer's reaction. A suggested order plus an alternative on the quantity to purchase have been proposed. Does the quantity seem high? It may be high, just right, or low, but it is the buyer's decision. The salesperson is saying that, given past sales and the customer benefit plan, the customer can sell X amount.

Be realistic about your suggested increase in order size. Some salespeople double the size of the order, expecting the prospect to cut it in half. Your honesty builds credibility with the buyer.

The Colgate salesperson might suggest purchases not only of toothpaste but of all Colgate products. That same sales call could involve multiple presentations of several products that have promotional allowances plus the recommended purchase of 10 or more items based on present inventories and the previous month's sales.

The Guarantee

The guarantee is a powerful proof technique. It assures prospects that if they are dissatisfied with their purchase, the salesperson or the company will stand behind a product. The manufacturer has certain product warranties that the retail salesperson can use in a presentation.

Furthermore, the consumer goods salesperson selling to retailers might say, "I'll guarantee this product will sell for you. If not, we can return what you do not sell." The industrial salesperson may explain the equipment's warranties and service policies and state, "This is the best equipment that you can buy for your situation. If you are not 100 percent satisfied after you have used it for three months, I will return it for you."

Testimonials

Testimonials in the presentation as proof of the product's features, advantages, and benefits are an excellent method to build trust and confidence. Today, manufacturers effectively advertise their consumer products using testimonials. Professional buyers are impressed by testimonials from prominent people, experts, and satisfied customers about a product's features, advantages, and benefits.

Proof Statements: Companies routinely furnish data concerning their products. Consumer goods salespeople can use sales data such as test market information and current sales data.

Company Proof Results

Companies routinely furnish data concerning their products. Consumer goods salespeople can use sales data such as test market information and current sales data. Industrial salespeople use performance data and facts based on company research as proof of their product's performance.

A consumer goods manufacturer gave its salespeople test market sales information to use in their presentations on a new product being introduced nationally. Using this information, a salesperson might say:

> Our new product will sell as soon as you put it on your shelf. The product was a success in our Eastern test market. It had 10.8 percent market share only nine months after the start of advertising. Laboratory tests proved our formula superior to that of the leading competition in our consumer product tests. It had a high repurchase rate of 50 percent after sampling. This means increased sales and profits for you.

Independent Research Results

Proof furnished by reputable sources outside the company usually has more credibility than company-generated data. Pharmaceutical salespeople frequently tell

©SelectStock/Getty Images

physicians about medical research findings on their products published in leading medical journals by medical research authorities.

"On a typical day selling pharmaceuticals," says Sandra Snow of The Upjohn Company,

> I see as many physicians as possible and initiate a discussion with them about one of our products that will have importance to them in medicine. I attempt to point out advantages that our drugs have in various states by using third-party documentation published in current medical journals and texts. The information has much more meaning to a physician who knows that it is not me or The Upjohn Company that has shown our drug to have an advantage, but rather a group of researchers who have conducted a scientific study. All of the material that we give to the physicians has been approved for our use by the Food and Drug Administration.

Publications such as *Road Test Magazine* and *Consumer Reports,* newspaper stories, and government reports such as Environmental Protection Agency publications may contain information the salesperson can use in the presentation. For a proof statement referring to independent research results to be most effective, it should contain (1) a restatement of the benefit before proving it, (2) the proof source and relevant facts or figures about the product, and (3) expansion of the benefit. Consider the following example of a salesperson's proof statement:

> I'm sure that you want a soundbar that's going to sell and be profitable for you (**benefit restatement**). Figures in *Consumer Guide* and *Consumer Sales* magazines indicate that the Sony XL-100 soundbar is the newest product innovation on the market and the third largest in sales (**source and facts**). Therefore, when you handle the Sony XL line, you'll find that soundbar sales and profits will increase, and more customers will come into your store (**benefit expansion**).

Proof statements must be incorporated into the presentation. They provide a logical answer to the buyer's challenge of "prove it!"

Exhibit 10.6 shows four examples of using proof to support what is said about *FAB*s—features, advantages, benefits. Proof statements are a great way to substantiate your sales claims. Often, proof statements are presented through visual aids.

The Visual Presentation—Show and Tell

In giving a sales presentation, as a salesperson you do two things: You *show* and *tell* the prospect about a proposal. You *tell* using persuasive communications, participation techniques, and proof statements. You *show* by using visual aids.

EXHIBIT 10.6

Proof statements help prove what you say.

Feature	Advantage	Benefit	Proof
■ New consumer product	Early results show it will be a big seller	Drives revenues in comparison to competitors	Test-market results demonstrates sales success versus competitors
■ High energy-efficiency rating	Uses less electricity	Saves 10% on energy costs	*Consumer Reports* magazine
■ Mobile CRM (customer-relationship management) phone app.	Gets information to sales force instantly	Increases closing of sales by 5% and customer retention by 8%	Testimonials from other firms regarding the effects of application on their sales forces
■ Buy 100 cases	Reduces out-of-stocks	By enhancing in-stock levels, increases sales, profits, customer satisfaction	Customer's past sales data and research on other customer's success

People retain approximately 10 percent of what they hear but 50 percent of what they see. Consequently, you have five times the chance of making a lasting impression with an illustrated sales presentation than with words alone.

Visuals are most effective when you believe in them and have woven them into your sales presentation message. Use them to

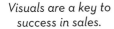

Visuals are a key to success in sales.

- Increase retention.
- Reinforce the message.
- Reduce misunderstanding.
- Create a unique and lasting impression.
- Show the buyer that you are a professional.

The visual presentation (showing) incorporates the three remaining elements of the presentation mix: visual aids, dramatization, and demonstration. There is some overlap among the three; for example, a demonstration uses visuals and has some drama. Let's examine each of the elements and consider how they can be used in a sales presentation.

Visual Aids Help Tell the Story

Visuals, or visual aids, are devices that chiefly appeal to the prospect's vision, with the intent of producing mental images of the product's features, advantages, and benefits. Many companies routinely supply salespeople with visuals for their products. Some common visuals are

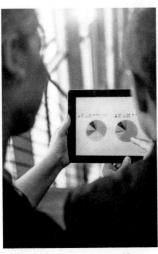

©suedhang/Image Source/Getty Images

- Slides, such as those made from Microsoft PowerPoint or Prezi
- The product.
- Charts and graphics illustrating product features and advantages such as performance and sales data.
- Photographs and videos of the product and its uses.
- Models or mock-ups of products, especially for large, bulky products.
- Equipment such as videos, slides, and computers.
- Sales manuals and product catalogs.
- Order forms.
- Letters of testimony.
- A copy of the guarantee.
- Flip boards and posters.
- Sample advertisements.
- Research whitepapers.

Before each sales call, ensure that all visuals necessary for the presentation are organized in a manner that allows the salesperson to easily access needed visuals. Only new, top-quality, professionally developed visuals should be used. Tattered, torn, or smudged visuals should be routinely discarded. The best visual aid is the actual product.

A Checklist for Visuals

As a salesperson, you may be called upon to conduct a presentation and need to create visuals, such as slides. Visuals should not only garner attention, but should also have an objective. For instance, a visual's objective could be to: (1) reinforce a benefit, (2) provide an interpretation of important data and analysis; or (3) provide a key takeaway (an important point that should be reinforced to the audience). The following list provides direction regarding best practices for developing a visual.

The Value of Your Visuals To The Buyer

- In some instances, your buyer will use your visuals to sell your product or service to their supervisor or management team. Therefore, your visuals should contain succinct, logical information that will help the customer remember key benefits and the value of your service.

Headlines

- The headline should always communicate the essence of the slide. For example, you may want to ask yourself, "What is the goal of this slide?" You may want to place some form of the answer in the headline.
- Effective headlines use active verbs and communicate clearly a point to the audience. Salespeople use headlines to guide the conversation and communicate important aspects that garner the attention of the customer. For instance, your headline might communicate:
  - **A method or action that may allow the customer to receive a benefit**
    (By _____, XYZ Increases Revenue by X%)
  - **A critical trend that the customer could take advantage of**
    (XYZ Leverages Consumer Trend by Stocking 5 Organic Items)
  - **A current situation that the customer can benefit from** if it is lessened or reduced
    (By Reducing Expenses, XYZ Enhances Profit Margin by 8%)
  - **An approach to reach a new productive state** of their business
    (Increasing Productivity through Supply Chain Process Enhancement Adds $3 million in Cash Flow)

Data

- Effective visuals interpret data and analysis. As a knowledge broker, the salesperson should present knowledge rather than information. This means that placing a bar chart or line chart without numbers would not be acceptable. Instead, the data should be easy to read and an interpretation of the data should be contained on the slide.

Bullet Points

- Effective bullet points are logical and provide information. If a slide has a bullet point with one or two words, the reader is forced to guess about the information on the slide. Instead, ensure each bullet point communicates something important.
- Logically order bullet points. In this chapter, we discuss the sequence of major premise, minor premise, and conclusion. Consider adapting this approach to order your bullet points to ensure they offer a logical argument to the customer.

Clip-art and Photographs

- Effective visuals tend to reduce the clutter on the slide. While pictures and graphics are a great means of communication, they should be selected to assist in telling the narrative or story that is on the slide rather than distract attention away for the slide's main communication points.

In Exhibit 10.7 and Exhibit 10.8 we provide two visuals and a few best practices to consider when developing visuals.

EXHIBIT 10.7

Best practices for a slide

Action verbs are used in the headline

The headline states a specific benefit

The bullet points explain the benefit touted in the headline

The bullet points are arranged in a logical sequence

The language is specific and professional

Increase XYZ Manufacturing's Efficiency Via Waste Reduction System

- **Manufacturing waste significantly decreased by new process**
  - **82%: Average waste decrease in first year**
  - **Waste decrease experienced by 300 of 303 customers**
- **Decreased expenses led to bottom-line profit improvement: 2.5% (average)**

Average Waste Reduction
■ Average Waste – Dollars/Year

1000

180

Year before process implemented

Year after process implemented

Data source: 303 customer case studies

Implementing Proposed Process Leads to Profit Enhancement

- The visual layout is aesthetically appealing
- The chart contains a specific title and the axes are labeled
- The bar chart contains specific data (numbers) and explains their importance
- An interpretation of the data is placed below the bar chart

EXHIBIT 10.8

Best practices for a business proposition slide

Action verbs are used in the headline

The headline states a specific benefit

The bullet points are arranged in a logical sequence

The language is specific and professional

Margins Per Unit Exceed Annual Goal

Suggested Retail Pricing for XYZ Lumber Line

- **Suggested retail pricing strategy drives incremental profit**
  - **Markup on cost exceeds 65% for product lengths**
- **All product lengths exceed average markup/cost by 10 to 22 points**
- **Using pricing strategy enables penny profit and margin growth**

	Pine 2 inch × 4 inch 6 foot	Pine 2 inch × 4 inch 8 foot	Pine 2 inch × 4 inch 10 foot
MSRP (suggested retail price)	$2.89	$3.49	$4.59
Cost of Goods Sold	$1.75	$2.00	$2.60
Penny Profit	$1.14	$1.49	$1.99
Markup/Cost	65%	75%	77%
Your Firm's Average Markup/Cost	55%	55%	55%

- The title of the chart describes the content
- The chart is easy to read and understand
- The chart contains specific titles for the columns and rows

Dramatization Improves Your Chances

Dramatics refers to talking or presenting the product in a striking, showy, or extravagant manner. Thus, sales expertise can involve **dramatization** or a theatrical presentation of products. However, dramatics should be incorporated into the presentation only when you are 100 percent sure that the dramatics will work effectively. This was not considered by the salesperson who set the buyer's trash can on fire. When the salesperson had difficulty extinguishing the fire with a new fire extinguisher, the buyer ran out of the room because of the extensive smoke. However, if implemented correctly, dramatics are effective. One of the best methods of developing ideas for the dramatization of a product is to watch television commercials. Products are presented using visuals, many products are demonstrated, and most products are dramatized. Take, for example, the following television advertisements:

- "We challenged the competition . . . and they ran!" says the Heinz tomato ketchup advertisement. Two national brands of ketchup and Heinz ketchup are poured into paper coffee filters held up by tea strainers. The competition's ketchup begins to drip and then runs through the filter. The Heinz ketchup does not drip or run, which indicates the high quality of Heinz ketchup relative to the competition.
- Bounty paper towel advertisements show coffee spilled and how quickly the product absorbs the coffee relative to the competitive paper towel.
- The STP motor-oil additive advertisement shows a person dipping one screwdriver into STP motor-oil additive and another screwdriver into a plain motor oil. The person can hold with two fingers the end of the screwdriver covered with plain motor oil. The screwdriver covered with STP motor-oil additive slips out of the fingers—indicating STP provides better lubrication for an automobile engine.

George Wynn the Showman

Use a dramatic demonstration to set yourself apart from the many salespeople whom buyers see each day. Buyers, such as industrial purchasing agents, like to see you, as they know you will have an informative and often entertaining sales presentation. One salesperson known for his effective presentation was George Wynn. George was an industrial salesperson for Exxon, and he was responsible for sales of machine lubricating oils and greases in Dayton, Cincinnati, and Columbus, Ohio.

George Eats Grease

One group of products Wynn sold were oils and greases for the food-processing industry. These lubricants had to be approved by the federal Food and Drug Administration (FDA) for incidental food contact. One of the products was a lubricating grease, Carum 280. Wynn ordered a number of one-pound cans for customer samples. As Wynn started his sales presentation of these FDA-approved products, he would take one of the cans from his sample case, open it, and spread this grease on a slice of bread. After taking a bite of bread spread with the grease, he then offered a bite to the buyer. The buyer generally refused the offer. However, in the mind of the buyer, this dramatic demonstration set Wynn's presentation apart from others. It helped prove to the buyer the product was safe to use in a food-processing plant.

George Lights Up

Another of Wynn's dramatic demonstrations involved lubricating greases used by the steel industry. Greases that resist high temperatures are desirable for most applications in the steel industry. Exxon developed a line of temperature-resistant greases that used a new thickener that held the oil in suspension better than competitive products. To demonstrate this product attribute, Wynn used a pie tin held at a 45-degree angle centered over a small lighted alcohol lamp. A small glob of the Exxon grease and globs of several better-known competitors were placed on the pie tin. As the pie tin was heated, the oil separated from each of the competitive greases and ran down the pie tin. The oil did not separate from the Exxon product, dramatically demonstrating the high temperature resistance of this steel-mill grease as compared with leading competitive products.

Demonstrations Prove it

One of the best ways to convince a prospect that a product is needed is to show the merits of the product through a **demonstration** as George Wynn did. If a picture is worth a thousand words, then a demonstration is worth a thousand pictures. Therefore, it is best to show the product, if possible, and have the prospect use it. If this is not feasible, then pictures, models, videos, films, or slides are the best alternatives. Whatever the salesperson is attempting to sell, the prospect should be able to see it.

Psychological studies have shown that people receive 87 percent of their information on the outside world through their eyes and only 13 percent through the other four senses.

Psychological studies have shown that people receive 87 percent of their information on the outside world through their eyes and only 13 percent through the other four senses. What this says to the salesperson is to make a product visible. Also, let the prospect feel, see, hear, smell, and use the product. The dynamic demonstration appeals to human senses by telling, showing, and creating buyer–seller interaction.

Demonstrations are part of the dramatization and fun of your presentation. Do not underestimate their ability to make sales for you, no matter how simple they may appear. For example, a glass company once designed shatterproof glass. This was not standard equipment in automobiles at the time, as it is now. The company had its salespeople going around the country trying to sell shatterproof glass. One of the salespeople completely outsold the rest of the sales force. When they had their convention, they said, "Joe, how come you sell so much glass?" He replied, "Well, what I've been doing is taking little chunks of glass and a ball-peen hammer along with me on sales calls. I take a little chunk of glass, and I hit it with the hammer. This shows that it's shatterproof. It splinters, but doesn't shatter and fall all over the ground. This has helped me sell a lot of glass."

So, the next year they equipped every salesperson with a ball-peen hammer and little chunks of glass. But an interesting thing happened. Joe still far outsold the rest of the sales force. So when the convention occurred the next year, they asked, "Joe, how is it you're selling so much? You told us what you did last year. What are you doing differently?" He replied, "Well, this year, I gave the glass *and* the hammer to the customer to let *them* hit it." You see, the first year Joe had dramatization in his demonstration; the second year he had dramatization and participation. Again, it's often not what you say but how you say it that makes the sale.

A Demonstration Checklist

There are eight points to remember as you prepare your demonstration. These points are shown in Exhibit 10.9. Ask yourself if the demonstration is really beneficial and

EXHIBIT 10.9

Eight points to remember about demonstrations.

✓ Is the demonstration *needed* and *appropriate*?

✓ Have I developed a specific demonstration *objective*?

✓ Is the demonstration tied to a benefit that is important to the customer?

✓ Have I properly *planned* and *organized* the demonstration?

✓ Have I rehearsed to the point that the demonstration *flows smoothly* and appears to be *natural*?

✓ What is the probability that the demonstration will go as *planned*?

✓ What is the probability that the demonstration will *backfire*?

✓ Does my demonstration present my product in an *ethical* and *professional* manner?

appropriate for your prospects. Every sale does not need a demonstration nor will all products lend themselves to a demonstration.

If the demonstration is appropriate, what is its objective? What should the demonstration accomplish? Next, be sure you have properly planned and organized the demonstration; rehearse it so the demonstration flows smoothly and appears natural. Take your time in talking and going through your demonstration; make it look easy. Remember, if you, the expert, cannot operate a machine, for example, imagine how difficult it will be for the prospect.

The only way to ensure a smooth demonstration is to practice. Yet, there is always the possibility that the demonstration will not go as planned or will backfire no matter how simple. Be prepared. A former student was demonstrating his new overhead projector. Two bulbs in a row burned out as he demonstrated the product to a buyer for a large retail chain. He anticipated what could go wrong and always carried extra parts in his sales bag. When the first bulb went out, he talked of how easy it was to change bulbs, and when the second one blew, he said, "I want to show you that again," with a smile. He always carried two spare bulbs; now he carries three.

Finally, make sure your demonstration presents the product in an ethical and professional manner. You do not want to misrepresent the product or proposal. A complex product, such as a large computer system, can be presented as simple to install with few start-up problems, yet the buyer may find the computer system difficult to operate.

Use Participation in Your Demonstration

Confucius, the Chinese philosopher (551–479 B.C.), is often credited with saying, "Tell me and I'll forget. Show me and I'll remember. Involve me and I'll understand." By having the prospect participate in the demonstration, you obtain a buyer's attention and direct it where you want it. It also helps the prospect visualize owning and operating the product. The successful demonstration aids in reducing buying uncertainties and resistance to purchase. Also, when determining a demonstration, start with a goal—a benefit. Ask yourself, "What are the key benefits that I want to demonstrate?" This approach allows your demonstration to focus on solving the buyer's needs. A successful demonstration involves the prospect in four ways; it

1. Lets the prospect do something simple.
2. Lets the prospect work an important feature.
3. Lets the prospect do something routine or frequently repeated.
4. Has the prospect answer questions throughout the demonstration.

First, ask the prospect to do something simple with a low probability of foul-ups. Second, in planning the demonstration, select the main features that you will stress in the interview and allow the prospect to participate on the feature that relates most to an important buying motive. Again, keep it simple.

A third way to have a successful demonstration is by having the prospect do something with the product that is done frequently. Finally, receive feedback from the prospect throughout the demonstration by asking questions or pausing in your conversation. This is extremely important, as it will

- Determine the prospect's attitude toward the product.
- Allow you to progress in the demonstration or wait and answer any questions or address any objections.
- Aid in moving the prospect into the positive yes mood.
- Set the stage for closing the sale.

Little agreements lead to the big agreement and saying yes. Phrase questions in a positive manner such as "That is really easy to operate, isn't it?" instead of "This isn't hard to operate, is it?" They ask the same thing, yet the response to the first question is positive instead of negative. The best questions force the prospect to place the product in use mentally, such as the question phrased, "Do you feel this could increase your employees' productivity?" This yes answer commits the buyer to the idea that the feature will increase employee productivity. Remember, it is often not what you say but how you say it.

Reasons for Using Visual Aids, Dramatics, and Demonstrations

As we have seen, visual aids, dramatics, and demonstrations are important to the salesperson's success in selling a prospect. The reasons to use them include wanting to

- Capture attention and interest.
- Create two-way communication.
- Involve the prospect through participation.
- Afford a more complete, clear explanation of products and the benefits that are important to the customer.
- Increase a salesperson's persuasive powers by obtaining positive commitments on a product's single benefit.

Guidelines for Using Visual Aids, Dramatics, and Demonstrations

Although visual aids, dramatics, and demonstrations are important, their proper use is critical to their effectiveness. When using them, consider

- Rehearsing by practicing in front of a mirror, and/or on video. Once you are ready to make the presentation, begin using it with less important prospects. This allows you time to refine the presentation before contacting more important accounts.
- Customizing them to the sales call objective—the prospect's customer profile and the customer benefit plan—and concentrating on the prospect's important buying motives, using appropriate multiple appeals to sight, touch, hearing, smell, and taste (see Exhibit 10.10).
- Making them *simple, clear,* and *straightforward.*
- Being sure you control the demonstration by not letting the prospect divert you from selling. It can be disastrous to have the prospect not listen or pass up major selling points you wished to present.

Which buyer senses are being appealed to by the seller?

©Graham Oliver/Getty Images

- Making them *true to life*.
- Encouraging *prospect participation*.
- Incorporating *trial closes* (questions) after showing or demonstrating a major feature, advantage, or benefit to determine if the prospect believes the presentation and considers it important.

Technology Can Help!

Technology provides excellent methods of presenting information to the buyer in a visually attractive and dramatic manner. Using a computer tablet in front of the buyer can be impressive. Today, technology enables the presentation of video clips, sound bites, and beautifully illustrated graphics and can be connected to projection equipment for great presentations. Analytical software can quickly crunch data—providing instant solutions to buyers' questions. Salespeople selling products such as services real estate, and industrial equipment can quickly show buyers a product's cost when considering different installment payment schedules at various interest rates. Remember, it's often not what you say but how you say it that makes the sale.

Video Conferencing

Technology has truly expanded and improved video conferencing. For the average person, options like Skype and FaceTime are prevalent. However, a number of vendors ranging from WebEx, GoToMeeting, to Adobe Connect provide businesses and their salespeople with opportunities to interact over video, share screens, and provide more interactive conversations across the world. Salespeople can hold client meetings, introduce new products, and demonstrate key benefits and features. However, the increased use of video conferencing also means that that many salespeople will need to develop their communication skills specific to the video arena. In Exhibit 10.11, we provide a few considerations for the salesperson using video-conferencing technology in the sales process.

EXHIBIT 10.11

Considerations for Using Video Conferencing Technology

Software Accessibility: Make sure everyone has the software or access to the software application for the video conference.

Practice using the video technology. Conduct a practice round and then watch your practice.

Place yourself in the viewer's shoes. If possible, watch the practice round ahead of time. Take note of the elements that were difficult to understand, hear, or interpret.

Contingency Plan: Ensure you have established a backup plan in case of a technical glitch.

Interaction Planning: Understand how people will interact with you.

- If it's a demonstration, will you use video technology that allows users to electronically signify they have questions?
- If it's a webinar with multiple attendees, will you use video technology that allows users to be muted to reduce the opportunity for paper ruffling, movement, etc?

Environment: Consider your background. Do the participants see a natural view of you or do you appear scrunched behind a webcam?

Sound: Is the room you are using quiet? Will your microphone pick up background noise?

Lighting: Where should you place the lighting to ensure the video captures you in an appealing manner?

Clothing: What types of patterns on your clothing should you wear to create a great impression on video?

The Sales Presentation Goal Model

"Wow!" you say. There are many things to consider when creating a sales presentation. Persuasive communication, participation, proof statements, visual aids, dramatization, demonstration that may or may not include technology. How do you decide what elements of the sales presentation mix to use in a sales presentation? It depends on the goal of your presentation and the answers to six questions.

Exhibit 10.12 will help you decide whether to use some or all of the sales presentation mix ingredients. You need to answer these six questions:

1. What is your objective?
2. Who is your audience?
3. How will you structure your presentation?
4. How will you create impact?
5. How will you design and display visual aids?
6. How will you stage your presentation?

Your sales presentation goal(s) and the answers to these six questions will be your guide to skillfully show and tell your customers how your product will fulfill their needs.

The Ideal Presentation

In the ideal presentation, your approach technique quickly captures your prospect's interest and immediately identifies signals that the prospect has a need for your product and is ready to listen. The ideal prospect is friendly, polite, and relaxed; will not allow anyone to interrupt you; asks questions; and participates in your demonstration as planned. This allows you to move through the presentation skillfully.

The ideal customer cheerfully and positively answers each of your questions, allowing you to anticipate the correct moment to ask for the order. You are completely relaxed and sure of yourself when you come to the close. The customer says yes, and

EXHIBIT 10.12

The sales presentation goal model.

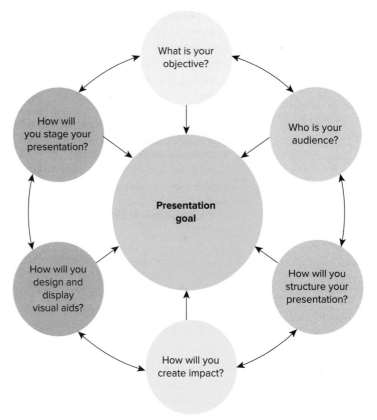

The Presentation Goal Model

enthusiastically thanks you for your valuable time. Several weeks later, you receive a copy of the e-mail your customer wrote to your company's president glowing with praise for your professionalism and sincere concern for the customer.

Be Prepared for Presentation Difficulties

Yes, a few sales presentations are like the previous example; but most presentations have one or more hurdles you should prepare for. While all of the difficulties you might face cannot be discussed here, three main problems that are encountered during sales presentations are handling an interruption, discussing your competition, and making the presentation in a less-than-ideal situation.

How to Handle Interruptions

It is common for interruptions to occur during the presentation. The administrative assistant comes into the office or the telephone rings, distracting the prospect. What should you do?

First, determine if the discussion that interrupted your presentation is personal or confidential. If so, by gesture or voice you can offer to leave the room—this is always appreciated by the prospect. Second, while waiting, regroup your thoughts and mentally review how to return to the presentation. Once the discussion is over, you can

1. Wait quietly and patiently until you have regained the prospect's attention completely.
2. Briefly restate the selling points that had interested the prospect, for example: "We were discussing your needs for a product such as ours and you seemed especially interested in knowing about our service, delivery, and installation. Is that right?"
3. Do something to increase the prospect's participation, such as showing the product, using other visuals, or asking questions. Closely watch to determine if you have regained the prospect's interest.
4. If interest is regained, move deeper into the presentation.

Should You Discuss the Competition?

Competition is something all salespeople must contend with every day. If you sell a product, you must compete with others selling comparable products. How should you handle competition? Basically, remember three considerations: (1) do not refer to a competitor unless absolutely necessary; (2) acknowledge your competitor only briefly; and (3) when necessary make a detailed comparison of your product and the competition's product.

Do Not Refer to Competition

First of all, lessen any surprises the buyer may present by properly planning for the sales call. In developing your customer profile, chances are that you will learn what competing products are used and your prospect's attitude toward your products and competitors' products. Based on your findings, you can develop the presentation without specifically referring to competition.

Acknowledge Competition and Drop It

> *Many salespeople feel their competition should not be discussed unless the prospect discusses it. Then, acknowledge competition briefly and return to your product.*

Many salespeople feel their competition should not be discussed unless the prospect discusses it. Then, acknowledge competition briefly and return to your product. "Yes, I am familiar with that product's features. In fact, the last three of my customers were using that product and have switched over to ours. May I tell you why?"

Here, you do not knock competition, but acknowledge it and in a positive manner move the prospect's attention back to your products. If the prospect continues to discuss a competing product, you should determine the prospect's attitude toward it. You might ask, "What do you think about the IBM 6000 computer system?" The answer will help you mentally determine how you can prove that your product offers the prospect more benefits than your competitor's product.

Make a Detailed Comparison

At times, it is appropriate to make a detailed comparison of your product to a competing one, especially for industrial products. If products are similar, emphasize your company's service, guarantees, and what you do personally for customers.

If your product has features that are lacking in a competitor's product, refer to these advantages. "Our product is the only one on the market with this feature! Is this important to you?" Ask the question and wait for the response. A yes answer takes you one step closer to the sale.

You are in the competitive business of selling office machines. You have an appointment with the senior partner of a large medical center. She has already studied several competitive products. Her hot buttons are low operating costs and low maintenance. You know that four competitors have demonstrated their products to your prospect.

After you have shown her the benefits of your product, she asks you, "Tell me, what makes your machine better than Brand X?" You restate some of your obvious product benefits and she comes back with, "The salesperson with Company X told me that they use a special kind of toner that is superior to what you use for your machine by 20 percent." You know that this is an obvious lie, so you ask, "What evidence did this salesperson give you to prove the claim?" She shows you a customer testimonial letter that talks about satisfaction with the machine, but it says nothing about a longer lifetime. You reply carefully, "That's the first time I have ever seen a letter praising a Brand X machine."

Next, she shows you another piece of paper, a chart that graphically illustrates the operating costs of five different brands. The chart says on the bottom, "Marketing Research Brand X, 2002." It shows your machine with the highest operating costs over a five-year period, and it shows Brand X in the leading position with 50 percent lower operating costs. You are stunned by this unfair comparison. You try to control your temper.

What would be the most ethical action to take?

1. Tell your customer that you have never heard or seen the information she is showing you. Offer to do some additional research into the matter so that she can make her decision based on the most accurate information possible.
2. Do your best to refute the information on the chart. It is not your job to tell the customer that your competitor is being untruthful. It is only your job to sell your product.
3. Tell your customer that you believe that the Brand X research is misleading. Based on everything you have seen or heard, Brand X does not meet the standards it states.

Often the prospect can use both your product and a competitor's product. For example, a pharmaceutical salesperson is selling an antibiotic that functions like penicillin and kills bacteria resistant to penicillin. However, it costs 20 times more than penicillin. This salesperson would say, "Yes, Dr. Jones, penicillin is the drug of choice for . . . disease. But do you have patients for whom penicillin is ineffective?" "Yes, I do," says the doctor. "Then, for those patients, I want you to consider my product because. . . ."

Competition Discussion Based on the Situation. Whether or not you discuss competition depends on the prospect. Based on your selling philosophy and your knowledge of the prospect, you can choose how to deal with competition. If you are in doubt due to insufficient prospect knowledge, it is best not to discuss competition.

Be Professional

No matter how you discuss competition with your prospect, always act professionally. If you discuss competition, talk only about information that you know is accurate, and be straightforward and honest—not belittling and discourteous.

Your prospect may like both your products and the competitor's products. A loyalty to the competitor may have been built over the years; by insulting competition, you may insult and alienate your prospect. However, the advantages and disadvantages of a competitive product can be demonstrated acceptably if done professionally. One salesperson relates this story:

> Several customers I called on were loyal to my competitors; however, just as many were loyal to my company. I will always remember the president of a chain of retail stores who flew 500 miles to be at one of our salesperson's retirement dinners. In his talk, he noted how 30 years ago, when he opened his first store, this salesperson extended him company credit and made him a personal loan that helped him get started.

It would be difficult for a competing salesperson to sell to this loyal customer. When contacting customers, especially ones buying competitive products, it is important to uncover why they use competitive products before discussing competition in the presentation.

Be a Professional. Everything you do and say should be based upon your professionalism, especially as it relates to competitors. Take a minute to review the section titled "Others Includes Competitors" in the appendix to Chapter 1.

In everything, you want to do to others what you would have them do to you. Remember the George Wynn story discussed earlier in this chapter. Assume, for example, you are a purchasing professional for a food-processing plant and this week the FDA passed a new law on the type of lubricating oils and greases that you can use for manufacturing ice cream. You do not have this type of lubricant. A salesperson calls on you and says his lubricants are not FDA approved. Wouldn't you want the salesperson to tell you where you could quickly buy the product you need? Sure you would! George Wynn would be happy to help his customer. What would you do?

Where the Presentation Takes Place

The ideal presentation happens in a quiet room with only the salesperson, the prospect, and no interruptions. However, at times the salesperson may meet the prospect somewhere other than a private office and need to make the presentation under less than ideal conditions.

For short presentations, a stand-up situation may be adequate; however, when making a longer presentation, you may want to ask the prospect, "Could we go back to your office?" or make another appointment.

Diagnose the Prospect to Determine Your Sales Presentation

You have seen that in contacting prospects you must prepare for various situations. That is why selling is so challenging and why companies reward their salespeople so well. A major challenge is adapting your sales presentation to each potential buyer. In Chapter 3, you read about selling based on personality. Reexamine that discussion to better understand how and why you should be prepared to adapt your presentation.

SUMMARY OF MAJOR SELLING ISSUES

The sales presentation is a persuasive vocal and visual explanation of a proposition. While there are numerous methods for making a sales presentation, the four common ones are the memorized, formula, need-satisfaction, and problem–solution selling methods. Each method is effective if used for the proper situation.

In developing your presentation, consider the elements of the sales presentation mix that you will use for each prospect. The proper use of persuasive communication techniques, methods to develop prospect participation, proof statements, visual aids, dramatization, and demonstrations increases your chance of illustrating how your products will satisfy your prospect's needs.

It is often not what we say but how we say it that results in the sale. Persuasive communication techniques (questioning, listening, logical reasoning, suggestion, and the use of trial closes) help uncover needs, communicate effectively, and pull the prospect into the conversation.

Proof statements are especially useful in showing your prospect that what you say is true and that you can be trusted. When challenged, prove it by incorporating facts in your presentation on a customer's past sales—guaranteeing the product will work or sell, testimonials, and company and independent research results.

To both show and tell, visuals must be properly designed to illustrate features, advantages, and benefits of your products through graphics, dramatization, and demonstration. This allows you to capture the prospect's attention and interest; to create two-way communication and participation; to express your proposition in a clearer, more complete manner; and to make more sales. Careful attention to development and rehearsal of the presentation is needed to ensure it occurs smoothly and naturally.

Always prepare for the unexpected, such as a demonstration that falls apart, interruptions, the prospect's questions about the competition, or the necessity to make your presentation in a less than ideal place, such as in the aisle of a retail store or in the warehouse.

The presentation part of the overall sales presentation is the heart of the sale. It is where you develop the desire, conviction, and action. By giving an effective presentation, you have fewer objections to your proposition, which makes for an easier sale close.

If you want to be a real professional in selling, acquire or create materials that convey your message and convince others to believe it. If you try to sell without using the components of the sales presentation mix, you are losing sales not because of what you say but how you say it. Exhibits, facts, statistics, examples, analogies, testimonials, and samples should be part of your repertoire. Without them, you are not equipped to do a professional job of selling.

Quick Review for Students

The quick review sections provide key questions to help you develop a greater level of conceptual understanding. We suggest that after you read the chapter, you try to answer the following questions without looking back at the textbook.

1. What are the three essential steps in the presentation section of the sales process?
2. What are five best practices when developing *FAB* statements?
3. What is a trial close? What are two examples of trial closes? What is the value of a trial close?

4. What is a proof statement? Why is a proof statement valuable? What are examples of data that could be incorporated into a proof statement?
5. What is a dramatization? When would a salesperson use dramatization?
6. What are three best practices that would aid a salesperson during the development of visuals, such as slides?
7. How should a salesperson handle a discussion about the competition?

MEETING A SALES CHALLENGE

The carpet's ability to resist fading is important to the customer who needs proof your carpet will not fade. In this situation, the proof statement should be authoritative, using independent research results, if possible. Here is an example of an effective proof statement:

"Mr. Jones, a carpet made of our new XT-15 synthetic fibers will not fade" (**restatement of the benefit**). "A recent study conducted by the Home Research Institute and reported in the *Home Digest* proves that our fibers hold their colors much better than natural fibers" (**a proof of the benefit**). "And since Superior's carpets are made with synthetic fibers, you'll never hear any complaints about these carpets fading" (**an expansion of the benefit**). "What do you think?" (**trial close**).

KEY TERMS FOR SELLING

autosuggestion   365
benefit expansion   370
benefit restatement   370
countersuggestion   365
demonstration   375
direct suggestion   365

dramatization   374
indirect suggestion   365
logical reasoning   365
prestige suggestions   365
proof statements   368
sales presentation mix   364

source and facts   370
suggestive
   propositions   365
visuals   371

SALES APPLICATION QUESTIONS

1. You plan to give a demonstration of the Dyno Electric Cart to the purchasing agent of a company having a manufacturing plant that covers 200 acres. Which of the following is the best technique for your demonstration? Why?
   a. Let your prospect drive the cart.
   b. You drive the cart and ask the prospect to ride so that you can discuss the cart's benefits.
   c. Leave a demonstrator and return a week later to see how many the prospect will buy.
2. When contacting a purchasing agent for your Dyno Electric Carts, you plan to use your 10-page visual presenter to guide the prospect through your benefit story. This selling aid is a binder containing photographs of your cart in action along with its various color options, a guarantee, and a testimonial. Should you
   a. Hand over the binder? Why?
   b. Hold on to it? Why?
3. Assume you were halfway through your presentation when your prospect had to answer the telephone. The call lasted five minutes. What would you do?
4. Discuss the various elements of the sales presentation mix, and indicate why you need to use visuals during your presentation.

5. In your proof statement of the benefit, cite your proof source, in addition to relevant facts or figures about your product. Which of the following is a correct proof of a benefit?

    a. Well, an article in last month's *Appliance Report* stated that the Williams blender is more durable than the other top 10 brands.

    b. You'll get 10 percent more use from the Hanig razor.

    c. *Marathon* is the most widely read magazine among persons with incomes over $25,000 per year.

    d. Figures in *Marathon* magazine indicate that your sales will increase if you stock Majestic housewares in your store.

6. Examine the following conversation:

    Customer: What you say is important, all right, but how do I know that these chairs will take wear and tear the way you say they will?

    Salesperson: The durability of a chair is an important factor to consider. That's why all Crest chairs have reinforced plastic webbing seats. *Furniture Dealer's Weekly* states that the plastic webbing used in Crest chairs is 32 percent more effective in preventing sagging chair seats than fabric webbing. This means that your chairs will last longer and will take the wear and tear that your customers are concerned about.

    Look at each sentence in this conversation and state if it is

    a. An expansion of the benefit.

    b. A restatement of the benefit.

    c. A proof of the benefit.

7. After a two-hour drive to see an important new prospect you stop at a local coffee shop for a bite to eat. As you look over your presentation charts, you spill coffee on half a dozen of them. You don't have substitute presentation charts with you. What should you do?

    a. Phone the prospect and say that you'd like to make another appointment. Say that something came up.

    b. Keep the appointment. At the start of your presentation, tell the prospect about the coffee spill and apologize for it.

    c. Go ahead with your presentation, but don't make excuses. The coffee stains are barely noticeable if you're not on the lookout for them.

FURTHER EXPLORING THE SALES WORLD

1. What is one thing in this world on which you are an expert? Yourself! Develop a presentation on yourself for a sales job with a company of your choice. Relate this assignment to each of the 10 steps of the selling process.

2. Visit several retail stores in your community such as an appliance, bicycle, or sporting goods store and report on the demonstration techniques, if any, that were used in selling a product. Suggest ways that you would have presented the product.

3. Report on one television advertisement that used each of the following: a proof statement, a demonstration, unusual visual aids, and a dramatization.

4. In your library are magazines in which companies advertise their products to retail and wholesale customers, along with information about current price discounts. Find at least three advertisements containing current price discounts manufacturers offer to wholesalers and/or retailers. How might you use this information in a sales presentation?

STUDENT APPLICATION LEARNING EXERCISES (SALES)

An important part of consultative selling is the use of questions to uncover the customer's needs. You have planned some of your questions in constructing your **SELL Sequences**. **SELL Sequences** should be contained in your discussion of the product, marketing plan, and business proposition.

SALE 5 of 7—Chapter 10

Every important sales presentation should contain most—if not all—of the presentation mix ingredients shown in Exhibit 10.5 on page 364. To make **SALE 5:**

1. Construct and write out one SELL Sequence. After your trial close, the buyer questions what you have just said. The buyer sounds as if unsure what you are saying is true. Create a proof statement that shows your claim is true. See pages 368–370.

   SELL SEQUENCE:

   Buyer's skeptical remark:

   Proof statement:

2. Describe a demonstration you could do of one of your product's benefits. If possible, add dramatization. Remember: simply showing the product is not a demonstration.
3. Describe three visual aids you could use in your presentation. Flip charts and notebooks are easy to develop, or you can place your visuals in a folder and pull out one at a time as you discuss it.

   Visual 1:

   Visual 2:

   Visual 3:

NOTES

1. Adapted from David Jeremiah, "The Salesman," *State of Grace* (San Diego, CA: Turning Point), p. 39.
2. Rosemary P. Ramsey and Ravipreet S. Sohi, "Listening to Your Customers: The Impact of Perceived Salesperson Listening Behavior on Relationship Outcomes," *Journal of the Academy of Marketing Science,* Spring 1997, pp. 127–137.
3. Patricia M. Doney and Joseph P. Cannon, "An Examination of the Nature of Trust in Buyer–Seller Relationships," *Journal of Marketing,* April 1997, pp. 35–51.

CASE 10.1

©Ron Chapple Stock/FotoSearch/
Glow Images

Dyno Electric Cart Company

As you'll remember, we used the example of the Dyno Electric Cart to demonstrate a memorized presentation (Chapter 8, Exhibit 8.4) and the SPIN process (Chapter 9). The buyer was Conway Pride and the salesperson represented Dyno Electric Cart. Let's review the background information that was already discussed in the chapter.

Situation: You call on a purchasing manager to elicit an order for some electric carts (like a golf cart) to be used at a plant for transportation around the buildings and grounds. The major benefit to emphasize in your presentation is that the carts save time; you incorporate this concept in your approach. For this product, you use the memorized stimulus–response presentation.

Salesperson: Hello, Mr. Pride, my name is Karen Nordstrom, and I'd like to talk with you about how to save your company executives' time. By the way, thanks for taking the time to talk with me.

Buyer: What's on your mind?

Salesperson: As a busy executive, you know time is a valuable commodity. Nearly everyone would like to have a few extra minutes each day and that is the business I'm in, selling time. While I can't actually sell you time, I do have a product that is the next best thing . . . a Dyno Electric Cart—a real time-saver for your executives.

Buyer: Yeah, well, everyone would like to have extra time. However, I don't think we need any golf carts. [First objection.]

Salesperson: Dyno Electric Cart is more than a golf cart. It is an electric cart designed for use in industrial plants. It has been engineered to give comfortable, rapid transportation in warehouses, plants, and across open areas.

Buyer: They probably cost too much for us to use. [Positive buying signal phrased as an objection.]

Salesperson: First of all, they cost only $2,200 each. With a five-year normal life, that is only $400 per year plus a few cents for electricity and a few dollars for maintenance. Under normal use and care, these carts require only about $100 of service in their five-year life. Thus, for about $50 a month, you can save key people a lot of time. [Creative pricing—show photographs of carts in use.]

Buyer: It would be nice to save time, but I don't think management would go for the idea. [Third objection, but still showing interest.]

Salesperson: This is exactly why I am here. Your executives will appreciate what you have done for them. You will look good in their eyes if you give them an opportunity to look at a product that will save time and energy. Saving time is only part of our story. Dyno carts also save energy and thus keep you sharper toward the end of the day. Would you want a demonstration today or Tuesday? [Alternative close.]

Buyer: How long would your demonstration take? [Positive buying signal.]

Salesperson: I only need one hour. When would it be convenient for me to bring the cart in for your executives to try out?

Buyer: There really isn't any good time. [Objection.]

Salesperson: That's true. Therefore, the sooner we get to show you a Dyno cart, the sooner your management group can see its benefits. How about next Tuesday? I could be here at 8:00 and we could go over this item just before your weekly management group meeting. I know you usually have a meeting Tuesdays at 9:00 because I tried to call on you a few weeks ago and your secretary told me you were in the weekly management meeting. [Close of the sale.]

Buyer: Well, we could do it then.

Salesperson: Fine, I'll be here. Your executives will really be happy! [Positive reinforcement.]

SPIN example:
Dyno Electric Cart salesperson to purchasing agent: "How large are your manufacturing plant facilities?"

Dyno Electric Cart salesperson to purchasing agent: "Have your executives ever complained about having to do so much walking in and around the plant?"

Dyno Electric Cart salesperson to purchasing agent: "It sounds as if your executives would have an interest in reducing their travel time and not having to exert so much energy in transit. Doesn't it seem that if they could do so, they would get to the plant as quickly as they need to, saving themselves time and energy, and saving the company money?"

Dyno Electric Cart salesperson to purchasing agent: "If I could show you how you can solve your executives' problems in getting to and from your plant, and at the same time save your company money, would you have an interest?"

In this exercise, we examine the next steps in the process.

You plan a call-back on Conway Pride and the president of his company to sell them several of your electric carts. The company's manufacturing plant covers some 200 acres, and you have sold up to 10 carts to many companies smaller than this one. Since Pride allows you to meet with his company's president and maybe other executives, you know he is interested in your carts.

You are determined to make an effective presentation of your product's benefits using visual aids and a cart demonstration. Mr. Pride raised several objections on your last presentation that may be restated by other executives. Your challenge is to develop a dramatic, convincing presentation. You also have the following information and research that may assist you in developing your presentation.

Investment (Cost of one Dyno Cart)	$2,200	Amount of time saved riding vs. walking	30 seconds per 300 feet
Expected Lifetime of Cart	5 years	Average amount walked in normal facility (200 acres)	10,000 steps (2 feet per step) 20,000 feet per day
Cost of Service (over lifetime) of Cart	$100	Average executive compensation	$150,000
Electricity cost (per year)	$12.00	Number of hours in average work year	2,000 hours
		Compensation per hour (Executive)	$75.00
		Compensation per minute (Executive)	$1.25

Prospect's Facility

| Number of Executives | 12 | Additional Executives Expected To Be Hired In Next 3 Years | 4 |

Questions

1. How would you demonstrate the cart to Pride and the president? What would you specifically plan?
2. Consider crafting a proof statement for Dyno Electric Cart that you would provide to Pride and the president. What would your proof statement specifically state?
3. Consider crafting a testimonial for Dyno Electric Cart that you would provide to Pride and the president. What would it specifically state?
4. Develop two visuals that you would present Pride and the president. What benefits would they focus on? Ensure your visuals follow the best practices outlined in the chapter.

CASE 10.2

©Ron Chapple Stock/FotoSearch/
Glow Images

Dumping Inventory: Should This Be Part of Your Presentation?

Ron Kapra is sales manager at Electra Toy Company, a retail toy store specializing in electronic games. Ron's brother-in-law Jerry works for the company that manufactures the Lasertron electronic game. Jerry mentioned to Ron that the company is coming out with the Lasertron II in three months. However, it will not be announced to retailers for another two months.

Lasertron II will have advanced technology over the present model. The new game cartridges will not be compatible with Lasertron I. Once Lasertron II comes on the market, consumers will want it and not the present model. Jerry explains that for any of the present models the retailer returns after the introduction of Lasertron II, the manufacturer will refund to the retailer the retailer's original cost of Lasertron I.

The Way to Make Extra Sales

Kapra has decided to run a special sale offering 20 percent off the regular price of Lasertron I. With 1,000 cases in stock, Ron wants to sell as many of the present model as possible to his customers. Then when the new model comes out, the same customers will come in and purchase Lasertron II. This will greatly increase sales, Ron feels.

Salesperson Is Unsure

Bill Corrington has been a top salesperson with Electra Toy for about two years. Although excited about the new model, Bill questions Ron's idea. Bill feels his customers trust him. If he sold them Lasertron now and the new model came out in a few months, customers would be upset with him. Bill feels this is no way to treat customers. However, Ron sees nothing wrong. "The loss of a few customers will be offset by the increase in sales," says Ron.

Questions

1. What are the ethical considerations, if any, in this case?
2. At what level of moral development are Ron and Bill operating in this business situation? Explain your answers.
3. What would you do if you were Ron?
4. What would you do if you were Bill?

Welcome Your Prospect's Objections

Main Topics

The Core Principles: Objections

What Are Objections?

Welcome Objections!

When Do Prospects Object?

Objections and the Sales Process

Basic Points to Consider in Meeting Objections

Meet the Objection

Six Major Categories of Objections

Techniques for Meeting Objections

After Meeting the Objection—What to Do?

LEARNING OBJECTIVES

When you learn how to skillfully handle your prospect's questions, resistance, and objections, you are a professional. After studying this chapter, you should be able to

11–1   Explain why you should welcome a prospect's objections.

11–2   Describe what to do when objections arise.

11–3   Discuss seven basic points to consider in meeting a prospect's objections.

11–4   Explain six major categories of prospect objections, and give an example of how to handle each of them.

11–5   Present, illustrate, and use in your presentation several techniques for meeting prospect objections.

11–6   Describe what to do after meeting an objection.

FACING A SALES CHALLENGE

As you drive into the parking lot of a top distributor of your home building supplies, you recall how only two years ago the company purchased the largest opening order you ever sold. Last year its sales doubled, and this year you hope to sell the distributor over $100,000 of supplies.

As you wait, the receptionist informs you that since your last visit, your buyer, Mary Smalley, was fired and another buyer, Nonnie Young, was transferred to her place. Mary and you had become good friends over the past two years, and you hated to see her go.

As you enter the new buyer's office, Young asks you to have a seat and then says: "I've got some bad news for you. I'm considering switching suppliers. Your prices are too high."

What would you do in this situation? What would you say to the buyer? Salespeople commonly face challenges; in most presentations, they experience objections. How does a professional salesperson handle a potentially difficult situation?

Be prepared! No two sales calls are exactly alike. You never know when the customer will say something that makes you wonder if you will be allowed to give the presentation you have worked on for hours.

This chapter examines resistance a saleperson may receive during a sales call (i.e., objections). It discusses how to meet objections, communication techniques to use in overcoming objections, and how to proceed after addressing an objection. Many of these same communication methods can be used with your friends, family, and people you meet every day. Try them out this week. See if they help you better understand why someone gives you an objection and if the communication technique provides a smooth transition into telling your side of the story.

Welcome objections! Think of them in positive terms. In sales, always reflect on why you are calling on this prospect or customer. As discussed in Chapter 7, focus on your purpose and plan for the sales call.

> *"Listen first, speak last."*
>
> PETER F. DRUCKER

The Core Principles: Objections

A customer gives you an objection saying your product is not what is needed. What do you do if you consider yourself a professional salesperson? Would you state, "OK, thanks for your time," and leave? Maybe, maybe not. It depends upon whether the other person is correct. If correct, you politely leave. If not correct, you politely, professionally, and ethically strive to show the person how your product will help her or him. Is this being pushy?

It depends on your purpose. Is your purpose to help or make the sale? Both, you say! What is your main purpose for the sales call? If it is to make the sales, you are being self-centered and only thinking of you. Probably over time you will lose interest in your sales career even if you are earning a high income. If your purpose is to help others, you will be rewarded with results and you will be energized by playing a role in helping your customers and your employer succeed. Chances are you will love selling. Thus, when objections arise, view them as challenges to help your customer. Helping through providing ethical service builds long-term relationships. Remember, professionals welcome objections!

What Are Objections?

Opposition or resistance to information or to the salesperson's request is labeled a **sales objection.** Objections are natural because you are often asking buyers to make some type of change. It may be a change in a product, a change in their actions, a change in a belief, or a change in a process. Change is difficult and it is natural to expect a customer to ask questions, express hesitation, or to even procrastinate in making a decision. Welcome sales objections because they indicate prospect interest and help determine what stage the prospect has reached in the buying cycle—attention, interest, desire, conviction, or readiness to close.

Welcome Objections!

Interestingly, prospects who present objections often are easily sold on your product. They are interested enough to object and express their concerns; they want to know what you have to offer. When a prospect first gives an objection, *smile,* because that's when you start earning your salary. You want to receive personal satisfaction from your job and at the same time increase your salary—right? Well, both occur when you accept objections as a challenge that, handled correctly, benefit both your prospect and you. The more effectively you meet customers' needs and solve their problems, the more successful you will be in sales. If you *fear* objections, you will *fumble* your response, which often causes *failure.*

Remember, although people want to buy, they do not want to be taken advantage of. Buyers who cannot see how your offering will fulfill their needs ask questions and raise objections. If you cannot effectively answer the questions or meet the objections, you will not make the sale. If you sincerely believe your offering fulfills a need but the prospect will not buy, it your fault, not the buyer's fault that the sale was not made. The salesperson who can overcome objections and smoothly return to a presentation will succeed.

When Do Prospects Object?

The prospect may object at any time during your sales call—from introduction to close. Imagine walking into a retail store, carrying your materials, and the buyer yells out, "Oh no, not another salesperson. I don't even want to see you, let alone buy from you!" What do you say?

One salesperson said, "I understand. I'm not here to sell you anything, only to check your stock, help stock your shelves, and return any old or damaged merchandise for a refund." As the salesperson turned to walk away, the buyer said, "Come on back here; I want to talk to you."

If the salesperson had simply said OK, he would not have made that sale. The salesperson knew that he could benefit that customer, and his response and attitude showed it. The point is always to be ready to handle a prospect's objections, whether at the approach, during the presentation, after a trial close, after you have already met a previous objection, or during the close of the sale.

> *Objections can occur any time throughout the sales conversation.*

Objections and the Sales Process

Objections can occur at any time. Oftentimes, however, the prospect allows you to make a presentation, asking questions along the way. Inexperienced salespeople traditionally finish their presentation and wait for the prospect's response.

Experienced, successful salespeople have learned to use the system shown in Exhibit 11.1. After the presentation, they use a trial close to determine the prospect's attitude toward the product and if it is time to close.

Remember, the *trial close* asks for the prospect's opinion, not a decision to buy. The trial close asks about what was said in the presentation. Since you may not know the prospect's opinion, it is too early to close. Typically, the trial close causes the prospect to ask questions and/or state objections.

Let's say that, after the presentation and the trial close, the person gives an objection. First determine the objection. Use one of the objection-handling techniques to transition back into the product, marketing plan, business proposition, or suggested order presentation materials. Address the person's objection. Now ask a trial close to determine if you have handled the objection. If you receive a positive response and no other objection or request for more information occurs, close again using a different closing technique. If an objection, resistance, or request for more information occurs, cycle back through the above sequence. This is the reason you need to be prepared to use several objection-handling techniques and to close multiple times using different closing techniques. Properly executed it will seem natural and professional. You are there solely to help the person and organization fulfill their need or to fix their problem. Again you plan your follow-up and service to the prospect or customer. Off you go to see your next prospect or customer.

When objections occur,
quickly determine what to do.

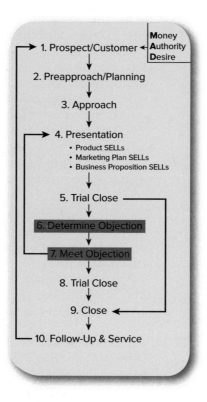

Thus, there are several strategies that a salesperson needs to handle objections. It is important to adapt to the situation. A big help to successfully handling objections is to thoroughly understand several points.

Basic Points to Consider in Meeting Objections

No matter what type of objections the prospect raises, certain basic points should be considered in order to meet them:

- Plan for objections.
- Anticipate and forestall.
- Handle objections as they arise.
- Be positive.
- Listen—hear them out.
- Understand objections.
- Meet the objection.

The salesperson can plan for each of these basic points for meeting objections.

Plan for Objections

Plan for objections that your customer might raise, as shown in Exhibit 11.2. Consider not only the reasons that prospects should buy but why they should *not* buy. Structure your presentation to minimize the disadvantages of your product. Do not discuss disadvantages unless prospects raise them in the conversation.

EXHIBIT 11.2

Prepare for objections.

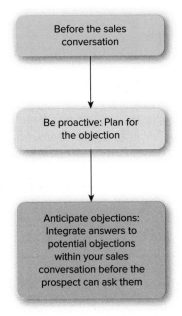

After each sales call, review the prospect's objections. Divide them into major and minor objections. Then develop ways to overcome them. Your planning for and rehearsal of overcoming objections allows you to respond in a natural and positive manner. Planning for and review of the sales call allows you to anticipate and forestall objections.

Anticipate and Forestall

Forestalling the objection has the salesperson discussing an objection before the prospect raises it. It often is better to forestall or discuss objections before they arise. The sales presentation can be developed to address anticipated objections directly.

For example, take an exterior house paint manufacturer's salesperson who learns that an unethical competitor is telling retail dealers that his paint starts to chip and peel after six months. Realizing the predicament, this salesperson develops a presentation that states, "Three independent testing laboratories have shown that this paint will not chip or peel for eight years after application." The salesperson has forestalled or answered the objection before it is raised by using a proof statement. This technique also can prevent a negative mood from entering the buyer–seller dialogue.

Another way to anticipate objections is to discuss disadvantages before the prospect does. Many products have flaws, and they sometimes surface as you try to make a sale. If you know of an objection that arises consistently, discuss it. If you acknowledge it first, you don't have to defend it.

On the other hand, a customer who has an objection feels compelled to defend that objection. For example, you might be showing real estate property. En route to the location you say, "You know, before we get out there, I just want to mention a couple of things. You're going to notice that it needs a little paint in a few places, and I noticed a couple of shingles on the roof the other day that you may have to replace." When you arrive, your customer may take a look and say, "Well, those shingles aren't so bad and we're going to paint it anyway." Yet, if you reached the house without a little prior warning of small defects, those items are often what a customer first notices.

> Proactively plan for potential objections and how you will handle them.

> Anticipate the objection: Consider discussing the buyer's potential concerns before they arise.

A third way of using an anticipated objection is to brag about it and turn it into a sales benefit. A salesperson might say, "I want to mention something important before we go any further. Our price is more than our competitors because our new software provides technology found in no other equipment. It will improve your operation and eliminate the costly repairs you are now experiencing. In just a minute, I want to fully discuss your investment. Let's first discuss the improvements we can provide. Take a look at this."

This takes the sting out of the price objection because you have discussed it. It is difficult for a buyer to come back and say, "It's too high," because you have mentioned that already. So, there are times when you can anticipate objections and use them advantageously.

Handle Objections as They Arise

Very infrequently, situations arise in which it is best to postpone your answer to an objection. When the objection raised will be covered later in your presentation, or when you build to that point, pass over it for a while. However, the best practice is to meet objections as they arise; postponement may cause a negative mental picture or reaction such as these:

- The prospect may stop listening until you address the objection.
- The prospect may feel you are trying to hide something.
- You also feel it's a problem.
- You cannot answer because you do not know the answer or how to deal with this objection.
- It may appear that you are not interested in the prospect's opinion.

The objection could be the only item left before closing the sale. So, meet the objection, determine if you have satisfied the prospect, use another trial close to uncover other objections, and if there are no more objections, move toward closing the sale. Exhibit 11.3 gives some good examples on how to handle objections during the sales conversation.

EXHIBIT 11.3

Process for handling an objection.

How to handle objections during the sales conversation

Don't delay in handling most objections. Handle objections as they arise.

Be positive: Use positive nonverbal body language.

Acknowledge the concern. Find an area in which you can empathize with the buyer.

Listen, listen, listen. Don't immediately respond. Learn about the underlying concern.

Ask questions about the objection before responding directly to the objection

Provide your answer to the objection. Then, use a trial close to ensure understanding.

Example:
The buyer states, "Well I'm a little hesitant to stock the quantity you are suggesting, Normally, we sell approximately one-half of that amount of your competitor's product. I just don't feel comfortable in moving forward with this quantity." [Objection]

Example:
The salesperson nods and acknowledges positively the customer's concern. The salesperson's body position is open and emits green signals (i.e., positive nonverbal communication signs). Remember, the objection is a gift. It shows that the buyer is still engaged in the conversation.

Example:
The salesperson states, "I understand it is very important to align your inventory with your sales. It totally makes sound business sense." [Empathize with the buyer.]

Example:
The salesperson asks, "Can you share with me how often the competitor's product is supported with advertising and promotional initiatives?" [Ask question about objection before responding directly.]

Example:
The customer answers, "Actually, very rarely. In fact, only during the holidays." [Customer answer.]

Example:
Now with a better understanding of the concern, the salesperson answers the objection, "That makes sense, as the holidays are an important time. However, I'd like to show you our promotional calendar for our product. As you will note, we have five months of national advertising throughout the year. Additionally, we distribute coupons every four months to drive traffic into your store. As such, we will invest in marketing to ensure our product moves off your shelves and into your customer's shopping carts." [Answer the objective.]

"What are your thoughts on how this type of promotional plan could drive faster turnover of our product?" [Use a trial close to ensure you have reduced the customer's concern.]

Be Positive

> *Objections are a natural element of the sales process; all solutions will have drawbacks.*

When responding to an objection, use positive body language such as a smile. Strive to respond in a manner that keeps your prospect friendly and in a positive mood. Do not take the objection personally. Never treat the objection with hostility. Take the objection in stride by responding respectfully and showing sincere interest in your prospect's opinion.

At times, the prospect may raise objections based on incorrect information. Politely deny false objections. Be realistic; all products have drawbacks, even yours. If a competitor's product has a feature your product lacks, demonstrate the overriding benefits of your product.

Listen—Hear Them Out

> *Don't respond immediately. The key to handling objections is to LISTEN and then ASK QUESTIONS to understand the customer's perception.*

Many salespeople leap on an objection before the other person has a chance to finish. The prospect barely says five words—and already the salesperson is hammering away as though the evil thing will multiply unless it's stomped out. "I have to prove he is mistaken, or he won't take the product" is a panicky reaction to the first hint of any objection.

Not only does the prospect feel irritated at being interrupted, but the prospect also feels pushed and uneasy. Your prospect will ask, "Why's he jumping on that so fast and so hard? I sense something is wrong." Suppose you run south when the prospect heads north, and you answer the wrong objection or even raise one that the prospect hadn't thought of?[1] Review the listening guidelines discussed in Chapter 5; they apply.

Understand Objections

When customers object, they do one of several things, as shown in Exhibit 11.4. They are requesting more information, setting a condition, or giving a genuine objection. The objection can be hopeless or true.

EXHIBIT 11.4

What does a prospect mean by an objection?

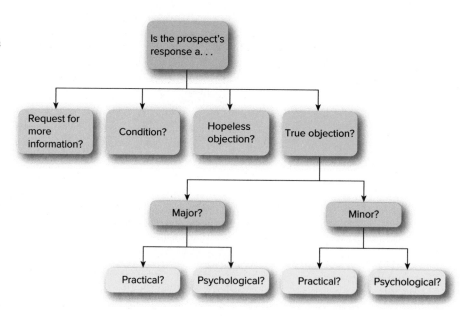

Request for Information

Many times, prospects appear to make objections when they are requesting more information. That is why it is important to listen. If prospects request more information, chances are that they are in the conviction stage. You have created a desire; they want the product, but they are not convinced that you have the best product or you are the best supplier. If you feel this may be the case, supply the requested information indirectly.

A Condition

At times, prospects may raise an objection that turns into a **condition of the sale.** They are saying, "If you can meet my request, I'll buy," or "Under certain conditions, I will buy from you."

If you sense that the objection is a condition, quickly determine if you can help the prospect meet it. If you cannot, close the interview politely. Take the following real estate example:

> **Prospect:** It's a nice house, but the price is too high. I can't afford a $2,000 a month house payment. [You do not know if this is an objection or a condition.]
>
> **Salesperson:** I know what you mean [acknowledging the prospect's viewpoint]. If you don't mind my asking, what is your monthly salary?
>
> **Prospect:** My take-home pay is $2,700 a month.

In this case, the prospect has set a condition on the purchase that cannot be met by the salesperson realistically; it is not an objection. Continuing the exchange by bargaining would waste time and possibly anger the prospect. Now that the prospect's income is known, the salesperson can show a house in the prospect's price range.

Negotiation Can Overcome a Condition. Often, conditions stated by the prospect are overcome through negotiation between buyer and seller. **Negotiation** refers to reaching an agreement mutually satisfactory to both buyer and seller. Prospects may say things like, "I'll buy your equipment if you can deliver it in one month instead of three," or "If you'll reduce your price by 10 percent, I'll buy."

If you determine that this type of statement is a condition rather than an objection, through negotiation you may make the sale with further discussion and an eventual compromise between you and the buyer. In the example above, you might ask the manufacturing plant if equipment can be shipped to the prospect in two months instead of three. This arrangement may be acceptable to the prospect. You may have a current customer who has that piece of equipment but is not using it. You might arrange for the prospect to lease it from your customer for three months.

If the prospect sets a price condition saying, "I will buy your product only if you reduce your price by 10 percent," determine if your company will reduce the price if the buyer will purchase a larger quantity. Consider this example. As a state agency, Texas A&M University purchased much of its office equipment on a bid system. The IBM salesperson could not sell the Texas A&M Marketing Department a certain type of computer hardware because the cost of a single machine was too high for the department's budget. The department wanted the machine; however, it could not afford it. Instead of giving up, the salesperson went to other departments in the

"Seek first to understand, then to be understood."

STEPHEN COVEY

university and found a need for a total of 16 machines (at a lower price of $4,000 per unit, less than the price of one machine). IBM could lower the price substantially because of the large number of machines purchased. The salesperson determined that price was a condition, found a way to overcome the condition, and made the sale. Through initiation and inquiry, a potentially lost sale became a multiple victory beneficial to all parties.

There are two broad categories of objections. One of them is called *hopeless.* A hopeless objection is one that cannot be solved or answered, such as I already have one, I'm bankrupt, and I'd like to buy your life insurance, but the doctor gives me only 30 days to live. Hopeless objections cannot be overcome.

If your prospect does not buy, and no condition exists or the objection is not hopeless, it is your fault if you did not make the sale because you could not provide information to show how your offering would suit the buyer's needs.

The second category is the objection that can be answered. Called a true objection, it has two types: major and minor.

Major or Minor Objections

Once you determine that the prospect has raised a true objection, determine its importance. If it is of little or no importance, quickly address it and return to selling. Do not provide a long response or turn a minor objection into a major discussion item. The minor objection is often a defense mechanism of little importance to the prospect. Concentrate on objections directly related to the prospect's important buying motives.

Practical or Psychological Objections

Objections, minor or major, can be **practical** (overt) **objections** or **psychological** (hidden) **objections** in nature. Exhibit 11.5 gives some examples. A real objection is tangible, such as a high price. If this is a real objection, and the prospect says so, you can show that your product is of high quality and worth the price, or you might suggest removing some optional features and reducing the price. As long as the prospect states the real objection to purchasing the product clearly, you should be able to answer the objection.

However, prospects do not always clearly state their objections. Rather, they often give some excuse why they are not ready to make a purchase, which conceals real objections. Usually, the prospect cannot purchase the product until hidden objections are rectified. You must uncover a prospect's hidden objections and eliminate them.

EXHIBIT 11.5

Examples of objections.

Practical	Psychological
■ Price	■ Resistance to spending money
■ Product is not needed	■ Resistance to domination
■ Prospect has an overstock of your or your competitor's products	■ Predetermined beliefs
■ Delivery schedules	■ Negative image of salespeople
■ Level of profitability	■ Dislikes making a buying decision
■ Ability to integrate the solution into current processes	■ Resistance to change
■ Ability of solution to meet buyer's goals	■ Concerned with how others in the organization will perceive the decision

Meet the Objection

Once you fully understand the objection, you are ready to respond to the prospect. How to respond depends on the objection. During the year, a salesperson will hear hundreds of objections. Prospects object to various items in different ways.

Generally, objections fall into six categories. By grouping objections, you can better plan how to respond. Let's examine these six categories and discuss specific techniques for meeting objections.

Six Major Categories of Objections

Most objections that salespeople encounter can be placed into the six categories shown in Exhibit 11.6. Know how you will handle each situation before it occurs. An advance idea about how you handle these objections will help you become a better salesperson by improving your image as a problem solver.

The Hidden Objection

Prospects who ask trivial, unimportant questions or conceal their feelings beneath a veil of silence have **hidden objections.** They do not discuss their true objections to a product because they may feel they cannot trust you, they are afraid objections will offend you, or they may not feel your sales call is worthy of their full attention.

Such prospects may have a good conversation with you without revealing their true feelings. You have to ask questions and carefully listen to know which questions to ask in order to reveal their true objections to your product. Learning how to determine what questions to ask a prospect and how to ask them are skills developed by conscious effort over time. Your ability to ask probing questions improves with each sales call if you try to develop this ability.

Smoke Out Hidden Objections

With prospects who are unwilling to discuss their objections or who may not know why they are reluctant to buy, be prepared to smoke out objections by asking questions. Do what you can to reveal the objections. Consider the following questions:

- What are the major benefits you need in order to move forward?
- What causes you to say that?
- Let's consider this, suppose my product would [do what prospect wants] . . . then would you consider it?
- Tell me, what's really on your mind?
- Can you lead me through your decision process?

Uncovering hidden objections is not always easy. Observe the prospect's tone of voice, facial expressions, and physical movements. Pay close attention to what the prospect is saying. You may have to read between the lines occasionally to find the buyer's true objections. All these factors will help you discover whether objections are real or simply an excuse to cover a hidden objection.

> "Every adversity carries with it the seed of an equivalent or greater benefit."
>
> NAPOLEON HILL

EXHIBIT 11.6

Six major categories of objections.

| 1. Hidden objections | 2. Stalling objections | 3. No-need objections | 4. Money objections | 5. Product objections | 6. Source objections |

Prospects may not know consciously what their real objections are. Sometimes they claim that the price of a product is too high. In reality, they may be reluctant to spend money on anything. If you attempt to show that your price is competitive, the real objection remains unanswered and no sale results. Remember, you cannot convince anyone to buy until you understand what a prospect needs to be convinced of.

If, after answering all apparent questions, the prospect is still not sold, you might subtly attempt to uncover the hidden objection. You might ask the prospect what the real objection is. Direct inquiry should be used as a last resort because it indirectly may amount to calling the prospect a liar, but if it is used carefully, it may enable the salesperson to reveal the prospect's true objection. Smoking out hidden objections is an art form skillful salespeople develop over time. Its successful use can greatly increase sales. This approach should be used carefully, but if it enables the salesperson to uncover a hidden objection, then it has served its purpose.

The Stalling Objection

When your prospect says, "I'll think it over," or "I'll be ready to buy on your next visit," you must determine if the statement is the truth or if it is a smoke screen designed to get rid of you. The **stalling objection** is a common tactic.

What you discovered in developing your customer profile and customer benefit plan can aid you in determining how to handle this type of objection. Suppose that before seeing a certain retail customer, you checked the supply of your merchandise in both the store's stockroom and on the retail shelf and this occurs:

Buyer: I have enough merchandise for now. Thanks for coming by.

Salesperson: Ms. Marcher, you have 50 cases in the warehouse and on display. You sell 50 cases each month, right? I'm a little concerned about missed sales for your firm.

You have forced her hand. This buyer either has to order more merchandise from you or tell you why she is allowing her product supply to dwindle. An easily handled stall is illustrated in Exhibit 11.7. When the prospect says, "I'm too busy to see you now," you might ask, "When would be a good time to come back today?"

The six types of objections: hidden, stalling, no-need, money, product, and source.

EXHIBIT 11.7

Imagine walking into your prospect's office, who says, "I'm too busy to see you now." What would you say?

©Huntstock.com/Shutterstock

One of the toughest stalls to overcome arises in selling a new consumer product. Retail buyers are reluctant to stock consumer goods that customers have not yet asked for, even new goods produced by large, established consumer product manufacturers. The following excerpt is from a sales call made by an experienced consumer goods salesperson on a reluctant retail buyer. This excerpt begins with an interruption the buyer makes during a presentation of a new brand of toothpaste:

Buyer: Well, it sounds good, but I have seven brands and 21 different sizes of toothpaste now. There is no place to put it. [A false objection—smoke screen.]

Salesperson: Suppose you had 100 customers walk down the aisle and ask for Colgate 100 Toothpaste. Could you find room then?

Buyer: Well, maybe. But I'll wait until then. [The real objection.]

Salesperson: If this were a restaurant and you did not have your restaurant sign outside, people wouldn't come in because they wouldn't know it was a restaurant, would they?

Buyer: Probably not.

Salesperson: The same logic applies to Colgate 100. When people see it, they will buy it. You would agree that our other heavily advertised products sell for you, right? [Trial close.]

Buyer: Yeah, they do. [Positive response; now reenter your selling sequence.]

The salesperson eliminated the stall in this case through a logical analogy.

A third common stall is the alibi that your prospect must have approval from someone else, such as a boss, buying committee, purchasing agent, or home office. Because the buyer's attitude toward purchasing your product influences the firm's buying decision, it is important that you determine the buyer's attitude toward your product.

When the buyer stalls by saying, "I will have to get approval from my boss," you can counter by saying, "If you had the authority, would you go ahead with the purchase," If the answer is yes, chances are that the buyer will positively influence the firm's buying decision. If not, you must uncover the real objections. Otherwise, you will not make the sale.

An additional response to the "I've got to think it over" stall is, "What are some of the issues you have to think about?" Or you may focus directly on the prospect's stall by saying, "Would you share with me some things that are holding you back?"

Another effective response to "I've got to talk to my boss" is, "Of course you do. What are some things that you would talk about?" This allows you to agree with the reluctant prospect. You are now on the buyer's side. It helps encourage the buyer to talk and to trust you. This empathic response ("Of course you do") puts you in the other person's position.

Sometimes, the prospect will not answer the question. Instead, the response is, "Oh, I just need to get an opinion." You can follow-up with a multiple-choice question such as, "Would you explore whether this is a good purchase in comparison with a competitor's product or would you wonder about the financing?" This helps display an attitude of genuine caring.

As with any response to an objection, communicate a positive attitude. Do not get demanding, defensive, or hostile. Otherwise, your nonverbal expressions may signal a defensive attitude—reinforcing the prospect's defenses.

Your goal in dealing with a stall is to help prospects realistically examine reasons for and against buying now. If you are absolutely sure it is not in their best interest to buy now, tell them so. They will respect you for it. You will feel good about yourself. The next time you see these customers, they will be more trusting and open with you.

Objections are a gift. The customer is still engaged in the conversation and sharing a concern.

Stalling Objections

A. I have to think this over.
   1. I would be happy to help you consider the opportunity now while it is fresh in your mind. What are some of the items you need to know more about?
   2. I understand that you want more time to think. I would be interested in hearing your thoughts about the reasons for and the reasons against buying now.
   3. You had mentioned that this is a terrific opportunity, you noted that you liked the product, and our calculations show it will save you money. Right? [If prospect says yes:] Would you consider moving forward with this today?

B. I'm too busy.
   1. I appreciate how busy you are. When could we visit for just a few minutes? [Stop or add a benefit for seeing you.]

C. I'm too busy. Talk to _____ first.
   1. Can you share with me her responsibilities with the buying process? Does he/she have the authority to approve the purchase? [If prospect says yes:] Thank you. I'll tell him/her you sent me. [If prospect says no:] Well, then why should I talk with him/her?
   2. This is an executive-level decision and has the opportunity to assist your firm. Might I suggest that we discuss the potential of this opportunity?

D. I plan to wait until next fall.
   1. Can you share with me your timeline?
   2. I totally understand. Some of my best customers have expressed something similar. However, once they bought, they were sorry they waited.
   3. Would you be willing to approve the commitment today for this fall? [If prospect says yes, then:]
      a. OK, let's finalize the order today and I'll have it ready to arrive October 1.
      b. Great! Should I call you in September or October so we can make the final arrangements?
   4. What if I could arrange for it to be shipped to you now but you didn't have to pay for it until the fall?

However, the main thing to remember is not to be satisfied with a false objection or a stall; see the box "Selling Tips: Stalling Objections." Tactfully pursue the issue until you have unearthed the buyer's true feelings about your product. If this does not work, (1) present the benefits of using your product now; (2) if there is a special price deal, mention it; and (3) if there is a penalty for delay, mention it. Bring out any or all of your main selling benefits and keep on selling!

The No-Need Objection

The prospect says, "Sounds good. I really like what you had to say, and I know you have a good product, but I'm not interested now. Our present product [or supply or merchandise] works well. We will stay with it." Standing up to conclude the interview, the prospect says, "Thanks very much for coming by." This type of objection can disarm an unwary salesperson.

The **no-need objection** is used widely because it politely gets rid of the salesperson. Some salespeople actually encourage it by making a poor sales presentation. They allow prospects to sit and listen to a sales pitch without motivating them to participate by showing true concern and asking questions. Therefore, when the presentation is over, prospects can say quickly, "Sounds good, but. . . ." In essence, they say no, making it difficult for the salesperson to continue the call. While not always a valid objection, the no-need response strongly implies the end of a sales call.

A. I'm not interested.
1. Would you be willing to share your hesitation?
2. What elements would a product need in order for you to purchase it?
3. I wouldn't be interested if I were you, either. However, I know you'll be interested when you hear about. . . . It is very exciting! [If prospect still says no:] What would be a better time to talk?
4. Some of my best customers first said that until they discovered . . . [state benefits].
5. You are not interested? Then who should I talk to who would be interested in . . . [state benefits]?

B. The . . . we have is still good.
1. Would you be willing to share what you like about your current product and what you wish it had?
2. I understand how you feel. Many of my customers said that before they switched over. However, they saw that this product would . . . [discuss benefits of present product or service versus what you are selling].

3. That's exactly why you should buy—to get a good trade now.
4. What are some of your concerns about moving forward with our solution?

C. We are satisfied with what we have now.
1. Satisfied in what areas?
2. Would you share with me what do you like most about what you have right now? [Then compare to your product.]
3. I know how you feel. Often we're satisfied with something because we have no chance [or don't have the time] to compare it with something better. I've studied what you are using. Would you be willing to invest a few minutes to compare products and show you how to . . . [state benefits].
4. Many of our customers were happy with what they had before they saw our product. There are three reasons they switched . . . [state three product benefits].

The no-need objection is especially tricky because it also may include a hidden objection and/or a stall. If your presentation was a solo performance or a monologue, your prospect might be indifferent to you and your product, having tuned out halfway through the second act. Aside from departing with a "Thanks for your time," you might resurrect your presentation by asking questions. See the box "Selling Tips: No-Need Objections" for ways to respond to the no-need objections.

The Money Objection

The **money objection** encompasses several forms of economic excuses: I have no money, I don't have that much money, It costs too much, or Your price is too high. These objections are simple for the buyer to say, especially in a recessionary economy.

Often, prospects want to know the product's price before the presentation, and they will not want you to explain how the product's benefits outweigh its costs. Price is a real consideration and must be discussed, but it is risky to discuss product price until you can compare it to product benefits. If you successfully postpone the price discussion, you must eventually return to it because your prospect seldom forgets it. Some prospects are so preoccupied with price that they give minimal attention to your presentation until the topic reemerges. Other prospects falsely present price as their main objection to your product, which conceals their true objection.

By observing nonverbal signals, asking questions, listening, and positively responding to the price question when it arises, you can easily handle price-oriented objections.

A. Your price is too high.
1. Can you share with me your current target price?
2. How much would you be willing to invest in this solution?
3. We can lower the price right now, but we need to decide what options to cut from our proposal. Is that what you really want to do?
4. Our price is higher than the competition. However, we have the best value. [now explain]
5. How high is too high?
6. If it were lower priced, would you want it?

B. I can't afford it.
1. Would you share with me the constraints you are facing?
2. If I could show you a way to afford this purchase, would you be interested?
3. I sincerely believe that you cannot afford *not* to buy this. The benefits of . . . far outweigh the price.
4. My greatest concern regards all the business you can lose, the productivity you can lose, that lost income from not having the latest, best, and most reliable technology. You'll love it! You'll wonder how you've done without it! Let's discuss how you could make this investment.
5. Do you mean you can't afford it now or forever?

C. Give me a 10 percent discount, and I'll give you an order today.
1. I always quote my best price.
2. If you give me an order for 10, I can give you a 10 percent discount. Would you like to order 10?
3. [Prospect's name], we build your product up to a certain quality and service standard—not down to a certain price. We could produce a lower-priced item, but our experience shows it isn't worth it. This is a proven product that gives 100 percent satisfaction—not 90 percent.

D. You've got to do better than that.
1. Can you explain further what you would like in terms of value?
2. When you say better, can you describe to me what you mean?
3. Do you mean a longer service warranty? A lower price? Extended delivery? Share with me exactly what you want.

Many salespeople think that offering the lowest price gives them a greater chance of sales success. Generally, this is not the case. Once you realize this, you can become even more successful. You might even state that your product is not the least expensive one available because of its benefits and advantages and the satisfaction it provides. Once you convey this concept to your buyer, price becomes a secondary factor that usually can be handled successfully.

Do not be afraid of price as an objection; be ready for it and welcome it. Quote the price and keep on selling. It is usually the inexperienced salesperson who blows this often minor objection into a major one. If the price objection becomes major, prospects can become excited and overreact to your price. The end result is losing the sale. If prospects overreact: slow down the conversation, let them talk it out, and slowly present product benefits as they relate to cost.

See the box "Selling Tips: Money Objections" for ways to respond to the money objection. One way to view the money objection concerns the price/value formula.

How to Handle the Price Objection: The Price/Value Formula

The price objection is a bargaining tool for a savvy buyer who wants to ensure the best, absolutely lowest price. But there is often more to it than shrewd bargaining.

If the buyer is merely testing to be sure the best possible price is on the table, it's a strong buying signal. But perhaps the prospect sincerely believes the price is too high.

A. Your competitor's product is better.
 1. I must tell you, that's a little surprising based on our testing results. [Act surprised.]
 2. Can you please help me understand in what way? [Have customer list features liked in the other product; then show how your product has the same or better features.]
 3. I'm interested in hearing your unbiased opinion of the two products.
 4. You've had a chance to look at their product. What did you see that impressed you?
 5. Are you referring to quality, service, features, or the product's value after five years of use?
B. The machine we have is still good.
 1. I understand how you feel. Many of my customers have said that before they switched over. However, they found that the reason a new model makes an old model obsolete is not that the old one is bad, but that the new one is so much more efficient and productive. Would you like to take a look at what these businesses found?
 2. That's exactly why you should trade now. Since your machine is still good, you still have a high trade-in value. When it breaks down, your trade-in value will go down, too. It's less expensive to trade in a workable machine than to wait for it to fail.

C. I'll buy a used one.
 1. When you buy a used product, you take a high risk. You buy something that someone else has used and probably abused. Do you want to pay for other people's mistakes?
 2. You may save a few dollars on your monthly payments, but you'll have to pay much more in extra service, more repairs, and downtime. Which price would you rather pay?
 3. Many of our customers thought about a used product before they decided to buy a new one. Let me show you why they decided that new equipment is the best buy. The cost comparisons will make it clear.
 4. I understand you want to save money. I like to save money. Perhaps you should consider the smaller model for starters. It provides you with the first start on cost savings.
D. I don't want to take risks.
 1. Can you share with me what you mean by risky?
 2. "Risky" compared to what?
 3. What could we do to make you feel more secure?
 4. [Prospect's name], it may be more risky for you not to buy. What is the price you may pay for low productivity in your plant?

Let's define why one buyer might already be convinced the product is a good deal—fair price—but is just testing to make sure it's the best price, whereas another buyer may sincerely believe the asking price is more than the goods are worth.

Remember that cost is what concerns the buyer, not just the price. Cost is computed in the buyer's mind by considering what is received compared with the money paid.

In other words, price divided by value equals cost:

$$\frac{\text{Price}}{\text{Value}} = \text{Cost}$$

In this price/value formula, the value is what the prospect sees the product doing for them and/or their company. *Value* is the total package of benefits you have built for the prospect. Value is the solution you provide to the buyer's problems.

The price will not change. The company sets that price at headquarters. The company has arrived at the price scientifically—computers were used—based on costs, competition, and other salient factors. It is a fair price, and it's not going to change.

So, the only thing to change is the prospect's perception of the value. For example, assume the buyer viewed the cost as follows:

$$\frac{\text{Price } 100.}{\text{Value } 90.} = \text{Cost } 1.11$$

The price is too high. You have to solve the prospect's problem with the product by translating product benefits into what it will do for the buyer. You have to build up the value:

$$\frac{\text{Price } 100.}{\text{Value } 110.} = \text{Cost } .90$$

Now that is more like it. The cost went down because the value went up.

The price/value formula is not the answer to "Your price is too high." It is only a description of the buyer's thinking process and an explanation of why the so-called price objection is heard so often. It tells us what we must do to answer the price objection.

The salesperson is usually the one who identifies a statement or question from the prospect as an objection. Rarely does the prospect say, "This is my objection." So, you need to ask, "Why did the buyer say that?" If you ask that question, you can ask the prospect to say more about why he or she made the objection.

Remember, at one extreme, the buyer may be sold on the product and is simply testing to see if there is an extra discount. At the other extreme, the buyer may not see any benefit in the product or service but only see the price. When this is the case, "it costs too much" is a legitimate objection to be overcome by translating features into advantages into benefits for the buyer. Use the SELL Sequence technique.

The Product Objection

All salespeople encounter **product objections** that relate directly to the product. Everyone does not like the best-selling product on the market. At times, most buyers have fears about risks associated with buying a product—they are afraid that the product will not do what the salesperson says it will do, or that the product is not worth either the time and energy required to use it or the actual cost.

What seems fair to you may not seem fair to others.

You also sell against competition. The prospect already uses a competitive product, has used one, would like to use one, has heard of one, or knows people who have used one. Your reaction to a product objection must use a positive tone. The use of a guarantee, testimonial, independent research results, and demonstrations helps counter the product objection. See the box "Selling Tips: Handling Product Objections" for ways to respond to the product objection.

The Source Objection

The **source objection** is the last major category of objections salespeople typically face. Source objections relate loyalty to a present supplier or salesperson. Also, the prospect may not like you or your company.

Prospects often discuss their like for a present supplier or salesperson. They may tell you that they do not like your company. Seldom, however, will someone directly say, "I don't want to do business with you."

Usually, handling a source objection requires calling on the prospect routinely over a period. It takes time to break this resistance barrier. Get to know the prospect and the prospect's needs. Show your true interest. Do not try to get all of the business at once—go for a trial run, a small order. It is important to learn exactly what bothers the prospect. Some examples are shown in the box "Selling Tips: The Source Objection." Choose one of these responses to handle the objection illustrated in Exhibit 11.8.

A. I'm sorry; we won't buy from you.
   1. Would you be willing to share with me your concern? Why not?
   2. You must have a reason for feeling that way. May I ask what it is?
   3. Are you not going to buy from us now or forever?
   4. What could we do to win your business in the future?
   5. Is there anyone else in your company who might be interested in buying our cost-saving products? Who?
   6. I respect the fact you aren't buying from us this one time. However, I suspect that as you hear more about our fantastic products in the news and from customers, you will buy something from us in the future. Do you mind if I stop by periodically to update you on our new products?
   7. Would you like to work with someone else in our company?
   8. Is there anything about me that prevents you from doing business with our company?

B. I want to work with a more established company. We've done business with . . . for five years. Why should I change?
   1. I understand how safe you feel about a relationship that goes back five years. And yet, I saw your eyes light up when you looked at our products. I can see that you're giving serious consideration to diversity. Just out of curiosity, could we compare the pros and cons of the two choices? Let's take a piece of paper and list the reasons for and against buying from us. The first reason against us is that we haven't worked with you for the past five years. What are some reasons for giving us a chance to prove ourselves?
   2. I can only say good things about my competitor, and if I were you, I would go with him or her—unless, of course, you want a better product at a better price.

EXHIBIT 11.8

Imagine that this customer says, "I like your proposal but we are happy with our present supplier." What would you say?

©Izabela Habur/Getty Images

We provide two examples to overcome objections.

Example 1

Buyer: Before we move forward, I'm concerned about how much money I will need to invest in your recommended retirement plan? [Money Objection]

Seller: I understand. Any sizable investment like this one requires careful consideration. [Empathize]

Seller: When you examine investments like this one, what financial metrics do you commonly review? [Ask questions to understand concern]

Buyer: Well honestly, I didn't prepare my budget with an opportunity like this in mind. I'm a little worried about the investment returns, such as the timing of the dividend income.

Seller: That's very understandable. I've brought a document that shows the expected timing of the investment returns, including the dividend date and the total amount of dividends expected per year. As you can see, you will receive quarterly returns that exceed your current returns. [Meet the objection]

Seller: Is this the type of information you needed, or are there any additional items we should review and discuss? [Trial close to ensure understanding]

Buyer: This is great. Thank you for the information.

Example 2

Buyer: I'm unsure if your solution makes sense for us at this time. There is a great deal of pressure on my team to reduce costs. It seems silly to invest more money when our management is asking for us to reduce our expenses [Money Objection]

Seller: I understand you feel stretched. You feel compelled by your management to reduce costs and at the same time you want to make sure you are making the right investments to enable these long-term cost savings. [Empathize]

Seller: Would you be willing to share your three biggest apprehensions about our proposed plan to reduce your electricity costs? [Ask questions to understand concern]

Buyer: Well first of all, the cost for the 2,500 units is a big investment. Second, I'm not sure if we can implement all of your products in our stores immediately. And third, how do I finance all of this investment within this fiscal year?

Seller: Thanks. These are all major areas we need to address. Let's review this document. In the first section, it provides the expected cost savings for the next five years for your project. As you see, you will not only pay for your investment in the first two years, you'll receive ongoing cost savings. The second section details the implementation timelines. We have a recommended action plan to ensure we have everything installed in your stores by the end of the fiscal year. In the final section, you will find three ways in which we can help your firm finance the project.

Seller: What are your thoughts? Are there any other elements of this project that are creating additional concerns? [Trial close to ensure understanding]

Buyer: Actually, this document is very helpful. It looks like this plan is very manageable.

Techniques for Meeting Objections

Having uncovered all objections, a salesperson must answer them to the prospect's satisfaction. We highly suggest using the technique of empathizing, listening, asking questions, answering the concern, and using a trial close. However, different situations require different techniques; several techniques are presented in the following sections. In some situations you may be able to integrate multiple techniques. Again, it is important to adapt the technique to the situation and the customer. Techniques used by salespeople include

1) Let a third-party answer.
2) Ask questions to smoke out objections.

3) Rephrase an objection as a question.
4) Compensate for the objection.
5) Boomerang the objection.
6) Postpone the objection.
7) Dodge the objection.
8) Pass up the objection.
9) Indirectly deny the objection.
10) Directly deny the objection.

Let a Third Party Answer

An effective technique for responding to an objection is to answer it by giving a **third-party answer** such as data, proof statement, or someone else's experience as your proof of testimony. Salespeople use a wide range of proof statements today. Therefore, it's important to be prepared to present a range of proof, including case studies, market data, white papers, research from industry thought-leaders, and the customer's sales data. You might respond to a question in this way: "I'm glad you asked. Here is what our research has shown," or, "EPA tests have shown," or, "You know, my best customer brought that point up before making the purchase . . . but was completely satisfied." These are examples of proof statement formats. If you use a person or a company's name, be sure to obtain their approval first.

Providing buyers the necessary information to make a decision can frequently overcome objections. A wide range of data can provide information to overcome buyers' objections.

Frito-Lay salesperson June Steward frequently uses her laptop to show buyers their past purchases of products and to project future sales. Using his laptop computer while in the buyer's office, Fisher Electronic's salesperson John Berry checks with his warehouse daily on available products and shipment schedules. Merrill Lynch salesperson Sandy Lopez uses software to display her client's present investments, past earnings, and recommendations on how much money should be put into stock and bond mutual funds.

Technology can be incorporated easily into most, if not all, of the techniques for meeting objections. Anytime you need to provide information to buyers, you can create a technological method of presenting data in an accurate and dramatic manner.

Secondary data or experiences, especially from a reliable or reputable source, are successful with the expert or skeptical prospect. If, after hearing secondary testimony, the prospect is still unsure about the product, one successful equipment salesperson asks the buyer to contact a current user directly:

Salesperson: I still haven't answered your entire question, have I?

Buyer: Not really.

Salesperson: Let's do this. Here is a list of several people (or companies and their buying representatives) currently using our product. Would you be willing to contact them *right now* and ask them that same question? They have used our product for several years and are willing to share their candid opinions with you.

A salesperson should use this version of the third-party technique only when certain that the prospect is still unsatisfied with how an objection has been handled, and that positive proof will probably clinch the sale. This dramatic technique allows the salesperson to impress a prospect. It also shows a flattering willingness to go to great lengths to validate a claim.

Ask Questions to Smoke Out Objections

Intelligent questioning impresses a prospect in several ways. Technical questions show a prospect that a salesperson knows the business. Questions relating to a prospect's particular business show that a salesperson is concerned more with the prospect's needs than with just making a sale. Finally, people who ask **intelligent questions,** whether they know much about the product, the prospect's business, or life in general, are often admired. Buyers are impressed with the sales professional who knows what to ask and when to ask it. Examples of questions are

Prospect: This house is not as nice as the one someone else showed us yesterday.

Salesperson: Would you tell me why?

or

Prospect: This product does not have the [feature].

Salesperson: If it did have [feature], would you be interested?

[This example is an excellent questioning technique to determine if the objection is a smoke screen, a major or minor objection, or a practical or psychological objection. If the prospect says no to the response, you know the feature was not important.]

or

Prospect: I don't like your price.

Salesperson: Will you base your decision on price or on the product offered you . . . at a fair price?

[If the prospect says "Price," show how benefits outweigh costs. If the decision is based on the product, you have eliminated the price objection.]

Five-Question Sequence Method of Overcoming Objections

Buyers state objections for numerous reasons. From time to time, all salespeople sense that a buyer will not buy. As you gain sales experience, you will be able to feel it. It may be the buyer's facial expressions or a tone of voice that tips you off. When this occurs, find out quickly why a prospect doesn't want to buy. To do this, consider using a preplanned series of questions as shown in Exhibit 11.9.

EXHIBIT 11.9

Five-question sequence method of overcoming objection.

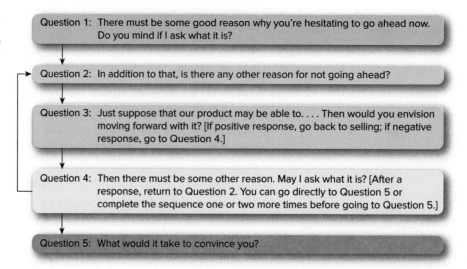

Question 1: There must be some good reason why you're hesitating to go ahead now. Do you mind if I ask what it is?

Question 2: In addition to that, is there any other reason for not going ahead?

Question 3: Just suppose that our product may be able to. . . . Then would you envision moving forward with it? [If positive response, go back to selling; if negative response, go to Question 4.]

Question 4: Then there must be some other reason. May I ask what it is? [After a response, return to Question 2. You can go directly to Question 5 or complete the sequence one or two more times before going to Question 5.]

Question 5: What would it take to convince you?

Let's assume you have finished the presentation. You try to close the sale and see that the buyer will not go further in the conversation. What do you do? Consider using the following **five-question sequence.**

First, use this question: "There must be some good reason why you're hesitating to go ahead now; do you mind if I ask what it is?" When the buyer states a reason or an objection, immediately double-check the objection with one more question by using question number two: "In addition to that, is there any other reason for not going ahead?" The buyer may give the real reason for not buying, or the buyer may give the original objection. No matter what the customer says, you have created a condition for buying.

Now, use question number three, a "just suppose" question: "Just suppose you could. . . . Then you'd want to go ahead?" If the answer is yes, discuss how you can do what is needed. If you receive a negative response, use question number four: "Then there must be some other reason. May I ask what it is?" Respond with question number two again. Then ask, "Just suppose. . . . You'd want to go ahead?" If you receive another negative response, use question number five by saying, "What would it take to convince you?"

What often happens will surprise you. The buyer often will say, "Oh, I don't know. I guess I'm convinced. Go ahead and ship it to me." Or, you might be asked to go back over some part of your presentation. The important point is that this series of questions keeps the conversation going and reveals the real objections, which increases your sales. Imagine you are the salesperson in this example:

> "Just suppose you could convince yourself that. . . . Then would you want to go ahead with it?"

Salesperson: Should we ship the product to you this week or next?

Buyer: Neither; see me on your next trip. I'll have to think about it.

Salesperson: You know, there must be some good reason why you're hesitating to go ahead now. Would you mind if I asked what it is? [Question 1.]

Buyer: Too much money.

Salesperson: Too much money. Well, you know, I appreciate the fact that you want to get the most for your money. In addition to the money, is there any other reason for not going ahead? [Question 2.]

Buyer: No.

Salesperson: Well, suppose that you could convince yourself that the savings from this machine would mean it pays for itself in just a few months, and that we could fit it into your budget. Then you'd want to go ahead with it? [Question 3.]

Buyer: Yes, I would.

Now, return to selling by discussing the return on investment and affordable payment terms. You went from the first objection to the double-check question. ("In addition to the money, is there any other reason for not going ahead?") Then, you used the just suppose question. You met the condition, the machine's cost. Then, you used the convince question. The buyer said yes, so you can keep selling. Now, let's role-play as if the buyer had said no. (Again, you are the salesperson.)

Buyer: No, I wouldn't go ahead.

Salesperson: Well, then there must be some other reason why you're hesitating to go ahead now. Do you mind if I ask what it is? [Question 4.]

Buyer: It takes too much time to train my employees in using the machine.

Salesperson: Well, you know, I appreciate that. Time is money. In addition to the time, is there any other reason for not going ahead? [Question 2.]

Buyer: Not really.

Salesperson: Suppose that you could convince yourself that this machine would save employees time so that they could do other things. You'd find the money then, wouldn't you? [Question 3.]

Buyer: I'm not sure. [Another potential negative response.]

Salesperson: Money and time are important to you, right?

Buyer: Yes, they are.

Salesperson: What would it take for me to convince you that this machine will save you time and money? [Question 5.]

Now you have to get a response. The buyer has to set the condition. You, as the salesperson, are uncovering the real needs. The buyer is answering the questions. Remember, you want to help the person buy. When you get an objection, it tells you what you must do to make the sale happen. So do not fear objections; welcome them!

Rephrase an Objection as a Question

Since it is easier to answer a question than to overcome an objection, counter an objection with a **rephrasing question** when you can do so naturally. Most objections are easily rephrased. Exhibit 11.10 presents examples of several procedures for rephrasing an objection as a question. Each procedure, except when the objection is based on a bad previous experience with the product by the prospect, has the same first three steps: (1) acknowledging the prospect's viewpoint, (2) rephrasing the objection into a question, and (3) obtaining agreement on the question. Here is an example:

Buyer: I don't know—your price is higher than your competitors'.

Salesperson: I can appreciate that. You want to know what particular benefits my product has that make it worth its slightly higher price. [Or, What you're saying is that you want to get the best product for your money.] Is that correct?

Buyer: Yes, that's right.

EXHIBIT 11.10

Examples of rephrasing objections as questions.

Facts Are Incorrect	Facts Are Incomplete	Facts Are Correct	Based on Bad Personal Experience
■ Acknowledge prospect's viewpoint.	■ Acknowledge prospect's viewpoint.	■ Acknowledge prospect's viewpoint.	■ Thank prospect for telling you.
■ Rephrase objection.	■ Rephrase objection.	■ Rephrase objection.	■ Acknowledge prospect's viewpoint.
■ Obtain agreement.	■ Obtain agreement.	■ Obtain agreement.	■ Rephrase objection.
■ Answer question providing information supported by proof—a third party.	■ Answer question by providing complete facts.	■ Answer question; outweigh it with benefits.	■ Obtain agreement.
■ Ask for prospect's present viewpoint.	■ Ask for prospect's present viewpoint.	■ Ask for a present viewpoint.	■ Answer question.
■ Return to selling sequence.	■ Return to selling sequence.	■ Return to selling sequence.	■ Return to selling sequence.

Now discuss product benefits versus price. After doing so, attempt a trial close by asking for the prospect's viewpoint to see if you have overcome the objection.

Salesperson: Do you see how the benefits of this product make it worth the price? [Trial close.]

A variation of this sequence is sales training consultant Bruce Scagel's Feel-Felt-Found method, where he first acknowledges the prospect's viewpoint, saying, "John, I understand how you *feel.* Bill at XYZ store *felt* the same way, but he *found,* after reviewing our total program of products and services, that he would profit by buying now."

Scagel refers to rephrasing the objection to a question as his Isolate and Gain Commitment method. He gives as an example: "Mary, as I understand it, your only objection to our program is the following. . . . If I can solve this problem, then I'll assume that you will be prepared to accept our program."

Scagel knows that he can solve the problem or he would not have asked the question. When Mary says yes, he has isolated the main problem. He is not handling an objection; he is answering a question. He now shows her how to overcome the problem and then continues selling. If Mary says no, Bruce knows he has not isolated her main objection. He must start over in uncovering her objections. He might say, "Well, I guess I misunderstood. Exactly what is the question?" And now, when Mary responds, it usually will be a question. "Well, the question was about. . . ." Involve the customer and find out what is happening internally. You can do this with the proper use of questions.

Compensate for the Objection

Sometimes a prospect's objection is valid and calls for the **compensation method.** Several reasons for buying must exist to justify or compensate for a negative aspect of making a purchase. For example, a higher product price is justified by benefits such as better service or higher performance. In the following example, it is true that the prospect can make more profit on each unit of a competing product. You must develop a technique to show how your product has benefits that will bring the prospect more profit in the long run.

Prospect: I can make 5 percent more profit with the Stainless line of cookware, and it is quality merchandise.

Salesperson: Yes, you are right. The Stainless cookware is quality merchandise. However, you can have an exclusive distributorship on the Supreme cookware line, and still have high-quality merchandise. You don't have to worry about Supreme being discounted by nearby competitors as you do with Stainless. This will be the only store in town carrying Supreme. What do you think? [Trial close.]

If the advantages presented to counterbalance the objection are important to the buyer, you have an opportunity to make the sale.

Boomerang the Objection

Always be ready to turn an objection into a reason to buy. By convincing the prospect that an objection is a benefit, you have turned the buyer immediately in favor of your product. This is the heart of the **boomerang method.** Take, for example, the wholesale drug salesperson working for a pharmaceutical firm, who is selling a pharmacist a new container for prescription medicines. Handling the container, the prospect says:

Prospect: They look nice, but I don't like them as well as my others. The tops seem hard to remove.

Salesperson: Yes, they are hard to remove. We designed them so that children couldn't get into the medicine. Isn't that a great safety measure? [Trial close.]

Be Positive in Discussing Price

All prospects are sensitive to how price is presented. This is a typical list of negative and positive ways to deal with price issues during the business proposition phase:

Negative Words:

- This costs $2,300.
- Your down payment . . .
- Your monthly payment . . .
- You can pay the purchase price over a series of months.
- How much would you like to pay us every month?
- We'll charge you two points above the prime rate.
- We'll take off $6,700 to trade in your used equipment.

Positive Words:

- This is only $2,300.
- Your initial investment . . .
- Your monthly investment . . .
- We would be happy to divide this investment into small monthly shares.
- What monthly investment would you feel comfortable with?
- Your rate will be only prime plus two.
- We are offering you $6,700 to trade your existing equipment.

Or, consider the industrial equipment salesperson who is unaware that a customer is extremely dissatisfied with a present product:

Prospect: I have been using your portable generators and do not want to use them anymore.

Salesperson: Why?

Prospect: Well, the fuses kept blowing out and causing delays in completing this project! So get out of here and take your worthless generators with you.

Salesperson: [with a smile] Thank you for telling me. Say, you and our company's design engineers have a lot in common.

Prospect: Oh yeah? I'll bet! [Sarcastically.]

Salesperson: Suppose you were chief engineer in charge of manufacturing our generators. What would you do if valued customers—like yourself—said your generators had problems?

Prospect: I'd throw them in the trash.

Salesperson: Come on, what would you really do? [With a smile.]

Prospect: Well, I would fix it.

Salesperson: That's why I said you and our design engineers have a lot in common. They acted on your suggestion—don't you think? [Trial close.]

You have used reverse psychology. Now, the prospect is listening, giving you time to explain your product's new features and to make an offer to repair the old units. You are ready to sell more products, if possible.

Another example is the industrial salesperson who responds to the prospect's high price objection by saying, "Well, that's the very reason you should buy it." The prospect was caught off guard and quickly asked, "What do you mean?" "Well," said the salesperson, "for just 10 percent more, you can buy the type of equipment you really want and need. It is dependable, safe, and simple to operate. Your production will increase so that you will pay back the price differential quickly." The prospect said, "Well, I hadn't thought of it quite like that. I guess I'll buy it after all."

Boomeranging an objection requires good timing and quick thinking. Experience in a particular selling field, knowledge of your prospect's needs, a positive attitude, and a willingness to stand up to the objection are necessary attributes for successful use of this technique.

Postpone the Objection

Often, the prospect may skip ahead of you in the sales presentation by asking questions that you address later in the presentation. (See Exhibit 11.11.) If you judge that your customary method will handle the objection to your prospect's satisfaction, and that the prospect is willing to wait until later in the presentation, you politely **postpone the objection.** Five examples of postponing objections are

Prospect: Your price is too high.

Salesperson: In just a minute, I'll show you why this product is reasonably priced, based on the savings you will receive compared to what you presently do. That's what you're interested in, savings, right? [Trial close.]

or

Salesperson: Well, it may sound like a lot of money. But let's consider the final price when we know the model you need. OK? [Trial close.]

or

Salesperson: There are several ways we can handle your costs. If it's all right, let's discuss them in just a minute. [Pause. This has the same effect as the trial close. If there is no response, continue.] First, I want to show you. . . .

EXHIBIT 11.11

Suppose you show your prospect your business proposition, and the prospect asks, "How much does this software cost?" What would you say?

©Xavier Arnau/Getty Images

or

Salesperson: I'm glad you brought that up [or, I was hoping you would want to know that] because we want to carefully examine the cost in just a minute. OK? [Trial close.]

or

Salesperson: High? Why, in a minute I'll show you why it's the best buy on the market. In fact, I'll bet you a Coke that you will believe it's a great deal for your company! Is it a deal? [Trial close.]

Tactfully used, postponing can leave you in control of the presentation. Normally, respond to the objection immediately. However, occasionally it is not appropriate to address the objection. This is usually true for the price objection. Price is the primary objection to postpone if you have not had the opportunity to discuss product benefits. If you have discussed the product fully, then respond to the price objection immediately.

Dodge the Objection

Central Michigan University students in Professor Dean Kortge's personal selling class created a communication technique for handling a sales objection. Here's how. When the buyer said, "I think your price is a little high," Scott Dodge replied, "Before you decide to buy let me tell you about the value that goes with this product." It is called the **dodge** because the salesperson neither denies, answers, nor ignores the objection, but simply temporarily dodges it.

Notice how the phrase is structured in a positive manner: "Before you decide to buy. . . ." This positive communication technique now allows the seller to effectively make a smooth transition into a proper response to the buyer. Done in a calm, natural manner it is a very professional technique.

You can use the dodge by itself or in combination with one of the other techniques, such as the pass up, rephrase, postpone, boomerang, or third party. As you study the following objection handling techniques, see if you could first use the phrase "Before you decide to buy. . . ." You would use it only once in a presentation.

Pass Up an Objection

Occasionally, you may have a prospect raise an objection or make a statement that requires not addressing it. After introducing yourself, for example, a prospect may say, "I'm really not interested in a service such as yours."

You have two options. First, you can say, "Well, if you ever do, here is my card. Give me a call." Or second, you could take the **pass up** approach used by top salespeople and say something that allows you to move into your presentation, such as immediately using the customer benefit approach or simply asking "Can you explain to me your concerns?"

As you gain selling experience, you will be confident in knowing when to pass or to stop and respond to the objection. If you pass up an objection and the prospect raises it again, then treat this as an important objection. Use your questioning skills to uncover the prospect's concerns.

Indirectly Deny the Objection

An **indirect denial** is different from a direct denial in that it initially appears as an agreement with the customer's objection but then moves into a denial of the fundamental issue in the objection. The difference between the direct denial and the indirect denial is that the indirect denial is softer, more tactful, and more courteous. Use the direct denial judiciously, only to disconfirm especially damaging misinformation.

The typical example of indirect denial is the "yes, but" phrase. Here are several examples:

- Yes, but would you agree that it takes information, not time, to make a decision? What kind of information are you really looking for to make a good decision?
- I agree. Our price is a little higher, but so is our quality. Are you interested in saving $1,200 a year on maintenance?
- Sure, it costs a little more. However, you will have the assurance that it will cost much less over its lifetime. Isn't that the way your own products are made?
- Your point is well taken. It does cost more than any other product on the market. But why do you think we sell millions of them at this price?
- I appreciate how you feel. Many of our customers made similar comments prior to buying from me. However, they all asked themselves: "Can I afford not to have the best? Won't it cost me more in the long run?"

The indirect denial begins with an agreement or an acknowledgment of the prospect's position: Yes, but; I agree; Sure; Your point is well taken; and, I appreciate how you feel. These phrases allow the salesperson to tactfully respond to the objection. Done in a natural, conversational way, the salesperson will not offend the prospect.

Try this yourself: when a friend says something you disagree with, instead of saying, "I don't agree," say something like "I see what you mean. However, there's another way to look at it." See if this, as well as the other communication skills you have studied, helps you to better sell yourself—and your product.

Directly Deny the Objection

You will face objections that are often incomplete or incorrect. Acknowledge the prospect's viewpoint; then answer the question by providing the complete or correct facts:

Prospect: No, I'm not going to buy any of your lawn mowers for my store. The Bigs-Weaver salesperson said they break down after a few months.

Salesperson: Well, I can understand. No one would buy mowers that don't hold up. Is that the only reason you won't buy?

Prospect: Yes, it is, and that's enough!

Salesperson: The BW salesperson was not aware of the facts, I'm afraid. My company produces the finest lawn mowers in the industry. In fact, we are so sure of our quality that we have a new three-year guarantee on all parts and labor. [Pause.]

Prospect: I didn't know that. [Positive buying signal.]

Salesperson: Are you interested in selling your customers quality lawn mowers like these? [Trial close.]

Prospect: Yes, I am. [Appears that you have overcome the objection.]

Salesperson: Well, I'd like to sell you 100 lawn mowers. If even one breaks down, call me and I'll come over and repair it. [Close.]

As you see by this example, you do not say, "Well, you so-and-so, why do you say a thing like that?" Tact is critical in using a direct denial. A sarcastic or arrogant response can alienate a prospect. However, a **direct denial** based on facts, logic, and politeness can effectively overcome the objection.

A mind once stretched by a new idea never regains its original dimensions.

If I say to you, "You're wrong. Let me tell you why," what happens to your mind? It closes! So, if I tell you that you are wrong and this closes your mind, what would I have to tell you to open your mind? That you are right! But, if what you said was wrong, do I tell you it was right? No, instead, do what the example illustrated by saying, "You know, you're right to be concerned about this. Let me explain." You have made the buyer right and kept the buyer's mind open. Also, you could say, "You know, my best customer had those same feelings until I explained that. . . ." You have made the customer right.

After Meeting the Objection—What to Do?

As shown in Exhibit 11.12, your prospect has raised an objection that you have answered and overcome; now what? First, as shown in Exhibit 11.13, use a trial close; then either return to your presentation or close the sale.

EXHIBIT 11.12

Imagine you are this salesperson and you just answered an objection. What should you do now?

©Amble Design/Shutterstock

EXHIBIT 11.13

The procedure to follow when a prospect raises an objection.

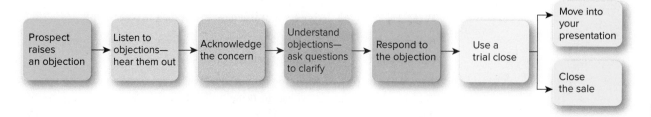

Prospect raises an objection → Listen to objections—hear them out → Acknowledge the concern → Understand objections—ask questions to clarify → Respond to the objection → Use a trial close → Move into your presentation / Close the sale

You are a salesperson for a large, national company that publishes and sells college textbooks. Three days ago you talked with Dr. Bush, the department head, about adopting one of your books in a sophomore course of 2,000 students. He said the book is a good one but there were three others that were just as good.

Before leaving, Dr. Bush said the department would use your book if the publisher donates $1,000 and provides a new computer and printer to the English department. You tell your boss about this and she says, "Do it, but keep it quiet so none of your other schools hear of it. This will be a $100,000 sale. The home office will approve this expense if we don't do it for too many schools."

What would be the most ethical action to take?

1. Tell your boss that you do not think that the situation is fair but go ahead and do it anyway—it is ultimately her call in the end.
2. Tell your boss that you are uncomfortable making that type of sale and that you no longer want to be involved. It is not only unfair to your customers but also unfair to you by asking you to keep it quiet.
3. Go ahead—take the sale and donate the computer and the money.

First, Use a Trial Close—Ask for Opinion

After meeting an objection at any time during the interview, you need to know if you have overcome the objection. If you have not overcome it, your prospect may raise it again. Whether it resurfaces or not, if your prospect believes that an objection was important, your failure to handle it, or your mishandling of it, will probably cost you the sale. Ideally, all objections raised should be met before closing the sale. So, after responding to the objection, use a trial close to determine if you have overcome the objection. Remember, open-ended trial closes provide an opportunity for customer feedback. A few examples are provided:

- Does this help clarify your concern? Are there any other concerns in this area I can address?
- Are there any additional areas that we haven't covered?
- With that question out of the way, would it be acceptable to continue?
- Have we adequately covered the question you raised and given you a way to handle it? Are there any concerns we've missed?
- Now that's settled entirely, isn't it?
- That solves your problem, doesn't it?

Once you have confirmed overcoming an objection, immediately go to the next SELL Sequence step. To signal that the last step is over, and that you are moving on, use body language as you speak. That is, make an appropriate gesture, look in a new direction, turn the page of your proposal, or shift in your chair—make some physical movement. Now, do one of two things (assuming you have handled the objection): either return to your presentation or close the sale.

Move Back into Your Presentation

When you have answered and overcome an objection, make a smooth transition back into your presentation. As you nonverbally signal that the last step is over, let the

423

prospect know you are returning to your presentation with a phrase such as, "As we were discussing earlier." Now, you can continue the presentation.

Move to Close Your Sale

If you had finished your presentation when the prospect raised an objection, and the prospect's response to your trial close indicates that you overcame an objection, your next move is to close the sale. If the objection was raised during your close, then it is time to close again.

As you move on to the close with a gesture, you might summarize benefits discussed previously with a phrase such as, "Well, as we have discussed, you really like. . . ." Then, again ask the prospect for the order. Chapter 13 gives you other ideas on how to ask for the order.

If You Cannot Overcome the Objection

If you cannot overcome an objection or close a sale because of an objection, be prepared to return to your presentation and concentrate on new or previously discussed features, advantages, and benefits of your product. If you determine that the objection your prospect raises is a major one that cannot be overcome, admit it, and show how your product's benefits outweigh this disadvantage.

If you are 100 percent sure that you cannot overcome the objection and that the prospect will not buy, go ahead and close. *Always ask for the order.* Never be afraid to ask your prospect to buy. The buyer says no to the product—not you. Someone else may walk into the prospect's office after you with a product similar to yours. Your competitor also may not be able to overcome this person's objection, but he or she may get the sale nonetheless just by asking for it!

SUMMARY OF MAJOR SELLING ISSUES

People want to buy, but they do not want to be misled, so they often ask questions or raise objections during a sales presentation. Your responsibility is to be prepared to logically and clearly respond to your prospect's objections whenever they arise.

Sales objections indicate a prospect's opposition or resistance to the information or request of the salesperson. Basic points to consider in meeting objections are to (1) plan for them, (2) anticipate and forestall them, (3) handle them as they arise, (4) listen to what is said, (5) respond warmly and positively, (6) make sure you understand, and (7) respond using an effective communication technique.

Before you can successfully meet objections, determine if the prospect's response to your statement or close is a request for more information, a condition of the sale, or an objection. If it is a real objection, determine whether it is minor or major. Respond to it using a trial close, and if you have answered it successfully, continue your presentation based on where you are in the sales presentation. For example, if you are still in the presentation, then return to your selling sequence. If you have completed the presentation, move to your close. If you are in the close and the prospect voices an objection, then you must decide whether to use another close or return to the presentation and discuss additional benefits.

Be aware of and plan for objection. Objections are classified as hidden, stalling, no-need, money, product, and source objections. Develop several techniques to help overcome each type of objection, such as stalling the objection, turning the objection into a benefit, asking questions to smoke out hidden objections, denying the objection if appropriate, illustrating how product benefits outweigh the objection drawbacks, and developing proof statements that answer the objection.

Welcome your prospect's objections. They help you determine if you are on the right track to uncover prospects' needs and if they believe your product will fulfill those needs. Valid objections are beneficial for you and the customer. A true objection reveals the customer's need, which allows a salesperson to demonstrate how a product can meet that need. Objections also show inadequacies in a salesperson's presentation or product knowledge. Finally, objections make selling a skill that a person can improve constantly. Over time, a dedicated salesperson can learn how to handle every conceivable product objection—tactfully, honestly, and to the customer's benefit.

Quick Review for Students

The quick review sections provide key questions to help you develop a greater level of conceptual understanding. We suggest that after you read the chapter, you try to answer the following questions without looking back at the textbook.

1. What is a sales objection?
2. Why should salespeople welcome objections?
3. What are the key points to consider in meeting sales objections and why?
4. What are the six major categories of sales objections?
5. What are the key techniques for meeting sales objections?
6. What are the logical steps a salesperson should take immediately after meeting the objection?

MEETING A SALES CHALLENGE

Before handling an objection, it's important to find out what the *exact* objection is. Is price a stall or bona fide reason for changing suppliers? Is the competitor's cheaper price attractive, or does the problem exist with the salesperson and the possible inability to sell a high-priced line? There could be many problems, so before you answer the objection, do some probing and find out what the real one is. A good question would be, "Would you mind telling me exactly why you're considering this move?" Then continue to probe until you totally understand the buyer's reasoning for wanting to change suppliers.

Listen carefully to what the buyer says. This person may be a tough negotiator wanting to see if you will lower your prices. Nonnie Young may be happy with your prices.

KEY TERMS FOR SELLING

boomerang method 417	intelligent questions 414	psychological
compensation method 417	money objection 407	objection 402
condition of the sale 401	negotiation 401	rephrasing question 416
direct denial 421	no-need objection 406	sales objection 394
dodge 420	pass up 420	source objection 410
five-question sequence 414	postpone the objection 419	stalling objection 404
hidden objection 403	practical objection 410	third-party answer 413
indirect denial 420	product objection 410	

SALES APPLICATION QUESTIONS

1. Halfway through your sales presentation, your prospect stops you and says, "That sounds like a great deal and you certainly have a good product, but I'm not interested now; maybe later." What should you do?

2. Assume you are a sales engineer for a cloud computing company. You have finished your presentation, and the purchasing agent for a big oil firm says, "Well, that sounds real good and you do have the lowest price I have ever heard of from a cloud computing vendor. In fact, it's $200,000 less than the other bids. But we have decided to stay with our current supplier, mainly because $200,000 on a $1 million system is not that much money to us." Let's further assume that you also know that other than price, their current supplier has significant advantages in all areas over your service. What would you do?

3. When a customer is not receptive to your product, there is some objection. In each of the following situations, the customer has an objection to a product:
   a. The customer assumes she must buy the whole set of books. However, partial purchases are permitted.
   b. The customer does not like the color and it's the only color your product comes in.
   c. The customer doesn't want to invest in a new set of books because she doesn't want to lose money on her old set. You have not told her yet about your trade-in deal.

   In which of these situations does the objection arise from a misunderstanding or lack of knowledge on the customer's part? In which situation(s) does the product fail to offer a benefit that the customer considers important?

4. Which response is best when you hear the customer reply, "I'd like to think it over"? Why?
   a. Give all the benefits of using the product now.
   b. If there is a penalty for delaying, mention it now.
   c. If there is a special-price deal available, mention it now.
   d. None of the above is appropriate.
   e. Depending on the circumstances, the first three choices are appropriate.

5. Cliff Jamison sells business forms and he's regarded as a top-notch salesperson. He works hard, plans ahead, and exhibits self-confidence. One day, he made his first presentation to a prospective new client, the California Steel Company.

   "Ladies and gentlemen," said Jamison, "our forms are of the highest quality, yet they are priced below our competitor's forms. I know that you are a large user of business forms and that you use a wide variety. Whatever your need for business forms, I assure you that we can supply them. Our forms are noted for their durability. They can run through your machines at 60 per minute and they'll perform perfectly."

   "Perfectly, Mr. Jamison?" asked the California Steel executive. "Didn't you have some trouble at Ogden's last year?"

   "Oh," replied Jamison, "that wasn't the fault of our forms. They had a stupid operator who didn't follow instructions. I assure you that if our instructions are followed precisely you will have no trouble.

   "Furthermore, we keep a large inventory of our forms so that you need never worry about delays. A phone call to our office is all that is necessary to ensure prompt delivery of the needed forms to your plant. I hope, therefore, that I can be favored with your order."

   Did Jamison handle this situation correctly? Why?

6. One of your customers, Margaret Port, has referred you to a friend who needs your Hercules Shelving for a storage warehouse. Port recently purchased your heavy-duty, 18-gauge steel shelving and is pleased with it. She said, "This will be an easy sale for you. My friend really needs shelving and I told him about yours."

Port's information is correct and your presentation to her friend goes smoothly. The customer has asked numerous questions and seems ready to buy. Just before you ask for the order, the customer says, "Looks like your product is exactly what I need. I'd like to think this over. Could you call me next week?" Which of the following would you do? Why?

a. Follow the suggestion and call next week.
b. Go ahead and ask for the order.
c. Ask questions about the reason for the delay.

FURTHER EXPLORING THE SALES WORLD

1. A national sales company is at your school wishing to hire salespeople. What are some objections that such a company might have toward hiring you? How would you overcome them during a job interview?
2. Visit three different types of business (such as a grocery store, a hardware store, and an apparel retailer), and pick out one product from each business. If you were that store's buyer, think of the major objections or questions you would ask a product salesperson if you were asked to buy a large quantity and promote it. Now, as that salesperson, how would you overcome those objections?

STUDENT APPLICATION LEARNING EXERCISES (SALES)

Sales objections are defined as opposition or resistance from the buyer. To make **SALE 6**

SALE 6 of 7—Chapter 11

1. List three objections a buyer might give you. See examples of various types of objections on page 403. Make certain you use objections that relate to your product. Do not use general objections, such as "I do not like it." The objection should be specific, such as "I do not like the color."

   Objection 1:

   Objection 2:

   Objection 3:

2. Now, write the actual process (i.e.. dialogue) for handling each of the above objections. The process and examples for handling objections are on Exhibits 11.3 and 11.13, pages 399 and 422, respectively.

   Dialogue 1: _____

   Dialogue 2: _____

   Dialogue 3: _____

3. Write the buyer–seller dialogue for each objection. State the buyer's objection and then your response to it. Each time you respond to an objection use a trial close (see page 423) to determine if you have overcome the objection or correctly answered the buyer's concern or question. After your trial close, label it using parentheses (Trial Close).

Buyer's objection 1:

Your response:

Buyer's objection 2:

Your response:

Buyer's objection 3:

Your response:

Role-play the buyer giving you the above objections and your responses. If possible, use a tape recorder to play back the dialogue. Does what you say sound natural and conversational to you? If not, adjust it. If it does, go with it.

NOTES

1. Adapted from Tom Hopkins, *How to Master the Art of Selling* (New York: Warner Books, 1994), p. 191.

CASE 11.1

Ace Building Supplies

©Ron Chapple Stock/FotoSearch/
Glow Images

This is your fourth call on Ace Building Supplies to motivate them to sell your home building supplies to local builders. Joe Newland, the buyer, gives every indication that he likes your products.

During the call, Joe reaffirms his liking for your products and attempts to end the interview by saying: "We'll be ready to do business with you in three months—right after this slow season ends. Stop by then, and we'll place an order with you."

Questions

1. Which one of the following steps would you take? Why?
   a. Call back in three months to get the order as suggested.
   b. Try to get a firm commitment or order now.
   c. Telephone Joe in a month (rather than make a personal visit) and try to get the order.
2. Why did you not choose the other two alternatives?

©Ron Chapple Stock/FotoSearch/
Glow Images

Electric Generator Corporation (B)

George Wynn is a salesperson for EGC whose primary responsibility is to contact engineers in charge of constructing commercial buildings. One such engineer is Don Snyder, who is in charge of building the new Ivy College of Business facility at Iowa State University. Don's Des Moines-based engineering firm purchased three new EGI portable generators for this project. George learned that Don's company will build four more buildings on the Iowa State University campus, and he felt that Don might buy more machines.

Salesperson: Don, I understand you have three of our new model electric generators.

Buyer: Yeah, you're not kidding.

Salesperson: I'm sure you'll need additional units on these new jobs.

Buyer: Yeah, we sure will.

Salesperson: I've gone over the building's proposed floor plans and put together the type of products you need.

Buyer: They buy down in Des Moines; you need to see them!

Salesperson: I was just in there yesterday, and they said it was up to you.

Buyer: Well, I'm busy today.

Salesperson: Can I see you tomorrow?

Buyer: No need; I don't want any more of your lousy generators!

Salesperson: What do you mean? That is our most modern design!

Buyer: Those so-called new fuses of yours are exploding after five minutes' use. The autotransformer starter won't start. . . . Did you see the lights dim? That's another fuse blowing.

Questions

George Wynn feels pressured to sell the new EGI. Don Snyder's business represents an important sale both now and in the future. If you were George, what would you do?

1. Have EGC's best engineer contact Don to explain the generator's capabilities.
2. Come back after Don has cooled down.
3. Get Don to talk about problems and then solve them.

©Monkey Business Images/Shutterstock

Closing Begins the Relationship

Main Topics

The Core Principles: Closing

When Should I Pop the Question?

Reading Buying Signals

What Makes a Good Closer?

How Many Times Should You Close?

Closing Under Fire

Difficulties with Closing

Essentials of Closing Sales

Get Ready for Closing

Closing Techniques

Prepare a Multiple-Close Sequence

Research Reinforces These Sales Success Strategies

Keys to Improved Selling

Closing Begins the Relationship

When You Do Not Make the Sale

Learning Objectives

If everything has been done to properly develop and give a sales presentation, then closing the sale is the easiest step in the presentation. After studying this chapter, you should be able to

12–1 Explain when to close.

12–2 Describe what to do if your prospect asks for more information, gives an objection, or says no when you ask for the order.

12–3 Explain why you must prepare to close more than once.

12–4 Present, illustrate, and use several techniques for closing the sale in your presentation.

12–5 Construct a multiple-close sequence.

12–6 Discuss the 12 keys to a successful close.

FACING A SALES CHALLENGE

John made his presentation for in-office coffee service to the office manager. As he neared the end of it, the office manager asked, "What's your price?" John quoted the standard price, and immediately the manager said, "Way out—your competitor's price is $10 cheaper!"

As Lisa, who represented a medical laboratory equipment company, finished her presentation, the pathologist asked her about the cost. She stated the list price and heard, "Your price is too high. I can get the same type of equipment for a lot less."

Ralph, selling a line of office copying machines, was only halfway through his presentation when the director of administration asked for the cost. When Ralph quoted the price on the top-of-the-line model, the administrator closed off the interview with the familiar phrase, "Your price is too high."

John, Lisa, and Ralph are facing a real challenge. Their buyers said, "Your price is too high," indirectly saying, "No, I'm not interested." In each situation, what would you do now?

This chapter wraps up our discussion of the main sales presentation elements. We discuss when to close, showing examples of buying signals and discussing what makes a good closer. Next we discuss the number of times you should attempt to close a sale, along with some problems associated with closing. A range of closing techniques is presented, followed by an explanation of the importance of being prepared to close several times based on the situation.

To be a good closer, you must be able to handle objections. Objections frequently arise as the salesperson nears the end of the presentation, as in the case of John, and after the close, as Lisa experienced. However, as Ralph found out, price objection can pop up anytime. This chapter and the previous chapters on objections will help you solve the "Sales Challenge" above.

The Core Principles: Closing

You have spent hours preparing your sales presentation. The discussion of your product, marketing plan, and business proposition went well. You feel it is now time to ask the person to buy. Before you ask someone to buy, you should answer an important question: "Should the person buy this product?" The traditional salesperson will sell it to the person even if she or he does not need it (refer back to Exhibit 1.2). The professional salesperson would like to know if this product fulfills the need or solves the problem. If not, the salesperson may say something like "You may know something I do not, Mr. Buyer, but it does not appear this product is what you need." The buyer may reply, "I feel it fits my needs, I want to buy." Would you believe a very small number of salespeople would not sell the product to the person? Most people would. What would you do? A book cannot say what to do in all situations, since all facts are not known. You are asked to remember the purpose of contacting the customer in making your decision.

Take a look at the title of this chapter. Let's say you close the sale and the person buys. Soon the buyer will know if what you said is true. Will the correct product be received on time at the agreed-upon price? Will the product do what you promised? Your relationship begins with this first sale and continues on into the future.

Have you had someone you trusted lie to you? Have you had someone you trusted cheat you? Why did the person lie or cheat you? How did it make you feel? It is hard to forgive, isn't it? Well, in industry you lie and lose the sale, maybe your job, and possibly go to jail. But some people use unethical practices to sell—usually motivated by greed. They are hopeful of not getting caught. But in the end the customer wins!

In closing, it is extremely important to think about the purpose of the sales call—unselfish service to the other person. Placing the other person's interest first builds long-term relationships. The question is, "When should you pop the question?"

When Should I Pop the Question?

Closing is the process of helping people make a decision that will benefit them. In effect, closing is the process of facilitating a decision by the buyer. In some instances, you help people make the decision by asking them to buy. In other instances, you ask them to serve as your advocate and set a meeting with another decision-maker, such as a chief financial officer or senior leader. As successful salespeople know, there are no magic phrases and techniques to use in closing a sale. It is the end result of your presentation. If everything has been done to properly develop a sales presentation, closing the sale is the next step in a logical sequence.

Although it seems obvious, some salespeople forget that prospects know that the salesperson is there to sell them something. So, as soon as they meet, the prospect's mind already may have progressed beyond the major portion of the salesperson's presentation. At times, the prospect may be ready to make the buying decision early in the interview.

So when should you attempt to close a sale? Simply, *when the prospect is ready!* More specifically, when the prospect is in the conviction stage of the mental buying process. A buyer can enter the conviction stage at any time during the sales presentation. As Exhibit 12.1 shows, you might ask someone to buy as early as the approach stage or as late as another day. Much of the time, however, the close comes after the presentation. The ability to read a prospect's buying signals correctly helps a salesperson decide when and how to close a sale.

> *Closing is about helping the buyer with a decision point.*

Reading Buying Signals

After prospects negotiate each stage of the mental buying process and are ready to buy, they often give you a signal. A **buying signal** refers to anything that prospects say or do indicating they are ready to buy. Buying signals hint that prospects are in the conviction stage of the buying process. Prospective buyers signal readiness to buy when they

- **Ask questions—**"How much is it?" "What is the earliest time that I can receive it?" "What are your service and returned goods policies?" At times, you may respond to a buying signal question with another question, as Exhibit 12.2

EXHIBIT 12.1

Close when the prospect is ready.

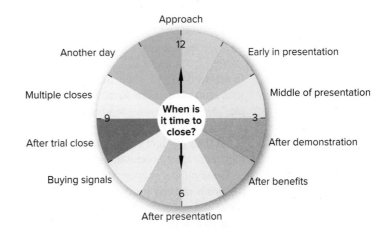

EXHIBIT 12.2

Answering a prospect's buying signal question with a question.

Buyer Says:	Salesperson Replies:
■ What's your price?	■ Can you share with me the quantity that you were considering?
■ What kind of terms do you offer?	■ What are the typical terms that your vendors provide your firm?
■ When can you make delivery?	■ When do you want delivery?
■ What size copier should I buy?	■ How many copies do you make during the year?
■ Can I get this special price on orders placed now and next month?	■ Would you like to split your shipment?
■ Do you carry 8-, 12-, 36-, and 54-foot pipe?	■ Are those the sizes you commonly use?
■ How large an order must I place to receive your best price?	■ What size order do you have in mind?
■ Do you have Model 6400 in stock?	■ Is that the one you like best?

shows. This helps determine your prospect's thoughts and needs. If your question is answered positively, the prospect is showing a high interest level and you are nearing the close.

■ **Ask another person's opinion**—The executive calls someone on the telephone and says, "Come in here a minute; I have something to ask you." Or the wife turns to her spouse and asks, "What do you think about it?"

■ **Relax and become friendly**—Once the prospect decides to purchase a product, the pressure of the buying situation is eliminated. A state of visible anxiety changes to relaxation because your new customer believes that you are a friend.

■ **Pull out a purchase order form**—If, as you talk, your prospect pulls out an order form, it is time to move toward the close.

■ **Carefully examine merchandise**—When a prospect carefully scrutinizes your product or seems to contemplate the purchase, this may be an indirect request for prompting. Given these indications, attempt a trial close: "What do you think about . . .?" If you obtain a positive response to this question, move on to close the sale.

■ **Display positive body language**—The buyer may use positive nonverbal communication. This may include leaning forward, smiling, or nodding her head.

> *Ask and people will buy.*

A buyer may send verbal or nonverbal buying signals at any time before or during your sales presentation (remember Exhibit 12.1). The accurate interpretation of buying signals should prompt you to attempt a trial close.

What Makes a Good Closer?

In every sales force, some individuals are better than others at closing sales. Some persons rationalize this difference of abilities by saying, "It comes naturally to some people," or, "They've just got what it takes." Well, what does it take to be a good closer?

Good closers have a strong desire to close each sale. They have a positive attitude about their product's ability to benefit the prospect. They know their customers, and they tailor their presentations to meet each person's specific needs.

> *Effective salespeople learn to be comfortable asking for the buyer's decision.*

Good closers prepare for each sales call. They take the time to carefully ascertain the needs of their prospects and customers by observing, by asking intelligent questions, and, most of all, by earnestly listening to them. To be successful, salespeople should know their ABCs. ABC is an acronym for *Always Be Closing*. Be alert for closing signals and close when the prospect is ready to buy.

The successful salesperson does not stop with the prospect's first no. Effective salespeople understand that purchasing a solution requires a change—a change in the buyer's beliefs, or their firm's processes, or the buyer's habits. Change is difficult. Therefore, it's best to not always expect an immediate "Yes" from the buyer. If a customer says no, determine the nature of the objection and then return to the presentation. After discussing information relative to overcoming the objection, use a trial close to determine if you have overcome the objection, and then determine if there are other objections. If resistance continues, remain positive and remember that every time you attempt to close, you are closer to helping the prospect make a decision. In addition, always ask for the order and then be silent.

Ask for the Order and Be Quiet

No matter when or how you close, remember that when you ask for the order, it is important to be silent. Do not say a word. If you say something—anything—you increase the probability of losing the sale.

You must put the prospect in a position of having to make a decision, speak first, and respond to the close. If you say anything after your close, you take the pressure off the prospect to make that decision.

Imagine this situation: The salesperson has finished the presentation and says, "Would you want this delivery in two or four weeks?" The average salesperson cannot wait more than two seconds for the prospect's reply without saying something like "I can deliver it anytime" or starting to talk again about the product. This destroys the closing moment. The prospect does not have to make the decision. There is time to think of reasons not to buy. By keeping quiet for a few seconds, the prospect cannot escape making the decision.

All individuals experience the urge to say no, even when they are not sure of what you are selling or when they may want what you propose. At times, everyone is hesitant in making a decision. To help the prospect make the decision, you must maintain silence after the close.

The professional salesperson can stay quiet all day, if necessary. Rarely will the silence last more than 30 seconds. During that time, do not say anything or make a distracting gesture; merely project positive nonverbal signs. Otherwise, you will decrease your chances of making the sale. This is the time to mentally prepare your responses to the prospect's reaction.

It sounds simple, yet it is not. Your stomach may churn. Your nerves make you want to move. You may display a serious look on your face instead of a positive one. You may look away from the buyer. Worst of all, you may want to talk to relieve the uncomfortable feeling that grows as silence continues. Finally, the prospect will say something. Now, you can respond based on the reaction to your close.

Constantly practice asking your closing question, staying silent for 30 seconds, and then responding. This will develop your skill and courage to close.

Get the Order—Then Move On!

Talking also can stop the sale after the prospect has said yes. An exception would be if you ask the customer for names of other prospects. Once this is done, it is best to take the order and move on.

In continuing to talk, you may give information that changes the buyer's mind. So, ask for the order and remain silent until the buyer responds. If you succeed, finalize the sale and leave.

How Many Times Should You Close?

"I will persist until I succeed."

OG MANDINO

Courtesy and common sense imply a reasonable limit to the number of closes a salesperson attempts at any one sitting. But you say, "I'm afraid to ask the person to buy the first time. I'm certainly not going to ask again." Yet what if you think the product is exactly what the customer needs? When the customer says, "I don't think so," do you say "OK" and leave? Are you unselfishly helping by taking the first no and leaving? To help others by selling your product, you must be able to use multiple closes. If needed, you should come back another day to present and close again. This is why salespeople need to be persistent.

However, it depends on the situation. The salesperson must consider their relationship with the buyer as well as the nature of the buying process. In more transactional types of situations, three closes is a minimum for successful salespeople. Attempting several closes in one call challenges a salesperson to employ wit, charm, and personality in a creative manner. In a more relationship-based situation, the salesperson may need to schedule another meeting to revisit the buying decision.

Example of Closing More than Once

You go through your presentation, as shown in Exhibit 12.3. Everything seems great! You verify with your trial close before asking for the order. You receive a positive response, so you close. During the close, an objection occurs that causes you to determine the objection, meet it by going back to the product, marketing plan, or business proposition in the presentation, and use that information to meet the objection. You ask a trial close to determine if the objection has been met. If so, close again. There are other scenarios, but this gives you idea of the situations faced by salespeople. Plan your follow-up and service to this prospect or customer for your next business meeting. Now head out to see your next prospect or customer.

EXHIBIT 12.3

A positive response to the trial close indicates a move toward the close; a negative response to indicates the need determine the prospect's objections.

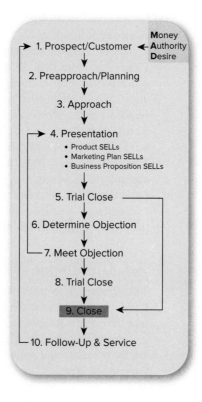

Mark Twain attended a meeting where a missionary had been invited to speak. Twain was deeply impressed. Later he said, "The preacher's voice was beautiful. He told us about the sufferings of the natives and pleaded for help with such moving simplicity that I mentally doubled the fifty cents I had intended to put in the plate. He described the pitiful misery of those savages so vividly that the dollar I had in mind gradually rose to five. Then that preacher continued. I felt that all the cash I carried on me would be insufficient. I decided to write a large check. Then he went on," added Twain, "and on and on about the dreadful state of those natives. I abandoned the idea of the check. Again, he went on, and I was back to five dollars. As he continued, I went to four, two, and then one dollar. Still, he persisted to preach. When the plate finally came around, I took ten cents out of it."[1]

Closing under Fire

To close more sales effectively, never take the first no from the prospect to mean an absolute refusal to buy. Instead, you must be able to close under fire (see Exhibit 12.4). In other words, you must be able to ask a prospect who may be in a bad mood or even hostile toward you to buy.

Take the experience of a consumer goods salesperson who suggested that a large drug wholesaler should buy a six-month supply of the company's entire line of merchandise. Outraged, the purchasing agent threw the order book across the room. The salesperson explained to the furious buyer that the company had doubled its promotional spending in the buyer's area and that it would be wise to stock up because of an increase in sales. The salesperson calmly picked up the order book, smiled, and handed it to the buyer saying, "Did you want to buy more?"

EXHIBIT 12.4

Closing under fire.

You can tell this customer is unhappy with your product or you. How do you save the sale and close?

©Image Source

The buyer laughed and said, "What do you honestly believe is a reasonable amount to buy?" This was a buying signal that the prospect would buy, but in a lesser quantity. They settled on an increased order of a two-month supply over the amount of merchandise normally purchased. This example illustrates why it is important for the salesperson to react calmly to an occasional hostile situation.

Difficulties with Closing

Closing the sale is the easiest part of the presentation. It is a natural wrap-up to your sales presentation because you solidify details of the purchase agreement. Yet, salespeople sometimes have difficulty closing the sale for several reasons.

One reason salespeople may fail to close a sale and take an order is that they are not confident in their ability to close. Perhaps some earlier failure to make a sale has caused this mental block. They may give the presentation and stop short of asking for the order. The seller must overcome this fear of closing to become successful.

Second, salespeople often determine that the prospect does not need the quantity or type of merchandise, or that the prospect should not buy. So, they do not ask the prospect to buy. The salesperson should remember that *it is the prospect's decision and responsibility whether or not to buy.* Do not make the decision for the prospect.

Finally, the salesperson may not have worked hard enough in developing a customer profile and customer benefit plan—resulting in a poor presentation. Many times, a poorly prepared presentation falls apart. Be prepared and develop a well-planned, well-rehearsed presentation.

Closing requires preparation. When the salesperson is well-prepared for the sales conversation, she increases the opportunity to close the sale.

Essentials of Closing Sales

Although there are many factors to consider in closing the sale, the following items are essential if you wish to improve your chances:

- Be sure your prospect understands what you say. Clear communication is critical.
- Always present a complete story to ensure understanding. Your ability to tie your solution's benefits to the buyer's true needs will assist you in closing the sale.
- Tailor your close to each prospect. Eighty percent of your customers will respond to a standard close. It is the other 20 percent of customers that you need to prepare for. Prepare to give the expert customer all facts requested, to give the egotistical customer praise, to nurture the indecisive customer, and to slow down for an analytical thinker.
- Consider the customer's point of view in everything you do and say.
- Never stop at the first no. Seek to understand their concerns.
- Learn to recognize buying signals.
- Before you close, ask a trial close. Once the buyer says no, it is hard to change the person's mind. A famous proverb says "A fool finds no pleasure in understanding but delights in airing his own opinions." This can mean that once the prospect adopts an objection, the person tends to defend it and builds on it rather than seeking the truth. If you close too early and you have not answered the objection, the prospect may say no, and there will be no way to change the person's mind. So you come back another day!
- After asking for the order—be silent.
- Set high goals for yourself and develop a personal commitment to reach your goals.
- Develop and maintain a positive, confident, and enthusiastic attitude toward yourself, your products, your prospects, and your close.

"Don't think or say 'I.' Think and say 'we.'"

PETER F. DRUCKER

Too many salespeople regard the close as a separate and distinct part of the sales call. "I've discussed benefits, advantages, and features, answered some objections, handled price, and now it's time to close."

Chronologically, of course, the close does come at the end. However, you must close all along. Closing is the natural outgrowth of the sales presentation. If the rest of the sales call has been a success, closing simply means working out terms and signing the order.

What about the salesperson who says, "I always have trouble closing. Everything's fine until it's time to close the sale." Chances are, there's no basis for the sale. "Everything's fine . . . " may merely be a way of saying, "I stated my case and the prospect listened. At least she never told me to pack up and go."

Before we discuss specific techniques on how to ask for the order or close the sale, remember that you will increase your sales closings by following 12 simple keys to success. The keys are shown in Exhibit 12.5.

As you see from these 12 keys, a successful close results from a series of actions that you have followed before asking for the order. Closing is not one giant step.

Should you not make the sale, always remember to act as a professional salesperson and be courteous and appreciative of the opportunity to present your product to the prospect. This allows the door to be open another time. Thus, key number 12 cannot be overlooked—always remember to leave the door open!

Often, salespeople believe that there is some mystical art to closing a sale. If they say the right words in the appropriate manner, the prospect will buy. They concentrate on developing tricky closing techniques and are often pushy with prospects in hopes of pressuring them into purchasing. Certainly, salespeople need to learn alternative closing techniques. However, what they need most is a thorough understanding of the entire selling process and of the critical role that closing plays in that process.

> *The race is not always won by the swift but by those who keep on running.*

EXHIBIT 12.5

Twelve keys to a successful closing.

1. Think *success!* Be enthusiastic.
2. *Plan* your sales call. Be prepared to assist your customer with your knowledge, understanding, and willingness to truly listen.
3. Confirm your prospect's *needs* in the approach. Ask open-ended questions.
4. Give a *great* presentation. Focus on tying your solution's benefits to your buyer's needs.
5. Use *trial closes* during and after your presentation. Try to use open-ended questions as trial closes.
6. Use open-ended questions to understand the prospect's *real* objections.
7. *Overcome* real objections. Empathize, listen, ask questions, and then provide an answer.
8. Use a *trial close* after overcoming each objection.
9. Summarize *benefits* as related to a buyer's *needs*.
10. Use a *trial close* to confirm step 9.
11. Ask for the *order* or the next step in the decision-making process and then be quiet.
12. Leave the door *open*. Act as a professional.

Often the seller does not have to close.

In this case, the product sold itself. After examining the business proposition, the prospect bought without the salesperson asking for an order.

©Blend Images/Alamy Stock Photo

A memorized presentation and a hurriedly presented product will not be as successful as the skillful use of the 12 keys to a successful close. A close look at the 12 keys illustrates that a lot of hard work, planning, and skillful execution of your plan occurs before you reach number 11 and ask for the order. The point is that if salespeople understand how each of the 12 applies to them and their customers, and if they perform each successfully, they earn the right to close.

In fact, many times the close occurs automatically because it has become the easiest part of the sales presentation. Often, the prospect will close for the salesperson, saying: "That sounds great! I'd like to buy that" (see Exhibit 12.6). All the salesperson has to do is finalize the details and write up the order. Often, though, the prospect is undecided on the product after the presentation, so the skillful salesperson develops multiple closing techniques.

Get Ready for Closing

Before you learn about different closing techniques, we present one important element to consider. Many salespeople have learned that it's important to confirm the buyer doesn't have any additional concerns (i.e., objections) and the buyer understands the value of the proposed solution. Therefore the salesperson uses a final trial close that ensures they did not miss any important issue. In the next section, we present a few methods to ensure you don't miss an important element before you begin closing the sales.

Did I Miss Anything?

To effectively close, the buyer must believe the solution is a valuable and credible option. Therefore, a buyer needs to feel comfortable that the solution solves the problems or meets the needs. Before formally closing, it's important to clear the air. That is, the salesperson should ask if he missed anything or if the buyer perceives any risks. A few great questions to ask the buyer before formally closing may include

- Are there any areas about this solution that we have not addressed adequately?
- Do you have any specific concerns about the solution?
- What areas are you unsure of at this time?
- What am I missing to ensure this meets your needs?
- Are there any areas that we haven't addressed in order to make a decision?

Closing Techniques

To successfully close more sales, you must determine your prospect's situation, understand the prospect's attitude toward your presentation, and be prepared to select instantly a closing technique from several techniques based on your prospect. By using a closing technique that fits the situation, you can save the sale and keep your customer satisfied.

Successful salespeople adapt a planned presentation to any prospect or situation that may arise. Some salespeople practice more than 10 closing techniques, each designed for a specific situation. In the next section, we will discuss a range of closing techniques.

In this section, we begin with a number of commonly used techniques. Then, we move to a number of techniques that may be applied in *specific types of situations.* (See Exhibit 12.7.) Since different closing techniques work best for certain situations, salespeople prepare several options. By being prepared for each sales call, you are able to adapt to your customer and the specific situation. This level of preparation provides you with increased confidence and an increased opportunity to close the sales.

Commonly used techniques include the

- Summary-of-benefits close
- Direct close
- Question close
- Probability or rating close
- Negotiation close
- Technology close
- Visual aids close

EXHIBIT 12.7

Techniques for closing the sale: Which close should be used?

Common Closes	Speciality Closes (Specific Situation)
Summary-of-benefits close	Assumptive close
Direct close	Alternative-choice close
The question close	Minor-points close
The probability close	Compliment close
The negotiations close	Standing-room-only close
The technology close	Continuous-yes close
Using visuals to close	T-account or balance-sheet close

Techniques used in specific situations are the

- Assumptive close
- Alternative choice close
- Minor points close
- Compliment close
- Standing room only close
- Continuous yes close
- T account or balance sheet close

Summary-of-Benefits Close

During the sales presentation, remember the main features, advantages, and benefits of interest for the prospect and use them during the close. Summarize these benefits in a positive manner so that the prospect agrees with what you say; then ask for the order. The summary close is possibly the most popular method to ask for the order. Emmett Reagan, sales trainer at the Xerox Training Center, says the major closing technique taught consists of these three basic steps of the summary close:

1. Determine the key product benefits that interest the prospect during the presentation.
2. Summarize these benefits.
3. Make a proposal.

Here is an example of using the **summary-of-benefits close** on a prospect. Assume that the prospect indicates during your sales presentation that she likes your profit margin, delivery schedule, and credit terms.

Salesperson: Ms. Stevenson, I'd like to recap our discussion. At the beginning of our discussion, you mentioned that any new product needed to meet your profit margin goals. Our new product delivers 48 percent. You also mentioned fast delivery. And I can commit to you that you will have the product in your distribution center within three weeks of the initial order. Finally, you mentioned you needed your vendors to provide favorable credit terms, and our firm offers a generous 2/30 net 90 payment policy. Am I missing anything? [Summary and trial close.]

Prospect: No. Those are the areas that I need for a new product.

> *The summary close is likely the most popular type of close.*

Salesperson: With the number of customers in your store and our expected sales of the products due to normal turnover, along with our marketing plan, *I suggest you buy* [state the products and their quantities]. This will provide you with sufficient quantities to meet customer demand for the next two months, plus provide you with the profit you expect from your products. I can have the order to you early next week. [Now wait for her response.]

You can easily adapt the *FAB* statements and SELL Sequence for your summary close. The industrial equipment salesperson might say, "As we have discussed, our model's high-speed assembly system [feature] produces twice as many units in a similar amount of time as your current manufacturing system [advantage], saving you 15 to 30 percent in your manufacturing process [benefit] and helps you meet the pressures imposed upon you by your senior management to increase your plant's productivty [benefit of benefit]. What are your thoughts? [Trial close. If positive response, say:] "Would you like to move forward with this opportunity today?"

The sporting goods salesperson might say, "As we have said, this golf ball will give you an extra 10 to 20 yards on your drive [advantage], helping to reduce your score [benefit] because of its new solid core [feature]. How would it feel to take off a few golf strokes and improve your golf game? [Trial close. If positive response, say:] Will a dozen be enough?"

The air-conditioning salesperson could say, "This air conditioner has a high efficiency rating [feature] that will save you 10 percent on your energy costs resulting in a monthly savings of over $1,000 [benefit] because it uses less electricity [advantage]. What are your thoughts on this type of monthly savings? [Trial close. If positive response, say:] We can provide delivery within the week. Would you want the air-conditioning system delivered this week or do you prefer next week?"

One of the most popular methods of closing the sale, the summary-of-benefits technique, could be especially useful when you need a simple, straightforward close rather than a close aimed at a specific prospect's personality.

Direct Close

The **direct close** describes an explicit manner of closing. The salesperson asks the customer for a decision in a straightforward, candid manner. For example, the salesperson may ask the customer, "Do you feel comfortable moving forward and signing the agreement now?" or "Well, the next step in the process would be sign the agreement and begin the implementation process. Shall we move forward at this time?"

It is very important for a salesperson to address all the objections prior to attempting a direct close, because the direct close can only be done successfully if the salesperson feels confident that the customer will surely say yes to her offerings. Once a salesperson gets the idea that the customer understands the benefits of her product, then it is a good time to pose a direct question such as "So, Mike, can I enter your purchase details into my system and get this process started?" or "Mike, when would you like the first delivery of the product?"

Although it requires a lot of courage and confidence to ask a direct question, the outcome could be very rewarding as it may simplify the process for both sides. The basic tenet of direct close is to take control of the situation by assuming the deal is already closed. If a salesperson has done her job of highlighting the benefits of the product and addressing all the concerns of the customer, direct closing could probably be the simplest yet most effective technique to close the sale.

Question Close

The **question close** uses questions to generate a decision point. While the situations may vary, the question close focuses on having the buyer make a key decision. For instance, some salespeople may need to receive multiple approvals within a customer's organization before a purchase can be finalized. First, they may have a sales conversation with a purchasing manager. Upon the purchasing manager's approval, the next step may be a chief procurement officer. In these situations, the salesperson is navigating throughout the organization. In this example, critical closing questions may include

- "In terms of next steps, what needs to happen next in the decision-making process?"
- "What do we need to discuss about this proposal before it could be moved forward?"

- "Would you be willing to set a meeting with John, you, and me next week to discuss the next steps in the process?"
- "It sounds like you feel comfortable moving forward with this recommendation. How do you suggest we proceed in moving this opportunity forward through the organization? Whom do we need to include in our next meeting?"

In other situations, you may be able to ask directly for the business at the present meeting. In these instances, a salesperson may ask the buyer the following questions:

- "It sounds like you would like to move forward. Shall we sign the investment agreement at this time?"
- "With all of this information, is there anything else I can answer or shall we move forward with the purchase order?"
- "Shall we move forward with the agreement at this time?"
- "Would you be willing to invest in testing the software for a 30-day test period?"

The question close technique can be an effective way for a salesperson to handle unsettled objections while securing a commitment simultaneously. This technique provides a rep with an opportunity to ask either for close or for additional information as to why the customer is not fully convinced to buy. So, notably, it's win-win for a salesperson.

Probability or Rating Close

What is the probability we will be doing business?

In some sales situations, the salesperson needs to assess the buyer's level of comfort or risk with certain solutions. In the **probability or rating close,** you ask buyers to share their level of perceived risk on the entire solution or certain elements of the solution. This close may be used when the product or service is very technical or requires a sizable investment. The value of the probability close is that it allows the salesperson to understand the customer's ongoing concerns. We show an example of the probability close below. Please note that in the second element of the close, the buyer expresses some hesitation about distribution timelines. As you can see, this provides the salesperson with an opportunity to better meet the buyer's needs and move forward later.

Salesperson: We have covered a great deal of information in this discussion. If I may, I'd like to propose that we take the three major elements of this proposal and ensure you are comfortable with them. Would this be acceptable to you?

Customer: That sounds great.

Salesperson: Fantastic. Now in terms of the promotional campaign, I'd like to understand your thoughts. On a scale of 1 to 10, how does the proposed campaign meet your business objectives in terms of driving the sales you need to meet your quarterly revenue numbers?

Customer: I really like the heavy investment of in-store promotions. This is exactly what I want my vendors to enact. I give it a 9.

Salesperson: Great. Now, let's transition to the implementation plan, primarily focused on the distribution timelines. We mentioned that your distribution centers can have the product within 11 business days of the first order date. Based on this timeline, what are your thoughts on a scale of 1 to 10 of this meeting your internal requirements?

Customer: About a 6, I'd ideally like it in the distribution centers within 9 business days.

Salesperson: Okay, this sounds like something we should discuss before we move forward.

Asking Questions Regarding Comfort and Level of Risk

Perhaps the purchase requires a sizable investment, you could ask buyers to rate their level of perceived risk in making the investment. For instance, a salesperson might ask, "I want to understand your thoughts at this time. On a scale of 1 to 100, what's your level of comfort in making this investment and moving forward today?"

Asking Questions Regarding the Probability of Conducting Business Together

When the prospect gives the famous "I want to think it over" objection, or some variation, try saying, "Ms. Prospect that would be fine. I understand your desire to think it over, but let me ask you this—when I call you back next week, what do envision as the probability, in percentage terms, out of a total of 100 that you and I can work together to help you meet your needs with this solution?" Then pause, and don't say another word until the prospect speaks.

The prospect's response will be from three possible categories:

1. More than 50 percent but less than 85 percent for buying. If your prospects respond in this range, ask what the remaining percent is against buying, then pause and be silent. When you become skilled in this technique, you will see prospects blink as they focus on their real objections. Many times, we hear that prospects want to think it over. It is not because they want to delay the decision; it is because they don't fully understand what bothers them. The probability close permits your prospects to focus on their real objections. Once you have a real objection, convert that objection with a persuasive sales argument.
2. Above 85 percent but not 100 percent for buying. If they're in this range, recognize that there is a minor probability against you. You might want to say, "As it is almost certain that we'll do business together, why wait until next week? What concerns do you have at this time? Or could we get a running start on this project together and move forward today?"
3. Less than 50 percent for buying. This is a signal that there is little, if any, chance that you will ever close this particular sale. The only appropriate tactic is returning to square one and starting the reselling process. It is amazing how many professional salespeople in a closing situation expect the prospect to say 80–20 as a probability in their favor, and instead they hear "80–20 against."

The probability close permits prospects to focus on their objections. It allows the true or hidden objections to surface. The more prospects fight you and the less candid they are about the probability of closing, the less likely they will buy anything.

Negotiation Close

Every sale is a negotiation. Most sales negotiations focus on two major themes: value and price. Customers often demand more value and lower prices. In their quest for more value at a lower cost, prospects often resort to unfair tactics and put heavy pressure on the salesperson. The purpose of a good sales **negotiation close** is not to haggle over who gets the larger slice of pie, but to find ways for everyone to have a fair deal. Both the buyer and seller should win. In order for this to occur, the salesperson should understand the areas in which she can compromise. This requires a substantial knowledge of your firm's processes, policies, products, and implementation. Here are two examples of a salesperson using a negotiation close:

- If we could find a way in which we would eliminate the need for a backup machine and guarantee availability, would you be happy with this arrangement?

- Why don't we compromise? You know I am unable to offer you a discount, but I am more than happy to defer billing until the end of the month. Would you be willing to move forward with the agreement using these terms?

When you hit a tennis ball over the net, the kind of spin put on the ball determines the type of return shot received. In a negotiation, the attitude that you project determines the attitude you receive. Be positive! Be helpful! Be concerned! Show your interest in helping the prospect.

Technology Close

Picture this! You have just completed the discussion of your product, marketing plan, and business proposition. You summarize your product's main benefits to your customer. Now you bring out your laptop computer or tablet, placing it on the buyer's desk so she can see the screen, or you prepare to project the screen onto the wall. Using graphs and bar charts, you show the buyer past purchases and sales trends. Then you call up your recommended purchase suggestion. If appropriate, you can show payment schedules considering different quantity discounts. This **technology close** is very impressive to buyers.

The exact use of technology in closing a sale depends on the type of product and customer you're selling. Without a doubt, incorporating technology into your presentation will help you close more prospects and customers.

Visual Aids Close

Effective salespeople develop their sales presentation to build credibility and demonstrate that their solution meets the buyer's needs. Throughout their presentation, they convey their product's FABs, marketing plan, and business proposition to justify the adoption of their solution (i.e., by directly meeting the needs of their buyer). At the end of the conversation, they may include an action plan that integrates a suggested order and incorporates a closing statement.

Often, salespeople use visual aids in their closing. They integrate visuals, such as documents, slides, and sales sheets. It is an effective way to visually convey or reinforce a point. The visuals may also be introduced at a point to allow the buyer to make a decision—an ideal opportunity to close the sale. In the next sections, we discuss the use of visual aids and their value in the closing process.

Visual Aids Focusing on Your Solution's Financial Elements

The use of the visual aid works well in discussing the business proposition and when closing. Immediately after discussing the marketing plan for a national brand cereal, the salesperson provides a visual (on her laptop) to demonstrate the sales and profits for the suggested order.

It has been personalized by typing the account's name at the top. The salesperson discusses each item on the profit forecaster (as shown on her laptop screen). Then the salesperson says, "Based on your past sales, the profits you will earn, and our marketing plan, I would recommend an initial order of 100 cases for your three stores. Would you feel comfortable moving forward with this opportunity?" The suggested order is also included on the profit forecaster visual. Now the salesperson remains silent. The buyer will respond with yes, no, or that is too much to buy. While waiting, the salesperson should mentally go over what to say for each response that can be made by the buyer.

EXHIBIT 12.8

Examples of a personalized visual.

Using a visual is an excellent way to close. After discussing the financial information on the visual, close by suggesting what and how much should be ordered.

Mila Supinskaya Glashchenko/Shutterstock.

Visual Aids Focusing on Your Solution's Action Plan

The use of visual aids is often helpful to show a timeline or steps in a process. For instance, a salesperson may provide an action plan after the business proposition. The action plan details the steps required to implement the product, service, or solution. Within the action plan, the salesperson may include a suggested order, timelines, major steps or tools needed, and a closing statement. By using an action plan, the salesperson provides a natural conclusion for the buyer to make a decision. We provide an example of the discussion that integrates the action plan and a visual (Exhibit 12.9).

Salesperson: I'm delighted that our solution meets the financial objectives you need to accomplish [transition]. Now, I'd like to review the opportunity to execute this solution within your firm. I've developed a potential timeline for the implementation process. As you can see, if we move forward on this agreement today, the first action item will be completed within one week. During this time, we meet with your technology group to learn about your existing technology and manufacturing system. The next step is the integration period. This will require a two-week testing period and a three-week integration period. In summary, a signed agreement allows us to integrate the total solution within a six-week time period and allows your team to begin capturing cost savings. Would you be amenable to starting the implementation process and moving forward with this initiative today?

Visual Aids Focusing on Your Solution's Ability to Meet the Buyer's Needs

As we have stressed throughout the book, your sales conversation must adapt to the buyer and the situation. For example, consider the situation in which you have met with a customer on numerous occasions. In the past conversations, you have discussed needs and the requirements that any solution needs to meet. In your final meeting, you need to provide a solution. During these situations, a visual aid serves as an effective

EXHIBIT 12.9

Visual aids help the salesperson close.

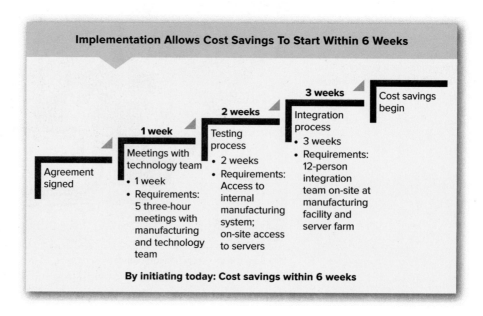

method to close the meeting. After you have presented your solution, you use a visual aid with a summary of benefits close. The visual aid outlines each specific need and then ties a specific benefit to each need. As you summarize your solution's value, you direct your buyer's attention to the need and associated benefit as a means of reinforcement. We provide an example of this conversation along with a sample of the visual (Exhibit 12.10).

Salesperson: Ms. Stevenson, just to recap our past discussions, you wanted to ensure you had always had the financial ability to cover three main goals, that of housing, college, and daily expenses if anything happened to you. Did I miss any items or goals?

Customer: You are right. Those are exactly the areas I'm concerned about.

Salesperson: Fantastic. Then the $1 million insurance policy that we've discussed provides the certainty and ability to make that happen. The policy's amount allows us to provide the $300,000 remaining on your mortgage, $200,000 for college costs for your son, John, and $2,000 for the monthly expenses that your spouse, Jeff, may require for the next two years? Knowing that we have a financial tool that can provide you with the ability to meet your goals in a secure manner, would you be willing to move forward with the policy process?

Close Based On the Situation

Since different closing techniques work best for certain situations, salespeople often identify the common objections they encounter and develop specific closing approaches designed to overcome these objections. In developing your sales presentation, review your customer profile and develop your main closing technique and several alternatives. By being prepared for each sales call, you experience increased confidence and enthusiasm, which results in a more positive selling attitude. You can help the customer *and* reach your goals. Exhibit 12.11 shows how to use different

EXHIBIT 12.10

Using a visual to close the sale.

A salesperson directs a buyer's attention to the goals and associated benefits using a visual aid.

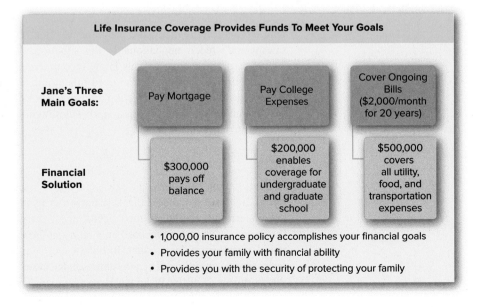

EXHIBIT 12.11

Examples of closing techniques based on situations.

Situation	Alternative	Compliment	Continuous-yes	Minor-points	Assumptive	T-account	Standing-room-only	Reason why
Customer is indecisive	X		X	X		X	X	Forces a decision
Customer is expert or egotistical		X				X		Lets expert make the decision
Customer is hostile		X	X					Positive strokes
Customer is a friend					X			You can take care of the small things
Customer has predetermined beliefs						X		Benefits outweigh disbeliefs
Customer is greedy, wants a deal							X	Buy now

closing techniques to meet objections. Next, we discuss different situation specific closing techniques in detail.

Assumptive Close

Many times the salesperson has worked with a customer for a long time. In these instances, the salesperson has earned a high level of the customer's trust, and the salesperson can recommend and even place an order for the customer. Here, the assumptive close is especially effective. With the **assumptive close,** the salesperson assumes the prospect will buy. Statements can be made such as "I'd like to move forward with the recommendation and call your order in tonight" or "To meet the deadline we discussed, I'll have this shipped to you tomorrow." If the prospect does not say anything, assume the suggested order has been accepted.

In other instances, the customer may believe the salesperson is a valued partner. Due to this level of trust, the customer is often willing to move forward with the salesperson's recommendations. In this situation, the salesperson may state the following assumptive closes, "This is my recommendation for the product assortment and quantities that I suggest you need this month. I'd like to move forward with the order today," or "I'd like to send the following items to your distribution centers by the end of the week." Again, the assumptive close tends to be used within a more trust-based, long-term relationship.

Alternative-Choice Close

In some selling situations, the salesperson possesses a strong relationship with the buyer. In these instances, the salesperson may be more straightforward because she understands the buyer, their needs, and their past buying history. Additionally, the conversation may be focused on a rebuy situation—when the buyer intends to buy the identical or similar product. In this type of situation, the alternative-choice close may serve as an option. The **alternative-choice close** was popularized in the 1930s as the story spread of the Walgreen Drug Company's purchase of 800 dozen eggs at a special price. A sales trainer named Elmer Wheeler suggested to the Walgreen clerks that when a customer asked for a malted milk at a Walgreen fountain, the clerk should say, "Do you want one egg or two?" Customers had not even thought of eggs in their malteds. Now, they were faced with the choice of *how many eggs*—not whether or not they wanted an egg. Within one week, all 800 dozen of the eggs were sold at a profit. Two examples of the alternative close are

- Which do you prefer—our current version of software or the version with the upgraded features?
- Would you prefer the Xerox 6200 or 6400 copier?

As you see, the alternative choice does not give prospects a choice of buying or not buying, but asks which one or how many items they want to buy. It says, "You are going to buy, so let's settle the details on what you will purchase." This approach assumes that a sale is imminent, such as the rebuy situation.

Take, for example, the salesperson who says: "Would you prefer the Xerox 6200 or 6400?" This question (1) assumes the customer has a desire to buy one of the copiers; (2) assumes the customer will buy; and (3) allows the customer a preference. If the customer prefers the Xerox 6400, you know the prospect is ready to buy, so you begin the close. A customer who says, "I'm not sure," is still in the desire stage, so you continue to discuss each product's benefits. However, you see that the customer likes both machines. Should the prospect appear indecisive, you can ask: "Can you share with me the areas you are unsure of?" This question probes to find out why your prospect is not ready to choose.

If used in an appropriate situation, the alternative-choice close is an effective closing technique. It provides a choice between items, never between something and nothing. By presenting a choice, you either receive a yes decision or uncover objections, which, if successfully met, allow you to come closer to making the sale.

Minor-Points Close

It is sometimes easier for a prospect to concede several minor points about a product than to make a sweeping decision on whether or not to buy. Big decisions are often difficult for some buyers. By having the prospect make decisions on a product's minor points, you can subtly lead into the decision to buy.

The **minor-points close** is similar to the alternative-choice close. Both methods involve giving the buyer a choice between two options. The alternative-choice close asks the prospect to make a choice between *two* products, which represents a high-risk decision to some people that they may prefer not to make. However, the minor-points close asks the prospect to make a low-risk decision on a minor, usually low-cost element of a *single* product such as delivery dates, optimal features, color, size, payment terms, or order quantity.

Single- or multiple-product element choices may be presented to the prospect. The automobile salesperson says, "Would you prefer the premium quality speakers or digitally integrated speakers within your new automobile?" The Xerox Business Products salesperson asks, "Are you interested in buying or leasing our equipment?" The home security system salesperson asks, "Would you like to install the 18- or the 24-camera system?"

This close is used widely when prospects have difficulty in making a decision or when they are not in the mood to buy. It is also effective as a second close. If, for example, the prospect says no to your first close because of difficulty in deciding whether or not to buy, you can close on minor points.

Compliment Close

Effective salespeople adapt to their buyer. The **compliment close** is especially effective when you talk with a prospect who is a self-styled expert, who is quite dominant in the discussion, or who has a big ego. Would-be experts and egotistical prospects often desire recognition. By complimenting them, they listen and respond favorably to your presentation. The prospect with low self-esteem or one who finds it difficult to decide also responds favorably to a compliment. Here is an example of a consumer packaged goods salesperson closing a sale with a grocery retail buyer. Please note that the compliment should be sincere and targeted. Buyers can usually sense a false or insincere comment.

> *"Kind words are short and easy to speak, but their echoes are truly endless."*
>
> MOTHER TERESA

Salesperson: Obviously, you have a wealth of experience within the grocery business. You have every linear foot of your store creating strong revenue gains and providing substantial profit levels. Ms. Stevenson, our products also will assist your store and your personal goals of increasing profitability. In fact, our profit will exceed your store's average profit-per-linear-foot by 25 points. And, the inventory turnover is 1.5 times greater than the average product in the competitive set. This added benefit of high turnover will further increase your cash flow—which you have said is important to you. [He pauses, and when there is no response, he continues.] Given the number of customers coming into your store, and our expected sales of these products due to normal turnover, along with our marketing plan, I'd like to recommend that you purchase 45 units per store. This will provide you with sufficient quantities to meet your customers' demands for the next two months, plus provide you with the expected profit from your products. [Now he waits for the response or again asks for the order using the alternative choice or assumptive close.]

All buyers appreciate your recognition of their better points. Conscientious merchants take pride in how they do business; customers entering the retail clothing store take pride in their appearance; people considering life insurance take pride in looking after their families. So compliment prospects relative to something that will benefit them as you attempt to close the sale. Remember, always make honest compliments. No matter how trusting you may think people are, nearly anyone can detect insincerity in a compliment. When a compliment is not in order, summarize the benefits of your product for a specific customer.

Standing-Room-Only Close

For the right product, person, and situation, this is an appropriate close. Both retail and industrial salespeople can use this technique in situations in which deadlines, time constraints, inventory availability, or limited access to products and resources exist.

For instance, imagine you are representing a clothing manufacturer. You will need to communicate the time constraints associated with the availability of certain seasonal clothing lines. Prospects realize that factors such as seasonality, high sales demand, labor strikes, weather, transportation, inflation, and inventory shortages, could make it difficult to buy in the future. In some instances, it is appropriate to communicate the deadline and convey a greater level of urgent action by using the standing room only close.

How does the standing room only close work? What happens if someone tells you that you cannot have something that you would like to have? You instantly want it! When you face an indecisive prospect that may not be able to access a product if they wait much longer or if you believe it is in a prospect's best interest to purchase a larger quantity due to limits on production or inventory, communicate that if they do not act now they may *not* be able to buy in the future. You can communicate this sense of urgency by using a **standing-room-only close:**

- This is the fastest selling style in our fall product line. Would you want them if I have them in stock?
- My customers have been buying all we can produce. If we don't act quickly, I'm not sure if we will have any inventory left to sell you.
- Well, I know you are thinking of ordering *X* amount, but would you please consider ordering (a larger amount) because we now have it in stock and I don't think we will be able to keep up with demand and fill your November order.
- Due to the increasing costs of commodities, the cost of this equipment will increase 10 percent next week. Would you consider writing the purchase order today so you can avoid the price increase that goes into effect next week?

By using the standing-room-only close at the appropriate time, you may do your prospects a favor by encouraging them to buy now and thus avoid future uncertainties. However, it should be used honestly.

Continuous-Yes Close

The **continuous-yes close** is like the summary close. However, instead of summarizing product benefits, the salesperson develops a series of benefit questions that the prospect must answer. When using this approach, it's important to tie the buyer's needs with your solution.

Salesperson: Ms. Stevenson, I'd like to review with you some key elements of our discussion to ensure I'm meeting your needs. First, you mentioned that the quality of our products met your firm's quality expectations. Is that safe to say?

Prospect: Yes, that's right.

Salesperson: And you also mentioned that our delivery schedule aligns with your key time periods for stocking. Is that correct?

Prospect: Yes, it does.

Salesperson: Finally, you mentioned that profit productivity and financing terms were also key requirements. Would it be safe to say that the product's profit margin and credit terms align with your needs?

Prospect: That's correct.

Salesperson: Ms. Stevenson, our quality products, fast delivery, profit margin, and good credit terms will provide you with an excellent profit. With the number of customers in your store and our expected sales of the products due to normal turnover, along with our marketing plan, I suggest you buy [state the products and their quantities]. This will provide you with sufficient quantities to meet customer demand for the next two months, plus provide you with the profit you expect from your products. I can have the order to you early next week. [Now wait for her response.]

In this example of the continuous-yes close, the salesperson recognized four product benefits that the prospect liked: (1) the product's quality, (2) fast delivery, (3) profit margin, and (4) favorable credit terms. After the presentation, the salesperson used three questions to reaffirm key needs and also to give the prospect the opportunity to agree that she was impressed with each of the four product benefits. By stacking these positive questions, the salesperson kept the prospect continually saying, "Yes, I like that benefit."

The prospect has placed herself in a positive frame of mind. Her positive stance toward the product makes it more likely that she will continue to say yes when asked to buy.

However, the key to any closing approach is to make it conversational and a natural outcome from your conversation. Therefore, consider integrating the buyer's needs with a key product benefit. Why is this important? If buyers feel as though you are trying to manipulate them with a consistent set of questions that require a "yes," you may lose the opportunity. Therefore, use this type of closing approach wisely and in the appropriate situation.

T-Account or Balance-Sheet Close

The **T-account close** is based on the process that people use when they make a decision. Some sales trainers refer to it as the Benjamin Franklin close. In his *Poor Richard's Almanac,* Franklin said, "You know, I believe most of my life is going to be made up of making decisions about things. I want to make as many good ones as I possibly can." So, in deciding on a course of action, his technique was to take pencil and paper and draw a line down the center of the paper. On one side he put all the pros, and on the other side he put all the cons. If there were more cons than pros, he would not do something. If the pros outweighed the cons, then he felt it was a good thing to do; it was the correct decision.

This is the process a customer uses in making a buying decision, weighing the cons against the pros. At times, it may be a good idea to use this technique on paper. Common column headings are pros and cons, debits and credits, or to act and not to act. For example, on a sheet of paper, the salesperson draws a large *T,* placing *to act* (asset) on the left side and *not to act* (liability) on the right side (debit and credit, in accounting terms). The salesperson reviews the presentation with the prospect, listing the positive features, advantages, and benefits the prospect likes on the left side and all negative points on the right. This shows that the product's benefits outweigh its liabilities, and it leads the prospect to conclude that now is the time to buy. If prospects make their own lists, the balance-sheet close is convincing. Here is an example:

> *Life is like a field of newly fallen snow; where I choose to walk, every step will show. Tell the truth.*

Salesperson: Ms. Stevenson, here's a pad of paper and a pencil. Bear with me a minute and let's review what we have just talked about. Could you please draw a large *T* on the page and write "To Act" at the top on the left and "Not to Act" on the right? Now, you said you liked our fast delivery. Is that right?

To Act	Not to Act
Fast delivery	Narrow assortment
Good profit	
Good credit	

Prospect: Yes.

Salesperson: OK, please write down "fast delivery" in the To Act column. Great! You were impressed with our profit margin and credit terms. Is that right?

Prospect: Yes.

Salesperson: OK, how about writing that down in the left-hand column? Now is there anything that could be improved?

Prospect: Yes, don't you remember? I feel you have a narrow assortment with only one style of broom and one style of mop. [Objection.]

Salesperson: Well, write that down in the right-hand column. Is that everything?

Prospect: Yes.

Salesperson: Ms. Stevenson, what in your opinion outweighs the other—the reason to act or not to act? [A trial close.]

Prospect: Well, the To Act column does. But it seems I need a better assortment of products. [Same objection again.]

Salesperson: We have found that assortment is not important to most people. A broom and mop are pretty much a broom and mop. They want a good quality product that looks good and that holds up continuously. Customers like our products' looks and quality. Aren't those good-looking products? [Trial close showing broom and mop.]

Prospect: They look OK to me. [Positive response—she didn't bring up assortment so assume you have overcome objection.]

Salesperson: Ms. Stevenson, I can offer you a quality product, fast delivery, excellent profit, and good credit terms. I'd like to suggest this: Buy one dozen mops and one dozen brooms for each of your 210 stores. However, let's consider this first: The XYZ chain found that our mops had excellent drawing power when advertised. Their sales of buckets and floor wax doubled. Each store sold an average of 12 mops. [He pauses, listens, and notices her reaction.] You can do the same thing.

Prospect: I'd have to contact the Johnson Wax salesperson, and I really don't have the time. [A positive buying signal.]

Salesperson: Ms. Stevenson, let me help. I'll call Johnson's and get them to contact you. Also, I'll go see your advertising manager to schedule the ads. OK? [Assumptive close.]

Prospect: OK, go ahead, but this stuff had better sell.

Salesperson: [Smiling.] Customers will flock to your stores [he's building a picture in her mind] looking for mops, polish, and buckets. Say, that reminds me, you will need a dozen buckets for each store. [Continuous-yes, keep talking.] I'll write up the order. [Assumptive.]

Some salespeople recommend that the columns of the T-account be reversed so that the Not to Act column is on the left and the To Act column is on the right. This allows the salesperson to discuss the reasons not to buy first, followed by the reasons to buy, ending the presentation on the positive side. A contrary idea in the prospect's mind is like steam under pressure—explosive. So, when you remove the pressure by openly stating an objection, opposition vaporizes. An objection often becomes minor or disappears. Remember, however, if the customer says, "Well, I'm going to buy it," do not say, "Well, let's first look at the reasons not to buy." Instead, finalize the sale.

People may dislike you, be unhappy, and hard to get along with; be caring, joyous, and a pleasure to be with anyway.

Modified T-Account or Balance-Sheet or Checklist Close

Some salespeople modify the T-account close by only listing reasons to act in one column. They do not want to remind the prospect of any negative reasons not to buy as they attempt to close the sale. This is similar to a summary-of-benefits close or a continuous-yes close. The only difference is that the product benefits are written on a piece of paper. For instance, think about a checklist written on a piece of paper. The checklist would contain the buyer's needs. As you review the buyer's needs, you would relay the way in which your solution meets each need.

This is a powerful sales tool because the prospects are mentally considering reasons to buy and not to buy anyway. Put the reasons out in the open so that you can participate in the decision-making process.

This close is especially useful as a secondary or backup close. For example, if the summary close did not make the sale, use this type of close. By doing so, you can ask the buyer to provide feedback on each element of your solution and how each element meets the needs.

Prepare a Multiple-Close Sequence

> It takes courage to stay the course when life gets hard.

By keeping several different closes ready in any situation, you are in a better position to close more sales. Also, the use of a multiple-close sequence, combined with methods to overcome objections, enhances your chance of making a sale.

For example, you could begin with a summary close. Assuming the buyer says no, you could rephrase the objection and then use a question close. If again the buyer says no and would not give a reason, you could use a number of visuals to aid you in closing.*

Closing Begins the Relationship

When you make a sale for the first time, you change the person or organization from a prospect to a customer. You have helped the customer. You have contributed to the customer's welfare. Yes, you should feel good about the sale because you have served someone. What a wonderful feeling!

Now, how do you earn the opportunity to sell to the customer in the future? You do it by making sure you have followed the Core Principles in selling the correct product for the customer's need and providing exceptional service. It is now that the customer will find out if you told the truth about what the product will do, gave the best price, delivered on time, and provided great service.

> The enjoyment you receive from selling is equal to the service you put into it.

Revisit Exhibit 1.8 and the personal characteristics needed to sell for building long-term relationships. Hopefully you can see more clearly why today's salesperson needs these personal characteristics. "Which is the most important?" you might ask. All are important; yet if there is one that is most important, it is the "caring for the customer" characteristic. Did you place the customer's interests before yours? Do you truly care that what you sold will benefit the customer? The strong desire to help the customer is the most important ingredient to building a long-term relationship. All of the other eight personal characteristics will occur if you truly "care."

*See Chapter 11 for correct procedures on overcoming objections.

You have been seated in the president's office of a large bank in your town for an appointment you had worked six months to obtain. The president begins your meeting by saying that he is in the market for more insurance and that he had spoken with one of your competitors earlier in the day.

After your presentation and proposal, you begin to close, and he tells you that he is convinced and you get the sale. But, there is one condition. He will only accept a policy with preferred nonsmoker rates. A dirty ashtray is on his desk, and he is obviously at least 25 pounds overweight. You know it is impossible to obtain preferred nonsmoker rates for him if you complete the application truthfully. You also know your company relies on your information when it underwrites the policy.

Purposely submitting false information on an application is grounds for agent termination. If the client dies during the policy's two-year contestable period, death benefits are reduced to the amount of premiums paid if the application had been submitted falsely.

However, if he dies you can say that he told you he did not smoke. He also has to take a physical, so you can blame it on the doctor. This is a big sale, with high commissions. You know he will buy and that you can get away with falsifying the application. If you do not do it, someone else will.

What would be the most ethical action to take?

1. Tell the customer that you will fill out the preferred nonsmoker application if he agrees to try to quit smoking. However, let him know that if the doctor disagrees with your application type, you will have to go with the doctor's recommendation.
2. Go ahead with the preferred nonsmoker application, falsifying information where you need to. Chances are that no one will find out and you can get the commission.
3. Tell the customer that you cannot submit the preferred nonsmoker application. You might lose the sale, but at least you did not compromise your job or your values.

After Closing, Discuss Action Steps

If you successfully close a sale, remember to discuss the next steps. This process initiates the follow-up and service stage. In this step, your goal is to describe the action steps you will immediately accomplish as well as any action steps the buyer has agreed upon. We provide two examples of how a salesperson may communicate action steps to the customer.

Example 1: "Thank you so much for the order. If I can, I'd like to share our next steps in the process. First, I'll submit the order to our distribution department so that your materials will be prepared for shipment and then sent to each of your seven distribution centers. Next, I'll contact and confirm with our internal logistics group that we will deliver all of the products to your distribution centers by your deadline of 15 business days. I will also contact you via e-mail with updates within eight working days. In addition, you kindly agreed to submit the contact information for your firm's new accounts payable manager to us tomorrow. Finally, I wanted to provide you with another one of my business cards. Feel free to contact me with any questions or concerns that you might have throughout this process. Are there any items that I'm missing?"

Example 2: "I really appreciate your willingness to use our financial services. To ensure we are on the same page, I'd like to recap our agreed-upon action steps. First, I'll submit your financial application to our processing specialists by 5:00 p.m. today. The process usually takes five working days, so you can expect an answer via e-mail no later than Wednesday evening. Second, I will contact you via phone on Thursday to ensure you received the documents. You had mentioned that you would be available between 10:00–11:00 a.m. on Thursday. At 10:00 a.m., we'll review the next steps and discuss additional financial information that may be required. In addition, we'll also ask for your decision on the title company that you would like to use for the business transaction. Are there any other steps or key areas of information that I need to capture?"

When You Do Not Make the Sale

Should the person not buy, do not take it personally. Try to discover why before leaving. This helps you prepare for your return visit. However, chances are the reason for not buying will come out in your presentation. (See Exhibit 12.12.)

Act as a professional. Leave the door open for a return visit. You might using the **exit technique** conclude by saying, "Mr. Smith, would you do one thing for your company? Would you please think about what we discussed? Please look over this material and the price sheet. I know (product name) is needed by your organization. Please call me if you have any questions. Would it be all right, Mr. Smith, if I come by in a month or so to see what you think about (product name)?" Stand, smile, and compose yourself. While looking the buyer in the eyes and giving a firm handshake, say something like, "Thank you very much, Mr. Smith. I really enjoyed visiting with you! I look forward to seeing you next month!" Do not leave the room as if it is on fire. Leave slowly, professionally, with a smile on your face, a song in your heart, and a spring in your step. Be friendly with everyone you pass as you go to your vehicle. Call them by name if known.

EXHIBIT 12.12

Sometimes the salesperson will not make the sale, but it is important to leave the door open.

If this software salesperson had not made a sale, she would have left the door open for a return sales call by being just as friendly leaving as when she came.

©Dan Dalton/Getty Images

Research Reinforces These Sales Success Strategies

Although it is difficult to summarize all sales success strategies discussed throughout this book, one research report reinforces several key procedures that improve sales performance. This research sought to examine two key questions all salespeople frequently ask themselves: What makes one sales call a success and another a failure? Do salespeople make common mistakes that prevent success?

To answer these questions, Xerox Learning Systems enlisted a team of observers to monitor and analyze more than 500 personal sales calls of 24 different sales organizations. The products and services sold ranged from computers to industrial refuse disposal.

Mike Radick, the Xerox senior development specialist overseeing the study, stated that the average successful sales call lasted 33 minutes. During that call, the salesperson asked an average of 13.6 questions and described 6.4 product benefits and 7.7 product features. Meanwhile, the customer described an average of 2.2 different needs, raised 1.0 objection, made 2.8 statements of acceptance, and asked 7.7 questions.

The observers noted that it does not seem to matter whether the salesperson is 28 or 48 years old, male or female, or has 2 or 20 years of experience. What matters is the ability to use certain skills and avoid common errors. These six common mistakes have prevented successful sales calls.

- **Tells instead of sells; doesn't ask enough questions.** The salesperson does most of the talking. Instead of asking questions to determine a customer's interest, the salesperson charges ahead and rattles off product benefits. This forces the customer into the passive role of listening to details that may not be of interest. As a result, the customer becomes increasingly irritated.

  For example, a person selling a payroll system may tell a customer how much time this service could save. However, if time is not a concern, then the customer has no interest in learning how to reduce payroll processing time. On the other hand, the same customer may have a high need for more accurate record keeping and be extremely interested in the reports the system generates.

- **Overcontrols the call; asks too many closed-end questions.** This sales dialogue resembles an interrogation, and the customer has limited opportunities to express needs. The overcontrolling salesperson steers the conversation to subjects the salesperson wants to talk about without regard to the customer. When the customer does talk, the salesperson often fails to listen or respond, or doesn't acknowledge the importance of what the customer says. As a result, the customer is alienated and the sales call fails.

- **Doesn't respond to customer needs with benefits.** Instead, the salesperson lets the customer infer how the features will satisfy his or her needs. Consider the customer who needs a high-speed manufacturing machine. The salesperson responds with information about heat tolerance, but doesn't link that to how fast the equipment manufactures the customer's product. As a result, the customer becomes confused, loses interest, and the call fails.

  Research shows a direct relationship between the result of a call and the number of different benefits given in response to customer needs; the more need-related benefits cited, the greater the probability of success.

- **Doesn't recognize needs; gives benefits prematurely.** For example, a customer discussing e-commerce software mentions that some clients complain that their website is hampered by slow credit-card processing. The salesperson demonstrates the

> *Have an attitude of gratitude.*

benefits of his service, but the customer responds that slow credit-card processing is not that important since people will probably wait for a purchase confirmation. In this case, the customer is not concerned enough to want to solve the problem.

- **Doesn't recognize or handle negative attitudes effectively.** The salesperson fails to recognize customer statements of objection (opposition), indifference (no need), or skepticism (doubts). What isn't dealt with effectively remains on the customer's mind, and left with a negative attitude, the customer will not make a commitment. The research also shows that customer skepticism, indifference, and objection are three different attitudes. Each attitude affects the call differently; each one requires a different strategy for selling success.
- **Makes weak closing statements; doesn't recognize when or how to close.** In one extreme case, the customer tried to close the sale on a positive note, but the salesperson failed to recognize the cue and continued selling until the customer lost interest. The lesson is that successful salespeople are alert to closing opportunities throughout the call.

The most powerful way to close a sales call involves a summary of benefits that interest the customer. Three out of four calls that included this closing technique in Radick's study were successful.

Keys to Improved Selling

How is the bridge from average to successful salesperson made? Xerox found that it involves learning and using each of the following skills:

- Ask questions to gather information and uncover needs.
- Recognize when a customer has a real need and how the benefits of the product or service can satisfy it.
- Establish a balanced dialogue with customers.
- Recognize and handle negative customer attitudes promptly and directly.
- Use a benefit summary and an action plan requiring commitment when closing.[2]

Learn and use these five selling skills, use the other skills emphasized throughout the book, and develop your natural ability and a positive mental attitude to become a successful, professional salesperson.

SUMMARY OF MAJOR SELLING ISSUES

Closing is the process of helping people make decisions that will benefit them. You help people make those decisions by asking them to buy. The close of the sale is the next logical sequence after your presentation. At this time, you finalize details of the sale (earlier, your prospect was convinced to buy). Constantly look and listen for buying signals from your prospect to know when to close. It is time to close the sale any time the prospect is ready, whether at the beginning or end of your presentation.

As you prepare to close the sale, be sure you have presented a complete story on your proposition and that your prospect completely understands your presentation. Tailor your close to each prospect's personality and see the situation from the prospect's viewpoint. Remember that you may make your presentation and close too early, which causes a prospect to say no instead of "I don't understand your proposition and I don't want to be taken advantage of." This is why you should never take the first no. It is another reason to use a trial close immediately before the close. But, no matter when or how you close, do so in a positive, confident, and enthusiastic manner to better serve your prospect. Learn and follow the 12 steps to a successful closing.

Plan and rehearse closing techniques for each prospect. Develop natural closing techniques or consider using closes such as the summary-of-benefits close, direct close, question close, probability or rating close, negotiations close, the technology close or the visual aids close. Consider the situation and switch from your planned close if your prospect's situation is different than anticipated. Some of the situations specific closings techniques are the assumptive close, alternative-choice close, minor-points close, compliment close, standing-room-only close, continuous-yes close, or the T-account or balance-sheet close.

A good closer has a strong desire to close each sale. Rarely should you accept the first no as the final answer. If you are professional, you should be able to close a minimum of three to five times.

Do not become upset or unnerved if a problem occurs when you are ready to close. Keep cool, determine any objections, overcome them, and try to close again—you can't make a sale until you ask for the order!

Quick Review for Students

The quick review sections provide key questions to help you develop a greater level of conceptual understanding. We suggest that after you read the chapter, you try to answer the following questions without looking back at the textbook.

1. What does buying signal refer to? Why is reading buying signals important for salespeople?
2. What are the 12 keys to a successful closing?
3. What are some commonly used closing techniques?
4. What are some closing techniques that can be utilized in specific type of situations?
5. How can using visual aids add value in the closing process?
6. What are the action steps a salesperson should take after closing?
7. What are the five skills that salespeople should learn and use to improve their selling success rate?

MEETING A SALES CHALLENGE

Lisa had finished her presentation. John and Ralph had not. At least Lisa was able to tell her whole story. John and Ralph should have postponed discussing price. They may have lost all hope of making the sale.

In all three cases, the prospect said, "Your price is too high." Many buyers learn or are trained to say this to see if the seller will decrease the price.

When the buyer said, "What's your price?" John could have said, "It will depend on the type of service you need and the quantity purchased. Let's discuss that in just a minute." When the buyer said, "Way out—your competitor's price is $10 cheaper!" John could say, "I quoted you our base price. Your actual price will depend on the quantity purchased. We can meet and beat that price [the competitor's price]."

Lisa needs to find out more, such as what specific equipment and from whom. Equipment is different. So are service, terms, and delivery.

When Ralph's buyer said, "Your price is too high," he needs to find out what the buyer is comparing his price to. Ralph's buyer may not need his top-of-the-line model. So he must get back to a discussion of the buyer's needs before determining the model and price.

KEY TERMS FOR SELLING

alternative-choice close 450	exit technique 458	standing-room-only
assumptive close 450	minor-points	close 453
buying signal 433	close 451	summary-of-benefits
closing 433	negotiation close 445	close 442
compliment close 452	probability or rating	T-account close 454
continuous-yes close 453	close 444	technology close 446
direct close 443	question close 443	visual aids close 446

SALES APPLICATION QUESTIONS

1. A salesperson must use a closing technique that is simple and straightforward, and ask the prospect only to buy rather than something in addition to buying. In which of the following examples, if any, is the salesperson suggesting something to the buyer that is a close, rather than something the buyer must do in addition to buying?

   a. If you have no objection, I'll go out to the warehouse now to see about reserving space for this new item.

   b. To get this promotion off right, we should notify each of your store managers. I've already prepared a bulletin for them. Should *I* arrange to have a copy sent to each manager, or do *you* want to do it?

   c. To start this promotion, we should notify each of your store managers. I've already prepared a bulletin for them. On my way out, I can drop it off with the secretary.

   d. We should contact the warehouse manager about reserving a space for this new item. Do you want to do it now or after I've left?

2. Buying signals have numerous forms. When you receive a buying signal, stop the presentation and move in to close the sale. For each of the following seven situations, choose the appropriate response to your prospect's buying signal that leads most directly to a close.

   a. "Can I get it in blue?" Your best answer is
      (1) Yes.
      (2) Do you want it in blue?
      (3) It comes in three colors, including blue.

   b. "What's your price?" Your best answer is
      (1) In what quantity?
      (2) To quote a specific price.
      (3) In which grade?

   c. "What kind of terms do you offer?" Your best answer is
      (1) To provide specific terms.
      (2) Terms would have to be arranged.
      (3) What kind of terms do you want?

   d. "How big an order do I have to place to get your best price?" Your best answer is
      (1) A schedule of quantity prices.
      (2) A specific-size order.
      (3) What size order do you want to place?

   e. "When will you have a new model?" Your best answer is
      (1) A specific date.
      (2) Do you want our newest model?
      (3) This is our newest model.

     f. "What is the smallest trial order I can place with you?" Your best answer is
        (1) A specific quantity.
        (2) How small an order do you want?
        (3) A variety of order sizes.
     g. "When can you deliver?" Your best answer is
        (1) That depends on the size of your order. What order size do you have in mind?
        (2) A specific delivery date.
        (3) When do you want delivery?

3. Which of the following is the most frequently committed sin in closing? Why?
    a. Asking for the order too early.
    b. Not structuring the presentation toward a closing.
    c. Not asking for the order.

4. Is a good closing technique to ask the customer outright (but at the right time), "Well, how about it? May I have the factory ship you a carload?" Why do you agree or disagree?

5. After completing a presentation that has included all of your product's features, advantages, and benefits, do not delay in asking the customer, "How much of the product do you wish to order?" Is this statement true or false? Why?

6. Each visual aid you use during your presentation is designed to allow the customer to say yes to your main selling points. What should your visual aids include that allows you to gauge customer interest and help move to the close? What are several examples?

7. "Now, let's review what we've talked about. We've agreed that the Mohawk's secondary backing and special latex glue make the carpet more durable and contribute to better appearance. In addition, you felt that our direct-to-customer delivery system would save a lot of money and time. Shall I send our wall-sample display or would you be interested in stocking some 9 by 12s?"
    a. The salesperson's closing statement helps ensure customer acceptance by doing which of the following?
        (1) Summarizing benefits that the customer agreed were important.
        (2) Giving an alternative.
        (3) Assuming that agreement has been reached.
    b. The salesperson ends the closing statement by
        (1) Asking if the customer has any other questions.
        (2) Asking if the product will meet the customer's requirements.
        (3) Requesting a commitment from the customer.

8. "Assuming agreement has been reached" reflects the kind of attitude you should project when making a closing statement. When you make a close, nothing you say should reflect doubt, hesitation, or uncertainty. Which of the following salesperson's remarks assume agreement?
    a. If you feel that Munson is really what you want.
    b. Let me leave you two today and deliver the rest next week.
    c. Well, if you purchase.
    d. Well, it looks as if maybe.
    e. We've agreed that.
    f. When you purchase the X-7100.
    g. Why don't you try a couple, if you like.

9. A good rule is, "Get the order and get out." Do you agree? Why?

10. The real estate salesperson is showing property to a couple who look at the house and say, "Gee, this is great. They've taken good care of this place and the rugs and drapes are perfect. Do you think they'd be willing to leave the rugs and drapes?" What should the salesperson do or say? Why?

FURTHER EXPLORING THE SALES WORLD

1. Assume you are interviewing for a sales job and there are only five minutes remaining. You are interested in the job and know if the company is interested, they will invite you for a visit to their local distribution center and have you work with one of their salespeople for a day. What are several closing techniques you could use to ask for the visit?

2. Visit several retail stores or manufacturing plants in your local area and ask their purchasing agents what they like and do not like about the closing when they are contacted by salespeople. See if they have already decided to buy or not to buy before the salesperson closes. Ask how a salesperson should ask for their business.

3. Develop a complete sales presentation that can be given in eight minutes. Include the buyer–seller dialogue. Make sure the appropriate components in Exhibit A are contained in the presentation. Use one of the three approaches shown in Exhibit A depending on your situation. For example, use the SPIN approach if

EXHIBIT A

Format of your sales presentations.

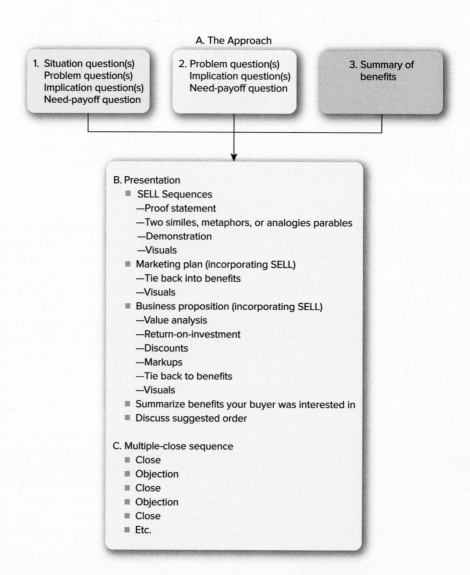

this is the first time you have called this prospect. Use the SPIN or summary-of-benefits approach if this is a repeat sales call on a prospect or customer.

Your presentation must use several SELL Sequences and should contain a minimum of one proof statement; two similes, metaphors, or analogies; and a demonstration of important benefits. The marketing plan also must incorporate one or more SELL Sequences that tie the marketing plan back to the information uncovered in the approach and the first SELL Sequence.

The business proposition is last and contains the appropriate discussion on price and value. Relate the business proposition to the information uncovered earlier in the presentation. Develop visuals for presenting your benefits, marketing plan, and business proposition. Anywhere within the presentation prior to the close, use a minimum of one objection and answer one of the buyer's questions with a question.

Now, ask for the order using a summary-of-benefits close that includes a suggested order if appropriate for your product or service. Use a minimum of three closes. This requires you to develop a *multiple-close sequence* since the buyer has raised an objection or asked for more information after each close. Use three different closes, the first being the summary-of-benefits close. Also, use different methods of handling objections. In the presentation, be sure to (1) have a professional appearance; (2) firmly shake hands and use direct eye contact before and after the presentation; (3) project positive nonverbal signs; and (4) use a natural level of enthusiasm and excitement in conversation.

STUDENT APPLICATION LEARNING EXERCISES (SALES)

SALE 7 of 7— Chapter 13

Now it's time to ask for the order! Frequently, questions and objections arise when you ask someone to buy. Thus, you should anticipate questions and/or objections and be prepared to use several different closing and objections-handling techniques. To make **SALE 7**

1. List the main benefits discussed in your presentation.
2. Select a closing technique, such as the summary-of-benefits close on page 000. Write out your close and label it with the name of the closing technique in parentheses. Use a trial close after completing the close to verify that these benefits are important to the buyer. Write out your trial close and label it using parentheses as shown on page 000 (trial close).
3. Create a visual aid showing your suggested order. See page 376 for an example. This visual aid may be similar to the one you developed for discussing your price(s).
4. Now you are ready to construct your multiple-closing sequence. First carefully study Exhibit 12.3 on page 000. Now look at the example of a multiple-closing sequence on page 000. The multiple-closing sequence should be composed of the following:
   a. Use the summary-of-benefits close.
   b. Use the trial close.
   c. Suggest an order.
   d. Use the assumptive or alternative close.

  e. Have the buyer ask a question or give an objection.
  f. Respond using another objection-handling technique.
  g. Ask a trial close to see if you successfully handled the objection.
  h. Ask for the order again using an unused closing technique. Don't be pushy. Use a calm, laid-back, friendly, conversational style.
  i. Repeat the close–objection–close–objection sequence if appropriate.

5. To complete **SALE 7,** write up the above *a–i* in a script format. Role-play this dialogue until it sounds natural to you. This may require replacing the used techniques with new ones. Once the manuscript is finalized, type it and turn it in to your instructor.

NOTES

1. Adapted from John L. Johnston, *Works of Mark Twain* (New York: Harper & Row, 1989), p. 133.

2. Gerhard Gschwandtner, "How to Sell in France," *Personal Selling Power,* July/August 1991, pp. 54–60.

CASE 12.1

©Ron Chapple Stock/FotoSearch/
Glow Images

Skaggs Omega

Linda Johnson, the purchasing agent of Skaggs Omega has e-mailed you an inquiry regarding hardware items. Skaggs Omega is a large chain of supermarkets that is very particular about the quality of the products they place on their shelves. In her e-mail, Linda mentioned that she is interested in learning more about your firm's hammers, screwdrivers, and nails. Although the news is good, you were a bit surprised. The vast majority of potential buyers usually approach your company to ask about the power tools that your company distributes. The power tools are very popular among residential as well as industrial users. Conversely, hammers, screwdrivers, and nails require a very active (and somewhat expensive) promotional investment from your sales team.

As you start planning the presentation, you begin to query your sales colleagues. You hope to learn whether any of your colleagues will share their insight on the Skaggs Omega's buying process. Although you gather very little information about the organizational buying process, you collect some background information about the purchasing agent. You are told that she is not very talkative, she chooses her words carefully, and she pays attention to the details.

Upon arrival at the Skaggs Omega's headquarters, you make a sales presentation to Linda Johnson and a store manager who was invited to give his perspective. You state that you had visited several of their stores. You discuss your revolving retail display, which contains an assortment of the three items of interest. You also attempt to directly tie your products' benefits to the needs Johnson had mentioned in her inquiry.

During your presentation, you notice that the information you gathered about Ms. Johnson was true. She listened diligently and took a great deal of notes. It appears that she is interested in your product line because she has asked a number of insightful questions; and she was very interested in understanding some of the challenges other retailers have faced when distributing the products. She did not object to any of the pricing or margin information in your business proposition. The end of your presentation is nearing; and now is the time to close.

Questions

1. Please write two specific closing sequences that could be used in this sales conversation. Please explain why you believe both sequences would be appropriate.
2. On a scale of 1 to 5 (1 = poor and 5 = excellent), please rank the following questions that could be asked during closing. Further, explain what you believe would be the buyer's response to each question close.
   a. How do you like our products, Ms. Johnson?
   b. What assortment do you prefer, the A or B assortment?
   c. Can we go ahead with the order?
   d. If you'll just OK this order form, Ms. Johnson, we'll have each of your stores receive a display within two weeks.
3. Now, prepare a multiple-close sequence that would be appropriate for this scenario. Write it down.

CASE 12.2

Central Hardware Supply

©Ron Chapple Stock/FotoSearch/ Glow Images

Sam Gillespie, owner of Central Hardware Supply, was referred to you by a mutual friend. Gillespie was thinking of dropping two of its product suppliers of home-building supplies. "The sale should be guaranteed," your friend had stated.

Your friend's information was correct and your presentation to Gillespie convinces you that he will benefit from buying from you. He comments as you conclude the presentation: "Looks like your product will solve our problem. I'd like to think this over, however. Could you call me tomorrow or the next day?"

Questions

1. The best way to handle this is to
   a. Follow his suggestion.
   b. Ignore his request and try a second close.
   c. Probe further. You might ask: "The fact that you have to think this over suggests that I haven't convinced you. Is there something I've omitted or failed to satisfy you with?"
2. What would be your second and third choices? Why?

CASE 12.3

©Ron Chapple Stock/FotoSearch/
Glow Images

Furmanite Service Company—A Multiple-Close Sequence

Chris Henry sells industrial valves and flanges, plus tapes and sealants. He is calling on Gary Maslow, a buyer from Shell Oil, to sell him on using Furmanite to seal all of his plant's valve and flange leaks. Chris has completed the discussion of the product's features, advantages, and benefits, plus the marketing plan and the business proposition. Chris feels it is time to close. Chris says:

Salesperson: Let me summarize what we have talked about. You have said that you like the money you will save by doing the repairs. You also like our response time in saving the flanges so that they can be rebuilt when needed. Finally, you like our three-year warranty on service. Is that right?

Buyer: Yes, that is about it.

Salesperson: Gary, I suggest we get a crew in here and start repairing the leaks. What time do you want the crew here Monday?

Buyer: Not so fast—how reliable is the compound?

Salesperson: Gary, it's very reliable. I did the same service for Mobil last year and we have not been back for warranty work. Does that sound reliable to you?

Buyer: Yeah, I guess so.

Salesperson: I know you always make experienced, professional decisions, and I know that you think this is a sound and profitable service for your plant. Let me schedule a crew to be here next week or maybe in two weeks.

Buyer: Chris, I am still hesitant.

Salesperson: There must be a reason why you are hesitating to go ahead now. Do you mind if I ask what it is?

Buyer: I just don't know if it is a sound decision.

Salesperson: Is that the only thing bothering you?

Buyer: Yes, it is.

Salesperson: Just suppose you could convince yourself that it's a good decision. Would you then want to go ahead with the service?

Buyer: Yes, I would.

Salesperson: Gary, let me tell you what we have agreed on so far. You like our online repair because of the cost you would save, you like our response time and the savings you would receive from the timely repair of the leaks, and you like our highly trained personnel and our warranty. Right?

Buyer: Yes, that's true.

Salesperson: When would you like to have the work done?

Buyer: Chris, the proposition looks good, but I don't have the funds this month. Maybe we can do it next month.

Salesperson: No problem at all, Gary; I appreciate your time, and I will return on the fifth of next month to set a time for a crew to start.

Questions

1. Label each of the selling techniques Chris used.
2. What were the strengths and weaknesses of this multiple-closing sequence?
3. Should Chris have closed again? Why?
4. Assume Chris felt he could make one more close. What could he do?

CASE 12.4

©Ron Chapple Stock/FotoSearch/
Glow Images

Steve Santana: Pressured to Close a Big Deal

Steve Santana works for a pharmaceutical manufacturer. Steve's company is pressuring his division to increase sales. Presently Steve is working on closing a big deal with the Danson HMO. This sale would be huge for the company. The sale would allow Steve to reach not only his sales goals but also his entire sales division's sales quota.

Rob, the divisional sales manager and Steve's boss, is understandably anxious about making the sale to Claire Manford, Danson's purchasing agent. In their conversation about Claire, Rob suggests Steve go around Claire and talk with Danson's chief medical adviser. This might help close the sale. Steve is against this suggestion. Rob then suggests they place Claire on their consulting board, which pays a nice fee to board members. Rob feels this would help close the deal. However, Steve is against this idea.

After meeting with Rob, Steve calls on Claire at her business. During their visit, Claire mentions her son is learning disabled and she is the new fund-raising chairperson for an information and referral center for people with learning disabilities. Her fund-raising group will need $100,000 just to get the center started. As Steve is getting ready to leave, Claire also says that she likes Steve's proposal but his prices seem a little too high.

That afternoon Steve visits with Rob about his sales call on Danson and the conversation with Claire. When Rob hears about her interest in the learning disabilities center he immediately suggests that their company make a $10,000 donation. Rob feels this would greatly increase the probability of making the sale. Again, Steve is reluctant and thinks this is bad business. However, Steve can see Rob is very nervous. At the end of their meeting Rob says, "Steve, I rarely let someone in your position handle such a big sale. But I am going to leave this up to you. It is your responsibility."

Questions

1. What are the ethical considerations, if any, in this case?
2. At what level of moral development are Rob and Steve operating in this business situation? Explain your answers.
3. What would you do if you were Rob?
4. What would you do if you were Steve?

©Caia Images/Glow Images

Service and Follow-Up for Customer Retention

Learning Objectives

Providing service to the customer is extremely important in today's competitive marketplace. After studying this chapter, you should be able to

13–1 State why service and follow-up are important to increasing sales.

13–2 Discuss how business friendships are developed.

13–3 Discuss how follow-up and service result in account penetration and improved sales.

13–4 List the eight steps involved in increasing sales to your customer.

13–5 Explain the importance of properly handling customers' returned goods requests and complaints in a professional manner.

FACING A SALES CHALLENGE

As a construction machinery salesperson, you know that equipment malfunctions and breakdowns are costly to customers. Your firm, however, has an excellent warranty that allows you to replace a broken piece of equipment with one of your demonstrators for a few days while the equipment is repaired. King Masonry has called you four times in the past three months because the mixer you sold them has broken down. Each time you have cheerfully handled the problem, and in less than two hours they have been back at work. Your company's mixer has traditionally been one of the most dependable on the market, so after the last breakdown, you let King Masonry keep the new replacement in hopes of solving any future problems.

The owner, Eldon King, has just called to tell you the newest mixer has broken down. He is angry and says he may go to another supplier if you cannot get him a replacement immediately.

If you were the salesperson, how would you handle this situation?

The last but not least cliché applies to this chapter, which ends our discussion of the elements of the selling process. Follow-up and service to customers is the salesperson's most important activity for future sales. Planning the sales presentation may take hours, days even. Giving the sales presentation may take only minutes. Follow-up and service never end.

Many salespeople's interest declines after the sale. Yet the customer's interest in the product and desire to interact with the salesperson increases. This is one of the reasons service after the sale is so important to the seller–buyer long-term relationship. Please pay close attention to the discussion of this important chapter.

The Core Principles: Post-Sales Service

Sales is hard work. Effective salespeople understand that sales is about taking care of the customers. Often, serving customers presents challenges like the Eldon King example described in the scenario, "Facing a Sales Challenge." Salespeople do not earn the big bucks for nothing. If all you had to do was give a presentation and they bought, everyone would be in sales. The fact is many people do not make it in sales because they do not have the ability to put someone's interests before their own needs for money, power, and influence. All they want to do is make the sale and move on to the next conquest. However, sales is about relationships and problem-solving—two elements that require understanding, communication, and ongoing attention.

Sales is not for everyone. Due to unethical or short-term perspectives, some salespeople should not be employed in their current positions. The inwardly focused salesperson often creates a negative perception of the sales profession by treating customers as transactions rather than individuals requiring assistance. This type of behaviors reduces trust between the salesperson and the customer. In addition, customers are likely to share their negative experiences with their colleague and friends, which contributes to a general mistrust of salespeople.

Creating a long-term relationship requires trust, and trust is based on long-term communication. Therefore, closing a sale is only the start of the relationship.

Service and follow-up present challenges to the salesperson. Often, salespeople are tunnel-focused on closing the sale and interacting with the next customer. Some salespeople view selling as a competitive sport. They have to win. After all, salespeople are only human. They want to be successful. They have bills to pay and people to support. Many feel under pressure to sell, and others are driven by greed. "Yes, I am here to help," said a saleswoman, but "I am here mainly to sell."

However, it is worth repeating that the business relationship begins after you sell someone (i.e., close the sale). Service and follow-up after the sale show you truly care. If the salesperson is to have the privilege of selling again, the customer must answer positively to questions like these:

1. Can I trust this person?
2. Did the product and salesperson do what was presented?
3. Does the salesperson truly care about me?

If the customer answers yes to these questions, certainly he or she will allow the salesperson to make future presentations. Will the customer always buy? No. But if the customer feels the salesperson is trustworthy and cares, the customer often will give the salesperson the benefit of the doubt and buy rather than taking a chance on another salesperson.

The Importance of Service and Follow-Up

In Chapter 1 we defined service as making a contribution to the welfare of others. Most of the book refers to service in the context of helping others, and that is the emphasis of this chapter. How does a salesperson help customers? The salesperson demonstrates **follow-up** and ongoing customer service by maintaining contact with a customer (or prospect). By following-up with the customer, the salesperson attempts to understand the customer's perception of the product and the customer's level of satisfaction.

But what is satisfaction? We next describe customer satisfaction and explain the key elements of the customer satisfaction process.

What Is Customer Service and Satisfaction?

When a customer buys a product, what is being purchased? Remember from Chapter 1 that a product (good or service) is a bundle of tangible and intangible attributes, including packaging, color, and brand, plus the services and even the reputation of the seller. People buy more than a set of physical attributes. They buy want-satisfaction such as what the product does, its quality, and the image of owning the product.

Please note the phrase *plus the services.* Buyers usually believe an organization ought to deliver a certain level of service to the customers when they purchase something. Here are several expected services:

- Product—the product purchased has no defects.
- Price—fair value for the price.
- Place—the product is available when and where needed and promised.
- Promotion—correct, honest information in advertisements, from salespeople, and on product labels.
- Exchange transaction—handled correctly, quickly, and professionally the first time.
- After the sale—warranty honored, repairs or exchanges made cheerfully; written information or company representative available to discuss how to put together, hook up, or use the product.

When buying something, you have certain expectations of what you are receiving for your money. So do organizations. Did the customer receive what was expected? The answer to this question determines the level of service quality perceived by the buyer.

Customer service helps drive customer satisfaction.

Customer service refers to the activities and programs the seller provides to make the relationship satisfying for the customer. The activities and programs add value to the customer's relationship with the seller. Warranties, credit, speedy delivery, invoices, financial statements, computer-to-computer ordering, parking, gift wrapping, and having items in stock are services designed to satisfy customers.

Expectations Determine Service Quality

Who determines the quality of the salesperson's customer service and follow-up? The customer does. The quality of service an organization and its salespeople provide must be based on its customers' expectations. Customers expect a certain level of service from the seller. Their expectations frequently are based on information the salesperson provides, past experiences, word of mouth, and personal needs.

When buyers perceive the service they have received meets or exceeds their expectations, they are satisfied. Thus, service quality describes how well the service provided meets customers' expectations.

Building a Long-Term Business Friendship

In order to ensure the customer perceives the salesperson is providing a high quality of services, sales professionals strive to create long-term business relationships. This implies that a personal relationship with clients is often formed. And in fact, salespeople often develop more than just a casual relationship with the client; they frequently develop business friendships.

What Is a Business Friendship?

The relationship between a salesperson and a client that revolves around business-related issues is referred to as a **business friendship.** A good business friendship is a relationship much like any of your personal friendships.

How to Build a Business Friendship

Do you build a friendship with a business client, or do you expect it to just happen? Most of the time salespeople are in too big a hurry to make a sale and move on to the next customer. Even after calling on the same person over a long period of time, the salesperson may not know the customer.

The answer is that you build a business friendship in much the same way that you build a personal friendship. Think about your present friends. You consider some better friends than others. Usually we have one of three levels of relationships with both business and personal friends: acquaintances, friends, and intimate friends (see Exhibit 13.1).

EXHIBIT 13.1

Trust and wisdom in a relationship grow over time. Years may pass before an intimate friendship develops between buyer and seller.

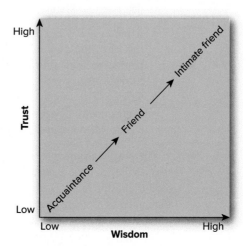

Level 1. Acquaintances are people whose names you know, whom you see occasionally, and whom you may know little about even if you've known them for a long time. This is where all friendships must start. Usually these people turn out to be friends we meet along the way in our life. In the business world, as well as in one's personal life, acquaintances are viewed as having low levels of wisdom and trust.

Level 2. Friends are people whom we spend more time with and with whom we share common interests and/or hobbies. We know not only who they are but also what they are about. These people are good for a long walk in our life. In industry, business friends are trusted. They have earned loyalty by demonstrating their caring for the customer over time.

> *Provide service after the sale and customers will buy again.*

Level 3. Intimate friends, often called "best friends," are the people we know on a deeper level. We know about their family. We know many of their deepest thoughts and feelings. They confide in us. They ask our advice. We may have shared personal hardships. We share deep mutual interests. These wonderful people are friends for our life's journey. In the customer–seller relationship, personal interests of each other and their families have top priority.

Building any friendship takes time, especially in the business world. It can often take three years or more to build a truly good level 2 friendship. Usually several things happen between people before they become friends:

- Self-disclosure—sharing a few things about yourself and allowing your client to share a few things about him- or herself. If your client is not immediately responsive to your efforts, don't worry. Remember, building friendships takes time.
- Acknowledgment—Take time to listen to your client. Everyone has a desire to be heard, acknowledged, and understood. Remember these three steps to acknowledgment:

  Step 1: Repeat back—You might want to repeat, in a summarized fashion, what your client tells you.
  Step 2: Don't invalidate—Avoid telling or making your clients feel that they are wrong.
  Step 3: Don't try to change—Do not attempt to change clients' minds on an issue. Simply listen to what they say and formulate a solution based on their perceived problems.

- Attending—Pay attention, or attend, to your client. Your eyes, ears, body, and thought should all be focused on them and what they are saying. Make eye contact to show your client that you are really listening to what he or she has to say.
- Talking—The foundation for any relationship is good communication. This means that to develop a good business friendship with your client, you must be a great listener. Share information and allow information to be shared.

The previous steps provide a good start to building a friendship with your business client. But once a relationship has begun, it must be maintained. To maintain a good friendship requires structure, not trying to control or outdo your client, and not attempting to pressure your friend to buy.

Structure for Survival

A good relationship needs structure to survive. Define your and your business friend's responsibilities, expectations, and roles at the outset and follow them accordingly. What responsibilities will you or won't you take on? What can your client reasonably expect from you, and what can you reasonably expect from her or him? What role will you play in his or her life? These questions are important to answer early in the relationship and to continually reaffirm in order to avoid confusion.

Avoid Control and One-Upmanship

What you do speaks so loud that I cannot hear what you say.

There is often a tendency for one person to take control in a relationship. This can be damaging, and it should be avoided. Do not try to control your client, and do not allow yourself to be controlled. Allow your client his own point of view, and listen to it.

Another tendency in relationships is to try to outdo, or one-up, your friend. This creates tension and can cause your client to feel threatened, neither of which adds to a healthy, productive business relationship. Try to avoid this snag by listening to your client and responding in terms of potential solutions to the problem.

Do You Pressure a True Friend?

Would you pressure a true friend to buy from you? If you do, whose interest is first, your self-interest or your business friend's needs? Would you be tempted to pressure your friend to buy? Most of us would. Yet to maintain a healthy and lasting business relationship, the needs of the people you serve should come before your own self-interest. However difficult it may be in practice, you should never abandon the effort to put others' interests before yours. Does this relate to any of your personal relationships?

What Is Most Important?

The most important ingredients in building a lasting friendship are truly caring for the other person and placing their interests before your interests. Friendship is based on their needs, not on your needs. Otherwise it will not work. Why?

If a friendship is based on your needs, at times you will take advantage of your so-called friend. True friendship, instead, is based upon how you can help the other person. This makes it possible to build a relationship! Am I this person's friend because I need something from him or her? If so, at times your feelings may be hurt, such as when the person buys from a competitor. This is why you want to be a friend without expecting something in return.

How Many Friends?

A wise old proverb says a person with too many friends comes to ruin. If you have many friends, your friendships become broad but not deep. In this case, when the going gets tough, they get going. Will they stick by you no matter what? Will you stick by them no matter what?

Friends are wonderful! Real friends are one of the greatest assets you have in your life. Yet three true, intimate business friends may be all you can handle and have time for. This is not talking about casual business acquaintances, but true intimate friendships.

Relationship Marketing and Customer Retention

As you are probably noticing, developing and maintaining relationships with customers is critical. And while salespeople understand the value of relationships because they deal directly with customers, others within the salesperson's organizations may not. They may think in general terms about customers. Therefore, it's important to discuss the three levels of customer relationship marketing.

- *Transaction selling:* the salesperson sells to customers and does not contact them again.
- *Relationship selling:* after the purchase the seller finds out if the customer is satisfied and has future needs.
- *Partnering and consultative selling:* the seller works continually to improve the customer's operations, sales, and profits.

Take a moment to compare transaction selling, relationship selling, and partnering/consultative selling to the three levels of business friendship. Do you see any similarities? Becoming a partner takes time just as developing an intimate friendship does. It takes time to build a personal, sales, and marketing friendship between seller and buyer. Let's take a moment to review relationship marketing in an effort to better understand the importance of follow-up and service, ways of keeping customers, methods of helping customers increase sales, and how to handle customer complaints.

Relationship Marketing Builds Friendships

Relationship marketing is the creation of customer loyalty and retention. Relationship marketing is based on the idea that important customers need continuous attention. Organizations use combinations of products, prices, distribution, promotions, and service to achieve this goal.

An organization using relationship marketing is not seeking simply a sale or a transaction. It has targeted a major customer that it would like to sell to now and in the future. The company would like to demonstrate to the customer that it has the capabilities to serve the account's needs in a superior way, particularly if a *committed relationship* can be formed. The company's goal is to get customers and, more important, to retain customers. Customer relationship marketing provides the key to retaining customers.

Customer Satisfaction Enables Retention

Customer satisfaction refers to feelings toward the purchase. As illustrated in Exhibit 13.2, purchase satisfaction reflects the customer's feelings about any differences between what is expected and actual experiences with the purchase. If the customer is satisfied, the chances of selling to the customer in the future increase. If the customer is satisfied with the repeat purchases, the customer will tend to continue to buy from the salesperson.

When a customer is highly satisfied, it's likely they will become very loyal; and it will be very difficult for another seller to attain the customer's business. Hence, customer retention serves as an important goal for the professional salesperson. Customer retention enables long-term success.

People buy from you for many reasons, but primarily because of your excellent products and the service you and your company provide to customers. You follow the Core Principles of Professional Selling: "Do unto others as you would have done unto you." You feel customers put the meat and potatoes on your table. They are responsible for the good income you earn. You appreciate that and always try to show how much you appreciate their trust and business.

You occasionally have been taking one of your customers, whom you like personally, out to lunch. Recently, this customer's purchases have increased from $50,000 to $650,000 a year. You want to show your appreciation by buying your customer two season tickets for the local professional basketball team. The buyer and his spouse are great basketball fans. However, if your other clients and co-workers find out, they may view the gift as unprofessional.

What would be the most ethical action to take?

1. Get a season ticket for yourself and for your client. That way, you can always justify it as a "business meeting" if people ask.
2. Buy your client and his wife the season tickets. You are just trying to show your appreciation for his business.
3. Do not buy the season tickets. It is unprofessional to mix work and social ties. Instead, write your client a nice thank-you letter stating that you appreciate his continued business.

EXHIBIT 13.2

Customer retention occurs when the buyer is satisfied with purchases over time.

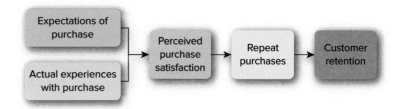

What Do Customers Expect of Salespeople?

If meeting or even exceeding the buyer's expectations are important, what are common buyer expectations? For instance, what do professional buyers expect of business salespeople? A survey of purchasing professionals showed that they expect results. The following list shows the most important traits that purchasing professionals found in their top business salespeople:

- Willingness to go to bat for the buyer within the supplier's firm.
- Thoroughness and follow-through after the sale.
- Knowledge of the firm's product line.
- Market knowledge and willingness to "keep the buyer posted."
- Imagination in applying one's products to the buyer's needs.
- Knowledge of the buyer's product line.
- Preparation for sales calls.
- Regularity of sales calls.
- Diplomacy in dealing with operating departments.
- Technical education—knowledge of specifications and applications.
- Now that you have learned about the expectations of buyers regarding service, it's important to incorporate them into your professional selling behaviors.

EXHIBIT 13.3

Technology may provide a means to enable the salespeople to communicate in a more responsive manner.

58% consumers who expect a company to respond to their complaint post on a social networking site

22% report receiving a response

42% expect a response within one day

39% expect a response within one week

7% expect a response within 1 h

2% expect a response within 1 min

Technology Aids Salesperson's Post-Sale Service Behaviors

Throughout the book, we have been discussing how sales technology such as CRM systems could help salespeople throughout the sales process—whether it be for prospecting or for gaining customer knowledge. It is important for you to understand that post-sales service also requires technology and automation. For instance, CRM technology and social media tools help facilitate activities and behaviors that salespeople perform after closing the initial sale.[1]

CRM technology helps salespeople monitor inbound and outbound communications with customers. A salesperson may use the technology to track a customer's inbound calls that ask for support and thus help resolve a service issue.

As shown in Exhibit 13.3, customers often visit social media platforms such as Facebook and LinkedIn to post their grievances and expect the selling organizations to respond quickly.[2] Another popular social media platform, Twitter, is used by customers to express their dissatisfaction with products and services they purchased. Experts suggest that "one bad Twitter 'tweet' can cost companies as many as 30 customers."[3] Therefore, it is important for salespeople to listen to negative feedback and respond appropriately.

Technology-savvy salespeople can now track and respond to customers' Tweets and LinkedIn posts. Such information can be integrated with other data captured in CRM systems to assist salespeople to develop appropriate and timely responses to their customers' post-sale service needs. In summary, the salesperson's responsiveness is critical to meet customers' expectations and ultimately gain their trust (Exhibit 13.3). As an emerging salesperson, it's important to understand how technology can aid your responsiveness—because responsiveness impacts customer satisfaction.[4]

So, How Does Service Increase Your Sales?

Take a look at Exhibit 13.4. By now you are very familiar with it! Can you answer the question noted in this section's heading, "How does service increase your sales?"

EXHIBIT 13.4

Sales come from existing and new customers. Salespeople are constantly involved in follow-up and service, plus planning their next sales call on the customer; some also spend time prospecting.

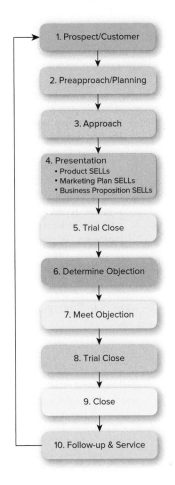

1. Prospect/Customer

2. Preapproach/Planning

3. Approach

4. Presentation
   • Product SELLs
   • Marketing Plan SELLs
   • Business Proposition SELLs

5. Trial Close

6. Determine Objection

7. Meet Objection

8. Trial Close

9. Close

10. Follow-up & Service

The circular relationship in managing a sales call.

Planning — Implementation — Evaluation

You—the salesperson—increase sales by obtaining new customers and selling more products to present customers. What is the best method for obtaining new customers? For many types of sales, customer referrals are best! Customers provide referrals when they are satisfied with the salesperson. So how important is it to your success and livelihood to take care of your customers? Even though it is last in the selling process, step 10 is extremely important to a salesperson's success.

What has occurred after you have completed step 9 of Exhibit 13.4 and are no longer with the customer? You have either made or not made a sale. Now what do you do? You evaluate why you made the sale or did not make the sale. Why? It prepares you for making the next sales call.

Salespeople are continually planning, implementing, and evaluating their purpose, plans, and success for contacting each customer. Wow, is this important to your success in sales and in the classroom!

As also illustrated in Exhibit 13.4, after step 10 of the selling process the salesperson moves back to the first step, to plan the next sales call on a customer or prospect. Meanwhile, the salesperson also is prospecting if needed in his or her type of sales. Thus, the salesperson is involved in the ongoing process of finding new customers and taking care of present customers. With this review in mind, let's discuss several service and follow-up techniques.

Satisfied Customers Are Easier to Sell To

Taking care of existing customers yields a number of benefits. It is easier to sell to an existing customer than to a prospect—especially a satisfied customer. That's why building a relationship—keeping in touch after the sale—is so important to a salesperson's success. Sally Fields of California Office Supply says.

> It took me five tough years to build up my customer base. Now selling is easy and fun. But the first months were terrible. Calling only on strangers got old, but I hung in there. I was going to succeed—no matter how hard I had to work.
>
> The more strangers I sold, the more friends (customers) I had. It is easy to sell a friend. So in the mornings I contacted possible new customers and in the afternoons I visited customers to make sure they were happy with their purchases and sell them more office supplies. Today, 80 percent of my monthly sales come from existing customers. I still make cold calls to keep sharp. By next year my goal is to have 95 percent sales come from these customers. To do that I must do all I can to make sure customers are happy plus find new customers. The relationships I build today will take care of my tomorrow!

Fields owes her success to doing everything she can to ensure her customers are happy with their purchases and her organization's service. Her yearly income is now more than $100,000. She has built her business through hard work, selling, and service.

Turn Follow-Up and Service Into A Sale

Following-up with customers also provides an opportunity to learn about additional needs. High-performing salespeople can convert follow-up and service situations into sales (see Exhibit 13.5). Jack Pruett, a jewelry retailer, gives several examples:

> I send customers a thank-you card immediately after the sale, and after two weeks, I call again to thank them and see if they are pleased with their purchase. If the purchase is a gift, I wait on contacting the customer or contact the spouse. This has been a key to my success in building a relationship and in farming or prospecting. Very often I get a lead.

EXHIBIT 13.5

Follow-up is critical for ensuring that the customer is satisfied.

Here, a customer feels good when the salesperson follows up with a phone call describing additional uses for the product purchased.

©Kate Kunz/Glow Images

Here is how it works. In two weeks they have shown it around to someone who has made a comment. I start with, "Is everything OK?" Then I say. "Well, I know Judy [or Jack] is real proud of it, and I'm sure she's [he's] shown it to someone—parents, family, friends. I was curious if there is anyone I could help who is interested in something. I'd like to talk to them or have you call and see if they'd like me to call them." If I've done a good job, the customer feels good about letting me call this individual and will help me. If I wait too long to call, they say. "Well, someone was asking about it, but I've forgotten who it was."

My biggest sale to a single customer was $120,000. It took about two weeks. A man initially called asking for 12 diamonds to give 2 stones to each of his children. In handling this, I found some other pieces I felt were good for him—a ruby ring, a 4.62 sapphire ring, a gold and diamond bracelet, and two other rings. He bought everything. Thus, much of my success comes from follow-ups, suggestion selling [when someone comes in for something and they buy other things], or service situations. Once you realize you can turn routine situations into sales, retail selling becomes exciting and challenging.[5]

Pruett realizes follow-up and service help satisfy the needs of his customers. This approach really works. Over the years, we have had a series of discussions regarding post-sales service needs with professional buyers. Exhibit 13.6 describes a few of the most common expectations conveyed from professional buyers. Another way to help customers involves account penetration.

What's the Plan after the Sale: Making Sure Everything Happens

As you have read, the sale is simply the start of the customer service process. The salesperson often needs to lead, coordinate, or confirm that all of the processes and resources are available to meet the customer's timelines.

EXHIBIT 13.6

What are some best practices to excellent post-sales service?

Buyers want their salespeople to	
Understand the policies of the buying firm. Firms often have specific policies regarding delivery, shipping, billing, and acceptance of materials. The buyer wants the salesperson to know this information so that implementation of the solution is flawless.	Outline important next steps (i.e., an action plan) at the conclusion of each meeting. The next steps include the actions the salesperson will accomplish and the actions the buyer will accomplish to make the project successful.
Coordinate the needed resources (within the salesperson's firm) to enable excellent execution. This may include managing the project and coordinating with other departments within the salesperson's firm. The buyer wants the salesperson to ensure the process is seamless and does not require needless work from the buyer.	Be accurate. Buyers want to the salesperson to accurately input orders, billing, and other information. The buyer does not want to be responsible for correcting the salesperson's mistakes.
Follow-up with the buyer. Examples of follow-up include e-mails, phone calls, or text messages regarding the progress on a project or an order. Buyers do not want to be responsible for ensuring the salesperson has accomplished agreed-upon next steps.	Be proactive with any good or bad news. Many buyers do not want to be surprised. They expect their salesperson to communicate any changes to product, pricing, delivery, etc.
Provide updated information on the buyer's market or industry. Buyers want to understand if market conditions are changing—regardless of the timing.	Continually learn about the customer's business. Buyers seek business partners that they can trust. Buyers often evaluate the credibility of salespeople through the salesperson's understanding of their business.

For example, let's consider the salesperson who recently gained distribution of a new soda product line within a major grocery store chain. This salesperson may meet with his firm's merchandising team to ensure everyone understands delivery schedules. The salesperson may develop a planning calendar with the customer service team to ensure timely phone calls are made to each store to guarantee in-stock rates; and the salesperson may communicate with the accounts receivable team to confirm billing and payment terms. Finally, the salesperson may work with someone on the promotions team to plot a schedule for in-store sampling. As you can see, for some salespeople coordinating resources, planning, and project management are important skill sets.

Next, let's examine the role of an industrial salesperson. In this example, the salesperson closed the sale of a new lighting system for 10 manufacturing plants. Now, the salesperson meets with the internal projects team to develop a timeline for implementation. Next the salesperson consults with the internal procurement department to order all of the needed items. Further, the billing team is consulted to ensure the payment and billing terms are confirmed; and this is simply just the start of the process.

As you can see from these very brief vignettes, a salesperson may need to use management and communication skills to ensure the commitments made to the customer are met.

Account Penetration Is a Secret to Success

Follow-up and service create goodwill between a salesperson and the customer, which increases sales faster than a salesperson who does not provide such service. By contacting the customer after the sale to see that the maximum benefit is derived from the purchase, a salesperson lays the foundation for a positive business relationship. Emmett Reagan of Xerox says:

> Remember that there is still much work to be done after making the sale. Deliveries must be scheduled, installation planned, and once the system is operational, we must monitor to assure that our product is doing what is represented. This activity gives us virtually unlimited access to the account, which moves us automatically back to the first phase of the cycle. We now have the opportunity to seek out new needs, develop them, and find new problems that require solutions. Only this time, it's a lot easier because, by now, we have the most competitive edge of all, a satisfied customer.[6]

The ability to work and contact people throughout the account, discussing your products, is referred to as *account penetration*. Successful penetration of an account allows you to properly service that account by uncovering its needs and problems. Achieving successful account penetration is dependent on knowledge of that account's key personnel and their situation. If you do not have a feel for an account's situation, you reduce chances of maximizing sales in that account.

Tailor the presentation to meet buyers' objectives and benefit them. By knowing your buyers, their firms, and other key personnel, you uncover their needs or problems and develop a presentation that fulfills the needs or solves the problems. Account penetration is determined by several factors:

- Your total and major-brand sales growth in an account.
- Distribution of the number of products in a product line, including sizes used or merchandised by an account.

- Level of cooperation obtained, such as reduced resale prices, shelf space, advertising and display activity, discussion with their salespeople, and freedom to visit with various people in the account.
- Your reputation as the authority on your type of merchandise for the buyer.

As a general rule, the greater your account penetration, the greater your chances of maximizing sales within the account. Earning the privilege to move around the account freely allows you to better uncover prospect needs and to discuss your products with people throughout the firm. As people begin to know you and believe that you are there to help, they allow you to take action that ultimately increases sales, such as increasing shelf space or talking with the users of your industrial equipment in the account's manufacturing facilities. A good sign that you have successfully penetrated an account is when a competitor dismally says, "Forget that account; it's already sewn up." You have created true customer loyalty.

Service Can Keep Your Customers

You work days, weeks, and sometimes months to convert prospects into customers. What can you do to ensure that they buy from you in the future? After landing a major account, consider these six factors:

1. Concentrate on improving your account penetration. As discussed earlier, account penetration is critical in uncovering prospect needs or problems and consistently recommending effective solutions through purchasing your products. This allows you to demonstrate that you have a customer's best interests at heart and are there to help.
2. Contact new accounts frequently and on a regular schedule. In determining the frequency of calls, consider

   - Current sales and/or potential future sales to the account.
   - Number of orders expected in a year.
   - Number of product lines sold to the account.
   - Complexity, servicing, and redesign requirements of the products the account purchases.

   Because the amount of time spent servicing an account may vary from minutes to days, be flexible in developing a call frequency for each customer. Typically, invest sales time in direct proportion to the actual or potential sales represented by each account. The most productive number of calls is reached at the point at which additional calls do not increase sales to the customer. This relationship of sales volume to sales calls is referred to as the *response function* of the customer to the salesperson's calls.

3. Handle customers' complaints promptly. This is an excellent opportunity to prove to customers that they and their businesses are important, and that you sincerely care about them. The speed with which you handle even the most trivial complaint shows the value you place on that customer.
4. Always do what you say you will do. Nothing destroys a relationship with a customer faster than not following through on promises. Professional buyers do not tolerate promises made and subsequently broken. They have placed their faith (and sometimes reputation) in you by purchasing your products, so you must be faithful to them to ensure future support.
5. Provide service as you would to royalty. By providing your client with money-saving products and problem-solving ideas, you can become almost indispensable.

Always do what you say you will do. Nothing destroys a relationship with a customer faster than not following through on promises.

Handle customers' complaints promptly. This is an excellent opportunity to prove to customers that they and their businesses are important.

Customer: May I speak to Frank, please? I want to reorder.

Supplier: Frank isn't with us anymore. May someone else help you?

Customer: What happened to Frank? He has all my specs; I didn't keep a record.

Supplier: Let me give you Roger; he's taken over Frank's accounts.

Customer: Roger, you don't know me, but maybe Frank filled you in. I want to reorder.

Salesperson: You want to reorder what?

Customer: I want to repeat the last order, but increase your number 067 to 48.

Salesperson: What else was in the order?

Customer: Frank had a record of it. It's got to be in his file.

Salesperson: Frank isn't here anymore, and I don't have his records.

Customer: Who does?

Salesperson: I don't know. I'm new here, so you'll have to fill me in on your requirements. Are you a new customer?

Customer: Does four years make me new?

Salesperson: Well, sir, you are new to me. How long ago did you place your order?

Customer: Last month.

Salesperson: What day last month?

Customer: I don't remember; Frank always kept track of it. Maybe I could speak to the sales manager?

Salesperson: You mean Mort?

Customer: No, I think his name is Sam.

Salesperson: Sam left us about the same time as Frank. I can ask Mort to call you, but I'm sure he doesn't have your file either.

Customer: Roger, have you ever heard that your best prospect is your present customer?

Salesperson: Is that true?

Customer: I don't think so. Multiply this conversation by the millions of times it happens each year, and you have the biggest deterrent to sales in America.

You are an adviser to listen to rather than an adversary to haggle with. A insurance agent, for example, sells business insurance to the physician shown in Exhibit 13.7. The doctor relies on the salesperson for expert knowledge and ethical service.

6. Show your appreciation. A buyer once said to a salesperson, "I'm responsible for putting the meat and potatoes on your table." Customers contribute to your success, and in return, you must show appreciation. Thank them for their business and do them favors. Here are several suggestions:

- Although you may be hundreds of miles away, consider calling whenever you've thought of something or seen something that may solve one of your customer's problems.
- E-mail links to information that may interest your customers even if the material has no bearing on what you're selling. They could be items from trade journals, magazines, newspapers, or newsletters.
- Write congratulatory notes to customers who have been elected to office, promoted to higher positions, given awards, and so on.
- Send newspaper clippings about your customers' families such as marriages, births, and activities.

EXHIBIT 13.7

Customers expect their salespeople to work as advisers to them.

©BSIP SA/Alamy Stock Photo

- Send holiday or special-occasion cards. If you limit yourself to just one card for the entire year, send an Easter card, a Fourth of July card, or a Thanksgiving card. This makes a big impression on customers.
- Send annual birthday cards. To start this process, subtly discover when your prospects were born.
- Prepare and e-mail a brief newsletter, perhaps quarterly, that keeps customers informed on important matters.
- E-mail information to prospects and buyers.

These are just a few of the many practical, down-to-earth ways you can remember customers. The important point is to personalize whatever you send.

Specifically, it doesn't take much thought, energy, or time to send a card, newspaper clipping, or copy of an article. The secret to impressing customers is to personalize the material with a couple of sentences in your handwriting. Be sure it's legible!

Returned Goods Make You a Hero

One of the best ways to help customers is through careful examination of merchandise you have sold in the past to see if it is old, out-of-date, or unsalable due to damage. If any of these conditions exist, the salesperson should cheerfully return the merchandise following the company's returned goods policies.

Handle Complaints Fairly

Customers may be dissatisfied with products for any number of reasons:

- The product delivered is a different size, color, or model than the one ordered.
- The quantity delivered is less than the quantity ordered—the balance is back-ordered (to be delivered when available).
- The product does not arrive by the specified date.
- Discounts (trade or promotional payment; see Chapter 5) agreed on are not rendered by the manufacturer.
- The product does not have a feature or perform a function that the customer believed it would.
- The product is not of the specified grade or quality (does not meet agreed-on specifications).

Whenever you determine that the customer's complaint is honest, make a settlement that is fair to the customer. Customers actually may be wrong, but if they honestly believe they are right, no amount of haggling or arguing will convince them otherwise. A valued account can be lost through temperamental outbursts.

You Lose a Customer—Keep on Trucking

All salespeople suffer losses through the loss of either a sale or an entire account to a competitor. Four things can win back a customer:

1. Visit and investigate. Contact the buyer and your friends within the account to determine why the customer did not buy from you. Find out the real reason.
2. Be professional. If you have lost the customer to a competitor completely, let the customer know you have appreciated past business, that you still value the customer's friendship, and that you are still friendly. Remember to assure this lost account that you are ready to earn future business.
3. Don't be unfriendly. Never criticize the competing product that your customer has purchased. If it was a bad decision, let the customer discover it. Sales is never having to say, "I told you so!"
4. Keep calling. Treat a former customer like a prospect. Continue to make calls normally; present your product's benefits without directly comparing them to the competition.

Build bridges, not walls.

Like a professional athlete, a professional salesperson takes defeat gracefully, moves on to the next contest, and performs so well that victories overshadow losses. One method of compensating for the loss of an account is to increase sales to existing accounts.

Is the Customer Always Right?

So you might ask, "Is the customer always right?" What do you think? Is the customer always right? You might say yes because this book has stressed that the salesperson puts the interest of the customer first.

Always is the key word in this phrase. What if the customer wanted the salesperson to do something illegal or unethical? What if a customer demanded that a seller provide illegal price kickbacks? What if a customer requested terms that would produce results harmful to the employer, yet beneficial to the customer?

Salespeople are often placed in positions of determining what is right and what is wrong. As discussed in Chapter 2, it is critically important to have a fixed frame of reference for making morally ethical decisions. While others will disagree, your author feels the customer is *not* always right.

This Customer Is Not in the Right!

Occasionally, a dishonest customer may require you and your company not to honor a request. Retailer A once purchased some of my firm's merchandise from Retailer B, who had a fire sale and eventually went out of business. Retailer A insisted he purchased it from me and that I return close to $1,000 of damaged goods to my company for full credit. He actually had paid 10 cents on the dollar for it at the fire sale. I told Retailer A that I would have to obtain permission from the company to return such a large amount of damaged goods.

That afternoon, a competitive salesperson told me that Retailer A had asked him to do the same thing. I informed my sales manager of the situation. He investigated the matter and found out about Retailer B, who sold most of his merchandise to Retailer A—who happened to be my customer. I went back and confronted Retailer A with this and said it was company policy only to return merchandise that was purchased directly from me. This was a rare situation; yet you must occasionally make similar judgments considering company policy and customer satisfaction.

Customers should get the benefit of the doubt. Always have a plan for problem solving. Some procedures you can use include

- Obtain as much relevant information from your customer as possible.
- Express sincere regret for the problem.
- Display a service attitude (a true desire to help).
- Review your sales records to make sure the customer purchased the merchandise.
- If the customer is right, quickly and cheerfully handle the complaint.
- Follow-up to make sure the customer is satisfied.

Take care of your customers—especially large accounts. They are difficult to replace and are critical to success. When you take care of accounts, they take care of you. However, the salesperson does need to be prepared to handle the demands of a dishonest customer.

Dress in Your Armor

Each day before leaving for work, the salesperson should prepare to meet a few unethical and dishonest people. This requires a person to have tough skin, even armor. To withstand the attacks of unethical prospects and customers requires speaking the truth, being prepared to do what is right, readiness to discuss what is the ethical action, and trust that you are doing right. These traits will save the salesperson from doing something that is illegal or unethical.

The salesperson is often required to use a double-edged sword in dealing with customers. One edge represents dealing with the ethical customer. It is used to cut through the red tape that might hinder proper servicing of the customer, such as speeding up delivery.

You may need to use the other edge of the sword to cut ties to dishonest or morally unethical customers. Occasionally a prospect or customer may lie, cheat, steal, or want the seller to do something that is morally wrong or unethical. The salesperson's attitudes and actions should exemplify the proper way to do business. The salesperson serves as a role model to all encountered during the day. By conducting oneself

> *"People are often unreasonable, illogical and self-centered; forgive them anyway."*
>
> MOTHER TERESA

so as to set an example worthy of imitation by your spouse, children, grandmother, and others, you will be seen as a person of integrity and character. This helps build professionalism.

THE PATH TO SALES SUCCESS: SEEK, FOCUS, ASK, SERVE

Selling is challenging. And similar to other occupations, selling is not for everyone. Yet for those who assist in solving problems and helping others reach their objectives, they may hear the call to be a salesperson. For those individuals, sales is a wonderful way of life. So in any type of sales, please remember to

1. Seek customers to serve and you will find them.
2. Become focused on assisting others and people will open their doors.
3. Ask how you may assist others and people will buy.
4. Provide service after the sale and customers will buy again.

Selling takes faith, focus, and follow-through—the three *F*s. Never give up. Always continue to seek more knowledge, patience, wisdom, caring, and understanding of others' situations. Focus on caring for others' needs. This takes the spotlight off your challenges and struggles. Consider all hardships as character builders. Your character will grow as you endure the ups and downs of the sales life. If you take care of your character, your reputation will grow. In the end, you will be rewarded. It takes courage to stay the course when life gets hard and sales do not come. Yet success comes to the people who get up, even when they feel they cannot go on.

Developing Service Recovery Skills

Salespeople are being asked to create and maintain relationships as well as ensure the implementation of the agreed-upon action steps (i.e., post-sales service).[7] For today's salesperson, the combined expectation of sales and service means developing a wide-ranging skill set of relationship skills. One critical skill set lies in service recovery. A service recovery focuses on resolving customer problems when a mistake happens or when a breakdown in sales execution occurs (i.e., service failure).[8] (Relatedly, a service failure describes when a customer's expectations are not met by a company when it carries out a service.)

Understanding the service recovery process is important because the world of sales and business are not perfect. As a salesperson, you can reasonably expect some level of errors, gaffes, and oversights. People make mistakes, technological glitches occur, customer service personnel have bad days, and sometimes we simply forget about a commitment.

The following service recovery process helps us focus on the action steps to take when a mistake occurs or when our customer is not pleased with the implementation of a program.[9]

1. First research, isolate, and describe the problem in the customer's terms. The problem is what the customer perceives it to be. It's important to understand how the customer describes the problem, what terms they use in describing the problem, and how it impacts their needs. Therefore, your skills in questioning, probing, and discovering needs will be important in this stage. Also, it's vital to consider the personal side of the business relationship. A sincere apology or an expression that the customer is important are crucial communication steps in this stage.

2. Second, try to understand what the customer perceives is triggering the service failure. When you meet with your customer, ask them to describe to you how the problem began, how it evolved, and how it impacts them. Then, begin to examine your firm's processes and your actions to determine what might be additional elements that may impact the perceived problem.

3. Third, prepare a range of action options and develop an action plan that allow you to respond to your customer. A number of broad options are available for you to consider, including: (a) compensating the customer in some way, (b) allowing the product to be returned or replaced, (c) reimbursing the customer, and (d) expressing apologies.[10]

4. Fourth, discuss the alternatives with your customer and implement the mutually agreed-upon recovery plan. One key to any service recovery process lies in consistent follow-up and excellent execution. Communication is critical. Make sure your buyer understands you are resolving the problem, the steps you have or are undertaking, and the next steps you project in the process.

5. Try not to let it happen again. The final step is to work with your team to ensure the service failure does not occur again. This includes sharing best practices with your colleagues, making sure processes are followed, and creating monitoring systems to ensure the problem does not happen again.

Words of Sales Wisdom

Salespeople are often guided by their eagerness to sell. Some salespeople view selling as a competitive sport. They have to win. After all, salespeople are only human. They want to be successful. They have bills to pay and people to support. Many feel under pressure to sell, and others are driven by greed. "Yes, I am here to help," said a saleswoman, but "I am here mainly to sell."

This book, however, offers sales wisdom the reader can use to learn how to help others through the purchase of their products and services rather than how to sell in pursuit of their own self-interest. Caring for people is the beginning of sales wisdom. The purpose of this book is to teach people how to become an effective salesperson and experience long-term career success by doing what is right and just and fair. This book strives to help new salespeople gain knowledge and discretion and to help seasoned salespeople add to their learning.

Sales Proverbs

A **proverb** is a short, wise, easy-to-learn saying that calls a person to think and act. The following are a few proverbs of sales wisdom:

- Customer choice among suppliers has never been greater.
- You lose X percent of sales or customers per year.
- People do not care how much you know until they know how much you care.
- You do business with the one you trust and you trust the one you know.
- 80 percent of your profits comes from about 20 percent of your customers.
- Obtaining new customers and selling more products to present customers are the ways to increase sales.
- Like a ripple in water, satisfied customers will tell others about their positive experiences.
- It is always easier to sell a satisfied customer than an unsatisfied one or a prospect.
- The cost of acquiring a new customer is higher than keeping a present customer.

What does this mean to the salesperson? Take excellent care of your current customers!

Knowledge versus Wisdom

This knowledge is good, but there is a vast difference between **knowledge** (having these facts) and **wisdom** (applying these facts to taking care of customers). We may amass knowledge, but without wisdom, our knowledge is useless. We must learn how to live out what we know. In this age of information, knowledge is plentiful, but wisdom is scarce. Wisdom means far more than simply knowing a lot. It is a basic attitude that affects every aspect of life. The foundation of knowledge and wisdom is to honor and respect people. All people!

Wisdom Is Learned

In sales, one gains wisdom through a constant process of growing. First, we must trust and honor people. Second, we must realize that our purpose is to help people. Third, we must make a lifelong series of right choices and avoid moral pitfalls. Fourth, we must learn from our errors and recover. People do not develop all aspects of sales wisdom at once. The sales career involves both science and art that takes time to learn.

Exhibit 13.8 helps illustrate the importance of follow-up and service. The business relationship begins after you sell someone. This is referred to in Exhibit 13.8 as commitment. If the salesperson is to have the privilege of selling again, the customer must answer positively to questions like these:

1. Can I trust this person?
2. Did the product and salesperson do what was presented?
3. Does the salesperson truly care about me?

If the customer answers yes to these questions, certainly he or she will allow the salesperson to make future presentations. Will the customer always buy? No. But if the customer feels the salesperson is trustworthy and cares, the customer often will give the salesperson the benefit of the doubt and buy rather than taking a chance on another salesperson.

True Caring Builds Relationships and Sales

What is the purpose of the sales call? Is it solely to make a sale? Or is the sales call meant to help someone? There is a big difference! The potential buyer can often see this difference.

EXHIBIT 13.8

If customers are truly important, their needs come first. Sellers should care about customers as much as themselves.

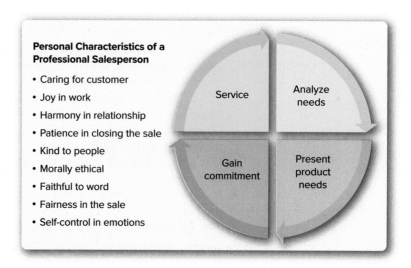

Personal Characteristics of a Professional Salesperson

- Caring for customer
- Joy in work
- Harmony in relationship
- Patience in closing the sale
- Kind to people
- Morally ethical
- Faithful to word
- Fairness in the sale
- Self-control in emotions

Service — Analyze needs — Present product needs — Gain commitment

Exhibit 13.8 shows that the salesperson first analyzes the prospect's, customer's, or organization's needs. This can take time. Yet it is critical. It is somewhat like a medical doctor getting someone to have X-rays and blood analysis before determining the exact problem and prescribing a course of action. Once the prospect feels the salesperson understands needs, confidence improves in what the salesperson recommends.

After the sale, customers look to see if you are the same as before the sale. People like to buy and be remembered, not sold and forgotten. A relationship should be stronger, not weaker, after the sale. This is why Chapter 1 pointed out that today's salespeople need personal characteristics allowing them to

- Care for the customer, take joy in work, and find harmony in the relationship.
- Have patience in closing the sale, kindness to all people, and moral ethics.
- Be faithful to one's word, fair in the sale, and self-controlled in emotions.

Do these success characteristics describe you? Do you have all, or part, of them? Can you develop the missing ones? The desire to serve others is a quality we all admire. However, only when we enjoy serving others does our service take on a radiant goodness that gives a contagious glow. This glow shows you care!

Caring Is Seen!

Caring about the customer is more than simply warm feelings; it is an attitude that reveals itself in action. How can sellers care about a customer as much as themselves? By helping when it is not convenient, by giving the best price, by devoting energy to their welfare, by making sure the customer is satisfied. These are just a few ways the seller shows caring for the customer.

Caring Is Hard to Do!

This kind of caring is hard to do. That is why people notice when the seller does it. This is how customers know the salesperson places their welfare first. This is how customers know the seller can be trusted. This is how a long-term relationship begins and extends into the future. Through caring comes exceptional service to the customer, which in turn brings peace to the relationship. Buyer and seller care for and trust each other. Wow! Live from day to day in a self-forgetful way so you focus on others, not yourself. Let "live for others" be your personal motto.

SUMMARY OF MAJOR SELLING ISSUES

Salespeople increase sales by obtaining new customers and selling more product to current customers. Customer referrals are the best way to find new prospects. Thus, it's important to provide excellent service and follow-up to customers. By building a relationship and partnership, you can provide a high level of customer service.

Customers expect service. When you deliver service, customers are satisfied and continue to buy; this results in retention and loyalty. Providing service to customers is important in all types of selling. Follow-up and service create goodwill between salesperson and customer that allows the salesperson to penetrate or work throughout the customer's organization. Account penetration helps the salesperson better service the account and uncover its needs and problems. A service relationship with an account leads to increases in total and major brand sales, better distribution on all product sizes, and customer cooperation in promoting your products.

To serve customers best, improve account penetration. Contact each customer frequently and regularly; promptly handle all complaints. Always do what you say you will do, and remember to serve customers as if they were royalty. Finally, remember to sincerely thank all customers for their business, no matter how large or small, to show you appreciate them.

Should customers begin to buy from a competitor or reduce their level of cooperation, continue to call on them in your normal professional manner. In a friendly way, determine why they did not buy from you, and develop new customer benefit plans to recapture their business.

Always strive to help your customers increase their sales of your product or to get the best use from products that you have sold to them. To persuade a customer to purchase more of your products or use your products in a different manner, develop a sales program to help maximize sales to that customer. This involves developing an account penetration program; increasing the number and sizes of products the customer purchases; maintaining proper inventory levels in the customer's warehouse and on the shelf; achieving good shelf space and shelf positioning; communicating clearly with persons who directly sell or use a product; being willing to assist wholesale and retail customers' salespeople in any way possible; being willing to help customers; and developing a positive, friendly business relationship with each customer. By doing these things, your ability to help and properly service each customer increases.

Today's professional salesperson is oriented to service. Follow-up and service after the sale maximize your territory's sales and help attain personal goals.

Quick Review for Students

The quick review sections provide key questions to help you develop a greater level of conceptual understanding. We suggest that after you read the chapter, you try to answer the following questions without looking back at the textbook.

1. What does post-sales service mean?
2. Why do service and follow-up play such an important role to sale?
3. What are the three levels of customer relationship marketing?
4. What does customer service refer to?
5. What does customer satisfaction refer to? How do satisfied customers help salespeople?
6. What are some best practices to excellent post-sales service?
7. What are the six key factors that a salesperson should consider after closing the sale?

MEETING A SALES CHALLENGE

What a tough situation! You have to keep servicing the equipment if you want to keep King Masonry as a customer. If the customer is misusing the mixer, causing it to break down, you must train the operators of the mixer and explain to Eldon King what is happening. Before saying anything to King, get his permission to talk with the mixer operators. Find out why the machine is breaking down.

KEY TERMS FOR SELLING

acquaintances   476
business friendship   475
customer satisfaction   478
customer service   474

follow-up   474
friends   476
intimate friends   476
knowledge   492

proverb   491
wisdom   492

SALES APPLICATION QUESTIONS

1. Compare the relationships between customer service and follow-up to a business relationship. Include in your answer why the customer's interest should come before the seller's.
2. What is account penetration? What benefits can a salesperson derive from it?
3. List and briefly explain the factors salespeople must consider to ensure that customers buy from them in the future.
4. What must a salesperson do after losing a customer?
5. A good way for a salesperson to create goodwill is by helping customers increase their sales. What steps should the salesperson attempting to increase customer sales take?
6. This chapter discussed several reasons why a salesperson must project a professional image. Why is being a sales professional so important?
7. You have just learned that one of your customers, Tom's Discount Store, has received a shipment of faulty goods from your warehouse. The total cost of the merchandise is $2,500. Your company has a returned goods policy that allows you to return only $500 worth of your product at one time unless a reciprocal order is placed. What would you do?

   a. Call Tom's and say you will be out to inspect the shipment in a couple of days.
   b. Ask Tom's staff to patch up what they can and sell it at a reduced cost in an upcoming clearance sale.
   c. Send the merchandise back to your warehouse and credit Tom's account for the price of the damaged goods.
   d. Go to Tom's as soon as possible that day, check the shipment to see if there are any undamaged goods that can be put on the shelf, take a replacement order from Tom's manager, and phone in the order immediately.
   e. Call your regional sales manager and ask what to do.

FURTHER EXPLORING THE SALES WORLD

1. Contact the person in charge of the health and beauty aids department of a local supermarket. In an interview with this person, ask questions to determine what service activities salespeople perform in the department. For example, do they build product displays, put merchandise on the shelves, straighten products on the shelves, and keep a record of how much product is in the store? Also, determine how the department head feels salespeople can provide the best service.
2. Contact the person in charge of marketing in a local bank. Report on the role that service plays in attracting and retaining bank customers.

SELLING EXPERIENTIAL EXERCISE

Providing excellent customer service often requires a special person—someone who quietly enjoys interacting with people even when they are upset. To help you better understand yourself, respond to each statement by placing the number that best describes your answer on a separate sheet of paper.

1 Never   2 Rarely   3 Sometimes   4 Usually   5 Often

What's Your Attitude toward Customer Service?

1. I accept people without judging them.
2. I show patience, courtesy, and respect to people regardless of their behavior toward me.
3. I maintain my composure and refuse to become irritated or frustrated when coping with an angry or irate person.
4. I treat people as I would want them to treat me.
5. I help others maintain their self-esteem, even when the situation requires negative or critical feedback.
6. I do not get defensive when interacting with other persons, even if their comments are directed at me.
7. I realize that my attitude toward myself and others affects the way I respond in any given situation.
8. I realize that each person believes his or her problem is the most important and urgent thing in the world at this time, and I attempt to help each one resolve it immediately.
9. I treat everyone in a positive manner, regardless of how they look, dress, or speak.
10. I view every interaction with another person as a golden moment, and I do everything in my power to make it a satisfactory win–win situation for both of us.

Total Score

Total your score: If your score is more than 40, you have an excellent service attitude; if it is 30–40, you could use improvement; and if you scored less than 30, you need an attitude adjustment.[11]

NOTES

1. R. Agnihotri, K. J. Trainor, O. S. Itani, & M. Rodriguez, "Examining the Role of Sales-Based CRM Technology and Social Media Use on Post-Sale Service Behaviors in India." *Journal of Business Research* 81 (December 1, 2017), pp. 144–154.

2. Right Now Technologies (2010), Customer Experience Report: North America, 2010, Harris Interactive.

3. S. Shannon, "One Bad Twitter 'Tweet' Can Cost 30 Customers," Bloomberg. com, November 26, 2009.

4. R. Agnihotri, R. Dingus, M. Y. Hu, & M. T. Krush, "Social Media: Influencing Customer Satisfaction in B2B Sales," *Industrial Marketing Management* 53 (2016), pp. 172–180.

5. Charles M. Futrell, *ABC's of Relationship Selling through Service* (Burr Ridge, IL: McGraw-Hill/Irwin, 2005), p. 418.

6. Ibid., p. 67.

7. R. Agnihotri, C. B. Gabler, O. S. Itani, F. Jaramillo, & M. T. Krush, "Salesperson Ambidexterity and Customer Satisfaction: Examining the Role of

Customer Demandingness, Adaptive Selling, and Role Conflict," *Journal of Personal Selling & Sales Management* 37, no. 1 (January 2, 2017), pp. 27–41.

8. "Pursuing Success in Service Recovery: A Conceptual Framework of Salesperson's Power in Selling Centre," Prabakar; Kothandaraman, Raj; Agnihotri, and Rebecca E. Dingus, *Journal of Services Research; Gurgaon* vol. 14, no. 1 (Apr–Sep 2014), pp. 141–159.

9. R. Gabriel, K. Gonzalez, Douglas Hoffman, and Thomas N. Ingram, "Improving Relationship Selling through Failure Analysis and Recovery Efforts: A Framework and Call to Action," *Journal*

of *Personal Selling & Sales Management* 25, no. 1 (Winter 2005), pp. 57–65.

10. Ibid.

11. Adapted from Richard F. Gerson, *Beyond Customer Service: Keeping Customers for Life* (Menlo Park, CA: Crisp Publications, 1992), p. 79.

12. Adapted from *Marketplace Ethics: Issues in Sales and Marketing* (Westport, CT: J/S Productions, 1990), pp. 15–35.

13. This exercise was created by Professor Jeffrey K. Sager of the University of North Texas, Richard Langlotz of Minolta Business Systems, and Professor Charles M. Futrell of Texas A&M University.

CASE 13.1

©Ron Chapple Stock/FotoSearch/ Glow Images

California Adhesives Corporation

Marilyn Fowler recently became a sales representative for the California Adhesives Corporation and covers the states of Oregon and Washington. After completing a three-week training program, Marilyn was excited about the responsibility of reversing a downward sales trend in her territory, which had been without a salesperson for several months.

The previous salesperson was fired due to poor sales performance and had not left behind any information regarding accounts. After contacting her first 20 or so customers, Marilyn came to a major conclusion: None of these customers had seen a CAC salesperson for six to nine months; they had CAC merchandise, which was not selling, and they had damaged merchandise to return. These customers were hostile toward Marilyn because the previous salesperson had used high-pressure tactics to force them to buy, and as one person said, "Your predecessor killed your sales in my business. You said you would provide service and call on me regularly, but I don't care about service. In fact, it's OK with me if I never see anyone from your company again. Your competition's products are much better than yours, and their salespeople have been calling in this area for years trying to get my business." Marilyn was wondering if she had gone to work for the right company.

Questions

1. If you were Marilyn, what would you do to improve the sales in your territory?
2. How long would your effort take to improve sales, and would you *sell* it to your sales manager?

CASE 13.2

©Ron Chapple Stock/FotoSearch/
Glow Images

Sport Shoe Corporation

You are a salesperson for the Sport Shoe Corporation. At the office, there is a letter marked urgent on your desk. This letter is from the athletic director of Ball State University, and it pertains to the poor quality of basketball shoes that you sold to him. The director cited several examples of split soles and poor overall quality as his main complaints. In closing, he mentioned that since the season was nearing, he would be forced to contact the ACME Sport Shoe Company if the situation could not be rectified.

Question

What actions would be appropriate for you? Why?

a. Place a call to the athletic director assuring him of your commitment to service. Promise to be at Ball State at his convenience to rectify the problem.
b. Go by the warehouse and take the athletic director a new shipment of shoes and apologize for the delay and poor quality of the merchandise.
c. Write a letter to the athletic director assuring him that SSC sells only high-quality shoes and that this type of problem rarely occurs. Assure him you'll come to his office as soon as possible, but if he feels ACME would be a better choice than Sport Shoe he should contact them.
d. Don't worry about the letter because the athletic director seems to have the attitude that he can put pressure on you by threatening to switch companies. Also, the loss in sales of 20 to 40 pairs of basketball shoes will be a drop in the bucket compared to the valuable sales time you would waste on a small account like Ball State.

CASE 13.3

©Ron Chapple Stock/FotoSearch/
Glow Images

Wingate Paper

George McGinnis, a marketer for Wingate Paper, is jogging with Tom Cagle.[12] Tom is a longtime distributor for Wingate Paper and has a good relationship with the company and its owners. George asks Tom about the status of the

Orkand contract. Tom explains that he has nearly sold them on going with Wingate for all of their paper products needs, both administrative and production. George remarks that the Orkand contract could not have come at a better time. He has never seen Wingate squeeze the numbers so hard. He also states that he is counting on his bonus to pay his daughter's tuition. Tom admits that he needs this contract badly, as well, to pay off a bank loan.

In Wingate Paper's warehouse, George is talking with Kyle Cross, a new distributor. Kyle is impressed with Wingate Paper and informs George that he is going after the Orkand account for Wingate and to establish himself in the business. He remarks that he knows Orkand is interested in Wingate Paper products. Kyle implies that he might win the account in part to help Orkand increase its minority contracting but that he does not want the decision to be based solely on that factor and is therefore offering them a 10 percent discount. George questions if Kyle knows that Tom Cagle has also been pitching Orkand. Kyle acknowledges that Tom is a good competitor, but he is confident of success because of the low price he offered.

A week later, Tom is complaining to George that he may lose the Orkand account because of Kyle Cross. Tom questions why George did not tell Kyle that the Orkand account was his, and George explains that Kyle is a legitimate competitor. Tom warns that Orkand may question the way Wingate Paper operates because of the two very different price quotes, but George reminds Tom that he cannot tell distributors what to charge.

Orkand has given Tom one week to meet Kyle's price, but Tom claims he cannot do it and tells George that he needs his help. First, Tom requests a price break, but George explains that he has to give all the distributors the same price. Next, Tom asks for a portion of the design fund for distributors, and George refutes this possibility, stating that the fund is only used for developing a product. Tom then wants part of the ad budget, but George explains the budget is already committed. Frustrated, Tom acknowledges that he understands why George wants to do business with Kyle, but he threatens to take away his other accounts from Wingate Paper. George tries to salvage the situation, but Tom argues that George should remember about all the times he pushed Wingate Paper instead of other brands to help George get rid of inventory or promote a new line. George tries to express his appreciation for Tom's help, but Tom does not want appreciation, he wants money. He tells George to find a way to help him, if he really cares. George contemplates his decision.

Questions

1. What are the main ethical issues, if any, in the Wingate Paper case? Describe each ethical issue.
2. What are George's options?
3. How do the three levels of moral development relate to George's situation?
4. What would you do?

Apply Your Skills: Sales Role-Plays

How would you like to take a computer class without ever using a computer? To learn, you need an instructor, a textbook, and a computer. To learn to sell, you need an instructor, a textbook, and one or more role-plays. Role-plays are where the true learning takes place, where you see how to use all of the classroom instruction materials your instructor and textbook provided.

We have worked with thousands of people to help them develop role-plays similar to those presented in a sales training class. The following role-plays have been created from actual organizations' sales information provided to their salespeople. The names of the companies and their products have been changed to provide anonymity.

Role-Play One: Consumer Sales

You are a salesperson for a multibillion-dollar consumer goods manufacturer. Today you will be calling on Amy, the cereal buyer for ABC Grocery Stores. ABC is a chain of 20 large grocery stores. You have known Amy since last year about this time, when she became the buyer. Since then you have called on Amy about every month to sell her your various new items, talk about reordering your other products ABC currently carries, and create marketing plans for your major items.

Amy's office is in the largest city in your area. ABC currently carries about 100 different products of yours, with each of these 100 products available in various sizes and flavors. Thus ABC has 450 SKUs (stock-keeping units) of yours that it sells. (Each item carried in the store is given a tracking, or stock-keeping, number referred to as an SKU.)

You will be selling Amy one size of a new ready-to-eat cereal. For your role-play choose any cereal in your favorite grocery store to use in this exercise. Incorporate the following information that relates to the role-play's product, promotion, pricing, and sales objectives.

Product Description

Select any ready-to-eat (RTE) cereal of your choice to use in your role-play.

- Although the sales of ready-to-eat cereal in the U.S. has been declining for a good number of years, it still is the largest dry grocery category with sales of $8.66 billion in 2017.

Category/Segment Performance

The following information is based on AC Nielsen information and test markets.

- 93 percent of consumers will buy your cereal in addition to their normal cereal.
- Your cereal focuses on people nine years of age to older adults.

Item Fit and Uniqueness

- 60 percent of category growth comes from new cereal products.
- Your product attracts your key consumer group—households with kids.
- 67 percent of households that tried your cereal in test markets said that it would be their first or second favorite cereal.
- 61 percent of households with kids said they would buy your cereal in test markets.

Introductory Promotional Period (IPP)

- 95 percent of adults 18 to 49 years of age will see your cereal's advertising an average of 10 times.
- 64 percent of kids age 9 to 14 will see your cereal an average of six times.
- Advertising, consumer promotions, and a public relations blitz will run for two and one-half months, beginning in two months; $16 million will be spent on advertising, with over 50 percent of spending in network prime time: three FSIs (free-standing inserts) will appear, one every other week, with a high coupon value.
- A large-scale social media campaign engaging users on Twitter, Facebook, and Instagram through visual storytelling would run parallel to traditional promotional activities.
- Trade promotion pricing is available two months from today.
- 12 boxes of cereal in each case.
- Estimated number of cases the average individual grocery store will sell: 7 cases for three-day special at a featured price of $1.79; 20 cases per two-week promotion at a featured price of $1.99; 2 cases per average week with no promotion at a normal store price of $3.40.

Normal Pricing		Introductory Pricing Promotion*	
Case pricing	$33.24	Case pricing	$33.24
Net unit	2.77	Introductory discount rate	−13.56
Suggested retail	3.39	Net case cost	19.68
Normal store price	3.40	Net unit cost	1.64
% Margin	18%	Suggested retail	1.99
		% Margin	18%

*Requires feature and display.

Sales Objectives

- Purchase enough cereal for a three-day special with feature price of $1.79; two-week special with feature price of $1.99; and four-week normal sales period with a $3.40 suggested retail price.
- Have an in-store aisle display and $1.79 shelf-talker for the three-day special.
- Have an in-store shelf-talker showing the $1.99 price for two weeks.
- For either the three-day or the two-week period have one advertisement in ABC's weekly in-store printed ad newspaper.
- Have a normal store price of $3.40.

After reviewing the product, promotion, pricing, and sales objectives, you listed the features, advantages, and benefits for the cereal that you will use in the product discussion, the marketing plan, and the business proposition phases of your presentation. These features, advantages, and benefits are shown in the three tables—product discussion, marketing plans discussion, and business proposition discussion. In addition to the FABS provided, carefully analyze the FABs that are unique to the cereal you select, and incorporate those and the given FABs into your presentation as if this were a new cereal.

You feel certain Amy will buy from you today. Both you and Amy know your organization will withdraw future special pricing deals if ABC buys the new cereal at the low introductory price and does not reduce the initial price and promote it. You feel Amy will buy some cereal to promote. The question is, How much?

Product Discussion

Features	Advantages	Benefits
- 93% of consumers will buy your cereal in addition to their normal cereal - Your cereal attracts your store's key consumer group—households with kids	- Consumers will buy more boxes of cereal each time they shop at your store - Your store's customers will purchase your cereal	- Increased sales - Increased profits

Marketing Plan

Features	Advantages	Benefits
- Prime time TV advertising blitz for 2½ months - 3 coupon inserts - In-store aisle display and shelf talker	- Increase in brand awareness before product is on shelves - Increase in trial purchase - Increase in store traffic during special	- Increase in sales - Increase in profits

Business Plan

Features	Advantages	Benefits
- Normal store price of $3.40	- 18% Margin	- Increase in profits

Your goal is to sell her on the idea of running two price specials. This will allow you to sell her more product, plus the grocery stores' customers will buy more, resulting in a large reorder once the four-week supply of cereal is sold.

Role-Play Two: Distributor Sales

You are a new sales representative for Creative Solutions and its, Technology Division. The Technology Division is a distributor of cutting-edge tools and gadgets for sale to businesses. Creative Solutions' primary clients include businesses that maintain a large sales force, require constant communication, and demand the latest technology.

You are taking over for Alex Jones, who recently moved on to a management position. This afternoon you have your first appointment with one of Creative Solutions' largest clients, Greg Johnson. Mr. Johnson is a regional manager for a large commercial real estate firm, Urban Properties. He is responsible for managing 16 sales representatives in three states. Mr. Johnson is concerned with maintaining the most prepared sales force while keeping costs to a minimum.

The material Alex Jones collected on this account follows. Use this material to prepare your first sales call on Mr. Johnson. He has allowed only 10 minutes of his busy schedule to meet with you. Remember to give him your business card and ask for his.

Information on Greg Johnson

Greg Johnson is a regional manager with Urban Properties, one of the nation's largest commercial real estate firms. He maintains a sales force of 16 people spread over five states and understands the importance of effective and efficient communication. Mr. Johnson is interested in having his sales force use new technology to improve performance. He has recently expressed concerns about the increasing costs of travel for his salespeople.

Mr. Johnson used Creative Solutions' products in the past because he thought they were high quality. He was a salesperson before his advancement to regional manager and loves the tools of the trade. In fact, he takes pride in the quality of the technology his sales force uses.

Mr. Johnson likes to be given all the information on a product. He is interested in hearing the benefits of a product, rather than just being told about a long list of available products. He likes salespeople who get straight to the point. Mr. Johnson is a very busy man. His relationship with the previous Creative Solutions' salesperson, Alex Jones, was a good one.

Annual Call Report Summary (*Prior Year*) Sales Representative: Alex Jones Client: Greg Johnson (*Urban Properties*)

Month 1

Spoke to Mr. Johnson for 25 minutes to introduce our 360-degree, fish-eye camera exclusively built with the needs of real estate professionals in mind. I mentioned the savings on large purchases for his sales force. No purchase was indicated.

Month 2

Talked with Mr. Johnson for about 10 minutes. Answered some questions about the product and market trends. He indicated some interest in the camera for his salespeople.

Month 3

The special on the fish-eye camera was about to end. I tried to sell Mr. Johnson one more time. He was impressed with the quality but decided his budget was too tight this month.

Month 4

Spent about 15 minutes discussing the 360 degree fish-eye camera. These cameras can help salespeople show prospects everything they'd like to see in a 3-D tour of a property. He mentioned he would like to know more about the camera. A sale is getting closer.

Month 5

Stopped in to talk with Mr. Johnson for 10 minutes. Discussed some key value-added features of the product that would allow salespeople to do sharper low-light photography in their customers' basements (or any poorly lit rooms) and far less image noise when shooting the outdoor images. This interested him, so we began discussing price. A decision would be made next month.

Month 6

Met with Mr. Johnson for 35 minutes. We agreed that the convenience and quality of the new 360-degree fish-eye camera were worth the price. He purchased 16 cameras for $5,700.

Month 7

Mr. Johnson met with me for 20 minutes this morning. He conveyed to me that salespeople are very impressed with the working of the cameras. I solved a couple of technical problems with one of the cameras.

Month 8

Mr. Johnson was on a business trip for the month. I stopped by his office to drop off some donuts for his administrative associates.

Month 9

Spent 15 minutes with Mr. Johnson this morning. He seemed especially interested in a way to cut down on travel costs to visit potential properties. He frequently travels with his salespeople to look at commercial real estate property. Mr. Johnson said he would like to spend more time in the office but still be able to approve new real estate ventures. He asked about tools and technologies that might help him out. I mentioned our portable backup drive and editor, designed especially for organizing photos and video content from any camera or smart device. The product has the wifi capability to stream data.

Month 10

Spent 30 minutes with Mr. Johnson this afternoon. I mentioned the convenience and compatibility of our portable backup drive and editor when used with the 360-degree fish-eye camera he bought in July. He liked the easy editing of videos and the data-streaming capability. Apparently, traveling to view properties is getting expensive, and the Backup Drive and Editor is the best alternative to being there. He wanted to wait a few months because of new computer hardware they were purchasing soon. I left him some information on the new Backup Drive and Editor. I plan to discuss it with him again in a few months, once their new computer system is in place.

Month 11

Spent about 15 minutes discussing some of the challenges Urban Properties was facing in promoting large and unique real estate properties that don't photograph well from the ground. I mentioned exploring our CreateView mini-drone, an unmanned aerial vehicle (UAV) camera. CreateView mini-drone is ideal for sales professionals who are new to aerial listing photography. I informed him that drones are now approved for commercial use and they are appealing to real estate professionals. He was very interested in the ability to do aerial listing photography. He mentioned he would like to learn more about this product. I told him I'd set an appointment for a product demo.

Month 12

Stopped by Mr. Johnson's office in the morning and dropped off some donuts for his administrative associates. I talked to Mr. Johnson for about five minutes, just long enough to schedule a product demonstration meeting. He seemed excited about the mini-drones.

Your Sales Call

You are planning your sales call on Mr. Johnson. Your sales call objective is to sell the CreateView mini-drones for all of his salespeople. You have reviewed your customer profile showing past sales calls and what went on. Next you created the FABs for the product, marketing plan, and business proposition as shown below. You came up with several ideas for demonstrations and proof statements and wrote down how you would discuss them. Before you begin to finalize your presentation, you want to review the table of features, advantages, and benefits for the product, marketing plan, and business proposition discussions. You have also planned two demonstrations to incorporate into the sales call. Now you want to create your visuals to use in the presentation. With much practice you will give a great sales presentation and sell Mr. Johnson. You know he needs this product for his sales force.

Product discussion.

Features	Advantages	Benefits
– Takes high definition aerial video and photos of the property. – Programmed flight paths capture up to 20 minutes of 12 megapixel footage. – Automatically creates a 15-second final edit of the flight path – Allows salespeople to stream images to their devices or save them on an SD card – Bigger, more stable, with more expansive range	– Gets prospective buyers' attention more easily and enables them to spend more time looking at the property – Effectively provides more visual information at a reasonable cost – Enables quick-hit marketing on social media or listing landing pages	– Increase in sales – Higher return on investment

"Drones are modernizing the buying and selling process in the real estate industry. This technology creates an opportunity to further educate buyers about the property they're interested in purchasing and creates a greater opportunity for quicker sales for your clients. "What are your thoughts on this technology?"

"Salespeople do not have to rely on grainy satellite images (like those found on Google Earth). Moreover this could reduce the cost for your operations as you do not have to conduct those expensive aerial photography sessions with a hired airplane or helicopter. Often aerial photography exceeds $2,000 per session. Would you like to see what type of video can be made using this tool?" Play a video clip for Mr. Johnson on your smart phone or tablet.

Marketing plan discussion.

Features	Advantages	Benefits
– Easy to use by salespeople – Generates more visual information at a reasonable cost for buyers to make quicker decisions	– Removes the need for expensive aerial photography sessions with a hired airplane or helicopter – Enables salespeople to better market their listings – Saves time as videos filmed by drones can easily capture the whole area of large properties and surroundings – Provides buyers with a better idea of the property by means of videos and photos before they visit for a showing	– Increase in sales – Higher return on investment – Increase in profits – Decrease in costs

"Wasn't that cool and impressive? In fact, one of the biggest appeals of using such drones is simply the buzz it brings to the real estate listing. This product is new and trendy. Our CreateView mini-drones would raise your sales professionals' profiles." Tell a story about a real estate agent who recently used CreateView mini-drone to showcase a large property with a beautiful water view that had previously been on-and-off the market and how CreateView helped the agent in selling the property by showcasing the scope of the property.

Business Proposition Discussion

Features	Advantages	Benefits

■ Quantity pricing
  ■ 1–4 units $400 each
  ■ 5–14 units $350 each
  ■ 15 units $300 each
■ For 16 units the total cost would be $4,800
	■ Savings of $100 per unit
	■ $1,600 in savings if buy 16 units
		■ Increase in profits
		■ Increase in sales
		■ Decrease in costs

Role-Play Three: Business-to-Business

Last Friday was your first day on the job.[13] You completed your initial one-week training course. Your boss now wants you to make several sales calls this week before you attend the upcoming four-week sales training program. She feels this will help you relate better to the class materials.

You talked with Chris Hammond, owner of Travel Xpress, for about five minutes last week when he visited the district sales office. You mentioned visit to your boss that you would like to call on Chris. She said, "Go for it!" The following are some of the main things you learned from talking to Chris.

Travel Xpress—A Small Business

Travel Xpress (TX) is a personalized travel agency located in your town. TX has been in business since 2008. Chris bought the agency from the original owner in 2014. He worked at the agency as a part-time (college student) employee since its beginning. He makes all business decisions for the company.

TX has one full-time and one part-time employee. The full-time employee is going to have a child and will shortly become a part-time worker.

Business has been growing for Chris. Two years ago sales were about $5,000 per week. Last year, sales increased to $10,000 per week because of the opening of another active-adult community in the area. This year's sales are expected to be about $12,000 per week.

Four years ago, Chris purchased a Futrell 300 at a cost of $675. At that time Chris had just purchased the agency. Sales were about $2,500 per week. Although the Futrell works well for incidental copying, it is a bit slow (10 copies per minute). In addition, the Futrell can print only single copies—so Chris or one of his employees has to stand by the machine to make multiple copies. Since TX has begun group sales, it is often necessary to issue multiple itineraries. In addition, Chris now provides multiple-page information sheets to customers and to attendees at travel seminars. Chris estimates he makes about 5,000 copies a month.

Chris has called DataMax, the Futrell dealer, several times about upgrading his machine. DataMax encouraged Chris to deal with a telemarketer who specializes in small businesses. The telemarketing representative talked with Chris for about 10 minutes. The representative sent Chris a bid on another Futrell machine. However, the bid did not mention the toner cost or copy speed. The representative stressed that the machine was lightweight and easy to use. The bid price is $595. Chris likes this price! Chris asked the representative how long he could expect the copier to last and was told about five years.

Chris is concerned with the copy quality and durability of the machine. Last year, Chris had to send the copier out for repairs three times. One time the copier shut off and would not restart. The auto shut-off mode had short circuited. That repair took three days and cost TX about $400. On another occasion, a customer got upset with Chris's full-time employee because the copy the customer was given was too light to read. The customer threw a fit, screaming at the full-time employee and telling the other customers on site that TX was a "rinky-dink, small-time operation." Shortly thereafter, the full-time employee indicated that she would go part-time after the birth of her child.

Three weeks before, the copier jammed late one evening. Chris decided to fix it. After opening the copier case with a screwdriver, he failed to dislodge the jammed paper. Chris was unable to reassemble the copier. Paul, owner of Office Machine Repair, told Chris that it would cost more to fix the Futrell 300 than the machine was worth.

So Chris is stuck with a dead, four-year-old copy machine. Chris wants to buy another machine but is skeptical about all copiers.

Preparation for the Sales Call

Excited, yet nervous, about making your first sales call, you wonder how to prepare for meeting Chris. Your boss suggested you find the answer to these three questions:

1. How many copies does Chris make a year? Chris told you he makes about 60,000 copies a year.

2. How many years does Chris think he will keep the copier? You guess about five years.

3. What are the costs associated with the copier you will recommend and the Futrell copier? A bottle of Futrell copier's toner lasts for 1,600 copies and costs $100.95. Your machine's toner costs $14.50 and produces 1,500 copies.

You also create a table showing how your Minolta copier compares with the Futrell copier on six items. Also, you feel, maybe wrongly, that Chris will not want to know about all the items in your comparative analysis. However, you need to be prepared to discuss all items Chris may consider in his buying decision. Use the Competitive Information table to compare the two machines.

After reviewing the customer profile you made for Chris, you listed the FABs for the Minolta that you will use in the product discussion, the marketing plan, and the business proposition phases of your presentation. These features, advantages, and benefits are shown below. In addition, you thought of a way that you could demonstrate the Minolta's high-quality copy capabilities to the customer and collected a testimonial proof statement. Before you finalize your presentation, you want to review the features, advantage, and benefits of the Minolta thoroughly, become comfortable with the demonstration and proof statement, revisit your competitive analysis of the Futrell 300 and the Minolta, and create the visuals you wish to use in the presentation.

| | **Competitive Information** | |
	Minolta	Futrell
Price	$2,295	$595
Type		
Mfn Rec Mo/vol	500 to 2,500 copies	Up to 500 copies
Configuration	Desktop, stationary	Desktop, moving
Toner	Dry, dual component	Dry, monocomponent
Optics	Lens and mirror	Fiber optics
Speeds		
First copy	5.9 sec	15 sec
Multicopy	13 cpm	Single sheet
Warm-up	30 sec	None
Paper		
Paper feed	Single tray	User feeds single sheets
Paper capacity	250 sheets	Single sheets
Maximum original size	8½″ × 14″	8½″ × 11″
Supplies		
Copy toner yield	1,500 copies	1,600 copies
Toner price	$14.50	$100.95
Imaging cartridge (drum)	$365 for 21,500 copies	Included in toner price
Comments	Can produce up to one set of 50 copies; imaging unit contains organic drum, cleaning blade, remote meter reading	Maintenance-free—user replaces PC cartridges, no warm-up time, portable, desktop unit with pop-up carrying handle
Specifications		
Dimensions (H × W × D)	14″ × 25″ × 21″	14⅛″ × 15½″ × ¼″
Weight	70 lb	17 lb
Power requirements	120V, 11A	115V, 6A

Minolta Product Discussion

Features	Advantages	Benefits
■ Makes 22 copies per minute ■ Paper capacity of 250 sheets ■ 10-year warranty ■ Advanced lenses and mirror optics*	■ No need for constant paper feeding by employee ■ Less time spent on printing ■ Employees have more time to spend on work ■ Greater productivity ■ No need to spend money on copier repairs in the next 10 years ■ Higher quality photocopy	■ Increase in profitability ■ Decrease in service and maintenance expenses ■ Increase in customer satisfaction

*Demonstration.

"The advanced lens and mirror optics provide a higher quality photocopy process, which gives you superb copy quality. Here, compare these two copies that I made this morning: I made one from the Minolta and the other from a brand that is very similar to the Futrell. Notice the difference in quality and clarity. Wouldn't you say the Minolta looks much more high-quality and professional?"

Minolta Marketing Plan

Features	Advantages	Benefits
■ Free copier training ■ Basic model ■ Full-service customer support team	■ Reduction in time and cost it takes to train employees ■ High value and reliability* ■ Knowledgeable techniciams	■ Increase in profits ■ Increase in productivity ■ Decrease in service costs

*Testimonial proof.

If customer objects to needing all the features of the Minolta.

"I can understand where you're coming from. This copier is actually the basic model that we market to small businesses. In fact, most of my small business clientele initially chose this model because of its high value and reliability, but most actually found that they do get a great deal of use out of its advanced features which make them more productive. They were a little uncertain about the same things you are before they purchased it, but I actually have copies of letters from some of these local business owners stating how much they use these advanced features. Would you like to see them?"

Minolta Business Plan

Features	Advantages	Benefits
■ Dual component toner	■ Allows more copies to be produced per cartridge ■ Cheaper price per cartridge	■ Decrease in toner expense ■ Increase in profits

Your biggest challenge is to overcome the initial price objections. In fact your sales manager said that getting a small business owner to part with $1,000 is sometimes harder than getting a purchasing agent of a large corporation to pay $100,000 for equipment. Small business owners seldom look past actual price, whereas buyers for large businesses consider the overall long-term cost. With this in mind, you calculate the total cost of each product over the five-year expected life of the copier in order to show Chris the value of the Minolta.

Price Breakdown—60,000 copies a year (*5-year life of copier = 300,000 copies over product life)

	Futrell		Minolta
Price per unit		$595	$2,295
Toner per cartridge	$100.95		$14.50
Refill cartridge in 5-year span*	188		200
Total toner cost		$18,928.13	$2,900
Total cost		**$19,523.13**	**$5,195.00**

*Minolta = 300,000 copies in = years/1,500 copies each toner yields
 Futrell = 300,000 copies in = years/1,600 copies each toner yields

With all this information and practice, you will be prepared to make your sales call on Chris. Your sales call objective is to convince Chris to buy a Minolta instead of replacing his copier with another Futrell. You are sure that Travel Xpress could benefit greatly from the product, and with a polished presentation, you can show these benefits to Chris and sell him on the Minolta.

Role-Play Four: Business-to-Business Sales XDT's RoboPhone+ (XDT)

It is the end of third quarter of a very successful year for Travolta Engineering. Jason Blake, president and CEO of Travolta, announced the end-of-quarter numbers and was delighted to see the results. He expressed his desire to take Travolta to the number one global position in the diesel engine manufacturing industry in the next 10 years.

Michael Hansen, the vice president of sales at Travolta, is happy about his team's performance. However, he feels that some room for improvements still exists within the sales division. He knows that every division in Travolta Engineering is required to perform at its best in order to reach the number one position in the engine manufacturing industry.

Your Role

Congratulations! You have recently been hired and appointed to the sales group of X Dot Technologies (XDT) after successfully completing a six-month training program. You have been assigned to work with John Firestone, who has worked with XDT for five years. Your first sales call with John was with Michael Hansen, VP of sales at Travolta Engineering. He discussed some problems which decrease the efficiency of his sales team. After further research on the company and its problems, you and John feel Mr. Hansen and his team could be potential customers for the newly released RoboPhone+ product manufactured by XDT. Before you approach Mr. Hansen to make a sale, it is important that you understand the company he works for and how they could benefit from the RoboPhone+.

Company Background

Travolta Engineering, founded in 1952, is a corporation that designs, manufactures, distributes, and services diesel engines and related technologies. Headquartered in College Station, Texas (USA), Travolta serves customers in approximately 200 countries and territories through a network of more than 250 company-owned distributor locations. Travolta reported a net income* of $2.06 billion last year.

Travolta manufactures and markets a wide range of diesel-powered engines for on-highway and off-highway use. It markets high-, medium-, and low-speed engines used in passenger cars, diesel-electric locomotives, motorcycles, aircrafts, navy, and military vehicles. The high reliability and durability of diesel engines has helped the diesel engine industry and Travolta grow exponentially.

Travolta Engineering has five major functional groups—design, manufacturing, distribution, sales, and service—which generate revenue for the company. The design and manufacturing groups completely operate out of the United States of America. The distribution group is located in 250 different locations across the globe. The sales and service groups operate in four regions, namely America, Africa, Asia-Pacific (APAC), and Europe and the Middle East (EMEA). One regional sales team handles the sales for each region.

Sales Division at Travolta

Michael Hansen's sales team has 276 salespeople who are the industry's top performers. This sales team contributes 52.8% of the revenues generated by Travolta. However, Mr. Hansen's concern is not the revenue generated but the expenses his team incurs. Last week during your meeting, he expressed his concerns about these additional unavoidable expenses.

Translator Expenses

Travolta has regional sales offices in the continents of Africa, America, Asia, and Europe. The regional offices handle the sales activities for customers situated in the same continent. This business model has proved to be very efficient for Travolta in the past. However, this approach has some shortcomings. Travolta has customers from over 100 countries who speak 87 different languages. It is not possible to hire employees who speak all of the 87 languages. Because of the language barriers, the sales team currently hires translators and interpreters on a contractual basis. This is one of the major expenses incurred by the sales team, and unfortunately it looks like this expense is unavoidable. Last year, Travolta's sales team spent around $970,000 on translators and interpreters.

Keeping Up with Technology Advancement

The sales team at the new technological advancements in the sales field such as using automated systems to find customer information and create background reports. Therefore, the business processes are inefficient and obsolete. Due to lack of technical resources, the salespeople spend a significant amount of time researching their customers' business, background, and interests. Hansen is not happy about this waste of valuable time and resources. According to a report submitted by Arthur Knight, a salesperson at Travolta, each salesperson at the company spends around 22 hours a month researching his customers and prospects which is 13.5 hours above the industry

*Net Income = Revenue − Expenses.

average. Hansen told you that "Although prospecting is an important stage in the selling process, we spend over 20 hours researching our customers and prospects. If we can save these 20 odd hours, we can boost our sales revenue by at least $2 million. I am sure the time spent on researching can be significantly reduced by the use of technology. We are now looking at technology solutions which can help us reduce this wastage of time."

Sales Presentation Challenge

Hansen is also troubled about the difficulty his team faces during the sales presentations. Because diesel engines are huge and difficult to carry, product demonstrations are not always feasible. It is often difficult to explain the features to the clients with just a two-dimensional image of the product. Because of this limitation, most clients request a meeting with the technical team to better understand the product. In such a case, another meeting is set up in which the technical team and salesperson both participate. This additional meeting greatly increases the travel costs. Also, not all customers are cooperative. Some clients demand live demonstrations of the product. In this situation, either the engines are shipped to the client location or the clients are flown to the nearest distribution center. These unanticipated expenses added up to $376,000 last year and are expected to rise by 12.7% in the next year.

Paying Salespeople on Time

Hansen also mentioned their legacy time-tracking system, which requires the salespeople to fill in paper-based timesheets. Since commissions are a huge component of a salesman's paycheck, Hansen's team uses a different time-tracking system and payroll system as compared to the rest of the company. This led to a lot of confusions and time-delays because of erroneous and late timesheet submissions. Often, the salespeople were not paid on time, which led to dissatisfaction and low employee morale. Hansen believes that adopting an automated system can help his team save $250,000 every year.

Sales Opportunity

John and you have realized XDT's RoboPhone+ will solve all of the problems faced by the sales team at Travolta. RoboPhone+, a salesperson's best friend, is much ahead of its time both in innovation and technology. You can give the device a name; let's say you name it Moon Pie. To use the device you simply say "Moon Pie I want this or that," and it will be done. No typing required. Moon Pie can also talk back to you. The device allows you to use voice commands to send messages, schedule meetings, place phone calls, and more. Hansen's sales force is currently using the Red Phone 800, which is created by one of XDT's competitors. Red Phone 800 is a basic smartphone with call, Internet, and e-mail features. It fails to compete with RoboPhone+ when it comes to advanced features like global voice translator, generating customer reports, and projecting a 3-D image.

Global Voice Translator

The global voice translator can eliminate the language barrier the sales team at Travolta is experiencing today. This will save the company almost $1 million every year, which will directly add to their bottom-line. RoboPhone+ will help Hansen streamline his sales process. It is not just money that can be saved by RoboPhone+ but time as well. This revolutionary phone makes prospecting easier for the salesperson and saves them hours of research time. On average, a salesperson at Travolta spends 22 hours per month researching customers. RoboPhone+ can do this within minutes or maybe even seconds. If 276 salespeople save 22 hours every month, do the math to find the number of days saved per year! Now the salespeople can sell more and earn more.

Sales Presentation in 3-D

You know that RoboPhone+ can make sales presentations a great experience! Currently, Hansen's team is not content with their sales presentation tools. Robo-Phone+ 's built-in projector and presentation editor make sales presentations easier. Product demonstrations are now trouble-free with the hologram technology used to project 3-D images and product demo videos. The video conferencing feature makes collaboration between the technical team and customers possible at any time of the day. This helps the sales team save at least $430,000 every year.

Time Tracking

RoboPhone+ 's time-tracking functionality will help the salespeople submit their timesheet virtually from any part of the world. This automated time-tracking system can be integrated with the company's existing payroll system to ensure that salespeople are paid the correct amount on their pay date. This will reduce costs for Travolta as well as increase satisfaction among the salespeople.

There are other features (see the features and functions section for details) like voice commands, social networking integration, and business card scanners that come with RoboPhone+ that will make life easier for the salespeople. And the best part is every employee can attend a free training session to learn how to use this fully loaded device to the fullest. Remember, if your salespeople are happy, your customers are happy! With the RoboPhone+ there are opportunities for cost savings, time savings, and process improvement. What other reasons do you need to sell RoboPhone+ to a troubled manager?

Further Research

Most people are not comfortable with change. This might be the case with Mr. Hansen. In order to ease Mr. Hansen's reluctance to change phones, you conducted further research to compare the Red Phone 800 and RoboPhone+. You found the following quote from *Sales Management Journal,* a popular trade journal in the sales industry:

> *The RoboPhone+ will completely revolutionize the technology in the sales industry. The think tank of geniuses at XDT has come up with another technological breakthrough that could change the way we all live our lives. It has simultaneously filled the need for a phone and a laptop. The RoboPhone+ can do everything the Red Phone 800 can do and more. It's innovative and yet easy to use functions and features will give salespeople all the tools they need to be efficient on the job. While the details are a closely guarded secret, the RoboPhone+ is thought to be based upon new Nano technology. If this rumor is true, this means RoboPhone+ is the first device of its kind.*

—Bob Holtzer, President of the Sales Association of America

Current Situation

Last night you received a telephone call from your district sales manager saying John Firestone had left the company for a better job. You are now responsible for the Travolta account. That means you will have to recheck everything done by John.

Features and Functions of RoboPhone+

1. **Sales**
   - Global language translator: Instantly speak in any global language. Just speak from the front of the phone and the language of your choice is spoken from the speaker in the rear. You can now do business in any country you wish! Language is never a barrier.
   - Projector screen for business presentations: RoboPhone+ 's built-in projector helps you project your presentations up to a 72-inch screen size. Simply point the phone to the screen or wall and it projects in a vivid widescreen format.
   - Presentation editor: RoboPhone+ helps you create and edit presentations on the go. A very intuitive interface allows you to create business presentations in one voice command.
   - Compile background reports on customers and prospects: RoboPhone+ can compile reports on customers and prospects. All you need to do is say their name and it finds a complete background report. Prospecting is no longer a pain.
   - Product information with video: You can ask RoboPhone+ for a video that includes the product information. Simply say the name of the product and the phone will retrieve the video of the product for your customers. You can use the projector and speaker features to present this video to your customers.
   - Quick check-in: RoboPhone+ helps you check in to flights and hotels in less than five seconds. Just say the confirmation number and you are checked in. Traveling is always now stress free.
   - Hologram technology: RoboPhone+ can project 3-D images of the product to both you and the buyer. Now your customers can see the product as if it was real. No need to carry the product for sales presentations anymore!
   - Video conference call capabilities: Short of time to travel to a client location? Just use the video conferencing feature of RoboPhone+. The 3-D video conferencing technology allows you to see and hear your customer as if he were sitting right in front of you. Now, you can see the buyer and the buyer can see you. You can make a sale without ever leaving your office.

2. **Service**
   - Enhanced voice search: Tell the phone what to search for and it will report the information back to you within seconds.
   - Email/fax via voice dictation: Sending e-mail and fax has never been easier. Just speak into phone the message you want to send and the RoboPhone+ will type up the e-mail or fax and send it.

TABLE 1

Features, Advantages, and Benefits for Sales

Features	Advantage	Benefits
- Global language translator - Hologram technology - Video conferencing	- Makes communication between the salespeople and customers much easier	- Improves customer service - Reduces costs
- Projector - Presentation editor - Product demo video	- Enables the sales team to deliver a great sales presentation	- Increases sales and profits
- Background reports compiler	- Helps salespeople to learn their customers better	- Increases sales and profits - Saves time

TABLE 2

Features, Advantages, and Benefits for Service

Features	Advantage	Benefits
■ Enhanced voice search ■ Voice dictation ■ Voice reminders	■ User-friendly interface	■ Improves customer service ■ Saves time
■ Instant communication	■ Easier communication between the salespeople and customers	■ Improves customer service ■ Reduces costs

■ Instant communication: The salesperson can use the video-conferencing feature and connect the customers with anyone in X Dot including the various technical support departments.

■ Voice reminders: RoboPhone+ saves your appointments in the phone so you have a sales call appointment book with vocal reminders of upcoming meetings. No need for a planner!

3. **Territory Management**

■ Time-tracking: Employees can track time spent to report to HR. All they need to do is hold the phone in front of their face. The phone scans the retina so that nobody else can enter time for you. The location is obtained from the GPS and time from the time server. This system can easily be connected with your payroll application. So, people can now get paid on time for the hours they have worked. Less paperwork, more accuracy, and more security!

■ Print documents: Salespeople can print documents from anywhere in the world. Just say the document name that you wish to print, and the printout is ready to be picked up at the nearest connected printer.

■ Video sales call recording: Salesperson can record sales call video for critique, feedback, and performance review. RoboPhone+ records and stores the videos in the home office, and the salesperson and manager can access it any time.

4. **Sales Promotion**

■ Social networking integration: Connect with customers and prospects through the RoboPhone+ 's social networking interface. You are connected to all networking sites such as LinkedIn, Twitter, and Facebook. Update just once and everything is synced. No more managing multiple pages.

■ Contact book: RoboPhone+ has a great contact book that stores all the details of any person you meet. Store the pictures, phone numbers, e-mail accounts, websites, social network IDs, preferences, and so on. It is much easier to remember a person by face now!

■ Business card scanner: Isn't it difficult to manage business cards? Forget the hassle; simply snap a picture of the business card with your RoboPhone+. All the information on the card is stored and integrated with the contact book.

TABLE 3

Features, Advantages, and Benefits for Territory Management

Features	Advantage	Benefits
■ Time-tracking ■ Video sales call recording	■ No more paperwork thus eliminating human errors ■ Helps the salespeople improve their sales skills	■ Improves employee satisfaction ■ Reduces costs ■ Improves customer service

Features	Advantage	Benefits
■ Social network integration ■ Contact book ■ Business card scanner	■ Builds strong customer relationships	■ Improves customer service

5. **General**
   - Charging: No recharging is required. Research says RoboPhone+ has a battery life of up to 10 years.
   - Entertainment: Upload music to the phone and play it out loud using the 5.1 channel speakers. Experience the home theater by projecting 1080p HD movies using the projector feature.
   - Waterproof/shockproof: Research shows that RoboPhone+ can be submerged in up to 45 feet of water for six hours without damage. Also, dropping the RoboPhone+ from the seventh floor caused no damage to the phone.

All of the above looks correct. Now you must carefully check the pricing.

Pricing

Currently, the sales team at Travolta uses GRW as its cellular service provider for the Red Phone 800 handsets. Travolta pays a $110 monthly fee per handset for unlimited calls, text, and web for its 276 salesmen and 34 managers. They pay $25 fixed charge monthly for the Red Phone 800 handsets under the current deal.

If Travolta adopts RoboPhone+ , it can continue to use GRW as their cellular service provider; however, XDT has a tie-up with Race wireless which offers the unlimited package for just $80 monthly fee per handset for RoboPhone+ users. RoboPhone+ is comparatively a little expensive as it offers a wide range of advanced features to its users. The cost per handset depends on the number of RoboPhones purchased and the contract length. Table 5 gives you a brief idea about the monthly fixed charge for the handsets:

Let's say Travolta pays for 310 handsets (276 for salespeople and 34 for managers) and enrolls for the one-year contract with Race wireless; the cost and pricing structure will be as shown in Table 6.

Mr. Hansen may not be thrilled about this $148,800 annual increase in the total expenses of the sales team. To combat this you decided to highlight the financial advantages that RoboPhone+ will bring to his sales team. The return on investment (ROI) analysis that you conducted could be summarized as shown in Table 7.

| Number of devices | Monthly cost per handset | |
	6-month contract	1-year contract
1–50	$150	$135
51–00	$140	$125
10–200	$130	$115
201–300	$120	$105
301+	$110	$ 95

TABLE 6

Pricing Comparison—Red Phone 800 vs. RoboPhone+

	Monthly wireless service fee per employee	Monthly handset fixed cost per employee	Total monthly cost per employee	Total annual cost* (handsets + wireless service)
Red Phone 800	$110	$25	$135	$502,200
RoboPhone+	$ 80	$95	$175	$651,000

*Total annual costs = total monthly cost per employee × number of employees × 12

TABLE 7

Net Increase on Bottom Line

RoboPhone+ ROI components	Annual costs
Savings on translator service	$ 970,000
Increase in sales revenue due to less time spent prospecting	2,000,000
Savings on sales presentation techniques	430,000
Savings on time-tracking	250,000
Additional expenses incurred (Table 6)	(148,800)
Net increase on bottom line	**$3,501,200**

TABLE 8

Annual ROI Analysis

Total cost of investment (Table 6)	$ 651,000
Tota gains from investment (Table 7)	$3,650,000
ROI%	**460.68%***

*ROI = (Total sales gains − Total costs)/Total costs

Role Play Five (Part One): Consumer Packaged Goods Sales

You are a salesperson for an entrepreneurial, emerging company in the consumer packaged goods world, Ag-Kru Foods. Your flagship product is called the Pizza-Munch, a portable, healthy pizza product.

Ag-Kru Foods has gained distribution in a number of well-known grocery stores and mass merchandisers. However, the next step for sales growth targets club super-stores. These type of stores tend to sell in large quantities and offer limited assort-ments. Instead of offering a variety of the same type of product, such as 15 flavors and sizes of ketchup, the club stores only offer one or two types of that particular product, usually in larger packing size (such as 22 ounces). In order for consumers to purchase at a club store, they pay an annual membership fee.

Gaining distribution within a club superstore is a major benefit for consumer pack-aged goods manufacturers. The club business model provides limited competition within a food category and provides the potential for a high volume of sales (i.e., due to strong inventory turnover).

The major benefits of distribution in a club superstore also pose a distinct chal-lenge. Due to the limited assortment policy, gaining distribution is very competitive. In order to gain distribution within a club superstore or wholesale warehouse, it is important to provide a product and service that aligns with the club's business and member needs.

Therefore, clubs and wholesale warehouses seek products that will sell well in bulk, provide unique benefits to their members, are innovative, and capture impulse purchases from the member base.

You have scheduled a meeting with Pat, a buyer at the Super-Club. You have met with Pat at a few industry trade-shows. Pat has expressed interest in learning more about PizzaMunch. From your discussions with Pat, you notice that Pat relies on quantitative analysis. Pat is interested in the analytics and metrics. Therefore, your discussion should incorporate market data, consumer data, and financial data. You want to develop a very strong fact-based presentation that provides a strong business-based case for including PizzaMunch into Super-Club's distribution plans.

About Super-Club

Super-Club was initiated in the Midwest. It currently owns 250 clubs across the United States. Its members pay a $200 membership fee to access the clubs. Super-Club states that the average member saves an estimated $2,200 per year due to its prices on its products and services. Super-Club has a clean store policy. This means the store does not allow manufacturer displays or signs in its stores. Therefore, in-store promotions are limited to in-store sampling.

The pizza category within Super-Club is very competitive. Super-Club only allows six types of frozen-pizzas—four manufacturer brands and two of its private label offerings. All of the pizzas are currently 12-inch diameter frozen pizzas or larger. The club mandates margins (markup on cost and markup on price exceeding 15% on all products). Super-Club is also very protective of its private label offerings. Manufacturers must demonstrate that their products will not cannibalize (impact market share of) Super-Club's private label products.

Sales Objectives

Your sales objective is to gain distribution of either the 12-pack or 24-PizzaMunch within Super-Club. You would like to have shipping begin in 6 weeks and the packing to be in Super-Club stores in 8 weeks. You would like distribution in all 250 Super-Club stores. You would also like to have Super-Club approve in-store sampling of PizzaMunch during Saturday and Sunday from August to November (i.e., to align with football season and national advertising). You would like to suggest an introductory order of four cases per store. You would also like to monitor inventory turnover for the first six months and provide e-mail updates to the buyer every four weeks.

Your product

- PizzaMunch are smaller, hand-friendly pizzas
- Each PizzaMunch is 6 inches in diameter
- All components are vegetable based
- No high-fructose corn syrup
- Two PizzaMunches have 400 calories or less
- Minimal sodium
- Baked instead of fried
- Vegetable-based filling
- Recognized by leading health magazine and leading consumer magazine as one of top three healthiest options in pizza category

Key Consumer Trends (Source: Ag-Kru Internal Market Research)

- *Consumption:* Approximately 55% of all pizza consumers purchase a frozen pizza for consumption every 7.23 days.
- *Consumption:* Approximately 1 in 8 American consumers eat pizza each day.
- *Mobility:* Approximately 28% of all pizza consumers eat pizza while standing, multitasking, or riding in some form of transportation.
- *Health:* Approximately 30% of all pizza consumers are seeking a lower-calorie pizza alternative.

Strategic Positioning of PizzaMunch

Target consumer	Males and females, approximately 25 to 39, who consistently feel time constrained. They are frequently frustrated by the trade-offs between healthy foods that taste good (or are even indulgent). Their above-average incomes ($48,000 plus) provide them a willingness to pay more for convenience. They also seek greater mobility with their foods, as they often eat when they are physically moving (be it walking to a meeting or in a vehicle).
Positioned against	Direct comparison to existing "healthy" food category and its consistent "dullness" of food options.
	Second direct comparison to pizza that is decadent but not guilt-free.
Emotional benefit	Reduction in guilt of eating what everyone else eats (i.e., pizza) and aligning eating with lifestyle choices. PizzaMunch ensures you are eating good, tasty, and healthy.
Functional benefit	Assurance that the consumer who eats pizza doesn't have to make the trade-off between indulgence and healthy. Easy, quick, healthy value.
Communication of value	All vegetable-based materials (from crust to filling)
	Awards from leading healthy eating magazines
	All varieties have calorie content under 400 calories
	All varieties can be cooked in oven or microwave in 10 minutes or less

Marketing Goals for PizzaMunch (2 Year Plan):

- Current year goal: Drive nationwide penetration to 45% U.S. households
- Create trial of product in 22 million households over next 104 weeks
- Pull consumers into retail partners for product purchase

Marketing Investments Made by Ag-Kru Foods

- $3,000,000 in sampling (in-store partners).
  - Over 4,000,000 total samples available (to be distributed in national retailers).
- $1,500,000 in social media targeting pizza consumers
- $1,000,000 in mobile marketing coupons
- $4,500,000: 1 SuperBowl commercial
- $3,000,000 in TV advertising (professional and college football times), Fall of upcoming year

PizzaMunch Flavors (8 varieties)

Garlic and spinach	Pineapple and anchovy	Peppers & mushrooms	Eggplant parmesan
BBQ onion and olive	Pepperoni (soy-based)	Sausage (soy-based)	Vegetable pack

PizzaMunch Packings

Club packings	12-pack economy size (individually wrapped). Assorted flavors (4 pepperoni, 4 sausage, 4 vegetable)	24-pack club size (individually wrapped) Assorted flavors (8 pepperoni, 8 sausage, 4 vegetable, eggplant parmesan, 4 garlic & spinach)
Grocery store and mass merchandiser packings	Doubles (2 per package; individually wrapped)	4-pack family size 4 per package

Packings & Pricings of PizzaMunch

Packings	12-Pack Economy Size (individually wrapped)	24-Pack Club Size (individually wrapped)	Doubles (2 per package) (individually wrapped)	4-pack Family Size 4 per Package
MSRP (manufacturer's suggested retail price)	$17.49	$34.99	$2.99	$5.99
Per unit	1.46	1.46	1.50	1.50
Investment (list price)	13.20	26.40	2.24	4.48
Margin	4.29	8.59	.075	1.51

Consumer Taste Panel (PizzaMunch vs. Competitive Offerings)

	PizzaMunch	Leading Home Pizza (frozen)	Leading Take-Out Pizza	Leading Healthy Meal
Very good taste	60%	40%	50%	45%
Average taste	30	30	30	25
Very poor taste	10	30	20	30

*Internal market research survey based on 5,000 pizza consumers.

Percentage Sales Increases (year-over-year) for PizzaMunch
(mass merchandisers and grocery stores: past year)

	Eastern	Western	Southern	Midwest-Great Plains
Dollar sales	4%	6%	12%	18%
Unit sales	5	8	14	16

Benefits from Sampling Initiative (PizzaMunch)

Sampling	Volume Increase During Sampling (same week)	Volume Increase 1 Week after Sampling Initiative	Volume Increase 2 Weeks after Sampling Initiative	Volume Increase 3 Weeks after Sampling Initiative	Volume Increase 4 Weeks after Sampling Initiative
Eastern	8%	6%	4%	3%	2.5%
Western	6	6	4	2.5	2
Southern	9	10	11	11	10
Midwest-Great Plains	12	13	14	15	16

Overlap Analysis (PizzaMunch's impact on retailer's private label pizza)

	1 Month after Introduction of PizzaMunch	3 Months after Introduction of PizzaMunch	6 Months after Introduction of PizzaMunch	12 Months after Introduction of PizzaMunch
Private-label share in Eastern retailers	33%	32%	33%	33%
Private-label share in Western retailers	28	29	28	28
Private-label share in Southern retailers	42	40	41	43
Private-label share in Midwest-Great Plains retailers	18	18	19	17

Pizza Category (all pizza sales) Growth after Introduction of PizzaMunch into Retailers

	1 Month after Introduction of PizzaMunch	3 Months after Introduction of PizzaMunch	6 Months after Introduction of PizzaMunch	12 Months after Introduction of PizzaMunch
Eastern retailers	0.8%	1.2%	3.0%	3.3%
Western retailers	2.0	1.8	2.0	1.9
Southern retailers	2.8	2.6	2.7	3.0
Midwest-Great Plains retailers	4.0	4.5	5.0	5.2

(Source: Ag-Kru Foods Internal Market Research)

Role Play Five (Part Two): Consumer Packaged Goods Sales

Congratulations. You have gained distribution within Super-Club. (For this scenario, you can decide whether you gained distribution of the 12-pack or 24-pack.) You have had distribution within Super-Club for six months. Last night, you received a voice-mail from your Super-Club pizza category buyer. The buyer sounded very upset and wants to meet with you in two days. The buyer stated that Pizza Munch sampling was a "major frustration." Your buyer also relayed that sampling has gone awry in one of her clubs. While your company, Ag-Kru Foods contracts through a third party,

Sampling-R-Us, for in-store sampling initiatives, the Super-Club buyer still considers you responsible for what the buyer termed a "fiasco."

You have made a number of background calls to learn about the challenge. You've made some preliminary notes and have surmised the following:

- Customers called the manager of one Super-Club (store #187) and relayed a very unprofessional sampling representative.
- The sampling representative did not adhere to the sampling procedures and did not adequately cook the PizzaMunch samples. The product was still frozen in the center.
- When customers provided feedback to the in-store sampling person, the sampling representative was rude and told them, "It's free isn't it?"
- The sampling occurred on the first Saturday of the month. The first day of the month is the largest revenue and consumer traffic day of the month for the club.
- During that day, the manager received over 100 complaints via telephone calls, e-mails, and personal visits.
- The manager attempted to talk with the sampling representative. However, the person was rude and walked out of the club and left immediately. The Super-Club manager was forced to remove the PizzaMunch sampling station.
- Super-Club may be considering no longer doing business with your firm.

You asked your category manager to examine PizzaMunch sales at Super-Club. The following data was provided. Based on the sales data, you want *and need* to retain distribution within Super-Club.

Pizza-Munch Market Share in Super-Club

Sampling	Week 4	Week 8	Week 12	Week 16	Week 20	Week 24
Eastern clubs	2.0%	4.0%	6.1%	6.3%	7.1%	7.5%
Western clubs	1.0	1.5	2.0	2.5	3.0	3.5
Southern clubs	1.5	3.5	4.0	5.0	6.6	8.0
Midwest–Great Plains clubs	2.0	5.0	6.0	8.0	9.0	10.0

Super-Club Pizza Category Performance* (all pizza sales) after Introduction of PizzaMunch

Sampling	Week 4	Week 8	Week 12	Week 16	Week 20	Week 24
Eastern clubs	1.0%	2.0%	3.1%	3.3%	3.7%	4.0%
Western clubs	0.5	0.5	1.0	1.0	1.5	2.0
Southern clubs	0.5	1.0	1.0	2.0	2.0	2.5
Midwest–Great Plains clubs	1.8	4.0	5.0	6.0	7.0	8.0

*Growth in dollar sales

When these types of service failures occur, you always want to prepare contingency plans for the meeting. You are meeting with your supervisor to talk about your contingency plans. Your supervisor calls these contingency plans, "what we have in our back-pocket." Depending on the tenor of the meeting with the Super-Club buyer, you might offer one or a combination of the following three remedies. You also plan to share the impact of PizzaMunch sales at Super-Club.

Contingency Plans

1. Provide free goods as a "make-good" for the time and effort invested by the Super-Club (#187) manager to address the sampling professional. Super-Club would not be charged for a one-month supply of PizzaMunch for the club (#187). You estimated this quantity is approximately 387 units.
2. Suspend all sampling for four weeks until a new vendor is located. Provide a promise that a new sampling vendor will be used for all Super-Club demonstrations (within the next four weeks). In addition, you will personally meet with the Super-Club (#187) manager to provide a face-to-face apology within the next five (5) working days.
3. You will work with Super-Club and its manager for the store (#187) to gain a comprehensive list of all affected club members. You will personally call all of the affected members in the next 7 business days and alert them that you will be sending them two free cases of PizzaMunch delivered directly to their household. You will ensure that delivery is scheduled to arrive at a convenient time (i.e., such as in the evening when they are home).

As you review all of this information with your supervisor, she jots it all down on a whiteboard. This systems allows you to see all of the sales call objectives. Together, you review the multiple goals for the upcoming meeting, including: (a) to use your needs-discovery (questioning) skills to understand and confirm all elements of the buyer's frustration, (b) to provide an acceptable remedy to the buyer, (c) to reinforce the value of PizzaMunch at Super-Club by providing important data and interpretation of the sales and category data, and (d) to ensure the relationship recovers from the service failure, thereby retaining the PizzaMunch business at Super-Club.

It's time to begin developing your pre-approach and sales strategy, including the visuals and all other materials you will use. Good luck.

Role Play Five (Part Three): Consumer Packaged Goods Sales Business Review

You are a salesperson for an entrepreneurial, emerging company in the consumer packaged goods world, Ag-Kru Foods. Your flagship product is called the Pizza-Munch, a portable, healthy pizza product.

Ag-Kru Foods has gained distribution in a number of well-known grocery stores and mass merchandisers. In addition, you have recently gained distribution (i.e., the 24-pack club size—individually wrapped) within your first chain of club superstores, Super-Club.

Your product, PizzaMunch, has been distributed by the Super-Club chain for the past 10 months. Your buyer has asked you to provide a business review. A business review often integrates a product's performance within a specific business (i.e., Super-Club) along with a comparison of the product's performance in competitive trade channels (such as grocery stores and mass merchandise). Specifically, she has asked you to compare the first five months of distribution versus the second five-month period. The business review also provides updates on key marketplace trends. Your buyer has also asked for a promotional recommendation. Super-Club limits the forms of in-store promotions. Beyond sampling, the chain is open to 30-day price alerts. The

30-day price alerts are a month-long sale on the product. The buyer would want to discuss a promotional price point and the associated margins.

The timing of the business review appears to be fantastic. Your national sales trends are very favorable (i.e., nationally). However, it does appears that the sales growth within Super-Club lags behind sales growth in grocery stores. You will need to find a way to proactively address this issue with the buyer.

In your meeting with your sales manager, you write down two meeting objectives:

1. To provide a quantitative, fact-based business review that reaffirms Super-Club's decision to distribute PizzaMunch; and to proactively overcome any hesitation of Super-Club's sales growth in comparison to other channels of trade.
2. To provide a recommendation and gain acceptance for a 30-day price alert for PizzaMunch. Upon acceptance by the buyer, the promotion would begin eight weeks after your meeting with the buyer.

Your product

- PizzaMunch is smaller, hand-friendly pizzas.
- Each PizzaMunch is 6 inches in diameter.
- All components are vegetable based.
- No high-fructose corn syrup is used.
- Two PizzaMunch products have 400 calories or less.
- Sodium content is minimal.
- They are baked instead of fried.
- Recognized by leading health magazine and leading consumer magazine as one of the top three healthiest options in the pizza category.

Key Consumer Trends (Source: Ag-Kru Internal Market Research)

- *In the past 12 months:*
  - Mobile snack consumption has increased by 6%.
  - Mobile meal consumption has increased by 5%.
  - Pizza consumption has increased by 4%.
  - Healthy frozen-food options have increased by 12%.
  - Healthy frozen-food consumers' preference to "taste new flavors" has increased by 7%.

PizzaMunch Flavors (8 varieties)

Garlic and spinach	Pineapple and anchovy	Peppers & mushrooms	Eggplant parmesan
BBQ onion and olive	Pepperoni (soy-based)	Sausage (soy-based)	Vegetable pack

Pizza Munch Packings

Club packings	12-pack economy size (individually wrapped). Assorted flavors (4 pepperoni, 4 sausage, 4 vegetable)	24-pack club size (individually wrapped) Assorted flavors (8 pepperoni, 8 sausage, 4 vegetable, eggplant parmesan, 2 garlic & spinach)
Grocery store and mass merchandiser packings	Doubles (2 per package; individually wrapped)	4-pack family size 4 per package

Packings & UNIT Sales Growth of PizzaMunch
(Second 5 month period compared against first 5-month period)

Packings	12-Pack Economy Size (individually wrapped)	24-Pack Club Size (individually wrapped)	Doubles (2 per package) (individually wrapped)	4-Pack Family Size 4 Per Package
Super-Club	N/A	12%	N/A	N/A
Grocery store channel	N/A	N/A	14%	13%
Mass merchandise channel	N/A	N/A	11.5	10.9
Drugstore channel	N/A	N/A	11.7	12

Packings & DOLLAR Sales Growth of PizzaMunch
(Second 5-month period compared against first 5-month period)

Packings	12-Pack Economy Size (individually wrapped)	24-Pack Club Size (individually wrapped)	Doubles (2 per package) (individually wrapped)	4-Pack Family Size 4 Per Package
Super-Club	N/A	15%	N/A	N/A
Grocery store channel	N/A	N/A	17.5%	16.1%
Mass merchandise channel	N/A	N/A	12.4	11.7
Drugstore channel	N/A	N/A	14.5	13.5

Updated Consumer Taste Panel (PizzaMunch vs. competitive offerings in each class of trade) Completed within Past Month

	PizzaMunch*	Leading Frozen Pizza (Grocery Store Channel)	Leading Frozen Pizza (Club Channel)	Leading Frozen Pizza (Mass Merchandiser Channel)
Very good taste	61%	52%	57%	58%
Average taste	29	30	22	18
Very poor taste	10	18	21	24

*Internal Market Research Survey based on 5,000 pizza consumers

Percentage Sales Increases (Second 5-month period compared against first 5-month period) for PizzaMunch (ALL varieties/packings) (Grocery Stores—Based on Region)

Super-Club	Eastern	Western	Southern	Midwest—Great Plains
Dollar sales	9%	12%	19%	27%
Unit sales	7	9	16	18

Interpretation: Suggests dollar sales increased 9% in Eastern U.S. in second five-month period vs. first five-month period for grocery store.

Percentage Sales Increases (Second 5-month period compared against first 5-month period) for PizzaMunch (ALL varieties/packings) (Super-Club Stores—Based on Region)

Super-Club Stores	Eastern	Western	Southern	Midwest—Great Plains
Dollar sales	10%	18%	15%	15%
Unit sales	8	16	13	12

Interpretation: Suggests dollar sales increased 10% in Eastern U.S. in second five-month period vs. first five-month period for Super Club stores.

Overlap Analysis (PizzaMunch's impact on Super-Club private label pizza market share)
(First 5-month period compared against second 5-month period)

	First 5-Month Period after PizzaMunch Distribution	Second 5-Month Period after PizzaMunch Distribution
Private-label share in Eastern region	22%	21%
Private-label share in Western region	31	33
Private-label share in Southern region	18	22
Private-label share in Midwest–Great Plains region	26	24

Interpretation: Private-label share in the Eastern region was 22% during the first five months and 21% in the second five months that PizzaMunch was distributed.

Role-Play Six (Part One): Business-to-Business

Technology Sales

Overview

You are a territory manager representing Pro-Customer Focused Solutions, a firm specializing in customer relationship management technology and other complementary software. You serve as a key contact for customers; and provide fact-based business conversations to prospects and existing customers to identify their needs and grow their business.

Your Product

Customer relationship management (CRM) is a technology system that helps companies manage information about existing and potential customers. Your CRM system includes contact management technology, a listing of all the customer contacts that a salesperson makes in the course of conducting business. The form of the technology is like an electronic collection of business cards and includes such information as the contact's name, title, company, address, phone number, fax number, and e-mail address. It also includes additional information such as the particular industry, date of last order, name of administrative assistant, other key decision makers, and so on.

The value of your CRM system lies in its ability to manage knowledge. Your CRM software combines sales, marketing, and customer service data into one information technology platform. For example, your CRM system includes insight from the salesperson's colleagues. Your CRM system allows a firm's customer service department to document the interactions and communications with customers, and the firm's marketing department to track all of its marketing communication activities with potential customers. Hence, CRM technology not only provides a tracking mechanism, it also allows salespeople and their colleagues to share critical information throughout their organization and more effectively collaborate.

Sales Scenario

You are calling upon a Midwestern-based firm, ABC Industries, Inc. They manufacture products for the home remodeling industry. ABC Industries, Inc. has been in operation for decades. When the organization started as a small manufacturer, they designed and paid for an account management software specifically developed for their firm. Over the past 12 years, the company has experienced tremendous growth and expanded its sales and marketing organization. ABC Industries, Inc. now

Pro-Customer Focused Solutions Cloud-Based CRM	Benefits
	Reduces complexity typically tied to • Implementation of updates, upgrades, and security • The internal processes and time invested in determining types of upgrades, project planning, and implementation
	Provides online expertise • For your IT resources • For all users This online expertise can be reached through e-mail, on-line chats, and telephone calls
	Reduces internal costs tied to • IT resources devoted to upgrading CRM systems • IT resources devoted to problem-shooting • IT hardware (such as servers) and infrastructure to house servers and technology • Developing upgrades and updates • Implementing upgrades and updates on all user's computers • IT processes to maintain CRM infrastructure
	Provides stability and accuracy in • Understanding technology costs tied directly to CRM • Understanding technology costs tied to upgrades • Forecasting technology investment and ongoing costs • Understanding technology costs tied to employee new-hires
	Provides users with 24-hour • Access to data, regardless of location • Technology assistance and questions • Access to the latest software updates, upgrades, and versions
	Provides the firm with the opportunity to • Access all data, regardless of location • Integrate all information regarding prospects to existing customers • Understand all communication touch-points and interactions with customers • Track interactions and customer responses

Investment	
Investment	$44.50 per user per month (monthly subscription) or $500.00 per user per year (if customer prepays for annual subscription)
ABC number of estimated subscriptions (i.e., users)	150
One-time training and account transition investment	$7.00 per account *This expense includes moving all customer data to the CRM system. This also includes on-line tutorials for all users and a 3-hour one-to-one session with all users.
ABC number of accounts to transfer	14,000 unique accounts

understands that their legacy system will not adapt to today's business environment. Hence, it has made a call to Pro-Customer Focused Solutions to learn about its Pro-Customer Focused Solutions Customer Relationship Management product.

The firm needs some type of CRM system that enables better coordination between its marketing and sales divisions. In addition, it needs to ensure a greater level of automation of its marketing activities. With the current legacy system, the sales organization has some difficulty tracking leads, including referrals. In addition, the legacy system does not have the capability to track any marketing activities.

Your sales objective is to develop a sales proposal and solution that shows the value of Pro-Customer Focused Solutions CRM. Ideally, you would like ABC Industries, Inc. to commit to signing an agreement that begins a subscription for the online Pro-Customer Focused Solutions Customer Relationship Management product. However, this means you will need to understand ABC Industries, Inc.'s goals and provide a comprehensive solution.

Your Customer: ABC Industries, Inc.

ABC Industries, Inc. was established in 1996 in Manhattan, Kansas, as a manufacturer in the home remodeling industry. ABC Industries, Inc. is a fast-growing manufacturer serving the home remodeling industry. Its primary products include the manufacture of cabinetry, large decks, custom windows, and stainless steel siding.

The firm has salespeople that call on all 50 states, and it distributes its products in the United States, Mexico, and Canada. This diversified manufacturing base has allowed steady growth over the past 20 years. However, as the firm has grown, it has experienced growing pains, especially in its technology systems. As previously noted, it is attempting to find a CRM system to enable greater coordination and integration of its marketing and sales efforts.

The firm is notorious for attempting to project its returns and paybacks on any technology or capital investment. Your key contact person is the IT manager. The IT manager is responsible for both integration of technology and training. Hence, the individual wants a full solution rather than simply hardware or software. The salesforce exceeds 100 individuals and many of the individuals have tenures exceeding 15 years with the company. The marketing division is primarily tasked with prospecting for potential customers (i.e., home improvement centers, remodeling companies, and contractors) and providing qualified leads to the salesforce.

You've heard that your buyer, the IT manager, likes to get to the point. The buyer is extremely analytical and desires data-based decisions. You also have noticed that the buyer downloaded a trial of your product. You should assume that your buyer continually feels pressured to provide a strong return on the firm's technology investment. Finally, you understand that both the marketing and the sales departments are placing pressure on the IT manager to move the buying process along quickly. This will be the first meeting with IT manager. However, you have met the buyer before at a few civic events. Your goal is to prepare your needs discovery and a sales presentation.

Internal Data

Pro-Customer Focused Solutions CRM Internal Research. The following information has been tracked by Pro-Customer Focused Solutions and its customer base (approximately 480 firms). All data are in the form of ranges experienced by customers.

> Return on investment. For every $1.00 spent, return on investment:
> $1.33 to $3.50 (range)
> Revenue increases for customer (within 24 months of implementation):
> 3.7%–9.2% (range)

Reduction in cost of sales (within 24 months of implementation):
5%–12% (range)
Average decrease in sales (within 24 months of implementation:
8–22 days (average range)
Average increase in customer satisfaction (within 24 months of implementation):
3 to 6 points (range)
Average reduction of total IT costs (within 24 months of implementation):
2%–8% (range)

Your Pre-Call Research

In preparation for your sales conversation, your research has allowed you to identify the following key metrics:

ABC Data (or industry estimates)	
ABC Customer Satisfaction Levels (based on industry estimates)	68%
Projected IT Costs (cost accounting estimates tied to legacy CRM product) (based on industry estimates)	$60,000 (annual)
Number of Potential Users at ABC (estimate based on ABC website)	150
Projected ABC Sales Cycle (based on industry estimates)	180 days
Average Customer Sale (based on industry estimates)	$8,700
Average Cost of Sales (based on industry estimates)	$4,700
Estimated: ABC's Customer Base (per year) (based on industry estimates)	12,000 customers
% of Customer Attrition per Year (industry estimates)	9.3% (i.e., 9.3% of customers no longer conduct business with the firm)
Estimated Cost of Upgrades to Legacy System on a quarterly basis (industry estimates)	$12,000
Numbers of Upgrades (estimated)	4 (once per quarter)

Role-Play Six (Part Two): Business-to-Business

Prospecting & Technology Sales

Estimating Effort and Professional Communication

Overview

You are a territory manager representing Pro-Customer Focused Solutions, a firm specializing in customer relationship management technology and other complementary software.

Background

Pro-Customer Focused Solutions has an annual business objective of increasing sales by 12%. Your supervisor, the vice president of sales, has asked you to develop a sales forecast of your territory. She would like to understand how many sales leads you need to contact each month in order to reach a monthly sales goal of $42,000. Your supervisor has provided the following template to each of her territory managers. She would like you to complete the template and provide a one-page e-mail summarizing the number of leads that you would need to contact to reach the sales goal.

As you read your supervisor's e-mail, you are a little apprehensive. The template assumes that you will be able to close a deal within 30 days. However, you know that the time from introduction to the lead accepting a business proposal is 45 days (minimum). In your e-mail, you have decided to *also* include a polite but direct reminder to your supervisor that the assumption in the template may not be exactly correct. You know it is important to provide professional business communication; and you know your supervisor will want to know about any inherent inconsistencies in the calculations.

Now, it's time to complete the template and also draft the e-mail. Good luck.

Descriptions of Actions (Sales Funnel)	Percentage of Leads That Proceed to Next Step	Number of Leads Contacted Each Month				
Sales Leads (number of introductory e-mails sent to leads)	**100%**	**35** (example)	**70**	**105**	**140**	**175**
· Territory manager: Uses CRM system to send customized e-mails to leads						
Leads respond & inquire about additional information from your firm	30	10.5				
· Territory manager: Sends a customized e-mail with attachments. The attachments provide information focused upon inquiry.						
Leads respond again and ask for more detailed, specific information	60	6.3				
· Territory manager: Sends second customized e-mail with attachments. The attachments provide information focused upon inquiry.						
Meeting set with prospect for needs discovery	50	3.15				
· Territory manager: Sets web conference meeting. During meeting, learns about prospect and defines specific needs and goals.						
Second meeting set and business proposal provided to prospects	75	2.3625				
· Territory manager: Sets an on-site meeting at prospect's facility. You provide a comprehensive proposal focused on prospect's needs.						
Customers accept proposals (closed sales)	45	1.063125				
· Territory manager: Finalizes all necessary paperwork and submits a final implementation timeline to customer.						
Average sale (value of proposal)		$12,000	$12,000	$12,000	$12,000	$12,000
Total sales generated (rounded down)		12,000				

For example, if you calculated that 3.8 customers accept proposals, assume that only 3 customer accepted the proposal (3 × $12,000).

Role-Play Six (Part Three): Business-to-Business

Technology Sales

Overview

You are a territory manager representing Pro-Customer Focused Solutions, a firm specializing in customer relationship management technology and other complementary software.

Background

Congratulations! As a Pro-Customer Focused Solutions territory manager, you successfully gained acceptance of your CRM product into your customer's firm. Your customer feels the product was a great addition and productivity tool for his/her firm.

Sales scenario

It is one year later and your client has called to express a new concern. The client has communicated to you that their firm would like to enhance the productivity of the Pro-Customer Focused Solutions CRM technology. Your client has done their research on your website. They have found that Pro-Customer Focused Solutions offers a number of software add-ons that help firms gain greater productivity from their CRM technology.

Your client has asked you to set a meeting in two weeks. During the meeting, the client would like you to present a two-page overview (proposal). The proposal should recommend a solution regarding a suite of add-on software services. You may also develop a number of visuals (i.e., slides, marketing collaterals, etc.) if you so choose. However, the two-page proposal is a mandatory.

In the client's e-mail to you, they noted the proposal should include the following areas:

- The proposal should assist the client in leveraging their existing Pro-Customer Focused Solutions CRM solution.

- The options (i.e., software add-ons) that you recommend must aid the client achieve no less than one (minimum) of the following objectives:
  - Locating leads
  - Qualifying leads and developing them into clients
  - Tracking customer interactions with the client firm
  - Gaining insight and understanding customers
  - Consistently communicating with the firm's customers and/or leads

In order for the client to accept any of your recommendations, each option (on its own individual merit) *must meet one additional financial criteria*:

- You must be able to demonstrate each recommended option has a return on investment exceeding 50% in year one. Please do not discuss any options that do not meet this threshold.

To meet this opportunity, you will review your four major software add-ons. You will evaluate each option and propose only the software add-on option(s) that meet the client's criteria. You've decided that you will recommend individual options as well as a portfolio of options (i.e., a combination of the options).

Through your past interactions with the client, you know that this individual is very particular in their evaluation of options. You remind yourself of the following:

- Your client believes that it is important to evaluate a variety of options. Therefore, your proposal should provide multiple options (i.e., more than one).

- You will want to align with your client's mandatories. You will need to explain how each proposed option meets their goals of further leveraging the CRM technology. In addition, you will need to ensure the recommendation meets the prescribed financial metric.

Now it's time to develop a sales strategy, develop a formal proposal, and provide specific recommendations to meet the targeted metrics as well as the other goals expressed by your client.

The four software add-on options follow. In order to incorporate an option into your proposal, you will need to evaluate it and ensure it meets the client's goals.

Four Options

All software add-on options can be purchased. Each option provides additional capabilities to leverage the CRM systems capabilities. The formal names and descriptions of the product follow:

1. **Pro-Customer Focused Solutions Leader:** Lead and Prospect Management Add-On
2. **Pro-Customer Focused Solutions Tracker:** Marketing Communication Add-On
3. **Pro-Customer Focused Solutions Marketing Metric:** Business Intelligence Add-On
4. **Pro-Customer Focused Solutions Customer Access:** Customer Intelligence Add-On

Pro-Customer Focused Solutions Leader: Lead and Prospect Management Add-On
The Leader software add-on provides an expansive understanding of a firm's customers. When your firm needs a better understanding of its potential and existing customer base, the Leader add-on software provides the information you need. Information about all of your customers is easily accessed and displayed in an easy interface. Further, your entire firm can access information on any customer at any time. Additional capabilities include:

- An ability to visualize the progress salespeople are making in transitioning a lead into a prospect and finally a customer

- An ability to understand all interactions between your firm and its customers—from e-mails, website interactions, white paper downloads, and any other communications

- An ability to consistently score each prospect and customer. Your sales team can develop scenarios regarding different lead scoring systems and their associated metrics. The scenarios allow you to examine what, how, and where your sales resources (i.e. time, people and financial) could be deployed

Pro-Customer Focused Solutions Tracker: Communication Add-On

The Tracker software add-on provides an online real-time communication agency at your fingertips. Consider all of the communication that is typically targeted to your clients (newsletters, direct mail, surveys, telephone communication, webinars, blogs, white papers, etc.). Now imagine a software add-on that aids in its content and visual development. With over 10,000 marketing communication templates, the Tracker makes it easy to develop content.

The Tracker not only develops content, it also tracks it. Regardless of the marketing communication format, the Tracker enables your firm to understand customer feedback, behaviors, and actions. With this understanding, you'll be able to evaluate the impact of each marketing communication tool and its ability to move prospects closer to making a sale.

Pro-Customer Focused Solutions Marketing Metric: Business Intelligence Add-On

The Marketing Metric software add-on provides your firm with an ability to evaluate your CRM data, to statistically analyze it, and to visually present the results.

Plus, Marketing Metric's visual capability allows to develop a wide range of visual and analytic tools such as dashboards, graphs, charts, tables, maps, etc. If your firm and its senior leadership need instant reporting that is easily understandable, the Marketing Metric software add-on is the solution. The system allows you to quantify business opportunities in a variety of ways, including the number of leads in your system, the number of prospects in your system, buying trends of your current customer base, and forecasted business opportunities for each month, each quarter, and each year. If you need the data in a quick, easily accessible, reportable format, the Marketing Metric software add-on is a fantastic investment.

Pro-Customer Focused Solutions Customer Access: Customer Intelligence Add-On

The Customer Access software add-on provides your front-line salespeople with instant understanding of their customer. When a customer contacts your firm (via phone, web, webinar, etc.) our technology provides a visual representation of key customer data. This data includes major purchases, data on the customer's firm, previous interactions, marketing communication and associated responses, and any other important aspect about the customer. With this arsenal of easily accessible information, you assist your sales representative in serving your customer and enhancing customer satisfaction. In addition, the software also provides tips on serving the customer. These tips range from questions to ask the client about their needs to confirming follow-up actions occurred on recent mishaps and service recovery incidents. The Customer Access software add-on provides instantly-accessible information at your salesperson's fingertips and enables your employees to better serve your customers.

	Training and Installation* (one-time cost) Occurs only during First Year	Investment in Technology per User (annual subscription per user) Occurs Every Year	Number of Subscriptions Needed† (users of technology)	Example: Total Investment Required for Year 1 (one-time training and installation + yearly subscription × users)	Forecasted Productivity Impact (Return) (annual revenue increase or expense reduction per subscription) Savings Realized Annually— every year
Pro-Customer Focused Solutions Leader: Lead and Prospect Management Add-On	$ 20,000	$ 800	5	$24,000	$2,200
Pro-Customer Focused Solutions Tracker: Marketing Communication Add-On	80,000	1,000	35	?	4,000
Pro-Customer Focused Solutions Marketing Metric: Business Intelligence Add-On	150,000	1,200	22	?	5,500
Pro-Customer Focused Solutions Customer Access: Customer Intelligence Add-On	200,000	2,200	44	?	4,000

Hint:

Total Investment in Technology/Year 1:	
(Investment in tech per user × number of subscriptions) + training and installation	($800 × 5) + $20,000 = $24,000
Return: Forecasted productivity impact × number of subscriptions	($2,200 × 5)

*Due to the one-time installation cost (which only occurs during the first year), the customer would only pay the training and installation cost in year 1 (i.e., one-time investment).

†The customer would pay the annual subscription per user every year (i.e., ongoing investment).

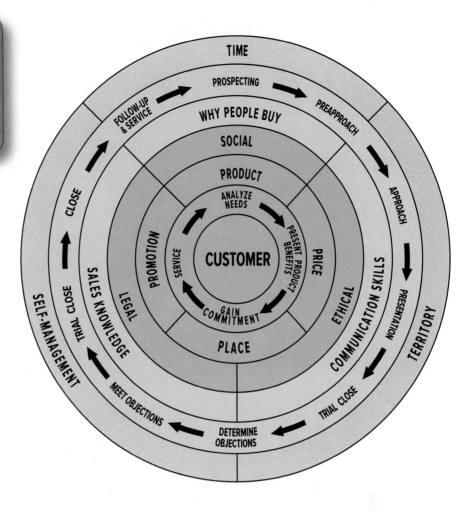

Time, Territory, and Self-Management: Keys to Success

Sales professionals are managers of themselves, their time, and when they contact their customers. The last chapter of the book introduces you to several key factors in managing a sales territory.

chapter
14

Time, Territory, and Self-Management: Keys to Success

Main Topics

The Core Principles: Time

The Management of Time

Customers Form Sales Territories

Elements of Territory Management

Technology Use Can Enhance Time Efficiency

Self-Management

What's Happening in Sales

Learning Objectives

A salesperson's ability to manage time and territory is important to success. After studying this chapter, you should be able to

14–1 Elaborate on the value of time management in the sales profession.

14–2 List and explain the time management skills.

14–3 Discuss the importance of the sales territory.

14–4 Explain the major elements involved in managing the sales territory.

14–5 Explain why salespeople need to segment their accounts by size.

14–6 Calculate a salesperson's break-even point per day, hour, and year.

14–7 Discuss the use of technology in managing time and territory.

FACING A SALES CHALLENGE

"How can I manage my time to take better care of my customers?" thought Alice Jenson. "It seems each day I work I get further and further behind."

Alice had recently taken over the sales territory of Mike Batemen, who retired and moved across the country after 35 years of calling on customers. He kept all records in his head. Alice had to contact the 200 customers in the sales territory with no information other than their past sales. After several weeks, Alice had seen 95 percent of the customers once and 25 percent of them a second time. Two weeks ago, complaints started coming in that Alice had not followed up on her last calls or that she had not been back to see them.

Alice started telephoning people. That helped some, but customers wanted to see her. She almost stopped prospecting for new customers because she felt it was easier to keep a customer than get a new one. However, as sales started to decline, Alice realized customers were beginning to buy from her competitors.

Alice is in trouble, and it is getting worse. What can you suggest Alice do to keep customers, have time to prospect, and increase sales?

Managing time and territory is an important factor in selling. "Facing a Sales Challenge" illustrates that Alice is certainly having a challenging time doing all she needs to do in a day. Because of such things as the rapidly increasing cost of direct selling, decreasing time for face-to-face customer contact, continued emphasis on profitable sales, and the fact that time is always limited, it is no wonder that many companies are concentrating on improving how salespeople manage time and territory. Time is money. That is what this chapter is about—how to effectively use time.

Pretend you are given a bank account that receives a fresh deposit of $86,400 every day. You are free to spend the money any way you want, but the unspent balance is not carried forward to the next day. Regardless of what you have spent by the end of the day, the balance is reset daily at $86,400. What would you do with such a bank account?

Now consider the fact that each dollar represents the number of seconds in one day: $24 \times 60 \times 60 = 86,400$ seconds. Once they are "spent," they disappear; and the balance is reset at 12:00:01 A.M. every day. How do you spend your time?[1]

The Core Principles: Time

Time is money because time is limited. There is only so much time in a day, week, month, year. People spend time doing what is most important in their lives. That is why living with "purpose" is the only way to really live. Everything else is just existing. You need purpose to get out of bed in the morning. You need purpose to get in your car and drive to see a stranger or someone you hardly know to try and help them. You need purpose in your life for guidance in your job.

Who am I? Do I matter? What is my purpose in life? What job is best for me? Why am I in this job? Serious questions we ask ourselves as we decide our purpose and how to spend the time in our lives and career in order to fulfill our purpose.

Today the average life span is 28,700 days. That's how long you will live if you are typical. Chances are you will work over 12,000 of those days as an adult in a full-time job. Don't you think it would be best to spend your time wisely? How you spend your time determines your life. It greatly influences the level of your success in sales—and school. Time encompasses the time spent with customers and your life activities. Using your life's time in a career to help others, and get paid for it, results in a wonderful life. Using ethical service as a guide for actions allows one to spend time doing what one loves. It allows you to find your purpose.

The Management of Time

"Time is money" is a popular saying that applies to our discussion because of the costs and revenue the individual salesperson generates. A good salesperson is a skilled time manager who knows how to manage time wisely to maximize territorial profits. Thus, the effective salesperson consistently uses time well. How does the effective salesperson manage time?

Plan by the Day, Week, and Month. Many salespeople develop daily, weekly, and monthly call plans or general guidelines of customers and geographical areas to be covered. The salesperson may use them to make appointments with customers in advance, to arrange hotel accommodations, and so forth. Weekly plans are more specific, and they include the specific days that customers will be called on. Daily planning starts the night before, as the salesperson selects the next day's prospects, determines the time to contact the customer, organizes facts and data, and prepares sales presentation materials.

"In our initial training we teach people how to be organized, set a list of priorities and plan their activities, and we encourage them to think outside of the box. They need to think about tomorrow, next week, down the road and to set objectives and anticipate needs before they occur," explains Jeff DeRoux, information and technology manager for the Preston, Washington-based SanMar Corporation. DeRoux believes that good organization, long- and short-range planning, and setting priorities are absolutely necessary in eliminating time wasting.[2]

Exhibit 14.1 lists six time management skills that can help sales professionals in achieving productivity and efficiency.

"It's been said," says Tupperware's Terry Fingerhut, "21 days make a habit—good or bad. In three weeks, the results of the work I did or didn't do today will show up. If I spent my time well, three weeks from today I'll have positive results. If I wasted my time, three weeks from today I'll have negative results. The conclusion—each day, every day—is produce *now* at your best. In three weeks and every week thereafter you'll have a string of truly positive results."

You reap what you sow.

Qualify the Prospect. Salespeople must be sure that their prospects are qualified to make the purchase decision, and they must determine whether sales to these accounts are large enough to allow for an adequate return on time invested. If not, they do not call on these prospects.

Alvin Perez, sales executive with Total Graphics in Norwalk, Connecticut, feels that the biggest time waster of all is spending time with a prospect who isn't qualified.[4] "It's important that you gather, within reason, as much information as possible about prospects and determine whether they are serious about doing business with you," he says. "After all, in the sales business, time is money."

EXHIBIT 14.1

Six time management skills that can help sales professionals in achieving success.[3]

©Rawpixel Ltd/Alamy Stock Photo

1. Be selective in prioritizing time

2. Spend time on high-priority tasks

3. Have a better sense of the time needed to complete tasks

4. Avoid overcommitting to nonessential tasks at the expense of core work tasks

5. Develop an effective plan to allocating efforts across goals, activities, and time periods

6. Have a systematic account for the outcomes you aim to achieve before allocating time to achieve these outcomes

Use Waiting Time. Have you seen salespeople waiting to see buyers? Have you ever noticed their actions? They work while waiting: studying material about their products, completing call reports, or organizing material for the sales presentation. Also, they quickly determine whether buyers they wait for will be free within a reasonable time. If not, they contact other customers.

Have a Productive Lunchtime. Salespeople often take prospects to lunch. However, the results of one study show that the business lunch does not lead directly to a sale, but to the buyer and seller knowing each other better, which builds confidence and trust. In turn, this may lead to sales in the long run.

During a business lunch, salespeople must keep an eye on the clock and not monopolize too much of the buyer's time. They should not have a lunchtime cocktail. In fact, in some companies, a luncheon cocktail or any use of alcohol or other drugs is against company policy. A salesperson's lunch is time to review activities and further plan the afternoon. It is a time to relax and start psyching up for a productive selling afternoon.

©filmfoto/Alamy Stock Photo

Records and Reports. Records and reports are a written history of sales and of the salesperson's activities. Effective salespeople do paperwork during nonselling times; evenings are best. Many companies note these records and reports in performance evaluations of salespeople, and the salesperson should keep them current. The company, however, should hold paperwork to a minimum.

So you see, time is important for salespeople. Yesterday's the past, tomorrow's the future, but today is a *gift*. That's why it's called the *present*. Life is like the sands of time slipping through the hourglass. Use your time wisely!

Return on Time Invested

Time is a scarce resource. To be successful, the salesperson uses time effectively to improve performance. In terms of time, costs also must be accounted for. That is, what is the cost both in time and money of an average sales call?

Break-even analysis determines how much sales volume a salesperson must generate to meet costs. The difference between cost of goods sold and sales is the gross profit on sales revenue. Gross profit should be large enough to cover selling expenses. **Break-even analysis** is a quantitative technique for determining the level of sales at which total revenues equal total costs. Break-even point is computed in dollars with this formula:

$$\text{Break-even point (in dollars)} = \frac{\text{Salesperson's fixed costs}}{\text{Gross profit percentage}}$$

To illustrate the formula, let us use the values shown here for sales and costs, with gross profit being the difference between a salesperson's sales revenue and costs of goods sold in the territory, expressed as a ratio of gross profit to gross sales in percentage form:

Sales	$600,000
Cost of goods sold	
Gross profit	$180,000
Gross profit (percentage)	(180,000 ÷ 600,000), or 30 percent

Assume the salesperson's direct costs are as follows:

Salary	$60,000
Transportation	12,000
Expenses	15,000
Direct costs	$87,000

and substitute in the formula:

$$\text{BEP} = \frac{\$87,000}{.30} = \$290,000$$

If the salesperson sells $290,000 worth of merchandise, it exactly covers the territory's direct costs. A sales volume of $290,000 means that the salesperson produces a gross margin of 30 percent, or $87,000. Sales over $290,000 contribute to profit.

Assume that the salesperson works 46 out of 52 weeks (considering time off for vacations, holidays, and illness) for 230 days each year; also assume a five-day week and an eight-hour day in which six calls are made. There are 1,840 working hours per year and 1,380 sales calls (230 × 6 calls) made each year in the territory. To determine a salesperson's cost per hour, divide direct costs ($87,000) by yearly hours worked (1,840 hours). The cost per hour equals $47.28. The break-even volume per hour is as follows:

$$\frac{\text{Break-even}}{\text{volume per hour}} = \frac{\text{Cost per hour}}{\text{Gross profit percentage}} = \frac{\$15.76}{.30} = \$157.60$$

Thus, the salesperson must sell an average of $157.60 an hour in goods or services to break even. Carrying this logic further, the salesperson must sell an average of $1260.80 each day, or $210.13 each sales call to break even.

Customers Form Sales Territories

A **sales territory** comprises a group of customers or a geographic area assigned to a salesperson. The territory may or may not have geographic boundaries. Typically, however, a salesperson is assigned to a geographic area containing present and potential customers.

Why Establish Sales Territories?

Companies develop and use sales territories for numerous reasons. Next, we discuss the seven important reasons listed in Exhibit 14.2.

EXHIBIT 14.2

Reasons companies develop and use sales territories.

- To obtain thorough coverage of the market.
- To establish each salesperson's responsibilities.
- To evaluate performance.
- To improve customer relations.
- To reduce sales expense.
- To allow better matching of salesperson to customer's needs.
- To benefit both salespeople and the company.

To Obtain Thorough Coverage of the Market

With proper coverage of territories, a company will reach the sales potential of its markets. The salesperson analyzes the territory and identifies customers. At the individual territory level, the salesperson better meets customers' needs. Division into territories also allows management to easily realign territories as customers and sales increase or decrease.

To Establish Each Salesperson's Responsibilities

With technology-based reporting systems, the salesperson can efficiently monitor individual territory and customer sales.

Salespeople act as business managers for their territories. They are responsible for maintaining and generating sales volume. Salespeople's tasks are defined clearly. They know where customers are located and how often to call on them. They also know what performance goals are expected. This can raise the salesperson's performance and morale.

To Evaluate Performance

Performance is monitored for each territory. Actual performance data are collected, analyzed, and compared to expected performance goals. Individual territory performance is compared to district performance, district performance compared to regional performance, and regional performance compared to the performance of the entire sales force. With computerized reporting systems, the salesperson and a manager can monitor individual territory and customer sales to determine the success of selling efforts.

To Improve Customer Relations

Customer goodwill and increased sales are expected when customers receive regular calls. From the customer's viewpoint, the salesperson is, for example, Procter & Gamble. The customer looks to the salesperson, not to Procter & Gamble's corporate office, when making purchases. Over the years, some salespeople build such goodwill with customers that prospects will delay placing orders because they know the salesperson will be at their business on a certain day or at a specific time of the month. Some salespeople even earn the right to order merchandise for certain customers.

To Reduce Sales Expense

Sales territories are designed to avoid duplicating efforts so that two salespeople do not travel in the same area. This lowers selling cost and increases company profits. Such benefits as fewer travel miles and fewer overnight trips, plus regular contact with productive customers by the same salesperson, can improve the firm's sales-to-cost ratio.

To Allow Better Matching of Salesperson to Customer's Needs

Salespeople are hired and trained to meet the requirements of the customers in a territory. Often, the more similar the customer and the salesperson, the more likely the sales effort will succeed.

To Benefit Both Salespeople and the Company

Proper territory design aids in reaching the firm's sales objectives. Thus, the company can maximize its sales effort, while the sales force can work in territories that allow them to satisfy personal needs, such as a good salary.

Why Sales Territories May Not Be Developed

In spite of advantages, there are disadvantages to developing sales territories for some companies, such as in the real estate and insurance industries. First, salespeople may be more motivated if not restricted by a particular territory; they can develop customers anywhere. In the chemical industry, for example, salespeople may sell to any potential customer. However, after the sale is made, other company salespeople are not allowed to contact that client.

Second, the company may be too small to be concerned with segmenting the market into sales areas. Third, management may not want to take the time or may not have the know-how for territory development. Fourth, personal friendships may be the basis for attracting customers. For example, life insurance salespeople may first sell policies to their families and friends. However, most companies establish territories, such as the one assigned to Alice Jenson in "Facing a Sales Challenge."

Elements of Territory Management

For the salesperson, territory management is a continuous process of planning, executing, and evaluating the sales and service provided to customers. By completing each of the seven key elements involved in territory management, as shown in Exhibit 14.3, the salesperson ensures customers will be provided excellent service. Additionally, prospects will be found in the territory that may eventually become customers.

Building relationships with customers requires spending time with them. As discussed in Chapter 12, a good business friendship is like a personal friendship. Time is required to get to know each customer and his or her needs. But there is only so much time in the day, week, month, and year. This requires you to make the hard decision on how to spend your business time. Using the Core Principles of Selling as a guide in creating your strategic plan for your territory, you will find these seven elements will help increase sales by obtaining new customers and selling more to present customers. The first step is to set goals or quotas.

Salesperson's Sales Quota

A salesperson is responsible for generating sales in a territory based on its sales potential. The salesperson's manager typically establishes the total sales quota that each salesperson is expected to reach.

Once this quota is set, it is the salesperson's responsibility to develop territorial sales plans for reaching the quota. Although there is no best planning sequence to follow, Exhibit 14.3 presents seven factors to consider in properly managing the territory for reaching its sales quota.

EXHIBIT 14.3

Elements of territory management for the salesperson.

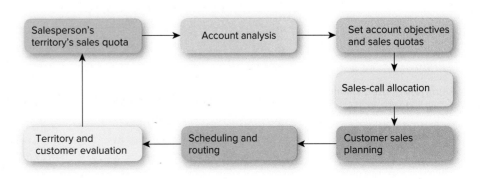

Account Analysis

Once a sales goal is set, the salesperson must analyze each prospect and customer to maximize the chances of reaching that goal. First, a salesperson should identify all prospects and present customers. Second, a salesperson should estimate present customers' and prospects' sales potential. This makes it possible to allocate time between customers, to decide what products to emphasize for a specific customer, and to better plan the sales presentation.

Two general approaches to **account analysis**—identifying accounts and their varying levels of sales potential—are the undifferentiated selling approach and the account segmentation approach.

The Undifferentiated Selling Approach

An organization may see the accounts in its market as similar. When this happens and selling strategies are designed and applied equally to all accounts, the salesperson uses an **undifferentiated selling** approach. Notice in Exhibit 14.4 that the salesperson aims a single selling strategy at all accounts. The basic assumption underlying this approach is that the account needs for a specific product or group of products are similar. Salespeople call on all potential accounts, devoting equal selling time to each of them. The same sales presentation may be used in selling an entire product line. The salesperson feels he or she can satisfy most customers with a single selling strategy. For example, many door-to-door salespeople use the same selling strategies with each person they contact (a stimulus–response sales presentation).

Salespeople whose accounts have homogeneous needs and characteristics may find this approach useful. The undifferentiated selling approach was popular in the past, and some firms still use it. However, many salespeople feel that their accounts have different needs and represent different sales and profit potentials. This makes an account segmentation approach desirable.

The Account Segmentation Approach

Salespeople using the **account segmentation** approach recognize that their territories contain accounts with heterogeneous needs and differing characteristics that require different selling strategies. Consequently, they develop sales objectives based on overall sales and sales of each product for each customer and prospect. Past sales to the account, new accounts, competition, economic conditions, price and promotion offerings, new products, and personal selling are among the key elements in the analysis of accounts and territories.

Salespeople classify customers to identify profitable ones. This classification determines where the salesperson's time is invested. One method of segmenting accounts is by

1. Key account.
   a. Buys over $200,000 from us annually.
   b. Loss of this customer would substantially affect the territory's sales and profits.

EXHIBIT 14.4

Undifferentiated selling approach.

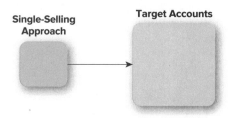

2. Unprofitable account.
   a. Buys less than $1,000 from us annually.
   b. Little potential to increase purchases to more than $1,000.
3. Regular account.
   a. All other customers.

The salesperson would not call on the unprofitable accounts. The **key accounts** and regular accounts become target customers.

Once the accounts are classified broadly, categories or types of accounts are defined in terms such as extra large (key), large, medium, and small, which we refer to as the **ELMS system.** For example, management may divide the 3,000 total accounts in the firm's marketing plan into these four basic sales categories, as shown in Exhibit 14.5. There are few extra large or large accounts, but they often account for 80 percent of a company's profitable sales even though they represent only 20 percent of total accounts. This is known as the **eighty/twenty principle.** The number of key accounts in an individual territory varies, as does responsibility for them. Even though the key account is in another salesperson's territory, a key account salesperson may call on the extra-large customer. Typically, this approach is taken because of the account's importance or because of an inexperienced local salesperson.

Accounts can be segmented whether or not the firms are actual customers or prospects. As shown in Exhibit 14.6, actual customers are further segmented based on sales to date and sales potential. Prospects also are segmented into the ELMS classification, and each account's potential sales are estimated.

Multiple Selling Strategies

Exhibit 14.7 illustrates how multiple selling strategies are used on various accounts. Salespeople know the importance of large accounts; in fact, meeting sales objectives often depends on how well products are sold to these customers. As a result, companies often develop their sales force organizational structure to service these accounts—incorporating elements such as a key-account salesperson.

EXHIBIT 14.5

Account segmentation based on yearly sales.

Customer Size	Yearly Sales (actual or potential)	Number of Accounts	Percentage
Extra large	Over $200,000	100	3.3%
Large	$75,000–200,000	500	16.6
Medium	$25,000–75,000	1,000	33.3
Small	$1,000–25,000	1,400	46.6

EXHIBIT 14.6

Basic segmentation of accounts.

Account Classification	Customers		Prospect Potential Sales
	Sales to Date	Potential Sales	
Extra large			
Large			
Medium			
Small			

EXHIBIT 14.7

Account segmentation approach.

As Exhibit 14.7 illustrates, selling strategies vary depending on the account. The bulk of sales force resources (such as personnel, time, samples, and entertainment expenses) should be invested in the key accounts, and the needs of these large accounts should receive top priority.

Company positioning relative to competition must receive careful consideration. Competitors also will direct a major selling effort toward these accounts. Thus, salespeople should strive to create the image that they, their company, and their products are uniquely better than the competition. One way to accomplish this is to spend more time on each sales call and to make more total sales calls during the year, thus providing a problem-solving approach to servicing accounts.

Selling larger accounts is different from selling medium and small accounts. However, these smaller accounts may generate 20 percent, and sometimes more, of a company's sales and must not be ignored.

Multivariable Account Segmentation

Multivariable account segmentation means using more than one criterion to characterize the organization's accounts. Sales organizations use segmentation because they sell to several markets and use many channel members in these markets. Furthermore, they may emphasize different products, product sizes, or product lines to different channel members in various markets.

Exhibit 14.8 illustrates how firms might use several variables to segment their accounts. This allows sales personnel to develop plans for selling various products to

EXHIBIT 14.8

Multivariable account segmentation.

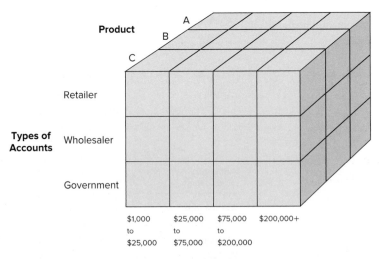

specific segments of their accounts. For example, they might develop different selling strategies for the extra-large and large accounts. There might be different sales plans for retailers, wholesalers, and government accounts. These three types of accounts might be further segmented. Retailers, for instance, could be segmented into mass merchandisers and specialty stores. Furthermore, different products might be emphasized in each account segment. The type of market, environment, account sales potential, and sales volume are major variables for segmenting accounts.

Develop Account Objectives and Sales Quotas

The third element of territory management is developing objectives and sales quotas for individual products and for current and potential accounts. Objectives might include increasing product distribution to prospects in the territory or increasing the product assortment current customers purchase.

Sales Call Allocation

The fourth element of territory management is **sales call allocation**, that is how salespeople develop a plan to allocate sales calls within territories. Increasing the number of sales calls each day and the number of new accounts obtained for the year are other examples of objectives salespeople develop to help meet sales quotas. In recalling his early days as a salesperson, Shelby H. Carter, Jr., former Xerox senior vice president of sales of U.S. field operations, said, "I placed a sign on my car's visor that read, 'Calls are the guts of this business.' We lived in Baltimore," he recalls, "and I drove 40 miles every day to get to Annapolis. You've got to make extra calls," he told his salespeople, "because 1 more call a day is 5 a week, 20 a month, and 240 calls a year. If you close 10 percent of the people you contact, you have an extra 24 sales a year. A sales territory is a cost- and revenue-generating profit center, and because it is, priorities must be established on account calls to maximize territory profits. These are seven basic factors to consider in call allocation:

Develop an effective plan to allocating efforts across goals, activities, and time periods

1. Number of accounts in the territory.
2. Number of sales calls made on customers.
3. Time required for each sales call.
4. Frequency of customer sales calls.
5. Travel time around the territory.
6. Nonselling time.
7. Return on time invested.

Analysis of accounts in the territory has resulted in determining the total number of territory accounts and their classification in terms of actual or potential sales. Now, the number of yearly sales calls required, the time required for each call, and the intervals between calls can be determined. Usually, the frequency of calls increases as there are increases in (1) sales and/or potential future sales, (2) number of orders placed in a year, (3) number of product lines sold, and (4) complexity, servicing, and redesign requirements of products.

Sales call efforts are in direct proportion to the actual or potential sales that the account represents.

Since the time spent servicing an account varies from minutes to days, salespeople must be flexible in developing call frequencies. However, they can establish a minimum number of calls they want to make on the various classes of accounts. For example, the salesperson determines that the frequency of calls for each class of account in the territory, as shown in Exhibit 14.9, should be one contact a month for all but the small accounts.

EXHIBIT 14.9

Call allocation by salesperson.

Customer Size	Calls per Month	Calls per Year	Number of Accounts	Number of Calls per Year
Extra large	1	12	2	24
Large	1	12	28	336
Medium	1	12	56	672
Small	1*	4	78	312
Total			164	1,344

*Every 3 months.

Typically, the salesperson's sales call efforts are in direct proportion to the actual or potential sales that the account represents. The most productive number of calls is reached at the point at which additional calls do not increase sales. This relationship of sales volume to sales calls is the **sales response function** of the customer to the salesperson's calls.

Customer Sales Planning

The fifth major element of territorial management is developing a sales-call objective, a customer profile, and a customer benefit program, including selling strategies for individual customers.* You have a quota to meet, have made your account analysis, have set account objectives, and have established the time you will devote to each customer; now, develop a sales plan for each customer.

Scheduling and Routing

The sixth element of territory management is scheduling sales calls and planning movement around the sales territory.

Scheduling refers to establishing a fixed time (day and hour) for visiting a customer's business. **Routing** is the travel pattern used in working a territory. Some sales organizations prefer to determine the formal path or route that their salespeople travel when covering their territory. In such cases, management must develop plans that are feasible, flexible, and profitable to the company and the individual salesperson, and satisfactory to the customer. In theory, strict formal route designs enable the company to (1) improve territory coverage; (2) minimize wasted time; and (3) establish communication between management and the sales force in terms of the location and activities of individual salespeople.

In developing route patterns, management needs to know the salesperson's exact day and time of sales calls for each account; approximate waiting time; sales time; miscellaneous time for contacting people such as the promotional manager, checking inventory, or handling returned merchandise; and travel time between accounts. This task is difficult unless territories are small and precisely defined. Most firms allow considerable latitude in routing.

Typically, after finishing a workweek, the salesperson fills out a routing report and sends it to the manager. The report states where the salesperson will work (see Exhibit 14.10). In the example, on Friday, December 16, she is based in Dallas and

"You've got to be careful if you don't know where you're going cause you might not get there!"

YOGI BERRA

*Refer to Chapter 7 for further discussion of customer sales planning.

EXHIBIT 14.10

A weekly route report.

Today's date December 16		For week beginning December 26
Date	**City**	**Location**
December 26 (Monday)	Dallas	Home
December 27 (Tuesday)	Dallas	Home
December 28 (Wednesday)	Waco	Holiday Inn/South
December 29 (Thursday)	Fort Worth	Home
December 30 (Friday)	Dallas	Home

plans to call on accounts in Dallas for two days during the week of December 26. Then, she plans to work in Waco for a day, spend the night, drive to Fort Worth early the next morning and make calls, and be home Thursday night. The last day of the week, she plans to work in Dallas. The weekly route report is sent to her immediate supervisor. In this manner, management knows where she is and, if necessary, can contact her.

Some firms may ask the salesperson to specify the accounts to be called on and at what times. For example, on Monday, December 26, the salesperson may write, "Dallas, 9 A.M., Texas Instruments; Arlington, 2 P.M., General Motors." Thus, management knows where a salesperson will be and what accounts will be visited during a report period. If no overnight travel is necessary to cover a territory, the company may not require any route reports because the salesperson can be contacted at home in the evening.

Territory and Customer Evaluation

Territorial evaluation is the establishment of performance standards for the individual territory in the form of qualitative and quantitative quotas or goals. Actual performance is compared to these goals for evaluation purposes. This allows the salesperson to see how well territory plans were executed in meeting performance quotas. If quotas were not met, new plans must be developed.

Many companies routinely furnish managers and individual salespeople with reports on how many times during the year salespeople have called on each account and the date of the last sales call. Management can monitor the frequency and time intervals between calls for each salesperson.

As an example, a national pharmaceutical company supplies its sales force with a net sales by customer and call report shown in Exhibit 14.11. The report lists each customer's name, address, and medical specialty. The desired number of monthly calls on a given customer and the actual number of calls to date are noted. Net sales are broken down into last year's sales, the current month's sales, and year-to-date sales. Finally, the date the salesperson last called on each customer is reported.

Using the report, one can see that H. L. Brown is a Houston physician in a general practice. He should be called on twice a month, and for the past four months, he has been seen eight times. He purchased $60 worth of merchandise this month, and his purchases so far are $50 more than last year. He was last called on April 20 of the current year. Using this type of information, which might include 200 to 300 customers for each salesperson, management and salespeople can continually review sales-call patterns and customer sales to update call frequency and scheduling.

ETHICAL DILEMMA

A Breakdown in Productivity

You are a hard worker, often putting in 60 hours a week. On your first sales job and with the company only five months, you realize the importance of getting off to a good start. You have sold an average of 30 percent over your sales quota for the past three months. One reason is your hard work. Another reason is that the salesperson that preceded you in this territory either neglected accounts or just renewed old orders, never striving to upgrade current accounts. Most customers complained that they hadn't seen a salesperson from your company for months before you began to call on them.

Last month one of the older salespeople jokingly suggested that you slow down—you are making everyone look bad. You have noticed a breakdown in productivity among your fellow salespeople, who seem to be goofing off to extremes. Although it doesn't affect you directly, it will ultimately have an adverse impact on the department's productivity. Your boss likes good news and frequently asks you for ideas on how to increase sales in other territories. Because you are new and have not yet established yourself as a loyal employee, you have kept quiet in the past, hoping to win the trust of your co-workers. Tomorrow you have a meeting with your boss about your territory's productivity and you are sure he is expecting input about the other territories.

What would be the most ethical action to take?

1. Tell your boss nothing. State that your territory must be particularly active right now and that you think the other territories must just be slow right now. It does not affect you, so why should you get involved?

2. Tell your boss that your numbers have been so high because you have been working very hard and putting in long hours. Let him know that you have noticed that the other salespeople have been slacking and, in fact, have told you to "slow down." After all, it isn't right that they are abusing their positions and hurting the company's profits.

3. Suggest to your boss that he have some type of new sales incentive plan. This way, maybe the other salespeople will stop "goofing off" and you don't have to say anything.

EXHIBIT 14.11

Net sales by customer and call frequency: May 1, 2017.

	Brown (GP, Houston)	Peterson (Pediatrics, Galveston)	Gilley (GP, Galveston)	Bruce (GP, Galveston)	Heaton (GP, Texas City)
Calls					
Month	2	1	1	0	2
Year-to-date	8	4	4	4	9
Last call	4/20	4/18	4/18	3/10	4/19
Net sales in dollars					
Current month	60	0	21	0	500
Year-to-date:					
This year	350	200	75	1,000	2,000
Last year	300	275	125	750	1,750
Entire last year	2,000	1,000	300	1,000	5,000

Technology Use Can Enhance Time Efficiency

Today's organizations understand the importance of technology to enhance the salesperson's time efficiency. With field sales costs still rising and no end in sight, more companies are investing in sales technology to supplement personal selling efforts. **Sales technology** is described as the transformation of manual sales activities to electronic processes through the use of various combinations of hardware and software applications.[5]

Sales technology tools assist salespeople with routine as well as strategic tasks, allowing them to focus on actual selling time. Examples of such automation tools include programs such as sales route planners and calendaring tools. Applications such as calendaring and routing tables can transform salespeople's typical sales routines and thus reduce downtime.

Sales technology aids salespeople by managing information about a larger number of customers. Salespeople equipped with such valuable information are able to relate to customers without as much difficulty and can be more responsive to critical issues, thereby shortening the duration of each sales call. Salespeople using the CRM system may be able to save time by speeding the process of sales call planning. For example, CRM use may help a salesperson configure product offerings that are better customized to customer needs. CRM systems also allow information sharing across a sales organization. Information sharing is important because it provides the knowledge about the customer throughout the organization, and therefore can reduce the potential for mistakes.

While each firm and its salespeople have to decide which sales technology is applicable to their sales process, most salespeople benefit from adopting the following practices:

- Ask yourself, "can this interaction be conducted virtually?" There is web conferencing and online meeting software (e.g., GoToMeeting) available that makes it simple and cost-effective to serve distant customers.
- Consider the resources invested in each customer. Consider assigning smaller accounts that contribute less than 5 percent of business mostly to inside-sales salespeople.
- Create a valuable information resource. Consider prospecting, marketing data gathering, and call scheduling with a CRM technology system.

Using Technology for Territory Management Activities

For today's salespeople, sales route planners and schedulers are offered through companies such as Mapline and Badger. Salespeople can quickly and easily visualize their sales territory by integrating important information, such as customer lists, maps, and their calendar, into one mobile app. With the help of such technology tools, it is easier for salespeople to adjust to schedule changes. For example, in the event of an appointment cancellation, a salesperson could use the technology to find potential appointments or leads in the same geographic areas. Salespeople also receive reminders when they are not meeting the timelines set on their daily schedule.

The next software technology used in territory management is called territory analysis. Territory analysis software helps a salesperson understand each customer within the territory, the cost to serve the customer, and the revenue each customer generates.

In addition, the software allows the salesperson to understand the performance of the entire territory. Territory analysis software allows salespeople to easily upload their customers' list and analyze data based on purchase volume, purchase types, and, purchase frequency. With this software, salespeople can continually see their sales performance, and it enables them to make adjustments based on the data.

Using Technology for Nonselling Activities

Sales technology tools can also provide an opportunity for salespeople to reduce their administrative tasks. A critical objective of the salesperson is to develop and maintain business relationships and revenue flows. Yet, in order to do so, the salesperson must manage a great deal of information about their customers, their distributors, and other key processes. Sales technology software provides a more automated, organized means to handle these activities and thereby reduce the administrative burden on the salesperson.

Self-Management

Apart from time and territory management practices, successful salespeople should also manage themselves. In a demanding and rewarding profession such as professional selling, it is critical for salespeople to pay attention to **self-management** that is develop a personal time management plan, set priorities based on their supervisors' expectations, keep a watchful eye on the industry trends, and have a vision for the future. In the following sections, we detail a number of areas that will be increasingly important for the emerging salesperson.

Personal Time Management

A salesperson views the time, the customers, and the relationships as critical resources. When salespeople manage their time effectively, they create opportunities to better serve their customers, to meet their post-sales service commitments, and to accomplish their objectives. Salespeople often use time management software, such as an online calendar application, to plan their time, to ensure they carry out their commitments to others, and to meet their responsibilities.

In many organizations, salespeople use calendar and time management systems such as Microsoft Outlook and Google Calendar. While these time management systems are continually improving their capabilities, the software provides the salesperson with the ability to

- Send invitations and appointments to customers.
- Reserve and schedule blocks of time to work on key projects.
- Reserve conference rooms within your company.
- Review the availability of your (internal) colleagues to meet on certain times and dates (i.e., search their schedules).
- Provide reminders of key deadlines.
- Receive meeting invitations from customers.
- Review their daily, weekly, and monthly meeting schedule.
- Access their list of internal and external contacts and their associated information.
- Develop and prioritize a task list or to-do list of their projects.

Regardless of your intended profession, we suggest that you begin using an online time management system. Time management is a critical skill to develop. Further, employers will be interested in knowing that you already possess the skill set.

What Might Your Sales Manager Tell You?

In our discussions with sales managers, we've found a number of consistent themes regarding new salespeople. In this section, we outline some of the reoccurring topics discussed with sales students and entry-level salespeople.

- **Take initiative.** Don't be afraid to act, make a recommendation, and get involved. Management wants you to become an active member in the organization.
- **Accept feedback and coaching.** The great sales organizations and sales managers want to help you develop your skill set and become more effective. In order to build your skill set, they will set up training as well as coaching opportunities. They believe in investing in you and hope you will accept the feedback in order to improve.
- **Do your due diligence.** In order to be a knowledge broker, you need to prepare, prepare, prepare. Don't take a customer relationship for granted. Your customer wants you to be a valued partner. The onus is on you to consistently create value for the customer.
- **Manage your time—well.** One of the fantastic elements of a sales career is the flexibility related to scheduling and time. You will need to develop your skills in managing your time and effort in order to meet the results expected from you.
- **Ask if you need help.** It's likely that most salespeople have confronted the same situations as you have. Be proactive and ask your colleagues and managers when you have a challenge or are unsure of the next step(s). You belong to a team.
- **Be honest and ethical.** Relationships are built on trust. Trust is extremely difficult to develop and easy to destroy. Be honest and ethical regardless of the situation—whether you are with the customer or you are alone. You have a long career to consider.
- **Meet deadlines.** We will all have milestones that we need to achieve. Set reasonable deadlines and be proactive when challenges occur. Forgiveness often comes easier when it's requested two weeks before a deadline rather than two hours before a deadline.
- **Understand the business—you are a key part of it.** You will need to be an ongoing learner. Business changes on an ongoing basis. Continually challenge yourself. Learn about your customer and your firm and understand key business processes—especially how your firm earns its money.
- **Understand your attitude.** Develop an earnest, appreciative attitude. Learn what bothers you and develop coping skills to manage frustration during challenging times.
- **Be careful with your use of technology.** Technology is advancing ahead of processes, protocols, and etiquette. Always consider the impact of your personal use of technology on the customer. Does your use of technology adhere to honest and ethical practices? Does your use of technology create trust or does it erode trust in the relationships with your customers and your colleagues?
- **You won't hit a home run every time.** It's impossible to close every sale. Instead, enjoy the successes and learn from the failures. However, keep an ongoing learning attitude. You will always be developing your sales skills.
- **Leverage the technology and tools.** Your company will provide a number of tools and technology to help make you more productive and effective. Don't be wary of learning and integrating sales technology into your skill set.
- **Leverage your internal resources.** You will have a group of colleagues that are invested in helping you and the business become successful. Use their collective

intelligence, skill sets, and capabilities to help you build and maintain strong customer relationships.

- **Be a professional.** Again, you have a long career to consider. Consider the impact of your actions, words, and deeds upon yourself, your customers, your colleagues, and your career. Always consider the little items that will make an impact on your career:
  - Are you on time for your meetings?
  - Do you follow the guidelines or processes required by your customer and your employer?
  - Do you submit quality work?
  - Do you meet expected milestones and deadlines?
  - Do you follow-up and ensure you meet your commitments?

Executive Presence

The term executive presence has entered a number of our discussions with senior sales professionals. **Executive presence** refers to a certain aura-that the salesperson is perceived as possessing. These qualities include professionalism, ability, and authority.

For instance, some salespeople meet with C-level executives (i.e., chief financial officers, chief operating officers, chief executives officers, chief marketing officers, and chief information officers). In these types of conversations, the salesperson needs to possess a certain level of executive presence. These salespeople must develop a level of professionalism and business presence; they must demonstrate that they are credible and bring value to the business relationship.

Some research suggests that executive presence is (a) the perception held by others about you; (b) the perception results from your initial interaction with a group as well as your ongoing interactions, and (c) the perception (held by others) that you have a certain level of gravitas and influence.[6]

As an emerging salesperson, you need to remember that executive presence is about how others perceive you. For instance, do your customers perceive you as being credible? Do your colleagues perceive you to be genuine; and do your supervisors perceive you as possessing the needed skills, attitudes, and attributes to accept increasingly levels of responsibilities?

Perhaps, the true question lies in asking yourself, "Am I developing the skills and qualities of a high performing professional?" As we discuss in the section "What Might Your Sales Manager Tell You?" your managers want you to be prepared, to be a lifelong learner, to be honest and ethical, to accept feedback, and to follow-up on your commitments. All of these qualities will serve you well in your interactions with customers, colleagues, and supervisors.

You have a long career to consider. Now is the time to set your goals for your professionalism, your goals for lifelong learning and development, and your understanding of business and the marketplace.

Emotional Intelligence

Emotional intelligence is another prevalent topic within the sales industry. **Emotional intelligence** (often called EI) is the combination of four abilities: (1) your ability to perceive other's emotions, (2) your ability to identify your emotions, (3) your ability to understand what's causing your emotion, and (4) your ability to manage your emotions.[7] EI serves as a skill the salesperson can utilize in interactions with customers, colleagues, and supervisors.

As you probably have guessed, a salesperson who can identify her customer's emotions and then suitably adapt their sales conversation has an opportunity to be more effective. Similarly, a salesperson may find a customer interaction overwhelming or frustrating. Rather than venting, the high EI salesperson can identify his emotion and its driver. By managing his emotions, the salesperson can better maintain his composure and continue the sales conversation.

Like any skill, enhancing your EI capacity requires practice, awareness, and coaching. However, it's becoming a skill that is increasingly valued within sales organizations; and EI serves as a skill that can increase your effectiveness with your customer base.

Networking

Sales is an interaction-based profession and **sales networking** is the continuous method of making and utilizing contacts. As a salesperson, you be will immersed in a series of relationships—relationships with your customers, relationships with your colleagues, relationships with your vendors, relationships with your business partners, and relationships with your family and friends.[8] Simply put, you will be working constantly with others—in face to face interactions, in virtual interactions through videoconferencing, and via teleconferences and individual phone calls.

As such, it's important to be able to build relationships, to maintain a wide array of relationships, and to be willing to assist those individuals within your network. These relationships will be invaluable to you throughout the course of your career. The people who make up your relationship network will allow you to

- Learn from them.
- Leverage their expertise to help you with your projects and customers.
- Ask for their assistance, guidance, and counsel.
- Experience greater levels of satisfaction with your job.[9]

But please remember, networking is your personal array of relationships—from those individuals you have met to those individuals you consider close friends and confidantes; and relationships are based on trust and communication. Effective salespeople remember that relationships are a mutual commitment. These salespeople ask themselves how they can help those in their network, how they can share their expertise, and how they can create value for others. Always keep in mind that building and maintaining relationships requires the **mutual investment** of effort, time, and resources.

What's Happening in Sales

Sales continues to evolve. In this section, we briefly highlight a few thoughts to consider as you are developing your vision for the future and start building your sales skill set.

Artificial intelligence and predictive analytics. Software provides an opportunity to learn more about your customers. Another evolving technology tool lies in artificial intelligence and predictive analytics. Firms are integrating the **artificial intelligence system** to better understand their customers and help their salesforce understand how they might help them. For instance, banks are integrating predictive analytics and artificial intelligence systems, such as Salesforce's Einstein software.[10] The goal is to better integrate and understand all of the ways that the firm and its customer base interact. With this learning, the **predictive analytics** software can predict the next plausible opportunity to assist the customers and provide their frontline salespeople with the needed tools to do so. For the upcoming salesperson, the software offers another tool to become more customer-focused and create value.

Inside sales provides an interesting growth opportunity. A number of firms continue to build their inside sales centers.[11] Rather than invest solely in a widely dispersed field sales force, firms are investing in more centralized inside sales centers. As discussed in Chapter 3, inside sales people sell remotely using a wide array of social media, web technology, video conferencing, and other technology tools. For salespeople, inside sales provides a unique learning opportunity to enhance their professional selling skill set by developing expertise in leveraging technology throughout the sales process.

Will marketing and sales departments integrate a little more? An opportunity exists to create more collaboration between the departments. Marketing and sales serve vital roles in a company's ability to drive sales. Now, the question lies in how to further leverage their collective value. While sales provide the capability to create relationships and drive revenue, marketing possesses the ability to differentiate a product and communicate its value. As firms increasingly develop strategies to attract new customers and cement relationships, an ideal time exists to create a collaborative relationship between marketing and sales. For the upcoming salesperson, this opportunity should open a number of opportunities in content strategy, digital prospecting, and customer-focused activities.

An ever evolving buyer. Buyers are leveraging technology to learn about options and services and to move forward with their decision-making processes. Technology has also impacted the buying process. Buyers and buying committees (i.e., buying centers) are leveraging technology to evaluate product options, seek expert opinions, and inform themselves—all from their desk, laptop, or even coffee shop. This has allowed the buying process to move forward, often without the involvement of the seller. For the upcoming salesperson, it's important to understand how to use technology to monitor and interpret new and existing customers' digital actions. Further, as the use of buying committees continues, the upcoming salesperson needs to be able to work with a broad array of buyers with distinct roles and responsibilities. Relationship adaptability will continue to be a critical skill set.

Customer-focused, value-creating, adaptable salespeople. Regardless of the changes in business, we believe it's a fantastic time for the upcoming salesperson. Undoubtedly, the upcoming salespeople will be asked to enhance their knowledge base on an ongoing basis, to learn how to muster internal and external resources, and to develop increasingly customized solutions for their customers. But despite the continued transformation in technology, buying processes, and business structure, we suggest that sales remains a fantastic career. For the earnest upcoming salesperson, the development of professional selling skills will remain a great investment across your career. The ability to communicate, to listen, to problem-solve, to share expertise, and to adapt to various buyers will continue to drive value in any relationship. We applaud your investment of time and effort in learning about professional selling and we sincerely hope you continue a lifelong development of your sales skill set.

SUMMARY OF MAJOR SELLING ISSUES

How salespeople invest their sales time is a critical factor influencing territory sales. Due to the increasing cost of direct selling, high transportation costs, and the limited resource of time, salespeople have to focus on these factors. Proper time management is essential for the salesperson to maximize territorial sales and profits.

A sales territory comprises a group of customers or a geographical area assigned to a salesperson. It is a segment out of the company's total market. A salesperson within a territory has to analyze the various segments, estimate sales potential, and develop a marketing mix based on the needs and desires of the marketplace.

Companies develop and use sales territories for a number of reasons. One important reason is to obtain thorough coverage of the market to fully reach sales potential. Another reason is to establish salespeople's responsibilities as territory managers.

Performance can be monitored when territories are established. A territory may also be used to improve customer relations so that customers receive regular calls from the salesperson. This helps reduce sales expenses by avoiding duplicated effort in traveling and customer contacts. Finally, territories allow better matching of salespeople to customer needs and ultimately benefit salespeople and the company.

There also are disadvantages to developing sales territories. Some salespeople may not be motivated if they feel restricted by a particular territory. Also, a company may be too small to segment its market or management may not want to take time to develop territories.

Territory management is continuous for a salesperson; it involves seven key elements. The first major element is establishing the territory sales quota. The second element is account analysis, which involves identifying current and potential customers and estimating their sales potential. In analyzing these accounts, salespeople may use the undifferentiated-selling approach if they view accounts as similar; or, if accounts have different characteristics, they use the account-segmentation approach.

Developing objectives and sales quotas for individual accounts is the third element. How salespeople allocate efforts in their territories is the fourth key element. Salespeople have to manage sales call plans and use spare time effectively.

The fifth element of territorial management is developing the sales-call objective, profile, benefit program, and selling strategies for individual customers. Salespeople have to learn everything they can about customers and maintain records on each one. Once this is done, they can create the proper selling strategies to meet customers' needs.

Another major element is scheduling sales calls at specific times and places and routing the salesperson's movement and travel pattern around the territory. Finally, established objectives and quotas are used to determine how effectively the salesperson performs. Actual performance is compared to these standards for evaluation purposes.

The increasing cost of a personal sales call and the increasing amount of time spent traveling to make personal calls are reasons for the efficient salespeople to look to the technology as a sales tool. Sales technology tools assist salespeople with routine as well as strategic tasks, allowing them to focus on actual selling time.

Quick Review for Students

The quick review sections provide key questions to help you develop a greater level of conceptual understanding. We suggest that after you read the chapter, you try to answer the following questions without looking back at the textbook.

1. Why does time management matter for salespeople?
2. List six time management skills that can help salespeople in achieving success?

3. What is a sales territory and why do organizations establish them?
4. List seven elements of territory management?
5. Why are organizations investing in sales technology?
6. How can technology help a salesperson enhance time efficiency during selling and nonselling activities?
7. Why is self-management critical for a salesperson and how can it be achieved?

MEETING A SALES CHALLENGE

How Alice Jenson manages her time will determine her productivity. Alice should tell her boss the situation. Then she should analyze her accounts to classify them according to past sales and sales potential. Now she can allocate her time by concentrating on her extra-large and large accounts, contacting each as often as necessary. The medium-size customers might be seen every one to two months, and the small ones less frequently or contacted by telephone. If needed, her boss could be asked to contact some customers. Alice's situation illustrates why companies require salespeople to do so much record keeping. After each sales call, Alice needs to develop a customer profile, as shown in Chapter 7, to have up-to-date information on all customers.

KEY TERMS FOR SELLING

account analysis 544
account segmentation 544
artificial intelligence
    system 555
break-even analysis 540
eighty/twenty
    principle 545
ELMS system 545

emotional intelligence 554
executive presence 554
key accounts 545
mutual investment 555
sales networking 555
predictive analysis 555
routing 548
sales call allocation 547

sales response
    function 548
sales technology 551
sales territory 541
scheduling 548
self-management 552
undifferentiated selling 544

SALES APPLICATION QUESTIONS

1. How could you use technology to better manage your customers and your territory? Explain how you could use technologies such as CRM system and other sales technology tools to save time and to manage a sales territory.
2. What is a sales territory? Why do firms establish sales territories? Why might sales territories not be developed?
3. Briefly discuss each of the elements of territory management and indicate how these seven elements relate to one another.
4. What is the difference between the undifferentiated selling approach and the account segmentation approach for analyzing accounts? When might each approach be used?
5. Assume a sales manager determines that in a given territory each salesperson sells approximately $500,000 yearly. Also, assume that the firm's cost of goods sold is estimated to be 65 percent of sales and that a salesperson's direct costs are $35,000 a year. Each salesperson works 48 weeks a year, eight hours a day, and averages five sales calls per day. Using this information, how much merchandise must each salesperson sell to break even?
    a. For the year?
    b. Each day?
    c. Each sales call?

6. What is a key account?
7. What are the factors to consider when a salesperson allocates time?
8. What is the purpose of customer sales planning?
9. Define *scheduling*. Define *routing*.

SELLING EXPERIENTIAL EXERCISE

Make a chart similar to the one below and record the time you spend on various activities for one week. Each day, place codes on your chart to indicate the time spent on each activity. Some codes are suggested here; add any codes you need. At the end of the week, write your total hours in that column. If any activity takes up a great deal of time—such as personal—subdivide it by assigning such additional activities as television, phone, and partying. Now that you have a good idea of how you spend your time, decide if you want to make some changes.

Name _____ Week beginning _____
(Date)

	Mon	Tue	Wed	Thur	Fri	Sat	Sun
7:00–7:30 A.M.							
7:30–8:00							
8:00–8:30							
8:30–9:00							
9:00–9:30							
9:30–10:00							
10:00–10:30							
10:30–11:00							
11:00–11:30							
11:30–12:00							

Activity	Code	Total Hours
Class	CL	_____
Sleep	SL	_____
Study	SU	_____
Work	W	_____
Personal	P	_____
_____	_____	_____
_____	_____	_____

	Mon	Tue	Wed	Thur	Fri	Sat	Sun
12:00–12:30 P.M.							
12:30–1:00							
1:00–1:30							
1:30–2:00							
2:00–2:30							
2:30–3:00							
3:00–3:30							
3:30–4:00							
4:00–4:30							
4:30–5:00							

	Mon	Tue	Wed	Thur	Fri	Sat	Sun
5:00–5:30 P.M.							
5:30–6:00							
6:00–6:30							
6:30–7:00							
7:00–7:30							
7:30–8:00							
After 8:00*							

*If you need to, make another sheet.

FURTHER EXPLORING THE SALES WORLD

1. Visit a large retailer in your community, and ask a buyer or store manager what salespeople do when they make a sales call. Determine the number of times the retailer wants salespeople to visit each month. Are calls from some salespeople preferable to others? If so, why?

2. Contact a salesperson or sales manager and report on each one's philosophy toward managing time and territory. Ask each person to calculate how much it costs to contact one prospect and, on the average, what amount must be sold each day just to break even.

NOTES

1. Adapted from David Jeremiah, "Who's Serving Whom?" *Turning Point,* January 2006, p. 33.

2. William F. Kendy, "Time Management," *Selling Power,* July/August 2000, pp. 34–36.

3. A. A., Rapp, D. G. Bachrach, & T. L. Rapp. "The Influence of Time Management Skill on the Curvilinear Relationship between Organizational Citizenship Behavior and Task Performance," *Journal of Applied Psychology* 98, no. 4 (July 2013), p. 668.

4. William F. Kendy, "Time Management," *Selling Power,* July/August 2000, pp. 34–36.

5. Mark L. Rivers, and Jack Dart. "The Acquisition and Use of Sales Force Automation by Mid-Sized Manufacturers," *Journal of Personal Setting and Sales Management* 19, no. 2 (Spring 1999), p. 59.

6. G. Dagley and C. Gaskin, "Understanding Executive Presence: Perspectives of Business Professionals," *Consulting Psychology Journal: Practice & Research* [serial online]. 66, no. 3 (September 2014), pp. 197–211.

7. John D. Mayer, and Peter Salovey, "What Is Emotional Intelligence?" *In Emotional Development and Emotional Intelligence: Educational Implications,* edited by Peter Salovey and David Sluyter (New York: BasicBooks, 1997), pp. 3–34.

8. Gerrard Macintosh, and Michael T. Krush, "Networking Behavior and Sales Performance: Examining Potential Gender Differences," *Journal of Marketing Theory and Practice* 25 (December 2017), pp. 160–170.

9. Gerrard Macintosh, and Michael T. Krush, "Examining the Link between Salesperson Networking Behaviors,

Job Satisfaction, and Organizational Commitment: Does Gender Matter?" *Journal of Business Research* 67, no. 12 (December 2014), pp. 2628–2635.

10. Penny Crosman, "U.S. Bank Bets AI Can Finally Deliver 360-Degree View," *American Banker* 182, no. 139 (December 2017), p. 1.

11. Jeff Green, "The New Willy Loman Survives by Staying Home," *Bloomberg Businessweek*, no. 4312 (January 14, 2013), pp. 16–17.

CASE 14.1

©Ron Chapple Stock/FotoSearch/ Glow Images

Your Selling Day: A Time and Territory Game*

Your sales manager is working with you tomorrow only, and you want to call on customers with the greatest sales potential (see Exhibit A). The area of your territory that you want to cover contains 16 customers (see Exhibit B). To determine travel time, allow 15 minutes for each side of the square. Each sales call takes 30 minutes. You can leave your house at 8:00 A.M. or later. If you take time for lunch, it must be in 15-minute time blocks (15, 30, 45, or 60 minutes). Your last customer must be contacted by 4:30 P.M. to allow you enough sales time. Your customers do not see salespeople after 5:00 P.M. You travel home after 5:00 P.M.

Questions

1. Develop the route that gives the highest sales potential for the day your boss works with you.
2. For the next day, develop the route allowing you to contact the remaining customers in this part of the territory.

EXHIBIT A

Distribution of sales.

Customer	Sales Potential	Customer	Sales Potential
A	$4,000	I	$ 1,000
B	3,000	J	1,000
C	6,000	K	10,000
D	2,000	L	12,000
E	2,000	M	8,000
F	8,000	N	9,000
G	4,000	O	8,000
H	6,000	P	10,000

*Case copyright © 2000 by Charles M. Futrell.

EXHIBIT B

A partial map of your sales territory.

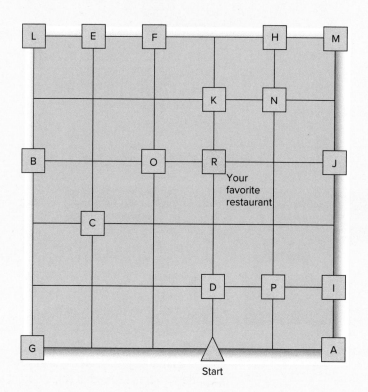

©Ron Chapple Stock/FotoSearch/
Glow Images

CASE 14.2

Sally Malone's District—Development of an Account Segmentation Plan

Sally Malone sat listening to her boss talk about the new time and territory management program being implemented by her company. Her boss was saying, "Since we wish eventually to establish priorities for our accounts in order to make time-investment decisions, we must classify the accounts into categories. A simple *A, B, C, D, E* designation of categories is the most commonly used approach, with *A* accounts the most valuable.

"The basis for setting the values or limits for each category is the distribution of sales or concentration patterns in most industries. In general, business in our company is distributed approximately as shown in Exhibit A. Generally, the top 10 percent of the accounts will generate 65 percent of sales, and the top 30 percent will generate 85 percent of the sales in any given territory. Salespeople may use this rule-of-thumb breakdown of accounts in

EXHIBIT A

Distribution of sales.

Customer Classification	Percentage of Customers	Percentage of Total Sales Volume
A	10%	65%
B	20	20
C	50	10
D	10	3
E	10	2
	100%	100%

determining the classification system for their accounts." Once the potential for all their accounts has been calculated, their territory should break down like this:

- *A* accounts = top 10 percent of the accounts
- *B* accounts = next 20 percent of the accounts
- *C* accounts = next 50 percent of the accounts
- *D* accounts = next 10 percent of the accounts
- *E* accounts = last 10 percent of the accounts

"Sally, I want you to have each of your salespeople take a close look at his or her sales-call cycles. As I have explained, a call cycle is a round of calls in which all *A* accounts are called on at least once and some, but not all, *B, C, D,* and *E* accounts are called on. When a salesperson has visited all of his or her *A* accounts, the cycle is completed. Then, a new cycle begins and the series of calls repeats. Since not all *B, C, D,* and *E* accounts are called on in every cycle, the specific accounts to be seen in these classifications differ from cycle to cycle. A call cycle, therefore, is established around the call frequency patterns of *A* accounts."

Suppose that a group of accounts is classified in this way:

Accounts	Expected Value
A	$100,000 and over
B	$50,000–100,000
C	$30,000–50,000
D	$20,000–30,000
E	Under $20,000

The call frequency patterns, therefore, based on potential and return on time invested, may be as follows:

Accounts	Weeks between Calls	Number of Accounts
A	2	10
B	4	20
C	6	45
D	8	12
E	10	10

Thus, a call cycle in this territory will cover two weeks. This means that in every two-week cycle the salesperson will call on these accounts:

- All of the *A*s.
- Half of the *B*s.
- One-third of the *C*s.
- One-fourth of the *D*s.
- One-fifth of the *E*s.

Questions

1. Develop a table showing a salesperson's call cycle using the call frequency patterns.
2. Discuss why this should be done.

Personal Selling Experiential Exercises

Sell Yourself on a Job Interview

You will play the roles of a sales job applicant and a recruiter.[1] You may interview any organization, but the hope is you will choose to interview an organization with which you would like to interview for a job sometime in the future. For your role as an applicant, develop a one- to two-page professional-looking résumé. Before you are to be interviewed, turn in a copy of the résumé to your instructor to give to your interviewer to go over before the meeting. Also give the instructor a one- to two-page description of the company at which you are applying for a beginning sales job. Assume this is your first interview with the company and you have never met the recruiter. It will last approximately five to eight minutes.

Recruiter

Create a business card to give to the applicant sometime during the interview.

Résumé

Bring an original copy of the résumé with you to the interview (see page 570). During the interview, be prepared to point out one or more selling points in the résumé that relate to the interviewer's question(s) or to major point(s) you will discuss about yourself during the interview.

Personal Business Card

Here are few format ideas for your business card (see Exhibit 1). Place your name in bold near the top. Underneath your name, have your address, telephone number, and e-mail address in a regular typeface. Now include the name of your school in bold, followed by your degree, such as BBA in Marketing, and graduation date. On the card's back you may consider including a bulleted list of items such as your GPA, courses relating to job, and main job(s). You are creating a creative mini-résumé.

EXHIBIT 1

John Smith
Marketing & Business Administration

515.555.5555
John.Smith@Agnikru.edu

Agnikru University

Jane Smith
Marketing Major

1234 Your Street
College Station, Texas 77840
Phone: (979) 555-7775
E-mail: janesmith@email.com

Portfolio

You may want to consider creating a bound portfolio of school projects you have completed during your work career and coursework (see pages 577–579). Or you may want to create a one-page summary of key projects and the skills that you learned from the projects. At the appropriate time during the interview, go over one or more of the projects that best relate to this job. If you have no projects, use a fake portfolio. Make up facts related to the project(s) for discussion with the recruiter.

The résumé and portfolio serve as visuals that aid in creating the image of you as a creative, highly motivated person who has thoroughly prepared for this interview and is very interested in obtaining a job with the organization. You will leave both the résumé and the portfolio with the interviewer. They will be returned to you after the interview. You are encouraged to develop other creative elements for your presentation.

I Want the Job

Before the interview is over, consider letting the recruiter know "you are very interested in the job." The interviewer may not feel this is true if you do not show knowledge about the organization and the job. However, if you can demonstrate in-depth knowledge about the company, the job, products, and customers, such a statement will be taken positively by the recruiter. Some organizations will not hire someone unless that person states: "I want this job." If true, you also would declare this in a later interview.

Grade Beginning and Ending

Your grade for this exercise begins when you shake hands for the greeting and ends when you shake hands to end the interview. You should act in a professional manner the entire time.

Follow-Up

After the interview, create a professional "thank you" letter or e-mail. (see page 574). In order to know the interviewer's address, ask for a business card sometime during the interview. Within one day after the interview, mail or e-mail the "thank-you" letter to your instructor. For the letter's inside address and salutation, use the recruiter's name as shown on the business card.

Two weeks after the interview send a follow-up e-mail to your recruiter (see page 575). Use the recruiter's name in the e-mail (To: Mr. Smith). The e-mail actually goes to your instructor. Assume you have not heard anything back from the recruiter after the interview, and you want to know if the recruiter has received your follow-up letter and has any other questions to ask you. Also, assume that you are interested in being further considered for the sales job and that the recruiter said she or he would let you know if you are still being considered for the job within two weeks after the interview.

You Are Selling

Whether you are an applicant or an interviewer, imagine that you have been placed in a sales situation. As an applicant you are selling yourself. As an interviewer you are selling not only yourself but also your company and the sales job as well.

Interviewers are looking for indications that the applicant can sell or can be trained to sell. How can you—the applicant—apply basic selling procedures to the job interview situation?

You can look, dress, and groom like, and have the attitude of, a successful person. Showing the interviewer you have prepared for the interview indicates how you might prepare to make a sales call on a customer. Using the résumé and portfolio during the interview helps distinguish you from others interviewing for the job. Finally, you should "close" the sale by asking for the order (job).

Sales Call Objective

An applicant typically goes through several interviews before being offered a job. Consider this your first interview. What is your sales call objective for the first interview? It is to be asked back for a second interview! The end of the interview is an excellent time for you to illustrate your sales skills.

Futrell's Closing Sequence

One way to demonstrate your sales skills is by using "Futrell's Two-Question Interview Closing Sequence." At the end of most first interviews the recruiter will ask something like, "Do you have any questions?" You should respond as follows:

- "Yes, I have two questions. What is the next step in the interview process?" Wait for the reply. Then ask,
- "Based on my background, my résumé, and what we have talked about today, how could I improve my skills to increase the chance of being asked back for a second interview?"

Should the interviewer not ask if you have a question, you should say something such as "I have two questions" or "May I ask two questions before I go?"

Résumé, Follow-Up Letter, E-Mail

There are many formats of résumés to choose from that will best highlight your qualifications and experience. No matter which of these you decide to use, there are some things that should be included in any format. The following is a checklist of these necessary items.

Résumé Checklist

- Personal Data: Include your name, permanent and local addresses, phone number, and e-mail address.
- Education: Begin with the most recent school attended. List the name and location of college or university (city and state are sufficient), degree received, your major and minor, and dates of attendance or month and year graduating. Include your GPA. May include relevant course work (six to eight important classes). Include honors achieved, such as dean's list, class rank, awards, and scholarships. Include special training, licensure, or certifications.
- Experience: Begin with the most recent. List full-time, part-time, internship, and co-op jobs. Do not include part-time work unless it's particularly relevant. Include dates of employment, company or organization name, city and state of location, and your job title. Describe your duties using phrases, beginning with action verbs, in present or past tense, depending on the time of the experience.
- Activities: List your professional affiliations, clubs/organizations, campus activities, and dates of involvement. Include any offices you held or committees you chaired. You may want to briefly describe the activity and what you did using action verbs.
- Skills: Include any technical skills, such as computer software applications, hardware, and/or languages. List any language fluencies.
- Personal Categories: These sections can be used to demonstrate valuable attributes, for example, military experience, publications and presentations, relevant projects completed, and major accomplishments.
- Miscellaneous: Optional information includes willingness to relocate, willingness to travel, dates of availability, and/or special interests.
- References: A statement "References available upon request" is common. However, if space is limited, this statement is not necessary. Rule of thumb: For the interview, have references available on a separate sheet.

Other Tips

- Use brief descriptive phrases instead of complete sentences. Avoid using personal pronouns—*I, me, my, their*.
- Have someone critique your résumé to check for spelling and/or grammatical errors.

Appearance Checklist

- Always buy good-quality paper for résumés.
- Select a subdued-colored paper: white, pale beige, light gray. Résumés are traditionally white. Print the résumé in *black ink* only.
- Limit résumé to one page unless a second page is essential for relevant details and extensive work experience.

Action Verbs

Use action verbs when describing your experiences/accomplishments on your résumé, in your letters, and during your interview. Skills you will bring to an employer will consist of three basic types: people, things, and ideas. The following are common verbs used to describe these skills.

- People: *administered, conducted, motivated, promoted, directed, coordinated, supervised, advised, explained, affected, managed, taught, activated, programmed, organized, conducted, stimulated, accomplished, adapted, adjusted, advertised, analyzed, assisted, cataloged, collaborated, calculated, consulted.*

- Things: *built, constructed, compiled, specified, designed, changed, improved, prepared, calculated, completed, invented, created, programmed, revised, expedited, drafted, edited, enlarged, established, evaluated, examined, expanded, facilitated, familiarized, formulated, generated, governed, guided.*

- Ideas: *established, wrote, proposed, coordinated, illustrated, modified, analyzed, adapted, investigated, explained, defined, devised, innovated, implemented, created, educated, synthesized, initiated, integrated, interviewed, maintained, manipulated, marketed, monitored, negotiated, obtained, persuaded, presented, presided.*

Résumé Formats

There are many different types of résumés. The most common type of résumé used is the chronological, which focuses on work history and experiences. A second type, which will become more widely used as technology expands, is the scannable. The scannable résumé is printed ready to be read by a computer. Here are suggestions for both of these types.

Chronological Résumés

The chronological résumé is the most common format and the one that is most familiar to employers (see Exhibit 2). It focuses on work history and experience and is organized by type of experience. Examples of categories of experience are education, technical experience, work experience, and activities.

This type of résumé has advantages and disadvantages. It can provide prospective employers with a clear and concise assessment of your experience. It also highlights most students' major asset: their education. On the downside, if you do not have a steady or relevant work history, this will be emphasized in the chronological résumé.

To write this type of résumé, first list your education, work experience, and activities. Then go beyond just listing the experiences and write what you gained in each experience that proves you have qualities that the employer desires.

Scannable Résumé

As technology advances, an increasing number of employers are requesting scannable résumés (see Exhibit 3). In many cases, your résumé will no longer be initially reviewed by an employer, but rather by a computer. **Remember: Computers read résumés differently than people do!** To make sure that no important information about you is lost in the scanning process and to increase your chances of

EXHIBIT 2

Example undergraduate résumé.

Jane Smith

OBJECTIVE

Sales in the fashion industry.

EDUCATION

Bachelor of Business Administration Degree in Marketing   May 20xx

Texas A&M University, College Station, Texas   GPA: 3.0 overall; 3.2 major

WORK EXPERIENCE

Department of Marketing, Texas A&M University

Student Worker,   January 20xx–May 20xx
- Worked for two professors within the department
- Duties included grading papers, making copies, typing, and editing

Recreational Center, Texas A&M University

Personal Trainer,   January 20xx–December 20xx
- Scheduled appointments with (# of) clients per shift
- Met with (# of) individual clients on a weekly basis
- Planned a workout schedule for each client to help client reach fitness goals

Payless Shoes, Houston, Texas

Buying Office Intern,   May 20xx–September 20xx
- Analyzed sales trends and markdowns and used data for merchandising
- Correlated with (# of) vendors the sending of samples and shipping orders
- Created and presented (# of) advertisements for newspapers and magazines
- Keyed and processed orders and distributions; approximately 3 per shift

LEADERSHIP ACTIVITIES

President, American Marketing Association   20xx–present

Vice-President, Retailing Society   20xx–20xx

Intramural Sports   20xx–20xx

Member, Business Students Society   20xx–20xx

HONORS

Alpha Mu Alpha, National Marketing Honor Society

Marketing Department Distinguished Student,   Fall 20xx

TECHNICAL EXPERIENCE

Microsoft Word, PowerPoint, Excel, Access

234 Your Street, College Station, TX 77840

(979) 555-7775

janesmith@email.com

EXHIBIT 3

Example scannable résumé.

Jane Smith
1234 Your Street
College Station, Texas 77840
Phone: (979) 555-7775
E-mail: janesmith@email.com

EDUCATION

Bachelor of Business Administration Degree in Marketing May 20xx
Texas A&M University, College Station, Texas
GPA: 3.0 overall; 3.2 major

COMPUTER SOFTWARE SKILLS

Microsoft Word, PowerPoint, Excel, Access

WORK EXPERIENCE

Department of Marketing, Texas A&M University
Student Worker, January 20xx–May 20xx
Worked for different professors within the department. Duties included grading papers, making copies, typing, and editing.

Recreational Center, Texas A&M University
Personal Trainer, January 20xx–December 20xx
Scheduled appointments with clients. Met with individual clients weekly to help them achieve their fitness goals.

Payless Shoes, Houston, Texas
Buying Office Intern, May 20xx–September 20xx
Analyzed sales trends and markdowns. Correlated with vendors the sending of samples and shipping orders. Created and presented advertisements for newspapers and magazines.
Keyed and processed orders and distributions.

ACTIVITIES & AFFILIATIONS

American Marketing Association
Retailing Society
Intramural Sports
Business Students Society

OTHER INFORMATION

Financed most of my college expenses, past 2 years 100%
Strong interest in languages and travel; willing to relocate

being electronically selected, the following are suggested guidelines for writing a scannable résumé:

- Use plain, white paper—8½″ × 11″.
- Do not fold—use large envelopes.
- Use no borders, graphics, or landscape printing.
- Select an unembellished typeface (such as Arial, Courier, Helvetica, ITC Bookman, ITC Avante Garde Gothic, New Century Schoolbook, Optima, Palatino, Times, Univers).
- Avoid *italics* and <u>underlining.</u>
- Use **bold** sparingly.
- Put name and address on each page.
- Clearly state functional and geographic preferences.
- Include degrees, majors, GPAs.
- List computer software and hardware skills.
- Include job titles, employers, dates, accomplishments, as usual, and additional sections for activities, honors, and the like.

Written Communication Is an Excellent Sales Tool

It may be necessary to write many letters during your job search. Some companies may prefer that you correspond by e-mail, and proper e-mail formats will also be discussed. Your best bet is to follow the lead of the recruiter in regard to communication.

You should always address letters to a specific person and include that person's job title. They should be only one page in length. There are several different styles of letter writing, but the favorite is the block style because it is the easiest. In block style, all lines begin at the left margin. Professional-looking business letters are very organized and contain standard parts (see Exhibit 4).

Return Address

In this section, beginning on line 11, you should type your street address and city, state, and ZIP code. Do not type your name as part of the address. On line 13, the next line after your address, you should type the date. Do not use abbreviations, except for the two-letter state abbreviation.

Inside Address

This part of the letter is where you type the address of the person receiving your letter. You should include the person's name and position in the organization. Be careful with the spelling of the recipient's name and always include a courtesy title such as *Mr., Ms.,* or *Mrs.*

Salutation

You should place the salutation two lines below the inside address. Type "Dear" followed by the person's courtesy title and last name. In block letter style, you do not add a colon after the person's name, unless you are on a first-name basis with that person.

EXHIBIT 4

Example follow-up letter format.

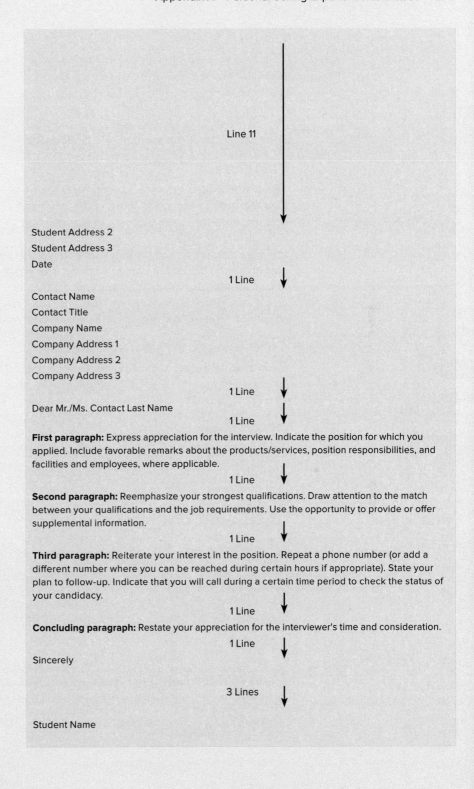

Line 11

Student Address 2
Student Address 3
Date

1 Line

Contact Name
Contact Title
Company Name
Company Address 1
Company Address 2
Company Address 3

1 Line

Dear Mr./Ms. Contact Last Name

1 Line

First paragraph: Express appreciation for the interview. Indicate the position for which you applied. Include favorable remarks about the products/services, position responsibilities, and facilities and employees, where applicable.

1 Line

Second paragraph: Reemphasize your strongest qualifications. Draw attention to the match between your qualifications and the job requirements. Use the opportunity to provide or offer supplemental information.

1 Line

Third paragraph: Reiterate your interest in the position. Repeat a phone number (or add a different number where you can be reached during certain hours if appropriate). State your plan to follow-up. Indicate that you will call during a certain time period to check the status of your candidacy.

1 Line

Concluding paragraph: Restate your appreciation for the interviewer's time and consideration.

1 Line

Sincerely

3 Lines

Student Name

Body

This portion of the letter should be single-spaced with double line spacing between paragraphs.

Complimentary Close

The complimentary close should come two lines after the last line of the letter. For a formal letter you should use a closing such as "Sincerely" or "Cordially."

Signature

Three to four lines below the complimentary closing, you should type your name. Sign the letter in the space above your typed name.

Enclosure Notation

If you are including something with your letter, such as your résumé, you should make a note of this two lines below your typed name. This serves as a reminder to the recipient to look for your attachment. You may type out the word "Enclosure" or "Attachment," or you can abbreviate it by typing "Enc." or "Att." You may indicate the number of attachments by adding a colon after the notation, for example. "Enclosure: 1 Résumé."

Thank-You Letters Are Important

Every time you meet with a recruiter, you should follow-up with a "thank-you" letter (see Exhibit 5). If you are interviewed by more than one person, then each

EXHIBIT 5

Example thank-you letter.

1234 Your Street
College Station, TX 77840
April 3, 20xx

Mr. John Doe
Manager of Human Resources
Industry Fashions

555 Main Street
Austin, TX 77543

Dear Mr. Doe

Thank you for the interview for the position of sales representative. Industry Fashions is a dynamic company with outstanding products. I would love to work as a sales rep for such a wonderful organization.

The interview strengthened my enthusiasm for the position and interest in working for Industry Fashions. Industry Fashions seeks only the most qualified recruits, and I believe that my education and experience are a good match for your company.

Hearing back from you would be very exciting. The phone number is (979)555-3418. Please call at your convenience.

Thank you again for your time and consideration.

Sincerely

Jane Smith

person should be written or thanked individually in a letter sent to the main contact person. A thank-you letter can be the final factor in the decision-making process. For example, if you and another recruit have practically the same skills and qualifications, and you sent a thank-you letter and the other recruit did not, chances are you will get the job. Your letter should reflect your desire to work for the organization and should once again highlight the skills and attributes that make you the best candidate for the job.

E-Mail Messages

In today's "e-world," some of the corresponding you do with future employees may be done by e-mail (see Exhibits 6 and 7). Because e-mail is constantly developing as a communications medium, its formatting and usage are always changing. The following suggestions are just a basic guide to help you construct your e-mail messages when you are unaware of the format the particular organization you are corresponding with uses.

To Line

In this portion of the e-mail, you should include the receiver's e-mail address. You may personalize this line by typing the name of the receiver first, followed by the receiver's e-mail address in angle brackets: John Smith <johnsmith@email.com>.

EXHIBIT 6

Example e-mail follow-up.

From: Student Name <student@email.com>

Sent: March 1, 20xx

To: Recipient Name <recipient@email.com>

Cc:

Subject: Type a concise but interesting subject here.

Dear Mr./Ms. Contact Last Name

First paragraph: Express appreciation for the interview. Indicate the position for which you applied. Include favorable remarks about the products/services, position responsibilities, and facilities and employees, where applicable.

Second paragraph: Reemphasize your strongest qualifications. Draw attention to the match between your qualifications and the job requirements. Use the opportunity to provide or offer supplemental information.

Third paragraph: Reiterate your interest in the position. Repeat a phone number (or add a different number where you can be reached during certain hours if appropriate). State your plan to follow-up. Indicate that you will call during a certain time period to check the status of your candidacy.

Concluding paragraph: Restate your appreciation for the interviewer's time and consideration. Make sure your message is not longer than two screens in length.

Sincerely

Student Name

From:	Jane Smith <janesmith@email.com>
Sent:	March 1, 20xx
To:	John Doe <johndoe@industryfashions.com>
Cc:	
Subject:	Thank you for the interview.

Dear Mr. Doe

Thank you for the interview for the position of sales representative. Industry Fashions is a dynamic company with outstanding products. I would love to work as a sales rep for such a wonderful organization.

The interview strengthened my enthusiasm for the position and interest in working for Industry Fashions. Industry Fashions seeks only the most qualified recruits, and I believe that my education and experience are a good match for IF.

Hearing back from you would be very exciting. The phone number is (979)555-3418. Please call at your convenience.

Thank you again for your time and consideration.

Sincerely

Jane Smith

From Line

This section contains your e-mail address and is automatically inserted by most systems.

Cc

Cc is an acronym for carbon copy or courtesy copy. The single *c* for any kind of copy is becoming the most commonly used copy notation. You should type the e-mail address, or addresses, of the people who need to receive a copy of the message in this line. There is also a *Bcc* function, which stands for blind carbon copy. This allows you to send a copy of your e-mail message to someone without the receiver's knowledge.

Subject

In this line you should briefly state the subject of your message. Include enough information so that the receiver will understand why you are writing and will be interested in reading what you have sent.

Salutation

You may include a brief greeting at the beginning of your message. Some writers use a salutation much like that of a letter, such as "Dear Mr. Smith." You may choose to include the receiver's name in the first line instead of using a salutation, for example, "Thanks, Mr. Smith, for meeting with me last week." There is a division in the way to treat an e-mail message: Some treat them more like letters (with a salutation), whereas others write them as if they were memos (with no salutation).

Message

Cover only one topic in your message. You should try to keep your message very concise and no more than two screens in length. To help you with this, many systems have features such as cut, copy, paste, and word-wrap. Do not get too carried away with formatting because the receiver's system may not support different fonts or colors.

Closing

You should close your message as you would a letter, with a closing followed by your name and e-mail address. If you do not include your e-mail address, and your system does not transmit your address to the recipient, then they will not be able to reply to you.

HOW TO CREATE A PORTFOLIO

A portfolio is a binder or book that shows off your work and abilities. It goes beyond a cover letter and a résumé. A portfolio is a job-hunting tool that you develop that gives employers a picture of who you are: your experience, your education, your accomplishments, and your skills. Not only does it show the employer who you are, but it displays what you have the potential to become. It is designed to do one thing: **support you as you market yourself!**

Top Six Reasons to Have a Portfolio

1. Distinguish yourself from the competition.
2. Turn the interview into an offer.
3. Increase the salary offer by impressing the interviewer.
4. Offer tangible proof of your abilities.
5. Potentially help you get promoted.
6. Help you find the position that is right for you!

Where to Begin

You should start developing your portfolio by first doing a self-assessment. Evaluate what you have to offer and what the best ways are to market your assets. You should decide which of your skills and experiences will relate to the needs of the interviewer, or what you would most like the interviewer to see. If you don't have much work experience—most students don't—you'll need to mine your schoolwork, volunteer work, and hobbies for evidence of the relevant skills you know you have. For example, if you did event promotions for a campus organization, include a copy of a flyer or poster you designed.

The following is a list of items you may want to include:

- **Table of contents** (for easy reference).
- **Career summary and goals:** A description of what you stand for (such as work ethic, organizational interests, and management philosophy) and where you see yourself in two to five years.

- **Traditional résumé:** A summary of your education, achievements, and work experience, using a chronological or functional format.
- **Scannable résumé:** A text-only version of your résumé should be included.
- **Skills, abilities, and marketable qualities:** A detailed examination of your skills and experience. This section should include the name of the skill area; the performance or behavior, knowledge, or personal traits that contribute to your success in that skill area; and the background and specific experiences that demonstrate your application of the skill.
- **Samples of your work:** A sampling of your best work, including reports, papers, studies, brochures, projects, and presentations. Besides print samples, you can include CD-ROMs, videos, and other multimedia formats.
- **Testimonials and letters of recommendation:** A collection of any kudos you have received from customers, clients, colleagues, past employers, professors, and so on. Some experts suggest including copies of favorable employer evaluations and reviews.
- **Awards and honors:** A collection of certificates of awards, honors, and scholarships.
- **Conferences and workshops:** A list of conferences, seminars, and workshops you've participated in and/or attended.
- **Transcripts, degrees, licenses, and certifications:** A description of relevant courses, degrees, licenses, and certifications.
- **Test results:** Professional or graduate school testing results (such as GRE subject test results).
- **Newspaper clippings:** Articles and/or photos that address your achievements.
- **Military records, awards, and badges:** A description of your military service, if applicable.
- **References:** A list of three to five people (including full names, titles, addresses, and phone/e-mail) who are willing to speak about your strengths, abilities, and experience. At least one reference should be a former manager.

Organize Your Portfolio

1. Keep your portfolio in a professional three-ring binder.
2. Come up with an organizational system of categories to put your items together. Sample categories are as follows: Work Experience, Education, Awards and Certificates, Special Skills, Personal Accomplishments, Background. Use tabs or dividers to separate the categories.
3. Your portfolio should be no more than 25 pages. The shorter it is the better, because an employer will really absorb only 6 to 10 samples.
4. Every page should have a title, a concise caption, and artifact. Captions should explain the process you went through and the resulting benefits, such as: "This is a flyer I designed for the promotion of the American Marketing Association Membership drive. We gained over 50 new members that year." Use the same type of action verbs you would use in a résumé.
5. Photocopy full-page samples to a smaller size, if needed.

6. Make the layout and design consistent, and don't get overly decorative—keep it clean and use lots of white space.

7. You may also consider including a disk or CD with samples of your work. An online portfolio is another option.

8. Once you have put together your portfolio, you should create a title page, a table of contents, and an introduction. The introduction provides an opportunity to tie together your portfolio contents and summarize your qualifications.

Finishing Touches

- Have a faculty member or someone at the career center review and critique your portfolio.

- Develop a condensed version of your portfolio that contains your most important accomplishments to leave with your interviewer. It could be in an inexpensive report cover or folder. This provides something physical to remind the interviewer that you were there. It also provides an occasion for an additional contact in a week or so to arrange for its pickup. Make sure you do not include original materials of which you only have one copy!

- Mention that you have a portfolio in the reference section of your résumé as well as in your cover letter.

How Do I Use My Portfolio during the Interview Process?

- Bring the condensed version of your portfolio with you to the interview and be prepared to present all the information within it to the interviewer. You may not always want to leave a condensed version of your portfolio. Level of interest in the position and cost should help you decide.

- Announce at the beginning of the interview that you have a portfolio and would like to present it at some point during the interview.

- You can use your portfolio to support your responses. For example, the interviewer might say, "I see that you have worked on your school newspaper. What were your favorite writing assignments?" You might reply, "My favorite assignments include this article (turn portfolio toward the interviewer and show the interviewer the article in the portfolio), which required a lot of research, and this creative writing piece (show article), which I wrote for a special edition."

- If you are unable to present it during the interview, begin the time allotted for questions by mentioning that you would like to present your portfolio.

NOTES

1. This exercise was created by Professors Charles M. Futrell of Texas A&M University and George Wynn of James Madison University. Copyright 2000.

glossary of selling terms

acceptance signals Signs that your buyer is favorably inclined toward you and your presentation.

account analysis The process of analyzing each prospect and customer to maximize the chances of reaching a sales goal.

account segmentation The process of applying different selling strategies to different customers.

acquaintance People you know little about.

adaptive selling Salespersons' ability to adjust and modify their behaviors to better align with their customers' needs

advantage The performance characteristic of a product that describes how it can be used or will help the buyer.

advertising The nonpersonal communication of information paid for by an identified sponsor, for example, an individual or an organization.

agenda The plan or a brief framework of the goals of the meeting or the targeted discussion areas.

alternative-choice close Gives the prospect a choice between two alternatives.

analogy A comparison between two different situations that have something in common.

approach Opening of the presentation from first talk with person to discussion of product.

artificial intelligence system The software system to better understand customers' behaviors and help salespeople understand how they might help their customers.

assumptive close A type of close that assumes the prospect will buy.

attention The first step in the prospect's mental steps. From the moment a salesperson begins to talk, he or she should try to quickly capture and maintain the prospect's attention.

autosuggestion A kind of suggestion that attempts to have prospects imagine themselves using the product.

benefit A favorable result the buyer receives from the product because of a particular advantage that has the ability to satisfy a buyer's need.

benefit selling A method of selling whereby a salesperson relates a product's benefits to the customer's needs using the product's features and advantages as support.

black box The unobservable, internal process taking place within the mind of the prospect as he or she reaches a decision whether or not to buy.

bonus Additional compensation given to the salesperson that is over what is usually earned.

boomerang method The process of turning an objection into a reason to buy.

breach of warranty A legal cause of action on which an injured party seeks damages. It arises when a salesperson makes erroneous statements or offers false promises regarding a product's characteristics and capabilities.

break-even analysis A quantitative technique for determining the level of sales at which total revenues equal total costs.

business friendship The relationship formed between a salesperson and client that revolves around business-related issues.

buying center A group composed of all of the people performing different roles in the buying process (e.g., user, buyer, decider, influencer, gatekeeper) based on their expertise and responsibilities within their firm.

buying signal Anything that prospects say or do indicating they are ready to buy.

calendar management Scheduling appointments, telephone calls, or "to-do" lists.

call reluctance Not wanting to contact a prospect or customer.

career path The upward sequence of job movements during a sales career.

caring Love; to show due concern or regard.

cash discounts Discounts earned by buyers who pay bills within a stated period.

caution signals Signs that a buyer is neutral or skeptical toward what the salesperson says.

CCC GOMES Acronym for the eight important stakeholders of an organization: customers, community, creditors, government, owners, managers, employees, suppliers.

center of influence method A method of prospecting whereby the salesperson finds and cultivates people who are willing to cooperate in helping find prospects.

centralized training programs Centrally located instruction of salespeople that supplements training conducted in the field.

character Who you are when no one is looking and what you are willing to stand for when someone is looking.

Clayton Act Prohibits the practice of tie-in sales when they substantially lessen competition.

closing The process of helping people make a decision that will benefit them by asking them to buy.

cloud A technology approach that enables a more mobile, portable opportunity for salespeople by allowing access to software anywhere, as long as the individual is connected to the Internet.

code of ethics A formal statement of the company's values concerning ethics and social issues.

cold canvass prospecting method A method whereby the salesperson contacts as many leads as possible with no knowledge of the business or individual called upon.

collect information The process by which buyers visit retail stores, contact potential suppliers, or talk with salespeople about a product's price, size, advantage, and warranty before making a decision regarding buying.

common denominator A common trait that distinguishes successful salespeople from unsuccessful salespeople.

communication The act of transmitting verbal and nonverbal information and understanding between seller and buyer.

compensation method The method of offsetting negative product aspects with better benefit aspects.

compliment close A close wherein the salesperson ends with a compliment to the prospect.

complimentary approach An approach that opens with a compliment that is sincere and therefore effective.

computer-based presentations Using the computer to present information to prospects and customers.

conceptual skills The ability to see the selling process as a whole and the relationship among its parts.

condition of the sale A situation wherein an objection becomes a condition of the sale, such that if the condition is met the prospect will buy.

conscious need level A state of mind in which buyers are fully aware of their needs.

consumer buying The purchasing activities of individuals and households for their personal use or consumption or to meet the collective needs of the household unit, such as a family or individual.

consumer discounts One-time price reductions passed on from the manufacturer to channel members or directly to the customer.

consumer products Products produced for, and purchased by, households or end consumers for their personal use.

consumer sales promotion A promotion that includes free samples, coupons, contests, and demonstrations to consumers.

continuous-yes close A kind of close whereby the salesperson develops a series of benefit questions that the prospect must answer.

conventional moral development level The second level of an individual's moral development. At this level, an individual conforms to the expectations of others, such as family, employer, boss, and society, and upholds moral and legal laws.

conviction In the conviction step of the prospect's mental buying process, the salesperson should strive to develop a strong belief that the product is best suited to the prospect's specific needs. It is established when no doubts remain about purchasing the product.

cooling-off laws Laws that provide a cooling-off period during which the buyer may cancel the contract, return any merchandise, and obtain a full refund.

cooperative acceptance The right of employees to be treated fairly and with respect regardless of race, sex, national origin, physical disability, age, or religion, while on the job.

cooperative (co-op) advertising Advertising conducted by the retailer with costs paid for by the manufacturer or shared by the manufacturer and the retailer.

core principles of professional selling The sales philosophy of unselfishly serving your customers and professionally representing the organization you work for.

core principles paradox One receives more than he or she gives to a customer or employer.

countersuggestion A suggestion that evokes an opposite response from the prospect.

creative imagery A relaxation and concentration technique that aids in stress management, in which a salesperson envisions successful coping in various sales situations.

creative problem solver A person with the ability to develop and combine nontraditional alternatives in order to meet specific needs of the customer.

credibility A salesperson's believability, established through empathy, willingness to listen to specific needs, and continual enthusiasm toward his or her work and the customer's business.

cumulative quantity discounts Discounts the customer receives for buying a certain amount of a product over a stated period, such as one year.

curiosity approach An approach whereby the salesperson asks a question or does something to make the prospect curious about the product.

customer benefit approach An approach whereby the salesperson asks questions that imply that the product will benefit the prospect.

customer benefit plan A plan that contains the nucleus of information used in the sales presentation.

customer contact person Another name for a salesperson.

customer profile Relevant information regarding the firm, the buyer, and individuals who influence the buying decision.

customer relationship management (CRM) A technology system that helps companies manage information about existing and potential customers.

customer satisfaction Feelings toward the purchase.

customer service Activities and programs provided by the seller to make the relationship a satisfying one for the customer.

decentralized training Training that comprises the main form of sales instruction.

decoding process Receipt and translation of information by the receiver.

demonstration The process of showing a product to a prospect and letting him or her use it, if possible.

denominator A common trait of salespeople.

desire The third step in the prospect's mental buying process. It is created when prospects express a wish or wanting for a product.

digital sales Uses all digital media, including the internet and mobile and interactive channels to develop communication and exchanges with customers and prospects.

direct close An explicit type of closing wherein the salesperson asks the customer for a decision in a straight-forward, candid manner.

direct denial The method of overcoming objections through the use of facts, logic, and tact.

direct-mail advertising Advertising that is mailed directly to the customer or industrial user.

direct-mail prospecting The process of mailing advertisements to a large number of people over an extended geographic area.

direct question A question that by and large can be answered with a yes or no response or at most by a very short response consisting of a few words.

direct sellers Sellers who sell face-to-face to consumers—typically in their homes—who use products for their personal use.

direct suggestion An approach that suggests prospects buy rather than telling them to buy.

directing The action of dealing with people positively and persuasively from a leadership position.

disagreement signals Signs that the prospect does not agree with the presentation or does not think the product is beneficial.

discretionary responsibility Actions taken by a company that are purely voluntary and guided by its desire to make social contributions not mandated by economics, law, or ethics.

distribution The channel structure used to transfer products from an organization to its customers.

diversity The difference between people due to age, religion, race, gender, and so on.

dodge Doesn't deny, answer, or ignore the objection, but simply temporarily dodges it.

dramatization The theatrical presentation of products.

economic needs The buyer's need to purchase the most satisfying product for the money.

eighty/twenty principle A situation in which a few key or large accounts bring in 80 percent of profitable sales although they represent only 20 percent of total accounts.

E-mail (electronic mail) Allows information to be sent electronically through a system that delivers the message immediately to any number of recipients.

ELMS system The process of dividing customers into varying size accounts.

emotional intelligence (EI) The combination of four abilities: (a) your ability to perceive other's emotions; (b) your ability to identify your emotions, (c) your ability to understand what's causing your emotion, and (d) your ability to manage your emotions.

empathy The ability to identify and understand another person's feelings, ideas, and circumstances.

employee rights Rights desired by employees regarding their job security and the treatment administered by their employers while on the job, irrespective of whether those rights are currently protected by law or collective bargaining agreements of labor unions.

employment planning The recruitment and selection of applicants for sales jobs.

encoding process One of the eight elements of the communication process. This is the conversion by the salesperson of ideas and concepts into the language and materials used in the sales presentation.

endless chain referral method A method of prospecting whereby a salesperson asks each buyer for a list of friends who might also be interested in buying the product.

enthusiasm A state of mind wherein a person is filled with excitement toward something.

Equal Employment Opportunity Commission (EEOC) The principal governmental agency responsible for monitoring discriminatory practices.

e-sales Is the strategic process of such as discovering the desires of customers, distributing, promoting, pricing products submitting orders, using digital media and digital marketing. It goes beyond the internet to include mobile phones, banner ads, digital outdoor marketing, and social networks.

e-sales call A sales call in which the seller and the customer meet using the computer screen.

ethical behavior Behavior demonstrating a willingness to treat others fairly and that shows one to be honest and trustworthy and that exhibits loyalty to company, associates, and the work for which one is responsible.

ethics Principles of right or good conduct, or a body of such principles, that affect good and bad business practices.

ethics committee A group of executives appointed to oversee company ethics.

ethics ombudsperson An official given the responsibility of corporate conscience who hears and investigates ethical complaints and informs top management of potential ethical issues.

evaluation Comparing actual performance to planned performance goals to determine whether to take corrective action if goals are not achieved or to continue using the same methods if goals are met.

exchange The act of obtaining a desired product from someone by offering something in return.

executive presence A certain aura—that the salesperson is perceived as possessing a quality of professionalism, ability, and authority.

exhibitions and demonstrations A situation in which a firm operates a booth at a trade show or other special-interest gathering staffed by salespeople.

exit technique A technique used by professional salespeople to keep the door open for future interactions with the prospect, in the event of not being granted the sale.

extensive decision making Decision-making characteristic of buyers who are unfamiliar with a specific product and who must therefore become highly involved in the decision-making process.

FAB selling technique A presentation technique stressing features, advantages, and benefits of a product.

fair Free from self-interest, prejudice, or favoritism.

faithful Firm in adherence; loyal; worthy of trust; devoted.

feature Any physical characteristic of a product.

feedback Verbal or nonverbal reaction to communication as transmitted to the sender.

firm An organization that produces goods and services.

five-question sequence The five-step process of overcoming objections in which facts, logic, and tact are used.

fixed point of reference Something that provides the correct action to take in any situation and never gets tailored to fit an occasion.

flaming The equivalent of a verbal lashing on the Internet.

FOB destination The point at which the seller pays all shipping costs and title passes on delivery.

FOB shipping point The shipping process in which the buyer pays transportation charges for goods, the title for which passes to the customer when the goods are loaded onto the shipping vehicle.

follow-up Maintaining contact with a customer (or prospect) in order to evaluate the effectiveness of the product and the satisfaction of the customer.

formula presentation A presentation by which the salesperson follows a general outline that allows more flexibility and tries to determine prospect needs.

friends People known for some time and with whom we share common interests and/or hobbies.

geographic information system (GIS) View and analyze customer and/or prospect information on an electronic map.

good A physical object for sale.

government An organization that provides goods and services to households and firms, and that redistributes income and wealth.

Great Harvest Law of Sales You reap what you sow.

green marketing Is part of an organization's strategic process that strives to maintain, support, and enhance the natural environment.

Green River ordinance This type of ordinance protects consumers and aids local firms by making it more difficult for outside competition to enter the market.

gross profit Money available to cover the costs of marketing the product, operating the business, and profit.

harmony State of calm; freedom from strife or discord; harmony in personal relationships; confidence that all is well, especially in times of hardship.

hearing The ability to detect sounds.

hidden objection An objection that disguises the actual objection with either silence or triviality.

household A decision-making unit buying for their personal use.

human skills The seller's ability to work with and through other people.

ideal self The person one would like to be.

indirect denial An apparent agreement with the prospect used by the salesperson to deny the fundamental issue of the objection.

indirect suggestion A statement by the salesperson recommending that the prospect undertake some action while making it seem that the idea to do so is the prospect's.

industrial advertising Advertising aimed at individuals and organizations who purchase products for manufacturing or reselling other products.

industrial products Products sold primarily for use in producing other products.

information evaluation A process that determines what will be purchased as the buyer matches this information with needs, attitudes, and beliefs in making a decision.

integrity The quality of being honest without compromise or corruption.

intelligent questions Questions relating to a prospect's business that show the salesperson's concern for the prospect's needs.

interest The second step in the prospect's mental buying process. It is important for the salesperson to capture the prospect's interest in their product. If this link is completed, prospects usually express a desire for the product.

Internet A global network of computers.

intimate friends People known on a deeper, more personal level than a friend.

intimate space A spatial zone up to two feet, about an arm's length, from a person's body that is reserved for close friends and loved ones.

introductory approach The most common but least powerful approach; it does little to capture the prospect's attention.

J K

job analysis The definition of a sales position in terms of specific roles or activities to be performed along with the determination of personal qualifications suitable for the job.

job descriptions Formal, written statements describing the nature, requirements, and responsibilities of a specific position.

job specifications The conversion of job descriptions into those people qualifications the organization feels are needed for successful job performance.

joint sales call A sales call that takes place when the manager accompanies a salesperson on the call.

joy Emotion evoked by well-being, success, or good fortune; gladness or delight.

key accounts Accounts the loss of which would greatly affect sales and profits.

kindness Benevolence; favorable disposition; showing sympathy and understanding; patient and compassionate.

KISS A memory device standing for Keep It Simple, Salesperson.

knowledge Knowing something gained through experience and/or training.

L

lead A person or organization who might be a prospect.

lead generation Establishing a group of firms and individuals that may be in the target market for a seller's product or service.

lead qualification Using some set of predefined criteria to determine whether the lead possesses an interest in the product as well as an ability to buy the product.

lead scoring system A system that grades each lead based on a range of criteria to help salespeople understand (a) which leads become prospects and (b) categorizes prospects into groups.

learning Acquiring knowledge or behavior based on past experiences.

limited decision making Decision-making characteristic of a buyer who invests a moderate level of energy in the decision to buy because, although the buyer is not familiar with each brand's features, advantages, and benefits, the general quality of the good is known to him or her.

list price A standard price charged to all customers.

listening Ability to derive meaning from sounds that are heard.

logical reasoning Persuasive techniques that appeal to the prospect's common sense by applying logic through reason.

looking-glass self The self that people think other people see them as.

M

manufacturer's sales representative A person who works for an organization that produces a product.

marketing The activity, set of institutions, and processes for creating, communicating, delivering, and exchanging offerings that have value for customers, clients, partners, and society at large.

marketing concept A philosophy of business maintaining that the satisfaction of customer needs and wants is the economic and social reason for a firm's existence and that the firm should therefore direct its activities toward fulfilling those needs and wants, yielding, at the same time, long-term profitability.

marketing mix The four main elements used by a marketing manager to market goods and services. These elements are product, price, distribution or place, and promotion.

markup The dollar amount added to the product cost to determine its selling price.

medium The form of communication used in the sales presentation and discussion, most frequently words, visual materials, and body language.

memorized presentation A type of presentation in which the salesperson does 80 to 90 percent of the talking, focusing on the product and its benefits rather than attempting to determine the prospect's needs.

memory The ability to recall information over time.

message Information conveyed in the sales presentation.

metaphor An implied comparison that uses a contrasting word or phrase to evoke a vivid image.

minor-points close A close in which the salesperson asks the prospect to make a low-risk decision on a minor element of a product.

mirroring When people take part in similar actions at relatively the same time (i.e., within three to five seconds).

misrepresentation A legal cause of action on which an injured party seeks damages. It arises when a salesperson makes erroneous statements or offers false promises regarding a product's characteristics and capabilities.

money objection A price-oriented objection.

morally ethical Good, morally right.

morals People's adherence to right or wrong behavior and right or wrong thinking.

motivation to purchase The "lack" of something in terms of a product, service, or solution, otherwise known as a *gap*.

multiple-question approach (SPIN) An approach in which the salesperson uses three types of questions—situation, problem implication, and need-payoff—to get a better understanding of the prospect's business.

mutual investment A requirement for building and maintaining relationships that involves effort, time, and resources.

national advertising Advertising designed to reach all users of the product, whether customers or industrial buyers.

need arousal A situation in which a salesperson triggers a psychological, social, or economic need in the buyer.

need awareness The stage at which the salesperson is aware of the buyer's needs and takes control of the situation by restating those needs to clarify the situation.

need development In a need-satisfaction sales presentation, the stage at which the discussion is devoted to the buyer's needs.

need fulfillment The last phase of a need-satisfaction sales presentation. Here, the salesperson shows how the product will satisfy mutual needs.

need-satisfaction presentation A flexible, interactive type of presentation in which a prospect's needs are thoroughly discussed.

needs The desire for something a person feels is worthwhile.

needs prioritization section Allowing buyers to prioritize their needs prior to needs-payoff section of the SPIN.

needs summary section Ensuring the salesperson totally understands the buyer's needs prior to needs-payoff section of the SPIN.

negotiation The process by which the buyer and the seller reach a mutually satisfactory agreement.

negotiation close A close in which buyer and seller find ways for everyone to have a fair deal.

net price The price after allowance for all discounts.

net profit Money remaining after costs of marketing and operating the business are paid.

netiquette Etiquette used on the Internet.

no-need objection An objection in which the prospect declares he or she does not need the product and implies the end of the selling effort, but which may actually be either a hidden or a stalling objection.

noise Factors that distort communication between buyer and seller, including barriers to communication.

noncumulative quantity discounts One-time reduction in price, usually for a short period of time such as one or two months.

nondirective question A question that opens up two-way communication by beginning the question with *who, what, where, when, how,* or *why.*

nonprofit clients Recipients of money and/or services from a nonprofit organization.

nonverbal communication Unspoken communication such as physical space, appearance, handshake, and body movement.

observation method The process of finding prospects by a salesperson's constantly watching what is happening in the sales area.

opinion approach An approach whereby a salesperson shows that the buyer's opinion is valued.

order-getters Salespeople who get new and repeat business using a creative sales strategy and a well-executed sales presentation.

order-takers Salespeople who only take orders by asking what the customer wants or waiting for the customer to order. They have no sales strategy and use no sales presentation.

organizational buying All of the activities of organizational members as they define a buying situation and identify, evaluate, and choose among alternative brands and suppliers.

organizational buying process The problem-solving procedure the firm uses to meet its goals and objectives as it relates to making purchases.

organizational buying situation The firm's perception of a business problem (also called a need).

orphaned customers Customers whose salesperson has left the company.

parable A brief story used to illustrate a point.

paradox A pair of opposing statements.

parallel referral sale Not only selling a product but also selling the idea of giving prospects' names as well.

partnering When the seller works continually to improve the customer's operations, sales, and profits.

pass up The option of a salesperson not to pursue a presentation or sale, or not to respond to an objection.

patience Endurance; hopeful forbearance; forbearance is to endure, do without; to hold oneself back from; to control oneself when provoked; to be patient; leniency.

people planning Planning how many and what type of people to hire.

perception The process by which a person selects, organizes, and interprets information.

performance criteria Bases for evaluating a salesperson's performance.

performance evaluation The formal, structured system of measuring and evaluating a salesperson's activities and performance.

personal productivity An effort by the salesperson to increase productivity through a number of tools including more efficient data storage and retrieval, better time management, and enhanced presentation.

personal space An area two to four feet from a person; it is the closest zone a stranger or business acquaintance is normally allowed to enter.

personality A person's distinguishing character traits, attitudes, or habits.

plan A method of achieving an end.

planning Establishing a broad outline for goals, policies, and procedures that will accomplish the objectives of the organization.

point-of-purchase (POP) displays Displays that allow a product to be easily seen and purchased.

postpone the objection The option of a salesperson to respond to an objection later during the sales presentation.

practical objection An overt objection based on real or concrete causes.

preapproach Planning the sales call on a customer or prospect.

preconscious need level The level at which needs are not fully developed in the conscious mind.

preconventional moral development level The first level of an individual's moral development. At this level, an individual acts in his or her own best interest and thus follows rules to avoid punishment or receive rewards. This individual would break moral and legal laws.

predictive analytics The software technology that can predict the plausible future opportunities to assist the customers and provide salespeople with the needed tools to do so.

premium An article of merchandise offered as an incentive to the user to take some action.

premium approach An approach in which the salesperson offers a prospect something as an inducement to buy.

prestige suggestions A technique in which the salesperson has the prospect visualize using products that people whom the prospect trusts use.

price The value or worth of a product.

price discrimination The act of selling the same quantity of the same product to different buyers at different prices.

principled moral development level The third level of an individual's moral development. At this level, an individual lives by an internal set of morals, values, and ethics, regardless of punishments or majority opinion.

probability or rating close A close that permits the prospect to focus on his or her real objections, which a salesperson attempts to reverse with a persuasive sales argument.

probing The act of gathering information and uncovering customer needs using one or more questions.

problem–solution presentation A flexible, customized approach involving an in-depth study of a prospect's needs, requiring a well-planned presentation.

product One of the four main elements of the marketing mix, it is a bundle of tangible and intangible attributes, including packaging, color, and brand, plus the services and even the reputation of the seller.

product approach An approach in which the salesperson places the product on the counter or hands it to the customer, saying nothing.

product objection An objection relating directly to the product.

professional selling The process and activities required to effectively develop, manage, enable, and execute a mutually beneficial, interpersonal exchange of goods and/or services for equitable value.

promotion One of the four main elements of the marketing mix, it increases company sales by communicating product information to potential customers.

proof statements Statements that substantiate claims made by the salesperson.

prospect A qualified person or organization that has the potential to buy a salesperson's good or service.

prospect pool A group of names, gathered from various sources, that represent prospective buyers.

prospecting The process of identifying potential customers.

proverb A short, wise, easy-to-learn saying that calls a person to think and act.

psychological objection A hidden objection based on the prospect's attitudes.

public relations The nonpersonal communication of information that is not paid for by an individual or organization.

public space Distances greater than 12 feet from a person.

purchase decision A buyer's decision to purchase something.

purchase dissonance Tension on the part of a buyer regarding whether the right decision was made in purchasing a product.

purchase or action The final step in the prospect's mental steps. Once the prospect is convinced, the salesperson should plan the most appropriate method of asking the prospect to buy or act.

purchase satisfaction Gratification based on a product that supplies expected, or greater than expected, benefits.

qualified prospect A prospect who has the financial resources to pay, the authority to make the buying decision, and a desire for the product.

question close A type of close wherein the salesperson asks questions to generate a decision point.

real self People as they actually are.

receiver The person a communication is intended for.

reciprocity An agreement whereby a person or organization buys a product if the person or organization selling the product also buys a product from the first party.

redirect question A question that guides the prospect back to selling points that both parties agree on.

referral A prospect who has been referred to a salesperson by another person.

referral approach An approach that uses a third person's name as a reference to approach the buyer.

referral cycle Provides guidelines for a salesperson to ask for referrals in four commonly faced situations experienced by salespeople.

rephrase as a question Turning an objection into a question in order to make the objection easier to answer.

rephrasing question A question in which the salesperson rephrases what the prospect has said in order to clarify meaning and determine the prospect's needs.

retail advertising Advertising used by a retailer to reach customers within its geographic trading area.

retail salesperson This individual sells goods or services to customers for their personal, nonbusiness use.

return on investment (ROI) The additional sum of money expected from an investment over and above the original investment.

Robinson-Patman Act An act that allows sellers to grant quantity discounts to larger buyers based on savings in manufacturing costs.

role-playing A process whereby a sales trainee acts through the sale of a product or service to a hypothetical buyer.

routine decision making The process of being in the habit of buying a particular product so attitudes and beliefs toward the product are already formed and are usually positive.

routing The travel pattern used in working a sales territory.

S

sales call allocation A plan to allocate sales calls within territories based on number of accounts in the territory, number of sales calls made on customers, time required for each sales call, frequency of customer sales calls, travel time around the territory, nonselling time, and return on time invested.

sales call objective The main purpose of a salesperson's call to a prospect or customer.

sales call planning The process of preparing to approach a prospect attempting to make a sale.

sales call purpose Sales call purpose is to make a contribution to the welfare of a person or organization.

sales networking The continuous prospecting method of making and utilizing contacts.

sales objection The prospect's opposition or resistance to the salesperson's information or request.

sales presentation The actual presentation of the sales message to the prospect.

sales presentation mix The key communication elements used by the salesperson in the presentation.

sales process A sequential series of actions by the salesperson that leads toward the prospect taking a desired action and ends with a follow-up to ensure purchase satisfaction.

sales promotion Activities and materials used to create sales of goods and services.

sales response function The relationship between sales volume and sales calls.

sales technology The transformation of manual sales activities to electronic processes through the use of various combinations of hardware and software applications.

sales territory The group of customers or a geographical area assigned to a salesperson.

sales training The effort put forth by an employer to provide the opportunity for the salesperson to acquire job-related attitudes, concepts, rules, and skills that result in improved performance in the selling environment.

scheduling The establishment of a fixed time for visiting a customer's business.

selection The process of selecting the best available person for a sales job.

selective distortion The altering of information when it is inconsistent with a person's beliefs or attitudes.

selective exposure The process of allowing only a portion of the information revealed to be organized, interpreted, and permitted into awareness.

self-concept A person's view of him- or herself.

self-control Restraint exercised over one's own impulses, desires, or emotions; temperance.

self-image How a person sees him- or herself.

self-management The development of a personal time management plan, setting priorities based on supervisors' expectations, keeping a watchful eye on the industry trends, and having a vision for the future.

SELL Sequence A sequence of things to do and say to stress benefits important to the customer: show the feature, explain the advantage, lead into the benefit, and let the customer talk by asking a question about the benefit.

service Making a contribution to the welfare of others; the product which is an action or activity done for others for a fee.

shelf facings The number of individual products placed beside each other on the shelf.

shelf positioning The physical placement of the product within the retailer's store.

shock approach An approach that uses a question designed to make the prospect think seriously about a subject related to the salesperson's product.

showmanship approach An approach that involves doing something unusual to catch the prospect's attention and interest.

SMART A technique to set the sales call objectives by making sure the objectives are specific, measurable, achievable, realistic, and timed.

social listening Monitoring, interpreting, and seeking understanding of buyer-based actions and communication.

social network Is a web-based meeting place for friends, family, coworkers, and peers that allow users to create a profile and connect with other users for the purposes that range from getting acquainted, to keeping in touch, to building a work-related network.

social networks Include Facebook, MySpace, LinkedIn, Twitter, blogs, wikis, photo sharing, video sharing, and podcasting, just to name a few.

social responsibility The responsibility to profitably serve employees and customers in an ethical and lawful manner.

social sales technology Any social interaction-enhancing technology that can be deployed by sales professionals to generate content and develop networks.

social space A zone that is 4 to 12 feet from a person and is the area normally used for sales presentations.

source The origin of a communication.

source objection A loyalty-related objection by which the prospect states a preference for another company or salesperson, and may specify a dislike for the salesperson's company or self.

space invasion A situation in which one person enters another person's personal or intimate space.

space threat A situation in which a person threatens to invade another's spatial territory.

stalling objection An objection that delays the presentation or the sale.

standing-room-only close A close whereby a salesperson suggests that if a prospect does not act now he or she may not be able to buy in the future, thus motivating the prospect to act immediately.

stimulus–response A model of behavior that describes the process of applying a stimulus (sales presentation) that results in a response (purchase decision).

storytelling in sales The approach that the salesperson uses to communicate and create understanding by describing some sort of sequence of events or a narrative.

strategic Programs, goals, and projects of great importance.

strategic customer relationship A formal relationship between the seller and customer with the purpose of being in joint pursuit of mutual goals.

success Setting a goal and accomplishing it.

suggestive proposition A proposition that implies that the prospect should act now.

summary-of-benefits close A close wherein the salesperson summarizes the benefits of the product in a positive manner so that the prospect agrees with what the salesperson says.

T-account close A close that is based on the process that people use when they make a decision by weighing the pros against the cons.

technical skills The understanding of and proficiency in the performance of specific tasks.

technology close A close in which the seller uses technology to present information.

tele-prospecting The process of reaching potential customers over the phone. The process tends to use a greater range of traditional selling elements, including needs discovery and solution provision.

telemarketing A marketing communication system using telecommunication technology and trained personnel to conduct planned, measurable marketing activities directed at targeted groups of consumers.

termination-at-will rule The employer's right to terminate sales personnel for poor performance, excessive absenteeism, unsafe conduct, and poor organizational citizenship.

territorial space The area around oneself that a person will not allow another person to enter without consent.

territory manager A person who plans, organizes, and executes activities that increase sales and profits in a given territory.

third-party answer The technique of responding to an objection with testimony from authoritative sources.

tie-in sale Prohibited under the Clayton Act, it occurs when a buyer is required to buy other, unwanted products in order to buy a particular line of merchandise.

trade advertising Advertising undertaken by the manufacturer and directed toward the wholesaler or retailer.

trade discounts Discounts on the list retail price offered to channel members.

trade sales promotion A promotion that encourages resellers to purchase and aggressively sell a manufacturer's products by offering incentives like sales contests, displays, special purchase prices, and free merchandise.

transitions Relating or linking two ideas or sections of the conversation.

trial close A question that checks the attitude and understanding of your prospect in regards to the sales presentation or its elements.

true Consistent with fact.

trust The belief that another will act as they are expected to act.

truth The facts needed to make ethical and moral decisions; to a person of faith—that which upholds and does not contradict what is fundamental to his or her faith and/or, frequently dependent on, what is stated in his or her sacred text.

unconscious need level The level at which people do not know why they buy a product.

undifferentiated selling The process of applying and designing selling strategies equally to all accounts.

unit cost A small component price of a product's total cost.

V

value analysis An investigation that determines the best product for the money.

value-added Benefits received that are not included in the purchase price of the individual good or service.

values One's moral code of conduct toward others: created through integrity, trust, and character.

virtual office A venue (home, vehicle, hotel room, or even local coffee shop) where salespeople are able to conduct business with the help of technology.

visual aids close Integrating visuals, such as documents, slides, and sales sheets as a way to visually convey or reinforce a point.

visuals Illustrative material that aids a prospect in increasing memory retention of a presentation.

W, Z

wants Needs that are learned by a person.

wholesale salesperson A person who sells products to parties for resale, use in producing other goods or services, or operating an organization.

wisdom Ability to make good use of knowledge.

worldview People's different beliefs about the world around them.

zone price The price based on geographic location or zone of customers.